MW01600854

Postcolonial Philosophy of Religion

Purushottama Bilimoria • Andrew B. Irvine

Editors

Postcolonial Philosophy of Religion

 Springer

Editors

Purushottama Bilimoria
SOPHIA, Inc.
School of Philosophy
Anthropology &
Social Inquiry (PASI)
The University of Melbourne
206-08 Old Law Quad
Parkville VIC 3052
Australia
p.bilimoria@unimelb.edu.au

Andrew B. Irvine
Maryville College
Division of Humanities
502 E. Lamar Alexander Parkway
Maryville TN 37804
USA
andrew.irvine@yahoo.com

ISBN 978-90-481-2537-1   e-ISBN 978-90-481-2538-8
DOI 10.1007/978-90-481-2538-8

Library of Congress Control Number: 2009928841

Printed on acid-free paper

9 8 7 6 5 4 3 2 1

Springer is part of Springer Science+Business Media (www.springer.com)

In memory of Bhibuti Yadav, Grace Jantzen, Ninian Smart.

Preface

The present collection of writings on postcolonial philosophy of religion takes its origins from a Philosophy of Religion session during the 1996 Annual Meeting of the American Academy of Religion held in New Orleans. Three presentations, by Purushottama Bilimoria, Andrew B. Irvine, and Bhibuti Yadav, were to be offered at the session, with Thomas Dean presiding and Kenneth Surin responding. (Yadav, unfortunately could not be present because of illness.)

This was the first AAR session ever to examine issues in the study of religion under the rubric of the postcolonial turn in academia. Interest at the session was intense. For instance, Richard King, then at work on the manuscript of the landmark *Orientalism and Religion*, was present; so, too, was Paul J. Griffiths, whose subsequent work on interreligious engagement has been so noteworthy. In response to numerous audience appeals, revised versions of the presentations eventually were published, as a "Dedicated Symposium on 'Subalternity'," in volume 39 no. 1 (2000) of *Sophia*, the international journal for philosophy of religion, metaphysical theology and ethics.

Since that time, the importance of the nexus of religion and the postcolonial has become increasingly patent not only to philosophers of religion but to students of religion across the range of disciplines and methodologies. The increased internationalization of the program of the American Academy of Religion, especially in more recent years, is a significant outgrowth of this transformation in consciousness among students of religion. Several other of the contributions to this volume grow out of work presented at the AAR in the past decade, including those of Grace Jantzen, Richard King, Nelson Maldonado-Torres, Arvind Mandair, Eduardo Mendieta, and Santiago Slabodsky.

We are grateful to all the contributors for their patience over the long course of the volume's completion. We extend our thanks also to the American Academy of Religion for supporting vital debate and conversation around postcoloniality. In addition, thanks are due to Springer SBM B.V., particularly to Floor Oosting, Ingrid van Laarhoven, and Willemijn Arts, for their enthusiasm and care for the project. We also thank Serena O'Meley, who assisted with the original symposium in *Sophia*, Amy Katherine Rayner, graduate student at the University of Melbourne, for help with editing many of the chapters and working on the index, and Emerald Kimber for additional assistance with the indexing. We are grateful to Gayatri Chakravorty Spivak, Dipesh Chakrabarti, Renuka Sharma, Morny Joy, Laurie Patton, and Devi & Rasa, among many others (some of whom may even be nameless or in worlds unseen), for their inspiration and encouragement.

This collection has been a long time coming. Indeed, in the course of its gestation, two of our colleagues were given to death. We wish to honour the memories of Bhibuti Yadav, Grace Jantzen, and Ninian Smart by dedicating this volume to them.

Contents

Contributors

Purushottama Bilimoria is Professor of Philosophy and Comparative Studies at Deakin University, Senior Research Fellow at the University of Melbourne, and Visiting Professor at State University of New York - Stony Brook and Columbia University. His research and publications cover classical Indian philosophy and comparative ethics, Continental thought, cross-cultural philosophy of religion, diaspora studies, bioethics, and personal law in India. He is Editor-in-Chief of the journal, *Sophia*. Recent publications are *Indian Ethics I* (Ashgate 2007; OUP 2008), *Sabdapramana: Testimony in Indian Philosophy*, revised edition (DK Print-World, 2008), and Nietzsche as 'Europe's Buddha' and Asia's Superman, *Sophia*, vol 47/3 2008.

Thomas B. Ellis (Ph.D., University of Pennsylvania) is an Assistant Professor of Religion in the Department of Philosophy and Religion at Appalachian State University. He specializes in the religious and philosophical traditions of South Asia, primarily Hindu, Buddhist, and Jain. Theoretically and methodologically, Ellis employs comparative philosophy, psychology, and biology in his research and teaching.

Jay Garfield (Ph.D., University of Pittsburgh) is Doris Silbert Professor in the Humanities, Professor of Philosophy and Director of the Logic Program and of the Five College Tibetan Studies in India Program at Smith College, Professor in the graduate faculty of Philosophy at the University of Massachusetts, Professor of Philosophy at Melbourne University and Adjunct Professor of Philosophy at the Central University of Tibetan Studies. His areas of expertise include philosophy of mind, philosophy of language, Buddhist philosophy, and ethics and epistemology. Garfield's most recent books are his translation, with the ven Prof Geshe Ngawang Samten of the Fourteenth-Fifteenth Century Tibetan Philosopher Tsong Khapa's commentary on Nāgārjuna's *Mūlamadhyamakakārikā* (Ocean of Reasoning) and *Empty Words: Buddhist Philosophy and Cross-Cultural Interpretation*, and *Fundamental Wisdom of the Middle Way: Nāgārjuna's Mūlamadhyamakakārikā* (Oxford University Press 2006 and 2006, 1995, respectively).

Andrew B. Irvine (Ph.D., Boston University) is currently Assistant Professor of Philosophy at Maryville College in Tennessee (USA). He previously directed the study abroad program in Comparative Religion and Culture at Long Island

University Global College. He is at work on a book with the working title, *God's Preferential Option for the Poor: Symbolic Liberation*.

Grace Jantzen (1948–2006) (Ph.D. in Philosophy, University of Calgary; D. Phil. in Theology, Oxford University) was Professor of Religion, Culture and Gender at the University of Manchester from 1996 to 2005 and Emeritus Professor until her untimely death. She wrote a series of studies on the philosophy of religion, including *Power, Gender and Christian Mysticism* (Cambridge University Press, 1995) and *Becoming Divine: Towards a Feminist Philosophy of Religion* (Manchester, 1998). Before she died she was working on a multi-volume study on Death and the Displacement of Beauty in Western philosophy and theology, including *Foundations of Violence* (Routledge, 2004) and two posthumous volumes *Violence to Eternity* (Routledge, 2008) and *A Place of Springs* (Routledge, 2009).

Richard King (Ph.D., Lancaster University) is Professor of Religious Studies at Vanderbilt University in Tennessee (USA). He is a specialist of classical Indian philosophies, postcolonial approaches to the study of religion, and the comparative study of mysticism. He is the author of four books: *Early Advaita Vedanta and Buddhism* (State University of New York Press, 1995), *Orientalism and Religion. Postcolonial Theory, India and "the Mystic East"* (Routledge, 1999); *Indian Philosophy. An Introduction to Hindu and Buddhist Thought* (Edinburgh University Press, 1999), and, with Jeremy Carrette, *Selling Spirituality. The Silent Takeover of Religion* (Routledge, 2005).

Nelson Maldonado-Torres (Ph.D., Brown University) is Associate Professor of Comparative Ethnic Studies in the Department of Ethnic Studies at the University of California, Berkeley, and current president of the Caribbean Philosophical Association. He is the author of *Against War: Views from the Underside of Modernity* (Duke University, 2008). In 2005, he co-edited with Ramón Grosfoguel and José David Saldívar the book *Latin@s in the World-System: Decolonization Struggles in the 21st U.S. Empire* (Paradigm Press). He is currently working on a book-length project entitled *Fanonian Meditations*, where he elaborates a theory of epistemic and material decolonization based on the work of W.E.B. Du Bois, Frantz Fanon, Gloria Anzaldúa, and other intellectuals of color.

Arvind Mandair (Ph.D. in Chemistry, Aston University; Ph.D. in Philosophy, The University of Warwick) teaches at the University of Michigan. His books include *Religion and the Specter of the West: Sikhism, India, Postcoloniality and the Politics of Translation* (Columbia, 2009), and, with C. Shackle, *Teachings of the Sikh Gurus* (Routledge, 2005). He is founding co-editor of the journal *Sikh Formations: Religion, Culture and Theory* published by Routledge.

Navdeep Mandair is presently completing his doctoral degree in the School of Philosophy, Theology and Religion, University of Birmingham, U.K.

Eduardo Mendieta (Ph.D., New School for Social Research) is professor of philosophy at the State University of New York, Stony Brook. He is the author of *The Adventures of Transcendental Philosophy* (Rowman & Littlefield, 2002) and *Global*

Fragments: Globalizations, Latinamericanisms, and Critical Theory (SUNY Press, 2007). He is presently at work on another book entitled *Philosophy's War: Logos, Polemos, Topos*. His most recent book publications are a collection of interview with Angela Y. Davis, entitled *Abolition Democracy: Beyond Empire, Torture and War* (Seven Stories Press, 2006), and an edited volume of interviews with Richard Rorty, *Take Care of Freedom, and Truth Will Take Care of Itself* (Stanford University Press, 2006).

Walter D. Mignolo (Docteur le Troisieme Cycle, L'École des Hautes Études, Paris) is William H. Wannamaker Professor of Romance Studies and Literature at Duke University and Director of the Center for Global Studies and the Humanities. His publications include *The Darker Side of the Renaissance: Literacy, Territoriality and Colonization* (The University of Michigan Press, 1995), *Local Histories/Global Designs: Coloniality, Subaltern Knowledges and Border Thinking* (Princeton University Press, 2000), and *The Idea of Latin America* (Blackwell, 2005), which received the Frantz Fanon Award from the Caribbean Philosophical Association. He also co-edits the web dossier, *WKO* (http://www.jhfc.duke.edu/wko/index.php).

Makarand Paranjape (Ph.D., University of Illinois at Urbana-Champaign) is a critic, poet, fiction writer, and literary columnist with over thirty books, 100 published academic papers, and more than 200 reviews, notes, and popular articles to his credit. He is currently Professor of English at Jawaharlal Nehru University, New Delhi. His latest book is *Another Canon: Indian Texts and Traditions in English* (Athem Press, 2009).

Santiago Slabodsky (Ph.D., University of Toronto) is assistant professor in Judaic Studies at St. Thomas More College, University of Saskatchewan. He holds previous degrees from Duke University, the University of Buenos Aires, and the Latin American Rabbinical Seminary. His work has been published in journals including *Majshavot, Paideia, Koinonia*, the *Journal of Human Architecture*, and in the edited volume, *Latin@s in the World System* (Paradigm Publishers, 2006).

Sharada Sugirtharajah (Ph.D., University of Birmingham) is Senior Lecturer in Hindu Studies in the School of Philosophy, Theology and Religion, University of Birmingham, United Kingdom. Her publications include chapters in edited volumes, journal articles, entries in reference works and contributions to resource packs on Hinduism. She is the author of *Imagining Hinduism: A Postcolonial Perspective* (Routledge, 2003).

Kenneth Surin (Ph.D., University of Birmingham) is Professor of Literature and Professor of Religion and Critical Theory at Duke University. He trained initially as an analytical philosopher. His teaching areas include anglophone literatures outside England, philosophy (both analytical and continental), critical theory, marxism, state theory, and international political economy. Recent publications include "Can a Chosen People have a True Politics?" *Angelaki* 12 (2007): 145–150, "World Ordering," *South Atlantic Quarterly* 104 (2005): 185–197, and "Rewriting The Ontological Script Of Liberation: On The Question Of Finding A New Kind Of Political Subject" in *Ontology in Practice*, ed. John Milbank, Slavoj Zizek and Creston Davis (Duke University Press, 2005): 240–266.

Bibhuti S. Yadav (1943–1999) (Ph.D., Banaras Hindu University) was Professor of Hindu and Indian Buddhist thought and Comparative Philosophy of Religion at Temple University, until his untimely death at 56, on October 10, 1999. Born in Tulasipur, India, he was educated at Banaras Hindu University, from which he received a B.A. in Sanskrit and philosophy, as well as an M.A. and Ph.D. (1970) in philosophy. He spent a year at McMaster University, then came to Temple University in 1972. As a member of the Department of Religion, he also taught at Temple University Japan during 1993–94 and 1996–98. He published widely in the area of Indian philosophy and served on the editorial boards of a number of journals and foundations. He received Temple University's Distinguished Teaching Award in 1992.

Introduction: The State of Philosophy of Religion and Postcoloniality

Andrew B. Irvine and Purushottama Bilimoria

The prominent philosopher of religion, Robert Cummings Neville, has recently argued that in late modern times, "the world's great religious cultures are confused by fragmentation in two directions." The first confusion stems from uncertainty as to how the religions relate to one another, the second from the failure of the religions to address the distinctive forces of a complex world society (Neville 2002: 137–138).

Neville commends philosophy as a way to clarify and perhaps transform the religious fragmentation of the times. However, even in doing so, Neville urges a vigorous critique of philosophy of religion as presently practised. We quote at length:

> [T]his discipline has almost incorrigibly insisted upon an eighteenth century angle of vision on religion, which sees little more than Christianity and through only epistemological perspectives. Ignoring the vast amount of information about other religions now available in English it is embarrassingly parochial, and innocent of so many other philosophical approaches to religion, many learned from other religio-philosophical traditions, that it is out of the loop for understanding religion in late modernity.... The real problem in philosophy of religion is not religion but philosophy. (Neville 2002: 5–6)

We do not here attempt to give an adequate description, let alone analysis, of the various ways in which "religion," as the object of an eponymous, heuristic category, is challenged by and active upon the times. That work, which is the multi-faceted labor of the academic study of religions, and related areas of inquiry, is not properly within the scope of this volume (although it finds its way into the essays gathered here in many ways, with robust impropriety).

What is offered here is a sustained examination, from a variety of viewpoints, of philosophy, particularly the philosophy of religion. All the essays share an interest in critically reconstructing that endeavor, to conduct it responsive to the postcolonial experience of various dispossessed communities.

Philosophy of religion today is, by and large, a discipline pursued by way of over-hauling a critically enfeebled Western tradition of philosophical theology. Different philosophers attempt to do this in different ways, but their efforts all may be understood as responses to the ground-shaking epistemological critique of Immanuel Kant.

P. Bilimoria and A.B. Irvine (eds.), *Postcolonial Philosophy of Religion.*
© Springer Science+Business Media B.V. 2009

Philosophical theology endures here and there, although its ability to survive in the current intellectual climate is uncertain. Some philosophers, such as Bernard Williams, believe that the days of philosophical theology are over, arguing that the conditions of its possibility collapsed under the twin onslaughts of positivism and criticism: thereafter, philosophical theology appears to be a science in much the same way that phrenology does.

On the other hand, some departments of religion and seminaries, mostly with Christian institutional affiliations, still concern themselves with philosophical theology. In some of these cases, at least, this is a matter of principle: a refusal to participate in modern errors. It represents a refusal to break with premodern traditions that felt no unbridgeable gulf between the things of nature and metaphysical realities. The persistent appeal of this kind of philosophical, or "natural," theology lies in the claim to offer rational justification of religious belief, even if the belief must be, ultimately, adopted on other grounds. In the traditional way of speaking, this is philosophy adducing truths of reason in support of truths *beyond* reason. We do not dismiss this venerable tradition of philosophical theology out of hand. Yet, we note the difficulty it faces to dissociate itself from a wider, "fundamentalist" vector in late modern, especially Anglo and Anglo-American societies (currently being helped along in the U.S.A. by the undermining of responsible public control of science in the name of "intelligent design").

In contrast to, and at least some times in direct reaction to, the practitioners of philosophical theology, contemporary philosophers of religion generally expect one another to represent themselves as free from apologetic preoccupations. If and when the "hard" analytic judgment on religion as meaningless activity is set aside, philosophers of religion are expected to concern themselves with critical investigation of claims that stem from or have their basis in vestiges of religious tradition and theological discourse, especially some persistent "problems" with a pedigree in the mainstream of Western philosophy, including God, (the) self, evil, faith and reason, and morality. But philosophy of religion does not presume doctrinal claims, one way or another, in the creation of its agenda. It does not hold on to positions which may be found insusceptible or resistant to the light of logical analysis, critical reflection, scientific discovery, even common sense. Philosophy of religion is a rational and universal, secular inquiry, then.

Precisely because of this secular stance, and in view of its strong concerns in the area of metaphysics and ontology, philosophy of religion is now more readily distinguished from the older, suspect philosophical theology, and is catching on in the academy with renewed vigour. Having repeatedly deflected identification with confessional disciplines, it attracts increasing interest among undergraduates and graduates, in teaching and research areas within the liberal arts faculties. Straddling philosophical, religious, and theological studies, it has broadened its base and its appeal. In this respect, it follows in the footsteps of contemporary ethics, which has been led by numerous thinkers, sensitive to the mounting urgency of global pressures, well and truly beyond the imaginative confines of its genealogical predecessor, moral philosophy, to become involved with the plight of future generations, of animals, mountains, forests, and so on.

Also precisely because of this secular stance, though, few contributions to the academic philosophy of religion hitherto have attempted to search the "soul" of the discourse, to consider what it excludes, and what it otherwise might be. The casual willingness of a Richard Rorty, say, to discount commitment to Christianity (or to "Judeo-Christianity") may have more to do with the rise in popularity of philosophy of religion among students in the West than we realize. After all, these are students looking to come to terms with the parental belief systems that impinge on their consciousness of every new decision they must make for themselves, and/or searching for deeper truth beyond teenage disillusionment. But – and this is rather a big but – the demographic profile of most of the societies thought of as the West has changed drastically in just a generation. Plurality and multiculturality are become givens. This is true in North America, the United Kingdom, Europe, Australia and New Zealand, and in a dramatic way in post-Apartheid South Africa. Israel, too, confronts these strains. Seemingly one of the conditions of Turkish accession to the European Union is that the state abandon its historically clear position and adamant role in the discourse on nation, culture, and religion.

However, even late capitalist marketing of ethnic and religious diversity has not yet succeeded in opening many doors inside, let alone between, discipline-based departments in Western universities. Political globalization, particularly of a cosmopolitan kind, advocating "world citizenship," with moral rights and responsibilities based on an at least minimal universalism of values does, in fact, attract interest across a range of disciplines. Yet economic globalisation, which is far more effective in the daily experience of every person on the planet, has only here and there provoked attempts at a systematic "crossing of boundaries" into non-western traditions. Interestingly, quite a few of the attempts that have been made are the initiative of confessionally committed theologians (e.g. Küng 1993; Knitter 1995; Cobb 1999). One of us in Australia has often heard it asked, why, simply because there are large numbers of fee-paying Asian students in the major Australian universities, should a department attend to philosophies of Asia? Either "Asian philosophers" cannot compete with "mainstream" philosophers, anyway, or "Asian Philosophy" is not based on anything fundamental and universal, like "reason." Of course, such preposterous excuses can only be sustained in virtually utter ignorance of so-called "Asian philosophers" and "Asian philosophy."

Postcolonial philosophy of religion, as we understand it, operates a critique of the secular self-representation of modern, post-Kantian philosophy of religion, which permits such indefensible ignorance to be passed off as deliberate sagacity. *That* version of philosophy of religion remains determined by the religious dogmatics of "the West." The experience of Europeans, and of Europe's colonizing emissaries to the Americas, Asia, Africa, and Oceania, norms the construction of categories and categorial schemes, the recognition of informants (or, on special days, interlocutors), and the selection and synthesis of relevant information. This in very rough terms is what it means for modern philosophy of religion to be *Eurocentric*. It regularly plays out in such topics as, "Hinduism and the Problem of Evil," or, "Daoism and Natural Law," or "The Spiritual Conquest of America," or "How Dreamtime became a Nightmare."

To put it differently, the religion and religious beliefs *not* presumed by Euro-centrically disciplined philosophers of religion continue to be Christian, and those particularly of a Christianity instilled in the exercise of colonial power over others. As Grace Jantzen puts it in her essay in this volume:

> The philosophy of religion in the west has largely assumed a male, "omni-everything" God. As a bishop wrote in *Church Times* a few years ago, "God is a relatively genderless male deity." We need only add that he is also white, and that he favours democracy, the free market economy, and the USA/UK. It is of course always immediately added that God does not have a body, and therefore has neither colour nor gender; and that God loves all people equally. But lurking behind the denial is the imaginary: the body that God does not have is male and white. And probably he speaks English.

The secularity of much contemporary philosophy of religion has been the basis for purporting the neutrality and universality of its judgments. However, what we see is that this secularity is peculiarly Western *secularism*. Moreover, this brand of secularism has operated in a tacit manner across the field of studies of "other" religions and the people that practice them. We see it beginning to be articulated already in the coimplication of Discovery and Evangelization, Gospel and Science, that shapes colonizations as different as those of Mexico and India. (It is telling in this respect, perhaps, that Columbus held that Spain's New World was none other than the old world of which Europe was a remote dependant; the novelty for him was a function of his intention to discover that world anew, by displacing it, as it were, to a European frontier.)

From the perspectives of colonized peoples, then, informed by "other" religious and philosophical traditions, much contemporary philosophy of religion evidently acquiesces to a Eurocentric ordering of the world and of knowledge. In doing so, the philosophers do Eurocentrism the favor of granting it foundational, if not absolute, importance. Thus philosophy of religion's very claim to secularity raises a phantom Christianity – shall we call it *religion; the religious?* – to wander the colonial order of things, its uncriticized and uncriticizable spirit, both certifier and subject of the terrifying and fascinating mystique of colonial power. Suppliant to Eurocentrism, philosophy of religion renders itself deaf to appeals and assertions of religion(s), not to mention philosophies of religion(s), pursued otherwise.

As Kenneth Surin writes in his Afterword: Religion and philosophy between the modern and postmodern, in this volume, "every culture generates for itself its own 'thinkability' (and concomitantly its own 'unthinkability' as the obverse of this very 'thinkability'), and its concepts are constitutive of that 'thinkability'" (327). The label, postcolonial philosophy of religion, refers to the variety of efforts (a fair selection of which are essayed in the pages that follow) to criticize cultures of coloniality, and thereby free other possibilities. The project shares genetic traits with modern and postmodern philosophy of religion in general. But it reflects critique, and refracts it, through what colonized peoples have experienced.

Tracking the spirit of colonial power through philosophy of religion is no easy task, of course. There is significant debate about the fitness of the term "postcolonial" itself. We opt to use the term, but mainly denotatively, to tie the essays into the ongoing debate without taking upon ourselves the pretense of settling it. Yadav's contribution to this volume offers a critique of postcolonial critique, branding it a permutation of "internal colonialism" for the benefit of a Brahmanic elite. We may also acknowledge the critiques of, say, Gayatri Chakravorty Spivak, J. Jorge Klor de Alva, and Enrique Dussel. Whether pro, con, or ambivalent, one can hardly ignore the term now; it is a core motif in the discursive consciousness shared, albeit imperfectly, by critics of actually existing world society. We offer the work of the contributors to this volume in hope of further enriching this consciousness, and rendering it more acute in the ways it may enter into the philosophy of religion as hitherto practiced. The vibrance of postcolonial experience is well reflected in the essays gathered here, and the volume should open up horizons for readers seeking an introduction to the philosophical implications of that experience for religious studies.

Reference

Neville, Robert Cummings. 2002. *Religion in Late Modernity*. Albany, NY: State University of New York Press.

Küng, Hang. 2002. *Trans. John Bowd Tracing the Way: Spiritual Dimensions of the World Religions*. London and New York: Continum.

Knitter, Paul F. 1995. *One Earth, Many Religions: Multifaith Dialogue and Global Responsibility*. Maryknoll, NY: Orbis Books.

Cobb, Jr., John B. 1999. *Transforming Christianity and the World: A Way Beyond Absolutism and Relativism*. Edited and introduced by Paul F. Knitter. Maryknoll, NY: Orbis Books.

Part I
Surveying the Scene

What Is the "Subaltern" of the Philosophy of Religion?

Purushottama Bilimoria

Philosophy of religion concerns itself with certain questions arising from the traditional tussle between the judgment of *reason* and the commitment to *faith*, augmented by disputes over whether it is language and conceptual analysis or some direct intuitive experience that provides access to the truth claims underpinning specific scriptural utterances, as articulated in philosophical (or "natural") theology. The late Ninian Smart lamented that philosophy of religion as conventionally practiced in discipline-bounded departments rested on two mistakes, namely its singular focus on problems of natural theology (in the context of Western theodicy) and, apropos of this, its inattentiveness to religion, even less to *religions*, as a totality of worldviews, ranging over a wide compass of doctrines, ideologies, myths and symbolic patterns, sacred practices, ultimate beliefs (that deeply inform human life rather than simply provide a basis for propositional assertions), and so on.[1] (An analogue to this is the tendency once, in philosophy of science, to be divorced from the history of science, not to speak of the laboratory itself.) Smart went on to suggest a three-tiered prolegomenon for the philosophy of religion, structured around the *comparative* analysis of religions, the *history* of religions, and the *phenomenology* of a range of (religious) experience and action (Smart 1995: 31).

Now, on the one hand, Smart has been applauded for raising concerns in this way about the parochialism of contemporary "analytic" philosophy of religion that has led virtually to its marginalization within philosophy – a field now "as inbred as the Spanish Bourbons" (Levine 1997: 11). But, on the other hand, Smart has been equally criticized for thinking that the way out of this impasse is to abandon traditional philosophical methods and concerns and, along with the history of religions and anthropology, to "go wild," that is, to take a structuralist approach and engage in what he calls "comparative systematics" (a strategy he adopts from "Biblical *comparare* or Systematics," implying exegetical hermeneutics and intratextual morphology more than redactive dogmatics).

There are merits, indeed, both in Smart's realist agenda and in the rebuff from his critics. However, in my brief essay here, I do not wish to get drawn too far into the Smart problematic; rather, I wish to come in from another direction and work out some implications elsewhere from Smart's revisionist prolegomenon. I want to suggest that, if taken seriously, Smart's position perpetuates rather than undermines at least one of the two central dogmas on which the comparative philosophy of religion

P. Bilimoria and A.B. Irvine (eds.), *Postcolonial Philosophy of Religion.*
© Springer Science+Business Media B.V. 2009

has been based, for better or for worse. The recent shift in emphasis toward a more "cross-cultural" philosophy of religion does not mitigate the situation all that much from the present concern, although it points in the right direction insofar as it allows the comparative phenomenon under purview to emerge in its uniqueness (although the similarity in meaning of "comparative" and "cross-cultural" could be a trifle overstressed).[2] My critique comes from what might be seen as more peripheral – or to the "left-out" – concerns within mainstream philosophy of religion; there are ramifications nevertheless. The focus here is more specifically on the comparative philosophy of religion in its historical genesis and its widespread impact across the board, as we have seen it echoing in Smart's prescription as well, more forcefully expressed in an earlier incarnation by Raimundo Panikkar (1980: 357–383). But much of what I argue in the end is to be seen as a supplement to, rather than a dismissal of Smart's critique. It is indeed an extension of his bold wake-up call, made very early on to philosophy of religion, to rethink its terms of reference vis-à-vis the persistent specter of logical positivism and the gradual collapse of colonial imperialism, signaling the arrival of pluralism, tolerance, and cross-fertilization of ideas and ideals (or "worldviews in tango," as I once heard Ninian say – which is not the kind of nuance that a Samuel Huntington would draw).

My own general claim is that comparative philosophy of religion mistakenly builds on the two dogmas of, for example, (1) comparative religion itself (within which I include Smart's aligned tier of the history of religions) and (2) natural (or philosophical) theology per se. To deal with the first, there is the popular belief that there are things common and therefore comparable between two or more traditions or systems, and that these objects of comparison are of scholarly significance. *Compare we must:* there seems to be an inexorable imperative to compare, simply because things present themselves as similar or as different, or both. But this enterprise is fraught with difficulties: just what does one compare, how does one choose what to compare or why, and through what methodological and epistemic tools, and *who* is it that carries out the tasks, arranges the comparative material, and sets the terms for the judgments to follow? There are epistemological questions of details, description, analysis, and explanation and the approaches or disciplines that inform the processes of religious investigation. Furthermore, how or what does one compare if categories in the typology of beliefs, crucial to understanding one side of the symbolic system being juxtaposed, are decisively absent in or irrelevant to the other tradition or system?[3] *Allgemeine Religionswissenschaft* thought it had the answers, but in recent decades the cards have been stacked against this enterprise, and comparative religion has looked elsewhere for succor.

For example, some have turned to comparative religion as a platform on which to build a basis for a *synthesis* of religions, drawing upon the insights and wisdom that they believe to be contained in all religions, large and small. The guiding principle in this approach has been the assumption that people everywhere have some basic, essential, religious needs that they all seem to share, and some have gone so far as to suggest that the varying quests lead ultimately to one destination: archetypal perfection or uniqueness ("God," the Transcendent, *Ur-Grund*). This is a prescriptive concern, in that it stipulates how religion *ought* to be. Many early Western studies of religion carried with them European ideas and presuppositions of what religion was or ought to be, whether in their quest for a "primordial" religion or in describing the "highest" religion. This subconscious bias was often manifested in the kinds of questions asked and in the categorization and classification of non-Western religions, which went hand in hand with the belief that religion can be studied "scientifically." This objectivist foray was further reinforced by the emergence of the disciplines of philology, mythology, folk studies, history, and the so-called social sciences, particularly anthropology, sociology, ethnology, and psychology. That is to say, comparative religion emerged as a discipline that used the method of objective description and impartial comparative analysis, eschewing all vested interests in any one religion. Like science itself, the "scientific" study of religion was believed to be "value free" and neutral. The evolutionary model characterized the development of religions as being like the development of living organisms.

During this period also, European thinkers were becoming increasingly aware of other cultures and their religions, and they thought it worthwhile to study and compare different religions in a systematic way comparable to the scientific study of different species of organisms on the evolutionary continuum. The model called for the study of the degree of development of each religion so as to indicate the place of each religion in this scale of development from a simple, undeveloped, "primitive" reality to the more complex, developed, and sophisticated forms in higher civilizations. But in its fetish with mythology, comparative religion was not unlike earlier attempts, for example by Megasthenes, to look for a prototype in all religions by tracing their mythologies and folklore back to their "origins" or "borrowed" roots. The nineteenth-century discovery by Europeans of Indian texts and the ancient traditions they recorded was a contributing factor to the development of the "comparative method" in its broad sense. The constant interaction between European orientalists and the absentee Indian writers (represented through the texts that reached Europe) fueled the hearth of comparative religion. Wilhelm Halbfass, in discussing the relation between India and the comparative method, made the following perceptive observation:

> It is a well-known and conspicuous fact that the development of comparative studies in the humanities has a special affinity with the development of Indian studies, and that later on the Indians themselves took a very active part in the business of comparison. The discovery of Indian materials stimulated the comparative instinct of European scholars from the end of the eighteenth century. At this time the word and concept of *comparison* itself became much more explicit and conspicuous than it had been before, and by the end of the nineteenth century, the "comparative method" had found at least a few advocates in most scholarly disciplines – comparative mythology, comparative philology, and soon-after comparative literature and comparative philosophy.[4]

Because of its imperialist genealogy – and not simply because *difference* had been forgotten in the obsession with similarity or *semblance* (cf. Cabezón 1998) – some scholars abhor the continuing fetish with "comparative x, y, z." These, then, are some of the problems and questions, well-rehearsed in the literature and numerous proceedings, that have continued to trouble the field of comparative religion (and, by implication, comparative theology and comparative systematics).

Coming to the second dogma, what has remained unasked and unanalyzed are the larger meta-questions concerning the motivation, civilizational presuppositions, cultural location, and legacies of orientalism and colonialism, or their persistent remnants, that together affect the boundedness of certain key categories and thematic issues taken up in the comparative enterprise such as, to name a few: God (the Absolute or the Transcendent), Creation, the Problem of Evil, the Afterlife, Immortality, Sin, Redemption, Purpose, and the End. As Garry Kessler has noted, philosophy of religion since Hegel has been the philosophy of theism, and it is Judaism, Christianity, and Islam that have provided the primary resources for reflection, also, on all religions and philosophies that refract off the *Ur*-Spirit (Kessler 1999: 7). But Kessler's foray toward a "global" perspective is, admittedly, shaped by his own Western philosophical "research tradition." I have had to look elsewhere, as I share a fragment only of that "research tradition," if this is what makes for a critique. Thus, in searching for a critique and alternative perspective, I have been moved to ask questions such as: what would an *after*-orientalist, postcolonial, gendered, and cross-cultural *Critique* look like if it were brought to bear on the comparative philosophy of religion in just the way in which this trend has triggered radical rethinking within the fields of comparative literature and history (or among other lesser social sciences) where it concerns "writing about the other"? I have been groping here, somewhat in the dark abyss of emptiness, for possible horizons, suggestions, criticisms, and a trajectory for the new millennium. Allow me to share some of my thoughts.

Let me go back to the first dogma noted above and ask a slightly different question with regard to it: is there anything left of comparative philosophy of religion that either has not been exhausted by an over-taxing, over-determination of the field, as has been the case with the parallel and in some ways related cross-disciplines of comparative philosophy and comparative religion? It might be instructive to note, incidentally, that unlike philosophy of religion in the narrow or mainstream sense, neither comparative philosophy nor comparative religion could claim for itself a strong disciplinary basis. This has been so partly because their progenitors and present-day advocates, who inherited eighteenth- and nineteenth-century orientalist preoccupations with mythology and *philosophia perennis*[5] – implying the universality across all religious philosophies – lacked both a critical-theoretical sensitivity to historiography anchored in radical historical consciousness and a deep sense of philosophical argumentation or poststructuralist critique and a critical, cross-cultural hermeneutics of suspicion. (See Bilimoria 2008a) The latter would entail a form of reflection and engagement with ideas that is distinct from just discerning mythic patterns of textual (inter-traditional) disputations and their interpretative ramifications from another felicitous perspective, usually theology mitigated by whatever remains "modern" in the arts.

Philosophy of religion, on the other hand, has remained heavily straddled – perhaps too stridently for its own good – over the rigors of logic, reason, analysis, dialectic, *reductio*, aggressive refutation, and dismissive rebuttals within established frameworks drawing from the other branches of philosophy, namely, again, logic, epistemology, ontology, and metaphysics. And the moves it makes are enacted in almost complete ahistorical, scholastic, and non-empirically grounded abstract reasoning or disquisitions, often without regard to developments in other fields, such as in the natural sciences and the empirical social sciences (history to psychoanalysis). Philosophy of religion has considered itself to be a branch of philosophy, but only just. What has distinguished philosophy of religion from other branches of philosophy, however, is that its subject matter, or rather the questions it takes upon itself, have been derived almost exclusively from theology, philosophical and natural. Philosophy of religion has always remained aloof, inward-looking, and immersed in its own Judaeo-Christian roots (with the occasional acknowledgment of Arabic scholastic *falāsifahs*, but where Ibn *Sīnā* becomes unrecognizably hellenized as Aviccena, and Ibn Rushd as Averroes), or occluded by the terms defined mostly since medieval (European) scholasticism, and has for the large part remained totally closed to possible responses and analyses that other traditions and cultures might have on the same "big questions" it sets out to solve or resolve. There is therefore an understandable movement to retrieve aspects of the "non-Western voices" in ancient and medieval scholasticism (such as those of the Muslim *mutakallimun*, Mu'tazilite, *khawari*, and Murji'ite theologians and Jewish rabbinic scholastics), especially where these "voices" were at the same time involved in comparative argumentation (or, better, the refutation of the adversaries' position both within and outside the "authoritative" tradition, and so on).

Comparative scholasticism, however, cannot provide an adequate model for philosophy of religion, as the latter is analytically narrower and conceptually broader than the "archivism" of scholasticism. The reason for this is that the simulacra of reason and rational disputation (the "intellectualist" thrust) within scholastic practices are too often geared toward apologetics (the rational triumph of "faith," "hope," and "charity") or "performatives" (redefining the "normative") or misological conversion – ending at times in a crusading or inquisitional dissimulation – of the rival theology and intellectual culture in confrontation with diverse religious worldviews or the emergent sciences or the Enlightenment (as in the case of "baroque scholasticism").[6] One may concede that in the contemporary chaos of epistemic relativism (where the postmodernist turn, along with postcolonialism, is viewed with an even greater hermeneutic of suspicion than modernism is) there may be good normative (meaning ethical) grounds for cultivating (or being in the pursuit of) an "ideal" or "paradigmatic" type of comparative scholasticism. I have no dispute with this wager and might even commend it in a different forum, but that is not the concern here (and not until scholasticism of whatever ilk has been liberated from its own historical condition or the scholars practicing the academic version are also deeply personally rooted in the very traditions they seek to unravel or interpret *qua comparare*) (cf. the chapter by Paul J. Griffiths in Cabezón [1998] and Cabezón's remarks on it, p. 245).

Coming, again, to the second question, a starting point for a critique on this point would obviously begin with the thesis of Orientalism, as popularized by Raymond Schwab (1984) and Edward Said (1978, 1985, 1993), wherein Orientalism is described as a "technology of power" (exemplifying the Foucauldian relation of power and knowledge, as developed in, for example, Foucault 1972, 1980) by which Europe or the Occident authorizes to itself the representation (in text) of its silent other, in the image of its own invulnerable essences and universalizing self (subject), but which it finds lacking, or lagging behind in the Oriental world that is the object. But Said in particular does not believe that there was or is any real discursive place called the "Orient," because Orientalism was through-and-through a Western construct (even though Said is aware that some European scholars, such as Max Müller and the Romantics, had traced a historical placenta between the birth of modern Europe and ancient Indo-Aryan language cultures, which is linked also to the "Aryanization" of the Indo-European *mentalité*).[7] Therefore, according to this non-foundationalist, anti-orientalist thesis, it is fruitless to look for "essentialist" answers as alternatives or counterpoints to Occidental discursive projections; it is sufficient that one de-centers the Western discourse by criticizing its discursive formation of the Orient, or the East, without necessarily substituting anything else in its place.

The bizarre consequence of this strategy would be – as with much of postmodern deconstructionism – that it eventually helps to wipe clean centuries, if not millennia, of *real* ideas of the sacred, community, and social organization, as well as aspirations to rationality, enlightened cultural development, intellectual ferment, and even resistance, in locations other than the mythic space constructed within the orientalist imaginary. Why, one is moved to ask, can there not be (or could not have been) indigenous attempts at writing their own narratives, histories, commentaries on literature, scholasticism if you will, social analysis, philosophies, and religious hagiographies, et cetera? The recognition (early on by Marxist scholars) that there have been such attempts, usually born out of resistance, even at the peak of European colonial domination, gave way to a series of critiques that stressed the shift away from colonial, nationalist, and, in the main, orientalist ways of seeing non-European cultures and how it might be possible to recover ("retrieve") the "voice" of nativist authorship in the postcolonial period.

Such a non-teleological and "hands-on-the-ground" strategy might even be called "contestatory" or "insurgent reading," as underscored in the enterprise of the subaltern studies group that has attempted to give prominence to the concept of *subalterneity* and the writing of "history-from-below" (Prakash 1990: 400), or from the "gaps." For instance, while most writers within this powerful genre would dispute the all-too-easy romantic demarcation of the East (India) as the cradle of spiritualism and the West (Europe) as the site of decadent materialism, others have quibbled about the extent to which nineteenth-century Indian nationalism was born out of religious revivalism (a nascent Hindu "renaissance"), ideological shifts within the caste hierarchy, peasant unrest, the exacerbation of class divisions under colonial reconfiguration, or the slow collapse of capitalism (or a bit of each) (see Chatterjee 1986, 1995–1996; Chakrabarty 2000). While the notion of *"difference"* is what might unite the often internecine strands of the radical critique emerging from a variety of such quarters, what seems common, and also instructive for the present purposes, is their power to question the unmitigated bias and, at certain critical points, the sheer hegemony of the European, colonial, modernist, and nationalist reinscription of a project that would remain for the most part alien to, if not oppressive of, the sensibilities of the other ("the other" not in Rudolph Otto's sense of the "The Wholly Other," or *Altarity*, but rather *alterity* as the "enslaved," "dispossessed," "displaced" other, which could peripheralize an entire civilization and cultures with the single brush of a pen, as it were).

So the general claim being contested in the kind of emergent critique just outlined is that each moment in the modernist onslaught structurally contributed to the suppression of indigenist insights, that is, an earlier or native rationality, the pluriform of worship or ritual discourse, a rich tapestry of iconography, diverse moral practices, customary legal or jurisprudential traditions and a magical cosmology undergirding much of these. The more specific concern is to test the observations of a handful of postcolonial Indian writers (Homi Bhabha, Partha Chatterjee, Ashis Nandy, Gayatri Spivak, and Gyan Prakash) that asymmetrical translations and transcreations of non-Western texts displace the indigenous understanding by reframing and reencoding the signs precisely within a Euro-centered imaging of the world whose cognitive claims are derived from the historical experiences of European (modernist) cultures (cf. Dutton, discussing Tejaswari Niranjana's critique). Roger Ames puts it elegantly in simpler terms, thus: "When a concept is assigned an English [or non-native] equivalent, much of the depth of the original concept tends to be lost: its word image, its allusive effectiveness, its morphological implications. At the same time, especially with philosophical vocabulary, inappropriate associations are evoked by the translated term to the extent that it is burdened by its own cultural history" (Ames 1989: 265).

Fine sentiments, one might remark, but how is all this particularly relevant to the concerns of philosophy of religion, and to a critique of comparative philosophy of religion? Precisely – since we are attempting to trace the "subaltern" of the comparative philosophy of religion. Let us begin with a simple example. The so-called problem of evil that has occupied the Western analytic philosophy of religion from Epicurus to J. L. Mackie, among others, has concerned itself with a conceptualization of evil at a very high level of abstraction supervenient upon the doctrine of God as omnipotent, omniscient, and perfectly good, which has allowed it to be succumbed to – what one of its own protagonists has dubbed a "value-theory imperialism of morals" (Adams 1999: 3–4; Zupko 2002). This monolithic model, when it gets transposed across to comparative (philosophy of) religion, has sent scholars scrambling for similar explanations or responses to paradoxes as rehearsed in the Western tradition (Bilimoria 1995a, especially pp. 1–5).

Apart from the patent misfit or disjuncture, especially in the case of traditions that entertain none of the supervenient doctrines, the tendency has been to ignore other kinds of evils – lesser but none the worse or more real for it – and also suffering that have been experienced by and, in certain instances, visited upon people, other sentient creatures, and ecosystems by the machinations of corporate exploitation or institutional colonization and through the psychophysical aberrations of individuals (from murder, rape, pornography, and other crimes against people to cruelty to animals). Marilyn McCord Adams calls these "horrendous evils" (as distinct from natural evils such as earthquakes, hurricanes, volcanic eruptions, and the like), but she also wonders whether the erstwhile freewill theodicy is all that is needed to reductively place responsibility squarely on human choice and, as it were, get God off the hook for these horrendous evils – *or vice versa?* There is something curiously phlegmatic about such a preoccupation. Even McCord Adams' suggestion to look for a way out of this impasse in the resources within one's own "faith" tradition does not get us far, either, toward a convincing philosophical solution or a dismantling of this construction from the perspective of non-faith-based traditions (which might look, for instance, to a sense of community to reason through the problematic – and here I am thinking of the Buddhist and, to an extent, the Mencian, Daoist, and Confucian systems of thought). How does it help us to come to terms with and heal the horrendous evils committed by one culture, or one civilization, upon groups of people from another who have apparently (in the eyes of the intending colonizers at least) not been equally blessed in the same measure by the design of natural law with the same divine goods?

To press the example of the problem of evil in a slightly different direction, consider that the junction of European-instigated Oriental-Indological research and British colonialism at times led to immensely fruitful outcomes, but it also resulted in producing a philosophic culture marked by what some writers have called *ambivalence and hybridity* under the ruse of "deep orientalism" (cf. Bhabha 1994; on "deep orientalism," see Pollock 1990: passim). Thus, the "law of karma," when confronted, again, with the (Western) scholastic problem of evil, evoked at best an utterly "fatalistic" interpretation and ambiguous *apologia* for the Indian moral life-world. This amoral trope proved even more alarmingly antinomous for those theodicies that gave no place or prominence to an all-loving, all-forgiving Supreme Deity – an omnipotent deity or Omni-God, to be sure, who might have had some well-intended purpose (*providential telos*) in creating the best of all possible worlds with "evil" as part of its ontological fabric rather than reducing this palpable recognition to a form of suffering, as a vain consequence or psychic and ontic trace-effect (*apūrva*) of human action or lapsed sacrifices, as was discovered to be the case in Buddhist thought and the Hindu Mīmāṃsā, respectively (Bilimoria 1995a). Likewise, the Buddha's First Noble Truth on the existential facticity of suffering stood transformed into the axiomatic edict: "*that* there is *Evil*, only so compounded with Suffering." (This effectively subverts the Buddha, turning him on his head; Raimundo Panikkar still recites this as an authentic comparativist or quaintly "imparativist" mantra, because it warrants space for Providence, which nontheist and pantheist cosmologies do not.) Outside a strong theistic (let alone monotheistic) framework, the problem of evil might wither away or be recast in less ontologically loaded terms, and the atheist (nontheist, pantheist, and Process theologues alike) would not be burdened with the onus of justifying the otherwise palpably obvious presence of evil in the absence of Providence to provide release from its sting.

Of course, the larger problematic (which is not my concern here) of the relation of European colonial philosophy with Indian thought generally has been examined by J. L. Mehta, Wilhelm Halbfass, and J. G. Arapura, and with Buddhist thought by Almond, Tuck, Lopez, and Cabézon, among others, and they all bring very helpful insights; however, the more specific terrain of a "deep orientalism" or colonialism operating within comparative philosophy of religion remains yet to be investigated.[8]

When applied to other disciplines beyond the excesses of Indian historiography, there are ramifications here also for the comparative history of philosophy and history of religions that focus on non-Western textual, so-called oral, and reconstructed premodern textualities of the "other."

The Postcolonial/Subaltern Critique Revisited

My purpose in setting up the debate in this way (and one or two symposia ensuing from it) is to press the following question: indeed, has not philosophy of religion, especially when such a discipline is touted among unsuspecting non-Western traditions in its comparativist guise, been guilty of similar epistemic crimes or a philosophic "evil" as we have been told with respect to the history of British India? And this problematic can then be generalized to the rest of the ("third") world space – hence the scourge of "third worldism." But what would it *mean* even to attempt to think in terms of the "postcolonial/subaltern critique" in the context of Asian philosophy of religion and of the broader cross-cultural enterprise? One can become equally restless here and rush into making judgments about the Eurocentric, hegemonic, and homogenizing tendencies in much of the standard practice of philosophy of religion (cf. the various essays in Dean [1995]).

Still, I am interested in exploring this judgment and critique in one area of its practice – to whit, the eighteenth-to-nineteenth-century model of philosophy of religion as it emerged in India – and that has been the focus of the historical sketch I have presented elsewhere (and I will draw liberally from that work for this report). I want to understand how this "comparative" model might have been linked with the overarching colonialist discourse, in what way it could be said to be interventionist, and what impact it has had on thinking about problems of religion in the writings of non-Western philosophers generally to the present day.

For a more systematic inquiry, such a move may begin simply with a quibble from some quarter within, say, tradition A about the way in which a supposed "truth claim" is represented in a first-order adjudication of its apparent conflict with truth claims in traditions B, C, D, et cetera, even though it could go on to champion a theoretical critique to the problematic of framing and privileging with the intent of grading *truth claims* in the first instance. How many truths are we to admit, even if provisionally? Whose truth(s)? Whose miracles? Whose ontology?

To be sure, comparative religion had already made forays into evaluative judgments about the "truth" of religious and normative judgments concerning the value of religions, and perhaps prescriptive judgments about the best route by which the ultimate aim of religion can be achieved. This concern has surfaced more notably in the current vogue of "interreligious dialogue" or ecumenism and "cross-cultural studies of religion." How should this task be carried out? But philosophy of religion has been more conscientious, and circumspect, about this because it has reminded itself constantly of the deep epistemological problems underpinning its problem areas, or else the discipline is made cognizant of the trappings of an uncritical enthusiasm by its sheer affinity to other research programs in philosophy, from logic to ethics – and quite a few lessons have been learned from developments in astronomy, physics, and other branches of natural philosophy, but perhaps most significantly from conceptual advances in metaphysics (transcendental and naturalized). Thus, drawing on the latter, it is noted that the "big question" is as much about *existence qua being* as it is about the possibility of there being (or not being) a Supreme Deity whose essence it might be (or, then again, it might not be) to claim this status; but what if there is a disjuncture between existence and essence (as Kant pointed out), and what if *nothingness* (or non-self-existing) were taken to be the ultimate *potency* of all being? (In other words, taking the Thomistic perspective, if God's *essentia* is the pure act of self-existence *[esse]*, and God is the *prima causa* of everything, of all being, one might show that the idea of self-existence as an intrinsic essence in all possible worlds is incoherent, and that all things are interdependently, contingently originated and related as many potencies, or that, in any event, the thesis about self-being as an *essentia* needs to be demonstrated before any such claim could be made with respect to a "highest" being beyond which no greater can be conceived.)

Likewise, the requirement of falsifiability is widely accepted among philosophers of religion as it has become axiomatic in the philosophy of science, but this criterion is shunned for its stringency and logical empiricist overlays by theological philosophers who prefer some deferred model of verifiability (and, by implication, falsifiability *hereafter*), as John Hick had advocated with respect to the claim of the Christian God and generalized under a sort of Hindu Advaita vision of "Nondual trans-theism."[9] Or, they maintain, like Hare, a "*blik*-out-all-options-open" for the time-being, as though in waiting (on the theory that there are fundamental assumptions that are not open to scientific testing, hence *blik*).[10] That might be a safer way to go, but we get nowhere nearer to the question of the criteria of truth and the basis for our acceptance of religious truth claims.

Furthermore, passing judgment on truth or falsity becomes a tricky task when religions all present themselves as alternative claimants to the ultimate truth. Are any of them right? By what tests do we evaluate competing religious traditions or subtraditions? Further, one might ask, can religions be evaluated as "better," "superior," "truer," et cetera, without making additional value judgments? Can one admit some gradation of "truth" in these religions without putting one's own religion in a compromised position? It is one thing to ponder the truth of religions (as a whole, under one paradigm, in contrast to its rival, say, science), but quite another to introduce the idea of "gradations of truth," for this latter move prejudges that there is some *truth* – from a modicum to a whole lot – shared by religions across the board, and the only problem facing the philosopher of religion is to arrange them accordingly along a sliding scale. What would the religion that makes it to the top end of the scale "taste like"? – as an Indian Mīmāṃsāka asked his adversary, who seemed to be suggesting that the ultimate truth has the quality of being perfectly beautiful!

Scholars like Paul J. Griffiths and Delmas Lewis have argued that it is a legitimate task of comparative philosophy of religion to look at ways in which the truth claims, values, normative concerns, and fulfillment possibilities of one religion can be measured against those of another from a vantage point outside all religions or from an objective frame of reference, such as might be provided by rationality or meta-cultural critique (Griffiths and Lewis 1983: 75–80; Bilimoria 1999). Evaluation may involve a grading of religions in terms of some agreed-upon criteria. Earlier on, R. C. Zaehner, for example, attempted to do this with the various forms of mysticism that he studied across different cultures. But in so grading and comparing religions, is one not presupposing that religions are somehow universal and not confined or localized to the particular people for whom they have unique meaning and value? Can one judge, for example, that the "Dreamtime," as a concept of the "transcendent" in Australian Aboriginal religion, is less sophisticated than the concept of Brahman in Hinduism, or even that all such notions belong to the loose cannon of what Streng called the transcendental reality. Do all religions necessarily have to make reference to one or another conception of ultimate reality in any trans-human, transcendental form? Here the nontheistic and noninstitutional Chinese "religion" of Taoism has continued to present problems to scholars who begin with such a hard conceptual approach. What is one comparing, if not the different ways in which the comparative paradigm has been set up with its own essentialist and universal presuppositions to boot!

So the question comes down to this: can religions in reality be compared? A positive answer to this presumes that (1) there is a multiplicity of religious phenomena across various cultures, (2) they can be grouped into "religions," and (3) they have something in common (e.g., a belief in the transcendent or in "sacred things" and in the possibility of salvation or liberation). But on the other hand, if we were to suppose that each religion is an organic whole and to that extent a system complete in itself in a way that no part of it can be isolated and considered separately from the other parts, how is comparison possible? If each part had a particular function that could not be explicable outside the system of which it is a part, then any assumptions about a "comparable" part in another religion might well be spurious. For example, to labor this point somewhat, can one isolate the ritual consumption of animal blood in Australian Aboriginal religion and compare it with the consumption of wine as the "blood of Christ" in the Christian Eucharist, or with the alleged bloodthirsty tendencies of the Hindu goddess Kali? Again, would it make sense to compare the Aboriginal Serpent-Rainbow with Vishnu-on-the-serpent in the Hindu pantheon? How far can we get with such comparisons?

If religions are organic wholes, then it would be difficult to make any meaningful comparisons of the sort mentioned in the examples above. Some have argued that we can look for common *themes* across religions, such as scriptures, worship, gods, incarnation, sacraments, mysticism, salvation, and enlightenment. Again, there are problems in lifting aspects or parts out of their context whereby their meaning might be lost. Now, if we cannot isolate and compare parts for fear of removing them from their specific setting (historical, cultural, theological, or simply functional), how can we compare religions as *whole* units? Similar kinds of problems bedevil the comparative philosophy-of-religion enterprise as well, for the range or pool of issues or themes is even more limited, confined mostly to questions of theodicy and certain select problems from theology, as the examples we have discussed attest to.

Hence, it comes down to this: how one positions oneself in philosophizing with or on behalf of the other must indeed be a critical question (I am tempted to say *the* critical issue for cross-cultural philosophy of religion). Questions like this are supplements rather than substitutes for the central concerns in mainstream philosophy of religion, but they would consciously displace the erstwhile preoccupations and ill-formulated questions within the field of comparative philosophy of religion modeled on or instigated by the once-popular enterprises of comparative philosophy and comparative religion or, to use its other name, the *history of religions*. This point needs elaboration.

When P. Masson-Oursel in 1923 articulated the discipline of comparative philosophy, from which arose comparative philosophy of religion, he was arguably thinking of comparing existing and known systems of thought broadly within Western civilization, with possibly some perfunctory reference to comparable or analogous traditions in the distant past of the Christian West, most notably Arabic Islam. The comparative thrust has had more of an impact in the study of religions and cultures than it has had in philosophy as such, although those more inclined toward non-Western thought have taken rather fervently to the comparative enterprise than have their counterparts in the Western philosophical enclaves.

Speaking of nineteenth-century influences, there is a story – which cannot be related in its entirety here – that while Hegel was wrestling with the Orient in his more historicized march of Reason, and Schopenhauer was confidently proclaiming that "Indian wisdom is flowing back into Europe and it will produce a fundamental change in our knowing and thinking,"[11] Nietzsche stepped back and urged that it was time the West tied the Gordian knot again, regained its Greek integrity, and dispelled the magic of the East (Bilimoria 2008: 364–70; see also Mistry 1981, among other works on Nietzsche in relation to Asian thought and Buddhism). He cautioned that certain dangers lay in wait for those who made the detour away from the safe harbor of their own way of thinking. (Heidegger, much later, seems to have taken this message to heart, but he also turned briefly to dabble in non-Western thought, if only to caution the East to be wary of the "Europeanization of the earth.")[12] Nevertheless, the ferment and excitement in Europe over Indian thought, the discovery of Sanskrit and the shared Aryan roots of Indo-European culture, and its possibilities as well as the negative downside for metaphysics, natural theology and philosophy, and aesthetics were to shape in a profound way a constructed "Indian renaissance," beginning with Raja Rammohan Roy and proceeding through the long chain of modern Indian philosophers until the present-day lacuna wherein there are virtually no departments for the study of religion and hardly much interest in philosophy of religion in Indian universities. J. L. Mehta narrates how even before the infamous 1835 Minutes on Education of Lord Macaulay, Rammohan Roy in 1823 protested against a government Sanskrit College in Calcutta on the grounds that this would encourage the perpetuation of ignorance, of a sort of pre-Baconian Dark Age (Jackson in Mehta 1992: 146; Sarkar 1975).

While Rammohan Roy mingled freely with British orientalists (he was friendly also with Jeremy Bentham and the Mills), he drew up his own agenda for the "modernizing of India" that drew philosophical, religious, social, and political sustenance more from a "bloodless cosmopolitanism" than it did from indigenous sensibilities (Bilimoria 1984).[13] Among the set of "creeds" promulgated by the Brahmos, polytheism and idol worship are definitely denounced, and "faith in the doctrine of karma and rebirth [made] optional" (Bilimoria 1984: 47). The noted Bengali lyricists Bankimchandra Chatterjee and Meghnad Madhusudan, through their writings, would "purify" the linguistic habits of the natives (or bring back ordinary language from its vacation), and together with Keshab Chunder Sen's "flaming enthusiasm" for the marriage of Eastern and Western religiosities, herald in a New Dispensation, modeled for all intents and purposes on (European) "classical" theism and its supporting ecclesia. Even to the ardent critics of their time, the linguistic monstrosities and the neo-Hindu congregation (Brahmo śamāj) looked more like a Calvinist Protestant reworking of Hindu śāstras into a rationally pragmatic-systematic worldview, with its philosophic theology sanitized of all the arcane magical, mystical, numinously ritualistic, and aberrant and superstitious tendencies of yore (Mehta 1992: 156).

In his numerous confrontations with orthodox and lay Hindu opponents, Rammohan Roy used the standard argumentative style and appealed to reason and Enlightenment morality to defend his own hybrid theology. This tradition of an articulate Hindu defense was already rife and mastered by Maharashtran *Pandits* like Vishnubawa Brahmachari in aggressive counterattacks against Christian doctrines in open confrontations with Christian missionaries like Dr. John Wilson,[14] or against the views of Ruskin, in circulation after the 1857 Mutiny, that were dismissive of Indian philosophy as "childish" or "restricted in their philosophies and faith," views that were echoed elsewhere in descriptions of Indian thought as pathetically illiterate, idiot-like, God-intoxicated, tantric aberrations,[15] a sure sign of "the grossest fetishism," as J. Murray Mitchell was wont to suggest (Mitchell 1885: 258).[16] But, on the other hand, these fervent symbols, insights, arguments, and tropes also served as prolegomena for the patriotic stirrings and the nationalist struggle looming on the horizon.

In 1917 Beni Madhab Barua became the first Indian to earn a D.Litt degree from the University of London, and a year later he published a treatise, *Prolegomena to a History of Buddhist Philosophy* (Barua 1974), in which he perpetrated a myth that "Divine Philosophy" had chosen two separate countries as "her sacred homesteads of which the earlier one was India" (p. 5). He went on to show the "decadence of Buddhism," which resulted from an excessive Yavana or Greek influence on the Indian mind. This subverts the German philological-philosophical ideology of the eighteenth and nineteenth centuries, which saw its roots in Greek origins, as distinct from Latin and Hebrew antecedents, to which it sought to return. But it is also arrogant in claiming such high purity for Hindu philosophism.

Other Bengali or short-term Calcutta-based savants who made their early careers on this rising tide of rationalism followed by the nationalist discourse that affected, wittingly or unwittingly, the twentieth-century philosophy of religion coming out of India emerged and immortalized themselves. Among them were: Akshay Sarkar,[17] Sri Aurobindo (whose works in this context are legendary), Surendra Nath Dasgupta (who began by comparing Bradleyian idealism with Indian metaphysics and was subsequently drawn to deist possibilities, publishing *Religion and Rational Outlook* in 1954), the very upright Sir Sarvepalli Radhakrishnan (busily saving appearances in Plato's academy),[18] and an underrated Jadhunath Sinha (with his tomes on Indian philosophy and psychology). The logical theism of Udayana, a medieval *Nyāya* scholar, came increasingly to the attention of Indian philosophers because he offered "proofs" that more resembled the Five Ways of Aquinas. Thus, Georg Chemparathy spent a good part of his Christian academic life in Utrecht translating and commenting on Udayana's theism for a Western theological interest, as did Indian Jesuit scholars in Pune, and John Vattanky chose to focus on God (*Īśvara*) in *Gaṅgeśa's* monumental work on logic, language, and epistemology.[19] Meanwhile Radhakrishnan practiced a pedigree of comparative philosophy of religion that drew India's wisdom equally close to the Gnostic insights of the West, which would go toward developing a rational Advaita metaphysics (a project still in the making between Varanasi, Hartford, and Montreal).

But what do we gain from such messengers, other than the glory of the medium? Do we need, for instance, to be told that Advaita *Vedānta* could be considered a strong metaphysical system on a par with McTaggert–Bradleyian idealism, et cetera, or with David Lewis' possible-worlds plurality (if there can be any comparison here at all)? Little wonder that the late and beloved Professor Bimal Matilal, who underwent the full classical training of a Sanskrit *Paṇḍit*-scholar (before he encountered Radhakrishnan in his own Sanskrit College and subsequently Quine and Ingalls at Harvard), was inspired to offer a thoroughgoing *logical* (meaning epistemological and linguistic) defense of "mysticism" in his inaugural lecture as the holder of the Spalding Chair at All Souls College of the Faithful Departed in Oxford (Matilal 2002; Bilimoria and Mohanty 1997). The imperative to show, as much as possible in rational terms, that Hindu philosophy was equal if not superior to all other philosophies, and the belief in some form of the Absolute (whether monist, monotheistic, dualistic, pantheistic, or the qualified variations in-between) gained increasing momentum, to the neglect or the undermining of those schools or systems that questioned the coherency of such beliefs. Thus, for instance, the *Mīmāṃsā* hardly received more than a passing mention in the works on Indologists of the more philosophical or theological bent. Dismissed as having "no philosophical doctrine" (Mitchell 1885: 201, 217), trading in exegetic scholasticism and ritual hermeneutics, it remained – as Kumārila Bhaṭṭa had complained back in the tenth century – reduced to the status of Lokayatā, or *Cārvāka-darśana*, of naturalistic materialism with its patently hedonistic ethic (*Ślokavārttika* I.i.10).

Yet, *Mīmāṃsā* presented a profound scope for an articulated critique of all theodicies, alongside the philosophical doubts of Guanilo, Hume, Kant, Bacon, and the logical positivists, about the reality of a supremely divine being and about the absolutes of metaphysics. Its predisposition toward the deconstruction of "onto-theo-logos" of the kind that had emerged from the historical Indian tradition was further crushed when in 1923 one Pasupathinath Sastri, invoking Max Müller, mounted a vehement defense of the Mīmāṃsā's apparent theism or "belief in God," for which he (mis)took *belief* in the supremacy of the Veda (*āstikatva*) to be the necessary and sufficient condition. (So it follows that those who do not subscribe to the Vedas – this includes Buddhists, but also Christians, Judaists, and Muslims – cannot be said to have a legitimate belief in God!) A profound category mistake that commits a theory of "Authorless Testimony" to an unabashed theodicy is an act of apologetics, not rational philosophizing. It was not until the early 1990s that papers such as "Hindu Doubts about God: Towards a Mīmāṃsā Deconstruction" (Bilimoria 1990; see also Krishna 1997) began to appear, showing that the key Mīmāṃsā protagonist, Kumārila Bhaṭṭa, was possibly a Humean in disguise who hounded crypto-Hindu theists and deists a few centuries before Hume was to upset the cart of philosophical theology in the West.

Dreamy Scenarios

Moving away from India to a nearby Pacific colony, I shall give a very brief example from a study of Australian Aboriginal culture in a little more analytical detail even as present-day Australians are still struggling to reconcile themselves to their colonialist ancestors' act of displacing native Aboriginal people from their spiritual identity with the land in the name of the exported Queen, Country, and God of the Church. Kenneth Maddock, a leading researcher on Aboriginal religion, commenting on earlier anthropological work on Aboriginal culture, notes that because Aborigines were "passive recipients of unmotivated gifts" that come through the powers of the All-Father/All-Mother in accordance with laws set down in the Dreamtime, they were morally denying "the creativity which is truly theirs." Thus, he adjudges this as "false consciousness," in contrast to the "true consciousness" that hermetically recognizes that "individuals are vehicles of their society's traditions." This "false consciousness" or unfounded beliefs of the Aboriginal people "abstracts imaginatively" what is "actually human creativity" as being "powers standing over and against men," according to Maddock (cf. 1987a, b; also Maddock's contributions in Morphy et al. 1989).

This amounts to saying that the Dreamtime is a figment of Aboriginal imagination, from the general premise that the idea of and belief in nonhuman powers (perhaps other than an almighty, freewill-respecting God) stems from imaginative abstractions. Hence, the All-Father/All-Mother and Rainbow Serpent of ambiguous gender, and the "Law" that they promulgate, merely provide a bridge between the imagined spirit ancestors and totems below. Note that Maddock has here locked himself into a "true-false"/"transcendental-totemic," "belief-myth" dichotomy, just as Emile Durkheim and Mircea Eliade could not see beyond the "sacred-profane" oppositional binary, or as Otto was unable to go past the holy numinous ideation delimited by his noninclusive categories of *mysterium, tremendum, et fascinans.* Conversely, R. C. Zaehner was insistent on the irreducibility of belief in a monotheistic God, whether encountered as the transcendent, differentiated entity (Omni-God, the theophanic Krishna, *spirit worlds, poly-heno-panentheism*) or the transcendent existing in the center within ("soul," *ātman, pudgala, totem, fetish*) (Zaehner 1957).[20] Or, for that matter, there is the suggestion that there has to be an uncompromising *rational* ordering of the world. But it augurs even less well to read into these beliefs fideist assumptions that renegade Swanseans like D. Z. Phillips would want to import into the nonnaturalistic theory. (A telling example of a fideist thesis is the following: *religious beliefs cannot be affected by personal, social, or cultural* events [Phillips 1986: 15].)

Radcliffe-Brown had known better that religious beliefs *qua beliefs* in Aboriginal Australian religion by themselves were of little significance when seen within the context of the larger mythological and cosmological picture – "worldview" in the sense in which Ninian Smart has championed it is probably closer to their predilection. Clearly, then, the Aboriginal consciousness in Maddock's Malthusian characterization is no more "false" than it is "true" that the alien Martians have green skin, or that if my Tibetan shitshu dogs were to conceive of the supremely transcendent in the dog-world *than that of which no larger herder can be conceived* that it will be a Super-Dog (*fido absconditus* notwithstanding). Must the rationality of the belief be dependent entirely or be modeled on the soundness of theistic or proto-theistic and ontological/metaphysical arguments (again, as in Anselm, or in Aquinas, Plantinga, Wolterstorff, Swinburne, and so on)?

Now here is a sound argument: "If two plus two equals four, then God exists; two plus two does equal four, therefore God exists" (cf. Nelson 1996: 7, and notes). Do people anywhere seriously base their beliefs on such arguments? Alternatively, need we even admit of the Barthian possibility, namely that the religious belief is properly *basic*, that is, is it rational to accept it without accepting it on the terms of any proposition or belief at all? But then Nāgārjuna, the second-century C.E. Buddhist dialectician, with a little help from J. N. Findlay, could argue that belief in the nonexistence of Omni-God is properly *basic*; or Charles Hartshorne, stretching Rigvedic insights on *asat* or Nonbeing, could justify Whiteheadean process-panentheism.[21] Need they, however, defer to any kind of rational justification – as necessary, essential, or basic? Wittgenstein, who became fond of Tagore's writings, chided both Bertrand Russell and the parson for trying to win the argument either way, lamenting that these (postwar days) were indeed "a sorry time for the philosophy of religion in the English-speaking countries."[22] But simply because Wittgenstein refused to look for philosophical foundations and justifications for religious belief, it does not follow that theology and its fragmented reincarnations in comparative religion should unrepentantly transmigrate to far-off colonies! One wonders, therefore, if looking for the soundness of either theistic or nontheistic (i.e., atheistic and agnostic) arguments is any longer a tenable enterprise. In other words, such beliefs as we are concerned with need not be viewed as first-order truth claims but rather located as part of a complicated "language-game" built up through accepted cultural experiences, or as part of a normative "form of life," as Wittgenstein would put it. Do people anywhere seriously base their beliefs on such arguments? As Nietzsche once complained, "I am afraid we are not rid of God because we still have faith in grammar" (quoted in Solomon 1995).

Kant and Wittgenstein, of course, denied the possibility of personal experience of the transcendent in terms of the categories acceptable to empirical and rational understanding, insisting that all our knowledge of the transcendent remains highly symbolic: the inarticulateness of the *unconditioned*, or that all our talk can only be talk of the *Sublime*, in supplemental discourses (as in the third *Critique*). But in those systems or traditions where personal experience of the transcendent is admitted, it is not intended to grant *universal* legitimacy to a particular cultural frame of reference and belief system. Rather one learns to negotiate different transcendent beliefs by interpreting them within a self-reflective epistemic discourse without the constraints of a limiting universal paradigm (See S. Akhtar, cited in Nielsen 1994: 11; see also Alston et al. 1992). It is important to pause for a moment at this juncture and really ask how concepts like necessity, universal, essential, analyticity, a prioricity, *ens realissimum*, the transcendent, and transcendental, enter into Western philosophy (and gradually affect philosophy of religion). It might not occur to many that each has a root in an earlier theological, even biblical, term expressive of notions, respectively, like eternity, immutability, distinguishing mark, predestined, never-before revelation (akin to the Sanskrit *apūrva*), identity of likenesses, God's will for the natural, and of heavenly, et cetera. Whence they become *sui generis* concepts and assume a life all their own in propositional and logical formulations is something of an enigma, but we get some clues from St. Anselm's so-called ontological preoccupations and from Augustine and Aquinas deferring to the ghosts of the philosophers, namely Plato, Aristotle, and Philo, among others.

Bringing these critiques and considerations toward a closure, I am tempted to say that the founders of natural theology, the precursor to classical and contemporary philosophy of religion, were ill aware that they had placed themselves in the half-self-deprecating *subaltern* position, as Gramsci might put it, and in this way invited the subordination of their own inner passions, cultural sensibilities, et cetera. But, simultaneously, this onto-theology instilled in them the desire or mission to civilize and uplift the moral and intellectual conditions of the near and remote pagans, barbarians, heathens, depraved, et cetera. The transcendent affirms its existence in and through arguments. Or perhaps natural theologians presupposed that Omni-God would like theistic arguments to succeed and nontheistic ones to fail. Even a disingenuous premise introduced stealthily into a prayer to stifle the Fool – as in Anselm's famous *reductio* that what is *in re* is greater than what is simply *in intellectu* – would be pleasing to Omni-God. But would an Omni-God true to His (non-gendered) ethical form be more on the side of *dis*honest theists than on the side of honest *non*theists (cf. Nelson 1996)? And it matters little what kind of Omni-God these arguments clinch "proofs" of – the God of classical philosophers, of *traditional* Christianity, of the revisionist rational reconstructivists (of the Alston and Hartshorne variety), of secularists in spite of themselves (like Hicks, Braithwaite, and D. Z. Phillips),[23] or of the Hindu theistic advocates (like Madhva, Caitanya, Krishnaism, Hindutva, Naipaul, and most modern-day Mahā-Gurus).

Finale

In closing I have one incident to report (with a useful background) that recounts and sums up the gist of the argument I have endeavored to sketch here. This comes from a symposium dedicated to a reappraisal of Gayatri Spivak's critique of "postcolonial reason"[24] that I think should help shed light on an issue raised earlier, namely: need one retreat to observations of faith, or an apologia for a superior position, when a charge is leveled from another tradition, A, that what is lacking in B is the full working out of the power, or "gift," of reason and rationality? Kant, Rousseau, and Hegel led the charge in the post-Enlightenment era. Foreshadowed in the first *Critique* and worked out more fully in subsequent essays, Kant had drawn a sharp line between those whose cognitive faculties are not yet mature and those whose cognitive faculties are informed by the categories of understanding (even erring on the side of misunderstanding) such abstractions as concepts, laws, theories, principles, axioms, antinomies, and more complex deductive postulates – of God, freedom, and immortality. It is by virtue of the "internal purposiveness of organization" (Spivak 1999: 30) that the person cultivated by reason unifies nature with inner ethical laws and pursues them as duty, with a *telos*.

By contrast, the "raw man of the Analytic of the Sublime" is stuck, as it were, in the down-under "*Abgrund*-affect without surreptitiously" being able to "shuttle over to *Grund*."[25] Kant would insist that the conditions of freedom are not for the *affective* (i.e., those given over to the passions, feelings, emotions – in short, to natural tendencies), even though their conduct may well appear to be morally innocuous and beneficial in other social respects – for instance child-rearing, community or filial cohesion, and friendliness (which rather signal their ready state for missionary colonization) – because even the principles and laws of practical workings must conform to and be derivable from the laws of pure reason, since theoretical reason alone knows or is the knowing Subject. Spivak captures this "foreclosure" perspicuously in this sentence: "The raw man has not yet achieved or does not possess a subject whose *Anlage* or programming includes the structure of feeling for the moral" (Spivak 1999: 14); he has not even fallen between the wedges of the *Critiques* (as the under-caste in a hierarchized order might be thought to be; he is not yet ready to be "cooked" by culture).[26] Would that the moral incentive of pure practical reason, which gives us moral laws, is forever debarred to them and also to their gods/goddesses. Rousseau and Hegel reinforced the divide in their own ways by invoking political-cosmopolitan registers and the trajectory of the historical march (or dialectic) of reason.

Recounting further the antics and textual moves by which the "Boys of Europe" foregrounded this radical-othering judgment in Enlightenment thinking, Spivak's response in the end has been to dismiss the privileging of reason that is at stake here, and to say "woe" to those who believe that the worth and dignity of one human group is to be adjudged by the extent to which it has or has not developed the faculty of reason, rationality, the art of argumentation, logic, and so on. It is rather the ethical commitments, the human values of decency, compassion, community-building and hospitality, perhaps, that count more than the achievements of the might of reason and the technologies that follow from its mathematical discoveries. Not surprisingly, Spivak further draws a complicitous link between the puritan culture of reason and what passes today as a self-styled postcolonial discourse (hence "postcolonial reason"), following its corruption at the hands of *bhadralok bābus*, or the motley of ex-colonial "native informants," displaced modernists, nationalist intelligentsia, and colored neocolonialists alike, at the ready, literally, to assume the seats vacated by the former European masters. And we also noted earlier the incongruity of the nineteenth-century Indian attempt to rationalize a sanitized form of elite religion on the basis of reason without any real regard for the history and social structures of lived religious traditions. Just as the European *philosophes* (barring perhaps Voltaire and Spinoza) had faith in sober rational discourse as the means for understanding other cultures without stopping to ponder that their system could be just one of the many possibilities of rational treatment that each tradition evolves in its own way, the Indian (and early twentieth-century Chinese) nationalists became convinced of the irrationality of their own societies and, hence, by parity, the superior standards of rationality exemplified in the West. This is simply an instance of ethnocentrism, where a constructed artifact (and a historicized rationality is just that) is imposed, for *good reasons* and *their own lack* on another culture.

Nevertheless, despite this recent history and the present-day ethnocentric mé-lange into which reason might have descended, I have attempted boldly to defend an unassailable commitment to rationality and theories of reason in classical Indian philosophy, as exemplified particularly in the works of the second-century Buddhist philosopher Nāgārjuna and the founders of the Nyāya schools (Gautama to Gaṅgeśa), as well as its sustained development in the works of recent Indian philosophers, from the Bhattacharyyas to Mohanty and Matilal (by far its most vocal advocate) (Ganeri 2001). Paying her respect to Matilal, Spivak nonetheless has retorted that this was an instance of *"civilizationism"* – the "we have been there before you" syndrome, as she put it, implying that the effect of reclaiming reason and the rhetoric of rationality as being one's own is on a par with such suspect suggestions as "We (let us, for argument's sake, say northern Indian Hindu Brahmins) discovered human rights" – before Hugo Grotius in the sixteenth century breathed a word about entitlements, or Thomas Paine penned *The Rights of Man* (but perhaps we suppressed or integrated this insight in the interest of a wobbly caste ordering of society). In other words, the move palpably smacks of rank orientalism of an even more sinister kind, which is precisely one of the targets of Spivak's assault on an unself-reflective faith in "postcolonial reason."

I, of course, have amicably disagreed with Spivak on this, and argued that the Buddha (and his ardent sincere followers) certainly did *reason* through the *śrāmaṇic* (Indian Stoics') disenchantment with aspects of the then dominant Brahmanical order (metaphysical, epistemic, and structural), such that Buddhist thinkers based their resistance to the orthodoxy on concepts (if not axioms) of decency, human dignity, and the desired equitable distribution of goods, if not on a fully articulated doctrine of human rights. A defense of precolonial reason is not in all instances a harkening back to the "Golden Age" and a recalling of the superiority of the Asian (and non-Western) civilizations, as has become a fashionable trend among fundamentalist and ultranationalist groups in many corners of the globe, who care less for reason and reasoning (whether analytical, dialectical, or ecological) and are single-mindedly interested in defending at all costs the truth of their own faith-tradition by whatever sort of epistemic violence rather than through dialogic argumentation. Nor is my (or Matilal's) defense, on the other hand, as disingenuous as the enthusiasm of the mercurial historian of religions to place "sex and psychology" or glamorous erotic intrigues in Asian cultural tracts ahead of "logic and episte- mology," as one writer has thought it prudent to claim.[27] There can be no dialogue from such positions where reason is muted or relegated to the dustbin of the fading post-Enlightenment and late-capitalist-hedonistic enterprise.

One must say, then, that Indian and comparative philosophy of religion fell into the lure of the concept and abstractions, in the Hegelian fashion – or, after Kant, with the idea of rationally ordering the world, but only on the Enlightenment model. The quest for perfection, for the goodness of the divinely gifted order, became an interminable project. Moving to the "cross-cultural" field, as the legacy of the ear- lier "comparative" enterprise following Max Müller and company should remind us, more often than not provokes *resentment* followed by a zeal to reform, and an even more sterile response from the appointed "native informants" of the other tra- dition as a means of overcoming the very othering (*alterity*) entailed in this process. This has been a welcome insight of postcolonial and subaltern studies scholars. The subaltern critique, therefore, on the margins of comparative philosophy of religion, must remain, like the symbol of the goddess in mainstream culture, a "disturbing presence," begging to differ and defer.

Notes

I dedicate this essay to the memory of Ninian Smart, who inspired it back in 1997. It has benefited from being heard and/or commented on (in part or in full) by Robert C. Neville, Sumit Sarkar, Gay- atri Chakravorty Spivak, Roger Ames, Arindam Chakrabarty, and Laurie Patton, among others, at two separate seminars: one at the International Association for the History of Religions Congress, Durban, August 2000, and the other at the Department of Philosophy, University of Hawai'i, Hon- olulu, November 2000. Note 31 below has reference to the larger project from which this article is in part derived.

 1 Smart (1997: 1–10), and also (1995: 17–31). Curiously, in his now classic little book *The Philosophy of Religion* (1970), Smart already gave some inkling of this by challenging the dogma that we can philosophize about religion without knowing anything about or having any experience of it; but there he was still battling against the excesses of logical positivists who had influenced the likes of A. J. Ayer, and he hadn't matured into nontheistic thinking as in Buddhism.
 2 Some scholars have argued for a resurrection of "comparative and cross-cultural perspective" in religious thought more generally and scholasticism or scholastic practice in particular, on the newfound recognition of the importance of "difference" as well as the common concerns across scholastic traditions *qua tradition* of certain other questions exegetical to epistemo- logical concerns. I have sympathy with this devil (from the standpoint of the modernist cultural-studies type of pursuits), but I am just not so sure that the "comparative" strategy advances the cause very far. See Cabezón (1998), one of the last monographs in the series "Toward a Comparative Philosophy of Religion." I was invited to serve as a coeditor of this series; however, I insisted on changing the name to "Cross-Cultural Philosophy of Religion" (just to get away from the hangovers of the Comparativist era), but the State University of New York Press management considered this to be a new proposal and asked for its jus- tification. Laurie Patton (continuing as editor from the previous series) and I were able to

muster up an argument underscoring some of the criticisms and positive aspects discussed herein. The series is now re-launched, albeit with Springer (publishers of *Sophia*, Journal of Metaphysical Theology, Philosophy of Religion & Ethics, which already has a cross-cultural focus), under the title: 'Sophia: Critical Dialogues in Philosophy, Religion and Culture'. www.springer.com/philosophy/philiosophy+of+religion/journal/11841.

3 Alasdair MacIntyre had raised this perspicuously in his 1964 essay "Is Understanding Religion Compatible with Believing?" reprinted in MacIntyre (1999), although I think that the problems go far beyond the "belief/understanding," "insider/outsider," "descriptive analysis/reductive explanation" polarities.

4 Wilhelm Halbfass (1985, 1988: 142) points out that the term "comparative philosophy" was actually not invented until after the 1923 publication of P. Masson-Oursel's *La philosophie comparée* (translated as *Comparative Philosophy* in 1926), although Al-Burini, as well as the nineteenth-century "Renaissance" Indian philosophes, was unquestionably practicing this art. Three of the greatest exponents of comparative philosophy in the twentieth century, who lifted comparative philosophy out of the sort of chess-pool that comparative religion had come unstuck in, were Charles Moore (famously associated with *Philosophy East and West*, based in Honolulu), P. T. Raju, and Archie Bahm. For a partial history see Larson and Deutsch (1989).

5 A term coined by Leibniz, for a more universal quest in philosophy (but appropriated and used by religionists to assert that all religions are species of a generic religion), emerged in India through the work of two powerful and influential writers, namely S. Radhakrishnan (1888–1974) and Ananda Coomaraswamy (1877–1947). The latter believed that a universal, primordial "tradition" informs all premodern cultures and that the search in each religion is for the recovery and a fuller expression of this "tradition." An interesting regeneration of traditionalists and transcendentalists (connected now with Walt Whitman and Ralph Waldo Emerson) carried over to the recent West, with writers such as Frithjof Schuon, René Guénon, Seyyed Hossein Nasr, and Frederick Streng, underscoring "The Transcendent Unity of Religions" (as Schuon's book by the same name makes plain). Streng took Buddhism to be a Southern Methodist mold of whiskey, while Schuon came to a dirty end; but others, even from yonder, appear to have kept alive a burgeoning movement in what is sometimes also called "Transcendent Philosophy" (there is, incidentally, now a good scholarly journal by that name as well).

6 See a fascinating account by Robert E. Goss, "Catholic and dGe lug pas Scholasticism," in Cabezón (1998); and Clooney's distinction between the "intellectualist" and "performative" types of scholasticism, which he projects onto the Indian scholastic systems of Mīmāṃsā, Vedānta, and Śrivaiṣṇavism, is summarized by Cabezón in Cabezón (1998: 243–244) (about which I have some reservations).

7 Or a convergence, as Frauwallner was to put it as late as 1944, of the "scientific character of Indian and European philosophy" (cited in Pollock 1990: 94); cf. Halbfass (1988: 70ff.).

8 To cite just a few such works: Mehta (1985, 1992), Larson and Deutsch (1988), Mohanty (1994); various papers by J. G. Arapura, Halbfass (1988), Inden (1990), Almond (1988), Tuck (1990), Lopez (1995). All of these attempt to show how the European colonial powers promoted a particular image of the Buddha as championing a simple ethical philosophy that was based on reason and restraint and opposed to ritual, superstition, and sacerdotalism.

9 See Hick (1968), and Tooley (1977). See also Hick (1983), and Sharma (1995, particularly 215ff.). Sharma discusses Hick's view in this light; note Sharma's ambitious reiterations of the problematic terms in Hick's title.

10 It goes back to the notion of "blik" introduced by John Wisdom, which he develops in this context also in his "Gods," reprinted in Santoni (1968).

11 I have developed this discussion more fully in Bilimoria (2000).

12 The phrase is, of course, Husserl's, who was more sanguine about this inexorable movement of the intentional rational mind than Heidegger, who was both more involved in and (dis-?) affected by the draconian imperialism of Nazism; he took this disquiet to Japan and sent a similar message to Charles Moore on the occasion of the first *Philosophy East and West* gatherings in Honolulu, circa 1954. Jung also would voice very similar concerns in view of

the twentieth-century interest in Eastern religions and a subsequent loss of belief in Western intellectual achievement, but he, more than most dilettantes, was responsible for the gross distortions, mystification, expropriation, and bastardization of Indian thinking.

13 The theosophical movement shortly after this should also be mentioned in this context.

14 For a fascinating account, see Conlon (1992: 17). I have a copy of a book published in 1858 by John Wilson, *India Three Thousand Years Ago,* in which he discusses the "social state of the Āryas... in the time of the Vedas"; he boasts of European learning and European ingenuity, with partial assistance from the natives of India, for securing the manuscripts and translating them (p. 17). But it is entirely derivative of the works of Müller and H. H. Wilson. Fifty or so years later Cowell put together a collection of essays by various British writers on themes covering "Ancient India," which was a vast improvement, but again the clear linkages with ancient Greek and European ancestral cultures is evident

15 First part cited in Singhal (1969), vol. 2: 249; second part in Chatterjee and Pendey (1993: 42–45).

16 See also two little books by F. B. Jevons, *The Idea of God in Early Religion* and *Comparative Religion* (both published in Cambridge ca. 1913), which together have only one index entry on "philosophy" and that, too, in the context of discussing the Buddha's substitution of philosophy for psychology!

17 Tapan Raychaudhuri discusses this intellectual in his unpublished Surrendra Paul Lecture 1995 for the Calcutta Ramakrishnan Institute for Culture, "Transformation of Religious Sensibilities in Nineteenth Century Bengal."

18 His idea of the playful Absolute (*Hiraṇyagarbha*) was halfway between the Brahman of Śáṅkara and the Concrete Absolute Spirit of Hegel. For passing discussion see Gopal (1989) and Bilimoria (1995b).

19 John Vattanky's *Gaṅgeśa's Philosophy of God* (1984) also comes to mind, and Vattanky continues to underscore the importance of *Īśvara* in Nyāya Philosophy – as a Thomist perhaps would in Aquinas' metaphysics – in his recent papers, e.g. Vattanky (2000). Most modern-day Naiyayikas tend to want to forget their Gods after the morning oblations and propitiation as they don their analytic vests for the office and desk-writing routine; Matilal and Mohanty left theirs behind in Calcutta or Calicut.

20 On Durkheim and Weber's intrusions into India see Romila Thapar, "Durkheim and Weber on Theories of Society and Race Relations to Pre-colonial India," in Thapar (1993).

21 On alternative strands in Indian thought derived from the *asat or Non-being* thesis since the R̥gvedic insight, see Avatarā (1986).

22 Cf. Phillips (1986: 1). Wittgenstein had blamed both "Russell and the parson" for the immense damage done to philosophy of religion. See Monk (1991: 410–415), where Ludwig narrates the virtues of a play by Tagore, "The King of the Dark Chambers," which he translates. Ludwig is happier that God remains unknown but yearned for.

23 See note 20.

24 Here, of course, the cracks and dissensions within the postcolonial following begin to show, as well as the heightened skepticism about the extent to which the "postcolonial" does not become just another aid-pumping and condescending trope such as "third worldism" or nationalist elitism, et cetera. This is powerfully argued by Spivak in her *Critique of Postcolonial Reason* (1999).

25 This is Spivak (1999: 30), in quotes extracting salient emphasis from Kant (pp. 15, 26), ignoring for now the resemblance that Spivak notes to the Freudian Oedipal scenario.

26 This is not a term Kant uses, but a metaphor that may have been suggested to her, as Spivak notes rhetorically in the footprint, from the Vedic idea of a higher priest-caste cooking the world in/as sacrificial fire (1999: 14 note 21).

27 Namely, Wendy Doniger, drawing up the division of labor that separated her from B. K. Matilal, which she gave as an excuse for declining to contribute to a volume of essays in memory of Bimal-da (personal correspondence). Although Professor Doniger has been very kindly disposed towards work on moral traditions of India and interactively chaired a symposium on *Indian Ethics, I* (Bilimoria et al. 2007; 2008b).

References

Adams, Marilyn McCord. 1999. *Horrendous Evils and the Goodness of God*. Melbourne: Melbourne University Press.

Almond, Philip C. 1988. *The British Discovery of Buddhism*. Cambridge: Cambridge University Press.

Alston, William P., et al. 1992. *Faith, Reason, and Scepticism: Essays*. Philadelphia, PA: Temple University Press.

Ames, Roger T. 1989. Confucius and the Ontology of Knowing. In *Interpreting Across Boundaries: New Essays in Comparative Philosophy*, edited by G. J. Larson and E. Deutsch. Princeton, NJ: Princeton University Press.

Avatarā, Antonio de. 1986 *Avatarā*, Antonio de. 1986 *The Humanization of Philosophy Through the Bhagavadgītā*. Stony Brook, NY: Nicolas Hay.

Barua, Beni Madhab. 1974 [1918]. *Prolegomena to a History of Buddhist Philosophy*. Second reprint edition. Delhi: Munshiram Manoharlal [Calcutta: Calcutta University Press].

Bhabha, Homi. 1994. *The Location of Culture*. London: Routledge.

Bhabha, Homi K. 1995. *The Location of Culture*. London/New York: Routledge.

Bilimoria, Purushottama. 1984. The Renaissance Reaction to *Sruti*. Annals of the Bhandarkar *Oriental Research Institute* (Poona) 65: 43–58.

Bilimoria, Purushottama. 1990. Hindu Doubts About God: Towards a Mīmāṃsā Deconstruction. *International Philosophical Quarterly* 30: 481–499.

Bilimoria, Purushottama. 1995a. Duḥkha and Karma: The Problem of Evil and God's Omnipotence. *Sophia* 34(1): 92–97.

Bilimoria, Purushottama. 1995b. Saving Appearances in Plato's Academy: Radhakrishnan on Philosophy. In *New Essays on Radhakrishnan*, edited by S. S. Rama Rao Pappu. Delhi: Satguru Publications/Indian Books Centre, pp. 327–344.

Bilimoria, Purushottama. 1999. A Problem for (Onto-theos) Radical Pluralism. In *Philosophy of Religion: Toward a Global Perspective*, edited by G. E. Kessler, pp. 575–582. Belmont, CA: Wadsworth Press.

Bilimoria, P., Prabhu, J., Sharma, R. (eds.). 2007, 2008b. *Indian Ethics Classical and Contemporary*. Aldershot: Ashgate; New Delhi: Oxford University, 2008.

Bilimoria, Purushottama. 2008. 'Nietzsche as "Europe's Buddha" and "Asia's Superman", Sophia, vol 47, no 3, November, pp. 359–376.

Bilimoria 2008a. Dialogic Fecundation of Western Hermeneutics and Hindu Mīmāṃsā in the Critical Era. In R. Sherma and A. Sharma (eds.) *Hermeneutics and Hindu Thought Towards a Fusion of Horizons*. Dordrecht: Springer, pp. 43–76.

Bilimoria, Purushottama and Mohanty J. N. (Eds.). 1997. *Relativism, Suffering and Beyond: Essays in Honour of Bimal K. Matilal*. Delhi: Oxford University Press.

Cabezón, José Ignacio (ed.). 1998. *Scholasticism: Cross-Cultural and Comparative Perspectives*. Albany, NY: State University of New York Press.

Chakrabarty, Dipesh. 2000. *Provincializing Europe: Postcolonial Thought and Historical Difference*. Princeton, NJ: Princeton University Press.

Chatterjee, Partha. 1986. *Nationalist Thought and the Colonial World – A Derivative Discourse*. London: Zed Books.

Chatterjee, Partha. 1995–1996. Plural Worlds Multiple Selves: Ashis Nandy and the Post-Columbian Future. *Emergences* 7–8.

Chatterjee, Partha and Gyanendra Pandey (Eds.). 1993. *Subaltern Studies* 7. Delhi: Oxford University Press.

Conlon, Frank, F., 1992. The Polemic Process in Nineteenth-Century Maharashtra Visnubawa Brahmachari and Hindu Revival. In *Religious Controversy in British India*, edited by K. Jones, pp. 5–26. Albany, NY: State University of New York Press.

Dean, Thomas (Ed.). 1995. *Religious Pluralism and Truth: Essays on Cross-Cultural Philosophy of Religion*. Albany, NY: State University of New York Press.

Dutton, Michael. Translating Theory: Orient-ing Postcolonialism. Draft paper, courtesy of author.
Foucault, Michel. 1972. *The Archaeology of Knowledge*. London: Tavistock.
Foucault, Michel. 1980. *Power/Knowledge: Selected Interviews and Other Writings 1972–1977*, edited by C. Gorden. New York: Pantheon.
Ganeri, Jonardon. 2001. *Philosophy in Classical India: The Proper Work of Reason*. London/New York: Routledge.
Gopal, Sarvepalli. 1989. *Radhakrishnan: A Biography*. New Delhi: Oxford University Press.
Griffiths, Paul and Delmas Lewis. 1983. On Grading Religions: Seeking Truth, and Being Nice to People – A Reply to Professor Hick. *Religious Studies* 19: 75–80.
Halbfass, Wilhelm. 1985. India and the Comparative Method. *Philosophy East and West* 35: 3–15.
Halbfass, Wilhelm. 1988. *India and Europe* Albany, NY: State University of New York Press.
Hick, John. 1968. Theology and Verification. In *Religious Language and the Problem of Religious Knowledge*, edited by R. E. Santomi. Bloomington, IN: Indiana University Press.
Hick, John. 1983. *The Philosophy of Religion*. Third edition. Englewood Cliffs, NJ: Prentice Hall.
Inden, Ronald B. 1990. *Imagining India*. Cambridge, MA: Blackwell.
Kessler, Garry E. (Ed.). 1999. *Philosophy of Religion: Toward a Global Perspective*. Belmont, CA: Wadsworth Press.
Krishna, Daya. 1997. *Indian Philosophy: A New Approach*. Delhi: Satguru.
Larson, Gerald J. and Eliot Deutsch. 1988. *Interpreting Across Boundaries: News Essays in Comparative Philosophy*. Princeton, NJ: Princeton University Press.
Levine, Michael P. 1997. Ninian Smart on the Philosophy of Worldviews. *Sophia* 36: 11–23.
Lopez, Donald. 1995. *Curators of the Buddha: The Study of Buddhism Under Colonialism*. Chicago, IL: University of Chicago Press.
MacIntyre, Alasdair. 1999. Is Understanding Religion Compatible with Believing? In *The Insider/Outsider Problem in the Study of Religion*, edited by R. T. McCutcheon. London/New York: Cassell.
Maddock, Kenneth. 1987a. All-Father. In *The Encyclopedia of Religion*, edited by M. Eliade et al., vol. 1, pp. 212–213. New York: MacMillan.
Maddock, Kenneth. 1987b. Australian Religions: A History of Study. In *The Encyclopedia of Religion*, edited by M. Eliade et al., vol. 1, pp. 566–570. New York: MacMillan.
Matilal, Bimal Krishna. 2002. Collected Papers. 2 volumes. Edited by J. Ganeri. New York: Oxford University Press.
Mehta, J. L. 1985. *India and the West: The Problem of Understanding – Selected Essays of J. L. Mehta*. Cambridge, MA: Center for the Study of World Religions.
Mehta, J. L. 1992. *J. L. Mehta on Heidegger, Hermeneutics and Indian Tradition*, edited by W. Jackson. Leiden: E. J. Brill.
Mistry, Freny. 1981. *Nietzsche and Buddhism: Prolegomenon to a Comparative Study*. New York/Bern: Walter de Gruyter.
Mitchell, J. Murray. 1885. *Hinduism Past and Present*. London: The Religious Tract Society.
Mohanty, J. N. 1994. *Essays on Indian Philosophy: Traditional and Modern*, edited by P. Bilimoria. Delhi: Oxford University Press. Reprinted 2002.
Monk, Ray. 1991. *Ludwig Wittgenstein: The Duty of Genius*. New York: Penguin.
Morphy, Howard, et al. (Eds.). 1989. *Religion in Aboriginal Australia: An Anthology*. Brisbane: University of Queensland Press.
Nelson, Mark T. 1996. Who Are the Best Judges of Theistic Arguments? *Sophia* 35. pp. 1–12.
Nielsen, Kai. 1994. Perceiving God. In *Faith, Scepticism and Personal Identity: Essays in Honor of Terence Penelhum*, edited by J. J. MacIntosh and H. A. Meynell. Calgary: University of Calgary Press.
Panikkar, Raimundo. 1980. Aporias of Comparative Philosophy of Religion. *Man and the World* 13: 357–383.
Phillips, D. Z. 1986. *Belief, Change and Forms of Life*. London: Macmillan.
Pollock, Sheldon. 1990. Deep Orientalism: Notes on Sanskrit and Power Beyond the Raj. *Asian Studies* 1990: 94.

Prakash, Gyan. 1990. Writing Post-Orientalist Histories of the Third World: Perspectives from Indian Historiography. *Comparative Studies in Society and History* 32 (1): 383–408.

Raychaudhuri, Tapan. 1995. Transformation of Religious Sensibilities in Nineteenth Century Bengal. Surendra Paul Lecture, Calcutta Ramakrishnan Institute for Culture. Unpublished.

Said, Edward. 1978. *Orientalism*. London: Penguin.

Said, Edward. 1985. *The Text, the World, and the Critic*. Cambridge, MA: Harvard University Press.

Said, Edward W. 1993. *Culture and Imperialism*. NY: Alfred A. Knopf, Inc.

Santoni, Ronald E. (Ed.). 1968. *Religious Language and the Problem of Religious Knowledge*. Indianapolis, IN: Indiana University Press.

Sarkar, Sumit. 1975. Rammohun Roy and the Break with the Past. In *Rammohun Roy and the Process of Modernization in India*, edited by V. C. Joshi, pp. 46–68. Delhi: Vikas.

Schwab, Raymond. 1984. *The Oriental Renaissance: Europe's Recovery of India and the East, 1680–1880*, translated by G. Patterson-Black et al. New York: Columbia University Press.

Sharma, Arvind. 1995. *The Philosophy of Religions and Advaita Vedānta: A Comparative Study of Religions and Reason*. University Park: Pennsylvania State University Press.

Singhal, D. P. 1969. *India and World Civilization*, 2 volumes. Delhi: Rupa.

Smart, Ninian. 1995. The Philosophy of Worldviews, or the Philosophy of Religion Transformed. In *Religious Pluralism and Truth: Essays on the Cross-Cultural Philosophy of Religion*, edited by T. Dean. Albany, NY: State University of New York Press.

Smart, Ninian. 1997. Does the Philosophy of Religion Rest on Two Mistakes? *Sophia* 36: 1–10.

Solomon, Robert C. 1995. Some Notes on Emotion, "East" and "West." *Philosophy East and West* 45: 171–202.

Spivak, Gayatri Chakravorty. 1988a. Can the Subaltern Speak? In *Marxism and the Interpretation of Culture*, edited by C. Nelson and L. Grossberg. Urbana, IL/Chicago, IL: University Press of Illinois. Originally published in *Wedge*, Winter/Spring 1985, pp. 120–130.

Spivak, Gayatri Chakravorty. 1988b. *In Other Worlds: Essays in Cultural Politics*. New York: Methuen.

Spivak, Gayatri Chakravorty. 1999. *A Critique of Postcolonial Reason: Towards a History of the Vanishing Present*. Cambridge, MA: Harvard University Press.

Thapar, Romila. 1993. *Interpreting Early India*. Delhi: Oxford University Press.

Tooley, Michael. 1977. John Hick and the Concept of Eschatological Verification. *Religious Studies* 12: 177–199.

Tuck, Andrew P. 1990. *Comparative Philosophy and the Philosophy of Scholarship on the Western Interpretation of Nāgārjuna*. New York: Oxford University Press.

Vattanky, John. 1984. *Gaṅgeśa's Philosophy of God*. Adyar: Adyar Library and Research Centre.

Vattanky, John. 2000. Is Theism Central to Nyāya? *Indian Philosophical Quarterly* 27: 411–420.

Wisdom, John. 1968. Gods. In *Religious Language and the Problem of Religious Knowledge*, edited by R. E. Santoni, pp. 295–314. Indianapolis, IN: Indiana University Press.

Zaehner, R.C. 1957. *Mysticism Sacred and Profane: An Inquiry into Some Varieties of Praeternatural Experience*. Oxford: Oxford University Press.

Zupko, Jack, 2002. Marilyn McCord Adams: Horrendous Evils and the Goodness of God, *Sophia*, Volume 41.1, May, pp. 135–138.

Philosophy of Religion as Border Control: Globalization and the Decolonization of the "Love of Wisdom" (*philosophia*)

Richard King

Abstract Mainstream philosophy of religion, particularly in its Anglo-American variant but also in the Continental tradition, is preoccupied by parochial questions that derive from its heritage in liberal Protestantism on the one hand, and the secular Enlightenment on the other. Yet the parochialism is masked by the material and intellectual history of colonial domination that permits "Western" philosophers to pose their questions as ostensibly universal questions asked *of* religion *by* philosophy. The process of globalization, however, recalls philosophy from such preoccupation with "border control" to be the loving pursuit of wisdom. The author examines how modern philosophy of religion, including some of the contributions of postcolonial theory, has, by classifying them as religions, subalternized many of the world's wisdom traditions. He concludes by advocating a renewed and more expansive form of philosophy of religion as loving pursuit of wisdom, nourished by a clearer self-critical grasp of its historic situation and limitations.

> Modernity produced both the illusion of the end of religion and the birth of the religious proper. Before modernity there was no religion, just as there was no "society". The fact is that modernity could not have come into being without the invention of religion. (Mendieta 2001: 46)
>
> Through the idea of religion, the West continuously speaks of itself to itself, even when it speaks of others. For when it does so, it is implicitly in relation to the perfected model that it thinks itself to be. This is narcissistic objectification. (Dubuisson 2003: 95)

The modern academic field of study known as the philosophy of religion is founded upon a central epistemological distinction – namely the cognitive separation of something readily identifiable as "philosophy" from that which it deems to examine, in this case "the religious". Mainstream philosophy of religion, particularly in an Anglo-American context, has been moulded by two key moments in Northern European history – the Protestant Reformation on the one hand and the separation of Church and State that led to the rise of the modern secular nation-state on the other. Consequently, the field continues to be dominated by a set of questions that derive from the concerns of liberal Protestant theology on the one hand, and by the anti-clerical and secular humanist philosophers of the Enlightenment on the other. Philosophy, as the love of wisdom, however, finds itself at a new juncture in its history, precipitated by the process of globalization. This is likely to have a profound long-term effect upon the shape and form of what counts as "wisdom" in this rapidly shifting context.

In the twentieth-century, philosophy of religion as a field of study has performed a key role in maintaining a link, however marginal, between philosophy as a modern secularized discipline and its longer history of engagement with a wide range of theological and metaphysical questions. Located uneasily between a hegemonic vision of modernity as secular, deriving from the European Enlightenment, and a much longer history of engagement by philosophers with the metaphysical preoccupations of the Hellenistic and Christian intellectual traditions, "philosophy of religion" as a field has functioned as a key mediator between modern secularized philosophical debates and the broader concerns of western philosophy's cultural heritage. Shifts in European culture and society have resulted in the discipline of modern philosophy generally turning away from what its modern practitioners have tended to see as the old "religious" or "metaphysical" questions of the past. Broadly speaking, in Anglo-American intellectual circles this has tended to involve re-modelling philosophy on one particular strand of its historical remit, namely, the questions and methods associated with "natural philosophy" – the "natural sciences". There has also been what has been called a "linguistic turn" in the discipline linked to the rise of what has become known as "Analytic Philosophy" – best exemplified in the twentieth-century by philosophers such as Bertrand Russell, the early Wittgenstein, Donald Davidson and Willard V. O. Quine. The emphasis within this "strand" of modern western philosophical practice has been upon the achievement of technical and definitional precision, an emphasis upon logical consistency and attention to linguistic analysis as a way of "moving forward" in solving philosophical problems.

In contrast to this, one often finds reference to a rival European phenomenon – most often called "Continental Philosophy," whose primary twentieth-century examples include Martin Heidegger, Jean-François Lyotard, Jacques Derrida, Michel Foucault, Gilles Deleuze and Jean Baudrillard. Here, and again I beg the reader's forgiveness for painting a picture with a very broad brush, the emphasis upon linguistic and analytic precision is generally eschewed in favour of a (no less rigorous) attention to deferred meanings, underlying sub-texts, and intellectual aporias within systems of thought, liberally sprinkled with a general scepticism about the role of instrumental rationality and logic as a means of discovering universal truths about reality. Both "genres" or "traditions" of modern western philosophy have had a tendency to speak across rather than to each other and to indulge in caricature. What they both share in common, generally speaking, however, is an indebtedness to a disenchanted and secularized vision of the world, grounded in the humanistic philosophies of the Enlightenment. This "secularist" tinge to modern philosophical debate in the West persists despite claims that there has been a "turn to the religious" in the late twentieth-century on the part of some key exemplars of these traditions.

Philosophy as a discipline and philosophy of religion as a field within that discipline find themselves at a new juncture at the beginning of the twenty-first century, precipitated by the end of European colonialism on the one hand, and the complex series of processes associated with the term "globalization" on the other. How philosophers respond to this new set of challenges will have a significant impact upon the way in which "the loving pursuit of wisdom" (*philosophia*) will be carried out in the future.

The End of European Colonialism and the Crisis of Western Philosophy

The second half of the twentieth-century has seen the era of European (though not necessarily western) domination of the world come to an end. As European impe-rialism and direct rule from overseas has ended, so has the myth that European world-views and epistemologies constitute the normative way of understanding the world. In the early period of European colonial exploration the primary ideological rationale for expanding European power and influence was the spread of the truth of the Christian gospel. This entered into a complex and sometimes antagonistic relationship with a new ideological configuration in the seventeenth and eighteenth centuries with the rise of "the Enlightenment project". The master narrative that emerged from this cultural shift continued to see European ideas and values as supreme and universal in import. Emphasis shifted in some circles away from the spread of Christianity per se as a rationale for colonial rule, and increasingly focused instead upon Europe as the apex of "civilization" modernity and the tools for estab-lishing "freedom" for the individual. In an age of globalization, this Eurocentric view of the world is now increasingly being seen for what it is – namely one of a number of competing cultural constructions of reality. In other words, in a world more conscious than ever before of the multicultural and post-colonial demands upon Occidental claims to universal truth, the provinciality of Euro-American ways of understanding the world is being highlighted with reference to the historical specificity of their origins and provenance.

This questioning of European and more generally western self-confidence is going on from a number of directions. Beyond the borders and on the margins we have seen the growth of a variety of interest groups, communities, movements, nation-states and social trends in the former colonies that are directly challenging what they see as the injustices of recent colonial history and ongoing examples of western cultural hubris. Mass immigration throughout the twentieth century, and again propelled by the destabilizing forces of an economically-driven model of globalization continue to have an impact upon European and American cultural sensibilities. As David Loy (2003: 14) suggests:

> The problem of immigration into Western societies, for example, is usually understood in terms of economics (cheap labor, competition for jobs), crime and occasionally differences in "lifestyle." This overlooks another dimension that in the long run may be more important: the anxiety produced when different worldviews are living next to each other.

There has also been a loss of self-confidence and guilt-ridden hand-wringing amongst "homegrown" westerners. After two world wars, the Holocaust, fears about nuclear devastation, concerns about genetic engineering and the damage being doing to the environment, many westerners have themselves become skeptical about some of the master narratives of their own culture. This two pronged assault – from outside the borders of the West (increasingly virtual in nature) and from within – has created fissures in the Enlightenment project of modernity in the latter half of the twentieth-century.

At an intellectual level this is no more evident than in the development of poststructuralist and so-called "postmodernist" trends and theories in the western academy. Such intellectual trends have directly questioned the universalist pretensions of Enlightenment models of rationality and modernity. In this way, European thinkers in the "continental philosophical tradition" such as Jacques Derrida and Michel Foucault represent the post-1968 intellectuals trying to make sense of the world at precisely the point in history when European colonialism was seen to have ended. In many ways, such thinkers can be seen as philosophers of the "death of Europe," or at least harbingers of its de-centering as the putative driving force of world history. Through their powerful theoretical works, Derrida and Foucault challenged the normativity of western claims to uncover universal truths, without being able to move beyond that frame themselves. In an interview with a Zen roshi during a visit to Japan in 1978, Michel Foucault was asked if he thought that "Eastern thought" might provide a way out of the contemporary crisis of Western thought. Foucault's reply is interesting, particularly since it opens up avenues of exploration that he himself did not follow. He remarks:

> It is true, European thought finds itself at a turning point. This turning point, on an historical scale, is nothing other than the end of imperialism. The crisis of Western thought is identical to the end of imperialism. The crisis has produced no supreme philosopher who excels in signifying that crisis.... For it is the end of the era of Western philosophy. Thus, if philosophy of the future exists, it must be born outside of Europe or equally born in consequence of meetings and impacts between Europe and non-Europe. (Carrette 1999: 113)

Foucault's knowledge of Asian religions and philosophies was very limited, as his discussion of Zen Buddhism in his 1978 Japanese interview demonstrates. However, what Foucault does here is explicitly link the dominance of European modes of thought to the might of European imperial power. A key factor in being able to make the claim that "western philosophy" constituted philosophy in toto was (and is) the sheer military, political and cultural dominance of Europe in the last few centuries of world history. The last 500 years of European colonialism enabled a whole network of European categories, ideas and paradigms to appear more universal and normative than they might otherwise have seemed. The local history and categories of one particular part of the world, projected onto others in the quest for a "Universal History", has tended, as Dipesh Chakrabarty (2000) has suggested, to place Europe and European civilization at its center. The end of this sustained period of overt imperial rule by European nations has slowly begun to impact upon debates about what counts as "philosophy," theory and indeed human wisdom in general.

More recently, the task of preserving Occidental (or more generally one might say Northern Hemisphere) supremacy in the world has been maintained by the social, political and economic might of the United States of America. This has been mostly achieved through new forms of "virtual colonialism" that do not necessitate direct political rule, but operate instead through the global spread of capitalism and the increasing power of transnational corporations to effect, even transform local societies and economies. Some theorists, such as Michael Hardt and Antonio Negri (2000), argue that this represents a new form of stateless sovereignty, dominated by the free transfer of Capital across borders. The deterrorialized and de-centred nature of "Empire," they suggest, make it all but impossible to locate within or be controlled by specific nation-states. The United States of America may be the sole superpower at the beginning of the twenty-first century, but it is clear that China and India (for example) are likely to exert considerably more socio-economic influence as the century progresses. How this will affect what counts as "wisdom" and its loving pursuit (*philosophia*) in the future one can only speculate. It is already clear, however, that the unhinging of the economic from the social that is occurring under neoliberal forms of economic globalization, is already having a profound effect upon our understanding of ancient wisdom traditions. Such "virtual" forms of colonialism transform indigenous wisdom traditions (popularly understood as "the world's religions") into individually customized "spiritualities" that can be consumed without the need for self-transformation (see Carrette and King 2004). Nevertheless, the emergence of neoliberal capitalism as the dominant (and economically driven) model of globalization, has also opened up spaces of resistance based upon a cosmopolitan engagement between "local" knowledge and wisdom-traditions.

Debates about globalization – arguably the philosophical issue of our era, colonialism and the impact of neoliberal forms of capitalism and consumerism upon human culture and identity remain conspicuously absent from mainstream philosophical debates. This deafening silence is strange given the apparent interest of philosophers in fundamental questions about ethics, personal identity, the nature of wisdom and, following Pierre Hadot's construction of the subject, "the pursuit of an authentic life". Similarly, challenges to the equating of "western philosophy" with philosophy in toto has rarely occurred amongst those professionally employed as philosophers in the academy. The claim to be motivated by a "love of wisdom," however, rings rather hollow when all that is ever discussed is framed by the epistemological paradigms and long-standing conversations of European intellectual history. Robert Bernasconi (1997: 224–225) describes this situation as philosophy's "paradoxical parochialism":

> One cannot understand why there has never been a serious debate about the origin of philosophy, unless one understands what is at stake in the question ... [Even] if the history of the discipline and the conception of the discipline that history supports is not racist in design, the question must still be addressed as to whether it is racist in its effects. Whole peoples experience themselves as excluded, in part because of the systematic diminishment of the achievements of their group. Philosophers almost everywhere are implicated. The problem must be addressed not just in research, but also at the institutional level in each and every department.

I have discussed many of the issues related to the exclusion of non-western intellectual thought (specifically Hindu and Buddhist thought) from the category of philosophy elsewhere (see King 1999b) and do not intend to rehearse that discussion here. However, it is worth pausing to reflect upon the parochialism that Bernasconi highlights here because it is philosophy, perhaps more than any other academic discipline in the West, that has been the primary standard bearer for western intellectual claims to be interested in the detached pursuit of truth. Philosophy is, after all, supposed to be the love of wisdom (*philosophia*) for its own sake and on its own terms, regardless of its cultural location. With the erosion of the "sacred canopy" of colonial rule that allowed the West to believe that it represented universal truth, western philosophers are now left exposed to their own rhetorical claims to be concerned with the pursuit of wisdom wherever it may have originated. In such a context, engagement with the intellectual traditions of the non-western world has become the single most important task for the philosopher in an age of globalization. Such a task, however, requires a willingness to provide a critical interrogation of the secularist and "post-Christian" limits of modern western philosophy. Challenging the narrowly secular and Eurocentric remit of contemporary philosophical debates, therefore, would seem to be a necessary step in the decolonization of philosophy.

Prima facie, "philosophy of religion" as a field would seem to be well placed to offer such a corrective to the Eurocentric horizons of western philosophy not only because of its potential openness to "other cultures" but also because of its unique place as a point of contact to the Christian legacy upon which much of contemporary western philosophical debate rests. Thus, in recent decades we have seen a few valiant attempts to move philosophy of religion into a multi-cultural or "world religions" space. This intellectual shift has been made partly in response to changes in the socio-political context which have proven amenable to such work being carried out. These include the growth of significant diaspora communities within western nations and shifts in academic institutions, such as the emergence of departments of Religious Studies (as opposed to traditional departments of Theology) seeking to examine a variety of "world religious traditions".

The multicultural, comparativist or multi-religious approach is often motivated by a liberal-minded desire to consider a wider range of viewpoints and cultures as pertinent to the remit of philosophical discussion. This, of course, is a laudable enterprise in many respects. However, before we all pat ourselves on the back for being so cosmopolitan and "enlightened", I wish to offer what may turn out to be a devastating caveat in terms of the longer-term prospects for "the philosophy of religion" as a legitimate field of study. In my view, the multi-religious or comparativist turn within the philosophy of religion will only achieve the desired effect of facilitating greater cross-cultural engagement if the basic terms and paradigms of its own discourse – namely the terms "philosophy" and "religion" and their relationship – are themselves subjected to critical and historical interrogation. What is the nature of the "of" in the "philosophy of religion"? Is it simply the application of the western philosophical gaze to an object called "religion"? Does it crumble under the weight of multicultural and postmodern relativism into a variety of isolationist philosophies deriving from the various "religions"? Is "philosophy of religion" the space for an intercultural engagement between western and non-western worldviews? What would the theoretical grounds for such a project be? Whose categories should one use in exploring such cross-cultural engagement?

These questions are challenging, but not as insoluble as a fatalistic appeal to cultural relativism might suggest. In an age of globalization, however, we should not expect a single answer to such questions, but rather considerable local and "glocal" responses. Failure to engage in this critical and cross-cultural enterprise, however, would seem to leave "the philosophy of religion" in its ancillary role as the disciplinary equivalent of immigration police – allowing foreign discourses and knowledge to enter the debate but only in the terms dictated by the authorities (in this case the dominant discourses of mainstream western philosophy).

The Paradoxical Parochialism of "Postcolonial Theory"

What help can philosophers seeking to respond to the challenge of globalization hope to gain from similarly inclined intellectual developments within the Academy? The end of overt European imperial rule and its political justification has also led to the development of postcolonial criticism and colonial discourse analysis as a growing intellectual trend within the western academy. "Post-colonial criticism," of course can mean different things to different people, ranging from a challenge to Eurocentrism (both from outside and within the western academy) to resistance to the totalizing conceptualization of history in terms of "the nation" or of traditional Marxist accounts of universal class-struggle (King 1999a: 214; Dayal 1996: 133–134). As Arif Dirlik (1994) has pointed out, much of this work is conceived within the western academic metropole and according to its own intellectual paradigms and canonical thinkers. Many of the key writers in this field are diaspora intellectuals from the two thirds world (e.g. Spivak, Bhabha, Chakrabarty), trained in the western academy and now based in the West. Indeed, there has been a marked dependence of much postcolonial criticism in the last 20 years on European poststructuralists such as Foucault and Derrida. This is especially so in the case of specialists in India and South Asia. There are a number of reasons for this.

Firstly, as argued above, poststructuralist thought provides an array of tools and concepts that have proven useful in challenging the universalist pretensions of western intellectual traditions. Secondly, such approaches have been increasingly in vogue in the western academic world – providing a way to bring postcolonial issues and concerns to the largely Eurocentric interests of mainstream academic debates. Thirdly, for some postcolonial critics poststructuralism has been seen as a way of reforming or even transcending some of the limitations of traditional (Eurocentric) Marxist analysis. The interest of many postcolonial writers within the Humanities in Gramsci's reading of Marx is another case in point here, since Gramsci's work represents a challenge to a narrowly economistic reading of Marx in favour of an appreciation of culture as a key driving force within human history.

Finally, for those influenced by the South Asianist strand of postcolonial criticism (exemplified by Spivak, Bhabha and the South Asian Subalternist historians), the post-structuralist critique of the European Enlightenment has a particular resonance, since it was precisely under the aegis of the eighteenth and nineteenth-century Enlightenment discourse of "civilizing the rest of the world" that the key transformation of South Asian societies and identities occurred. This point is aptly made by Mignolo (2000) who suggests that the enormous interest shown in poststructuralist thinkers such as Foucault and Derrida amongst South Asian postcolonial theorists is itself bound up with the impact of the European Enlightenment upon the colonial transformation of subjectivity in eighteenth and nineteenth-century South Asia. Mignolo, following the work of the Argentinian philosopher and liberation theologian Enrique Dussel (see for instance, Dussel 1996, 2001), refers to this as "the second stage of modernity" – denoting the eighteenth-century "Enlightenment" grounded in Northern Europe and its colonial exportation to Asia. For "Latin American" thinkers such as Dussel and Mignolo, however, the key stage to unravel in their own postcolonial projects is what they call "the first stage of modernity," conceptually and historically located in the sixteenth-century imperial project, initiated by Spain, to convert the heathens of "the New World" to Christianity. This project is to be distinguished (despite obvious continuities and overlaps) from the project of modernity initiated by the Northern European states, premised as it was upon the emergence of what was called "the Enlightenment" and the perceived need to universalize the fundamental values and principles of modern civilization to the colonies of Asia. It is not surprising then to find contemporary South Asian theorists attempting to interrogate this particular legacy with reference to the Enlightenment-centred critiques of thinkers such as Derrida, Foucault, and Gadamer.

One consequence of the interest in poststructuralist theory amongst the South Asianists has been that much of what passes for postcolonial theory today still remains dominated by categories and paradigms that are overwhelmingly derivative of European intellectual history. Postcolonial criticism, it seems, is in danger of remaining, like the theories that it seeks to challenge, a "derivative discourse". This is no more apparent than in the comparative lack of attention that has been paid to non-western systems of thought as a source for postcolonial theorizing. However, as Mignolo (2000: 9) has argued, "alternatives to modern epistemology can hardly come only from modern (western) epistemology itself."

For a great number of postcolonial theorists, many of whom are Marxist or "post-Marxist" in orientation, any perceived turn to indigenous "religiosity" or "tradition" as a source for the articulation of difference from western intellectual paradigms is a step too far. Such hesitancy, however, reflects an insufficiently rigorous interrogation of the Eurocentric inheritance that frames non-western intellectual traditions as essentially "religious" in nature. The central dichotomy that privileges Occidental conceptions of modernity is the dichotomy between the modern and the traditional. Any attempt to displace the pretensions of western conceptions of modernity, therefore, must interrogate the modernist and "secularist" assumptions that precondition us "moderns" in our engagement with all so-called "pre-modern" cultural traditions. Overcoming the polarization of "modernity" and "tradition" and the assumption that to offer a critique of one is to side uncritically with the other, is an important step in resisting not only western colonialism but also contemporary forms of atavistic indigenism (such as Hindutva and radical Islamism) which ride on the back of the postcolonial critique of the West. In an age of "glocalization" such projects represent a "critical cosmopolitanism" (Walter Mignolo) that, in its engagement with the diversity of human cultural expression, is at the same time a "critical traditionalism" (Ashis Nandy). It remains important to challenge the "global designs" of contemporary ethnocentrist movements not only by highlighting their own historical specificity but also by maintaining a commitment to some form of critical cosmopolitanism. This, however, requires an openness to "tradition" that engages indigenist movements on what they consider to be their own ground. Such a project as I understand it is not an attempt to recapture some distant utopian past that never existed (the indigenist goal), nor an attempt to homogenize cultural expression in the name of modernity, but rather an attempt to rethink postcolonial futures by paying attention to the rich diversity of traditions that have contributed to creating the present. It is to conceive, as the Zapatistas have put it, of "One World with Many Worlds Within It."

Nevertheless, challenging the polarization of modernity and tradition is insufficient if it does not also include critical engagement with the politics of representation involved in the translation of (non-western) traditions, through the category of "religion," into the lingua franca of "Universal History". This translation process remains an under-theorized aspect of both contemporary postcolonial thought and contemporary debates within philosophy and "the philosophy of religion" despite the interest of many of its modern practitioners in the workings of language.

The omission of an extensive engagement with the wisdom traditions of the non-western world amongst most postcolonial critics and theorists is even more remarkable, particularly when one realizes that, since the nineteenth-century, the main site for the negotiation and struggle to express difference from the colonial center has been through those movements, forms of life and traditions classified by the West as "religions". The trope of the modern, secular and liberal West in contrast to a more religious, spiritual and/or superstitious "non-west" has been a key feature in the construction of the West's sense of its own modernity. As the main point of entry into an engagement with western power, the category of "religion", therefore, has functioned as the main site of resistance to western models of modernity and civilization. Thus, the concept of "religion" has served as the conceptual location – the point of translation – of virtually all attempts to articulate an alternative to western Christian and secular (that is, post-Christian) models of what it is to be modern. Moreover, as we are all increasingly becoming aware in a post-Soviet and post-9–11 world, resistance to Euro-American models of modernity is finding its most potent articulations when it appeals to traditions and collectivities that are framed in western circles by the notion of the religious.

Translating Wisdom Traditions as "Religions" – The Price of Crossing the Border

An increasing number of writers (Smith 1962; Asad, 1993; McCutcheon 1997; Fitzgerald 2000; Balagangadhara 1994; Dubuisson 1998 [English translation, 2003], 2004; King 1999a, 2004; Peterson and Walhof 2002; Mandair 2003; Sharma 2004) have questioned the appropriateness of the concept of "religion" as a useful cross-cultural category on the grounds that it is the specific product of the cultural and political history of the west. The term reflects the localized, ideological imprints of western Christian and Enlightenment constructions of the subject-matter (King 1999a).

The category of "religion," of course, has almost universal currency in the con-temporary world. The universalization of the term almost renders transparent the translation process involved in its representation of diverse cultural forms and prac-tices. It is important to realize, however, that to use the term "religion" uncritically is already to re-present non-western traditions according to a culturally specific lin-guistic and conceptual scheme. The introduction of non-western traditions into the West as "religions" interpellates them into a long-standing, fractious and, highly localized debate that frames the parameters of articulation before such traditions have a chance to speak. For some thinkers, such as Daniel Dubuisson, the category of religion has itself come to function as the central pillar in the creation and sustenance of the identity of the West:

> Created by the West, enshrined in Western epistemology, and central to its identity, the concept of religion eventually came to be the core of the Western worldview. Since this notion is intrinsically linked to all the philosophies, complementary or competing, that have been invented in the West, the West cannot, at the risk of its own disintegration, do without it, because these global conceptions would then decompose into scattered or jux-taposed fragments. ... Would not abandoning the idea of religion be the equivalent for Western thought of abdicating part of its intellectual hegemony over the world? (Dubuisson 2003: 94)

Non-western movements and traditions that offer cultural resistance to western modes of life are translated into a *Latinized* frame of reference when they are represented in mainstream western culture. As Derrida puts it: "the world today speaks Latin (most often via Anglo-American) when it authorizes itself in the *name* of *religion.*" (Derrida 2000: 64). The process whereby expressions of cultural dif-ference become translated as "religions" in the western imagination is labelled by Derrida *mondialatinisation* (or in "Anglo-American" – *"globalatinization".*) This process of cultural translation is the epistemological equivalent of immigration and border control. It is the point at which "foreign" wisdom traditions become *natu-ralized* as "religions" and it is on these terms that such worldviews and forms of life are allowed to enter the mainstream world of western intellectual debate. Phi-losophy, as the pre-eminent discipline associated with "rationality" and the pursuit of wisdom in the West, has had a key role to play as a kind of intellectual bor-der police or "Homeland Security" office, making sure that any foreigners crossing the border are properly classified as "religious" rather than "philosophical" (that is, in the "proper" western sense of the term). In effect, indigenous wisdom traditions of the non-western world are separated from their western counterparts at customs and forced to travel down the red channel. This is because, unlike western philosophies, they are believed to have "something to declare" – namely, their "religious," dogmatic or "tradition-bound" features which mark them out as culturally particular rather than universal. Before being allowed to enter the public space of western intellectual discourse, such systems of thought must either give up much of their foreign goods (that is, render themselves amenable to assimilation according to western intellectual paradigms), or enter as an *object of* rather than as a *subject engaged in* debate. Through this process of cultural and ideological segregation, African, Australian aboriginal, native American, Buddhist, Confucian, Daoist, Hindu, Islamic and Sikh traditions enter the public space of academic discussion but only once they have been purified of much of their "foreignness" or naturalized as "religions". Through this translation process, which has been going on for so long now that it is largely taken for granted, western philosophy remains insulated from contestation by knowledge-traditions that might otherwise challenge its pretensions to open-ended enquiry, universal application and the detached pursuit of wisdom. As Jay Garfield notes in his discussion of the separation of "eastern philosophy" (classified as "religious") from western philosophy (classified as "philosophy" proper), such a distinction frequently fails, even on its own terms, to maintain the cultural (that is, *geo-political*) segregation that it sets out to achieve:

> This distinction [between religious and philosophical] is supposed to deliver the result that St. Thomas Aquinas's *Summa Theologica*, Descartes's *Meditations*, including the proofs for the existence of God, and Leibnitz's discussion of theodicy are philosophical, while Dharmakirti's investigation of the structure of induction and the ontological status of universals, Tsong khapa's account of reference and meaning, and Nagarjuna's critique of essence and analysis of causal relation are religious. Anyone who has a passing familiarity with all of the relevant texts will agree that something has gone seriously wrong if this distinction is taken seriously. (Garfield 2002: 252)

Academic philosophers in the west tends to be fiercely protective of the boundaries between their own disciplinary identity and its "significant other" – namely those cultural traditions that they associate with "the religious". In their inability to see this as a *peculiarly* western way of dividing up the world, their orientation is as unreflective as it is Eurocentric. Similarly, in general terms, modern western philosophers show little interest in continuing many of the intellectual debates of their own European Christian heritage. Leave that to the theologians. What is rarely recognized, however, is the extent to which western philosophical debates remain deeply soaked in the Christian history from which they arose. Even, or perhaps one might say *especially*, those who take an avowedly atheistic stance, seem peculiarly unaware of the saturation of their theories in a Christian (or, if you prefer, "post-Christian") view of the world.

The overarching secularism and eurocentrism of much of modern philosophy means that "philosophy of religion" as a specific field within philosophy has been generally devalued and given less and less institutional support, particularly in avowedly "secular" academic institutions. Let me illustrate this point with a personal anecdote on this topic. For many years I was located in a department of Religious Studies at the University of Stirling in Scotland. Religious Studies shared secretarial staff and a departmental office with the Philosophy department and had done so for many years. This reflected the usual kind of local, institutional arrangements that one would find in any university around the world. Historically, it also represented the fact that Religious Studies at Stirling University had emerged in the early 1970s as a sub-group within Philosophy that subsequently established its own autonomy. I remember my surprise when a relatively new member of the Philosophy department expressed his incredulity at the arrangement, for "what did philosophy and religion have to do with each other?" What surprised me most was not the attitude of my colleague across the corridor (a common prejudice I fear amongst Anglo-Saxon philosophers) but rather the historical myopia it represented. In what sense, I wondered, could one make sense of "western philosophy" as a tradition of intellectual discussions without appreciating the peculiarly Christian imprint upon its central debates, paradigms and fundamental questions.

If not underplayed as significant in the history of western philosophy, philosophy of religion as a field is sometimes viewed suspiciously because of its tendency to hover around the shadowy borders between philosophy, theology and religious studies. As such, contemporary philosophers of religion with an interest in exploring the global heritage of intellectual thought tend to be caught somewhere between the devil and the deep blue sea. Despite noble attempts to extend the range of philosophical debates beyond the limits of the western intellectual world, comparative or cross-cultural approaches to the philosophy of religion are in danger of acting as a handmaiden to the western colonial project so long as they fail to interrogate the geopolitics of knowledge involved in the construction of the category of philosophy itself (King 1999b; Maldonado-Torres 2000).

Sometimes comparative approaches to the philosophy of religion leave the impression that the issue is simply one of extending the range of religions to be examined philosophically. The same debates, forged in a context of a specifically western Christian history, are "adapted" to fit the other "world religions" which are thereby seen as correlates of Christianity (the "archetypal religion" in such debates.) Such approaches to the comparative philosophy of religion presume that we all know what counts as philosophy and what counts as religion, when in fact these very categories should themselves be the subject of the most rigorous critical interrogation from the outset. According to the liberal multiculturalist model, "foreign" wisdom traditions deserve to be examined, but not if this results in a reflexivity that might call the philosophical enterprise as understood in mainstream western circles into question. Simply put, "it wouldn't be philosophy anymore." The result of such resistance, however, is the perpetuation of a kind of intellectual apartheid. Indigenous wisdom traditions remain objects of study to which philosophy can be applied but are not allowed to enter (let alone change) the conversation or question its predetermined limits.

For comparative approaches to the philosophy of religion to avoid this trap, practitioners must be prepared to engage with non-western wisdom traditions in a way that will change the very nature of what counts as philosophy to occur.

Decolonizing philosophy as an act of reflexivity can never result in leaving the subject untransformed. As Raimundo Pannikar has argued:

[C]rosscultural studies do not mean to study other cultures, but to let other cultures impregnate the very study of the problem which by this very fact has already been transformed. In this sense a crosscultural Philosophy does not study other philosophies but changes the very perception of what philosophy is. (Pannikkar 1992: 236)

This cannot be done however, without paying attention to the role played by colonialism in allowed Europeans to present the local debates and categories of their own intellectual traditions as global in significance and application.

The Subalternization of Non-western Knowledges

Given some of the historical, cultural and political issues involved in searching for a way out of a Eurocentric framing of contemporary philosophical conversations, one might expect to find support for such an enterprise within the growing field of postcolonial studies. As we have seen, however, a peculiar lacuna in contemporary debates within "postcolonial theory" has been that, like mainstream debates within philosophy, it has generally failed to engage with the wisdom traditions of the non-western world. The subalternist approach within postcolonial studies, for instance, has been motivated by a concern not to erase the indigenous intentionalities of subaltern peoples and communities in terms of universalized categories such as class and nation. Since most forms of life on this planet continue to exhibit qualities that have been classified as "religious" by the West, any attempt to develop a subject-position that articulates the concerns of such groups must take these traditions, beliefs and practices seriously. "Religion" then simply cannot be ignored (even if we can question the usefulness of the term to render that which it deems to represent) if we are truly interested in moving beyond Eurocentric debates within both academic fields. This point has yet to sink in with any sense of depth in mainstream postcolonial circles. Some attempts have been made to engage with indigenous beliefs and practices (most notably Chakrabarty 2000) but, as Vinay Lal notes, Indian subalternist historians find it much easier to theorize about communalism than to reflect upon what they see as "religion and the supernatural." The result is that their accounts continue to juxtapose "faith" and "reason", "Enlightenment" and "superstition" (Lal 2003: 217–218).

As we have already indicated, the shunning of "the religious" is partly at least a reflection of the fact that so many postcolonial writers have been trained within the western academy and are either Marxist or "post-Marxist" by inclination. As such, there is a strong secularist suspicion of anything that smacks of "religion" and an understandable fear of appearing to align with authoritarian indigenist movements such as radical forms of Islamism and Hindutva. However, this abdication from the field of debate represents a failure to interrogate the European origins of the concept of religion and the secularist antipathy towards so-called "pre-modern" traditions.

Indeed, postcolonial theory necessitates a much greater engagement with the intellectual traditions of the non-western world if it is to carry its own intellectual project forward.

Subalternization and Resisting Cultural Essentialism

It should already be clear that pushing philosophy and the philosophy of religion in a postcolonial direction is not as straightforward as a simple turn to multiculturalism and a widening of the canon of thinkers. Developing a postcolonial perspective within philosophy and the philosophy of religion of course brings with it a number of problems, not least the question of representation itself. Whose agenda or tradition does one engage with when moving into a cross-cultural space? There is also the issue of the representation of the world-s intellectual traditions through the discourse of "the world religions". After all, the "-isms" that tend to be focused upon in most works on comparative philosophy of religion – Buddhism, Hinduism, Daoism etc. – are themselves already refracted through the lenses of western Orientalism (King 1999a: 67–69). Moreover, in so far as these "-isms" are upheld as "universalized systems of thought" (the so-called "world religions"), they also represent hegemonic discourses that have engaged in their own forms of internal colonialism "at home". With the "world religions" paradigm in question, are we left with no choice but to concede to the familiar quagmire of a self-defeating cultural relativism, paralyzed before we even start? Not quite, for as Uma Narayan has argued, what is required in cross-cultural philosophical debates is not an acceptance of cultural relativism but rather a concerted resistance to all forms of cultural essentialism, including those relativisms that privilege differences over similitudes:

> This critique of cultural essentialism would reject the idea that there is anything that can solidly and uncontroversially be defined as "Indian culture" or "African culture" or "Western culture" for that matter. It would proceed by challenging a "picture of the world" that some versions of cultural relativism assume to be true: that there are neat packages called "Different cultures" each of which is internally consistent and monolithic, and which disagrees only with "Other cultures". (Narayan 2000: 96)

The most striking modern example of cultural essentialism is perhaps Huntington's "clash of civilizations" thesis. Such a paradigm, however, is antithetical to the kind of nuanced "postcolonial" work that would be required in seeking to move beyond the "building block" mentality of a "world religions" approach to cross-cultural philosophical discussion. Much of the theoretical work for displacing the cultural essentialist approach has already been done by writers such as Edward Said, world systems theorists such as Immanuel Wallerstein, Anibal Quijano and Enrique Dussel and some of the work of the Latin American and South Asian subalternist writers. As we have seen, the subalternists have been particularly concerned with bringing the perspective of the subaltern or "non-elite" in pre- and post-colonial societies to the foreground of academic attention. Even here however there are significant problems in claiming to recapture the voice of the silenced, most famously captured in Spivak's question, "Can the Subaltern Speak?"

Moreover, what counts as "subaltern" in these contexts? The most interesting discussions of this term amongst postcolonial critics have paid attention to its context-relative nature (see King 1999a: 195, 251). As Florencia Mallon points out "no subaltern identity can be pure and transparent, most subalterns are both dominated and dominating subjects." From this perspective, something can be "subaltern" in one context and hegemonic in others (Mallon 1994: 1511). Such an approach obviates the tendency to represent "the subaltern" as some kind of homogeneous community devoid of internal hierarchies, hegemonies, and internal-politics of its own. In this sense, one can perhaps talk of subalternization as a process – denoting the flip-side of the development of hegemonies. If this is per-missible then one can also talk, in a specifically philosophical context, about what Walter Mignolo has called the *subalternization of knowledges*. It is in this sense, I would suggest, that a postcolonial perspective can bring important questions to bear upon philosophy and the philosophy of religions by drawing attention to their disciplinary role as a form of epistemological border control at the margins of "western civilization". Consideration of the embeddedness of knowledge claims in a field of power-relations, a stance firmly associated in western circles with the work of Foucault, but with a different resonance when considered in *geopolitical* and colonial terms, is crucial precisely because it challenges western (and western-ized) intellectuals to become more reflexive about their own complicity, whether tacit or overt, intentional or unintentional, in the subalternization or subordination of non-western traditions of knowledge.

In *Local Histories, Global Designs* (2000) Walter Mignolo, following a similar usage by the African philosopher Mudimbe, adopts the term "gnosis" as a catch-all term for the traditional wisdom traditions of non-western cultures that have been subject to "subalternization" by the last 500 years of European colonialism. As a scholar of "religion" I must admit to finding the use of the concept of "gnosis" prob-lematic here because it resonates too closely in my own mind with the historically specific network of movements and traditions known as Gnosticism, that prevailed in the Mediterranean and Near Eastern worlds of late Antiquity. Nevertheless, this caveat aside, Mignolo's use of the term "gnosis" is deliberately vague since what he means by it is any wisdom tradition or system of knowledge that has been "subalt-ernized" by the cultural domination of European modes of knowledge and therefore either silenced or relegated to the periphery of the modern/colonial world system. For Mignolo, the challenge to dominant (and Eurocentric) regimes of knowledge is to be met by transgressing the conditions of knowledge established by the modern notion of epistemology and through the exploration of knowledge systems and tra-ditions subalternized by European colonialism. There are two aspects to this: First, it involves challenging the culturally specific distinction between epistemology and hermeneutics, which Mignolo sees as the basis for the intellectual separation of the Humanities and the Sciences. At a more fundamental level, this also involves chal-lenging the central platform of epistemological discussion in Europe since Descartes and Kant – namely the cognitive separation of the knower from the known – of the

subject discipline (say in this case philosophy) and its object (those traditions translated as "the world religions"). To ask whether Buddhist thought, or African thought,
or Confucian or Daoist thought is philosophy or religion, is already to presuppose
a framework defined by the cultural horizons of post-Enlightenment secularism.
Arguably, as long as this particular form of intellectual apartheid is allowed to stand
uncontested, the wisdom traditions of non-western civilizations will continue to be
refused entry into the arena of philosophical debate, because they lack the apparent
secularized "purity" of their western counterparts.

Conclusion: W(h)ither the Comparative Philosophy of Religion?

What we are seeing in contemporary debates about multiculturalism and postcolonialism in philosophy and philosophy of religion circles is the intellectual
manifestation of a process that has taken on increasing force in the post-war era.
In the context of the end of European colonialism established regimes and disciplines of knowledge are being challenged and in some cases transformed by new
discourses in which previously subalternized knowledge traditions, once considered
only of interest as objects of study, become the very locus of enunciation themselves
(Mignolo 2000: 13). Mignolo calls this emergent phenomenon, "border gnosis"
since it occurs either at the exterior of established regimes of knowledge in the
modern western world (in the former colonized world), or represent elements of
forgotten or silenced knowledge from within western cultures that are also express-
ing resistance to subalternization. Feminist criticism and queer theory are perhaps
two cases of the latter.

The challenge of the geopolitics of knowledge for the philosophy of religion
is precisely to interrogate, to paraphrase Mignolo, the local histories that express
themselves as global designs. The question remains, however, whether "philosophy
of religion" is the most appropriate means of designating the field that might emerge
from an awareness of the coloniality of power and with the issue of the cultural segregation of "the West" from "the Rest" through the separation of "the philosophical"
from "the religious". Daniel Dubuisson, for instance, suggests that we discard our
obsession with the separation of "secular" and "religious" worldviews and consider
instead our object of study to be the variety of "cosmographic formations" through
which humans have made sense of their world (Dubuisson 1998 [English translation, 2003]). Such an approach, when applied to a subject such as "philosophy,"
would, in all likelihood, result in the demise of a specialized field such as "philosophy of religion," at least as traditionally understood, since the very distinction
between philosophy and religion (that keeps the field in existence but also renders
it a minority interest) would itself be rendered problematic. Such a move, however,
would seem to be necessary if one truly seeks to engender a form of intellectual
reflection that engages with the cross-cultural issues associated with an age of globalization. The philosophical analysis of Christian theology would no doubt continue
as a sub-field of "philosophy" as before. It is not clear however, whether "philosophy

of religion," so named, would continue to exist when conceived as a comparative or "border" enterprise, since the conceptual borders it is designed to preserve would already have been rendered problematic. Moreover, potentially the remit of such a reconstituted field would also be much wider. How are we to make sense of globalization as a phenomenon (perhaps the phenomenon) of our times? Why not consider the philosophical claims about human nature, reality and ethics that are embodied in contemporary neoliberal forms of capitalism as relevant to contemporary philosophical debates? If one wished to continue to interrogate and examine contemporary constructions of "the religious", why not consider the increasing impact of neoliberalism and consumerism as new forms of globalizing religions (Carrette and King 2004)?

For writers like Walter Mignolo the intellectual field emerging from the unravelling of the European colonial project would not be called Religious Studies or "philosophy of religion" but rather what he calls "Border gnoseology". This is a critical reflection upon knowledge production from both the interior borders of the modern/colonial world system and from its exterior borders (that is knowledge production related to the impact of the colonial encounter between cultures). Such approaches of course, do not involve some kind of wholesale rejection of the western intellectual heritage (as if one could erase the Christian theological assumptions or the Enlightenment from our own intellectual inventory), but it does open up the possibility of engagement with alternatives. As Mignolo himself notes, "the good news is that we have other choices (2000: 8) and as I have said elsewhere: "There are other ways of seeing the world than are dreamt of in post-Enlightenment Western philosophy" (King 1999a: 182). For such formulations and creative intellectual projects to emerge, however, requires those who consider themselves to be "philosophers" to pay attention to the issues associated with "globalization" and the "coloniality of difference" that continues to underlie the construction of their own disciplinary history and identity. It also requires that those interested in developing something called "postcolonial theory" engage more fully with the subalternized knowledge systems that have to date been largely excluded from theoretical consideration within the academy. This is not a call to "go native" but rather is a recognition of the need for a truly planetary approach to philosophical debate. This cannot occur, however, until there is a recognition of the provincial nature of Euro-American categories and paradigms and a willingness to explore what Enrique Dussel has called the "underside of modernity" – namely the global designs embodied in the European imperial project and the effect that this history has had upon our understanding of what counts as wisdom.

References

Asad, Talal. 1993. *Genealogies of Religion. Discipline and Reasons of Power in Christianity and Islam*. London: John Hopkins University Press.

Balagangadhara, S. N. 1994. *The 'Heathen in His Blindness...': Asia, the West and the Dynamic of Religion*. Leiden: Brill.

Bernasconi, Robert. 1997. Philosophy's Paradoxical Parochialism The Reinvention of Philosophy as Greek. In *Cultural Readings of Imperialism. Edward Said and the Gravity of History*, edited by Keith Ansell-Pearson, Benita Parry and Judith Squires, pp. 212–226. London: Lawrence and Wishart.

Carrette, Jeremy (Ed.). 1999. *Religion and Culture by Michel Foucault*. Manchester: Manchester University Press.

Carrette, Jeremy and Richard King. 2004. *Selling Spirituality. The Silent Takeover of Religion*. London/New York: Routledge.

Chakrabarty, Dipesh. 2000. *Provincializing Europe. Postcolonial Thought and Historical Difference*. Princeton, NJ: Princeton University Press.

Dayal, Samir. 1996. Postcolonialism's Possibilities: Sub-continental Diasporic Intervention. *Cultural Critique* 33: 113–149.

Derrida, Jacques. 2000. *Acts of Religion*, (edited with an Introduction by Gil Anidjar), London and New York: Routledge.

Dirlik, Arif. 1994. The Postcolonial Aura: Third World Criticism in the Age of Global Capitalism. *Critical Enquiry* 20: 328–356.

Dubuisson, Daniel. 1998. *L'Occident et la Religion. Mythes Science, et Idéologie*. Brussels: Complexe. (English translation: 2003. *The Western Construction of Religion*. John Hopkins University Press.)

Dubuisson, Daniel. 2004. *Les Sagesses de l'Homme: Bouddhisme – paganisme – spiritualité chrétienne*. Villeneuve D'Ascq: Septentrion Presses Universitaires.

Dussel, Enrique. 1996. *The Underside of Modernity: Apel, Ricoeur, Rorty, Taylor, and the Philosophy of Liberation*. Atlantic Highlands, NJ: Humanities Press.

Dussel, Enrique. 2001. 'The World System': Europe as 'Center' and Its 'Periphery' Beyond Eurocentrism. Translated by Eduardo Mendieta. In *Latin America and Postmodernity: A Contemporary Reader*, edited by Eduardo Mendieta and Pedro Lange-Churión, pp. 93–121. Atlantic Highlands, NJ: Humanities Press. Reprinted in Dussel, Enrique. 2003. *Beyond Philosophy. Ethics, History, Marxism and Liberation Theology*, edited by Eduardo Mendieta. Oxford: Rowman & Littlefield.

Fitzgerald, Timothy. 2000. *The Ideology of Religious Studies*. Oxford: Oxford University Press.

Garfield, Jay L. 2002. *Empty Words. Buddhist Philosophy and Cross-Cultural Interpretation*. Oxford: Oxford University Press.

Hardt, Michael and Antonio Negri. 2000. *Empire*. Cambridge, MA/London: Harvard University Press.

King, Richard. 1999a. *Orientalism and Religion. Postcolonial Theory, India and "the Mystic East"*. London/New York: Routledge.

King, Richard. 1999b. *Indian Philosophy. An Introduction to Hindu and Buddhist Thought*. Edinburgh: Edinburgh University Press; Washington, DC: Georgetown University Press.

King, Richard. 2004. Cartographies of the Imagination, Legacies of Colonialism: The Discourse of Religion and the Mapping of Indic Traditions. *Evam: Forum on Indian Representations* 3: 245–262.

Lal, Vinay. 2003. *The History of History. Politics and Scholarship in Modern India*. New Delhi: Oxford University Press.

Loy, David R. 2003. *The Great Awakening: A Buddhist Social Theory*. Somerville, MA: Wisdom.

McCutcheon, Russell T. 1997. *Manufacturing Religion: The Discourse on Sui Generis Religion and the Politics of Nostalgia*. New York: Oxford University Press.

Maldonado-Torres, Nelson. 2000. Latin American Thought and the Decolonization of Western Philosophy. *American Philosophical Association Newsletter on Hispanic/Latino Issues in Philosophy*, Fall 2000.

Mandair, Arvind-pal. 2003. What If 'Religio' Remained Untranslatable? In *Difference in Philosophy of Religion*, edited by Philip Goodchild, pp. 87–100. Burlington, VT: Ashgate.

Mallon, Florencia. 1994. The Promise and Dilemmas of Subaltern Studies: Perspectives from Latin American History. *American Historical Review* 99: 1491–1515.

Mendieta, Eduardo. 2001. Society's Religion: The Rise of Social Theory, Globalization, and the Invention of Religion. In *Religions/Globalizations. Theories and Cases*, edited by Dwight N. Hopkins, Lois Ann Lorentzen, Eduardo Mendieta and David Batstone, pp. 46–65. Durham, NC/London: Duke University Press.

Mignolo, Walter. 2000. *Local Histories. Global Designs. Coloniality, Subaltern Knowledges and Border Thinking*. Princeton, NJ: Princeton University Press.

Narayan, Uma. 2000. Essence of Culture and a Sense of History: A Feminist Critique of Cultural Essentialism. In *Decentering the Center. Philosophy for a Multicultural, Postcolonial and Feminist World*, edited by Uma Narayana and Sandra Harding, pp. 80–100. Indiana: Indiana University Press.

Pannikar, Raimundo. 1992. A Nonary of Priorities. In *Revisioning Philosophy*, edited by James Ogilvy,. Albany, NY: State University of New York Press.

Peterson, Derek and Darren Walhof (Eds.). 2002. *The Invention of Religion: Rethinking Belief in Politics and History*. New Brunswick, NJ: Rutgers University Press.

Sharma, Arvind. 2004. 'Religion' and 'Religious Freedom': Towards an Indic Understanding. *Evam: Forum on Indian Representations* 3: 55–70.

Smith, Wilfred Cantwell. 1962. *The Meaning and End of Religion*. New York: Macmillan.

The Third Eye and Two Ways of (Un)knowing: Gnosis, Alternative Modernities, and Postcolonial Futures

Makarand Paranjape

The starting point for this paper is the premise that "alternatives to modern episte-mology can hardly come from *modern* (Western) epistemology itself." This idea has been voiced quite forcefully in recent thinking, by scholars such as Walter D. Mignolo from whose book *Local Histories/Global Designs* the above phrase is taken. But even if we were to agree with such a premise, it still begs the question of where to look for these alternatives. For critics such a Mignolo, the challenge is to rehabilitate subaltern knowledge systems so as to bring about, to invoke a phrase from Foucault, "an insurrection of subjected knowledges." "Gnosis," "gnoseology" and "border thinking" have been used to describe those knowledge systems that are on the margins of or outside the world colonized by Western modernity. My project is to oppose the dominance of rationality (or, more recently, *ir*rationality) in modern and postmodern philosophy by invoking ideas of the supra-rational from Classical as well as modern traditions of thinking, especially in India. These traditions, for lack of a better word, may be called "wisdom traditions." That they share something with gnosticism should be obvious. I would like to focus on the work of one modern Indian thinker, Sri Aurobindo, particularly his idea of the Supermind, to suggest a slightly different way of conceiving postcolonial futures. Sri Aurobindo's thought has important implications for the discipline of consciousness studies because it posits the naturalization of a higher conscious than the mental. Is there, I ask, a bridge somewhere between the "secular" critics of Western modernity or colonial discourse, on the one hand, and their rather more "mystical" counterparts, on the other? If this missing link were to be discovered, it might contribute to a critical step forward in conversations on planetary futures and actually pave the way for a new global renaissance.

1

It is being increasingly acknowledged that colonial difference is a factor not just of economic or political power but also of contending knowledge systems. These knowledge systems, apart from being differentiated by the amount of power they enjoy, are also based on alternative epistemologies. Those who wish to critique

P. Bilimoria and A.B. Irvine (eds.), *Postcolonial Philosophy of Religion.*
© Springer Science+Business Media B.V. 2009

colonialism have usually done so in economic and political or, more infrequently, in philosophical and metaphysical terms. For instance, we might argue that modernity is imperialistic as an ideology and modernity in turn undergirds colonialism ideologically. This M. K. Gandhi realized only too well, which is why, when he attacked imperialism in *Hind Swaraj* (1909) he also attacked modernity. But Gandhi was one of the few to do so in so clear a fashion.

In the discourse of postcolonial studies, it has taken critics almost 100 years after Gandhi to make similar connections. In recent years a whole host of scholars and thinkers have begun to see that overthrowing imperialism requires a certain critique of what might be called Occidental reason. For instance, a recent book on the subject by Gayatri Chakravorty Spivak is tellingly entitled *A Critique of Postcolonial Reason*. Those who wish to make a connection between postcolonialism and postmodernism quickly leap to the conclusion that the anti-foundationalism of the latter informs the eclectic critique of power of the former. Thus Aijaz Ahmed castigates Edward Said of abandoning the teleology of history and the grand narrative of Marxian emancipation, in favour of a neo-Nietzschean critique of reality as linguistically constructed.

The Enlightenment project has its adherents both on the right and on the left – the classic debate has been between pro-market liberals and pro-statist socialists – both of whom accept the supremacy of reason as the arbiter of human destiny and as the primary tool to re-shape society. Those who debunk the Enlightenment project, on the other hand, resort to a sort anti-rationalism or irrationalism. What Mignolo and the others add to this debate is a different set of knowledge systems which are subaltern because they have been suppressed, or because they are generated on or from outside the borders of the dominant West. Mignolo has used the words "gnosis" and "gnoseology" to characterize these knowledge systems.

For Mignolo, alternatives to modernity are located in spaces outside the imperium, that is, outside the dominant West. He characterizes "colonial difference" as the space "where *local* histories inventing and implementing global designs meet *local* histories, the space in which global designs have to be adapted, adopted, rejected, integrated, or ignored. The colonial difference is, finally, the physical as well as imaginary location where the coloniality of power is at work..." (p. ix). Border thinking or border gnosis is "the fractured locus of enunciation from a subaltern perspective ... a response to the colonial difference" (p. x). So, gnosis here is a term given to knowledges which are suppressed by the dominant: "border thinking is more than a hybrid enunciation. It is a fractured enunciation in dialogic situations with the territorial and hegemonic cosmology" (p. x). One of Mignolo's interesting contributions to the discourse of decolonization is to propose a new kind of university, based on "*a critique of knowledge and cultural practices*" (p. xii) as opposed to the Kantian university based on *reason*, the Humboldtian university based on *culture* and the neoliberal university based on "*excellence* and *expertise*" (p. xii).

Speaking of the connection between imperialism and knowledge systems, Mignolo points out how Spanish missionaries judged and ranked civilizations in terms of whether they possessed alphabetic writing. They used *translation* (especially of the Bible into these languages) to absorb this difference; *border thinking* works to restitute that difference (p. 3). He alludes to border thinking not just from Latin America, but also to African *gnosis*. The key text here is Valentin Mudimbe's *The Invention of Africa: Gnosis, Philosophy and the Order of Knowledge* (1988). Mudimbe says that *gnosko* means "seeking to know, inquiry, methods of knowing, investigation, and even acquaintance with someone. Often the word is used in a more specialized sense, that of higher and esoteric knowledge" (p. ix). Mignolo, too, uses the word gnosis in a special sense that needs to be understood:

> Border gnosis as knowledge from a subaltern perspective is knowledge conceived from the exterior borders of the modern/colonial world system, and border gnoseology as a discourse about colonial knowledge is conceived at the conflictive intersection of the knowledge produced from the perspective of modern colonialisms (rhetoric, philosophy, science) and knowledge produced from the perspective of colonial modernities in Asia, Africa, and the Americas/Caribbean. Border gnoseology is a critical reflection on knowledge production from both the interior borders of the modern/colonial world system (imperial conflicts, hegemonic languages, directionality of translations, etc.) and its external borders (imperial conflicts with cultures being colonized, as well as the subsequent stages of independence and decolonization).... Finally, border gnoseology could be contrasted with territorial gnoseology or epistemology, the philosophy of knowledge, as we know it today (from Descartes, to Kant, to Husserl and all its ramifications in analytic philosophy of languages and philosophy of science): a conception and reflection on knowledge articulated in concert with the cohesion of national languages and the formation of the nation-state. (p. 11)

But I would like to invoke the older meaning of the word gnosis. Gnosticism, a religious sect dating back at least to the first century C.E. held that salvation came from knowledge or what in India would be called *jñāna*. But the moot question was knowledge of *what*. Hans Jonas in *The Gnostic Religion: The Message of the Alien God and the Beginnings of Christianity* says:

> As for *what* knowledge is about, the associations of the term most familiar to the classically trained reader point to *rational* objects, and accordingly to natural reason as the organ for acquiring and possessing knowledge. In the gnostic context, however, "knowledge" has an emphatically religious or supranatural meaning and refers to objects which we nowadays should call those of faith rather than of reason.... *Gnosis* meant pre-eminently knowledge of *God*, and from what we have said about the radical transcendence of the deity it follows that "knowledge of God" is the knowledge of something naturally unknowable and therefore itself not a natural condition.... On the one hand it is closely bound with revelatory experience, so that reception of the truth either through sacred and secret lore or through inner illumination replaces rational argument and theory .... on the other hand, being concerned with the secrets of salvation, "knowledge" is not just theoretical information about certain things but is itself, as a modification of the human condition, charged with performing the function in the bringing about of salvation. *Thus gnostic "knowledge" has an eminently practical object.* (p. 34)

Mignolo argues that the target of gnosis need not be God or salvation now but the "uncertainties of the borders" (p. 12): "Our goals are not salvation but decolonization" (p. 12). But, I would suggest, that decolonization is nothing but another name for a special kind of salvation, a secular salvation, perhaps, or salvation from oppression, from inequality, and therefore from ignorance.

The problem before us today is that of postcolonial or planetary futures. I agree with Mignolo, that "the future of a diverse planetary civilizations" cannot simply be "the universalism of either Western neoliberalism or Western neo-Marxism" (p. 8), and that "[a]lternatives to modern epistemology can hardly come only from *modern* (Western) epistemology itself" (p. 9). That is why I want to discuss the specific category of gnosis to ask if can be the basis for an alternative (post)modernity. Gnosis, which was a part of the Western semantics of knowledge, vanished after the ascendancy of rationality (p. 9). The word was associated with gnosticism, which was branded as an anti-Christian sect by the Church fathers, which it turn gave it a bad name. Mignolo uses "gnosis" and "gnoseology" to suggest these alternative knowledge systems. *Gignosko*, the verb "to know, to recognize" (like *jigñāsa*), and *epistemai*, "to know, to be acquainted with," suggest two different conceptions of knowledge and knowing (p. 9). In ancient Greek thought, gnosis emerges as a word to suggest a special or hidden kind of knowledge – but Greek philosophers do not establish a rigid distinction between gnosis and episteme (p. 10).

To invoke the ancient Gnostics for just a minute longer, it's fundamental to recognize that "The God of the Gnostics is not the God of this world." According to Gerd Lüdemann and Martina Janssen:

> The creator of the world to whom the Christians of the church pray is a 'lower God' who out of envy leaves the human soul in ignorance about its heavenly home. The God who brings the Gnostic redemption is the good, unknown Father. He cannot be understood by human efforts. Accordingly, it can only be said of him what he is not. This 'negative theology' occupies a good deal of space in all forms of Gnostic literature...(p. 17).

What this quotation actually suggests is that Gnostics had a totally different theology from the Christians, one that is closer to the Vedic view, which regards human beings as *amritasya putraha* or the children of immortality. In gnosticism there is no original sin, purgatory, or damnation, nor is God a vengeful and punishing deity.

Gnostics were branded as heretics by the Church and exterminated (p. 11). What makes them special for us is that they believed in salvation by knowledge, *jñana*, or *vijñāna* – the knowledge of the Self not by dogmas of belief or some prescribed set of ritual practices. "For the Gnostic, knowledge is primarily self-knowledge... This knowledge brings it salvation and reunites it with the Pleroma (=fullness) from which it comes" (Lüdemann and Janssen 1998: 12). Of course, it is important to remember that gnosticism is not uniform or homogenous, nor is it entirely Christian. There were Jewish, Iranian, Egyptian, and philosophical Gnosticisms (p. 12). Some sects include the Mandaeans of southern Iraq, the Manichaeans, the Hermeticists, and the Neoplatonists (pp. 12–13). For a long time, the Gnostics were known only by what was quoted against them by the heresiologists, until the discovery of the Nag Hammadi corpus around 1945, in a small town in Egypt by that name. Thirteen codices in Coptic were found which contain several Gnostic texts dating back to the fourth century C.E.

In his controversial book *Black Athena* (1987) Martin Bernal argues that much of the new knowledge, including the beginnings of modern science, that erupted after the renaissance was due to the Greek transmission of Egyptian wisdom (see chapter II, pp. 121–160). Bernal's thesis that the triumph of the "Aryan Model" and the defeat of the "Ancient Model" coincided with the emergence of a violent, racist, intolerant, and dominating Western modernity which saw itself as specially privileged and superior to the rest of the world. However, according to the "Ancient Model" which had prevailed right up to the first half of the nineteenth century, ancient Greece, which was the source of modern Europe, was itself a creature of the even more ancient Egypt, which was an Afro-Semitic civilization. What is pertinent to this paper in Bernal's argument is his positing a holistic wisdom tradition, derived from ancient Egypt, as both the precursor and the source of modernity itself, until it is overthrown by the regime of modern rationality after the Enlightenment. He identifies three strands of this tradition that influenced, even triumphed over, Europe until they were crushed: Hermeticism, Neo-Platonism, and Gnosticism. Before the advent of modern Egyptology, all of Egyptian wisdom was attributed to a single author, somewhat like Veda Vyas in India. Called Hermes Trismegistos, this mythical figure was thought to be older than Moses. Major figures of the renaissance such as Copernicus, Giordano Bruno, and even Newton were hermeticists (see chapter III, pp. 161–188). The other interesting aspect of Bernal's argument is that the European enthusiasm for India also served to diminish its regard for Egypt. Of course, like Egypt, India too had to be degraded and discarded in the nineteenth century for the emergence of a racist and supremacist imperial Europe (see chapter V, pp. 224–280).

2

My paper, however, is concerned primarily with India and what it has to contribute to this debate. What seems to me to be very important here is that India had a variety of knowledge systems in mutually supportive, dialogic relationships. In other words, it had smaller, localized, subaltern knowledge systems, some of which survive to this day among our so-called tribal populations. It also had extremely well-worked out systems of rational thought, called the *sastras*. But what is more, its deepest philosophical urges were grounded neither in empiricism or rational speculation, but on what might be called wisdom or gnosis. It is commonplace to claim that Indian philosophy is intuitive while Western philosophy is rationalistic. S. Radhakrishnan called it the contrast between "creative intuition" versus "critical intelligence" (quoted in Sinha 1981: 9). Both in Upanishadic and Buddhistic thought not *buddhi* but *prajna* take us to the Absolute (p. 4). And yet, as Ramesh Chandra Sinha puts it, "though Indian philosophical tradition does not regard reason as the supreme source of knowledge … it is reason which gives a coherent, systematic and consistent interpretation of intuitive experience" (p. 9).

If I were to sum up my argument I would say that this paper takes as its starting point Sri Aurobindo's critique of what might be termed Occidental reason. I first came across it in what was almost a textual aside in a long polemic that Sri Aurobindo first mounted in his periodical *Arya* from December 1918 to January 1921. These essays were later collected under the title *The Foundations of Indian Culture* and appeared as vol. 14 of the Sri Aurobindo Birth Centenary Library (SABCL). In the Collected Works of Sri Aurobindo (CWSA), designed to supersede the former, the title of the volume has been changed. The ostensible pre-text for Sri Aurobindo's critique was a wholesale dismissal of Indian culture by noted drama critic, William Archer. Archer's book, *India and the Future* is certainly forgotten today, though it was immortalized by Sri Aurobindo's detail rebuttal. The second series consisting of seven essays that Sri Aurobindo wrote against Archer was called "A Rationalistic Critic on Indian Culture." In essay 4 of this series, Sri Aurobindo says:

> Modern Europe separated religion from life, from philosophy, from art and science, from politics, from the greater part of social action and social existence. And it secularised and rationalised too the ethical demand so that it might stand in itself on its own basis and have no need of any aid from religious sanction or mystic insistence. (SABCL 14: 83)

But after this remarkably clear but somewhat expected assessment of modernity, there occurs the radical insight that is so carelessly tucked away in the corner of a larger polemic:

> At the end of this turn is an antinomian tendency, constantly recurring in the life-history of Europe and now again in evidence. This force seeks to annul ethics also, not by rising above it into the absolute purity of the spirit, as mystic experience claims to do, but by breaking out of its barriers below into an exultant freedom of the vital play. (ibid.)

This struck me as quite a prophetic pronouncement on the anti-foundationalism of postmodernist thought, with its emphasis on absolute freedom and play, but which is not supra-rational as much as *anti-* or *ir*-rational. Sri Aurobindo gives a more extended critique on reason as the sole arbiter of human destiny in another series of essays, first published in *Arya* from 15 August 1916 to 15 July 1918, and collected later as *The Human Cycle* (SABCL: 15). Here he states in detail why reason cannot deliver humanity:

> The whole difficulty of the reason in trying to govern our existence is that because of its own inherent limitations it is unable to deal with life in its complexity or in its integral move-ments; it is compelled to break it up into parts, to make more or less artificial classifications, to build systems with limited data which are contradicted, upset or have to be continually modified by other data, to work out a selection of regulated potentialities which is broken down by the bursting of a new wave of yet unregulated potentialities. (p. 102)

Sri Aurobindo concludes that only a widespread spiritual transformation that will usher in a universal Spiritual Age will be the natural culmination of the human quest for individual as well as social perfection.

What emerges from such a critique is that the central philosophical enterprise of the West proceeds in cycles of affirmation and negation of a certain kind of rationality. In the last 200 years or so, this has meant the enthronement of instru-mental reason and then its recent repudiation at the hands of several thinkers. Neo-classicism, romanticism, modernism, and, now, postmodernism also show traces of a similar cycle of affirmation and negation. Seeing its own history in terms of a progression from the pre-modern, to the modern, to the post-modern, the West has relegated other societies to a space equivalent to its own irrational past, thereby turning geography into history. However, I would like to argue that a civilization such as India is neither pre-modern, nor modern. In fact, one cannot call it post-modern or anti-modern either, though that is how some choose to see it. I would argue that India is best understood either as a traditional or a non-modern society. By this is meant that it does not subscribe to the logic of History that the West has invented. In a non-modern society, what is central is neither rationality nor its opposite, but something else, call it wisdom, which includes but supersedes rationality. The debate between the West and India is not between modernity and tradition or between modernity and pre- or anti-modernity, but between modernity and non-modernity. Indeed, in the ultimate analysis, this is a debate between two kinds of rationality, two ways of seeing, two visions and version of the world. A new global renaissance is possible not by rejecting or negating the West or by posting some kind of dissenting knowledge system against the dominant one, but by trying to change the world order on the basis of a mass inner awakening and transformation. In this process, wisdom, which is signified by the opening of the third eye, has to play a key role, not just the rationality – anti-rationality axis in which we seem to be ensnared at the present. The opening of the third eye is a symbolic way of suggesting the opening of higher consciousness; the third eye corresponds to the *ajnachakra* or forehead center, the sixth chakra in the yoga-tantra system. It suggests the awakening of inner sight, or insight, what Sri Aurobindo calls "occult vision and occult power" (*Letters on Yoga* SABCL 22: 372).

It seems to me that this aspect of Sri Aurobindo's thought has direct bearing on the crucial debate over the status and position of Enlightenment rationality within Western thought. The key text here is obviously Horkheimer and Adorno's *Dialectic of Enlightenment* (1944). Composed during World War II and in exile, this book is an anguished searching into the mind of Europe. How did fascism emerge in Europe in spite of the liberating ideals of the Enlightenment and the progressive Marxist doctrine of History? Their answer was sobering: "Enlightenment is totalitarian" (quoted in Young, p. 7). The project of the Frankfurt school was to rescue the promise of the Enlightenment from the instrumental rationality that led to the will to power and to asphyxiating collectivism. If the Frankfurt School showed that irrationality lurked within the hidden recesses of rationality, the French poststructuralists went further to interrogate in Foucault's words, "the relations between the 'Western' project of a universal deployment of reason, [and] the positivity of the sciences and the radicality of philosophy" (quoted in Young, p. 8): "In the history of the sciences in France, as in German critical theory, it is a matter at bottom of examining a reason, the autonomy of whose structures carries with it a history of dogmatism and despotism – a reason, consequently, which can only have an effect of emancipation on condition that it manages to liberate itself from itself" (quoted in Young, p. 9).

While most poststructuralists, postmodernists, and postcolonialists are in agreement that a new type of knowledge needs to be invented or discovered, its precise definitions or characteristics elude consensus. At best this auto-critique of the dominant has only produced various forms of negative dialectics, an example of which is Foucault's intriguing phrase that reason should "liberate itself from itself." Typically, a positive statement of what this alternative epistemology will be is avoided for the fear that a statement of it will prove to be oppressive and totalizing. This is what accounts for what I've called the *chakravyuva* of much of postal-thought: once you get in, you can't get out; it's a sort of prison-house of language, to invoke another famous phrase of Paul de Man's, from which there is no exit. Much of postal thought thus feeds off itself in a pathology of extreme self-reflexivity and narcissism. That is why it is useful to make it speak to another tradition, the so-called spiritual tradition of thought, which has addressed some of these concerns from a different location.

3

The remaining part of my presentation will be an exposition of exactly what this means in Sri Aurobindo's scheme of spiritual evolution.

In *Synthesis of Yoga*, Sri Aurobindo uses the words *vijñāna* and gnosis interchangeably, as synonyms (p. 457). He defines these terms carefully because they are central to his argument; in fact, he devotes several chapters to them (chapter XXII–XXIV). For Sri Aurobindo, "*vijñāna* or gnosis is not only truth but truth-power, it is the very working of the infinite and divine nature; it is the divine knowledge one with the divine will in the force and delight of a spontaneous and luminous and inevitable self-fulfillment. By the gnosis, then, we change our human into a divine nature" (p. 457). He clarifies that *vijñāna* is not the same as *buddhi*, neither is *buddhi* the same as reason (p. 457). He argues that those who consider *buddhi* to be the same as reason and consider these to be the highest mental faculty "pass at once from a plane of pure intellect to a plane of pure spirit" (p. 457); their error is in mistaking "the limited human means for facing truth ... for the highest possible dynamics of consciousness" (p. 457). "The opposite error" is to identify *vijñāna* with "the consciousness of the Infinite free from all ideation" (p. 457). But for Sri Aurobindo, *vijñāna* or gnosis is an *intermediate* power, at once "concentrated consciousness" and "infinite knowledge of the myriad play of the Infinite" (p. 458). In other words, "it contains all ideation ... but is not limited by ideation" (p. 458). Unlike reason, it is not "intellectual" or "mental" but "self-luminous, supramental" (p. 458). That is, it is not accumulative, consciously deductive or inductive, but direct and spontaneous. Of course, Sri Aurobindo tells us rather intriguingly that there is relation, even "a sort of broken identity between the two ... for one proceeds covertly from [the] other. Mind is born from that which is beyond the mind" (p. 458).

But having said this, he is quick to show how different the two modes are – they belong, as it were, to different planes of consciousness. To complicate matters farther, he posits other levels between them, for instance, "intuitive reason," which is akin to *buddhi* – higher than reason, but lower than *vijñāna*. Thought and its movements for Sri Aurobindo are slow, methodical, while intuition is swift and sure, a leap, a flash, "a supralogical process ... of rapid insight or swift discernment" (p. 459). But even this intuitive reason is not gnosis; "it is only an edge of light of the supermind finding its way by flashes of illumination" (p. 460). But the elevation of the mind from the rational to the intuitive is itself an important step up the ladder of consciousness. Sri Aurobindo believes that we can train our minds to attain it by "purifying the interfering intelligence" but this is difficult because the mind in nature is "bound by the triple tie of mentality, vitality, corporeality to its own imperfection and ignorance" (p. 461).

The difference between the two, between reason and gnosis is a fundamental one: the former proceeds from "ignorance to truth" but the latter from truth and "shows the appearances in the light of the truth" (pp. 462–463). "The reason proceeds by inference ... but gnosis proceeds by identity or vision" (p. 463). "To the reason only what the senses give is direct knowledge, *pratyaksa*... to the gnosis all its truth is direct knowledge, *pratyaksa*" (p. 463). To define gnosis thus in contradistinction to reason is, Sri Aurobindo realizes, still to adhere to the rational process. On its own terms, "it is hardly possible to speak of it except in figures and symbols" (p. 465).

For Sri Aurobindo, gnosis is the link which can give us back our lost divinity. It is the bridge between the Supreme Reality of Satchidananda and the lower reality of our world; both are triunes: infinite existence, consciousness, and bliss on the one hand and lower triad of matter, life, and mind on the other. That is why gnosis is not just light but force, "creative knowledge ... the self-effective force of the divine Idea" (p. 465). It is an embodiment of will as "conscious force of eternal knowledge" (p. 465). Described in the Vedas by the symbol of the sun, *tat savitur varennyam*, the whole creation has been inspired by this "divine delight, the eternal Ananda" (p. 466). Indeed, the supramental world that Sri Aurobindo wishes to harbinger is such a "true and happy creation, *rtam, bhadram*" (p. 466). It is for gnosis to reestablish the link between Divine Nature, Prakriti as it is, and fallen nature, prakriti as she seems to be. In order to do so, *vijñāna* has three powers: it receives supreme knowledge and transmits it; it concentrates supreme consciousness to act on matter; and a divine delight with which it harmonizes the "illimitable diversity" of manifestation (p. 466).

As evolutionary beings, the Purusha or conscious being in us must ascend into the *vijnanamaya* so as to transform Prakriti – this, according to Sri Aurobindo, is "the fundamental experience of the mental being transformed and fulfilled and sublimated in the perfection of the gnosis" (p. 467). According to Sri Aurobindo, a human being is constituted of multiple materials. Therefore, all of us carry the effects of these materials which have gone into building us. The human, the homo sapiens, or "man" – as the root of the word suggests – is primarily a mental being. That is we are distinguished from other species by our ability to think, by the fact that we possess what may be called a mind. Men and women, thus, are so called because of their minds, their *manas*. But we do not live in a mental world, except internally or occasionally. Our world is, in fact, primarily, physical. Our whole quest in the march of civilization which we call progress has been to gain greater and greater control over our physical environments. So, it is the physical existence that must be touched and transformed as the ultimate object of yoga. The proof of the pudding is in the eating-it is when this physical world around us is transformed that we can truly change the conditions of our existence.

How is this to be done? One step is to understand the nature of the physical itself. The body, made up of the gross elements, the same ingredients that make up matter, is nevertheless not untouched by something else, something other than itself and its own nature. The mental works on the body through the intermediacy of the nervous system. Even the most physical things that we experience are not without their mental component, or else we would never experience them. Between the mind and the body, connecting them both is the vital, the pranic. According to the Brihadranyaka Upanishad, prana is the essence, the subtle substance of life. It is indestructible and of the same material as the eternal divine. It may leave the body, but it does not perish.

By the same token, between the mind and what is above it, what is higher than it, are subtle connectors, sort of like an interface, which when activated, will help divinize our mental consciousness. That is the *vijnanamaya* sheath, or envelope. This transformation of consciousness is what all yoga wishes to accomplish, regardless of the different philosophical or theological bases from which it proceeds. The ancient truth that the kabala presents was, as above so below. As the Tantrics say, what is not here, meaning in the human body, is nowhere. In other words, there is a correspondence above the human to what we experience in the human plane. Gnosticism would mean an awareness of this correspondence. "All will be originated from above; from above, all that corresponds in gnosis to our present mental activity takes place" (p. 471). So there is already a higher mind that ours to which we have access if we wish. Between the mental and the absolute is the supramental or the gnostic; between the mental and the gnostic are a whole range of levels which Sri Aurobindo calls the overmind planes.

As we gradually ascend to higher levels of consciousness, the mental faculty expresses itself in a "differential rather than separative" fashion. The centre – the brain, the body – is still there, but it is merely for convenience, a point of reference as it were; the being is not tethered to it, but expands and diffuses over a larger area. This is a different form of individuality or personality, one that operates universally: "It has become the awareness of an infinite being who acts always universally though with emphasis on an individual formation of its energies" (p. 471). This state of consciousness may appear to be rather abnormal at first, but as Sri Aurobindo says, "it vindicates itself even to the mental intelligence by its greater calm, freedom, light, power, effectivity of will, verifiable truth of ideation and feeling" (pp. 471–472).

In this state, the ultimate truth, the infinite reality, becomes more true to us than the world of phenomenal existence: it becomes, as Sri Aurobindo puts it, "the primal, the actual reality" (p. 472). "In the plane of gnosis the infinite is at once our normal consciousness of being, its first fact, our sensible substance" unlike the "normal" state in which the finite, phenomenal world is our default mode of being, from which we rise only occasionally to glimpse "intimations of immortality." Once we are seized of and by this power of gnosis or *vijñāna*, Sri Aurobindo believes that it has the ability to transform and reshape the very physical and material aspects of our being in accordance with its own nature. Krishnamurti and David Bohm spoke of a similar process but in a different terminology. But the idea was that the higher energy of gnosis or intelligence, as Krishnamurti called it, can affect even the cells of the brain, altering them so that they function differently. This is the opening of the third eye, the rise of the *kundalini*, and the transformation of the *jīva* to Shiva or the *pashu* to *pashupati*.

According to Sri Aurobindo, in the *vijnanamaya*, "there is no place for sin; for all sin is an error of the will, a desire and act of the Ignorance" (p. 474). As in Buddhism, "When desire ceases entirely, grief and all inner suffering also cease" (p. 475). In the *vijñāna*, "the Divine is no longer veiled in Maya." Therefore, there is no *jīva* who says "I think I act, I desire, I feel" (p. 476); what is left, instead, is the infinite play of what Swami Muktananda called *chitshakti-vilāsa* or as Sri Aurobindo puts it "God himself by his Prakriti knows, acts, loves, takes delight through my individuality and its figures and fulfils there in its higher and divine measures the multiple *līlā* which the Infinite for ever plays in the universality which is himself for ever" (p. 476). The gnostic soul is akin to the supreme Godhead, free, but active, sovereign but taking delight in its apparent limitedness. The freedom that it enjoys is the same as nirvana: not an annihilation, but play.

An important distinction before I conclude this section: in Sri Aurobindo's scheme, this transformation is not just for a few select individuals, but for the whole human species. It will happen because the Supramental will be naturalized and normalized on earth just as mental consciousness was a few million years ago. So, when this happens, what the earth will see is a quantum shift in consciousness, which will ensure that every dimension of human life, political, social, economic, cultural, and so on, will be radically transformed.

4

This paper has been premised on the idea of a dynamic absolute that through its force of love and knowledge can act to transform this world. As such, it departs from notions of a static absolute aloof from this world or from ideas that regard the world itself as an illusion. This world as it appears may not be taken as the ultimate reality; indeed to do so would be to make a category error. Yet, whatever is and appears to be has some basis in reality. This much we must concede. Otherwise, any attempt to be agents of change in our world would be futile. In other words, we must act on the assumption that our collective efforts and intentions can, indeed, change the world for the better. What is more, we might even go on to assert that such a change can actually be proposed, explained, discussed, accepted or rejected by other actors and agents. It is only through such ceaseless interaction, even striving, that some breakthrough will occur. The path forward, moreover, may not be a single one, but may have multiple branches and possibilities. It would be an unfortunate error to attempt to impose one uniform prescription to the whole of humankind. My exposition of Sri Aurobindo's thought was to suggest one way forward, not to foreclose others.

The idea that the European renaissance of the fifteenth century was both incomplete and partial is not a new one. In the early nineteenth century, for instance, Friedrich Schlegel mooted the idea of an "Oriental Renaissance" (Clarke 1997: 55).

The phrase itself occurs as the heading of a chapter in a book Edgar Quinet published in 1841 (Schwab 1984: 11). Raymond Schwab picked it up again towards the end of the last century, using it as the title of his book. As he says at the opening of the book,

> An Oriental Renaissance – a *second* Renaissance, in contrast to the first: the expression and the theme are familiar to the Romantic writers, for whom the term is interchangeable with Indic Renaissance. What the expression refers to is the revival of an atmosphere in the nineteenth century brought about by the arrival of Sanskrit texts in Europe, which produced an effect equal to that produced in the fifteenth century by the arrival of Greek manuscripts and Byzantine commentators after the fall of Constantinople. (p. 11)

Of course, we might argue that what goes by the name of ancient wisdom was not especially Indian or Eastern, but prevailed in several parts of the world before the advent of modernity. What makes India special is the persistence of these traditions in a powerful and coherent form to this day.

Indeed, in the last 200 years, there have been repeated attempts to bring Western and all such esoteric knowledges or "inner sciences" into some sort of grand synthesis. Apart from the more spiritualist attempts, such as Theosophy or the New Age, such connections have existed in practically every branch of knowledge including literature, philosophy, religious studies, and even in certain aspects of the "hard" sciences (see Clarke for an account of some of these dialogues). Even if these attempts haven't succeeded entirely, we could argue that they haven't failed totally either. It is therefore not only possible but highly desirable to push such endeavours forward. The new global renaissance that Rajiv Malhotra and Robert F. Thurman wish to effect is thus very much the demand of our times. In this presentation I've argued against two ways of (un)knowing – the absolutist rationalism that characterizes the dominant strand of Western thought as well as the dissenting irrationalism of the postmodernists. Instead, a third way of knowing suggested by the opening of the third eye has been suggested as the way forward. The way points to the development of a gnostic being with an enhanced consciousness, a being that may be able better to shape a global future for our numerous planetary civilizations.

References

Ahmed, Aijaz. 1992. In Theory: Classes, Nations, Literatures. London: Verso.

Archer, William. 1917. India and the Future. London: Hutchinson.

Aurobindo, Sri. 1970. The Synthesis of Yoga. Sri Aurobindo Birth Centenary Library, Vol. 20. Pondicherry: Sri Aurobindo Ashram.

Clarke, J. J. 1997. Oriental Enlightenment: The Encounter Between Asian and Western Thought. London: Routledge.

Gandhi, Mohandas Karamchand. 1984. Hind Swaraj 1909. Ahmedabad: Navjivan.

Jonas, Hans. 1958. The Gnostic Religion: The Message of the Alien God and the Beginnings of Christianity. New York: Beacon.

Krishnamurti, Jiddu and David Bohm. 1986. The Future of Humanity: A Conversation. San Francisco, CA: Harper & Row.

Lüdemann, Gerd and Martina Janssen. 1998. Suppressed Prayers: Gnostic Spirituality in Early Christianity. Trans. John Bowden. Harrisburg, PA: Trinity Press International.

Mignolo, Walter D. 2000. Local Histories/Global Designs: Coloniality, Subaltern Knowledges and Border Thinking. Princeton, NJ: Princeton University Press.

Mookerjee, Ajit and Madhu Khanna. 1977. The Tantric Way: Art, Science, Ritual. London: Thames & Hudson.

Mudimbe, Valentin. 1988. The Invention of Africa: Gnosis, Philosophy and the Order of Knowledge. Bloomington, IN: Indiana University Press.

Muktananda, Swami. 1972. Chitshakti Vilas: The Play of Consciousness. Ganeshpuri: Sri Gurudev Ashram.

Schwab, Raymond. 1984. The Oriental Renaissance: Europe's Rediscovery of India and the East 1600–1880. Trans. Victor Reinking and Gene Patterson-Black. New York: Columbia University Press.

Sinha, Ramesh Chandra. 1981. Concepts of Reason and Intuition: With Special Reference to Sri Aurobind, K. Bhattacharya and Radhakrishnan. Patna/New Delhi: Janaki Prakashan.

Spivak, Gayatri Chakravorty. 1999. A Critique of Postcolonial Reason: Toward a History of the Vanishing Present. Cambridge, MA: Harvard University Press.

Part II
"India"

Mispredicated Identity and Postcolonial Discourse

Bibhuti S. Yadav*

Introduction

Key to the postcolonial discourse is an interpretation of the relation of identity and difference in which the terms of the relation are construed in a geocultural sense. The West is colonial in the sense that it silences difference in defence of its singular identity and eschatological economy. The postcolonial discourse has *an assumption and an aim*. It assumes that the modern, Western conception of knowledge is of an instrument for materialising a pre-determined end. Knowledge in Western hands is not descriptive, not a picture of how things are in themselves. It rather is *a utilitarian tool* with which the West establishes epistemic and ethical hegemony, and appropriates to itself the singular agency of global salvation. The European self is driven by a jealous cogito, one that reiterates its uniqueness and the concomitant dualism of the West and the rest. It is an entity that has ontological autonomy and it constitutes the boundary of thought. The Western singularity is intolerant of difference. It imagines difference *in contrast to* its identity, denies cognitive and ethical agency to the non-West, and reduces the civilizational other to a knowable object that can then be represented in discourse. Thus, Western colonialism entails dualism of the Orientalist sort. "Orientalism," said Edward Said, "is a style of thought that is based

*Editors' note: Following the author's sudden death, it proved an overwhelming task to trace the quotations and references contained in this challenging piece. Consequently, not all citations in the chapter can be provided with complete scholarly apparatus. A number are reproduced with less than full confidence as to the precise source from which Professor Yadav drew. We have attempted to document sources accurately where they could be accessed, and to create an overall consistency in citational format, while retaining as much as possible the author's own quotations, transliterations, and notes. Sources for which substantial bibliographical information was supplied are cited in parenthetical references. Certain classical sources in Sanskrit, for which we have been unable to trace the edition used, are, as a rule, cited in the endnotes or References. We are grateful to Sonam Kachru, of the University of Chicago, an editor of Yadav's papers, for additional assistance with resolving certain anomalous Sanskrit citations and diacritics, and providing editorial clarifications in footnotes.

P. Bilimoria and A.B. Irvine (eds.), *Postcolonial Philosophy of Religion.*
© Springer Science+Business Media B.V. 2009

upon ontological and epistemological distinction between the Orient and the Occident" (Said 1978: 2). West is West, East is East. The latter is an inert object and
must be silent, the former is a self-conscious subject and it alone can speak. Either
there *is* the singular agency of the West and a singular, Western discourse on global
ethos; or there *is no* West, *no* unifying categories of thought, and *no* human world.
The sovereignty of either/or logic is total.

The aim of the postcolonial discourse is to review the relation of identity and
difference. It insists that the Orient (in this article, I restrict myself to discussion of
India) must regain its right to centre itself in its own texts. Its mission is to undo
the colonial evil, to move the discourse to postmodern reality, and to emancipate
the Orient from the not-self that the West has imposed on it. Salvation lies in the
discourse of difference, in incarnating the cultural and historical identity of the East
through its own categories of thought. The point is to overcome the alienation of self
and self-representation, to reclaim the cognitive and ethical agency of the non-West,
and to recognise the multiple anchorages of world history. Mother India, too, must
write her own destiny. The postcolonial discourse does it all with a self-righteous
gesture that edges on the sacred. It claims to speak in defence of the non-Western
other, the marginalised majority, the voiceless subaltern, the silent victims of the
colonial cogito.

I must clarify my stance right away. Colonialism is a relational category. It entails
a subject so obsessed with its singular identity that it must invent difference, in
this case "India," as a site on which to impose itself. I believe that the modernity
that colonialism entails is actually as pre-modern as the theology of creation *ex
nihilo*. The mission of this theology is twofold: (a) to reduce history to a clean
slate by erasing all signs of a pre-Christian past and non-Christian present from
consciousness; and (b) to remember salvation as a future that implies christological
identity is universal in scope. The project of modernity, namely, "to post- the past,"
begins with this theology. The secular posture adopted during the Enlightenment
era involved the players changing their names, but the project remained the same.
Consciousness continued to be construed as *tabula rasa*, a clean slate, in which no
trace of the past was to be found and on which signs of universal salvation were to
be inscribed for the future.

I believe that Enlightenment and modernity had little to do with rationalism or
secularism. If anything, the civilizations of India and China were more rational and
secular than the West. The Enlightenment was actually an eschatological project,
one that conceived of identity in messianic terms and found salvation in the end
of difference. The state took on the same task that the church was supposed to
do. Euro-Christian identity provided the claim to common agency. The West alone
could inscribe the world historical future. As a modernizing project, colonialism
undertook to create, *ex nihilo*, the sacred and secular in the colonies.

I discern an irony here. The Euro-Christian subjectivity is obsessed with
"posting": its discourse is replete with expressions like "post-medieval," "post-
Enlightenment," "post-modern," "post-theistic," "post-cold war," even "postcolonial." Euro-Christian subjectivity defines itself in terms of what it does, and
what it does is invent difference, which can then be post-ed to clear the way for a

new beginning once again. Its point of reference is theological: it must begin with a nothing, yet it cannot affirm itself without the alien. Ironically, the posting mark is defined by the alien that is to be posted; the clearing identity is marked by the residual signs of difference so cleared. The object defines the subject, the not-self the self. The posting act necessitates a logical oddity, namely, defining identity in terms of the silenced difference. It is through such *mispredicated identity* that the West produces an ideology of power and, specifically, the right to write or erase cultures. In search of liberative universality, the West seems glued to mispredicated identity. The newer it makes a beginning, the more it identifies itself in terms of the past it believes has already been post-ed. *This* is modernity. Postmodernity is just as modern in this sense, which is to say, just as pre-modern and circular. The ghost of the past inevitably awaits its arrival in the future, only to invent one more difference that will have to be post-ed once again. The Euro-Christian self seems to be stuck with a samsaric facticity of its own, subjecting itself in an endless re-death and resurrection of its own mispredicated identity.

However, the Indian postcolonial consciousness, like Euro-Christian conscious-ness, is a case of mispredicated identity. It entails a subjectivity so obsessed with its liberated identity that it must offer itself as the site on which the alien can be initially placed and then subsequently erased. And it is as pre-modern as is the élite Vedāntism of Śaṅkarācārya, which reduced consciousness to a clean slate and found salvation through a utilitarian imposition and subsequent rejection of the not-self on the self (*adhyāropa-apavāda-nyāyaḥ*).* The postcolonial subjectivity is clearly self-colonising. It finds meaning in endless alienation of self and self-representation, in the strategic appropriation and subsequent posting of difference. In defence of its material interests, it must speak the language of the alien before returning to itself in spiritual silence. Like the colonial West, the self-colonising, postcolonial sub-jectivity must find salvation in the discovery and end of difference, be it Buddhist, Islamic or Euro-Christian. The irony is that such élite self-alienation does not truly alienate; it only reinforces the political and social hegemony of élite Brahmanism, lately known as Bhadraloka. There was, in the nineteenth century, a remarkable coincidence of interests between the colonial West and the self-colonising agency of the Bhadraloka. The convergence produced national heroes like Rammohan Roy, Keshab-Chandra Sen, Swami Vivekananda, Sri Aurobindo, Sarvepalli Radhakrish-nan, the Tagores and the Nehrus. Always postcolonial, one step ahead of the rest of society, the Bhadraloka embraced the colonial knowledge. With active support

---

*Sadānanda uses the phrase "*adhyāropa-apavāda-nyāya*" [unhyphenated] in his introduction to verse 31 in his *Vedānta-sāra*; and it appears to be most accessible reference for how Vedānta is often taught in India. See, M. Hiriyanna, *Vedānta-sāra of Sadānanda: A Work on Vedānta Phi-losophy* (Text, Translation, Detailed Introduction and Explanatory Notes), Varanasi: Chaukhamba Sanskrit Pratishtan, 2004. Tradition usually cites the paiṅgalopaniṣad? The reference to

adhyāropa-apavāda' as a technique occurs at II.12. "...adhyāropāpavādataḥ svarūpaṃ nichayatakartuṃ shakyate | = it is possible to determine the intrinsic nature [of the self] through adhyāropa and apavāda."

from Orientalists like Max Müller and William Jones, they also rediscovered the old Śaṅkarācārya, elevated the Upaniṣads to texts of salvation, and instituted the Neo-Vedāntic discourse of India as a spiritual civilization.

Today, the Bhadraloka write nationalistic histories and perform postcolonial discourse. They cannot forget the colonial, for they must define themselves in terms of what they appropriate and seek to post. Ashis Nandy, for instance, says, "colonialism tried to supplant the Indian consciousness to erect an Indian self-image which, in opposition to the West, would remain in essence a Western construction" (Nandy 1983: 72). True, the not-self is not the self, but it somehow comes to define the image that the self has of itself. But there is no point in bad faith, accusing Rudyard Kipling and the likes of so conceiving India that it needed the emancipatory agency of the West. The point is to recognise internal colonialism and the theory of consciousness it entails. The West did not unilaterally erect an alien image on India. It had powerful allies in the Bhadraloka. The Vedāntic tradition, for instance, insists that erection of alien images on consciousness is a utilitarian necessity. In cultural terms, this means that the colonial self-image of India would remain in essence a Vedantic construction.

Vedānta is a discourse of the loss and discovery of the self. Śaṅkarācārya called it *ātmakathā*, a reflective narrative conceived in the alienation of self and society. The subconscious presence of this Vedāntic ethos in Nandy's narrative is remarkable. In Nandy's case, the narrative conceives of the self as being in a place, and having to move West of it in pursuit of redeemed selfhood. *Ātmakathā* has become the condition of reflection, assuming cultural coherence and temporal permanence. It even controls Nandy's claim that "all interpretations of India are ultimately autobiographical" (Nandy 1983: 80). Postcolonial discourse on the slavery and salvation of India is *ātmalogical*, and it is to be done by those who are in the Indian social world but not of it, those who transcend society to assume "acquired Westernness" and then strategically predicate of themselves the alien they acquired. The Bhadraloka westernise in order to domesticate the colonial West. To discern the non-otherness of the (Western) other, they must view themselves as other. This means, as Nandy says, "controlled inner schism" resulting in deliberate alienation. But that is the price Nandy's "Unheroic Brahmin" must pay to ensure self-survival and self-interest (Nandy 1983: 109). It also affords him a higher order of cognition, a redeeming sense of the oneness of self and other, and a moral superiority with which to reconceive the childlike West in humanised terms. Nandy's Brahmin is physically weak, but he has cognitive weapons: the power of categories and of world construction. He uses these weapons strategically to inherit the earth and to keep doing what he has done throughout history, namely, reduce the victor to a manageable entity. With a proud gesture, Nandy chides Rudyard Kipling and the rest for being so naïve as not to recognise that the "crafty babus. . . . too. . . have a theory of the West" (Nandy 1983: 77; cf. Derrett 1979).

Yes, indeed the colonialists were naïve, but not quite in the sense Nandy thinks. There is no use chiding the colonialist, glorifying wounded pride, and deriving a psychopathology of victimised selfhood. It is more useful to bring the discourse back onto home turf, to thematise the self that must look at itself as other in order to

defend its self-interest. It is true that Euro-Christian colonialists centred their reflections of India in controlled inner schism, in the alienation of being and being in a
place. England was their home, but they had to be somewhere else for the good of the
world – thus they rationalised. But it is just as true that the "crafty babus" belonged
to a Vedāntic culture with a very old theory of strategic alienation that perpetuates
its hegemonic hold on society. I submit that the discourse of postcolonialism is not
between two "intimate enemies," as Ashis Nandy says. The discourse actually is
between two intimate friends: the colonizing liberal élite of the West on the one
end, and the self-colonising Neo-Vedāntic élite on the other. They need each other.
The supposed otherness of the two only illustrates the non-otherness of the one from
the other. They both find meaning in initial imposition and subsequent posting of the
not-self on the self. Two privileged identities are engaged in friendly fire in order to
reinforce mutual interest. What matters to the Indian postcolonial élite is national
identity, not social justice. The immense rural population of India, the poor and
the subaltern, remain as voiceless as ever. It is not surprising that the Neo-Vedāntic
postcolonialists now demand a return to the old Brāhmanic social order, by making
India a Hindu nation. And it is no small irony that the poor millions see more good
in modernity, the Enlightenment type of modernity, which at least affords them the
right to political self-representation in postcolonial India. Under that scenario, they
can at least now have a tryst with their own destinies.

In the following pages I reflect on the self-colonising agency of the Neo-Vedāntic
élite. Lest I be accused of cognitive slavery, I shall clarify my methodology. I believe
in immanent criticism, which means reflection in terms of Sanskrit categories of
thought. Nāgārjuna, the founder of Mādhyamika Buddhism, believed that criticism
is authentic only if it is immanent to its textual field, if it emanates from the problems
it seeks to understand, and if it is done in terms of indigenous categories of thought
(Yadav 1992). I will use the Vedāntic mirror to review the relation of identity and difference in the postcolonial discourse. The discourse is replete with expressions like
"impose," "superimpose," "plant," "supplant," "self," "other," "imagined," "manufactured," "bonding," "eroticised bonding," etc. It so happens that Śaṅkarācārya's
Vedānta is just that, both in theme and method of thought. The privileged category is
adhyāsa, meaning "mispredicated identity." I examine this category to discern how
Vedānta constructs the self as a site of which to predicate the not-self for utilitarian
reasons, and then to see how the ensuing self-alienation prepares the self to actively
receive the alien. The self is absolutely different from all its representations, but
the difference must be annulled in order to secure self-interest in the non-otherness
of the two. I then apply the category adhyāsa to the colonial self, showing how it
conceived of India in terms of absolute difference, and how it imposed its identity
on the alien in the name of utilitarian non-otherness. The colonial self is absolutely
different from the site on which it is imposed. That is the truth. But there is no good
in the truth, and the imagined non-difference of the two must be affirmed in order to
secure emancipatory interests. I then try to establish how these two mispredicated
identities, colonizing and self-colonising, converged in nineteenth century India.
The convergence gave birth to the postcolonial discourse. I end up listing a series of

questions that discourse ignores but which mother India nevertheless must face to define her future.

Śaṅkarācārya on *Adhyāsa*

Adhyāsa derives from a prefix, *adhi*, signifying a locus or site, and from the verbal root *as*, meaning, "to seat," "to place," "to let be." *Adhyāsa* means, not taking a thing as it is in itself and *mis*-taking it to be something else. It means placing an entity or its properties in a locus where the entity or properties are naturally absent (*abhūta-tad-bhāva*). The nature of the locus, its being in itself, is concealed. It is made to bear an altogether different sort of identity. *Adhyāsa* signifies an epistemic anomaly, for example, mistaking mother of pearl for silver. What is really present (the mother of pearl) is not perceived; something else is placed subjectively on it, and then is perceived, as in "I perceive silver." The anomaly consists in perceiving something that is simultaneously different from being and nonbeing. The silver is not present, for what is there is mother of pearl. It is not absent, for it actually is an object of sensory contact. Ontologically speaking, the silver is not the mother of pearl; and yet, phenomenologically speaking, it is none other than the mother of pearl. *Adhyāsa* consists in mistaking the actual for the real. The silver is an imagined entity, a categorial embarrassment standing between being and non-being, presence and absence. And yet it defines the real presence, the locus on which it is subjectively placed and perceived.

Adhyāsa entails logical oddity as well. "S is P" is a case of *adhyāsa* if P signifies properties that are alien to S, and which nevertheless ought to be imposed on S, if it is to be a site of material and moral interest. "S is S" is true, but it is also a tautology and meaningless. *Adhyāsa* means discovering meaning through mispredicated identity, which necessitates replacing "S is S" with "S is P". Logically speaking S and P are altogether different sorts of entity; the presence of one entails absence of the other in the same place. Difference is the truth, but in it there is no material and moral good. Therefore truth must make room for the false, difference for the imagined identity. Being must be altered into Being-as, self into self-as. There is no material or moral good in self-in-itself; it must be construed as something else. Imagined identity is logically odd, but it also is the condition for our being in the world. Life, after all, is larger than logic.

Śaṅkarācārya (788–820 CE) inaugurated the discourse of *adhyāsa* with his commentary on the *Brahmasūtra*, the *Brahmasūtra Śaṅkara Bhāṣya* (Cited hereafter as *BSB**). In the preface of his text he states that the difference of self and other is as evident as day and night, light and darkness. There is an absolute difference between the two, an infinite gap, and any appropriation of the one over the other cannot be logical. The appropriation can only be illogical, even erotically bonded

---

*Swami Yogindranand (ed.), *Brahmasūtra Śaṅkara Bhāṣya with Vācaspati's Bhāmatī*, Vol. 1 (Varanasi: Saddharma Prakasana Pratisthana), 6–8. Hereafter referred to as *BSB*.

(*mithunī-kṛtya*; cf. *BSB*: 6–8). But it is also natural, useful and efficacious. Śaṅkara emphatically asserts that it is in the eroticised non-otherness of the self and the other that the world is conceived and lived (*"satyānṛte mithunī-kṛtya itilokavyahāraḥ" BSB*: 15–16). The difference of self and other is the truth, but truth is useless for all practical purposes. This is so because the self (*Ātman*) by itself is worldless; it cannot say "I," it has no desire or body, and thus cannot define or represent itself in the world. The self is silence. Therefore the other, the not-self, must be imposed on the self in order that it may say "I," affirm or deny in terms of the other, and thus be able to bear a meaningful world. Through imposed identity, the eroticised bonding with the alien, the self assumes an epistemic gesture and says, "I know this." By the same imposition the self assumes an ethical agency and says, "I do this," assumes a political agency and says, "I am the king," and assumes a religious persona saying, "I do *yajña*." *Adhyāsa* is the prerequisite of epistemology and ontology, ethics and law, politics and culture, slavery and freedom, suffering and salvation, hell and heaven (*"Sarvāṇi ca śāstrāṇi vidhipratiṣeda-mokṣa parāṇi" BSB*: 42, 73). Where there is mispredicated identity, there is the world and, like the mother of pearl appearing as silver, all discourse entails mispredicated identity. Where there is no such identity, there is no world and no discourse (*"mithyājñānanimittaṃ vyavahāram iti/" Bhāmatī* 15–16. *BSB*: 428). The efficacy of *adhyāsa* is total. Śaṅkara's agenda is clear: being in the world means seeing oneself as other. It means letting the self be defined in alien terms, especially of an alien that promotes material and moral interests. Even a cow is driven towards a loving master with green grass in hand, let alone the philosopher (*"Viduṣāmapi ādhaya nibandhanaṃ vyavahāratvāt" BSB*: 45–46). Such is the power of self-alienating subjectivity, and it necessitates mispredicated identity. The self must first live through non-otherness with the other before it reclaims immediacy with itself in silence. Vedānta, says Śaṅkara, is a discourse on the utilitarian loss and spiritual discovery of the self (*BSB*: 52–53).

The key term in Śaṅkara's discourse is *atha*, the Sanskrit equivalent of our contemporary "post." It means "after," "auspicious," "departure," "new beginning," "new thinking," "decisive knowledge," "region," "location."[1] New thinking has to do with new location, the new location is auspicious, and that entails social transcendence. Śaṅkara devotes a whole chapter to *atha*/"post," using it to signify the condition for performing the new, Vedāntic discourse (*jijñāsādhikaraṇam; BSB*: 55–64). "Post" means post-Vedic forms of life and thought. The Vedic inquiry affirms the reciprocity of thought and action, self and self-representation, being and will. The Vedāntic inquiry, on the other hand, affirms the self-in-itself, one that cannot be an agent and to which all action, will, and representations are alien. The first conceives of the self as an agent of self-predication, and the other attributes no agency or subjectivity to the self and yet affirms it as the site of all predications (*BSB*: 65–83). The issue is not that there be no action. In that case there will be no world: being in the world means activity. The issue is whether the self incarnates its essence in will and representation, as the Vedic self does, or whether it is a locus of actions caused by the will of the self as the other. The Vedic self is immanent in its life-world, is happy or unhappy with the fruits of its own actions, and lives through the glory or humiliation of its own representation in history. The Vedāntic self transcends its life-world, and merely witnesses representations that are staged upon it for utilitarian reasons, not excluding slavery.

The discontinuity between the two visions of the self is evident. The prerequisite of Vedāntic discourse is to reject causal relations between self and society, being and history. It is necessary to take a geocultural stance, says Śaṅkara, to divide space categorically into east and west, and then to associate the Vedic discourse with the east and the Vedāntic discourse with the west. Performing this discourse of the self is like swimming the ocean. Unlike the Vedic folks, who swim towards the east, the Vedāntins must post the east and swim towards the west to produce the discourse of loosing and discovering the self ("*Nahi pūrvasamudraṁ jigamiśoh pratilomyena pratyaksamudram*").[2] The Vedāntins must discover meaning in self-alienation, that is, in being and belonging to a life-world. Vedānta means an "end," "devaluation," even "death," of the Vedic east. It also means "extreme west," the greatest "west that there is," so west that none further than it can be conceived (*paścimāt paścimaṁ*).[3] The knowledge of the loss and discovery of the self is produced there ("*Ātmakatve vidyā pratipattaye sarve Vedāntānta ārabhyate*" *BSB*: 53). This westward move occurs in scriptural reason, form of life and theme of thought.

The Upaniṣads, the reigning text in the Vedāntic west, are extremely secretive, exclusive and mystical. They contain the truth and good of society, but they affirm that people at large need not be aware of them. Being (*Ātman*) is a metaphysical presence; it equally resides in all beings but is hidden from them all (*anupraviśya tatah Bṛhadāraṇyaka Upaniṣad*: 1.5.14c). Hence the *bhāṣya* – the hermeneutics intended to bring the truth and good to light. Knowing Being or the self, bringing it out of hiding and seeing it face to face, satisfies emancipatory interests. But does it follow that the right to read the texts – and understand them – is enjoyed as universally as the universal presence of Being? Do the *śūdra* also have the right to read the texts? "*na tatra śūdrāya adhikāraḥ syāt*" If they are illiterate and cannot read, should not they have at least the right to hear them? Who is qualified to the *bhāṣya* asks Śaṅkara (*BSB*: 430–438)? Śaṅkara raises these questions, entwining ontology, social order, ideology and authorial location, in detail in *Brahmasūtra* 1.3.34–38. He answers in the negative. He acknowledges two kinds of rights: natural and morally acquired rights. He classifies the right to read the text as a morally acquired right, associating it with sociality test.[4] There is no text without the reading and reciting (hearing) of it, and neither activity has efficacy without the morally acquired right to perform them. Reading is not an act-in-itself; nor is it personal or natural. Reading the scriptures is a social act, whose efficacy lies in altruistic intention, which functions as the instrumental reason to materialise the desired end (*BSB*: 432). It also determines Śaṅkarācārya's authorial location. The reader-interpreter is qualitatively above the people, and they hear him because he discovers the meaning of their being in words. The right to read and interpret the scriptural texts is a matter of Brāhmiṇic exclusivity, and a *śūdra* violates the moral fabric of society if he appropriates to himself the right to read them. That is the law. Śaṅkara recommends severe punishment for those who violate the law. "The ears of him [*śūdra*] who hears the Vedas are to be filled with molten lead and lac...; his tongue is to be slit, if he recites it; his body is to be cut, if he possesses or preserves it" (*"Vedoccārane jihvācchedo dhāraṇe śarīrabheda iti"*).*

What about the Brahmins in general? Are they not authorised to read and interpret the scriptures? Śaṅkara says that authentic reading is consequent upon understanding, and this is what the Mīmāṃsā Brahmins, for instance, do not do. They reduce the scriptural meaning to syntactic structure, truth to form, life to social immanence. Śaṅkara insists the scriptural text is more than signs stilled in ink, that words bear meaning, and meaning transcends the sentences wherein it dwells. Śaṅkara views the relation between meaning and language as analogous with the relation between the self and the body. Self is qualitatively different from the body, although it dwells in the body. Similarly, the interpreter is the "head" of the social body, not only in the sense of being above the body, but also in the sense of being beyond it. Strictly speaking, the interpreter does not belong to the society, and the society is not his. Thus, Śaṅkara maintains the difference between Veda and Vedānta, between east and west. The Vedic east is a sphere of pre-reflective reason and linguistic formalism, tradition and social immanence, customs and conventions, rites and rituals, polytheistic prayers, and dualistic dogmas. It claims decisive knowledge of the sun by merely seeing it rise in the east. The Vedāntic west will have none of it.[5] Here reason has become reflective, consciousness emancipated from all cultural moorings. "Here a father is no longer the father, mother no longer the mother, world no longer the world, gods no longer the gods, Vedas no longer the Vedas. Having gone beyond good and evil, he has overcome all the woes of the heart."[6] Rising above cultural taboos is no flaw here; it actually makes the life of reflection all the more glorious.[7] The meta-Vedic Brahmin has become modern and enlightened, for he alone understands what society is and how it came into being. His cogito is like the sun that, having moved through the day, evokes decisive knowledge as it sets on the western horizon. Arriving in this western sphere, Vedāntic consciousness witnesses the difference between existence and essence; it affirms social inequality as a moral preference in the name of the universal presence and metaphysical perfection of Being. Having arrived there Vedānta responds to the egalitarian challenge of Buddhism by suspending the causal deduction of society from Being, and there it also meets the modernizing project of the Euro-Christian West.

And what has reflective reason discovered? Basically two things: the truth of silent Being and the merely utilitarian value of the alien subjectivity that *māyā* imposes on Being. It reduces Being to a thing-in-itself, to an immediacy forever glued to itself, an inert thereness unaware of its being there (*"Vastumātrasya sthitiḥ"* Śaṅkara 1918: 17 [cited hereafter as *SVS*]). Being is beyond cognitive thinking. A cognitive claim is about an X that implies a non-X that counts against X. To say, "This is a cow," is to imply that the subject that knows the cow is not a cow, and that cow is different from the rest of the world. Being cannot be affirmed or

---

*This is the text of Commentary to *BSB* 1, 3.38 | :
śravaṇādhyayanārthapratiṣedhāt smṛteś ca |
itaśca na śūdrasyādhikāraḥ .../

denied, and nothing can be affirmed or denied in its name ("*Niṣkalam niṣkriyam*" *SVS*: 27); "*vyaktavyaktasya vilakṣaṇaḥ*" Vidyaraṇya 1887: 997). Being transcends good and evil, and it devalues the world where questions of good and evil arise in the first place.[8] It excludes from itself the possibility of becoming otherwise than it is; it is ontological tautology. It cannot be a self-predicating subject ("*svātmasya avatiṣṭhataḥ*." Vidyaraṇya 1887: 982).

The notion of subjectivity to which everybody in Indian thought subscribed was that articulated by Pāṇini. A subject, according to Pāṇini, is free in the sense that it can visualise an end or purpose, has intentional consciousness, and appropriates the most efficient means to materialise its end.[9] The subject is *jīva*, the existing being, who is driven by a self-predicative project and whose consciousness is an intentional movement towards a willed end ("*kāmasya bījaḥ saṃkalpāḥ saṃkalpādeva jāyate.*" *SVS*: 11). Accordingly, an object is not a thing-in-itself. An object is that which the subject most ardently desires and which comes to exist through the appropriating act of the subject (*SVS*: 58). The identity of the object is constituted by the objectifying intentionality of the subject, who is driven to encounter its "I" as *this* "I" (*pradhānībhūta prayojana phalāśrayatvam*). Driven to say "I," it lands itself in an endless array of objects. Out to appropriate what it is not, desire lands the subject in a relational field, to a situation where meaning lies in "I know this", "I do this", "This is mine", and "I am this" (*BSB*: 43–44). But because the subject is appetitive, its desire is inevitably unfulfilled; it remains directional, living a life of self-transcendence (*saṃsarati iti saṃsāraḥ*). Man's being, the *jīva*, is committed to doing, and doing for the sake of having (*tattvam sampradhānatvam*). Desire drives the subject to an ablative form of life, to a life of self-distantiation (*vibhāga āśryatvam*). The subject is out to give everything to itself. This accounts for identity as a temporal unity, a process through which the subject arrives at himself only by first falling away from himself (*tad eva avadhitvam*). The subject's present, his being what he is, is only a passage to his becoming what he shall be ("*Bhrameti eṣaḥ jīvaḥ saṃsāra-maṇḍale.*" *SVS*: 55). Paradoxically, in this way the subject remains the same while the objects he appropriates are forever new. Desire commits the subject to a life of circular possibilities. The subject even denies his own death, but this denial only gives him back to the recurrence of rebirth and redeath (*punarapi jananam punarapi maraṇam*). The subject happens to arrive at himself by virtue of not being *there*, and each arrival inevitably necessitates one more departure ("*dūram duramito gattva... punaḥ punaḥ.*" Sharma 1975: 262). The subject is before himself, the subject is after himself, and in-between it remains himself. It is a strange bird, seeking to land while still flying. It is caught up in the paradox of opening and closing its own eyes. In its efforts to fulfil itself, it ends up more and more empty ("*Tataḥ kartā tato bhoktā.*" Śaṅkara 1973: 40; cited hereafter as *AV*). In sum, the subject is a karmic being, a self-predicative project in search of itself, a dialectic of action and consequence (*karma phala saṅghata*). Time is a burden that the karmic subject bears as an "I"; he does so in the hope of facing himself in the mirror of a decisive "this" (*abhimukha bhāva mātram sambandham viduḥ*). Such a burden is the world.

Śaṅkara subscribes to Pāṇini's view of the subject. However, he also insists that Being is not a subject. Being is pure consciousness, which for Śaṅkara means being unconscious of anything and everything, including itself. Being cannot appropriate to itself an "I" and a "not-I". It is voiceless, mindless, thoughtless, wordless, worldless, timeless presence. Being feels nothing, does or undoes nothing, affirms or denies nothing, loves or hates nothing.[10] Being is fullness, not in the sense that it desires and appropriates everything to itself, but in the sense that it desires nothing and therefore lacks nothing (*"Nasmyagantā nāpi gantā."* SVS: 128). Lack is not a thing, lack is not in things and, of course, lack is not nothing. Lack presupposes a subject who is self-conscious (*aham idam*) and whose mode of being is having (*mama idam*). Being is not conscious of itself; it blissfully sleeps (*sete iti puruṣaḥ*; 'puri sete iti puruṣaḥ' – "It is called 'puruṣaḥ' because it lies within the city/that is, the body". The association of city with body is Upaniṣadic.). It is too still to admit the alienation of "is" (*asti*) and "can" (*śakti*). It is devoid of self-transcendence and lacks a teleological destiny (*āptakāma*). It cannot begin to be in an act of self-negation, it cannot posit another that it seeks to subsume, and there is no question of it arriving at itself through the medium of history. Being is not in time, time is not in Being, and there is no relation between Being and time (*"Kāla bhedaṃ vastubhedaṃ "deśabhedaṃ kiṃcid bhedaṃ na tasya asti."* SVS: 151. *"Kālatrayepi naiva kaścana."* SVS: 117). Robbed of recognitive will, it has no idea of discovering itself through the rise and fall of civilization; it can have no society, history or nation. It cannot conceive of an alien with which it contrasts itself and which it could then overcome on the way to realizing its "concrete universality."[11] It is indifferent to "why" questions, and is itself without a "why." It is a pure given and, thus, it serves as a site on which the world can be erected (*ākāśo vai Brahma Chāndogya ūpaniṣad* 4.14).

Being need not be conceived this way. What *is* necessary is to see the social and political agenda in defence of which Śaṅkara proposed this conception of Being. The first item on the agenda that we may adduce is that Being does not happen as beings. There is a total difference, an absolute dualism, between Being and subject, essence and existence, self and society. Being is heartless like a stone (*pāṣāṇavat*); it does not care (*nirmama*). Being is not in society, although society cannot be without it. It is the ground on which *māyā*, through *adhyāsa*, places the world of subject and object. It is a classic case of "S is S" replaced by "S is P". *Māyā* is a transcendental cunning: wondrous and daring, it nevertheless dishonours Being and metaphysical reason (*"Vicārasahatvaṃ ca avidya ayaṃ alaṃkāram eva"*; *"Pramāṇa-vastu anadṛtya."* Vidyāraṇya 1888: 175, 176). Consequently, to ask for the "why" of *māyā* is naïve at best, and philosophers should certainly be aware of that (*"Na buddhirantaṃ pṛcchanti na jānāmi iti vādinaṃ"* Vidyāraṇya 1887: 933; also 932, 910). No less an authority than Vaśistha understands this; he asks Rāma, the ideal king and the most popular incarnation of God, to outgrow this naiveté on the ground that it serves no purpose (*"Kuto jāto 'yaṃ te rāma mā'stu te vicāraṇa."* Sharma 1975: 512; Vidyāraṇya 1888: 933). What serves the purpose of the Vedantin is not the genesis of *māyā* but its social efficacy, not where it comes from by what it does.

And what does *māyā* do? It turns Being into the site, the ground, on which society comes to pass. *Māyā* means to create and measure, to constitute and objectify, to identify and differentiate.[12] We have seen that Being has no intentionality, no will to represent itself, and all forms are alien to it. *Māyā* is the Other of Being, a transcendental subjectivity that cares. It makes possible that which is logically impossible (*caturā hi sā*). *Māyā* is *saṅgavasana*, which means, "being in relation to others." It is a subjectivity filled with will and eros, desire and representation ("*Vikṣepa nāmni rājastu... Pravṛtti hetu puruṣasya*" SVS: 77; "*piti saṃnkalpa jālasya nāmne'ti Rāghava.*" Sharma 1975: 260–261). It thankfully conceals Being and projects on it a subject that says "I" and "thou" and bears a world (*sambhāraṇam*). After all, being in the world, even as a mispredicated identity, is better than worldless Being and nothingness ("*Adhyasāt eva saṃsāraḥ.*" SVS: 78). Thus is erected a subject that places itself in bondage amidst objects, that binds itself through the alien in order to seize hold of itself and its world ("*Karyam eṣa janma mṛtyu paramparā; Pravṛtti eva saṃsāre.*" SVS: 8; "*pravṛtti eva samsare.*" SVS: 78). Such a subject is the *jīva*, his world the *saṃsāra* (*ātmakṛtiḥ sarvavṛttibhiḥ*). The world is a noetic density of temporal proportions. It is an aesthetic body that the *jīva* has constituted in *karma*, and a burden that it bears in mispredicated transcendence.[13] This transcendence requires a medium and a place. The medium is the body, and the world is the place. My body is the medium of my being in the world, the bearer of my embodied existence as a self-predicative existence ("*Samsarkarnam lingatmano bhoga sadhanam.*" SVS: 53). It is through my body that I am represented and recognised, related and separated, loved or hated. It is through my body that I have ritual purity or impurity, power or poverty, wealth or lack of social efficacy.[14] My birth into a caste is an intentional event, something that I cause in my self-predicative history.[15] I am a consequence of my own acts. My birth is an index to my will-to-be, and the moral of kārmic existence is measurable in terms of my caste duties. Therefore my rights and duties to society are determined by the social obligations of the caste in which I am born.[16] If I am born into a Brahmin caste, I should act like a Brahmin. I should mediate between text and society, kings and commoners. On the other hand, if I am born into a *sūdra* caste, I should act like a *sūdra*. It all has to do with my willed-being: I am bound by the consequences of my own will. The liberty of self-predication is the foundation of a moral society. Such a society is Sanātana Dharma.

Such is the Vedāntic vision of the world. Transcendentally speaking, there is no causal relationship between Being and society. Being has nothing to do with how we are in the world, except that it functions as a site on which *māyā* erects the existence of beings in relation to other beings. There is no intrinsic relationship between consciousness and language, Being and words. Being is a metalinguistic state, a clean slate, without any innate marks or signs (*amātram*). Vedānta is thus extraordinarily flexible. The meta-Vedic Brahmins actively adopt any linguistic structure on Being, be it Sanskrit, Persian or English. They are just as willing to erase the signs once their social and political agenda has been achieved. This makes the Vedāntic Brahmins extraordinarily progressive and modernistic, even postcolonial! The Brahmin caste will impose any language on consciousness that benefits its interest. In this way, it has been able to define the nation for its sole benefit. Vedānta justifies it all in the name of the Upanishads that say, "Whatever is an other, he does not perceive; even if he perceives, he does not witness it as an other."[17] The witnessed non-otherness of the other is more important than anything else. The Vedāntic west is the ontological site – not just the historical host – of all sorts of strategic imposition. *Māyā* has been used as a strategic category to impose dharmic society on the Vedāntic west. Historically speaking, this may imply all sorts of impositions, especially if, "in fact," society is not in Being and Being not in society. For instance, Swami Vivekananda understood it all with great clarity in the nineteenth century. "Let foreigners come," the Swami said, "and flood the land with their armies. Never mind. Up, India, and conquer the world with your spirituality. . . . the only condition of national life, of awakened and vigorous life, is the conquest of the world by Indian thought" (Thomas 1979: 22). By "Indian thought," Vivekananda meant Vedānta. Being, the pure consciousness, will be the site on which the drama of slavery and freedom, loss and discovery of the self is played, with the meta-Vedic Brahmins as the central players. These Brahmins exhibit a great deal of historical compassion for, and confidence in, Being – and a concomitant metaphysical denial of history. To be conquered and to conquer the conqueror, to appreciate the alien other and to surpass him in his own game: that is the leitmotif of the Vedāntic vision of history. Śaṅkarācārya understood the mission of mispredicated identity quite succinctly: willingly appropriate the alien in order eventually to erase the same (*adhyāropa-apavāda-nyāyaḥ*). In precolonial India, Vedantic subjectivity placed the Vedic east on the Vedāntic west; it even domesticated the categories of Buddhism in order to "post" Śākyamuni from India. In the nineteenth century the same subjectivity revived Śaṅkarācārya as the national philosopher; it was ready to willingly appropriate another alien, this time the Euro-Christian west. It wanted westernisation with a view to re-Vedāntise India. Colonialism entailed a coincidence of the interests of Euro-Christian and Vedāntic forms of west. Both wanted colonial imposition. Vedāntic subjectivity posted all history east of the Vedāntic west, posited absolute difference between the two, and placed itself in the middle in order to defend its hegemonic hold on society.

The Euro-Christian Colonial Project

Being in the world means being in relation with others, a moral bonding between cultures and cultures, nations and nations. The key word is "relation." The relation is not inherent in the *terms* of relation, and this accounts for what a perceived identity will do with difference. Colonialism is a relation between two fundamentally unequal entities, one that is unnatural and alien and symbolises "the strangest of all political anomalies", as Thomas Macaulay said. One term, the West, is the Euro-Christian light and redemption; the other, the East, is the dark and bloody superstitions (cf. Stokes 1989: 1–80; Darby 1987: 8–52; Metcalf 1994: 28–112). There is a "dangerous gulf" between the two; that is the truth. The gulf must be overcome in the interests of man; that is the good. The West must post East; that was the messianic call of history. Knowing the world was not enough; the need was to change it. Thus, colonialism was an ethical project. Colonialism insisted upon the return from metaphysics to history, speculative reason to liberative will. Filled with an "impulse for completion", the West in the eighteenth and nineteenth centuries demanded a new beginning on a universal scale. It called for a liberative colonialism. Scholar-statesmen like James Mill and Zachary Macaulay, Jeremy Bentham and Charles Grant, John Stuart Mill and Thomas Macaulay made the call. They all came from upper class backgrounds. They were part of an intellectual and moral aristocracy, and believed that politics was the noblest of professions. They believed that colonialism was a call of duty to humankind (Darby 1987: 32).

There were two sides to colonialism, sacred and secular, but both were utilitarian in aspect. Evangelical Christianity dominated the sacred side, represented by figures such as Charles Grant and Zachary Macaulay. "Upon what general principles," asked Grant, "may we best hope to make our connections with that country [India] permanent, and, as far as we are concerned, indissolvable?" (Grant 1832: 111). He took the difference between England and India as self-evident, and found good in the assimilation of the two. Grant insisted that the words of scripture command a conflictual stance against Hinduism, which, in his understanding, placed salvation in the other world. India must be emancipated from Hinduism, despite the truth that India is not England. Grant practiced liberation theology: creation is a liberative act, the act is universal, and it seeks a world historical univocity in Jesus Christ. The knowledge of God was to be found in his words, the Bible, and those words command men to work for the material and moral uplift of this world. The logos was made flesh to return the truth to the body, salvation to society (Grant 1832: 22). Yet Grant's justification for all this is intentionally utilitarian, and not speculative. "Those who conceive religions to be conversant merely about forms and speculative reason," he said, "may think that the world need not be troubled concerning it. No, the ultimate object [of religion(s)] is a moral government. The pre-eminent excellence of the morality which the Gospel teaches... cannot be denied by those who are unwilling to admit its higher claims" (Grant 1832: 99). In Grant's theology, doing is knowing, and seeing is believing. There is no such thing as a religion in itself. Not even Christianity is self-authenticating in this way. Religion must pass a utility test, must verify whether or not it promotes the material and moral happiness of people in this world. If it does not, it has failed the test and is not a religion. Truth must be good, that which is good must work. Of course, the Gospel has worked. Christianity has passed the utility test. It is the basis of the material and moral superiority of European nations, especially England, and Grant saw no reason why it could not do the same in India. Plainly, he was raising questions about identity and difference, the Christian I and the religious other.

Charles Grant had no patience with conservatives like Edmund Burke, who said of India: "Fault this nation may have, but God forbid that we should pass judgment upon people who framed their laws and institutions prior to our insect origin of yesterday" (Burke 1877: 46). Grant accused them of regressive utopianism, of taking religious plurality as a thing-in-itself, and of subscribing to an ideology of absolute difference (Grant 1832: 32). No matter how different, all cultures and religions should be subjected to the same utility test. He saw no good in difference and effectively proposed religious *adhyāsa*. Hinduism fails the test: it claims that truth may not be good, and good may not work. It dissolves the ethical in the metaphysical, the sociality of liberation in the spiritual immediacy with Being. Popular Hinduism is no better: it promotes servitude in a polytheistic border. It is "idolatry with all its rabble of impure deities, its monsters of wood and stone... its delusive hopes and fears, its ridiculous ceremonies and degrading institutions, its lying legends and fraudulent imposition" (Chand 1967: 238–239). Charles Grant wanted to replace this "fraudulent imposition" by liberative imposition, to replace the Hindu past with a Christian future. Convinced of the uniqueness of his kerygma, he essentialised the difference of East and West in geocultural terms, posited absolute difference between the two, and equated Hinduism with Vedantic illusionism and Christianity with liberal realism.

As indicated above, colonialism had a secular dimension as well, represented by great liberal thinkers like Herbert Spencer, Jeremy Bentham, Fitzjames Stephen, Thomas Macaulay and John Stuart Mill. Of these, Mill was most influential. He shared three things with sacred utilitarianism: (a) a distaste for metaphysical reasoning and logocentric discourse; (b) rejection of the conservative and orientalist claim that difference was good in itself, and (c) a view of knowledge as the means of utilitarian action. Human beings, said Mill, desire material and moral happiness, they ought to desire it, and the greatest happiness of the greatest number of people alone is desirable as the ultimate end. X should do Y if its consequence is Z, and only if none other than Y signifies the end to the same degree. Z signifies the utility test for Y as the most desirable moral act. X is the ethical agent by virtue of Y. In Mill's view, the ultimate source of moral actions is social conscience: denying oneself for the good of others is the greatest happiness, and the utilitarian agent is capable of this liberative end.

Turning this calculus into a colonial proposal, Mill advocated political *adhyāsa*. Like Grant, Mill had no faith in religious difference, cultural autonomy and national borders. For him, a nation is not an integral geocultural entity, a being-in-itself, that functions as the ontological locus of cultural identity. Nor is the nation a temporalised eternity, an *end*-in-itself, that vainly bears the memories of its past. Rather, a nation is the instrumental reason for actualising the material and moral happiness of its people. India failed Mill's ethical test and therefore had no reasons to exist as a nation (Hutchins 1967: 9). By equating salvation with transcendence of the social, Hinduism pre-empted reflection on ethics and politics, legislative authority and the common good. Mill demanded that India be emancipated from its illiberative memory of the Hindu past. Reduced in conception to *tabula rasa*, India's identity could be reconstituted in terms of a European future. By Mill's reasoning, that would be an ethical act. He saw no reason why what "England" had done as a utilitarian liberator for Tom, Dick and Harry in London could not be reproduced for Devadatta in Calcutta.

The Euro-Christian west had a noble aim. It made ethics the touchstone of politics. In the view of Macaulay, Mill, and others, salvation is material and social rather than spiritual or metaphysical and, furthermore, all human beings deserve it in the name of God. This West accordingly envisioned history as a self-predicative project, a relational existence in which England recognised its identity by conceiving and overcoming everything different. Two assumptions constitute that relation. One is liberative uniqueness: the belief that salvation is possible through Euro-Christian praxis alone. The other is universality: the belief that salvation is good for none unless it is good for all. Belief in uniqueness polarised the terms of the relation, that is, it was belief in the Euro-Christian I and the non-Christian other. It dualised the world as West and East, historical and mystical, linear and circular, this-worldly and otherworldly, mature and childish, sundown and sundawn (Nakamura 1965: 244–245; see also Brugman 1965: 221–232). The difference between West and East is qualitative and total, not quantitative and relative. Moreover, the difference is as evident as the difference between day and night, light and darkness. Of necessity, the uniqueness of Euro-Christian West is self-referential. It recognises itself only in relation to the different. However, "the different" is for it not an insurmountable limit but a project of "completion." This is the belief in universality. The different is not an independent subjectivity that can meditate on its presence in relation to its future by returning a critical gaze at its own past. If that were the case, it would pose an absolute limit to the Euro-Christian West. Nor is the different conceived as an instance of non-being. In that case, the West would have no object or locus of its liberative act. The different can only be an apparitional object, a definite presence that defies categories of being and non-being (*sat-asat-vilakṣaṇa**). That is, the difference is a product of *adhyāsa*. Derrida has described this prescriptive, Euro-Christian cogito very well. He says, "It institutes, declares, writes, inscribes, prescribes. A system of marks, it outlines space in order to assign forced residence or to close off borders. It does not discern; it discriminates" (Derrida 1986: 331; cf. Mudimbe 1988: 1–23, 44–97).

The Euro-Christian West cannot be content with absolute difference. That would undermine the christological promise of history, would ensnare uniqueness in particularity. It would make England infidel to God who says, "I am one who will be." The West must find meaning in concrete universality, which means enforcing its identity on others in order to make itself global. It could only find an India that suffers under "fraudulent imposition." Nonetheless, the so-called "imposition" really is anti-liberative in that it spiritualised salvation in a tautological Being that admits of nothing more than saying, "I am." And for all its transcendence, the imposition is nonetheless ideological, for it is salvation only to preserve a society of structural injustice and slavery, Brāhmiṇic monopoly and despotic government (Thomas

---

*This is a technical phrase associated with Śaṅkara's form of advaita vedānta: "something which cannot be defined as existing or as not-existing". It is a definition for mithyā, the manifest which is erroneous, but which is not non-existent. The doctrine as developed is not found in Śaṅkara's writings. It occurs, for the first time as doctrine, in the Brahma-siddhi, BS 9.11–10.2. Yadav most likely obtained this nuance from similar treatment in P. Sankaranarayanan, *What is Advaita?*, (Bombay: Bharatiya Vidya Bhavan, 1970)

1979: 38). Vedānta promotes the greatest good of the smallest number of people. In the Vedāntic view, India's liberation calls for two things. One is concealment (*āvaraṇa**) of the memory of her past, of her traditional form of saying, "I am this". The other is imposition (*prakṣepa*) on her consciousness of the Euro-Christian form of being, her predicating of herself a new self-consciousness and saying, "I am that". Charles Grant defended the doctrine of enforced identity on the ground that it would erase the "dangerous gulf" between West and East (Grant 1832: 204; Stokes 1989: 34). J.S. Mill did the same, and for the same reason. The doctrine of enforced identity, in his view was "not only the purest in intention, but one of the most beneficent acts ever known to mankind" (Stokes 1989: 284). The liberals in England were convinced that colonialism was a moral mantra, the emancipatory mission and co-project of the Crown and the Christ. Colonial law was raised to the sanctity of the Ten Commandments. Material and moral happiness of the people does not consist in political liberty, but in total obedience to the English laws. Later in the nineteenth century, Stephen Fitzjames summed up the colonial project with great simplicity. "It is so to speak," he said, "the gospel of the English, and it is a compulsory gospel which admits of no dissent and no disobedience" (Stokes 1989: 301–302). Happiness consists in political slavery.

The enforced identity has a structure and aim. The structure is logically odd, the aim is liberative. Let us say that India is S, the locus, on which P is placed. P signifies a fraudulent imposition associated with polytheism and structural injustice. "S is P" stands for political praxis that promotes the greatest good of the smallest number of people. Let us say that England is T, having the property Z, the greatest good of the greatest number of people. Now T imposes its political praxis on S. Logically speaking "S is T" (let alone "India is England") is odd. It mispredicates identity by placing alien properties upon S. But liberatively speaking, T must place Z on S. The important thing is the liberative aim in "S is T," not its formal coherence as a truth claim. The Euro-Christian cogito posited difference between West and East, England and India. It propounded salvation in mispredicated identity, implanting European memory in a consciousness to which the properties associated with the memory are alien (*atasmin tad buddhiḥ*).** Despite their difference, then, both the Euro-Christian and Vedāntic forms of West espoused the efficacy of *adhyāsa*. Both were engaged in cancelling difference and enforcing identity. Their quarrel was over which form of the West to impose on India. Macaulay, Mill, and the rest believed that the imposition of the Vedantic form of the West on India (that is, "the East") was a "fabric of error," a case of mispredicated identity without any sense of social justice or material or moral happiness. Their point was that India's self must appear as England's self. The original self had to be reduced to self-as. India must not have a sense of being other to the Euro-Christian West, although the truth is that the two

---

*In Later advaita vedānta, as traditionally explained, the manifest world is bodied-forth and this process of the bodying-forth of the word (*māyā*) operates through two powers (*śakti-s*):

āvaraṇa (the concealing of Brahman (Yadav's Being)) and vikṣepa (the projection of the manifold, manifest world)

**Cf Sankaranarayanan's (pp. 11–12), "it is the imposition of a thing on what is not that thing".

are totally other, like darkness and light. The concealment of truth and imposition of good entails intolerance of difference. Thomas Macaulay said very succinctly, "We are free to little purpose, if we grudge to any portion of the human race an equal measure of freedom and civilization" (Thomas 1979: 42).

But there is no enforced identity without language. Thomas Macaulay believed in the linguistic divide of East and West. India is enclosed in Sanskrit, a metaphysical language in which there is no place for temporal interests of man. It is a language of meaningless rituals and logocentric nonsense. English, though, is the language in which there is reciprocity of saying and doing, meaning and the means to bring the desired end. In English, all meaning is centred in material and moral happiness. A sentence is meaningful only if it serves as the means to materialise the utilitarian end. That is, English is the language of commands: through it alone has been conceived and acquired the political authority whose mission is to liberate India. "In India," Thomas Macaulay said, "English is spoken by the ruling class" (Thomas 1979: 43).

The latter assertion is fateful. It bespeaks a linguistic agency that needs a place to complete its mission. The "India" in Macaulay's locative phrase, "In India," bears a double meaning because of this location. There is a difference between being and being the locus of something, between being-in-itself and being the site of an alien agent that finds salvation in being with others. "India" signifies a mummified referent, an unmediated being or spatial presence in which there is no material or moral content. What makes "India" significant is its locative use in the sentence, its association with "in", in which case it denotes the locus of a self-predicative act ("*Jñāpaka-kriyāśraya-vācakād.*" Bhatta 1975: 372). The expression "in India" signifies a situation where India, the site, and England, the subject, are held together in an ostensibly liberative act. Given to being in doing good for others, driven by the belief that Euro-Christian uniqueness of necessity is universal, England moves from West to East. Her liberative will requires a space wherein, paradoxically, distance is reduced to a self-recognitive medium and a purposeful action. "In India" constitutes two kinds of relations. One is the relation that obtains between the subject and its site, between England and India (*adhiṣṭhāna*). This is a unilateral relation, having to do with praxis the subject performs in spite of the site. This relation is neither logical nor natural, but is directed to the liberation of India (Stokes 1989: 11). The other relation obtains between the agent and its acts, England and her political praxis. This relation is logical and natural, for with it England commits itself to historical self-transcendence, to an ablative form of life through which she mediates her identity in acts (Bhatta 1975: 355). Colonialism becomes a veritable sacred text: as one Neo-Vedāntin suggested, "The book which treats of moral, social and religious advancement of our great country... under the parental rule of the British nation is indeed a sacred book" (Keshab Chandra Sen, quoted in Heimsath 1964: 21). Colonialism is a sacred text in which England has expressed her identity in words. The privileged sentence in the text is "England in India is England." It unveils a liberated identity: England in India saying, "I am thou," to England in the Euro-Christian West.

Like the Upaniṣads, the colonial text is transcendent in two ways: spatially and linguistically. Spatially, its authors dwell seven seas away in the Euro-Christian West, giving distance an authoritative texture. It is written in English, a language that most Indians do not speak or understand, but it purports to contain the material and moral good for Indians. The content of the text is universality of liberation, although access to it is by no means universal. The text is for the people, although not of the people; it is regulative, not participative. The people may not handle "their" text. Like its authors, it can only be seen or accepted in reverence. Seeing presupposes distance between the seer and the seen, and encourages faith in the authority of the transcendent, whereas touching negates the distance between seer and the seen. Physical involvement creates cognitive intimacy, including loss of belief in the transcendent origin and authoritative voice of the text. Very much like the Upanishads, the colonial text cherishes linguistic secrecy (*guhyādeśa*). Colonialism opens itself only to Euro-Christian Brahmins, only to the moral minority, whose social worth is qualitatively different from that of the people. For, in order that the text command obedience, the representatives of the Raj, too, must be transcendent to the linguistic and social space of the people. They must be perceived as qualitatively different on moral grounds (Forster 1924: 50). It gives administrative authority to those "altruists" who know that political authority must not be shared if it is to be effective at all. Colonialism invites those who, in linguistic and cultural senses, reside West of society.

The Colonialist text has an assumption as well as an aim. It assumes that linguistic difference between Euro-Christian West and the East is total, but it aims to be understood on the site. The text needs mediators, those who can interpret its meaning to the people of India. Thomas Macaulay hoped to create this interpretive class through English education. In a letter to his father, Zachary Macaulay, he described his mission. "It is my belief that if our plans for education are followed up, there will not be a single idolater among the respectable classes in Bengal thirty years hence" (Panikkar 1963: 28). By "respectable classes" Macaulay meant Bhadraloka, the urbanised elite of the higher castes. He believed J.S. Mill's claim that every society has a gifted minority that is endowed with superiority of intellect, and that in India the Brahmins constituted that minority (Mill 1840: 178; cf. Hutchins 1967: 17). Macaulay wanted the men of superior intellect to learn English so that they could assume mediative authority and begin interpreting the colonial text to the people. "We must do our best to form a class of people who may be interpreters between us and the millions we govern, a class of people Indian in blood and colour, but English in taste, in opinion, in morals and intellect," he said (from the infamous "Minute on Education," quoted in Stokes 1989: 46). The colonial text can also be read from Fitzjames Stephen's later insistence that lack of political liberty is compatible with the principle of authority in India, that self-government is no substitute for good government, that power precedes liberty, that the government is always the rule of a gifted minority imposing its ideal of happiness on the majority, that man's work, whatever its worth, fulfils the gospel of duty formed in self-denial and obedience (Stephen 1874: 183, 239; cf. Stokes 1989: 288–313). Colonialism needed interpreters who could help post the "useless" and "fraudulent imposition,"

the Vedāntic cunning, and alter India's identity by imposing on her the useful mind
of the Euro-Christian West. But they first have to go through English education and
forms of thought, moral purgation and cognitive reconstitution. The Brahmins were
already the "head" of their society; they transcended their social body. The need was
to further distance their mind from their body, reconceive the mind in Euro-Christian
episteme, and place the mind on the body again. Thinking in Euro-Christian frames
of reference, living a post-conventional form of life and thought, the élite would
help liberate India by mediating and interpreting the colonial text to the people.

But mediation entails an alienated form of life. It seeks to overcome what it
assumes. It assumes a geocultural, even metaphysical, dualism between West and
East. The aim is to post what, in the first place, it posits; the aim is to overcome
difference by enforcing the European mind on a body that is tacitly admitted to be
different. The interpreter must bear a mispredicated identity – as all Vedāntins do.
He has a European mind on Indian body, but there is no organic relation between
the two. His body is not of his mind; his mind is not of his body, least of all the
extended social body. There is in the interpreter an alienation of being and body,
self and society. Conceived under an episteme that etches the difference of East
and West in either/or logic, the interpreter belongs to neither (*anirvācanīya*). He
cannot be described in terms of the categories that produced him; he is neither
Indian nor European. He is instead a cultural embarrassment, a category mistake.
He bears an enforced identity conceived in the eroticised bonding of East and West
(*mithunī-kṛtya*). However, his alienation is supposed not to cause estrangement. The
interpreter is in the middle that mediates text and society, rulers and the ruled. He
has gone West of his society to live in proximity with the colonial text, a privilege
denied to ordinary folks, including the Vedic Brahmins. He represents the moral
efficacy and power of the Raj, and gets to keep his precolonial hold on society. The
interpreter is a "sahib," bearing a logically odd but materially privileged between-
ness of Euro-Christian and Vedantic forms of West. Mispredicated identity bears the
world (*vyavahārasatya*).

Such is colonialism, the habit of suppressing difference in the name of identity.
The Euro-Christian West was the land of liberty and democracy; the East was to be
governed by the principle of authority and despotism. The East deserved happiness,
not freedom. Coming from upper class backgrounds, most colonialists practiced
liberalism to mediate their identity in terms of difference. Their subjectivity was
mispredicated in terms of the other; they wanted to say that "England in India" is
the same as "England in England." They met with the self-alienating subjectivity
of the "unheroic Brahmins," those who had the habit of ruling India by bearing the
alien. Theirs is not the subjectivity of the innocent and weak, and they certainly do
not suffer humiliation and violence. Nor is their alienation a case of personality failure, a psychosomatic reaction of an endlessly victimised self towards an oppressive
alien, as Ashis Nandy insists (Nandy 1983: 109). On the contrary, it is premeditated,
deliberate and willed. This "unheroic" subjectivity is rooted in the robust realism of
a Vedāntic philosophy that understands – and affirms – the pragmatics of mispredicated identity. It is the subjectivity of those who went West of their society only to
say, "India in England" is the same as, "India in India." They actively used the skill

of looking at themselves as someone else as a tool to preserve their mediating hold on society. It does not matter who is the king, as long as they alone have the privilege of mediating the ruler and the ruled. Their operative mantra is: How to appropriate the alien in order subsequently to erase the same in achievement of self-interest? The mantra called for initial colonization of India with a view to re-Vedāntise Hindu society. It is my contention that this is the beginning of the postcolonial discourse, and that it happened at three levels: linguistic, religious and socio-political.

Neo-vedāntic Colonialism

Thomas Macaulay was naïve. He did not have to create a "class of persons" on whose body the Euro-Christian mind then could be planted. The appropriate class is very old. Its members believe that the body is altogether different from consciousness, and that mind is the body that thinks (sūkṣma-śarīra). Raja Rammohan Roy (1772–1833), the pre-eminent Bhadraloka and father of "modern India" represented this class. In the Moghul era he was for Persian language, literature and thought. He even acquired the degree of "Raja" from the Moghul emperor in Delhi. But when colonialism was entrenched, Roy shifted towards everything British. Jeremy Bentham was proud to say that Roy has erased the "35 million gods" in Hinduism and become a utilitarian. At his funeral in 1833 in Bristol, the Reverend Lant Carpenter said that Roy was the "enlightened Brahmin from the British capital in Hindustan" who was undoubtedly a Unitarian (Knopf 1979: 3; Halbfass 1988: 197–216). Based on Śaṅkara's commentary on the Brahmasūtra, Roy wrote Vedāntagrantha and Vedāntasārā (1815), along with Bengali translations of the Kena, Īśā, Kaṭha, Muṇḍaka and Māṇḍukya Upanishads. He also wrote The Precepts of Jesus and The Ideal of Humanity of Jesus (1820). He established the Ārya Samāj in 1828 in Calcutta, to encourage affinity between Vedāntic self-understanding and utilitarian ethics.

Roy established linguistic adhyāsa. In a letter (1823) to Lord Amherst, the then-Governor General of the Raj, Roy demanded that English replace Sanskrit. "The Sanskrit language, so difficult that almost a life is necessary for its perfect acquisition, is well known to have been for ages a lamentable check on the diffusion of knowledge; and the learning concealed under this almost impervious veil is far from sufficient to reward the labour of acquiring it" (Karunakaran 1965: 125). Like Grant and Mill, Roy was for pastoral simplicity and utilitarian efficacy, both of which he found in the English language. Sanskrit was the language of logocentric discourse and metaphysical nonsense. It was not worth the effort. "The student of Nyāya Shāstra," he said, "cannot be said to have improved his mind after he has learned from it into how many classes the objects in the universe are divided, and what speculative relation the soul bears to the body, the body to the soul, the eye to the ear, etc." (ibid.). Roy had no interest in the logic of definitions, whether what one hears is in conflict with what one sees. He saw no good in determining whether conflict of knowledge and faith has anything to do with lack of reciprocity in seeing and hearing. It is not that he did not like empiricism; it is only that he preferred to learn it from Bentham and Mill, rather than from Dharmakīrti or Gaṅgeśa. Roy found irrelevant the mainstream Hinduism that insists that language is the mother of the world; that the originary word (*Vāk*) brought the consciousness from the silent cave in the ocean to the light of the sun; that the word is strewn with noetic nameability; that self-consciousness is caught up in the dialectic of words and objects to an unsurpassable degree, to becoming itself in such a way that something is inevitably left for it to be, and to say.[18] Roy had no idea that it is in language that the world is conceived, just as it is language that bears the mediation of Being with beings, truth and history.[19] He believed in the Upaniṣads, and in Śaṅkara's claim that language is merely a set of conventional signs, with no intrinsic relation to consciousness. Roy gratefully embraced the imposition of English on the meta-Vedic élite. "We looked forward with pleasing hope," he said, "to the dawn of knowledge thus promised to the rising generation.... We already offered thanks to providence for inspiring the most generous and enlightened of all nations of the West the glorious ambitions of planting in Asia the Arts and Sciences of modern Europe" (ibid.: 126). Roy offered his prayers to the providential theory of history, and in the interests of the Bhadraloka, those who understood the relation between language and power. He promoted English language and education for the "intelligent and respectable classes of the inhabitants," in the hope that they would help the colonial government in India (Gupta 1958: 142).

Roy inaugurated the tradition of anglicised Vedānta, also known as Neo-Vedānta. He still held firm to the old Vedāntic idea of metaphysical spirituality, the consciousness that is tabula rasa and on which any worldview may be planted for the interests of the mediating class. He made an exit from the Vedic East and demanded the imposition of the Euro-Christian on the Vedāntic consciousness. Keshab Chandra Sen (1838–1884), also known as Jesudas, pushed Roy's agenda a notch further. Raised in the anglicised culture of Calcutta, Sen had to live the agony of comparative consciousness. He found solace in the undoing of Christianity on its own terms. "I regard every European settler in India as a missionary of Christ," he said, "and I have a right to demand that he should always remember and act up to his high responsibilities. But alas! Owing to the reckless conduct of a number of pseudo-Christians, Christianity failed to produce any wholesome moral influence on my countrymen" (Sen 1979: 62–63). Christianity was out to achieve moral purgation in India, but had achieved none. Sen insisted upon the displacement of the old Father, the God of the Jewish people, and the old Mother, the deity of Vedic India. His proposal is stunning. The Euro-Christian had its own East in the religion of the Israelite people, just as the Vedāntic West had its East in the Vedic religion. Neither forms of the East would help; both of them had to be disowned. "The Father cannot be an example of sonship. Only the Son knows what the Son ought to be. In vain do I go to the Vedas or to Judaism to learn sonship. That I learn at the feet of my sweet Christ" (Sen, quoted in Narvane 1978: 40). Sen presented a theology of grandsonship, which disowns both the mother and the father. "Who rules India?... It is not politics and diplomacy that laid a firm hold of the Indian heart. Not politics and diplomacy but Christ. None but Christ ever deserved this bright, previous maiden India. And Jesus shall have it" (cf. Chatterjee 1993a: 38–39).* Born of Virgin Mary, Jesus deserved no less than a Virgin India.

The theology of grandsonship is an argument for a new beginning. Both Christ and India have to post their own past. Christ has to be emancipated from England, the Christian liberation from its medium. "England has sent to us, after all, a Western Christ. This is indeed to be regretted... It seems that the Christ that has come to us is an Englishman, with English manners and customs about him.... Why must we submit to one who is of a different nationality? Why must we bow before a foreign product?" (Chatterjee 1993a: 41). Keshab wanted to invent a Christ for India who was not a "gentleman," but an ascetic who seeks yogic communion with God on the mountains. "Behold, Christ cometh as an Asiatic in race, as a Hindu in faith.... He comes to fulfil and perfect a religion of communion for which India has been panting. Yes, after long centuries this communion will be perfected through Christ. For Christ is a true yogi, and he will surely help us realise our national ideal of a yogi" (Thomas 1979: 53). Christ comes to India after an exile in the terra incognita of the European West, and he achieves the eroticised bonding with India for which she has been panting. It is an India that has moved out of the Vedic East, and disowned the memory of how she was conceived in Sanskrit texts and how she lived in history. It is a brand new India and a brand new Christ. Out of their communion are born children like Keshab, members of the Brahmo śamāj. Keshab called his theology the "third dispensation," which advocates unitary pluralism and seeks to radically "complete" the old religion. "The Old Testament is for First Dispensation, the New Testament is for the Second; unto us these days has been vouchsafed the Third Dispensation. Unite and amalgamate these three, and you have the Trinity Church of the world" (Narvane 1978: 39–40; cf. also 38). Such is the universal *ecclesia* of the grandchildren. In it the sinful histories, emblematised in the divisive convention of nations, will go to the cross; and through her the nations shall be resurrected in their post-conventional, meta-sectarian identity. Keshab was very much influenced by Ramakrishna who was the mentor of Vivekananda, and has equated the catholicity of India with Vedāntic consciousness. "Truth," Ramakrishna said, "may be a reservoir of clean water. On one side of the reservoir a Hindu fills his pitcher with 'jala'; on another side a Muslim calls it 'pāni'; and yet on other side a sahib calls it 'water.' But the substance with which they all fill their pitchers remains the same" (Narvane 1978: 64). Keshab insisted that India is the home of all in Christ. "It will be contended," he said, "that to mix up Christ with a hundred and one creeds of the world is to deny and destroy Christ. But to mix Christ with what? With error? With impurity? No, mix Christ with all that is Christian in other creeds. Surely, that is not un-Christian, far less anti-Christian" (Narvane 1978: 40). The Indian Brahmo śamāj does not divide, it unites; it is not sectarian, it is unitarian.

There is an irony here. Keshab made a distinction between the spirit of Christianity and its cultural manifestation, between Christ and the European "gentleman."

---

*In fact, this apparent paraphrase does not match any quotation at the cited source. It does, however, clearly echo a quotation on p. 41 of Chatterjee's text. Perhaps the author was working from a combination of summary notes and memory.

We recall that Grant, along with Mill and Macaulay, wanted to reproduce India in christological dimensions, with England and her aristocracy as the means to the liberative end. Keshab emerged to 'complete' the episteme in which he was conceived. He, too, envisioned a Christ who appealed to the Indian sahibs, those who had Euro-Christian mind on their body, those who were the beneficiaries, even the proponents, of the Raj. True to the genealogy of his class, Keshab presented a Christianised Vedānta with a view to Vedāntise Christianity. Two themes were central to his theology: unity of religions and spiritual nationalism. He distinguished the "substantive" from what was "adjectival" in religion, associating the former with essence and the latter with contingent fashions. He ended up affirming the unity of religions by depriving them of their histories. Western Christianity is adjectival; driven by a materialistic ideology and anthropomorphic particularity, it imposes the adjectival on the substantive, the church on Christ. Christianity must be emancipated from its particularity before Christ can stand up for salvation on a universal scale. The Indian Christ will do what the real Christ stands for. "I am reminded," Keshab said, "of a passage in the Gospel in which he says, 'I am not come to destroy, but to fulfil.' The Mosaic dispensation only? Perhaps the Hindu dispensation also. In India he will fulfil the Hindu dispensation" (Thomas 1979: 52). Such a mission of Christ is consistent with Vedānta. We recall that Śaṅkarācārya built a hermeneutic of fulfilment (*ānantarya*), thus completing the dharmic law by dissolving it into metavedic consciousness, in *jñānayoga*. It is a yoga of unitive *kerygma*, of communion with Being by saying, "I am Brahman." Fond of yogi Christ, Keshab elevated "I and my Father are one" to emancipatory ultimacy, to the authority of the identity sentences of the Upanishads (*Mahāvākya*).

Thus Jesus Christ became yogi Christ. Christ is a true yogi, and he will help Indians to realise the national ideal of a yogi. The bitter irony is that Keshab spiritualises Christ, and with that, the Indian nation itself. His Christ has no memory of the historical Jesus, no appreciation of the truth that the logos was made flesh to socialise salvation, not to spiritualise it, and that Jesus dying on the cross was an answer to the question, "Does God care for the outcaste?" Keshab had accused the Euro-Christian West of reducing Christ to an "English gentleman". But his own Christ is a Bhadraloka, a Neo-Vedāntic "gentleman" who performs yoga in the Vedāntic West. And when he is done with the yogic routine, he moves in the circle of sahibs and babus, judges and lawyers, professors and politicians, doctors and journalists, swamis and civil servants of the Raj. He charmed those who carried a Euro-Christian mind in their body, who lived in European time and died in Indian space. He belonged to the culture of those Indians who thought it was impossible "to argue a man into slavery in the English language." (Kulkarani 1972: 44). These Indians, mostly Westernised Brahmins, affirmed Vedāntic spirituality in Christian categories, and did so in the English language. Heirs to the traditional spiritual aristocracy, they had acquired mediative privilege in the nineteenth century. The *sannyāsi* had become a modern swami, and fund-raising forums replaced his begging bowl. The so-called "gentlemen" felt discomfort with cow dung paint in the kitchen, eating with hands while sitting on the floor, the priestly profession and the sacred thread, the vernaculars and the rural folks (Bloomfield 1968: 318). The

Hindu Bhadraloka were proud of their achievement, but they also valued their high class status. They wished to develop their adopted institutions, which had served them so well in the nineteenth century, and they were concerned to preserve their social order, with its advantages for themselves. They knew that further institutional development would bring increasingly insistent demands from the lower orders for accommodation: for the wider opening of the doors of schools and colleges and offices to non-Bhadraloka. The Bhadraloka ventured categorial shift as well, expounding the spiritual superiority of Vedānta to European audience. They had inaugurated an ecumenical and comparative discourse in which there was no room for social justice, no historical or hermeneutical concern, and no technical vocabulary or methodological rigor of Sanskrit thought, not even of classical Vedānta. They had walked out of the Vedic East, the sphere of Dharmakīrti, Kumārila and Gaṅgeśa; and they could not get to the centre of the Euro-Christian West to which they thought they belonged. They remained mediators. They were, and they still are, ignorant of Sanskrit texts and traditions of thought. They confused their ignorance with modernity, of which they were proud. Whatever they knew of their heritage was conceived and imposed on them by the Euro-Christian West, a knowledge that humiliated them. The "gentlemen" lived through cognitive ambiguity, anguish of mispredicated identity, and the agony of being neither here nor there.

The divorce of Christ and mother India was inevitable. It was time for *apavādanyāya*, the realization that the imposition of the Euro-Christian *māyā* had served its purpose. It was time, by the end of the nineteenth century, to post the Christianised Vedānta and to re-Vedāntise India. There was a shift from Gospel to Gītā, from yogi Christ to yogi Krishna. Arjuna, after all, had confessed to Krishna: "Destroyed is my illusion and recognition has been gained by me through thy grace. I stand firm with my doubts dispelled. I shall act according to thy word." (*Gītā*, XVII 3). The need was to return to everything nationalistic (*svadeśi*), including a*dhyāsa*. The Vedāntic subjectivity was to embrace the doctrine of mispredicated identity of Śaṅkarācārya, to reclaim Being which is the ground of all beings, to reimpose Sanātana Dharma on the site of Being, and to practice the politics of *karmayoga* in order to defend the traditional Hindu social order. The caste structure of society is the nation, the nation is the body of God in history, and God asks to defend his body as an end-in-itself. The Vedāntic subjectivity reincarnated itself in the thoughts of Swami Vivekananda, Bhudeva Mukhopadhyay, Balgangadhar Tilak, Sri Aurobindo, and Sarvepalli Radhakrishnan. This was known as "Political Vedānta."

Vivekananda had the memory of a self-realised man. He had gone West of society in both Euro-Christian and Vedāntic senses of the term. The priests of his organization, the Ramakrishna Mission, would receive financial support from Rāni Rasmati, from a fisherman's caste, but they would not accept or eat food touched by her (Dhar 1977: 129–130). The tradition of the upper caste Bhadraloka had to be maintained. Vivekananda visited the princely states of India, such as Alwar, Ajamer, Jaipur, Khatiawar, Khetri and Travancore. Like Śaṅkarācārya, Vivekananda also visited holy places like Dwarika and Madurai, Kailash and Kanyakumari. Upon his return from the Parliament of Religion in Chicago, the Swami became an instant hit with the anglicised élite of India. The princes of major states pulled his carriage themselves, chasing the horses away.

Vivekananda's aim was to re-Vedāntise India. He said his consciousness was as motionless as the bottom of the sea, and that he was a witness to the deviations of Indian history. "Thus be thou calm, Sannyāsi bold; say '*om tat sat om*'" (Narvane 1978: 101). For Vivekananda, history is a collective memory of past events. To witness its mutations is the function of renunciative consciousness, and the consciousness has become one with Being. "I am," the Swami said, "the greatest God that there was or shall be. Christ and the Buddhas are just the waves of the boundless ocean that I am" (Narvane 1978: 99). The historical premises of the happenings of Buddhas and Christ are bubbles, and they merely have come to pass on Vedantic consciousness. That is how Vedānta exiled Buddhism from India. Vivekananda had a memory of how Śākyamuni returned as a monk to Kapilavastu, demanding social justice on religious grounds, and how Śaṅkarācārya silenced the Buddha by becoming a monk himself, and domesticating Buddhist categories into a Vedāntic scheme of things: there is no causal relation between Being and the world; in the world, karmic causation prevails. The same threat had appeared in the form of Jesus, and the Neo-Vedāntins would post him just as successfully. Vivekananda revived Śaṅkarācārya as the national philosopher of India, saying that he equated the emancipation of India with the historical sovereignty of dharmic society (Karunakaran 1965: 255). Not that the Swami did not criticise some of the trivial practices in the caste system. He did. But he opposed any structural changes in the caste system, insisting that it was the sign of the historical identity of India and it ought to be endlessly affirmed through the politics of *karmayoga*. National sovereignty was not an end-in-itself; it was only the means, the instrumental reason, to affirm the historical flow of the social identity of India. That is the affirmation Krishna asked Arjuna to make in the Gītā, and that Vivekananda asks Indians to make again. "This wonderful river of national life is flowing before us.... Who dares command its motion? Ours is only to work, as the Gītā says, without looking for results." (Karunakaran 1965: 252). What is true of individuals must be true of the nation. Individuals live through the karmic law of cause and effect. India, too, must be subjected to the same recurrence in a home grown *adhyāsa* than find salvation in the implanting of the Euro-Christian West. "We must revive the old laws of the Rishis.... We have to redivide the whole Hindu population, group it under the four main castes of Brahmin, Kṣatriya, Vaiśyas and Śūdras, as of old" (Vivekananda 1965: 405).

As of old, indeed. Sri Aurobindo, the great national yogi, also advanced a discourse of reclaiming precolonial, Brāhmaṇic India. People have their *swadharma*, a collection of attributes that makes them what they are and renders them different from others. I am before I am; I am after I am. In the present, I am only a passage to what I shall be. What I am depends on what I have been, and the two account for my future. That is the ideology of Sanātana Dharma, the Hindu social order: to each according to the ethical quality of his karmic will, and from each according to the caste worthy of that very will. Every experience in life is caused. My birth is the embodiment of my will to be; I wear a willed body; and that body is the cause of where and howsoever I shall be (*ihakāla o parakāla*). That explains why there is so much inequality in the world, and why inequality is moral. The Euro-Christians believe in *parakāla*, in the future that has nothing to do with the past. They have no historical consciousness. They must post the past, which was/is unethical. India, on the other hand, is an ethical and spiritual country, because of the inherent law of cause and effect, *karma* and *phala*. This law makes Indian society self-ordered, keeping people in their proper place. The *svarājatā*, the ownness of India, is the caste order of society, which is governed by the law of cause and effect. That accounts for the marginality of the state. The state is not central to Hindu society. Empires may rise and fall, but the structure of Hindu society remains the same. Should the state have an ordering power in the life of the people? No, said Sri Aurobindo. People should have power to rule themselves. In this Sri Aurobindo has the support of Bal Gangadhar Tilak who said: "The point is to have the entire control in our hands. I want to have the key of my house, and not merely a stranger turned out of it. Self-government is our goal" (Varma 1978: 203; see also Wolpert 1961: 197). It is a house where, as of old, the Braahmaṇas have legislative and judicial authority, the Kṣatriyas bear arms, the Vaiśyas run the markets, and the Śūdras serve in silence.

The key of this house is deemed to belong in the hands of those who have the memory of Vedāntic definition of the nation. Being, the Ātman, has not caused India; and yet there is no India unless it has Being as its site. "If the Vedāntic ideal is higher," said Tilak, "it is necessarily the national ideal which is lower. They are not irreconcilable if you know how to reconcile them" (Varma 1978: 444). There is no causal relation between Being and beings, between essence and existence. Being is the transcendental ground of all existence but it does not transform itself into the world. Being is a matter of *paramārtha*, of metaphysical beatitude and self-reflective reason. But *māyā* has concealed Being and brought society – the sphere of *vyavahāra*, which is subject to strict laws of cause and effect, will and action – into existence. India is a willed nation, one conceived in the transcendental imagination that is *māyā*. Thus, the political management of India ostensibly requires a purity of intention that incarnates itself in that particular caste that symbolises renunciative will and voluntary poverty. To deny political prerogative to that caste is to rob reflective reason of its rights to legislative authority. When that happens, disasters disrupt the core of the nation. The nation is displaced from its ground, and reason deviates from its mission to the self-ordering society (Varma 1978: 215–216, 478). Sri Aurobindo took Tilak seriously on these points. Accordingly, he reduced national identity to Sanātana Dharma, the caste order of society. He decisively shifted from the European discourse on nationalism to embrace the schemes of the Vedantic West. "I no longer say that nationalism is a creed, a religion, a faith," he said. "I say it is the Sanātana Dharma which for us is nationalism. This Hindu nation was born with the Sanātana Dharma, with it, it moves, and with it, it grows.... The Sanātana Dharma, that is our nationalism" (Aurobindo 1968: 16; cf. Varma 1976: 206). India was conceived in the caste order of society, the society is the body of God in history, and the mission of national sovereignty is to defend the body as an end-in-itself.

After saying this, Aurobindo left for *sannyāsa* in Pondicherry. He was elevated to national yogi, second only to the old Śaṅkarācārya.

Rammohan Roy, Keshab Chandra Sen, Swami Vivekananda, B.G. Tilak and Sri Aurobindo all embody the ironies of colonial and postcolonial discourse. Colonialism was not universalistic after all. It actually was a prophetic mission of Euro-Christian particularity, driven by a premodern faith that God ordains the destiny of world history through a national agency under Christ. Colonialism was a religious idea, a project of writing cultures in terms of Euro-Christian identity. It suppressed difference. Its problem was: How would a christological self think of the other in terms of itself? It talked of formal equality at a theoretical level, but it promoted inequality at the material level. Neo-Vedānta returned the favour in kind, driven as it was, and still is, by a social historicism of a premodern kind. It places the historical immortality of mother India under Sanātana Dharma, and it enshrines emancipating agency in the self-alienating sovereignty of meta-Vedic Brahmins. Colonialism, in a sense, created Neo-Vedānta in contrast to itself. It perceived itself and the other in terms of the real versus the illusionary. But it did not understand the staying power of illusion. Vedānta reincarnated in Neo-Vedānta, which also is a project of writing cultures. Its problem is this: How would the self alienate itself in terms of the other in order to return to itself its own identity? In tune with the Upanishadic *ātman*, the Neo-Vedāntic subjectivity is liberal and universalistic on a theoretical level (*paramārtha*). It even calls India the home of all that is possible in the world. For instance, even though he moved West of society, Śaṅkara worshipped all the Gods of the Vedic East. He did *pādayatra*, walking on foot all over India, and thus gave a sacred mantra to modern politicians. On account of this, Neo-Vedāntists can memorialise Śaṅkara as the prophet of nationalism and social unity. He visited from Badrinath in the north to Kanyakumari in the south, Dwarika in the west to Assam in the east. A modern scholar says this: "It was the positive spirit of Advaita which inspired Śaṅkara to organise society. He established four temples in the four distant corners of India, and initiated his disciples for the proper conduct of worship in those temples. His aim was social integration (*lokasaṅgraha*) on the basis of Vedāntic teachings" (Datta 1977: 134). But Neo-Vedāntic subjectivity is just as closed and particularistic at the social level (*vyavahāra*) as is Euro-Christian colonialism. The Neo-Vedāntins perhaps acknowledge that Being is present in all human beings and accounts for ontological equality. Socially speaking, however, they say, human beings are subject to their karmic will, which accounts for their inequality. The Neo-Vedantic subjectivity, despite its mysticism, is controlled by the Brāhmaṇic ideology of Manu and Śaṅkarācārya. Sri Aurobindo characterises the mission in these words: "I know my country as mother. I offer her my devotion, my worship.... I know I have the power in me to accomplish the deliverance of my fallen country.... It was the power of knowledge, *Brahmateja*, founded in *jñāna*. The feeling is not new to me..., With this feeling I was born.... God has sent me to earth to this work" (Nandy 1983: 92). India is closed in geo-cultural boundaries; its messianic mission equals the colonial nationalism of Charles Grant and John Stuart Mill.

Conclusion: Postcolonial Complicity and Dalit Protest

Almost all the (Indian) postcolonialists are the products of Neo-Vedāntic culture. They are all nationalists and are engaged in discussing the meaning of colonialism. They are out to post the Euro-Christian West in defence of their national identity. It is understandable that a nation should write its own culture, recovering its past, and mediating itself the future. But it is unfortunate that postcolonialists are shy of returning the critical gaze to the oppressive depth of mother India. They practice bad faith instead, accusing the oppressive Euro-Christian other and displacing the indigenous exploitation in psychoanalytic language. Ashis Nandy, for example, absolves Sri Aurobindo's pre-modernism with these questions: "Did Sri Aurobindo symbolise the larger suffering of his society under the colonial rule? Did his attempt to speak in a new language parallel his society's attempt to express – and protect – its secret awareness of its suffering?" (Nandy 1983: 97). A series of counter-questions must be put here. What larger suffering? Why must the awareness of suffering be secret, especially when the suffering is historical and social? And must the secret suffering be protected? Whose suffering does the awareness present anyway? Does the secrecy have anything to do with those who do not suffer but understand the suffering and put it in language that people who actually suffer do not understand? Is the secrecy rooted in the alienation of being and being in a place, in the cogito of the elite self that is in the world but not of it? Sri Aurobindo gave the appearance of speaking new language, but was it not precisely the same subjectivity the Vedantic elite has been practicing since Śaṅkarācārya's days? Ashis Nandy displaces the social suffering of India in a Bhadraloka psychology of the self, the "unheroic Brahmin," whom he believes was victimised by the colonial West and thus had to imitate the oppressor as a survival technique (Nandy 1983: 107). History shows that this was not the case. None of the Neo-Vedantins was a victim of colonialism. Not only did they inherit the aristocratic legacy of premodern India. They also were the greatest beneficiaries of the Raj, thanks to their self-alienating subjectivity. They all self-consciously imitated the Euro-Christian West in order to protect their interests. Valentine Chirol described the dominance of elite Brahmins in these words: "They sit in the Bench, they dominate the Bar, they teach in the schools, they control the vernacular press, they have furnished almost all the most conspicuous names in the modern literature and drama of Western India as well as in politics." (Chirol 1910: 322–323; cf. Cashman 1975, especially chapters I–I). Chirol was describing the Chitpavan Brahmins of Maharashtra. He might just as well have used the same language to describe the dominance of the elite in the whole of India.

I think the (Indian) postcolonialist discourse is evasive. Most of it is about what the colonial West did about thinking of India. The discourse has effectively ignored the Dalit voice of Jotirao Phule and Babasahib Ambedkar, the greatest exponents of the outcaste and marginalised majority. The élite writes culture, and they suppress the voice of the majority. Phule asked the privileged minority, the mediators between the East and the West, a few good questions. "How is it according to your Shāstras? To a good, honest pious Mahar will God say, you are a Mahar and therefore you must not come near me? And to a wicked Brahmin, will God say, you are a Brahmin, no matter how wicked you are, come and remain with me?" (O'Hanlon 1985: 72). The marginalised humanity has no scriptures like Vedas and Upaniṣads, so they are empty and naked and have nowhere to go. The circle of *ṛṣis*, the strength of dharma and the power of Vedas and Upaniṣads – they shower curses and they kick on the chest of humanity (O'Hanlon 1985: 210). What good is Gandhi's claim that the untouchables are the "children of God" when Krishna is incapable of giving a Gītā that would espouse social equality on religious grounds? Hindu God has not yet heard what Ambedkar said to Mahatma Gandhi. "Let me be brutally frank about it," Ambedkar famously said. "History tells us that Mahatmas, like fleeting phantoms, raise dust, but raise no levels. Why should the congressmen oppose our members and dub me a traitor? Gandhiji, I have no homeland." To be a traitor is to have a homeland, and Ambedkar has none. The postcolonialist Neo-Vedantin has to understand that meta-social spirituality, self-righteous nationalism, and Swami type mysticism will not do. Social reality is changing now. Thanks to modernism and colonialism, the majority now has a voice. They are asking the real civilizational questions: Whose Hinduism? Whose mother India? What kind of mother is India, that she would not listen to the overwhelming majority of children she herself has produced? What kind of a mother is she, that she listens to the children produced between her and Christ? Between her and Sanātana Dharma? Should not the texts that conceived her be burned? There is no point in doing the discourse on the colonial enemy, however intimate that enemy may be. It is time to recognise that the enemy is within India herself. If Orientalism means production of knowledge as an instrument of power, then it was Sanskrit discourse that invented it (cf. Pollock 1993). There certainly is an oriental Orientalism, a precolonial colonialism, and this is as systematically oppressive as any European colonialism. Did not Manu and Shankarācārya say that the hands and throats of the untouchable are to be cut if they cite the scripture? It is against this oriental Orientalism that Keshav Meshram, a Dalit poet of protest, wrote: "On my birthday, I cursed God. I cursed him again. Whipping with words, I said 'Bastard'" (Joshi 1986: 77). God's whipping is done in good faith, the severity of words notwithstanding. Meshram's intention is to refocus criticism in Sanskrit discourse from exogenous exploitation to indigenous violence, from European colonialism to Indian colonialism. In that field of writing culture, the response to the following question by a Dalit poet may determine the identity of mother India. The poet wrote: "My countrymen, to your court I brought you a complaint. Will you give me justice?" (Joshi 1986: 86). The postcolonial discourse has to return home. It has to be a discourse about authentic identity, not the mispredicated one.

Notes

1 Medini Kośa. 183:35. [Editors' note: No further reference is supplied by the author. We have discovered the following details regarding editions of Medini's late 13th century dictionary, all published in Banaras/Benares by the Chowkhamba Sanskrit Series Office: (1) Published in 1916. *Medini Kosha, or a dictionary of homonymous words by Medinikara* [I]. Kasi Sanskrit

Series, work 41 (Kośa section, 1); (2) Medinikara. 1940. *Nānārthaśabdakośāparaparyāyo Medinīkośaḥ*. Ed. Jagannāth Śāstri Hoshing; (3) 1968, other details the same.]
2 *Śaṅkara, Gītā Bhāṣyaṃ* 18.55 [Eds.: No indication regarding which edition of Sankara's commentary on the *Bhāgavad Gītā* was used by the author used was supplied.]
3 *Amarakośa*. 3.1.81; *Hemaśabdānuśāsana.* 2.159. [Eds.: Again, no further indication regarding the editions the thesaurus of Amarasimha (ca. fifth century) thesaurus and the grammar of Hemacandra (1089–1172) was supplied. For the former, perhaps A. Amarasiṃha. 1951. *Amarakośam*. Kadapa: Rayalu and Co. education publishers?]
4 *"Dvidharṃ hi sāmarthyaṃ nijaṃ cāgantukaṃ ca."* Bhāmatī on *BSB* 1.3.34.
5 *Amarakośa*, 3.1.81. [Eds.: See note 3 above.]
6 *Bṛhadāraṇyaka Upaniṣads (Bṛh. Up.)*, 4.3.22.
7 *"Alaṃkṛtvam sādhvi... Sureśvara," Samandhavārtika*, 1.238.
8 *"Na heyamupādeyaṃ vā,"* Śaṅkara's Commentary on Kaṭha Upaniṣad, 1.4.
9 *"Svatantraḥ kartā."* Pāṇini, *Aṣṭādhyāyi*, 1.4.54; Kauṇḍa Bhaṭṭa, Vaiyakarana Bhūṣana Sārā (Poona: Ananda Ashram, 1957), 183–184.
10 *"Tṛṣāṇi abhāvāt."* Śaṅkara on Chāndogya Upaniṣad. 7.23.1. [?]
11 Cf. Mehta 1985: 179–201, in connection with a contrast between Vedāntic consciousness and the Hegelian conception of Spirit.
12 *"Miyate anena iti māyā."* Atharva Veda 8.3.5.
13 *"Ahaṃ nāme'ti jīvabhimānaḥ kartā ca bhoktā ca."* (*SVS*: 55). *"Kartā-kṛtasya saṃcarati svakarmabhiḥ."* Śvetāśvatara Upaniṣad. 5.7.
14 *"Yathā manusasya adhikāra."* BSB 1. 3.34; *Bṛhadāraṇyaka Upaniṣad*, 1.4.15.
15 *"Śarira parigrahaṇa kena bhavati? Karmanā. Karma kena bhavati? Rāgādibhyaḥ."* Ātmanātma Viveka, 40; *"Jiva hetu phalātmakam."* Śaṅkara on Māṇḍukya Kārikā. 2.6.
16 *"Yathākāmo bhavati."* Bṛhadāraṇyaka. *Up.* 4.5.5; *"yathā saṅkalpitaṃ lokaṃ bhavati."* Praśna Upaniṣad. 3.10; cf. Adhisvarananda (1977: 23–58).
17 *"Yadvai tanna paśyati paśyanvai tanna paśyati."* Bṛhadāraṇyaka. *Up.* 4.3.23; Śaṅkara on *Māṇḍūkya Up.* 3.17.
18 *"Iyaṃ vā paramenisthini vāk daivi,"* Atharva Veda, 19.9.3; *"kāvyam ... mamara,"* Ṛg-Veda, 8.55.5.
19 *"Brahmedaṃ śabdanirmāṇaṃ śabda-sakti nibhaṇḍanam,"* Bhartṛhari, *Vākyapadīya*, 1.1; *"Sarvasya jagato bhāmāt,"* Nirukta 1.7; Bhāgavat, 10.27.4.

References

Adhisvarananda, Swami. 1977. Philosophy of History: The Hindu View. In *Contemporary Indian Philosophers of History*, edited by T.M.P. Mahadevan and G.E. Cairns, pp. 23–59. Calcutta: World Press.
Aurobindo, Shri. 1968. *Vitarapath Speech*. Pondicherry.
Bhaṭṭa, Kauṇḍa. 1957. *Vaiyakārana Bhūṣana Śārā*. Poona: Ananda Ashram.
Bhaṭṭa, Nagesh. 1975. *Vaiyakārana Siddhānta Paramalaghu Mañjuṣa*. Kapiladeva Shastri (Ed.). Kurukshetra: Kurukshetra Visvavidyalaya Prakashana.
Biderman, Shlomo and Ben-Ami Scharfstein (Eds.). 1992. *Interpretation in Religion*. Leiden/New York: E. J. Brill.
Bloomfield, J.H. 1968. *Elite Conflict in a Plural Society: Twentieth Century Bengal*. Berkeley, CA/Los Angeles, CA: University of California Press.
Breckenridge, Carol A. and Peter Van der Veer (Eds.). 1993. *Orientalism and the Postcolonial Predicament: Perspectives on South Asia*. Philadelphia, PA: University of Pennsylvania Press.
Brugman, Henry. 1965. The Uniqueness of Europe. In *The Glass Curtain Between Asia and Europe*, edited by Raghavan Iyer. With a foreword by the Dalai Lama. London/New York: Oxford University Press.

Burke, Edmund. 1877. *Works*, Vol. 2. London: Reprint services.

Cashman, Richard. 1975. *The Myth of The Lokamanya*. Berkeley, CA: University of California Press.

Chand, Tara. 1967. *History of the Freedom Movement in India*, vol. 2. New Delhi: The Publications Division, Ministry of Information and Broadcasting, GOI.

Chatterjee, Partha. 1993a. *The Nation and Its Fragments*. Princeton, NJ: Princeton University Press.

Chatterjee, Partha. 1993b. *Nationalist Thought and the Colonial World: A Derivative Discourse*. Minneapolis, MN: University of Minneapolis Press.

Chirol, Valentine. 1910. *Indian Unrest*. London: Macmillan. (Republished in 2007 [Charleston, S. C.: BiblioBazaar].).

Darby, Philip. 1987. *Three Faces of Imperialism: British and American Approaches to Asia and Africa 1870–1970*. New Haven, CT: Yale University Press.

Datta, Dhirendra Mohan. 1977. My Philosophy of History. In *Contemporary Indian Philosophers of History*, edited by T.M.P. Mahadevan and G.E. Cairns. Calcutta: World Press.

Derrett, J. Duncan M. 1979. Tradition and Law in India. In *Tradition and Politics in South Asia*, edited by R.J. Moore, pp. 32–59. New Delhi: Vikas.

Dhar, Nirjanan. 1977. *Vedānta and Bengal Renaissance*. Columbia, MO: South Asia Books.

Derrida, Jacques. 1986. Racism's Last Word. In *Race, Writing and Difference*, edited by H.L. Gates. Chicago, IL: University of Chicago Press.

Forster, E.M. 1924. *A Passage to India*. New York: Harcourt Brace.

Grant, Charles. 1832. Observations on the state of society among the Asiatic subjects of Great Britain, particularly with respect to Morals, and on the Means of improving it. In Parliamentary Papers (H.C.), Report from the Select Committee of the House of Commons on the Affairs of the East India Company, 16 August 1832, Appendix.

Gupta, Atula Chandra. 1958. *Studies in the Bengal Renaissance*. Calcutta: The National Council of Education.

Halbfass, Wilhelm. 1988. *India and Europe: An Essay in Understanding*. Albany, NY: State University of New York Press.

Heimsath, Charles. 1964. *Indian Nationalism and Hindu Social Reform*. Princeton, NJ: Princeton University Press.

Hutchins, Francis. 1967. *The Illusion of Permanence: British Imperialism in India*. Princeton, NJ: Princeton University Press.

Joshi, Barbara (Ed.). 1986. *Untouchable: Voices of the Dalit Liberation Movement*. London: Zed.

Karunakaran, K.P. 1965. *Religion and Political Awakening in India*. Delhi: Meenakshi Prakashana.

Knopf, David. 1979. *The Brahma Samaja and the Shaping of the Modern Indian Mind*. Princeton, NJ: Princeton University Press.

Kulkarani, V.B. 1972. *Problems of Indian Democracy*. Bombay: Bharatiya Vidya Bhavan.

Mahadevan, T.M.P., and Grace E. Cairns (Eds.). 1977. *Contemporary Indian Philosophers of History*. Calcutta: World Press.

Mehta, Jaswant Lal. 1985. *India and the West*. Chico, CA: Scholars Press.

Metcalf, Thomas. 1994. *The New Cambridge History of India*. Cambridge: Cambridge University Press.

Mill, James S. 1840. *The History of British India*, Vol. I. London: James Maden.

Mudimbe, Valentin Y. 1988. *The Invention of Africa*. Bloomington, IN: Indiana University Press.

Muni, Vidyāraṇya. 1888. *Vivarana Prameya Saṅgraha*. Kashi: Achyuta Grantha Mala, Samvat.

Nakamura, Hideki. 1965. The Uniqueness of Asia as Seen by an Asian. In *The Glass Curtain Between Asia and Europe*, edited by Raghavan Iyer. With a foreword by the Dalai Lama. London/New York: Oxford University Press.

Nandy, Ashis. 1983. *The Intimate Enemy: Loss and Discovery of Self Under Colonialism*. Delhi: Oxford University Press.

Narvane, V.S. 1978. *Modern Indian Thought*. Columbia, MO: South Asia Books.

O'Hanlon, Rosalind. 1985. *Caste, Conflict and Ideology*. London: Cambridge University Press.

Panikkar, K.M. 1963. *Foundations of New India*. London.

Pollock, Sheldon. 1993. Deep Orientalism: Notes on Sanskrit and Power Beyond the Raj. In *Orientalism and the Postcolonial Predicament: Perspectives on South Asia*, edited by Carol A. Breckenridge and Peter Van der Veer, pp. 66–133. Philadelphia, PA: University of Pennsylvania Press.

Said, Edward W. 1978. *Orientalism*. London: Penguin.

Sen, Keshab Chandra. 1979. Jesus Christ and Asia. In *Keshab Chunder Sen*, edited by David C. Scott. Madras: Christian Literature Society.

Śaṅkara. n.d. *Brahmasūtra Śaṅkara. Bhāṣya with Vācaspati's Bhāmātī*, ed. Swami Yogindranand. Vol. 1. Varanasi: Saddharma Prakasana Pratisthana. (Cited as *BSB*.)

Śaṅkara. 1918. *Sarva Vedānta Sārā Saṅgraha*. Varanasi: Govinda Matha, Sambavat. (Cited as *SVS*.)

Śaṅkara. 1973 *Atmanatma Vi-veka*, edited by J.C. Misha. Varanasi: Chowkhambha. (Cited as *AV*.)

Sharma, Shri Rama (Ed.). 1975. *Yoga Vaśiṣtha*, Vol. 1. Braeilly: Sanskrit Sansthana.

Stephen, James Fraternity. 1874. *Liberty, Equality, Fraternity*. London.

Stokes, Eric. 1989. *The English Utilitarians in India*. Delhi: Oxford University Press.

Thomas, George. 1979. *Christian Indians and Indian Nationalism: An Interpretation in Historical and Theological Perspectives*. Frankfurt: Peter Lang.

Varma, Vishwanath P. 1976. *The Political Philosophy of Sri Aurobindo*. Delhi: Motilal Banarsidass.

Varma, Vishwanath P. 1978. *The Life and Philosophy of Lokmanya Tilak*. Agra: Educational Publishers, NDT.

Vidyāraṇya, Swami. 1887. *Bṛhadāraṇyaka-Vārtika-Sārā* (BVS), Vol. 1. Kashi: Achyuta Grantha Mala, Samvat.

Vidyāraṇya, Swami. 1888. *Vivaraṇa-Prameya-Saṅgraha*. Kashi: Achyuta Grantha Mala, Samvat.

Vivekananda, Swami. 1965. *The Complete Works of Swami Vivekananda*, Vol. 2. Calcutta: Advaita Ashram.

Wolpert, Stanley A. 1961. *Tilak and Gokhale: Revolution and Reform in the Making of Modern India*. Delhi: Oxford University Press.

Yadav, Bibhuti S. 1992. Methodic Deconstruction. In *Interpretation in Religion*, edited by Shlomo Biderman and Ben-Ami Scharfstein, pp. 29–68. Leiden/New York: E.J. Brill.

On the Death of the Pilgrim: The Postcolonial Hermeneutics of Jarava Lal Mehta

Thomas B. Ellis

Abstract "Dialogue" has become a fashionable term of in many circles of comparative studies. The twentieth century German philosopher Hans-Georg Gadamer placed dialogue at the center of his philosophical hermeneutics. Proposing the accomplishment of a "fusion of horizons" between initially opposed parties, Gadamer outlined the structure of engagement between self and other. Situating the self in an irrevocable historical context, he argued that this self must encounter the other and through this encounter enrich its own position. Though ostensibly intended as a corrective to more openly colonial intentions and agendas, a close examination of Gadamer's philosophical hermeneutics betrays lingering colonial interests. These interests become pronounced when compared with what I call the postcolonial hermeneutics of the twentieth century Indian philosopher Jarava Lal Mehta. What distinguishes philosophical from postcolonial hermeneutics is the condition of the self subsequent to its encounter with the other. Where for Gadamer the other is a moment of the self's enrichment and edification – those elements of the other that do not facilitate such conservative agendas being discarded – the other for Mehta is a moment of the self's disruption. Mehta emphasizes an encounter wherein both parties are not edified but rather ruptured. Such rupture highlights the incompletion of all subjects subject to the "dialogue." Where philosophical hermeneutics emphasize edifying supplementation, postcolonial hermeneutics emphasize rupture, dislocation, and incompletion.

Philosophical hermeneutics harbors a colonial intention. Though perhaps not immediately obvious, Hans-Georg Gadamer's innocuous rhetoric of "dialogue" and "fusion of horizons" gives way to a subtle penchant for reducing the other to self. Paying particular attention to his particular choice of metaphor and analogy, I believe we detect a betrayal of Gadamer's ostensibly good intentions: the self/subject in philosophical hermeneutics heroically conquers its other and in turn augments its point of departure. These subtleties come to light when we compare Gadamer's hermeneutics with the hermeneutics of Jarava Lal Mehta, a Hindu thinker of the late twentieth century. A dedicated student of Martin Heidegger, Gadamer, and the Hindu tradition, Mehta suggests that philosophical hermeneutics may help the self understand itself, but it does not help the self understand the other. Offering the trope of the pilgrim to aid in his interpretation of interpretation, Mehta contests precisely the heroic supplementation of philosophical hermeneutics.

P. Bilimoria and A.B. Irvine (eds.), *Postcolonial Philosophy of Religion.*
© Springer Science+Business Media B.V. 2009

I propose that Mehta's pilgrim substitutes for the subject who is ruptured and destroyed rather than supplemented by the encounter with the other. Emphasizing such ruptures, destructions, and consequent dislocations, Mehta articulates a postcolonial hermeneutics predicated on the death of the pilgrim.

While the problem of alterity continues to exercise the (Continental) philosophical imagination, the indisputable presence of cultural others demands not only a continued effort to listen to these others but also and importantly a reflection on the history and theory of the cross-cultural encounter as such. We are of course quite familiar with the writings of the literary and culture critic Edward Said and the Indologist Ronald Inden (among many others), authors who particularly highlight the imperial legacy of this troubled encounter. Admittedly, the professed goal of such authors is a restoration of native agency. That is to say, if colonial powers essentialized the indigenous other, reducing thereby the other's agency to a static type, then the goal of postcolonial criticism is often a certain humanizing of the other. Yet some express a hesitation with regard to such a seemingly noble project. The historian of Indian philosophy Wilhelm Halbfass, for instance, suggests that Said and Inden fail to truly engage the other. He argues in particular that Inden speaks of dialogue and listening to the other (or at least letting the other speak), but in no way do we really hear the others' voices in his work. Halbfass notes:

> The critique of Orientalism, as presented by Said and Inden, is a thoroughly Western affair. In a sense, it is no less European and Eurocentric than Orientalism itself. The Indian "others" whom Inden wants to liberate from false European and Western claims do not really emerge as speakers and participants in a dialogue. He speaks about them, not to them; he is the Western authority dealing with their problems and losses. He wants to restore their identity and sovereignty; he never asks himself whether there is anything in the Indian tradition that might affect his own identity or sovereignty. In this sense, we may want to be not only beyond Orientalism, but also beyond the critique of Orientalism. (1997: 23)

Here Halbfass explicitly suggests that Inden forestalls any critical displacement of his own "identity or sovereignty" in his putative encounter with the "Indian 'others'." Such hesitance with respect to Inden (and Said) resonates directly with Mehta's concerns regarding philosophical hermeneutics, a point I will treat at length in what follows.[1] For now, and along similar lines, the literary and culture critic Gayatri Chakravorti Spivak asks whether or not the intention to restore native agency is not in some way a preservation of colonial agency: "some of the most radical criticism coming out of the West today … [reflects a] desire to conserve … the West as subject"(cited in Halbfass 1997: 21). In other words, the preservation of the West as subject rests not only in the usurpation of indigenous agency in the colonial period but also in the assumed capacity to restore such agency in the postcolonial period: the Western subject has the power to grant and take away agency, or so the argument goes. In this way, Halbfass and Spivak indirectly raise a most pertinent question: Is there a difference between merely talking about dialogical engagement and an actual dialogue? And on that note, how in fact do we conceive "dialogue"? Do we have (or better yet – and as will hopefully become clear in what follows – *can* we have) a *philosophy* of dialogue?

Hans-Georg Gadamer's *Truth and Method* certainly plays an essential role in discussions concerning the dynamics of the dialogical encounter. While recognizing of course the long history of hermeneutics in biblical and jurisprudential interpretation, Gadamer seeks to articulate the constitutive elements of the dialogical event as such. No longer interested in particular cases of interpretation, Gadamer's position defines the subject not as occasionally engaged in interpretative activities but rather constituted by the interpretive act. Here we see the philosophical in philosophical hermeneutics. As philosophy is often wont to articulate ontological elements and structures, Gadamer's *philosophical* hermeneutics conceptualizes the dialogical subject and its encounter with the provocative other. Philosophical hermeneutics "is concerned not so much with the art or methodology of interpreting texts as with understanding and interpreting as themselves basic moments in man's very way of being human, as forms of being and happening rather than as operations directed at an objectively given entity or happening"(Mehta 1985: 179).

While this is certainly one reading of "philosophical," I believe Mehta presents an elaboration that suggests a further conceptualization of the philosophical nature of philosophical hermeneutics. The seemingly apolitical nature of the philosophical in Mehta's characterization above turns out to be anything but apolitical. I believe the French philosopher Emanuel Levinas's reflections on (Western) philosophy anticipate the direction of our discussion:

> Western philosophy coincides with the disclosure of the other where the other, in manifesting itself as a being, loses its alterity. From its infancy philosophy has been struck with a horror of the other that remains other – with an insurmountable allergy. It is for this reason that it becomes philosophy of immanence and of autonomy, or atheism. (1986: 346)

According to Levinas, philosophy reduces the other to same, to self. The postcolonial theorist Robert Young similarly remarks, "In Western philosophy, when knowledge or theory comprehends the other, then the alterity of the latter vanishes as it becomes part of the same" (1990: 13). The present question thus asks to what extent this critique of philosophy and the philosophical applies to Gadamer's *philosophical* hermeneutics. I believe that for Mehta it is directly applicable. Though philosophical hermeneutics and its commitment to dialogue are couched in well-meaning intentions, Mehta is not seduced. The concern regards the nature of the self and the other during and after the encounter. I argue that Gadamerian *Bildung*, with its undeniably conservative bent, reflects an attempt to reduce the other to the same, the very same dynamic Levinas attributes to Western philosophy as such. Accordingly, the predominant sense in philosophical hermeneutics is, I propose, one of growth, accumulation, and expansion at the expense of the other, language and intentions preeminently associated with empire. For Mehta, an author who lived the colonial encounter and negotiated postcolonial spaces, the encounter with the other is anything but cumulative. Rather, we find throughout Mehta's writings a sense of rupture and irrevocable loss. It is here that I locate Mehta's postcolonial departure from the philosophical.

Hermeneutics is centripetal.[2] "To recognize one's own in the alien," writes Gadamer, "to become at home in it, is the basic movement of spirit, whose being consists only in returning to itself from what is other" (1997: 14). That the "basic movement of spirit" is to return to itself from what is other suggests that the idea of a journey is particularly apt for Gadamer's hermeneutics. To be sure, a journey suggests not only an end goal but a point of departure as well: the self departs from itself only to return to itself. The hermeneutic self, like a truly historical *Dasein* (Being-there), is always already in a world of understanding. Here we locate Gadamer's famous resuscitation of prejudice. While the Enlightenment envisioned a knowledge completely free of traditional bias and authority – witness Kant's *sapere aude* – Gadamer points out that prejudice is the positive starting point for any interpretation and understanding. Our prejudices enable our world: "Prejudices are biases of our openness to the world. They are simply conditions whereby we experience something" (Gadamer 1976: 9). This is not to suggest, of course, that Gadamer is numb to the negative aspects of prejudice. In fact, he at one point speaks of the "tyranny of hidden prejudice" (1997: 270). Philosophical hermeneutics certainly recognizes that the encounter with the other is an encounter with something that is not immediately resonant with self. If we therefore see the self in philosophical hermeneutics as an elaboration of the structure of *Dasein* – that subject for whom the world is a myriad of projected possibilities dependent upon an already established commerce with a tradition – then the other would appear to be that which the self cannot intend. In this regard, Gadamer proposes that in the genuine encounter the self, and significantly the other as well, must risk its prejudices.

Imagining dialogue as a game, Gadamer suggests that the ostensibly risky encounter overtakes the two parties and their concomitant prejudices. The dialogue, the game plays self and other. Any intentional method established prior to the encounter itself consequently distorts the movement of language and understanding (here of course we recognize that the conjunction in Gadamer's *Truth and Method* actually performs the role of a disjunction).[3] To this extent, Gadamer envisions the buoyancy of the two parties in a moment of freedom: "The back and forth movement of the game has a peculiar freedom and buoyancy that determines the consciousness of the player. It goes on automatically – a condition of weightless balance" (1976: 53). Elsewhere he writes, "the basic constitution of the game, to be filled with its spirit – the spirit of buoyancy, freedom and the joy of success – and to fulfill him who is playing, is structurally related to the constitution of the dialogue in which language is a reality" (1976: 66). Apparently, and perhaps ironically, there is an intentional suspension of method in this game, this journey from self to other and back to self, a process, note, intended "to *fulfill* him who is playing." We will have to return to this question of the game and its fulfilling nature, that is to say, just what kind of game does Gadamer have in mind here?

Concerning the hermeneutic return, Gadamer far more often than not describes a moment of growth. In other words, and perhaps like a good investment banker, the self broadens its horizons through its dialogical venture with the other. Implicit to this sense of broadening and enriching, I suggest, is a conservative commitment to maintaining and supplementing the principal. Gadamer's repeated use of words like "enriched," "broadening," and "expansion" suggests that the self is added on to rather than altered. Philosophical hermeneutics is a good bet. Gadamer notes, "The adventure is 'undergone,' like a test or trial from which one emerges *enriched* and more mature" (1997: 69; emphasis added). Elsewhere he writes, "Only the support of the familiar and common understanding makes possible the venture into the alien, the lifting up of something out of the alien, and thus the *broadening* and *enrichment* of our own experience of the world" (1976: 15; emphases added). Also, "We speak of narrowness of horizon, of the possible *expansion* of horizon ... the way one's range of vision is gradually *expanded*" (1997: 302; emphasis added). These emphases on the expansive nature of the dialogical encounter reflect the semantic load of *Bildung*. According to the philosopher of religion Mark C. Taylor:

> Bildung is the auto-telic process in which selves perpetually remake themselves through ongoing interrelationships.... From this hermeneutical point of view, we enter relationships with 'others' in order to become 'new beings.' The relation to the 'other' is, therefore, a self-relation that is self-transforming. The 'other' is not really other but is actually a moment in one's own self-becoming. (1990: 131)

In other words, the other for Gadamer's *Bildung* loses precisely its alterity in the encounter; the other becomes a constitutive moment in the enrichment of self. This, I suggest, is the heroic nature of philosophical hermeneutics. Indeed, for authors such as Levinas (not to mention Jacques Derrida and John D. Caputo), the hero is a trope of philosophical conquest and its attendant centripetal adventure. "The autonomy of consciousness," argues Levinas, "finds itself again in all its adventures, returning home to itself like Ulysses, who through all his peregrinations is only on the way to his native island," "an odyssey where all adventures are only the accidents of a return to self."[4] Even in moments in which the other is seemingly intractable, the self in fact returns once again to its agency, its sovereignty: "Openness to the other... involves recognizing that I myself must accept some things that are against me, even though no one else forces me to do so" (Gadamer 1997: 361). Indeed, notice that that which is adverse to self doesn't ultimately displace self as agential subject. In this way, the self's historical horizon is apparently challenged but not the sovereignty of the transcendental intention: the subject conserves itself. I believe Halbfass engaged a similar critique of Inden's position above. Taylor addresses what can be called an ironic self-negation:

> Irony entails a paradoxical strategy for relating to the world of experience in which one simultaneously sustains a certain attachment while remaining somewhat detached.... From the ironist's point of view, ironic self-consciousness is more complete and thus higher than nonironic awareness.... Though seemingly partial, the gaze of the ironist is ... panoptical. Affirming itself in every negation, the ironist extends rather than subverts the modern philosophy of the subject. (1990: 38–39)

In the moment of accepting the other as against the self, the self ironically maintains its authority as the adjudicating principle through a transcending detachment, that is to say, a persistent notion of choice betrays the deeper commitment to the self's agency.[5]

The result of the self's encounter with the other as found in Gadamer's texts thus suggests that the self ultimately makes what is other its own. The other supplements the self, enriches the self. This in turn invites a certain postcolonial hermeneutics of suspicion through a postcolonial suspicion of hermeneutics. The Hindu Studies scholar Richard King notes, "the general tenor of the arguments furnished by ...

Gadamer ... does seem to imply that the very act of interpretation by Western Orientalists when approaching the Orient inevitably involves an appropriation and 'colonization' of the material under consideration" (1999: 95).[6] Taylor similarly writes, "*Bildung* ... is identified with the cultural tradition of the West. Other cultural traditions are valued only insofar as they aid Westerners 'in becoming new beings'" (1990: 142). It would indeed seem that there are moments in Gadamer's texts that suggest that the other is a moment to be either conquered or perhaps miraculously brought back to life in the service of the self's expansion. *Bildung*, in fact, suggests just this: "In *Bildung*... that by which and through which one is formed becomes completely one's own" (Gadamer 1997: 11).

While Gadamer certainly characterizes the return to self as one of enrichment and edification, I don't believe this alone entails a heroic or colonial character to philosophical hermeneutics. Rather, if we question the motivation behind the hermeneutic journey, I believe we see the point both King and Taylor make. Gadamer's use of metaphor betrays the buoyant, free, and joyous dialogue. For instance, Gadamer speaks of the self in rather christological terms: "In deciphering and interpreting it, a miracle takes place: the transformation of something alien and dead into total contemporaneity and familiarity" (1997: 163). Elsewhere, Gadamer speaks of "the miracle of understanding" (1997: 311). Now of course such language suggests a good will, if not subtle self-congratulations through mission. But it also characterizes the other as mute, as passive, and as dead. The philosophical hermeneutic self miraculously resurrects the other. When applied to the cross-cultural encounter, this makes of the other an impotent, static, and ultimately lifeless object, implying in turn that the self is the potent, active, vibrant subject, all quite typical rhetorical flourishes in Orientalist discourse.

Though the idea of bringing a mute, alien other into the living, contemporary moment ostensibly reflects a good will, there are moments when Gadamer employs openly aggressive language: "The fact that a foreign language is being translated means that this is simply an extreme case of hermeneutic difficulty – i.e., *of alienness and its conquest*" (1997: 387; emphasis added). Here Gadamer in no uncertain terms equates the conquest of the alien with the hermeneutic task. Elsewhere he writes, hermeneutics "presupposed the foreignness of the content that is to be understood and thus made its task the overcoming of this foreignness by gaining understanding" (1976: 47). Again, the hermeneutic burden disburdens itself when the other is understood, that is, no longer other. While Gadamer undoubtedly characterizes such "conquest" as a game played between dialogue partners that are buoyant, joyous, and free, I suggest that the analogies he employs further disclose the latent aggression. I believe we see this best in his references to chess, and mongooses and snakes.

Far from an a-methodological, buoyant dialogue/game, I argue that chess involves concerned detachment and focused attention in order to lead one's opponent into a corner – checkmate: "To use the analogy of chess, everything is 'solved,' resembling a difficult chess problem where only the definitive solution makes understandable ... the necessity of a previous absurd position" (Gadamer 1976: 32). To be sure, unlike an unintended outcome forged by the willing participation of two parties, Gadamer suggests here a certain teleological determination of moments in pursuit of victory over the other. An absurd position is only so when taken out of context, a context suggesting that there is something other than a spontaneity of movements taking place. Elsewhere in speaking of the players being played, Gadamer writes, "the tension-filled situation in which the mongoose and the snake hold each other in check cannot be described as the reaction of one partner to the attempted attack of the other, but represents a reciprocal behavior of absolute contemporaneousness" (1976: 54). Again, far from buoyant, the self-other encounter is seen here as "tension-filled." Moreover, the contemporaneity to which the self brings the other back to life is explicitly aligned here to a life and death struggle. Neither the mongoose nor the snake desires the other's irreducible presence. Thus on the one hand, there is a dialogue theoretically envisioned as a moment of joy and weightlessness; on the other hand, we see a concerted effort to conquer the other through methodical manipulation and entrapment. This scheming aggression coupled with the notion that one returns home enriched suggests that Gadamer's philosophical hermeneutics resembles a colonial, imperial mission. Indeed, the self is supplemented precisely in the moment it conquers the other. Taylor notes in this regard, "When fully developed, hermeneutics tends to become culturally imperialistic.... The 'exotic' edifies only when it is first domesticated and then assimilated.... Other cultural traditions are valued only insofar as they aid Westerners 'in becoming new beings'" (1990: 142). It would appear that even Gadamer corroborates such a reading when he writes, "What we reject has nothing to say to us – or we reject it because it has nothing to say to us" (1976: 4).

These subtleties in Gadamer's work become pronounced when compared to the hermeneutics of J. L. Mehta. In his last public address on June 13, 1988, Mehta explicitly suggests that hermeneutics is unsatisfactory when it comes to understanding the other. Philosophical hermeneutics, he suggests, is good for "self-understanding":

> I am not so sure ... about the direct applicability of philosophical hermeneutics to the question of inter-religious understanding.... The principal value of philosophical hermeneutics seems to me to lie in clarifying the nature of self-understanding rather than in the understanding of others. (1992: 275)

Proposing here a pre-occupation with self at the center of Gadamer's philosophical hermeneutics, Mehta's interpretation resonates with Levinas's sense that philosophy has an allergy toward the other. Placed in the context of the empirical cross-cultural encounter, Mehta echoes here a comment he made in 1969 regarding Gadamer's take on the non-Western other:

> Gadamer's explication of the phenomenon of understanding, and his application of this to the philosophical present of the West as it has attained self-awareness in the thinking of Heidegger, is determined by an attitude towards the Western tradition which he shares with Husserl rather than Heidegger in its disregard of the existence, claim and world-historical viability of other traditions. (1985: 158; emphasis added)

Perhaps Gadamer's disregard of the non-Western traditions betrays his sense that these traditions have nothing to say to him. Of course, this would seem to imply that Gadamer already understood that which had nothing to say to him, otherwise how could he come to such a conclusion? (We see here the proximity of Gadamer's hermeneutics to Mircea Eliade's strange hermeneutics.[7]) Proposing an alternative model to such philosophical hermeneutics and its heroic *self*-understanding, Mehta suggests the trope of the pilgrim and the centripetal, and thereby still hermeneutic, journey of a pilgrimage.

In an explicit attempt to distance his hermeneutics from philosophical hermeneutics, Mehta suggests that we set aside "learned and bookish models for religious understanding" and look to "the model of a pilgrimage as more appropriate and helpful" (1992: 275). Why pilgrimage? How is pilgrimage different from heroic odyssey? Mehta suggests that people undertake a pilgrimage "to understand and experience the meaning of their lives, and of what remains to give completion to their pilgrimage through life, to be able to give the very name of pilgrimage to their lives" (1992: 276). Though Mehta speaks here of completion, itself seemingly resonant with chess's fulfilling solution, this completion is in fact ironic (and it may be precisely such ironic completion that illuminates Mehta's understanding of religion and the religious). Indeed, while completion suggests plenitude, and Mehta in fact writes that pilgrimage is a "last act [that] fills up a lack" (1992: 276), the fulfillment, I argue, is indeed ironic: pilgrimage is reconciliation to the incomplete, the unfulfilled, death. Mehta indicates this ironic fulfillment by suggesting that it will not occur "until living is transformed into a pilgrimage, which is nothing if not living in the face of death, one's own" (1992: 276–277). In this regard, I suggest that Mehta's pilgrimage presents a significant departure from the triumphant, supplementing, and thus enriching return to one's self found in Gadamer's philosophical hermeneutics. In fact, Mehta frames the encounter between India and the West in just this way:

> The only difference in this two-sided, mutual participation is that from the Western end it is in the nature of supplementing the substance of their mainstream culture, an assimilation of the alien and subordinating it within a more widely based totality. From the non-Western, including Indian ... the participation is an appropriation of the substance itself, not peripheral as in the Western case. (1990: 230; emphases added)

Notice that "an appropriation of the substance" stands opposed to a "more widely based totality." For Mehta, not to mention non-Western cultures in general, the other is not merely a supplement. It is just the opposite.

Mehta curiously suggests that destroying the other is sacred. Borrowing directly from the South Asian religious idiom, he characterizes the other as a tīrtha: "Understanding ... would be a pilgrimage toward oneself, others being the tīrtha, the sacred places one passes through on one's way to the final destination" (1992: 273). Here I believe Mehta directly contests Gadamer's christological characterization of the self as a miracle worker resurrecting the other, bringing the other to full transparency. Indeed for Mehta, the other as tīrtha retains a certain opacity, after all "otherness is overcome, to some degree" (1992: 268). Unlike Gadamer's chess partners reaching a point where "everything is 'solved'," and unlike the self handing the dead other life, here the other is not a moment within a "definitive solution," nor a lifeless object in need of the self's animating spirit. Rather, and significantly, the opaque other is a source of the self's destruction, the self's death. Mehta argues:

> Idols must be set up and idols must be broken, these same idols, our own, not those of
> others ... without the final perception of these symbols, including those called concepts,
> and of our very belongingness to a tradition, as idols to be discarded, down to the very last,
> there can be no arrival, no homecoming. (1985: 206–207; emphases added)

Explicitly contrasting Gadamer's self who gives the dead other life, Mehta's other, his tīrtha, gives the self death. The other is a moment of opacity that renders the self's search for definitive solutions mortally wounded.

Thus in direct contrast to Gadamer, Mehta recognizes precisely the loss of tradition and self through the encounter with the other: the other is the moment of the self's destruction. Pilgrimage, for Mehta, is therefore thoroughly iconoclastic, not supplementing and enriching. For this reason, I propose that Mehta's reading of hermeneutics intimately reflects his colonial experience as well as his postcolonial predicament. Historically speaking, Mehta is suspicious of *his* other. He is suspicious that the dominant other in his horizon (and that is unquestionably the colonizing other) is present for presents, that is, plunder, and not for dialogue. He writes (worth quoting at length):

> One "speech community" understands another ... to the extent to which it learns to live in
> the same "house of words" as the other. This is not just a question of scholarship nor, to use
> an expression much in favour these days, of "dialogue." This has mostly been an illdisguised
> monologue in which one partner is bilingual and the other (the initiator of the dialogue)
> knows or is at home in only one language, his own mother tongue. The conversation ...
> takes place in the latter's mother tongue and the poor bilingual traveler ... has already lost
> the dialogical battle before the exchange actually takes place.... What he sees in my speech
> is his own mirror image, reflected back to him in my words, an image enframed in a suitably
> exotic and "native" context.... [R]eligious encounters of this type are apt to leave us ruffled;
> they activate my sensitivity to the partner's talk as a kind of attack rather than a reaching
> out, they aggravate my sense of my religious identity, and leave us further apart than before
> the dialogue took place. (1992: 274)

Notice that for Mehta the cross-cultural dialogue is like a *battle* and that the partner's address is like an *attack* that leaves the interlocutors *further apart* than before. Certainly we have come a long way from buoyant games and fusions of horizons. In fact, and extending the notion of being at war with the other, Mehta writes of "(philosophical) hermeneutics as a weapon directed against the other" (1985: 194). He also suggests that this "ill disguised monologue" is undertaken in the name of one partner seeing himself in the other, thereby reassuring the one that his identity is not threatened by substantial alterity, a concern attributed to philosophical hermeneutics.[8] Directly contesting such dogged concern for one's identity, Mehta writes, "A dialogue can succeed only to the extent that the partners forget all about their specific religious identities for the moment and converse with each other like two wayfarers, who are thrown together for a while as companions on the same pilgrimage" (1992: 274).

While Mehta's polemical writings are directed primarily towards an imperial West, he is not blind to India's own history of philosophical hermeneutic activity, that is, its history of inclusivism.[9] Indeed, Mehta suggests that historically speaking India's traditions have been driven by the heroic predilection ascribed here to philosophical hermeneutics:

In its understanding of both itself and the other, India has followed the way of growth through absorption and assimilation, rejecting what could not be appropriated without its own disintegration, accepting from other cultures whatever could be suitably transformed to become part of its living body. (1985: 117)

Certainly this is a description of a heroic India. He continues:

It [i.e., India] must strive to comprehend the other in its otherness, let it speak to us in its difference from us.... I make bold to suggest that such an approach to what is other is somewhat alien to the genius of our entire tradition and the task ... correspondingly difficult and against the grain for us. (1985: 117)

Though speaking here as if India still has an agential role to play in opening up its horizons, Mehta far more often than not employs the rhetoric of accomplished rupture, especially in his reflections on Hinduism in modernity. For instance, he writes:

The major task which these attempts subserve is that of understanding how the Hindu life-world has been violently altered by India's entry into modernity in the early nineteenth century.... [T]he crucial problem is an examination of the cataclysmic change in the religious foundations of our old conception of social and political order. (1992: 220; emphases added)

Undeniably, "violently altered" and "cataclysmic change" in no way carry the same conservative connotations as "enrichment" and "expanded." Elsewhere he writes, characterizing the history of South Asian religious traditions: "the most dramatic changes and ruptures in their religious history – of which *the continuity and unity is all but lost from view*" (1992: 105–106; emphasis added). Here we see an unequaled example of what I am calling Mehta's *postcolonial* hermeneutics. As J. Weinsheimer and D. G. Marshall point out in their preface to *Truth and Method*: "What remains important is the concept [i.e., *Bildung*] that a self can be formed without breaking with or repudiating one's past" (Gadamer 1997: xii). In this regard, a continuity and unity that is all but lost from view is unquestionably antithetical to *Bildung*. Mehta provides further examples: "In the world of today, in this one world of 'world-civilization,' our relationship to tradition is an irreparably broken one" (1985: 261); "Our relation to tradition can no longer be one of conservation alone" (1985: 128); "The Hindu intellectual ... has ... witnessed and participated in ... a catastrophic alteration in his traditional life-world during the last half century" (1990: 216). Finally, Mehta characterizes "the cumulative religious tradition of India" as "comparable at the present time to a temple in ruins" (1985: 216). I thus propose that Mehta's meditations on hermeneutics reflect a colonial experience as well as a postcolonial predicament; the colonial and postcolonial experience enriches not, but violently alters everything. "We may start," writes Mehta, "with the basic fact of the crisis generated in our cultural and religious history by the British conquest of India, a crisis unique and unparalleled in all our previous history, and with its unresolved continuation beyond the termination of our colonial status" (1990: 143), a "basic fact" indirectly reflecting the conditions of "all non-Western civilizations, however decrepit or wounded" (1990: 31).

What, then, is the result of all of this talk of postcolonial hermeneutics? I believe it ultimately rests with a deconstruction/destruction of the philosophical self, that is, the self tied to a metaphysical notion of the subject, of identity.[10] Mehta notes:

> Ordinarily, the 'I' is regarded as that which remains identical in the midst of our varied behavior and experiences, thus standing as a point of reference for this manifold. Ontologically speaking, it is something that lies at the basis, the subjectum, which, as remaining the same in the midst of change, has the character of a self. (1976: 137)

It is this notion of the self that is at stake in Mehta's postcolonial hermeneutics. Indeed, if philosophical hermeneutics, like philosophy itself, is seemingly tied to the supplementation of self, that is, the ultimate buildup of self, then postcolonial hermeneutics rests on acquiescence to irretrievable loss and devastation. After all, "for the Oriental the restoration of a vanished autonomy is only a nostalgic dream" (Mehta 1992: 39–40). In this regard, Mehta suggests that it is one's acceptance of death that ultimately accounts for one's pilgrimage. An editor of one of the collections of Mehta's essays W. J. Jackson notes this as well:

> If one travels to colonize, manage, convert or sight-see as a tourist, one travels differently than if one goes on a pilgrimage seeking meaning.... 'Self knowledge' at the end meant being a pilgrim to one's Ur-revelation or spiritual mountain home, joined in postmodern communitas with fellow journeyers, all facing the common fate of losing their breath – inevitable death. (1992: 20)

Here Jackson points to something quite interesting – postmodern *communitas*. I believe Jackson is correct. In all his talk of loss, rupture, dislocation, Mehta did not intend all of this to end in despair. Rather, Mehta saw the need for a global community, a postmodern community. He nevertheless despaired that we had no way of envisioning this community: "we have no hermeneutic of a global 'we'" (1985: 199). Contrary to these expressed concerns, I believe Mehta in fact takes us quite a way towards such a hermeneutic. The question thus concerns how we are to interpret this hermeneutic of a global we, that is, this postmodern *communitas*.

If we were to follow the traditional *philosophical* hermeneutic approach we might expect some positive statement concerning the nature of this community. In this regard, we would broach the sense of community authors such as Jacques Derrida and John D. Caputo find most troubling. Caputo for instance writes:

> Derrida's use of the word 'guard' converges with the meaning of 'community,' which means of course a military formation, the wall of protection that the same builds against the other, the way a 'people' (the 'same') builds a common fortification (*com, munire*) around itself against the other, gathering itself together into One in order to keep safe the uniqueness of its archive. (1997: 271–272)

In other words, the etymology of "community" reflects a violent exclusion of the other in the name of a positive archive, identity. The horizons of philosophical hermeneutics and classical community fuse rather nicely. Mehta's community, his "global we" enlists, to the contrary, a "weak identity." Mehta's hermeneutic of a global we is his postcolonial hermeneutics. In this regard, "the global we" is predicated on a lack, on a common mortality, a community of mortals, a postmodern *communitas*. Mehta writes of the other's "identity with me in that which escapes the conceptual grasping of either of us" (1985: 195). Even more to the point:

> A dialogue between civilizations is certainly possible, is indeed urgently necessary ... even in the midst of an irretrievable loss by each of what once was. Today it is this sense of loss that alone can bring the legatees of great civilizations together in the philosophical endeavor. (Mehta 1992: 258; emphasis added)

In no uncertain terms, Mehta here points to the idea that what brings peoples of all civilizations together is not some common, positive type or character. Rather, it is the recognition of a loss of such essential determinations. This is a wounded community, a weak community, a postmodern community.[11] Moreover, while such loss was foisted upon certain cultures in the past, and Mehta would undoubtedly count among these the Indian cultures, he argues that in our postmodern world we must willingly embrace this loss, that is, we must "be willing to suffer change in one's inmost being" (1992: 263). Such change in "one's inmost being" directly resonates with the need to destroy one's concepts down to the very last. I suggest that such reflexive demolition in turn enables the recognition that we lack the master name/identity, the presumed possession of which more often than not facilitates violent appropriations and exclusions of the other. For Mehta, all of this is in fact a "religious activity," that is, "a form of mutuality and self-subordination" (1992: 269). We may thus conclude that for Mehta philosophy and philosophical hermeneutics reduce the other to self, while religious pilgrimage and postcolonial hermeneutics reduce the self to the humble state of being an other among others.

Mehta's conspicuous emphasis on rupture and loss, rather than on enrichment and gain, indicates a shift in hermeneutic focus. I argue that Mehta's work significantly contests philosophical hermeneutics' emphasis on *Bildung*. The pilgrim, for Mehta, is the tropic substitute (a religious trope at that) for the subject who, unlike the philosophical hero who returns only to an enriched home, recognizes, and is subsequently reconciled to, the death of its traditional identity, that is, its home. This death is not, however, a mere recognition that the self is changed in the encounter with the other. Indeed, the anguish for the pilgrim is that homecoming through pilgrimage is a ruinous destination – tradition is irreparably broken. Thus while both Gadamer and Mehta speak of a journey out to the other with an imminent return, that is, hermeneutics, it would appear that the former's heroic destination is enriched (philosophy) while the latter's violently and irreparably altered (religion). The death of the pilgrim thus reflects the postcolonial hermeneutics of Jarava Lal Mehta.

Notes

1 Assuming for the moment that this is in fact the case, it really should come as no surprise; after all, Halbfass and Mehta were themselves dialogue partners. I, in fact, suggest that at all the crucial theoretical reflections on hermeneutics found in Halbfass's *India and Europe* a quote from Mehta is more often than not cited in support. Moreover, the preface to the English edition of

India and Europe closes with the following: "Among those from whom I received intellectual and 'hermeneutical' inspiration during my work on both the German and the English versions of this book, I have to mention Jarava Lal Mehta. It would be difficult to imagine a better partner-in-dialogue" (1988: xi).

2 In this regard, I suggest that both the hero and the pilgrim are particularly apt hermeneutic tropes: both are homeward bound. In other words, both tropes represent a journey out to an other with an imminent return to self. Significantly, this is not the infinitely centrifugal journey of the deconstructive nomad. Elsewhere I suggest that Continental philosophy has employed certain "ethnotropes" to explicate certain philosophical critiques. I propose that Ulysses/the Greek Hero substitutes for Hegel's/Husserl's/Gadamer's imperial subject while Abraham/the Jewish Nomad substitutes for Derrida's deconstructive subject. Caputo notes in this regard, "Presents always come home, right away or after some time, like Ulysses, circling back economically to the *oikos*, as opposed to father Abraham who left the land of his fathers, never to return again" (1997: 162); also, "the figure of Ulysses Derrida learned from Levinas, where Ulysses is aligned with Hegel and set off from father Abraham who sets out from the land of Ur never to return. That would be to distinguish two kinds or figures of circumcision, between... a Ulyssean... which closes the circle of the same, and an Abrahamic circumcision, which cuts the cord of the same in order to be open to the other" (ibid.: 257). I believe Mehta's theory of the pilgrim adds a third possibility, a third ethnotrope. That is to say, the pilgrim like the hero and unlike the nomad returns, but like the nomad and unlike the hero the home to which the pilgrim returns is destroyed, a point I will argue in what follows.

3 It is interesting to note in this regard that Mehta once ascribed to Mircea Eliade a "stange hermeneutics." That is to say, Mehta found Eliade suggesting that in order for a dialogue to take place, one must first understand the other. For Mehta, the idea that understanding precedes dialogue is like putting the cart before the horse. Mehta quotes Eliade: "A true encounter implies a dialogue. In order to begin a valid dialogue with non-European cultures, it is indispensable to know and understand these cultures.... The will properly to understand the 'other' is rewarded by an enrichment of the Western consciousness" (cited in Mehta 1985: 180–181). To this Mehta replies: "Strange hermeneutics, in which a valid dialogue can begin only after understanding has first been achieved, rather than being itself the locus or the playground in which understanding has its very being" (ibid.: 181).

4 Here I have taken the liberty of juxtaposing two fragments from different sources; the full quotes from which these were taken are: "The God of the philosophers, from Aristotle to Leibniz, by way of the God of the scholastics, is a god adequate to reason, a comprehended god who could not trouble the autonomy of consciousness, which finds itself again in all its adventures, returning home to itself like Ulysses, who through all his peregrinations is only on the way to his native island" (1986: 346); "Philosophical knowledge is a priori: it searches for the adequate idea and ensures autonomy. In every new development it recognizes familiar structures and greets old acquaintances. It is an odyssey where all adventures are only accidents of a return to self" (1996: 14).

5 For postcolonial critics like Daya Krishna such irony continues the Western commitment to its own agency: "In a deep and radical sense ... it is only the West that has arrogated to itself the status of subjecthood in the cognitive enterprise, reducing all others to the status of objects" (1988: 78).

6 The psychoanalytic anthropologist Gananath Obeyesekere displays similar hesitancies in his methodological discussion of anthropological investigation: "Cultural consciousness ... involves a two-fold *critical* attitude. Often when we write about another culture there is an implied critique of it – sometimes we cannot handle this well. There is also another critique: a critique of one's own culture and traditions. This is, I believe, a very important part of our discipline – or should be – and must supplement the conservative notion of Gadamer's view of one's historical consciousness.... In studying another society it is the idea of 'cultural consciousness' that must supplement Gadamer's notion of effective history, historical consciousness, and the 'fusion of horizons' " (1990: 274). He continues this line of reasoning in an appended endnote:

"Fusion of horizons ... is appropriate when the text belongs to one's own tradition, but this model of the text is inadequate for studying an alien culture. Here, I believe, one must *resist* the fusion of horizons and try as best one can to restore in one's work the integrity of alien life-forms" (ibid.: 317). Implied in all of this is of course the idea that Gadamer's philosophical hermeneutics tends to see self in other much more quickly than self and other as other to each other.

7 On Eliade's "strange hermeneutics," see note 3 above. Whether or not Gadamer truly understood that which Mehta suggests he dismissed is debatable. In fact, Gadamer at one point suggests: "Although in the meantime the research in Eastern philosophy has made further advances, we believe today that we are further removed from its philosophical understanding.... What can be considered established is only the negative insight that our own basic concepts ... alter the essence of what is foreign" (cited in Halbfass 1988: 164).

8 This is precisely the role the "explanatory account" plays in Orientalist discourse according R. Inden: "Once the reader comes to know the natural reason for the Other's otherness, the threat of it is neutralized. The explanation is, thus, one which restores the unity of mankind, with Western man as its perfect embodiment" (1990: 43). With respect to Gadamer's fear of the other that remains other, Caputo addresses Gadamer's approach to modern art: "These art forms would seem on the face of it to resist traditional aesthetic categories like mimesis. They seem to represent a case not of the inexhaustibility of meaning but of a radical break with meaning and so to represent a rupture with the past history of art. But Gadamer's aim is to close this gap, to fuse these horizons, and to reconcile these differences. One might ask whether this is not a domesticative gesture, whether Gadamer is really ready to hear something new in modern art, something troubling and indigestible" (2000: 48).

9 For an extended discussion of India's history of inclusivism, see Halbfass (1988).

10 For an excellent discussion of the metaphysical self and its deconstruction, see Taylor (1984). For instance, he suggests that the metaphysical self is the self that is identical to itself: "identity includes two closely related elements: self-sameness at a particular time and continuity through time" (p. 37). My argument here is that Gadamer's self reflects this metaphysical notion. Granted, Gadamer's self grows through its encounter with the other, but the core never truly changes. After all, *Bildung* reflects a certain continuity through time.

11 In this regard, I believe Mehta anticipates the preeminent legal theorist and social philosopher Martha Nussbaum's reflections: "Liberal respect for human equality ... is inspired by Rousseau's profound contention that political equality must be sustained by an emotional development that understands humanity as a condition of shared incompleteness" (2004: 16); "a society of citizens who admit that they are needy and vulnerable, and who discard the grandiose demands from omnipotence and completeness that have been at the heart of so much human misery, both public and private" (ibid.: 17).

References

Caputo, John D. 1997. *The prayers and tears of Jacques Derrida: religion without religion.* Bloomington, IN: Indiana University Press.

Caputo, John D. 2000. *More radical hermeneutics: on not knowing who we are.* Bloomington, IN: Indiana University Press.

Franco, Eli and Karin Preisendanz (Eds). 1997. *Beyond orientalism: the work of Wilhelm Halbfass and its impact on Indian and cross-cultural studies.* Amsterdam: Rodopi.

Gadamer, Hans-Georg. 1976. *Philosophical hermeneutics.* Berkeley, CA: University of California Press.

Gadamer, Hans-Georg. 1997. *Truth and method.* Translated by J. Weinsheimer and D. G. Marshall. Second revised edition. New York: Continuum.

Halbfass, Wilhelm. 1988. *India and Europe: an essay in understanding*. Albany, NY: State University of New York Press.

Halbfass, Wilhelm. 1997. Beyond orientalism? Reflections of a current theme. In *Beyond orientalism: the work of Wilhelm Halbfass and its impact on Indian and cross-cultural studies*, edited by E. Franco and K. Preisendanz, pp. 1–25. Amsterdam: Rodopi.

Inden, Ronald B. 1990. *Imagining India*. Cambridge, MA: Basil Blackwell.

Jackson, William J. 1992. Steps towards the whole horizon. In *J. L. Mehta on heidegger, hermeneutics, and the Indian tradition*, edited by W. J. Jackson, pp. 1–24. Leiden: E. J. Brill.

King, Richard. 1999. *Orientalism and religion: postcolonial theory, India and 'the mystic East'*. London: Routledge.

Krishna, Daya. 1988. Comparative philosophy: what it is and what it ought to be. In *Interpreting across boundaries: new essays in comparative philosophy*, edited by G. J. Larson and E. Deutsch, pp. 71–83. Princeton, NJ: Princeton University Press.

Larson, Gerald James and Eliot Deutsch. 1988. *Interpreting across boundaries: new essays in comparative philosophy*. Princeton, NJ: Princeton University Press.

Levinas, Emmanuel. 1986. The trace of the other. In *Deconstruction in context: literature and philosophy*, edited by M. C. Taylor, pp. 345–349. Chicago, IL: The University of Chicago Press.

Levinas, Emmanuel. 1996. *Emmanuel Levinas: basic philosophical writings*, edited by A. T. Peperzak, S. Critchley and R. Bernasconi. Bloomington, IN: Indiana University Press.

Mehta, Jarava Lal. 1965. Existential Themes and Indian Thought. The Annual Humanities Lecture, Syracuse University. Unpublished.

Mehta, Jarava Lal. 1967. *The philosophy of Martin Heidegger*. Varanasi: [Published for the Centre of Advanced Study in Philosophy, Banaras Hindu University by] Banaras Hindu University Press.

Mehta, Jarava Lal. 1971. Commentary on Marc Galanter's "Hinduism, secularism, and the Indian judiciary". *Philosophy East and West* 21:489–492.

Mehta, Jarava Lal. 1985. *India and the west: the problem of understanding*. Chico, CA: Scholar's Press.

Mehta, Jarava Lal. 1990. *Philosophy and religion: essays in interpretation*. New Delhi: Indian Council of Philosophical Research.

Mehta, Jarava Lal. 1992. *J. L. Mehta on heidegger, hermeneutics, and Indian tradition*, edited by W. J. Jackson. Leiden: E. J. Brill.

Nussbaum, Martha. 2004. *Hiding from humanity: disgust, shame, and the law*. Princeton, NJ: Princeton University Press.

Obeyesekere, Gananath. 1990. *The work of culture: symbolic transformation in psychoanalysis and anthropology*. Chicago, IL: University of Chicago Press.

Said, Edward W. 1978. *Orientalism*. New York: Vintage.

Taylor, Mark C. 1984. *Erring: a postmodern a/theology*. Chicago, IL: University of Chicago Press.

Taylor, Mark C. (Ed.). 1986. *Deconstruction in context: literature and philosophy*. Chicago, IL: University of Chicago Press.

Taylor, Mark C. (Ed.). 1990. *Tears*. Albany, NY: State University of New York Press.

Young, Robert. 1990. *White mythologies: writing history and the west*. London: Routledge.

Western Idealism Through Indian Eyes: A Cittamatra Reading of Berkeley, Kant and Schopenhauer

Jay L. Garfield

Abstract I experiment with a non-standard approach to comparative philosophy, using Indian Buddhist cittamātra philosophy, as a lens for exploring the history of Western idealism.

Introduction: Metahermeneutic Preliminaries

This is an essay in metaphilosophy, in which I use one philosophical tradition as a lens through which to examine another. So it is already one level an abstraction from the already rarefied plane of metaphysics. But the principal agenda is yet one level more abstract: What I really aim to accomplish in this discussion is a reconception of the range of possibilities and the methodology of comparative philosophy and cross-cultural hermeneutics – a kind of meta-meta-metaphysics, if you will. So I begin with a discussion of the nature of and problems associated with cross-cultural hermeneutics and comparative philosophy in particular, and then we will get down to business at a number of more fundamental levels.

Comparative philosophy has acquired a somewhat deservedly bad reputation of late (e.g. Klein 1995; Tuck 1990; Larson and Deutsch 1989). It has been noted that it too often functions as an arm of Orientalism in the most pejorative sense of that term – as an appropriation of expertise on non-Western traditions by Western scholars, with a consequent disempowerment of their non-Western colleagues. Moreover, it has been noted, comparative philosophy often imports hermeneutical and philosophical methods to the study of non-Western texts that succeed in distorting or simply missing the significance of those texts or the meaningfulness of the claims they make and arguments they proffer in their home cultures. In addition it has been noted that the interpretive lens privileged in most comparative philosophy is a distinctively Western lens, taking for granted a horizon of interpretation which itself should be a matter for contention in comparing multiple traditions. Finally, and as a closely related matter, it has been charged that in comparing philosophical texts and views, the Western texts, views and arguments are typically taken as the standards against which non-Western texts are compared, and with respect to which are inevitably found either wanting, or, in the most generous case, found

P. Bilimoria and A.B. Irvine (eds.), *Postcolonial Philosophy of Religion.*
© Springer Science+Business Media B.V. 2009

to approximate – the latter serving as the highest (and most patronising) accolade vindicating the comparativist's attention to a tradition beyond his or her own.

All of these charges are, of course, overly broad, tarring with a single brush a wide range of philosophical activity. Nonetheless, there is enough truth in each of them, and truth in each case with respect to enough of the literature comprised under this rubric to take them all seriously. I have argued elsewhere (Garfield 2002) that the enterprise of cross-cultural interpretation, and inter alia comparative philosophy as a wing of that enterprise, is in need of a new model of scholarship – a conversational model that takes as its model not the interpretation of fixed canonical texts by readers, but rather discussion of texts-in-being-read by colleagues, in which active interchange between scholars with shared concerns and presumed comparable authority address questions of mutual interest. In such a conversation neither party can take his or her tradition, texts, or conceptual framework for granted as providing a privileged or Archimedean standpoint from which to approach the other. The goals of such interchange are then not simply to *compare* texts for the sake of comparison, but rather to further understanding to the benefit of participants in each tradition, and perhaps to erode the boundaries between traditions in a non-hegemonic fashion.

But such conversations require more than good faith, shared interests and mutual respect. They require the willingness of each participant to take seriously – as a moment in the dialectic, though not as its endpoint – the possibility of interpreting his/her own tradition and texts from the standpoint of the other. For even though the goal of conversational cross-cultural interpretation is the displacement of both text and tradition as the fundamental units of analysis in favour of scholarly interactions, and the abandonment of particular traditions as privileged contexts for those interactions, that is a goal to be achieved, and not a situation to be presupposed at the outset of hermeneutic practice. We must begin where we find ourselves, and that is in a situation in which Western scholars have succeeded in taking their own tradition as privileged, and have avoided the task of providing access to that tradition to their non-Western interlocutors, thus doubly impeding collegial progress. We must therefore strive to make our texts available on terms accessible to our cross-cultural colleagues, and strive self-consciously to see these texts from a distant point of view, the better to problematise them in the larger context we seek to create.[1]

It is therefore necessary first not entirely to *abandon* comparative philosophy, but to *use it*, albeit in a self-undermining way – in a way that will at the same time provide remedial equity to traditions too often placed in the object position under the comparative subjective lens and provide the kind of window into both the Western tradition and its hermeneutic practice for at least some of our non-Western colleagues. I therefore propose to take up the challenge implicit in this set of charges and to subject a slice of Western philosophy to the comparative method from the standpoint of an Indian tradition. I will take the Indian analysis for granted as the standard against which to measure the Western tradition; I will, insofar as is possible, adopt an Indo-Tibetan standard of interpretation and doxography as I approach the Western texts; and I will self-consciously adopt readings of the Indian text I use derived from the Indo-Tibetan doxographic/philosophical tradition.

Now, I cannot go all the way: I cannot shed my identity as a Western philosopher; I can pretend neither to the same distance from my target texts nor the same proximity to my lens presumed in ordinary comparative philosophy. And I come to the task with a self-conscious metaphilosophical agenda that is inevitably distorting of the ground-level project. The real philosophical activity I await will require practitioners of a non-Western tradition to have a go at ours themselves, as a prelude to an open dialogue among equals. Some of this is already happening, with interesting results (Chakrabarti 1996 is a good example). I believe – and I hope that this exercise will demonstrate – that we can learn a great deal about our own tradition and can prepare ourselves for such an open conversation by seeing it from the vantage point of another. Comparative philosophy, when done properly, can still be genuinely revelatory to all parties to the dialogue, and can assist in bringing the resources of all traditions in play in preparation for a circumstance when such comparative exercises will be passé and a plurality of traditions, each conscious of its own history and of the histories of those with which it interacts can interact through collective activity.

My case study will involve the examination of a fragment of the history of Western transcendental idealism, viz., the development of the account of representation beginning with Berkeley, going through Kant and concluding with Schopenhauer. The lens through which I intend to examine this history, and the framework in which I propose to reconstruct the story of this evolution is provided by the metaphysical account of phenomena developed by Vasubandhu in *Trisvabhāvanirdeśa*-that is, the doctrine of the three natures that forms the basis of the doctrine that came to be called *cittamatra*, or mind-only (sometimes also referred to as *vijñānavāda* or *vijñapta-matra*, the way of consciousness, or consciousness-only). I will argue that when we examine Western idealism (or this slice of it) from this classical Indian vantage point, we can discern a definite and somewhat surprising progressivity in the Western tradition, a progressivity invisible without that lens, and one which reveals this episode in the history of our tradition as a progressive approximation to Vasubandhu's own analysis.

In order to launch this venture, I must first defend what was once a noncontroversial claim – that cittamatra in Vasubandhu's formulation is in fact a Buddhist idealism. I will then briefly sketch the outlines of Vasubandhu's own formulation of that idealism, emphasising his analysis of phenomena as three-natured. With this framework in hand, I will argue that Berkeley's idealism respects the *parikalpita-svabhāva*; that Kant adds to this an appreciation of the importance of *paratantra-svabhāva*, and that Schopenhauer completes the tradition by emphasising the importance not only of these two natures, but of the *parinispanna-svabhāva* as well. Hence we will be able to see, through this Indian lens the respect in which the Western tradition can be seen as progressive. I hope we will then see both the value of privileging non-Western as well as Western traditions for the purposes of cross-cultural analysis, and the possibility of reading texts from very different traditions together, despite their different contexts.

Cittamatra Is Idealism

It has become something of a fashion lately to argue that cittamatra is not ideal-ist (Kalupahana 1987; Kochumuttom 1982; Dunne 1996; Lusthaus 1996; Powers 1996). Some argue that it is a form of pragmatism; others that it is a neutral monism; still others that it is completely continuous with Madhyamaka, as a doctrine of the emptiness of all phenomena. While it is true that simply saying that *all this is mind only* is not by itself, in a Buddhist context, enough to indict a school as idealist, given the plethora of metaphorical or qualified readings available for such formu-lae, I think that there are absolutely compelling internal and doxographic arguments for reading Vasubandhu and his fellow travellers as idealists in a strong sense of that term.

First let us be clear about what idealism in the relevant sense is, so that we do not find ourselves merely quibbling about terms. Idealism is a contrastive ontology: It is the assignment to the mind and to mental phenomena a fundamental reality inde-pendent of that of external objects, while denying to apparently external phenomena a merely dependent status – a second-class existence as objects of and as wholly dependent upon mind. Now there are different grades of idealism. As we shall see, Berkeley, Kant and Schopenhauer, for instance, diverge dramatically on points of detail, and if we were to add Hegel, Fichte, Bradley and the early Wittgenstein to the discussion still more divergence among idealists would be apparent. But these figures are unanimous in urging that the mind, or the transcendental subject exists prior to and independently of any of its objects, and that its objects exist only as its objects, and insofar as they are characterised as objects, in no way externally to consciousness.

When Kochumuttom, Anacker, Kalupahana, Lusthaus and Powers deny that Vasubandhu or Asanga are idealists, they intend to deny them precisely this view – that objects of consciousness have a special, lower-grade existence, while mind has a first-grade existence, is a necessary condition of the existence of those objects, and is independent of their existence. Consider these remarks:

> It [Yogācāra] is *not* idealism. The mind is not the only *reality* according to them...
>
> Unfortunately the standard *interpretation* of Yogācāra (especially of the Vimsatika) treats it as a form of idealism, which then renders all of the Yogācārin arguments silly.... [T]heir ontological position is neither materialist nor idealist, but rather ontological silence... (Lusthaus 26/6/1996)
>
> I have never read a Yogācārin text that ever made the claim that mind creates physical things...
>
> The point of refuting *objects* is to eliminate the appropriative consciousness that generates them qua appropriational goals. It is not to deny the objects in order to reify the conscious-ness. If Tibetan commentators say otherwise, they need to go back to school. (Lusthaus 27/6/1996)
>
> Tibetan commentators do in fact commonly characterise Yogācāra writers as holding a view that everything exists in the mind, but Asanga, Vasubandhu et al. never say this, as far as I'm aware.... [I]n my opinion their [Tibetan doxographers'] presentation of Yogācāra creates a view with which the proponents of the system would not agree. (Powers 30/7/1996)[2]

There are indeed passages in the Yogācāra literature which apparently support an idealistic monism. But I maintain that the entire system, when understood in terms of realistic pluralism, makes better sense and that, therefore, even those passages which apparently support idealist monism, have to be reinterpreted in accordance with realistic pluralism.... It positively holds that individuals are real as well as mutually independent beings. (Kochumuttom 1982: 3)

There was a time when one could simply take it for granted that the Cittamatra or Yogācāra school (I will use the terms interchangeably here despite good doxographic reasons for distinguishing both their intension and extension)[3] is the school of Buddhist idealism. However academic fashions and imperatives are such that once a position is regarded as obvious it seems that attacking it becomes mandatory. And so now we must defend the obvious. Taking John Dunne's (30/6/1996) and John Powers' (1/7/1996) point, and following on from various points made in Garfield (1996) I refrain from ascribing a common philosophical position to all of those referred to in Indo-Tibetan doxographies as Yogācārins. Here I restrict my gaze to Vasubandhu, and more particularly to the position he articulates and defends in *Vimśatika* and *Trisvabhāvanirdeśa*. These are probably his last two works and they present the most articulate and explicit statement of his ontology. I will also allude to *Madhyāntavibhaga-bhāṣya*, which presents the most complete elaboration of his ontology and epistemology. I would argue that Vasubandhu's idealism is shared by Sthiramati, and is accurately characterised by Candrakīrti, Tsong Khapa and mKhas grub, among others. Consider the following verses:

1. All this is appearance only
Because of the appearance of the non-existent.
Just someone with cataracts
Sees hairs, the moon and other nonexistents.
16. Perception is like a dream, etc.
That is, when it occurs
The object it distinguishes does not appear.
So, how can one call this perception? (*Vimsatika*)[4]

Vasubandhu in this text explicitly asserts that the entire phenomenal world is in fact *consciousness only* and that the objects that appear to us are *non-existent* like the hairs seen by the proverbial cataract patient. What is apparently the perception of external objects is actually more like a dream – the confusion of mere phantoms of the mind with physical objects.

20. Whatever is an object
Of conceptual thought,
That is thoroughly imaginary.
Without any entity, it does not exist. (*Trimskikakārikā*)
5. What is the imagination of the non-existent?
Since what is imagined absolutely never
Exists in the way it is imagined,
It is mind that constructs that illusion.

36. Through the perception of mind-only
One achieves the non-perception of objects;
Through the non-perception of objects
There is also the non-perception of mind. (*Trisvabhāvanirdeśa*)

In *Trisvabhāvanirdeśa* as well, Vasubandhu emphasises the illusory character of external objects and the reality of the mind as the source of that illusion. He further emphasises that the mind as it appears in introspection is no more real than external objects. It, too, is merely a phantom object of pure subjectivity which is the only reality.[5] This emphasis on the reality of consciousness and the unreality of its objects runs throughout to *Madhyāntavibhaga-bhāṣya* as well.[6] The following verse and its commentary is apposite:

I:3. Consciousness is the appearance of
Objects, sentient beings, self and representation.
Arising entirely this way, it is without object.
Being without that, it itself is non-existent. (Bi, 4b–c)

Here, when an object appears it appears as form, etc. When a sentient being appears it appears as sense powers in one's own and in others' mental continua. When the self appears, it appears as an afflicted mind, etc., and is like that because of having afflictions. The appearances of representations are the six consciousnesses. It says *It is without object*, since when objects and sentient beings appear they are all nonexistent, and when self and representations appear they appear falsely. Since it is without object, the grasping consciousness is nonexistent. (Bi, 4c–e)

I:4 Since it exists as the construction
Of the completely nonexistent,
It is thus not existent, yet not completely non-existent. (Bi, 4e)

So, how has appearance arisen, since it is non-existent – It is only illusion, but it is not completely non-existent. Therefore though it does not entirely exist, it gives rise to desire. So, (Bi 4e)

I:4d Through eliminating it, one can expect liberation. (Bi, 4e–f).

Note that Vasubandhu specifically asserts in these remarks and in many other points in these texts that the mind is real and persists even from the standpoint of nirvana – that is, in its guise as alaya-*vijñāna* the mind exists *per se* and not as an illusion. Moreover, he asserts that the nature of all apparently external phenomena, when they are correctly understood is seen to be mental – that they are purely appearances to the mind. Finally, he asserts that while the mind is a necessary condition for the appearance of phenomena, the mind exists anterior to – and will exist in a purified state posterior to – the appearance of objects:

27. Even the thought, *All this is appearance only*
Involves an object.
And anything that places something in front of it
Is not grounded in this-only.

28. When no object is apprehended
By consciousness,
Then grounded in appearance-only
With no object there is no grasping subject.
29. Then with no mind and no object
With supramundane knowledge,[7]
It is transformation of the basis,
And the end of the two adversities.
30. It is uncontaminated,
An inconceivable and stable sphere.
It is blissful, the liberation body,
And is called the Accomplished one's dharma body.

This position is as idealist as one can imagine. Indeed it is hard to imagine Vasubandhu being read in any other way. I emphasise here that this does not rely on any second or third hand authority of later doxographers (though to be sure it is in agreement of the unanimous verdict both of critics and followers of Vasubandhu in the Indo-Tibetan tradition). I am simply reading the texts themselves and taking Vasubandhu at face value.[8]

Vasubandhu's Cittamatra Idealism

While it is easy to clinch the argument in favour of reading Vasubandhu as an idealist, that does not tell us precisely what variety of idealist he is. For idealism comes in many varieties determined by the precise characterisation of phenomena and of their relation to the mind representing them. We will see this variety played out in the history of Western idealism in a moment. But let us first quickly present the distinctive features of Vasubandhu's own presentation. Here we rely on the precise articulation of *Trisvabhāvanirdeśa*.

We will not here present a complete exegesis of this complex work, but simply note the features of the idealism Vasubandhu presents that will be crucial for our comparative task. In this text Vasubandhu articulates his view of what it is for a phenomenon to be ideal. He argues that each phenomenon has three distinct natures, each of which is implicated by ideality.

First, each such object has an imagined nature (*parikalpita-svabhāva/kun btags kyi rang bzhin*). To have such a nature is to be merely imaginary. More precisely, for Vasubandhu insofar as any phenomenon is ideal, its status as an external object is merely imagined. We see physical objects, and even our mind as an object of introspection, as existing external to us. But that status is illusory. These things therefore – conceived as external to the mind – are imaginary in nature.

Second, each phenomenon is asserted by Vasubandhu to have an other-dependent *(paratantra-svabhāva/gzhen dbang gi rang bzhin)* nature. That is, for an object to be ideal is for it to exist in dependence upon the mind. If a thing were independent of mind, it would fail to be ideal in the requisite sense. This aspect of Vasubandhu's idealism emphasises the fact that while an object of consciousness may be imaginary *qua* external, independent object, it is a *real* object of consciousness, and has a kind of existence – existence as a mental act, or as the intentional – though not distinct and independent – object of a mental act, even though it fails to have the kind of existence it may be naively thought to have – *viz.*, external, independent existence.[9]

Finally, each object of consciousness has a consummate nature (*paranispanna-svabhāva/yong su grub pa'i rang bzhin*). This is the nature a thing is seen to have when it and its ideal status are completely understood. The consummate nature is the absence of the imagined nature – it is the fact of a thing's not existing as distinct from mind and the fact that even though a thing appears to exist in dependence upon mind, even the duality and distinction suggested by the relation of dependence is illusory – phenomena are not, when seen from this final perspective, as much *dependent upon* mind, as they are aspects of it. One way to sharpen this point is to say that the other-dependent nature from one standpoint distinguishes mind and object as mutually *other* (hence its name). That very distinction preserves part of the perspective of the imagined nature, *viz*, its duality of subject and object. But from the standpoint of the consummate nature it reveals the non-difference of object from mind, in virtue of its non-externality. The consummate nature hence reflects a complete understanding of objects *qua* ideal and an abandonment of the subject-object duality apparent in the imagined.[10]

Let us pause at this point for some clarifications and amplifications. First, while Vasubandhu presents these as three distinct natures that all phenomena have in virtue of their ideality, they are not presented as *independent*. Rather they are mutually implicative. It would be impossible to have one of them and not the others. They are, as it were, three aspects of ideality, which together make sense of that notion, and are made sense of by it. Second, they are as much epistemological in character as they are ontological. This is not surprising in virtue of the tightly intertwined relation between epistemology and ontology in the Buddhist philosophical tradition, a feature characteristic of idealistic philosophy quite generally, including the idealism of the West to which we will turn in a moment.

So, when we say that the consummate nature is the nature a thing is seen to have when it is completely understood we use an epistemological entree into an ontological insight – things as they *really are* are empty of the subject-object duality and are empty of any real distinction from the mind through which they are imagined. Likewise when we characterise the ontology of the imagined nature we approach it through consideration of the way things appear to consciousness. This interpenetration of epistemological and ontological concerns is unavoidable in this context and may be partially responsible for the erroneous view that there is no ontological import whatever in Cittamatra.[11]

Finally, let us emphasise that for Vasubandhu the central ontological-epistemological claim of *trisvabhāva* theory is not that all phenomena are ideal; that is almost taken for granted by this point (though it is defended at greater length in *Vimsatika* and its commentary). Rather that *what it is to be ideal is to be characterised by the three natures*. This text is hence an exploration of the structure of idealism itself.

Let us now use that exploration as a guide to the history of Western idealism and see what we can learn about our own traditions.

Berkeley and Parikalpita-Svabhāva

The history of modern Western idealism properly begins with Berkeley, and the *locus classicus* for the articulation of his brand of that doctrine, which we might, following Kant, call *dogmatic idealism* is the *Three Dialogues Between Hylas and Philonous*. There, Berkeley famously argues that "there is no such thing as matter" (p. 12) and that nothing exists but minds and the contents of those minds (pp. 77ff.). In the dialogues Berkeley castigates both the doctrine that we could have any knowledge of external phenomena and the doctrine that the conception of external phenomena is even coherent. All of this is by way of a defence of idealism, and the details of that defence can be left to one side for the moment and for the purposes of this investigation. For what concerns us is not so much the arguments Berkeley marshals for his ontological-epistemological position, or their success, but the structure of the position itself, and its historical relation to that which displaced it.

Berkeley's idealism is characterised by the following central principles: (1) Ideas are immediately perceived by the mind, and like the mind themselves in which they reside, they are real (pp. 45ff.). (2) Nothing external to a mind is ever perceived, and no such thing is even possible (ibid.). (3) Space and spatiality, and externality quite generally – though they may be thought to characterise the objects of our perception, are entirely illusory, and necessarily so (ibid.: 55ff.).

A crucial tenet that emerges from this cursory summary of Berkeley's views is the claim that to the extent that we represent the objects of our awareness as existing outside of us, in any sense, we are necessarily wrong. To put the point in Vasubandhu's terms, the externality of phenomena, in virtue of their ideality, is an imagined nature. Kant criticises Berkeley on just this point, referring to Berkeley as *degrading bodies to mere illusion* (p. B71) and arguing that he *regards things in space as merely imaginary entities* (p. B274). It is important for our purposes to note that whatever the merits of Berkeley's idealism, Kant is correct in pointing out that it goes no farther than this. Even if we grant Berkeley the conclusion that all phenomena are ideal, we see that his analysis of what it is to be ideal is unidimensional: He argues that for an apparent material object to be ideal is for it to be merely imaginary. From the standpoint of Vasubandhu this first stab at idealism in the West is a good start, but only one third of the story.

Kant and Paratantra-Svabhava

Kant, as we have already noted, criticises precisely this inadequacy in Berkeley's theory. With both Descartes' primitive representational realism (which he calls misleadingly "problematic idealism") and Berkeley's primitive dogmatic idealism in view, Kant sets out quite self-consciously to develop an idealism more sophisticated than either, which he calls "transcendental idealism." In the *Critique of Pure Reason* Kant argues that when we characterise a thing as a representation, and hence as an object for subjectivity we must represent it both as empirically real and as transcendentally ideal.

It would be folly in an essay of this scope to attempt to sketch even the vaguest outlines of Kant's entire system of transcendental idealism, or even of that part articulated in the transcendental aesthetic and transcendental analytic, which is most relevant to present concerns. Instead, I will make the necessary exegetical claims quickly and dogmatically: In recognising the compatibility – and indeed the mutual entailment between – transcendental ideality and empirical reality, Kant is acknowledging that any coherent account of representations must assign them at least (and in his case at most) a dual status. Kant emphasises that from one standpoint, our representations of objects in space and time (including our representations of ourselves in inner sense) must be thought of as empirically real. They are genuinely *outside* of us *qua* objects of representation. Yet at the same time, *qua* representations, they are, from the transcendental perspective, *in* us. Kant emphasises this *twofold* nature of representation in the Transcendental Aesthetic, and it is a central theme in his transcendental idealism:

> Our exposition therefore establishes the *reality*, that is, the objective validity, of space in respect of whatever can be presented to us outwardly as object, but also at the same time the *ideality* of space in respect of things when they are considered in themselves through reason.... We assert, then, the *empirical reality* of space, as regards all possible outer experience; and yet at the same time we assert its *transcendental ideality* – in other words that it is nothing at all, immediately we withdraw the above condition... (pp. A28/B44)

> What we are maintaining is... the *empirical reality* of time, that is, its objective validity in respect of all objects which allow of ever being given to our senses.... On the other hand, we deny to time all claim to absolute reality... This, then, is what constitutes the *transcendental ideality* of time. What we mean by this phrase is that if we abstract from the subjective conditions of sensible intuition, time is nothing... (pp. A35–36/B52)

The focus of Kant's complaint against Berkeley can be seen from this vantage point as a charge that Berkeley simply fails to note this dual character of representations, and so develops what from Kant's perspective can only be seen as a deficient, one-sided idealism. Kant takes himself to be the first to emphasise both sides of the coin of an idealist theory of representation: While things considered as they appear to us, when seen from a transcendental perspective, are, as Berkeley correctly noted, completely non-existent, Berkeley, according to Kant, failed to note the corollary of this truth, namely, that things, as seen from the point of view of subjectivity, are empirically real, and that their empirical reality and transcendental ideality are mutually implicative.

The two natures Kant distinguishes – empirical reality and transcendental ideality – are quite naturally mapped on to the imagined and the other-dependent nature as these are articulated by Vasubandhu. The empirical reality of objects as characterised by Kant, and hence the reality of space and time themselves, is a merely represented reality, and no part of the objects themselves. When seen from a transcendental point of view – a God's eye view as Kant himself would put it, and hence from the standpoint of omniscience – such objects and space and time themselves are *nothing at all*. On the other hand, the kind of reality they *do* have for Kant is reality *qua* representation, and that gives them a kind of *objective validity*. That is, as objects of the mind, as things dependent upon us, they are in fact real. Even God would assent to that. But *that* reality does not guarantee that the reality they *appear to have* is in fact actual. Hence for Kant, their dependent nature is a deeper fact about phenomena than their imagined nature.

Moreover, the relation between these two natures as it is sketched in the First *Critique* maps rather neatly onto the relations between these two natures as it is presented in *Trisvabhāvanirdeśa*. Vasubandhu emphasises that the imagined nature simply is the other-dependent nature as it appears to naive consciousness, and that when it is correctly understood, the appearance of things as they are imagined is seen to be merely illusory – that things when properly understood from a vantage point abstracting from the afflictions that determine ordinary subjectivity are completely devoid of the characteristics they are imagined to possess. Nonetheless, he emphasises that to be a phenomenon for an ordinary human consciousness simply *is*,*inter alia*, to appear through the imagined nature, and to do so *dependent upon* the structure of the human mind. Hence the imagined nature is the dependent nature become appearance. And so it is for Kant. Things appear to us in space and time in dependence upon the structure of human consciousness. So appearing as a real empirical object to consciousness is part and parcel of what it is to be an object of knowledge for a human being. This is what it is for something that is *in fact* a mere mental episode – and so, *as phenomenon* to exist only in dependence upon mind – to appear to us in space and time. But that appearance – though in one sense real *as appearance*, is in another completely illusory. *Parikalpita* and *paratantra svabhāvas* are two sides of the coin of appearance for Vasubandhu. Empirical reality and Transcendental ideality are two sides of the same coin for Kant.

We should note that though for Berkeley things *qua* appearance have only imagined reality, and though we have lined up Kant's empirical reality with Vasubandhu's imagined reality we cannot infer through transitivity that Berkeley and Kant agree that objects of experience are empirically real, as Kant himself emphasises. But that is not surprising. It is not as accurate to say that Berkeley's primitive form of idealism *omits* one of (at least) two characteristics that idealism forces us to ascribe to objects as it is to say that Berkeley *conflates* two characteristics, and in doing so fails to articulate the dependent reality that phenomena in fact have *as a characteristic of those phenomena*. We can hence see Kant as developing a very Vasubhandan critique of Berkeley – forcing a distinction between mutually implicative characteristics, while emphasising their non-duality in the very context of that distinction.[12]

Now a reader of Kant might be impatient at this point with the fact that I have not yet discussed Kant's doctrine of the thing-in-itself. For Kant argues that the phenomena we see have yet another nature, one hidden to us, and independent of their status as objects of experience – a noumenal nature as *Ding an sich*. And a reader of Kant familiar with Vasubandhu might impatiently argue that this noumenal character hints at *parinispanna-svabhāva*. And such a reader would be correct, as far as that goes.

However, I deliberately refrain from ascribing to Kant a doctrine of *trisvabhāva* for two reasons. First, Kant himself is inconsistent on this point.

Sometimes – consistent with the remainder of the critical theory – he asserts that the thing-in-itself is unknowable and uncharacterisable, not even subject to categories such as unity, plurality or existence:

> The true correlate of sensibility, the thing in itself, is not known, and cannot be known, through these representations; and in experience no question is ever asked in regard to it. (pp. A30, B45)
>
> ... [N]othing whatsoever can be asserted of the thing in itself... (pp. A49, B66)
>
> We cannot define any [category] in any real fashion, that is, make the possibility of their object understandable, without at once descending to the conditions of sensibility, and so to the form of appearances – to which, as their sole objects, they must consequently be limited. For if this condition be removed, all meaning... falls away. (pp. A241, B300)
>
> The pure categories, apart from formal conditions of sensibility, have only transcendental meaning; nevertheless they may not be employed transcendentally. such employment being in itself impossible, inasmuch as all condition of any employment in judgements are lacking to them, namely the formal conditions of the subsumption of any ostensible object under these concepts. (pp. A248, B305)

At other times he asserts that things-in-themselves exist, and that each phenomenon is an appearance of a thing-in-itself, in manifest contradiction to the framework of the *Critique*:

> But our further contention must be duly borne in mind, namely that though we cannot *know* these objects as things in themselves, we must yet be in a position to *think* them as things in themselves.; otherwise we should be landed in the absurd conclusion that there can be appearance without anything that appears. (p. Bxxvi)

Tracing, explaining and untangling Kant's unclarity on this point would take us far afield. But the most charitable reading of Kant takes the Transcendental Deduction seriously, and hence eschews *any* theorising regarding things-in-themselves.

Second, it is important to note that even if one does take seriously Kant's confused discussions of things-in-themselves, it is clear that this account plays no role in Kant's account of what it is to be an object of experience, and in particular no role in the discussion of the empirical reality of things or of their relationship to consciousness.[13] But for Vasubandhu this is precisely a central role that each of the three natures must play. For the three natures are each aspects of what it is to be an object in the context of idealism. Just as Kant criticises Berkeley for ignoring the empirical reality of phenomena we will see that Schopenhauer criticises Kant for failing to properly appreciate the reality and role of the thing-in-itself. In encountering Schopenhauer's account we will see what it is for Western idealism to live up to Vasubandhu's demands in this regard.

Schopenhauer and *Parinispanna-svabhāva*

Schopenhauer adopts and extends Kant's transcendental idealism, most notably by bringing the thing-in-itself into the field of knowledge, defending a fundamental non-duality of subject and object from a transcendental point of view, and by arguing that that non-duality appears as a subject-object duality only at the level of universal illusion. The appearance of that duality, he argues, reflects only our illusion about the truly non-dual nature of reality; the appearance of representations *as* representations is a consequence of that cognitive process grounded in fundamental ontological ignorance. Vasubandhu would be proud.

We can begin by noting Schopenhauer's thoroughgoing commitment to a Kantian idealism as a foundation for his more ambitious ontology and epistemology. Schopenhauer in fact explicitly (albeit a bit confusedly) connects this idealism with Indian views:

> That which knows all things and is known by none is the *subject*. It is accordingly the supporter of the world, the universal condition of all that appears, of all objects, and it is always presupposed; for whatever exists, exists only for the subject. (p. 5)

> [T]hese two halves [subject and object] are inseparable even in thought, for each of the two has meaning and existence only through and for the other... (p. 5)

> Past and future... are as empty and unreal as any dream; but the present is only the boundary between the two, having neither extension nor duration. In just the same way, we shall also recognise the same emptiness in all the other forms of the principle of sufficient reason, and shall see that, like time, space also, and like this, everything that exists... has only a relative existence...; it is Maya, the veil of deception, which covers the eyes of mortals, and causes them to see a world of which one cannot say either that it is or that it is not; for it is like a dream, like the sunshine on the sand which the raveller from a distance takes to be water, or like the piece of rope on the ground which he regards as a snake. (pp. 7–8)

Schopenhauer emphasises the two natures adumbrated by Kant, and indeed emphasises even more explicitly than does Kant their distinctness and mutual implication. He argues that while all representation, in being given as real and external is illusory, *qua representation* all that we experience (at least veridically) is indeed real:

> Only [through the] understanding... does the world stand out as perception extended in space. (p. 12)

> The whole world of objects is and remains representation, and is for this reason wholly and forever conditioned by the subject; in other words it has transcendental ideality. But it is not on that account falsehood or illusion; it presents itself as what is, as representation... (p. 15)

But whereas Kant stopped in his analysis of the character of representations with these two natures, Schopenhauer explicitly asserts not only the necessity of positing in thought the thing-in-itself,[14] but also its reality, and indeed *the more complete and genuine reality* of the thing-in-itself. Moreover, Schopenhauer, unlike Kant, but like Vasubandhu, regards this noumenal reality as essential to phenomena conceived as representations. This point must be put delicately: It is not that *qua phenomenon* a thing is represented *as thing-in-itself*. Rather, for Schopenhauer, in providing a full account of what it is to be a phenomenon, we must include its character as it is in itself, and not merely negatively. That noumenal nature is, of course, will.

> Phenomenon means representation and nothing more. All representation, be it of whatever kind it may, all *object* is *phenomenon*. But only the *will* is *thing-in-itself*... It is that of which all representation, all object, is the phenomenon, the visibility, the *objectivity*. It is the innermost essence, the kernel, of every particular thing and also of the whole... (p. 110)

To present Schopenhauer's entire metaphysics of the will would take us far afield. But we can say this much. For Schopenhauer will is far more than personal or psychological. It is an unconscious and undifferentiated force[15] – itself unitary – or at least not plural – which in its multiple manifestations becomes phenomenon. These manifestations include not only objects represented as external, but also the empirical selves we know. Schopenhauer, then, unlike Berkeley for whom our own minds are fundamental subjects, agrees with Vasubandhu that the evolving consciousness is itself as much representation as any of the phenomena it knows as exterior to itself. Ultimate reality is foundational to both empirical subject and empirical object, and is free of that merely apparent duality. Indeed, for Schopenhauer, as for Vasubandhu – and unlike either Berkeley or Kant – the distinction between duality and non-duality marks the distinction between appearance and ultimate reality.

> [The will] is free from all *plurality*, although its phenomena in time and space are innumerable. It itself is one, yet not as an object is it one, for the unity of an object is known only in contrast to possible plurality. (p. 113)

We can hence see that the will for Schopenhauer is indeed the consummate reality of (or at least *behind*) all phenomena. Indeed, in a paraphrase of Vasubandhu not at all unfaithful to the spirit of *The World as Will and Representation* we can say that will is what a representation is when its illusory character as external and independent phenomenon is discounted. That is, it is the dependent nature, emptied of the imagined. In Schopenhauer then we see idealism in the West in its fully evolved form. All three natures are present, and are related to one another in precisely the way Vasubandhu argues that they must be. They are represented as distinct, but mutually implicative, and the signal characteristic of the most real, the most fundamental, is the absence of all duality and plurality, and the absence of any external object of consciousness.[16]

The Progressive Character of Western Idealism

I have told the story of Western Idealism not as it is told in Western histories of philosophy, but as it would be told by a Cittamatra philosopher, or perhaps as it would be told *to* a Cittamatra philosopher, or perhaps more realistically to a philosopher whose entree into idealist thought was *through* Cittamatra. My aim in telling the story this way is not simply to demonstrate the possibility of *alternative* perspectives on our own tradition, or to show that turnabout can be fair play. Rather, I think that telling the story in this way is in fact illuminating. It shows that and how Western philosophy is progressive – revealing a dynamic at work in this strand of our intellectual history that may have been invisible to us.

The invisibility to which I allude is traceable to two sources: First, proximity and custom. We are simply so close to our own tradition, and so accustomed to the hermeneutic story internal to it that we do not countenance the need for or the possibility of an alternative reading of our history. This is not unique to us, of course. Our

Tibetan colleagues also inhabit a philosophical tradition that develops and understands itself through its own hermeneutic, a hermeneutic that we often challenge when we come as Westerners to the history of Buddhist philosophy. The point is simply that traditions do not problematise their own self-understanding until they come into dialogue not so much with other *ideas* but with other *ways of reading*.

Second, and at a more straightforwardly philosophical level, the construct that reveals this particular progressive dynamic is not thematised within our own tradition. We don't develop *trisvabhāva* theory as such. For that reason, lacking a vocabulary in which to distinguish theories in this way, we fail to see the distinction, and so miss a crucial dimension of our own increasing sophistication. It is in this sense that the alternative way of reading Vasubandhu offer us is not simply an *alternative*, but a *better* way of seeing our own history. We should not react to such a comparative exercise with shame at our own blindness but with a certain pleasure in the discovery of a deeper dimension to our own heritage than we might hitherto have suspected and the hope that we can contribute similar insights to our interlocutors if we tread with care on contested ground.

Comparative Philosophy as a Road to Conversation

I hope that this has been an example of comparative philosophy done right – providing a reading that sheds light from one tradition upon another. But a crucial component of *doing the right thing* as far as I am concerned is the motivation, the intended next step. For if the enterprise stops here, not enough has been accomplished to make it all worthwhile. We note a surprising relationship between two traditions; we discover a way of conceptualising our own not hitherto considered; we are on the way to understanding idealism itself more deeply. Not bad. The real dividend, however, is the philosophical progress this understanding makes possible. For up to this point, our gaze has been in the direction of the past – that of a historian or a curator of dead traditions. Philosophy is however a live enterprise, both in the West and in the East, and if cross-cultural philosophy is to mean anything and to contribute anything to philosophical progress, it must do so with its gaze turned towards ideas and their development.

To that end, I urge that the kind of exercise in which I have been engaging be seen as a prolegomenon. It is a stage in – to borrow a Gadamerian phrase – the fusion of horizons. The task is to provide a common horizon that can be a background for genuine collaboration and conversation in a joint philosophical venture. The possibilities for such a venture are enormous. The enlargement of the world scholarly community and the range of texts and resources on which it can draw portends a greater philosophical depth and rate of progress. But the condition of the possibility of such progress and of such a future is the establishment of genuine collegiality and conversation, as opposed to contact and the interrogation of informants. And the condition of the possibility of conversation is taking seriously the standpoint and hermeneutic method of one's interlocutor as well as his/her ideas themselves, and taking seriously one's own tradition not as a lens through which to view another's, but also as specimen under one's colleague's lens at particular moments in the dialectic. That is the point of the present examination and the value of comparative philosophy when it is conceived not as an activity in itself, but rather as a moment in a dialogical dialectic whose apogee is reached at the point where these previous moments are transcended in the collegiality they make possible.

Of course in any intercultural dialogue, and particularly at explicitly comparative moments in the dialectic, one must be alert to the dangers of procrustean beds. One can abuse the comparative method – and the cases of such abuse are legion and are the basis of the bad name comparative philosophy has earned of late. Such abuse leads to dramatic distortion of alien traditions through the imposition of hermeneutic and doxographic frameworks, or philosophical problematics or presuppositions entirely foreign to the traditions themselves. But the danger of abuse is not an argument against careful use. I have urged here that such careful use is not only possible, but desirable. In part this is because of the essential role of comparative philosophy as a rung in a ladder to be discarded by our descendants whose interlocution it may some day be seen to have enabled.[17]

Notes

1 See Garfield (1998) and Klein (1994) for more on cross-cultural hermeneutics and dialogue.
2 See also Powers (1/7/1996). Lusthaus (2/7/1996) even lumps Sthiramati in as a non-idealist exponent of Yogācāra and emphasises that in his view *no* early Yogācāra writer (anybody preceding Dharmakirti) is an idealist in any sense. Though it would take us well beyond the scope of this paper, it is hard to imagine how anyone reading Sthiramati's commentary on the *Trimsikakārikā* could come to this conclusion.
3 See Garfield (1997b) for more on this point.
4 Unless otherwise noted, all translations from Vasubandhu are my own, from Tibetan (sDe dge edition). The purpose of this essay is neither to engage in a philological examination of Vasubandhu's corpus or the commentarial literature it inspires (in any case, I work in Tibetan and not in Sanskrit, and so that goal is beyond my competence) nor to survey Vasubandhu's entire corpus for evidence of his idealism. I here restrict my gaze to those passages most directly relevant to the comparative enterprise at hand.
5 A full exposition of Vasubandhu's treatment of the dual character of mind is beyond the scope of the present essay. See Garfield (1997a) for a complete translation and detailed exposition of *Trisvbhāvanirdeśa*. For now suffice it to say that Vasubandhu, like Kant, argues that the mind figures both as subject and as object. Inasmuch as the mind appears to itself in introspection, it appears with subject–object duality, and the object that appears in such an awareness is for Vasubandhu of exactly the same status as any external object so appearing. On the other hand, he argues, in order to make sense of appearance at all, whether of an external object or the mind, we must posit an independently existing mental continuum in which the appearance is located. Vasubandhu argues that we come to realise the illusory character of the mind as object through first understanding the easier-to-grasp illusory character of external phenomena. But his analysis of the mind as it appears to itself does not undermine in any way his insistence on the reality of the more fundamental purely subjective mind.
6 While there is general agreement that Vasubandhu is the author of the commentary that comprises the bulk of this text, the authorship of the root verses of *Madhyāntavibāga* is uncertain. They are traditionally attributed to Maitreya, dictated to Vasubandhu's brother Asanga. They

may have been composed by a fifth or sixth century philosopher named Maitreyanatha. They may have been composed by Asanga. Or they may have been composed by Vasubandhu. I take no position in this debate, but note that Vasubandhu clearly endorses their content, and takes his commentary to provide both an exposition and defence of the position they articulate.

7 Here I agree with Anacker's reading of this verse, reading the Tibetan /'*jig rten 'das pa'i ye shes med*/ as /'*jig rten 'das pa'i ye shes*/. This appears to be the only coherent reading of this verse.

8 This position is quite different from the Madhyamaka position of Nāgārjuna/Candrakīrti according to which both subject and object are empty of essence yet conventionally existent. It would take us far afield to enter into a detailed comparison of these two philosophical schools or to explore their interchanges or the exquisite doxography they inspire. For now suffice it to say whereas the Madhyamaka assign identical ontological status to the mind and its objects and argue that both are empirically real, the Cittamatra sharply distinguish their status, assigning a more fundamental reality to the subject than to its objects. See Garfield (1995) for an exposition of Nāgārjuna's position and Huntington and Wangchen (1991) for an exposition of Candrakīrti's powerful refutation of Vasubandhu. See also Cabezon (1992) for a sense of the Tibetan doxography.

9 At this point it is worth noting another interesting difference between Cittamatra and Madhyamaka metaphysics. *Paratantra* involves the notion of causal dependence, and is importantly different from the *parikalpita* in this respect. As Sthiramati emphasises in his commentary on *Trimsika*, in the *parikalpita*, inasmuch as the imagined objects do not even exist, they are not connected by causal links to one another. *Paratantra-svabhāva*, though, is causal in two senses: First, the apparent objects are dependent upon psychological episodes; second the successive mental episodes which are the representations of the objects of experience are causally related to each other. This causal continuum of mental episodes is the evolving and endlessly transforming mind. For the decidedly non-idealistic Madhyamaka, on the other hand, all empirical phenomena, whether mental or physical, are linked in the endless webs of interdependence constituting the world of *pratitya-samutpada*, or dependent origination.

10 See Nagao (1991) for more on the Janus-like character of the *paratantra-svabhāva*.

11 See also Sellars (1992) for a fine discussion of the interpenetration of metaphysics and epistemology in the context of thinking about mental representation.

12 We should also at this point acknowledge a point at which Kant departs from Vasubandhu, and a respect in which he is perhaps closer to Candrakīrti: While Berkeley and Vasubandhu emphasise the *difference* in ontological status between external phenomena and mind, Kant (following Hume) like Candrakīrti, emphasises the *homogeneity* in ontological status between the outer an inner. Just as Candrakīrti emphasises that phenomena and the self are equally conventionally real and ultimately empty, in contradistinction to Vasubandhu's reification of self and consequent nihilism with respect to phenomena, Kant emphasises the empirical reality of both external objects and the self, as well as the transcendental ideality of both, arguing that Berkeley reifies the latter and is nihilistic about the former. Both Kant and Candrakīrti emphasise that these two extreme views are themselves opposite sides of the coin of a too-radical idealism. See Garfield (1993) for a more detailed discussion of this point.

13 I say this despite the fact that it is clear that for a variety of reasons – some of them good, and some a bit confused – Kant himself no doubt was committed to an ontological role for noumena.

14 See, e.g. Schopenhauer (1969: 98–99), 119).

15 To use the term *force* here is dangerous inasmuch as Schopenhauer himself (p. 111) explicitly eschews it. In that eschewal, however, he is concerned to avoid the implication that the Will is somehow on an ontological par with *forces of nature* of the kind posited in physics, either in virtue of being one of them or in virtue of being the single force of some future grand unifying theory. He would argue instead that *those* forces are all phenomenal manifestations of Will. He prefers terms such as *drive* or *impulse*. These, too, have their disadvantages, suggesting intentional content or consciousness, suggestions he also would wish to avoid. So it is important to take the term *force* here in a sense not indicating forces of nature, but rather a kind of metaphysical force prior to nature.

16 One should not be misled here into identifying Schopenhauer's will with the *alaya-vijñāna* of the Cittamatra. That would be a mistake. The will is not conscious. Nor is it personal. But then the *alaya-vijñāna* is not an aspect of representation. Rather I am identifying Schopenhauer's assertion that the fundamental nature of all phenomena is will, and hence non-dual, non-spatio-temporal, etc. with Vasubandhu's that the consummate nature of all phenomena is to be empty of externality, duality, etc., and their respective assertions that to be a representation is to have, in addition to an empirical, or imagined nature, and a nature as dependent upon mind a third nature more fundamental than these two in which the dualities implicated in those first two vanish. In fact, if space permitted, it would be fascinating to explore the relation between Schopenhauer's account of the transcendental subject – as opposed to the will – and Vasubandhu's account of the foundation consciousness.

17 I thank Dr. Moira Nicholls, Prof. Frank White and Ms. Angela Coventry Round for helpful comments on an earlier draft, and the late Ven. Gen Lobzang Gyatso, Prof. Janet Gyatso and Ms. Karin Meyers for many helpful discussions of Cittamatra and its relation to Western Idealism. I am also deeply grateful to the Ven. Prof. Gareth Sparham for comments on an earlier draft of this paper, for valuable suggestions regarding translations and for extensive interchange regarding Cittamatra philosophy and texts. Thanks also to two anonymous referees for *Sophia* for extremely helpful suggestions.

References

Anacker, S. (1984). *Seven Works of Vasubandhu: The Buddhist Psychological Doctor*. New Delhi: Motilal Banarsidass.

Berkeley, G. (1954). *Three Dialogues Between Hylas and Philonous*, C. Turbayne (ed.). Indianapolis, IN: Bobbs-Merrill.

Cabezon, J. (1992). *A Dose of Emptiness: The sTong thun chen mo of mKhas grub rje*. Albany, NY: State University of New York Press.

Chakrabarti, K. (1996). *Definition and Induction*. Honolulu, HI: University of Hawaii Press.

Dunne, J. (30/6/1996). Yogācāra Idealism. Contribution to Buddha-L, Buddhist Academic Discussion Forum (BUDDHA–L @ULKYVM.LOUISVILLE.EDU.

Garfield, J. (1993). *Eliminativism and Substantialism*. Levett-Spenser Lecture, Union College.

Garfield, J. (1995). *Fundamental Wisdom of the Middle Way: Nagarjuna's Mulamadhyamakakarika*. New York: Oxford University Press.

Garfield, J. (1997a). Three Natures and Three Naturelessnesses: Comments on Cittamatra Conceptual Categories. *Journal of Indian Philosophy and Religion*, Vol. I, No. 2, pp. 1–24.

Garfield, J. (1997b). Vasubandhu's *Trisvabhavanirdesa* with a Commentary. *Asian Philosophy*, Vol. 17, No. 2, pp. 135–154.

Garfield, J. (1998). Temporality and Alterity: Dimensions of Hermeneutic Distance. In P. Churchill (ed.), *Interpreting Across Boundaries*. New York: Humanities Press.

Garfield, J. (2002). Temporality and Alterity: Dimensions of Hermeneutic Distance, in Garfield, Empty Words, New York: Oxford University Press, 229–250.

Garfield, J. and Geshe Damdul Namgyal (2010). Sarnath: Central University of Tibetan Studies Press.

Huntington, C. and Geshe Namgyal Wangchen (1991). *The Emptiness of Emptiness*. Honolulu, HI: University of Hawaii Press.

Kalupahana, D. (1987). *Principles of Buddhist Psychology*. Albany, NY: State University of New York Press.

Kant, I. (1965). *Critique of Pure Reason*, N. Kemp-Smith (ed. and trans.). New York: St. Martins Press.

Klein, A. (1995). *Path to the Middle: The Oral Scholarship of Kensur Yeshe Thupden*. Albany, NY: State University of New York Press.

Kochumuttom, T. (1982). *The Buddhist Doctrine of Experience: A New Translation and Interpretation of the Works of Vasubandhu the Yogācārin*. New Delhi: Motilal Banarsidass.

Larson, G. J. and E. Deutsch, eds. (1989). *Interpreting Across Boundaries: New Essays in Comparative Philosophy*. Delhi: Motilal Banarsidass.

Lusthaus, D. (26/6/1996). Yogācāra Idealism. Contribution to Buddha-L, Buddhist Academic Discussion Forum (BUDDHA–L @ULKYVM.LOUISVILLE.EDU).

Lusthaus, D. (27/6/1996). Yogācāra Idealism. Contribution to Buddha-L, Buddhist Academic Discussion Forum (BUDDHA–L @ULKYVM.LOUISVILLE.EDU).

Nagao, G. (1991). *Madhyamika and Yogācāra*. Albany, NY: State University of New York Press.

Powers, J. (30/9/1996). Yogācāra Idealism. Contribution to Buddha-L, Buddhist Academic Discussion Forum (BUDDHA–L @ULKYVM.LOUISVILLE.EDU).

Powers, J. (1/7/1996). Yogācāra Idealism. Contribution to Buddha-L, Buddhist Academic Discussion Forum (BUDDHA–L @ULKYVM.LOUISVILLE.EDU).

Schopenhauer, A. (1969). *The World as Will and Representation*, E. F. J. Payne (ed. and trans.). New York: Dover.

Schopenhauer, A. (1974). *The Fourfold Root of the Principle of Sufficient Reason*, E. F. J. Payne (ed. and trans.). Chicago, IL: Open Court.

Sellars, W. (1992). *The Metaphysics of Epistemology*. Santa Cruz, CA: Ridgeview.

Tuck, A. (1990). *Comparative Philosophy and the Philosophy of Scholarship*. New York: Oxford University Press.

Vasubandhu. *Madhyantavibhagabhasya* (Tibetan translation: *Dbus dang mtha' rnam par 'byed pa'i 'grel pa*). Tibetan Buddhist Canon, Vol Bi, Paljor Press, Tibetan Government Printing Office, Dharamsala.

Vasubandhu. *Trimsikakarika* (Tibetan translation: *Sum cu pa*). Tibetan Buddhist Canon, Vol Shi, Paljor Press, Tibetan Government Printing Office, Dharamsala.

Vasubandhu. *Vimsatika* (Tibetan translation: *Nyi shu pa*). Tibetan Buddhist Canon, Vol Shi, Paljor Press, Tibetan Government Printing Office, Dharamsala.

Vasubandhu. *Trisvabhavanirdesa* (Tibetan translation: *Rang bzhin gsum gnes par bstan pa*). Tibetan Buddhist Canon, Vol Shi, Paljor Press, Tibetan Government Printing Office, Dharamsala.

An Approximate Difference: Proximity and Oppression in the West's Encounter with Sikhism

Navdeep Mandair

Abstract The work of John Hick represents a prominent trend in the philosophy of religion which is allegedly receptive to the epistemological concerns of religions other than Christianity. However, I will argue that this apparent latitude towards religious difference deploys a comparative idiom that is surreptitiously informed by Christian ideology and, thus, inscribes the same cultural chauvinism as other forms of Western discourse. This form of clandestine interventionism was also a feature of the colonial system. Among the most insidious regimes of control inaugurated by the British in India was the identification of racial kinship between themselves and other 'martial races' such as the Sikhs. I will suggest that this apparent commensurability of colonial and native traditions depended upon the Sikhs readily *appropriating* a martial signature which restricted the excesses of their warfare to the teleological calculation of British militancy, a solicitous gesture which surreptitiously testified to Sikh degeneracy. This ethnic cliché persists to this day and indicates that the Sikhs remain unacquainted with the lack organic to such stereotypes, prompting expressions of autonomy already prefaced by failure.

Introduction

> Look at the nigger!... Mama, a Negro!... Take no notice, sir, he does not know that you are as civilized as we... My body was given back to me sprawled out, distorted, recoloured, clad in mourning in that white winter day. (Fanon 1986: 113)

In this passage Fanon articulates the radical vacuousness of a colonized existence in which the subaltern cannot even lay claim to his own indignation against cultural prejudice, a victim whose protests are imprinted in advance by the fact of oppression. In contrast to those forms of cultural encounter in which the asymmetries of legitimacy and power are obviously defined by the discourse of racism ("look at the nigger...") Fanon indicates that modernity also deploys a more insidious form of prejudice which surreptitiously re-negotiates the space between cultures to its own advantage, an intervention which is facilitated by the concession of equality to the subaltern "...the Negro is a man, *like ourselves*..." (1986: 113; italics mine)

This apparent paradox constitutes, what will be termed in this essay, the problem of virtual alterity.

The primary concern of this essay is to highlight the disingenuousness of a pluralist discourse in which, despite the acceptance of religious difference, it is allowed that this does not present an obstacle to fluent dialogical exchange between traditions. The intellectual trend in the philosophy of religion associated with John Hick represents a conspicuous example of this pluralist treatment of religious difference. Hick has proposed a neo-Kantian hermeneutics of religious pluralism in which the "Real as manifested within the intellectual and experiential purview of [different religious] traditions" is a culturally perspectival understanding of "the Real *an sich*" (1989: 236). Thus, if the phenomenal organization of every religion reflects the same noumenal essence, a context of legitimacy may be proposed which does not restrict in advance the scope of religious truth claims.

Although, Hick's work indicates that the philosophy of religion has recently become more attentive to the question of religious difference it seems almost inconceivable that a discourse inaugurated as a critical appraisal of Christian belief, and which remains intimately concerned with the anxieties of the Christian subject, could do justice to the strange ontologies of the other. The emphasis it places on uncovering an identical significance in the diversity of religious idiom suggests a clear sanction of cultural difference, however, since the ciphers for this fideiography or, register of religious affinities, are provided by Christian theology a revisionary pressure becomes apparent which prompts other religions to substitute and elide concepts which contravene this discursive code. Thus, the philosophy of religion facilitates the clandestine retrieval of an unvexed Christian authority, in the process, reducing inter-religious dialogue to a mimetic event in which the babble of otherness is coordinated into a chorus of testimonies to Christian discourse.

This enquiry will attempt to sketch the vicissitudes of Khalsa[1] identity following colonial encounter in India, and highlights the continuity of perspective between the ethnographic scrutiny deployed during this period and recent efforts in the philosophy of religion to accommodate the views of (non-Christian) others. Given this degree of fidelity between these modes of Western cultural engagement it is not implausible to suggest that they simply represent proxy contexts for the interventionist horizon of modernity.

Among the main concerns of colonialism was to establish an index for defining legitimate identity. Since the indices which regulated admission to this register (race, gender etc.) reflected colonial values their appropriation by the native subject led inevitably to a clandestine revision of his identity. The failure to recognize that a revisionary intervention had occurred allowed the radical asymmetry informing cultural encounter to be dissembled as a relation between two autonomous subjects whose distance simply reflected an unequal share of power. Thus, colonial discourse appeared to concede the legitimacy of subject cultures, its oppressive effect being limited to the disenfranchising of the native other, a situation for which the facile intervention of increased political empowerment existed as a remedy.

The eliding of the other's identity corresponded to a substitution of its desire, an act which replaced an endless deferral of satisfaction with an economy of insatiable lack. This indigent desire, which demands a levelling of the disparity in power between the colonial self and its other, would seem to constitute the obvious point of departure for redressing the predicament of the subaltern; certainly, even Fanon, despite his suspicion of liberal society's concessionary gestures, is seduced by this desire when he situates his critique on the question, "(w)hat does the black man want?" (1986: 10) what else but to have his existence regarded by the self as the self regards its own.

This question has also exercised a profound influence on Sikh affairs, the traumas of the recent past,[2] in particular, exposing the radically unsatisfactory nature of a political course informed by perceived lacks. Ironically however, like every other marginalized group demanding admittance to the politico-economic centre it is in the satisfaction of this lack, a concession which appears to enable a real inter-subjective relation, that the dependence of the other unfolds, endlessly.

Incorporating the Foreign: On the Strange Convergence of Pluralism and Stereotyping

Perhaps the key assumption made about the other in the philosophy of religion is that is synonymous with the not-self. This synonymy, however, actually inscribes a slippage in the ontological status of the other qua other to a point where it exists pseudonymously or, under an assumed identity. The representation of the other as not-self positions it in an antagonistic exchange with Christian discourse, a mode of encounter which appears to establish the other's fidelity to its own sense of difference. Crucially, however, its negations signify, they are meaningful to the Christian self, which indicates that the otherness of the other, its radical incommensurability with the self, has suffered erasure. Therefore, he who speaks for the other is an impostor, but one for whom this imposture is indiscernible as such.

I will suggest that the disciplinary interventionism of the philosophy of religion, in respect of its encounter with others, is deployed through the act of cultural stereotyping. What this suggests, then, is the need for a more nuanced interpretation of a process which facilitates a rejection of the foreign through both the discourse of pluralism, as well as the more obvious regimes of exclusion.

Stereotyping is usually represented as a process which installs an irreducible 'difference' between a subject and its other. It involves displacing the other from a semiotic milieu in which it is enmeshed and ascribing prominence to corporeal and customary signs which, ordinarily, only signify within this referential system. The other is thus reified as a foreign body and perpetually excluded from the ontological domain circumscribed by the self. Gilman summarizes this perspective on stereotyping, observing that, "(s)tereotypes are a crude set of mental representations of the world... [which] perpetuate a needed sense of difference between the self and the object which becomes the 'Other'" (1985: 17).

Although the process of stereotyping tends to depict the other as a deviant figure, thus, highlighting the primary role of exclusion in defining self-identity, changes in the self's perception of the world may prompt a re-appraisal of its antagonistic relationship to difference, thereby facilitating an 'intimacy' with the other. "Thus," Gilman remarks "paradigm shifts in our mental representations of the world can and do occur, we can move from fearing to glorifying the other... (t)he most negative stereotype always has an overtly positive counterweight" (1985: 18). Despite this transition to a solicitous reception of difference it is clear that the 'good other' in this encounter is still a stereotyped object and, as such, is simply a cipher which alludes to the presence of the self. However, in contrast to the conspicuous interventionism which marks the other's encounter with the discursive regimes of racial and religious extremism, the eliding of its identity by the solicitous discourse of cultural pluralism escapes scrutiny, since, the stereotyped image it invokes is virtually the same, and therefore appropriated, as the other's own.

'Solicitous' stereotyping, like the installation of 'bad' stereotypes, proceeds through a suppression of the other's alterionomy, an identity whose meaning is arbitrated by the semiotic play of its milieu, and its substitution with a cluster of discrete bodily and cultural signs or, an alteriography. However, the crucial difference between them is that in 'solicitous' stereotyping this alteriography is appropriated by the other as its alterionomy. Thus, the other's semiotic context is rendered commensurable with the legislations prescribed by the arbiters of the stereotyping process (for instance the Christian or secular subject). However, these erasures of identity, and the radical asymmetry of power to which it testifies, are not detected, since a counterfeit difference (the 'good' stereotype) is installed in its place.

The other who stands in relation to the self then is nothing but a specious edition, it has been displaced from its strange corporeality and returned to a body which perfectly replicates its deformations, a virtual embodiment that speaks exactly like, but never as, the other. This experience of identity as the locus of a secret trauma, a mutilated body dissembled as whole, is appositely conveyed by Fanon when he describes the dislocation provoked by his encounter with the white Frenchman "... I took myself far off from my own presence" he remarks, "far indeed and made myself an object. What else could it be for me but an amputation, an excision, a haemorrhage that spattered my whole body with black blood. But I did not want this revision, this thematization, all I wanted was to be a man among other men" (1986: 112).

Thus, the solicitous mode of stereotyping exercises a more pernicious effect on the other than the reactionary regime which informs racial and religious chauvinism, since, its interventions are insinuated surreptitiously and, therefore, not readily contestable. Crucially this process continues to represent the other in the post-encounter stage as incommensurable with the self, given which, the other is never able to perceive itself as virtually embodied, this virtual difference is its 'proper' difference, that which situates it beyond the self. What this seems to suggest, then, is that the other will always remain unacquainted with is 'own' identity.

The disingenuous form of inclusion inscribed by 'solicitous stereotyping' provides an insight into the deceit and oppression which inform the encounter between the philosophy of religion and its other. According to John Hick one of the key issues in the philosophy of religion today is the need to address "... the problem [arising from] the conflicting truth claims made by different religious traditions"

(1990: 109). Given the multicultural nature of modern society the awkwardness of justifying interventions which privilege the Christian subject seems obvious. Thus, the circumstances of contemporary society require a context of religious encounter which is pluralist in scope, one that confers legitimacy on the other without prescribing in advance the limits of legitimate belief.

Hick's interpretation of pluralism invokes a fundamental affinity between every faith, thus, establishing a fideiography or an index which allows reference to all religious traditions. The cipher which facilitates this fideiographic organization of religion(s) is the allegedly universal belief in a distinction between the noumenal presence of God (the Real-in-itself) and the experience of this divinity in the world of phenomena. All "...the great religions [then]" observes Hick, "are at their experiential roots in contact with the same ultimate divine reality" (1990: 114) however, because this primitive encounter with the divine in se is mediated through the semiotic context of particular cultures, it prompts diverse and approximate representations of God.

This distinction between the noumenal and phenomenal experiences of God is, Hick claims, conspicuously attested in Hindu thought, which allegedly distinguishes "...between *nirguna* Brahman, Brahman without qualities, beyond the scope of human thought, and *saguna* Brahman, Brahman with attributes, encountered within human experience as Ishvara..." (1990: 117). Thus, Hick's pluralist thesis appears to affirm the strange legislations of the Hindu other and, since, this sense of difference is embedded within a fideiographic context, also avoids the tensions which arise from juxtaposing different truth claims. However, the real subtlety of Hick's pluralist solution lies in its clandestine re-negotiation of the other's difference, which facilitates a secret assertion of Christian authority. This is clearly indicated by Hick's profoundly misleading treatment of the Hindu conceptualization of 'God'.

In its Indian context the ultimate reality of the *nirguna* state is a vexed concept, since its presence must be traced through the endless play (*līlā*) or substitutions of phenomenal existence (*saguna*) itself. This intersection between divine and corporeal being is conspicuously attested in the beliefs of those traditions that comprise the *bhakti-marg*, a religious path in which "...the dominant mode of worship is one of devotion toward a divine being" (Lorenzen 1996: 1). Hindu bhakti tends to emphasize the *saguni* (embodied) aspect of the divinity; worship, therefore, involves the veneration of incarnations (*avatara*) of the gods who are represented in material images (*murti*). Whether the image is regarded as a vessel, or simply an icon, for the presence of the god, its veneration seems to involve the address of prayers and petitions to a divine object, thus, invoking the presence of a god who is qualitatively distinct from the physical register of existence, or identical to God. However, this onto-theological conception of divinity is challenged by the sheer physical familiarity which informs the Hindu worship of images, a body of acts which include "...bathing, feeding, clothing and fanning [the idol]" (Klostermaier 1999: 84). What the corporeal accent of this engagement between the devotee and his god signals is that the otherness of the deity must be traced in the fickle register of material acts itself, a context that invokes, not a substantive Being but, the presence of a world of others.

Sikhism represents the most obvious example of a bhakti tradition in which devotion is focussed on the formless or *nirguna* aspect of 'God'. Although conventional opinion indicates otherwise (Lorenzen 1996: 14) there seems to be a fundamental affinity between *saguni* and *nirguni* bhakti given that both traditions embed theistic experience in human intercourse with the world. In the *nirguni* context of Sikhism this is attested by the frequent references to 'God' that deploy the squalid imagery of corporeal existence. Thus, when Guru Nanak, composing in *raag dhanasri*, alludes to the enigmatic ontology of 'God' in the following terms "You have thousands of eyes and no eyes at all, You have thousands of bodies and no body at all" (Singh 2000: 663) the paradox invoked by the and in this passage may be 'decided' by positing the absolute otherness of 'God', what is beyond identification (*nirguna*), as an expression of the transcendence vested in a world in which every body (*saguna*) intimates the existence of others. The undecidable nature of human identity, then, places the Sikh in a world caught in an endless transition between absence and presence or, an intimacy with time which Guru Nanak, in the final line of the verse, describes as the seductive force of divine play (*chalth*).

What this brief excursus on the bhakti-marg illustrates, then, is that while Christianity consigns the encounter with 'God' to the compass of theology, for Indian traditions, given the role of the other in mediating this event, it falls within the ambit of ethical enquiry.

Thus, it is clear that Hick's appropriation of the other's culture involves a suppression of those beliefs which render it incommensurable with Christian tradition. The 'fuzzy' relationship between *nirguna* and *saguna* Brahman is conscripted by a regime which valorises the stark distinction of real and sensible existence, thus replacing an encounter with the 'divine' mediated through the intimacies of human contact with the ascetic economy of theism. However, the eliding of the other's difference escapes its attention, since the cultural object invoked by this disciplinary act is a virtual edition or 'good' stereotype, and therefore seems to rehearse the concerns proper to its own identity.

Hence, the utter disingenuousness of Hick's reference to "...the 'one world' of today [in which] religious traditions are consciously interacting with each other in mutual observation and dialogue...mov(ing) gradually on converging courses" (1990: 114) since it alludes to the counterfeit autonomy and future of subjects who have already converged with the chauvinistic presence of the Christian.

Given that the contexts of cultural encounter deployed by the West dictate an insidious oppression of the other, it is not surprising that the experience of non-Christian Diasporas in the Western world is marked by a profound sense of anxiety, a condition which is all the more troubling since it has no readily discernible cause. This anxiety signals the presence of an existential lacuna at the heart of the other's being; it reflects the burgeoning discrepancy between what the other as a virtual object believes itself to be following the assertion of its cultural difference and what it is in fact becoming, so that every positive enunciation of its identity by the other is always already a crypto-identification with the Christian subject. To put it another way, the sense of foreboding inaugurated following the surreptitious dislocation of the other's identity signals the proximity of an imminent, but amorphous, danger which always remains beyond thematization since this threat is immanent within the other itself conditioned as a virtual entity. Consequently every effort made to alleviate this tension is increasingly in vain since it serves merely to bring this lurking horror ever closer, until this fear and self loathing can only be contained by the consolation offered by the promise of a bullet in the head.

Violent Religion. Returning Sikhism to Itself

The penetrating brilliance of swords
Wielded by followers of the way
Strikes at the evil enemy
Lurking deep within
Their own souls and bodies. (Morihei Ueshiba[3])

There is nothing new about the clandestine interventionism of Hick's pluralist thesis, it is simply a contemporary example of the exclusionary discourse of modernity, and is thus ideologically contiguous with colonialism which had innovated the use of ciphers to surreptitiously regulate cultural difference. The colonial regime in India stipulated a variety of ethnographic signifiers which could be used to organize the baffling diversity of Indian society, of these perhaps the most prominent was caste (Metcalf 1995: 116).

Following the Indian Mutiny (1857) as categories such as manliness and martial disposition became emblematic of British identity (Van der Veer 2001: 88) the ethnological accent of the caste system changed to reflect the new emphasis on a muscular ethos. This served not only to organize Indian difference but also conscripted this order to the imperative of identifying those 'races' who could be relied upon to support the Imperial project. Thus, a "martial fitness" was perceived as organic to the character of 'races' such as the Sikhs, Pathans and Gurkhas which "...distinguish(ed) [them] from those elsewhere [in India] above all Bengal" (Metcalf 1995: 125).

However, this inscription of 'racial' kinship between the British and the Sikhs was not, contrary to appearances, an inclusive gesture, but rather dissembled the contempt and censure incurred by the allegedly effeminate culture of the Bengalis. The fact of victim hood eluded the Sikhs because of their complicity in this act of oppression. The Sikhs readily accepted the comparison between their own martial signature and the context for military action advocated by colonial discourse, and thus a world of severe intimacy was surreptitiously spurned for a territorializing of identity and the brutality of purpose.

A particularly distinctive feature of the religious compositions of Guru Gobind Singh[4] is the consistent representation of the 'divine' using the rhetoric of conflict. Thus, this 'divinity' is addressed as 'all-steel' (*sarbloh*) or as the 'revered sword' (*sri bhagauti*), a mode of expression that reveals a dark and turbulent presence which is only ever encountered through the convulsive events of battle and love, birth and death. One of the texts in which this thematization of the 'divine' as violent presence is conspicuous is *Jap Sahib*.[5] In couplet 52 of this work Guru Gobind Singh describes the fierce nature of this 'divinity' through expressions of obeisance:

> *namo sastarpaneh, namo astarmaneh, namo param geeata, namo lok mata.*
> "I bow before the wielder of the sword, I bow before the sender of arrows,
> I bow before the knower of the unknowable, I bow before the mother of the world".
> (Singh and Singh 1999: 116)

From this verse it is clear that approaching the other is always fraught with risk, since every such encounter unfolds violently. Yet, intriguingly, this perilous event also embraces a promise of love, since it occurs in the nurturing presence of the mother. Perversely, then, since the savage context of encounter with the other reflects a 'maternal' concern with the world what this intimacy inscribes is an act of despoliation, a prostration before a m(other) who loves us violently.

Surely, however, it is counter-intuitive to claim that a semantic continuity obtains between love and violence. Common sense dictates that these phenomena are mutually exclusive, thus, exposing a tension in Guru Gobind Singh's conception of the 'divine' or, a god at war with himself. This view is prompted by the acceptance of the idea that a utilitarian organization of the world is organic to the natural state of things. Acts of love and violence, then, become mere commodities in the economy of encounter between human objects and, as such, facilitate different ends within this process of exchange. For Bataille, however, human identity is determined by the play of 'economic forces' itself. This conclusion is attested by the accursed nature of love and violence, parts of which deflect ineluctably from productive organization, therefore exposing the capricious order of a world in which the 'economic' milieu itself assigns meaning. Thus, in the light of Bataille's observation that "(b)eyond our immediate ends, man's activity in fact pursues the useless and infinite fulfilment of the universe" (1988: 81) the possibility arises of the contradiction posited between violence and love overcoming itself.

The representation of *Jap Sahib* as a theological text tends to restrict the interpretation of its narrative to the optimistic order of a discourse in which every concern is conscripted into realizing this end. However, as a number of commentators have observed, a distinct awkwardness informs the attempt to conceive the 'god' of Sikh texts through the teleological language of conventional theology, a fact which is readily apparent from the contradictory descriptions which it invokes. Thus, 'God' is a wielder of the sword (*sastarpaneh*) and mother of the world (*lok mata*) (Singh and Singh 1999: 11), is cruel (*kalay*) and compassionate (*deealay*) and, exists in an excess of pleasure (*prabhogay*) and perfect austerity (*sujogay*) (Singh and Singh 1999: 4).

An early and much disputed commentary on Sikhism, 'Sketch of the Religion of the Sikhs' (1877), by the German Indologist Ernest Trumpp, had identified these contradictions as a recurrent feature of the Sikh scriptures. Trumpp claimed that the *Adi Granth Sahib*[6] sanctioned a pantheistic ideology which was inconsistent with a belief in "...an Absolute Being [who was] ...self-conscious...endowed with free will and act(ed) according to teleological principles" (Singh 1999: 129).

Yet, despite this alleged thread of pantheism in the text, the Sikh Gurus often alluded to the 'divine' in personal terms, prompting Trumpp to observe dismissively that"(c)ontradictory [ideas] of this kind we find a great many in the Granth" (ibid.).

The prevalence of these tensions within the texts encourages scepticism regarding the claim that a mature theology can be traced within Sikhism. However, what these contradictions signal is not a deviation from the standard inscribed by (Christian) theology but, rather, the accursed organization of a religion in which the remembrance (*jap*) of 'God' is facilitated by the intimate economy of human contact. In this light, then, the text of *Jap Sahib* resists identification as sacred literature and the view that repeating (*japna*) its contents is a devotional act. It attests, rather, to the context in which remembrance occurs, thus, snarling the student and the devotee in the web of social encounter inscribed by the act of reading itself. This shift of emphasis, from the logolatry of textual interpretation to the reading of texts, therefore, situates the 'reader' of *Jap Sahib* amidst the babble of an address to the (m)other, constantly venturing his body in a manner indistinguishable from the precarious style of encounter which informs battle play.

Engaging the Other: On the Solicitousness of Sikh Warfare

If reading, contrary to the way it is usually imagined, is inflected with a violent signature, then, the absolute validity of prevailing characterizations of violence may also be suspect. Is the contest of war, for instance, always as Clausewitz described it "... an act of violence intended to compel our opponent to fulfil our will" (1982: 101) or, in contrast to this instrumental perspective, is it possible to view conflict as an event defined by the context of the melee itself, thus obliging each party to trace its 'aims' among those of the other?

The idea that war could only be understood within a context of rational motivation has been challenged by, among others, the French ethnographer Pierre Clastres. Clastres' interrogation of conflict among tribal societies contested the conventional view which conscripted primitive warfare to the aims of economic or political activity. Economic anthropology, according to Clastres, traces the origin of primitive war to a "... weakness of productive forces" in 'savage' societies, prompting a scramble for scarce resources which inevitably "... ends in armed conflict" (1994: 146). Clastres, however, suggested that the alleged poverty of tribal societies only became apparent following the insinuation of a principle of accumulation into the descriptions of their economic activity. Since the primitive economy was organized simply to provide resources sufficient to the needs of the tribe, far from being destitute, this easy satisfaction of its requirements offered such societies an abundance and leisure which, paradoxically, promoted protracted episodes of warfare (1994: 147).

Clastres also questioned a genealogy of primitive warfare which emphasized political provocations. Thus, although Clastres conceded Levi-Strauss' description of the primitive political order as a system organized by exchange (of goods, women etc.) he challenged the idea that conflict was merely symptomatic of a failure in this politics of exchange, and therefore "...an accidental, uncertain, inessential characteristic of it" (1994: 152). However the 'quasi-universality' of tribal conflict signalled that it was an essential feature of the primitive world. The description of war, then, as a privative mode of politics exposed the role of exchange in Levi-Strauss' work as an absolute sociological explanation, a metanarrative which "...deform(ed) primitive social reality by mutilating it" (ibid.).

If the aims which provoke 'mature' societies to fight have no bearing on primitive conflict "(w)hy," asks Clastres, "are the tribes at war" (1994: 148)? Is this warfare, then, simply aimless savagery and a sign of an undeveloped mind or, are its 'aims' situated outside the order of teleological calculation?

Clastres claimed that what distinguished primitive society from the mature state was a radical impulse for dispersion which differentiated it into a multitude of autonomous communities each attesting an "irreducible freedom", an otherness, which was robustly expressed against neighbouring tribes. In this light, then, warfare was not precipitated by the alleged competition between the multiplicity of socio-political entities crowding the primitive world, it was, rather, the agent of this fractured political order. It would be inaccurate, however, to describe the organization of the primitive world as monadological, as a body of discrete cultural identities. Given that the political unity of the tribe is an expression of absolute difference, a resistance to self-identity, this 'we-ness' must be traced through an act of constant reference to the other. Warfare, then, is not primarily about killing or "...the compulsory submission of the enemy to [the tribe's] will" (Clausewitz 1982: 101), it is prefaced by the intimacy of the melee which obliges the tribal warrior to treat his opponent as an other, as an utterly incommensurable subject, if he is to intimate his 'own' difference. Far from inscribing contempt for the other primitive conflict is the necessary condition for engaging the other in his otherness. In this light, then, "(w)ouldn't war be, not the threat of death, but the condition of primitive society's life" (Clastres 1994: 156)?

Clastres' analysis of primitive war provides a clue to re-thinking the vexed relationship between Sikhism and violence. Sikh apologetics has tended to portray the belligerency of its tradition as a defensive act to maintain a righteous order (*dharma*)[7] thus signalling its commensurability with the solicitous discourse of world religion. However, the obligation to conform, pressed upon the other by the quasi-legality of religious consensus, exposes the fundamental symmetry between world religions ideology and the authoritarian structure of what Clastres refers to as "the State" (1994: 165). What distinguishes the State observes Clastres is a "...logic of unification...that embraces all differences in order to suppress them..." (ibid.) thus the easy passage of a turbulent Sikh tradition into the register of world faiths signals Sikhism's infidelity to itself, and the clandestine oppressiveness of a pluralist 'mega-machine'. The 'restoration' of a radical Sikh autonomy, then, requires the delineation of a notion of conflict that exceeds teleological regulation.

An alternative account of how violence intersects Sikh discourse will be sketched by reference to Guru Gobind Singh's composition *Chandi Charitra*. This text is a reworking in *Braj Bhasa*[8] of an important Hindu liturgical work known as the *Devi Mahatmya* and describes the acts of the great goddess Durga who recuperates the lost order (*dharma*) of the world by extinguishing, in a paroxysm of sanguinary violence, the invading presence of a swarm of degenerate monsters (*asuras*).

From the earliest passages in the text there is a recurring emphasis on the prodigious belligerency of the Goddess, who bursts upon the enemy with a spate of deadly shafts and murderous blows and rejoices in this act of perfect butchery:

> With Durga's assent, the pounding drums announced the onset of war,
>
> She grasped her sword, the mace of iron and the noose,
>
> Held ready the club and quoit,
>
> As cries of Slay! Slay them! broke from the field
>
> those eight mighty hands were poised, then
>
> she clove the heads of the enemy,
>
> Her mount, a savage lion, roared in the press of battle,
>
> And many warriors, ripped and rent, fell there,
>
> The demons raged as the mother's murderous barbs struck,
>
> Like a turbulent sky they shook their weapons furiously,
>
> Then, like a storm coming over the horizon the throng of demons surged on again,
>
> And the mother of the world crashed among them
>
> a bow in her hand, a smile upon her lips. (Singh and Singh 1999: 282)

It is customary in Sikh ideology to present the destructive figure of the Goddess, in compositions such as *Chandi Charitra*, as emblematic of the severe justice loosed by God to redress the world's slide into iniquity. This incorrigibly pedestrian interpretation of the text tends to reduce the savage excesses of Durga to a mere police action aimed at quelling a gang of diabolic ruffians, however, it is possible to read the credo of violence recounted in the narrative other than as teleologically organized. Its deviation from the instrumentality of conventional warfare is conveyed by the recurrent references to Durga's delight in conflict and carnage, a horrid pleasure attested in passages which describe her as smiling (*gigoh has ke*) (1999: 282), laughing mightily (*hasi kaprali*) (1999: 300) and jubilant (*harkan*) (1999: 306) amidst the bloody wreckage of battle. It is the gleeful accent of this onslaught that renders it excessive, a violence that exceeds the measures strictly necessary to restore *dharma*, and therefore regulated by the capricious tempo of divine play or *līlā*.

In a reference to the Hindu iconography of Durga Mahisamardini David Kinsley has also noted the excessive or playful context of her violence. This is attested by the radical antinomy between the murderousness of her attack and the composure of her expression, "(t)ypically she is shown bringing a blizzard of weapons to bear on the hapless demon [Mahisa]... (h)er face, however, is calm and shows no sign of strain. For her this is mere sport... a game... it is *līlā*. She enters into the cosmic struggle because it pleases her, not out of any sense of compulsion" (1987: 105).

It need hardly be said that Durga's enjoyment does not provide a vicarious purpose for her violence, this playfulness (*līlā*) invokes, rather, an alternative semiotics of conflict in which the play and press of the melee, not its outcome, give it meaning. This view is prompted by the awkwardness that informs the recovery of a state of order through an exuberant act of violence. Because play is organic to the organization of Durga's violence her belligerency exceeds the sober measures of the punitive act calculated to restore dharma to the world, and thus, paradoxically, reproduces the very waste(s) it was intended to erase. In this light, then, divine play-fulness (*līlā*) is simply a record of the fugitive tempo of dharma, a state of order contingent on the trespass against it by the ordure of the enemy.

Thus, the text of *Chandi Charitra* instructs the reader in a perverse art of war in which the Sikh warrior is obliged to establish 'his' order by identifying it among the legislations of his opponent. As such, Sikh subjectivity is regulated by an economy of reference to the adversary, who, therefore, exceeds any definition of it as a mere opposite and is revealed, rather, as an incommensurable other. Like the "primitive monad", then, Sikhism too inscribes a warlike signature which deviates incorrigibly from the conventional view of militant action, far from compelling the submission of an opponent it "... actually opens itself to others in the extreme intensity of the violence of war" (Clastres 1994: 156).

Given that Sikh subjectivity is shaped by the chaotic context of its struggle with the other then the play which orders this religious identity (dharma) amounts to a theophany of the goddess, it invokes the presence of the (m)other. Thus, for Sikhs, the practice of war is developed as a means to engage 'God', however, this divinity is not intimated as a substantive Being distinct from the world but, rather, in the intimacies which inform an embodied existence. Clearly, the otherness of Durga (the 'Unapproachable One' Skt.) does not coincide with the conventional theolog-ical descriptions of divine transcendence, which valorise it as reality-in-itself. Nor, however, is Durga's inapproachability simply an inversion of the prevailing onto-theological opposition, rather than immanence it invokes a state of imminence, where her theophany, in the endless contest of bodies that arbitrates existence, is conveyed simultaneously by the squalid presence of the carnal and a being that is never quite present.

Thus, the 'appearance' of the (m)other mediated by the Sikh ontology of violence is not a theological but an ethical event, and in conceding the absolute sovereignty of the other the Sikh warrior, like the practitioner of Zen archery described by Eugen Herrigel, "fundamentally... aims at himself and may even succeed in hitting himself" (1985: 14).

Sikh theology, then, suspends the restrictive order of contradiction by inscribing an economy of meaning in which any possibility of semantic authoritativeness is held in suspension by the recurrent trace of the other term in the substance of the original proposition. However, the idea of a discourse that resists the strict seman-tic regulation of the law of contradiction continues to attract the same censorious judgement from current trends in Western scholarship, which informed the view of Indologists such as Ernest Trumpp.

This is particularly true of the work produced by the eminent historian of Sikh religion W.H. McLeod, who draws attention to the apparent contradiction between the quietist ideology of early Sikhism (the *Nanakpanth*) and the militant signature of the Khalsa tradition. McLeod's answer to "... why a tradition built on Nanak's inte-rior practice of *nam simran* (meditation on the Divine Name) should have become a militant community" (1997: 111) emphasizes the importance of socio-historic factors in facilitating this change.[9] In 'The Evolution of the Sikh Community' McLeod claims that the militant politicisation of Sikhism in the seventeenth century coincided with a radical change in the social constituency of the community at this time to favour the agrarian and martial Jat caste (1976: 12). While the socio-historic changes sketched by McLeod are not implausible his interpretation of these events as a departure from an original practice is in dispute, since, a proximity between the early accent on meditation and the later concern with militancy is attested by reading both these phenomena as insinuating Sikhs in the play of the world or, an encounter with the (m)other.

Thus, the theological tension in Sikhism described by McLeod, far from being an obvious fact, comes already prefaced by the cipher of contradiction. This interventionism remains effectively immune from criticism because it is coupled with the idiom of objectivity, a mode of perception that is accepted as natural to all cultures, therefore, obliging Sikhs to sanction this revisionist view as their own. It is clear, then, that the objectivity of McLeod's historiographical discourse surreptitiously registers the restrictive order of an authoritarian encounter with the world.

The nature of this engaged perspective is signalled by McLeod's installation of interior religion at the core of Sikhism. By establishing the priority of intelligible over sensible being his thesis simply rehearses the ascetic ideal that informs Christian theology. It is this clandestine interpolation of a Christian cipher into the representation of Sikhism that exposes the recent interventions in the history of Sikh religion as in direct line of descent from colonial discourse. Their ideological proximity has been somewhat obscured, however, by the vicissitudes of this revisionism, current intellectual trends tending to emphasize interior religion, or more recently pluralism,[10] in place of the accent on militancy favoured by the discredited discourse of British colonialism.

From Battle Play to Playing Soldiers: Colonialism and the Reform of Sikh Militancy

There are many warlike races in India whose military qualities are of a high order but of these the Sikh indisputably takes the leading place as a thoroughly useful and reliable soldier (Bingley 1985 [1898]: 116).

Although, the purpose of British colonialism was to establish a politico-economic hegemony over non-European peoples the aggressive interventions deployed to achieve this end, the acts of territorial annexation and cultural expropriation, were not regarded as the sign of an abusive regime but, rather, one that was firmly paternalistic. Thus, the violent subjugation of allegedly immature races was merely a symptom of the proper function of colonialism, which was to facilitate the spread of civilization or, the inculcation of "Public Virtue" (Metcalf 1995: 8) in its subjects. Colonialism, then, was essentially, a process of pacification, inscribing both a subjugation of backward cultures and, as the imposition of a civilizing regime, the condition for the possibility of peace. This strict regulation of violence by the colonial regime was itself a conspicuous testament to the superiority of its values. In contrast to the capricious signature of Sikh warfare the military actions of the British were closely arbitrated by their civilizing remit. Thus, since the kind of force sanctioned by the colonial administration was never excessive to the condition(s) of peace, violence was simply that state of affairs occasioned by a deficiency of this pacific ideal. Although, this measured form of violence appears to be the obvious token of an enlightened society, this is contested by the representation of its pacifying signature in absolute, nonnegotiable terms. Thus, ironically, the restriction of violence by mature states contains the potential for unrestricted destructiveness.

Given that adherence to this narrowly defined form of militancy signalled a fidelity to a properly civilized condition the colonial regime in India was able to distinguish itself from those of their subjects whose alleged lack of martial vigour indicated their cultural degeneracy. This deviation from the normative standard imposed by colonialism was, Macaulay observed, most pronounced in the "... extraordinary effeminacy of the Bengali, whom no necessity would induce to fight" (Metcalf 1995: 127). By contrast, the British asserted the existence of an affinity between themselves and those Indian peoples, pre-eminently the Khalsa Sikhs, whose beliefs readily sanctioned the use of violence. Thus, because these "... 'martial races' were those who most closely resembled what the British imagined themselves to be" (ibid.) their cultural propriety seemed never to be in question.

However, contrary to prevailing opinion, I will suggest that this recognition of affinity surreptitiously imputed to the Sikhs the very same cultural deficiency that was conspicuously attributed to the Bengali Babu. On examination this proposition seems counter-intuitive; surely positing a cultural affinity between colonizer and colonized, what amounts to an expression of ontological parity, cannot be represented as an act of cultural prejudice. What this objection fails to register, however, is the abusive nature of all colonial encounter. The idea that a transparent exchange of meaning was possible between the Sikhs and the British is undermined by the fact that this affinity as the ideological gambit of colonialism must, therefore, have encrypted a colonial notion of militancy, one which was conceived in terms of teleological calculation. Given that Sikh warfare is informed by a gratuitous excess, then, its identification with the kind of restricted militancy prescribed by the British signals an ethnological departure which remains undetected, since, propriety is ascribed to this specious edition of military action. Thus, the affinity putatively obtaining between the Sikhs and the British, does not constitute a recognition of ontological parity but, rather, as a relation posited between a virtual reproduction of Sikhism and colonial identity, communicates a sense of Sikh degeneracy.

The economy of oppression that informed this form of colonial encounter went unrecognised because Sikhs themselves were closely implicated in facilitating this condition. The origin of this insidious oppression may be traced back to the more obvious act of subjugation inscribed by the annexation of Punjab to British India. The Sikh elites imputed this loss of sovereignty to a cultural malaise arising from the interpolation of Hindu religious and social observances into Sikhism. Inevitably, the act of reforming the messy tableau presented by pre-colonial Sikhism also tended to censure the excessive discourse of Sikh tradition.

The Sikhs were encouraged in the belief that the amelioration of their diminished plenitude could be achieved by identifying with the colonizing class, whose confident militancy seemed an obvious testament to ontological unity. This mimetic encounter was given theoretical expression in the work of reformist ideologues such as Bhai Kahan Singh Nabha (1861–1938) who sought to establish Sikhism's affinity to the colonial ideal by showing that its beliefs were equally distinctive from the perplexing and effeminate discourse of the Hindus. Among other opinions, Bhai Kahan Singh contested the Hindu assertion that Guru Gobind Singh was a votary of the Goddess who had "... written Chandi Charitra to eulogize Durga and acclaimed the meritorious ness of reflection on her Name" (2002: 76). This was, however, Kahan Singh claimed, a perverse reading of Durga's role in Sikh tradition, this turbulent Goddess did not represent an object of veneration but a trope for the punitive dispensation of a God of righteousness.

Thus, since Sikhs were not Hindus, and therefore not-effeminate, an affinity was indicated between Sikhism and the muscular ethos of colonialism. By establishing their place in the register of normative culture the Sikhs 'recovered' a uniform sense of identity, however, since the authoritative ness of this 'original' credo was determined by its proximity to colonial discourse, the return of Sikhism to itself simply rehearsed the concerns of the imperial regime. Given that Sikhs themselves sanctioned this revisionism as a native act of reform its oppressive force remained obscured. The slippage in emphasis of *Chandi Charitra*, from the battle play of the (m)other to the retributive justice of God, was not identified as a semantic restriction of the text's excessive signature, rather, as a return to the original teleological order of Sikh militancy and the sobriety of a monotheistic creed.

The colonial Sikh subject, then, was an impostor, or what Homi Bhabha refers to as a mimic man "..a reformed, recognizable Other... [the] subject of a difference that is almost the same, but not quite" (1994: 86). Because mimicry (re)produces the strange legislations of the other, the expression of its autonomy is always out of reach, every self-affirmation falling ever shorter in a sprawling deficit of being. The mimic man, then, "... conceals no presence or identity behind [his] mask" (Bhabha 1994: 88) and yet, the vacuous tempo of this imposture renders it incorrigible, thus, accounting for the bloated nullity of modern Sikhism.

Conclusion

The oppressive activity of colonialism constitutes what Clastres describes as ethnocide. In contrast to the obvious denial of difference which informs acts of genocide, an ethnocidal policy concedes the corrigibility of the other, which is negotiated through a regime of identification with the self. Thus, the authoritarian signature of ethnocide is elided because "... it is practiced for the good of the [other]" (Clastres 1994: 46).indeed, in its final refinement ethnocide becomes a 'good' to which the other subjects himself.

Ethnocide continues to characterize contemporary Sikh experience, and is, perhaps, most readily attested in the recent agitation by the Sikhs for full political sovereignty in the Punjab. One of the most notorious measures deployed by the Indian state to check the dissident ambitions of the Sikhs was the fake encounter, during which militants were killed while allegedly attempting an escape from the authorities. However, what such an encounter actually fakes is the idea that legislations are possible which can elude the authoritarian order of the State. Sikh dissidence was pre-eminently a desire for repatriation, a nostalgia for a state of ethnic purity (Khalistan) which was anticipated through the machismo and martyrdom proper to the theophany of an avenging God. By forfeiting a difference regulated by an encounter with the (m)other the Sikh's encounter with himself was fake, subject to the same mutilation of identity impressed upon him by colonialism. Perversely, then, the (Indian) State invites the kind of political trespass invoked by ethno-nationalism since, this expression of dissidence serves to conceal, the fundamental lack organic to the autonomy of the Sikh subject or, the fact that ethnocide requires the complicity of its victims.

This politics of ethnocide is also recorded in the pluralist idiom of John Hick's address to the other. Given that the context for dialogue with other religions is simply a proxy record of Christian concerns then, clearly, the encounter with traditions such as Hinduism and Sikhism is fake. Thus, Hick is a purveyor of the other side of modern State terror, deploying the intellectual register of the philosophy of religion as an instrument of repression, obliging the other to enter the field of religious consensus, where, his brutal task is facilitated by the victim's craving for a bullet.

Notes

1 The Khalsa are an order of Sikh initiates who are distinguished by their scrupulous maintenance of five articles on the body (*panj kakke*). The most visually significant of these corporeal pledges are the *kesh* or unshorn hair, which in the case of male Sikhs is draped by a turban (*pagh*), the *kirpan*, a curved, steel sword and the *kara*, a bracelet worn on the right wrist.

2 This trauma refers to the rise of Sikh ethno-nationalism in Indian Punjab during the 1980s and the brutal conflict that erupted between Sikh separatists and the national government.

3 This poem by Morihei Ueshiba, the founder of Aikido, is quoted in Fletcher and Scott (2001: 169).

4 Gobind Singh (1666–1708) was the tenth, and last, of the human Sikh Gurus. During his incumbency as Guru he was responsible for establishing the Khalsa. A highly capable military leader, Guru Gobind Singh was also a prolific author. His compositions were brought together in a volume known as the *Dasam Granth Sahib* (the Book of the Tenth Guru).

5 *Jap Sahib*, the first composition in the *Dasam Granth*, is one of Guru Gobind Singh's most important works and is ostensibly concerned with "describ(ing) the nature and qualities of God" (Cole and Sambhi 1997: 88). However, the conflicting representations of this 'divinity', which occur throughout the text, belie this interpretation. It may be more consistent to read this work as disclosing a 'God' who is always excessive to his own presence, this radical otherness signalling the inadequacy of any attempt to describe something that is never there to be described.

6 The *Adi* or *Guru Granth Sahib* is the principal Sikh scripture, the final recension of which was produced in the late seventeenth century. It contains the works of six of the ten Sikh Gurus (*Gurbani*) as well as writings by a number of Hindu and Muslim 'saints' (*Bhagat Bani*), the text being organised according to the musical measure (*raag*) deployed in composition.

7 Sikh tradition advocates the view that militancy was the obvious response to the oppressive rule of the Mughal Empire, enabling a blow to be struck in the defence of righteousness. A typical statement of this viewpoint is found in Harbans Singh, who declares that the purpose "... of the sword was to secure fulfilment of God's justice... (i)t stood for righteous and brave action, for the protection of truth and virtue. It was the emblem of manliness and self-respect and was to be used only in self-defence, as a last resort" (1994: 83).

8 *Braj Bhasa* is a vernacular associated with the district around Mathura in India and was used to compose the Krsna cycle of stories. The language of most of the texts in the *Dasam Granth Sahib* is Braj Bhasa recorded in the Gurmukhi script.

9 The polarisation of opinion between the advocates of the rigorously historical and traditional approaches to the question of militancy in Sikhism continues to be one of the key, and indeed most vituperative, debates within Sikh scholarship. This is, however, largely an artificial dispute, since the question of violence needs to be thought in terms of purposes or, the absence of them. Thus, the alleged differences between these two interpretations are disclosed merely as modifications of the idea that a purpose needs to be ascribed to militancy. If, as suggested, Sikh warfare is actually a gratuitous affair then, an entire tradition of thinking concerning this problem needs to be repudiated.

10 I am referring here to the work of Harjot Oberoi (1994) and Doris Jakobsch (2003).

References

Bataille, G. (1988) *The Accursed Share* (Volume 1). New York: Zone Books

Bingley, A.H. (1985) *The Sikhs*. Delhi: National Book Shop

Bhabha, H. (1994) *The Location of Culture*. London: Routledge

Clastres, P. (1994) *Archaeology of Violence*. New York: Semiotext(e)

Clausewitz, C. (1982) *On War*. Harmondsworth: Penguin

Cole, O. and Sambhi, P. (1997) *A Popular Dictionary of Sikhism*. Richmond: Curzon

Fanon, F. (1986) *Black Skin, White Masks*. London: Pluto

Fletcher, T. and Scott, D. (2001) *Way of Zen*. London: Vega

Gilman, S. (1985) *Difference and Pathology: Stereotypes of Sexuality, Race and Madness*. New York: Cornell University Press

Herrigel, E. (1985) *Zen in the Art of Archery*. London: Arkana

Hick, J. (1989) *An Interpretation of Religion: Human Responses to the Transcendent*. Basingstoke: Macmillan

Hick, J. (1990) *Philosophy of Religion*. New Jersey: Prentice Hall

Jakobsch, D. (2003) *Relocating Gender in Sikh History: Transformation, Meaning and Identity*. New Delhi: Oxford University Press

Kinsley, D. (1987) *Hindu Goddesses: Visions of the Divine Feminine in the Hindu Religious Tradition*. Delhi: Motilal Banarsidass

Klostermaier, K.K. (1999) *A Concise Encyclopaedia of Hinduism*. Oxford: Oneworld

Lorenzen, D. (1996) *Bhakti Religion in North India: Community, Identity and Political Action*. New Delhi: Manohar

McLeod, W.H. (1976) *The Evolution of the Sikh Community*. London: Oxford University Press

McLeod, W.H. (1997) *Sikhism*. Harmondsworth: Penguin

Metcalf, Thomas, R. (1995) *Ideologies of the Raj*. The New Cambridge History of India, III.4, Cambridge: Cambridge University Press

Nabha, K.S. (2002) *Hum Hindu Nahin*. Amritsar: Singh Brothers

Oberoi, H. (1994) *The Construction of Religious Boundaries*. Delhi: Oxford University Press

Singh, H. (1994) *The Heritage of the Sikhs*. New Delhi: Manohar

Singh, J. and Singh, D. (1999) *Sri Dasam Granth Sahib Text and Translation* (Volume 1). Patiala: Heritage

Singh, M. (2000) *Sri Guru Granth Sahib* (English and Punjabi Translation). Amritsar: SGPC

Trumpp, E. (1999) "Sketch of the Religion of the Sikhs," in Singh, D. (Ed.), *Western Image of the Sikh Religion: A Sourcebook*. New Delhi: National Book Organisation

van der Veer, Peter (2001) *Imperial Encounters: Religion and Modernity in India and Britain*. Princeton: Princeton University Press

Max Müller and Textual Management:
A Postcolonial Perspective

Sharada Sugirtharajah

Abstract The aim of this paper is to bring to the fore the hermeneutical presuppositions undergirding Max Müller's approach to the Veda. He constructs a textualized
Hinduism which is informed by nineteenth-century notions of evolution, historicism, and comparative philology. He forges a non-ecclesiastical Protestant form
of Hinduism which will eventually find fulfilment in Christianity. In other words,
Müller fashions a Hinduism that suits his own hermeneutical assumptions – a Hinduism that has much to do with his own nostalgia for an uncontaminated European
past. What he offers is a Veda that is still locked in its infancy, needing the help of
the evolved European culture. The Veda has glimpses of truth but these are those of
a child and should be treated as such.

First, a brief word about postcolonialism[1] Postcolonialism is one of the latest
theoretical categories to enter academic discourse. Each discipline has come up
with its own definition of postcolonialism and has appropriated it to suit its own
academic needs. Postcolonial theory has been used in many different ways – as a
methodological approach, as a resistant or oppositional strategy, or as a discursive
category. As with any critical category, postcolonialism is not without limitations,
but nevertheless it is a highly serviceable category. The aim of postcolonial criticism
is to interrogate textual, historical, ethnographic, visual and other representations of
societies which were badly affected by the historical reality of colonial presence and
domination. It is about how colonizers constructed images of the colonized, as well
as how the colonized themselves made use of these images as a counter-tool to com-
bat negative portrayals and to construct a new identity. Postcolonial theory is useful
in that it reveals the link between knowledge and power and between representation and mediation, and highlights homogenizing, essentializing and universalising
tendencies in varied discourses, reading and interpretative strategies. I will mainly
use postcolonialism as a hermeneutical tool to interrogate Max Müller's construction of Hinduism. This chapter[2] will look at Müller's treatment of the Veda, under
the following three theoretical categories: colonial patronage, trope of the child and
classification.

P. Bilimoria and A.B. Irvine (eds.), *Postcolonial Philosophy of Religion*.
© Springer Science+Business Media B.V. 2009

Colonial Patronage

Ever since the publication of Edward Said's *Orientalism*, the connection between knowledge and power cannot be ignored. Drawing on the Foucaultian thesis that knowledge is inextricably linked with power, Said shows that the production of knowledge about the Orient by the West, is not an innocent activity. The Orientalist pursuit of knowledge was inextricably bound up with the desire for colonial expansion and domination. A significant number of textual projects (from editing to translation of Sanskrit texts) were initiated, approved and authorized by the colonial government, from the eighteenth century onwards. In the first place, it is the West's power over the East that facilitated the production of knowledge about the East, and this in turn fortified the power of the West over the East. Müller's undertaking of textual production of the *Sacred Books of the East* falls into the category of what, in postcolonial discourse, is termed colonial patronage. The term Patronage "refers to the economic or social power that allows cultural institutions and cultural forms to come into existence and be valued and promoted. Patronage can take the form of a simple and direct transaction, such as the purchase or commissioning of works of art by wealthy people, or it can take the form of the support and recognition of social institutions that influence the production of culture" (Ashcroft et al. 1998: 43).

For example, Charles Wilkins's translation of the *Bhagavadgītā*, and Müller's translation and edition of the six-volume *RigVeda*, which had the financial backing of the East India Company, were not totally apolitical ventures.[3] Müller' translation project also had the support of royal patronage. In the colonial reversal of roles, the then Prince of Wales took with him numerous copies of Müller's *Sacred Books of the East* to be given as gifts to Indian kings during the Durbar.[4] True, early Orientalist-administrators such as Warren Hastings and Sir William Jones were more appreciative of India and its culture than many scholars were, but these Orientalists believed that the sound knowledge of Hindu beliefs and practices gained from their texts would be politically beneficial inasmuch as it would enable them to exercise effective control over the natives. As Eric Sharpe remarks: "The reason why East India Company in London had been prepared to fund the first translation of the Gītā was partly that they had allowed themselves to be persuaded that it might prove politically expedient for them to do so . . . Max Müller's text of the *Rig Veda* was funded by the same commercial company on the same grounds" (Sharpe 1985: 45).

Müller's translation projects not only legitimized British colonial rule but also justified intellectual and spiritual conquest. By the early nineteenth-century most of the Indian subcontinent came under the purview of the British East India Company, and by the middle of the nineteenth century British rule had been firmly established. Reflecting the mood of the time, Müller not only spoke approvingly of the establishment of British rule but also of the need to colonize India's minds. He spoke of "the conquest of the world by means of commerce, colonization, education, and conversion" (Müller 1902a: 289). Urging young British civil servants to undertake the study of Sanskrit, Müller declared that the material conquest of India alone will not suffice, and that Britain ought not to leave the intellectual conquest of India to other countries. In his letter to Cowell to whom the book *India: What Can It teach Us?* is dedicated, Müller remarks: "... You know that at present and for sometime to come *Sanskrit scholarship means discovery and conquest*" (Müller 1892: vi, emphasis mine).

Müller's translating activities are neither innocent nor altruistic. First, let me briefly spell out Müller's own attitude to the *Sacred Books of the East* to which he devoted most of his working life. Müller makes clear that one of the principal aims of translating the *Sacred Books of the East* is "to assist missionaries" (Müller 1920b: 455), although he was the subject of trenchant missionary criticism. In his letter to Lady Welby dated 25 July 1879, he assures her that the translation of the *Sacred Books of the East* "will do a great deal towards lifting Christianity into its high historical position" (Müller 1902b: 67). In his letter to the Dean of St. Paul's, Müller remarks: "I have myself the strongest belief in the growth of Christianity in India" (Müller 1902a: 332). As will be seen later, Müller values the Veda not so much for its spiritual import as for its archival worth. In his view, most of the material is unintelligible, that it is of no use except to an historian. "It cannot be too strongly stated," Müller remarks, "that the chief, and, in many cases, the only interest of the Sacred Books of the East is historical; that much in them is extremely childish, tedious, if not repulsive; and that no one but the historian will be able to understand the important lessons which they teach" (Müller 1902b: 11). It is ironical that Müller should have spent all his time and his energies on studying, translating and editing the *Sacred Books of the East* which he felt were worthless except as antiquarian documents. While speaking of his gratitude to the East India Company for the publication of the *Rig Veda*, Müller remarks that "such a publication would have ruined any bookseller, for it must be confessed, that there is little that is attractive in the Veda, nothing that could excite general interest. From an aesthetic point of view, no one would care for the hymns of the Rig-veda..." (Müller 1875: 367). He firms up his view by quoting Colebrooke who saw the Veda as being "too voluminous for a complete translation, and what they contain would hardly reward the labour of the reader, much less that of the translator" (ibid.: 368).

Trope of the Child

One of the significant features of postcolonial discourse is theorization of the trope of the child. The trope of the child functions as a useful hermeneutical device to represent the Other, and to establish a link between the invader and invaded. More importantly, it situates the former in a position of superiority. As Ashcroft remarks:

> The child, at once both other and same, holds in balance the contradictory tendencies of imperial rhetoric: authority is held in balance with nurture; domination with enlightenment; debasement with idealization; negation with affirmation; exploitation with education; filiation with affiliation. This ability to absorb contradiction gives the binary parent/child an inordinate hegemonic potency. (Ashcroft 2001: 36–37)

The trope of the child serves a number of purposes useful to the colonizer: it allows the colonizer to exercise his benevolent parental authority over colonial subjects. For the colonial parent the child symbolizes a state of innocence, unspoiled purity or a natural state, and therefore the child cannot exercise its rational faculties. The colonial parent now becomes the guardian into whose care colonial subjects are entrusted. In other words, the colonial parent takes upon himself/herself the responsibility of looking after the physical, mental, moral and spiritual welfare of colonial children. The problem is that the child is never allowed to grow; its identity is permanently fixed and frozen.

What I aim to demonstrate is that the trope of the child is at work in Müller's appropriation of the Veda. Firstly, Müller views the Veda from a nineteenth-century Western evolutionary perspective. He establishes an evolutionary link between the Veda and Kant's *Critique of Pure Reason*: the former representing the first "stammerings" of a child and the latter the mature thinking of a human being. He states that "while in the Veda, we may study the childhood, we may study in Kant's *Critique of Pure Reason* the perfect manhood of the Aryan mind" (Müller 1901: 249). In other words, for Müller, the religious journey begins with the Veda – symbolizing childhood innocence – and attains maturity in Kant's *Critique*. He remarks: "In the Veda we see how the Divine appears in the fire, and in the earthquake .... In Kant's *Critique* the Divine is heard in the still small voice – the Categorical Imperative – the I Ought – which Nature does not know and cannot teach" (ibid.: 249).

Müller fixes the historical value and meaning of the Veda by placing it at the lowest end of the evolutionary scale (starting not with the beast as in Darwin but with the child.[5] For him, the Vedic hymns represent "the lowest stratum in the growth of the human mind that can be reached anywhere by means of contemporaneous literature" (Müller 1902a: 271). He affirms the Veda but only as a product of an infantile mind which lacks the rationality of a mature adult. For Müller, the Vedic sage is but a child – a noble savage. Critiquing the anthropological significance attached to the term "savage," meaning primitive or uncivilized," Müller introduces two classes of savages – *"progressive"* and *"retrogressive"* – signifying "a hopeful and a hopeless barbarism"; "a growing and a decaying civilization" (Müller 1901: 156). In his view, "Man certainly began as a savage, but as a progressive savage" (1901: 178), regressing now and then, only to rise again. A "retrogressive savage" is one who has descended from a higher state but has the possibility of ascending again (Müller 1901: 156). Müller puts forward the much favoured Orientalist thesis – that Hindus had reached a higher stage of civilization but had regressed into a state of barbarism. Hindus in their present state have lost touch with their archaic purity which Müller seeks to recover for them, but his thesis does not end with this. Once the lost childhood is regained, Hindus need nurturing in order to grow into full maturity. Hindus could regain their ancient purity with the help of the evolved European culture. The Vedic child is always a child; it needs the nurturing parent to facilitate its growth into full maturity. The child lacks the necessary stimulus (reason and logic), which can be offered only by the European colonial parent. Whether the colonized cultures are thought of in terms of "primitive savage" or "progressive savage," the very concept "savage" itself legitimises colonial intervention and the exercise of authority over the colonized in the interests of those colonized. Müller's idea of "a progressive savage" implies the possibilities of evolution and fulfilment in a higher and universal truth, which, in his view, is no other than Christianity in its non-ecclesiastical form. In construing Hindus as locked in their infancy, Müller renders them powerless, in need of the help of enlightened cultures.

The construction of the Veda as an untainted document enables Müller to romanticize about Europe's supposed lost innocence. He is mainly interested in the Veda, not so much for its own worth but for the light it sheds on a supposed common Aryan ancestry whereby Indians and Europeans belong to the same race (Müller 1892: 116). He tells young British men that there is in the Veda "something that concerns ourselves, something of our own intellectual growth, some recollections, as it were, of our own childhood, or at least of the childhood of our race" (Müller 1892: 254). It is this innocent past that Müller is keen to resurrect or rather construct – an uncontaminated past free from any "foreign influence" (Müller 1892: 140). He sets himself the momentous task of recovering the Veda, which he calls Europess "oldest inheritance", and making it accessible to the European world (Müller 1902b: 74).

In brief, this section problematizes the conventional perception of Müller as a benevolent interpreter of the Veda. Müller's affirmation of the Veda has more to do with its significance as an antiquated document than with its spiritual content. For Müller, the Veda is significant for the study of the origin and evolution of religious ideas but only as an infantile document of great historical worth.

Classification

Naming or classifying the Other is not peculiar to any one culture; it occurs within and across cultures. In nineteenth century colonial discourse, classification was a way of domesticating and appropriating the Other on terms congenial to the colonizer. David Spurr regards classification itself as an ideologically charged rhetorical strategy. He remarks: "Within the realm of discourse, classification performs this policing function, assigning positions, regulating groups, and enforcing boundaries" (Spurr 1993: 63). Classification meant reordering and restructuring in terms of the modernist norms and values of the European Enlightenment. The collecting and cataloguing of texts, artifacts, trees, plants, seeds, and animals of non-western peoples were clear markers of colonial dominance in nineteenth-century India. Classification, naming and mapping the Other, was a way of asserting European supremacy. The invader worked on the assumption that the cultures of the invaded were "chaotic," in need of reordering and categorizing. Müller's theory of the science of religion resonates with the nineteenth-century discourse of colonial science. Gyan Prakash demonstrates that colonial science worked on the premise that the natives's knowledge of their agricultural products was muddled, requiring reorganization, and that the natives needed to be educated in the science of classification. He explains: "If one aim of colonial pedagogy was to instruct peasants by exhibiting their own products and knowledge organized and authorized by the science of classification, its other aim was to render manifest the principle of function so that it could be applied to improve production" (Prakash 1999: 23). A similar exercise is evident in Müller's classification of religions and their texts along evolutionary lines. Müller applies a modified version of the nineteenth-century evolutionary hypothesis in order to grade religious texts. He classifies the sacred texts of different religions in a hierarchical order. He places the New Testament at the top, and the Veda is assigned the second lowest position, followed by the Zoroastrian Avesta (1902b: 322). Commenting that such a classification may not be acceptable to others, he goes on to point out that in terms of ethical teaching Christian scriptures score higher than other sacred texts, and that this is what makes the Bible distinctive (Müller 1902b: 322–323). In his letter to Rev. Cox (June 1885), Müller states that "the Old Testament stands on a higher ethical stage than other sacred books – it certainly does not lose by a comparison with them" (Müller 1902b: 174). He uses the prevailing pietistic theology of the time (the Fall, punishment and redemption) as a hermeneutical key to compare the Christian texts with other texts, thereby establishing the primacy of the Christian texts. While other sacred texts have only a nominal value, Christian texts are seen as having a real value. Müller locates a purified form of Christianity in biblical texts and considers this to be the religion of humanity and the fulfilment of all religions. He declares that "if Christianity were not only preached, but lived in that spirit, it would then prove itself what it is – the religion of humanity at large, large enough itself to take in all shades and diversities of character and race" (Müller 1875: 276). In his estimation, Hinduism and other religions lack something that Christianity has, which is the special revelation of the love of God for humanity. It is this "Gospel which will conquer other religions" (ibid.: 278). He makes clear the hermeneutical aim of his science of religion, which is to compare and contrast religions and establish which of them is better than the other. Although Müller challenges the exclusive claims made for Christianity, by subjecting all religions including Christianity to a comparative and historical-critical method, his eventual aim is to demonstrate that such a scrutiny would not endanger Christianity but rather would place it higher in the evolutionary scheme. He remarks:

> The Science of Religion will for the first time assign to Christianity its right place among the religions of the world; it will show for the first time fully what was meant by the fullness of time; it will restore to the whole history of the world, in its unconscious progress towards Christianity, its true and sacred character. (Müller 1868: xx)

Müller's aim is to demonstrate that such a classification would give a clear insight into the origin and evolution of the religious ideas of humankind. To put it concisely, Müller's evolutionary hypothesis legitimates a hierarchical view of religions. Implicit in Müller's evolutionary paradigm is the modernist notion of a single universal standard of truth applicable to all cultures – a standard by which they can be evaluated. While Müller's inclusivist approach to other religions challenges Christian exclusivist attitudes, at the same time it denies them any independent agency.

Concluding Remarks

Finally, I would like to draw attention to some hermeneutical presuppositions undergirding Müller's appropriation of the Veda. One, Müller sees himself as having the hermeneutical key to unlock the original meaning of the Veda. The nineteenth-century European search for "origins" is reflected in Müller's approach to the Veda. In his introduction to the *Upanishads* which he translated, Müller states:

> But I know full well how much still remains to be done, both in restoring a correct text, and in discovering the original meaning of the Upanishads; and I have again and again had to translate certain passages tentatively only, or following the commentators, though conscious all the time that the meaning which they extract from the text cannot be the right one. (Müller 1884: xii)

He employs what was known at that time in biblical circles as higher criticism (later to be called historical criticism) in order to discern the "original" meaning of the Veda. Müller warns that any tampering with the meaning of the Veda would result in the loss of its real worth. One of the tasks of historical criticism is to look for the "Ur text." In his approach to the Veda Müller is engaged in a similar task of going back to an "Ur text" and recovering the "true Gospel" in it. He assumes the role of a Protestant reformer and wants to rescue the Veda and recover its "original" meaning for Hindus. In other words, he engages in a textual cleansing mission – he wants to restore Hinduism to its pristine form.[6] Like other Orientalists, Müller, too, constructs a picture of a magnificent age of Hindus which he locates in the Veda. He urges Hindus to go back to the Veda to recover the lost purity of their tradition but at the same time cautions that the purity of the Veda is of a primitive kind and therefore cannot provide a sound basis for reformed Hinduism. He exhorts the members of the Brahmo śamāj to look for guidance in the New Testament (1902b: 390). He reckons that Hindus will be able appreciate the true value of the Veda if they accept it "as an ancient *historical* document, containing thoughts in accordance with the character of an ancient and simple-minded race of men . . . ." (Müller 1902b: 110). Claiming that he has the necessary knowledge to make an historical assessment of the Veda, Müller urges Hindus to accept his verdict. Müller warns that to look for a rational religion or signs of modernity is contrary to the spirit of the Veda.[7] In other words, he cautions Hindus not to look in it for modern Western scientific, philosophical and rational categories or moral values (ibid.: 110).

Two, Müller brings his Protestant presuppositions about the written word to his study of the Veda. For most Hindus the meaning of a text is not confined to nor firmly entrenched in the written word. European Orientalists, for whom the written word is paramount, tended to view oral transmission of sacred knowledge not only as an inferior mode of communication but as a sign of backwardness. For Hindus, however, the orality of their texts (both *śruti* and *smṛti*) signified a highly developed spiritual culture. In fact, the act of writing was regarded as polluting. The sacrality of the Veda was retained in oral form before it was committed to writing, and even to this day oral recitation of the Veda and even *smṛti* texts such as the *Rāmāyaṇa* is highly preferred and valued.

European scholars have laid undue emphasis on the written word. It has been of utmost significance for Europeans since the seventeenth century, signifying a certitude of meaning, stability and security that orality was considered to be lacking. As Bernard Cohn states:

> Meaning for the English was something attributed to a word, a phrase, or an object, which could be determined and translated, at best with a synonym that had a direct referent to something in what the English thought of as a "natural world". Everything had a more or less specific referent for the English. With Indians, meaning was not necessarily constructed in the same fashion. The effect and affect of hearing a Brahman chant in Sanskrit at a sacrifice did not entail meaning in the European sense; it was to have one's substance literally affected by the sound. (Cohn 1996: 18–19)

What Müller's *The Sacred Books of the East* project did was to privilege the written word. That is, the printed page became the means of revelation. The written text was seen as a mark of modernity and progress, and the oral text as primitive. For missionaries, the written word was not merely a mark of civilization; salvation was to be mediated through the word. The outcome of such an exercise resulted in the production of textual knowledge about Hinduism that had little relevance to the vast majority of Hindus whose lives were not directly informed by written texts. As pointed out elsewhere, the link between the written and oral cultures has always been fluid in the Hindu tradition – the one impacting on the other in varying degrees.

Müller is the first European to edit and bring out the six-volume edition of the *Rig Veda*, together with the fourteenth-century commentary of Sayana. Both nineteenth century European scholarship and traditional Hindu scholarship have tended to rely heavily on the ritualistic interpretation of the Veda given by Sayana, thereby overlooking the inner symbolic import of the Veda (Aurobindo 1984: 17–18). The main drawback of Sayana's ritualistic interpretation, according to Sri Aurobindo, is that it "seeks continually to force the sense of the Veda into that narrow mould", thus obscuring the inner significance implicit in the hymns and rendering it in its minimalist sense (Aurobindo 1971: 18). He draws attention to how European scholars like Müller have made skilful use of traditional aspects of Sayana's commentary by subjecting the commentary to a comparative approach based on nineteenth-century Western notions of philology, mythology, history, and myth, thus constructing an elaborate body of Vedic mythology, history and culture (Aurobindo 1971: 23). Müller sees the Veda as a repository of natural revelation, and the Vedic deities as no more than mere personifications of the natural phenomena rather than as potent symbols or expressions of the One. In trying to fix the original meaning of the Veda, Europeans scholars like Müller have thus rendered the meaning of the Veda in its minimalist sense.

Three, in his approach to the Veda, Müller employs both the rhetoric of affirmation and of negation at one and the same time. He acknowledges that the Veda contains noble thoughts, but much in them appears to his Protestant perspective as "childish in the extreme, tedious'. low, common place" (Müller 1868: 27). He remarks that there is "much that is elevated and elevating, and much that is beautiful and sublime"; but at the same time there is much in them that is immature and repugnant that it can be of little interest to anyone except a historian (Müller 1902b: 11).

For Müller, even from an aesthetic point of view the Veda has nothing much to offer. He emphasizes that "there is little that is beautiful, in our sense of the word, to be found in the hymns of the *Rig-veda*" (Müller 1875: 369). Nevertheless, the hymns are seen as valuable, for "hidden in this rubbish there are precious stones" (Müller 1868: 27). Müller reckons that, in spite of the Upanishads containing some marks of "poetical eloquence" and philosophical worth, they are at the same time "utterly meaningless and irrational" and "utter rubbish." He goes on to say that "there will always remain in the Upanishads a vast amount of what we can only call meaningless jargon" (Müller 1884: xix–xx). In the same breath Müller praises the Bible as being far ahead of other sacred books (Müller 1884: xx).

Four, for Muller the Veda can offer only a fragile and insecure monotheism. As with other European scholars, Müller uses biblical monotheism as the yardstick to examine the Rig-Vedic affirmation of multiplicity of gods. Müller is struck by the fact that the *Rig Veda* affirms many gods whilst at the same time each god is given supreme importance in their respective hymns and becomes the sole object of devotion at given time while at another time another god is given similar attention. Neither the multiplicity of gods nor the affirmation of a particular god at a particular time diminishes the unique importance of other gods, even if the same attributes are ascribed to them. Müller finds such an understanding and treatment cumbersome, and characterises it as "chaotic theogony" (1892: 162). That is to say, the gods, in Müller's view, are not organized in any systematic manner but seemed to emerge with ease and occupy a supreme position. He coins two terms to describe what he considers the true nature of vedic religion: *Henotheism*, which is "the worship of single gods," and *Kathenothesim* which is "the worship of one god after another." He thus distinguishes it from Greek and Roman polytheism, and from Semitic monotheism. Preferring the term *Henotheism*, Müller draws a distinction between Semitic and Vedic monotheism: "This shorter name of *Henotheism* has found more general acceptance, as conveying more definitely the opposition between *Monotheism*, the worship of one only God, and *Henotheism*, the worship of single gods . . . " (Müller 1892: 147). Müller goes to great lengths to highlight this distinction in order to show that if at all there is any form of monotheism in the Veda, it is rather fragile and "defenceless," degenerating into polytheism. In his letter to the Duke of Argyll, Müller speaks of vedic religion being closer to untainted monotheism – a monotheism that is still in its infant state (Müller 1902a: 480). In brief, Müller locates in the Veda a "primitive monotheism" but not a distorted version of biblical monotheism, as Jones does. In Müller's view, the Vedic hymns, as we have seen, embody thoughts which are still in their infancy. In other words, the Veda in itself does not offer any room for the development of ideas for its true worth lies in its being the first sigh of a new born child. Therefore one should not look for a well-developed monotheistic conception of God in the Veda. To put it another way, one should not even try to look for anything other than natural revelation in the Veda (Müller 1901: 248).

Five, Müller privileges the Veda, thus disregarding other textual and oral forms of knowledge. He undermines any Sanskrit text that is not part of the *śruti* tradition.

In one of his 1882 lectures to British candidates for the Civil Service, Müller refers to the *Gītā* as "a rather popular and exoteric exposition of Vedantic doctrines"

(Müller 1892: 252). While William Jones rated the *Bhagavadgītā* highly, Müller lamented that a text of little importance had come to occupy an enormous significance in the West. In his reckoning, "It was a real misfortune that Sanskrit literature became first known to the learned public in Europe through specimens belonging to the second...period" (Müller 1892: 90). The *Gītā*, in his view, was a product of degenerate period whereas the Veda was a product of an uncorrupt period. "The only original, the only important period of Sanskrit literature," he remarks, "which deserves to become the subject of earnest study...is that period which preceded the rise of Buddhism..." (Müller 1878: 145). He regards Sanskrit works such as *Sakuntala* as no more than mere "literary curiosities," undertaken by men like William Jones, and which can "never become the object of a life-study" (Müller 1878: 142). Although the Veda is seen as the ultimate source of authority and has been drawn upon by various schools of Hindu philosophy and religious groups, its pre-eminent role has not been unanimously accepted by all Hindus, especially by *bhakti* sects. For Müller, only the Sanskrit Veda matters. Orientalists, like Müller, who are so obsessed with the Sanskrit language, fail to note that there is another Indian language, Tamil, which is essentially as old as Sanskrit and has its own sacred text. What is often not recognized is that the term Veda is also extended to the entire collection of Tamil Śrīvaiṣṇva devotional poems of *Aḻvars* (poet-saints), called *Nalayira Divya Prabandham*.[8] The point is that Divine revelation is not confined to the Vedic seers but is also seen as manifesting itself through the twelve *aḻvars*. Therefore Tamil devotional literature is regarded as the "Tamil Veda". The term is also applied to Nammalvar's *Tiruvaymoli* (meaning "word of sacred mouth") which is a significant part of *Nalayira Divya Prabandham*. The designation, "Tamil Veda", is particularly significant given that the term Veda was used solely with reference to revelation through the medium of the Sanskrit language. It was in the tenth century C.E. that a vernacular language for the first time became the medium of revelation. Furthermore, the notion of the Tamil Veda did not conflict in any way with the Sanskrit Veda or result in the former being treated as inferior. As Narayanan and Carman point out: "For the first time in Hindu consciousness, hymns in a language other than Sanskrit were considered to be revealed. The claim was also unique in that none of the teachers in the Śrīvaiṣṇva community felt that they were rebelling against the Sanskrit tradition; nor did they hold either Veda to be inferior to the other" but saw the two traditions in complementary terms – as a "confluence of two rivers" (Carman and Narayanan 1989: 4). In fact, some of the secondary texts such as the *Mahābhārata* and the *Bhagavadgītā* have been elevated to the status of *śruti*. The epic, the *Mahābhārata*, is designated "the fifth Veda".

Conclusion

What I have attempted to do is to draw attention to the hcrmeneuctical factors that influenced Müller's handling of the Veda. There is both negation and affirmation in Müller's treatment of the Veda, and it is only towards the end of his life that Müller came to speak highly of the Vedānta.

Notes

1 There are a number of volumes which deal with the subject. For a convenient entry into the origin, background, key practitioners, and debates from within and outside the field, see Ashcroft et al. (1989), Gandhi (1998), Mc Leod (2000) and Quayson (2000). For clarification of terms, see Ashcroft et al. (1998). For application of the theory for specific religions traditions, see King (1999) for Hinduism and Majid (2000) for Islam.

2 This is a slightly revised version of the paper presented at the AAR Meeting in Atlanta, 2003. For a more extended version of this subject matter, see chapter 2 in my book *Imagining Hinduism: A Postcolonial Perspective* (2003) London: Routledge.

3 Warren Hastings was highly impressed on reading Charles Wilkins's draft translation of the *Bhagavadgītā* and made a deliberate attempt to publicize it in Britain. He hoped that by showing that Indians were not a savage race but had a sublime text such as the *Gītā*, he could win the support of the British public for an oriental mode of government (Marshall 1970: 180).

4 See van der Veer (2001: 111).

5 Unlike Darwin, Müller does not see human evolution as beginning with the beast, but with the child. In his letter to the Duke of Argyll dated 22 February 1880, Müller states that he holds "that Man was evolved, not however, from a beast, but from a child, which actually represents a stage much lower than the highest beast, but potentially a stage out of the reach of any beast" (Müller 1902b: 81).

6 Müller states in his letter to the Duke of Argyll "that if the religion of India could be brought back to that simple form which it exhibits in the *Veda*, a great reform would be achieved" but this alone will not suffice. In his view the Veda lacks "the high and pure and almost Christian morality of the Buddha" but the redeeming fact is that "as far as the popular conceptions of the deity are concerned, the Vedic religion, though childish and crude, is free from all that is so hideous in the later Hindu Pantheon" (Müller 1902a: 362). Similarly in his letter to Professor Deussen of Kiel, Müller speaks of making *Vedānta* intelligible both to Europeans and Indians (Müller 1902b: 399).

7 Although Müller regards the Veda as having nothing to do with modernity, when the modern form of communication, the microphone, was invented, he used the medium, and recited the oldest Sanskrit hymn, the *Rig-Veda*, in order to sanctify and give the Veda a ritual welcome (Müller 1902b: 48–49).

8 See Sundaram (1996).

References

Ashcroft, Bill (2001) *On Post-colonial Futures: Transformations of Colonial Culture*. London: Continuum.

Ashcroft, Bill, Gareth Griffiths and Helen Tiffin (1989) *The Empire Strikes Back: Theory and Practice in Post-colonial Literatures*. London: Routledge.

Ashcroft, Bill, Gareth Griffiths and Helen Tiffin (1998) *Key Concepts in Post-colonial Studies*. London: Routledge.

Aurobindo, Sri (1971) *The Secret of the Veda*, Vol. 10. Pondicherry: Sri Aurobindo Ashram.

Aurobindo, Sri (1984) [1915] *Swami Dayananda*. Pondicherry: All India Books.

Carman, John and Vasudha Narayanan (1989) *The Tamil Veda: Piḷḷaṉ's Interpretation of the Tiruvāymoḻi*. Chicago, IL: The University of Chicago Press.

Cohn, Bernard S. (1996) *Colonialism and Its Forms of Knowledge: The British in India*. Princeton, NJ: Princeton University Press.

Gandhi, Leela (1998) *Postcolonial Theory: A Critical Introduction*. Edinburgh: Edinburgh University Press.

King, Richard (1999) *Orientalism and Religion: Postcolonial Theory, India and "The Mystic East."* London: Routledge.

Majid, Anouar (2000) *Unveiling Traditions: Postcolonial Islam in a Polycentric World.* Durham, NC: Duke University Press.

Marshall, Peter James (1970) *The British Discovery of Hinduism in the Eighteenth Century.* Cambridge: Cambridge University Press.

McLeod, John (2000) *Beginning Postcolonialism.* Manchester: Manchester University Press.

Müller, Max F. (1868) *Chips from a German Workshop : Vol. 1. Essays on the Science of Religion.* London: Longmans, Green & Co.

Müller, Max F. (1875) *Chips from a German Workshop : Vol. 1V. Essays Chiefly on the Science of Language.* London: Longmans, Green & Co.

Müller, Max F. (1878) *Lectures on the Origin and Growth of Religion as illustrated by the Religions of India.* London: Longmans, Green & Co.

Müller, Max F. (1884) "Introduction". In Müller, Max. F (ed.), *The Sacred Books of the East,* Vol. XV. Oxford: Clarendon.

Müller, Max F. (1892) *India: What Can It Teach Us?: A Course of Lectures Delivered Before the University of Cambridge.* London: Longmans, Green & Co.

Müller, Max F.(1901) *Collected Works of Right the Hon. F. Max Müller. Last Essays: Second Series XVII: Essays on Language, Folklore and Other Subjects.* London: Longmans, Green & Co.

Müller, Max F. (1902a) *The Life and Letters of the Right Honourable Friedrich Max Müller edited by His Wife,* Vol. 1. London: Longmans, Green & Co.

Müller, Max F. (1902b) *The Life and Letters of the Right Honourable Friedrich Max Müller edited by His Wife,* vol. 11. London: Longmans, Green & Co.

Prakash, Gyan (1999) *Another Reason: Science and the Imagination of Modern India.* Princeton, NJ: Princeton University Press.

Quayson, Ato (2000) *Postcolonialism: Theory, Practice or Process?* Cambridge: Polity.

Said, Edward W. (1985) *Orientalism.* Hammondsworth: Penguin.

Sharpe, Eric J. (1985) *The Universal Gītā: Western Images of the Bhagavagīitā.* London: Duckworth.

Spurr, David (1993) *The Rhetoric of Empire: Colonial Discourse in Journalism, Travel Writing and Imperial Administration.* Durham, NC: Duke University Press.

Sugirtharajah, Sharada (2003) *Imagining Hinduism: A Postcolonial Perspective.* London: Routledge.

Sundaram, P. (ed. & Trans.) (1996) *The Azhwars: For the love of God. Selection from the Nalayira Divya Prabandham,* New Delhi: Penguin.

van der Veer, Peter (2001) *Imperial Encounters: Religion and Modernity in India and Britain.* Princeton, NJ: Princeton University Press.

Auto-immunity in the Study of Religion(s): Ontotheology, Historicism and the Theorization of Indic Phenomena

Arvind Mandair

Questioning Post-colonial Theory in Light of the "Return of Religion"

Within the modern study of religion the division between philosophy of religion and the history of religions – long regarded as a truism insofar as it reflects the distinction between universal and particular – has become increasingly blurred in recent years with the growing influence of cultural and critical theory on the humanities and social sciences. Unlike the earlier paradigmatic split between theology and anthropology (or social science methodology), cultural theory has helped not only to dismantle well worn dualisms such as religion/politics, theism/atheism, sacred/secular, but more importantly has helped to narrow the gap between academic practices and cultural practices such as religion that scholars seek to study (Davaney 2002: 140). That is to say, cultural theory has simultaneously problematized and challenged essentialist and theological tendencies (such as dreams of absolute principles, supernatural origins, ahistorical authorities, pure traditions etc.) as well as scholars' claims to methodological objectivity and impartiality, since the academy far from being a site of neutral value-free analysis, is itself thoroughly implicated in cultural realities (Davaney 2002; Taylor 1999: 13–16). Indeed in what might seen as a reversal of critical theory's atheistic roots in the "masters of suspicion" (Marx, Nietzsche, Freud) contemporary cultural theory has been adapted by scholars not only to successfully dispute the atheistic presuppositions of modern secular thinking in the social sciences, thereby revitalizing religious and theological reflection in the Christian and Judaic traditions, but, more surprisingly perhaps, it has legitimized the use of phenomena from these particular traditions as resources for critical thinking about religion per se.

By contrast, however, the effects of critical theory on the study of non-Western religions has not only been far more modest, in many cases it seems also to have had precisely the opposite effect. In the study of South Asian religions, for example, the effect of critical theory (limited mainly to the work of social scientists) seems to have reinforced the priority of the secular. In his recent work "Provincialising Europe" Dipesh Chakrabarty points out the very different interventions of critical

P. Bilimoria and A.B. Irvine (eds.), *Postcolonial Philosophy of Religion.*
© Springer Science+Business Media B.V. 2009

theory in the two traditions. Whereas in the Western intellectual traditions fundamental thinkers who are long dead and gone are treated not only as people belonging
to their own times but also as though they were our contemporaries, the thinkers and
traditions of South Asia, once unbroken and alive in their native languages, are now
matters of historical research. These traditions are treated as truly dead, as history
(Chakrabarty 2000: 6). Few if any social scientists working in the history of religions
would ever try to make the concepts of these traditions into resources for contemporary critical theory. And yet "past Western thinkers and their categories are never
quite dead for us in the same way. South Asian(ist) social scientists would argue
passionately with a Marx or a Weber without feeling any need to historicize them
or to place them in their European intellectual contexts" (Chakrabarty 2000: 5).

Extending Chakrabarty's question, despite the fact that South Asian religion have
been part of the comparative study of religions for almost two centuries, why do the
ideas and phenomena of Indic traditions not find similar contemporaneity? Why
has critical theory's intervention in the modern study of religions been limited only
to Western forms of religion? What prevents Indic phenomena from being used as
resources for conceptual thinking rather than being regarded as relics?

A familiar answer to these questions plays on the artificial relationship between
the terms 'religion' and 'South Asia'. 'Religion', the argument might go, is not a
term native to South Asian cultures. Rather 'religion' came to be ascribed to Indic
cultures through an imperial dynamic in which colonized indigenous elites collaborated with Orientalists and Christian missionaries in the search for origin and an
identifiable theological core proper to the indigenous culture (King 1999: 120). To
avoid unnecessary repetition of the "religious effects" of colonialism within the
academic study of religion (either through the uncritical acceptance of relatively
recent constructs such as Hindu-ism or Sikhism, or, through being marginalized by
the overwhelming strength of representation of the hosting Western religious traditions) these *ethnic* traditions need a certain safety mechanism to be in place. Such a
mechanism is provided on the one hand by the uncompromising secularism of the
academic environment, and on the other by consignment of ethnic religions such as
Hinduism or Sikhism to an identifiable area: 'South Asia'. As an area, South Asia
represents a geopolitical entity and a viable object of knowledge formation based
on "South Asian first principles" which can be differentiated from the "received
dualisms of Western theology, philosophy and social theory that do not seem to prevail within South Asian cosmologies and conceptual logics" (Marriott 1976). Hence
the concept of South Asian religions can be regarded as a safety zone whose secularity protects its object from the hegemonic influence of Western religions, and
as a laboratory for generating empirical data about South Asian religions under the
horizon of history. In this way much of the research and teaching in South Asian
religions manages to avoid the truly self-reflexive moment that's crucial to theory
and thereby repeats a key procedure of Orientalism.

Ironically, though, few academics have been so vocal about giving back agency
to South Asians which was taken away through the undesirable "religious effects"
of Orientalist scholarship. It is precisely this move that will be problematised in this
chapter. The thrust of my argument is that the very form of critical theory invoked

for the protection of South Asian traditions from the religious effects of colonial-ism in fact repeats the design of a past imperialism. I refer specifically to the form of post-colonial critique inspired initially by Edward Said but refracted through the recent work of leading critical Indologists, social scientists and cultural theorists all of whom utilize South Asia as an archival resource. Unlike Said, who never seriously engaged with German Indology as the most powerful source of Oriental-ism pertinent to the case of India, scholars such as Ronald Inden, Johannes Fabian, Fred Dallmayr, Tejaswini Niranjana, Gayatri Spivak, Wilhelm Halbfass and Pheng Cheah, have more accurately tracked the ideological underpinnings of colonial Indology and its appropriation by native elites back to its German origins.[1] In what seems to have become a become a more or less consistent narrative, their studies have independently gravitated around the figure of G.W. F. Hegel, and specifically Hegel's influential *Lectures on the Philosophy of History* (*LPH* Hegel 1988) as an ur-text which provides the philosophical prototype for colonial and neo-colonial representations of India.

The genius of the *LPH* texts was that while perpetuating myths of a "religion-obsessed India" and a uniquely Indian "transcendental wisdom" (Pollock 2000: 302), they kept India and Indian thinking politically and intellectually imprisoned within this very representation which is always outside history. At the same time, however, their narrative expresses the hope that once the covertly Christocentric and overtly imperialistic tendencies of the *LPH* are dismantled, it would be possible to generate not only a post-Orientalist critique of the more blatant forms of Eurocen-trism, but, following Said, a *secular* anti-imperialist critique (Ansell-Pearson 1997). Any movement beyond Orientalism must therefore go through a secular purge, the aim of which is to guard against the "return of religion" or any form of repressed religiosity in its various guises. By removing the religio-spiritual underpinnings of the *LPH* it becomes possible to conceptualize agency on behalf of subaltern groups whose rights had been usurped by the religious nationalism of neo-colonial elites. Once historicism (minus religion) safely underpins the study of South Asian cultures we have a neutral zone that distances South Asian culture from the harmful and divisive influences of colonial and neo-colonialism both of which are religious in orientation. The concepts of area and historicism thus converge in a mutually benefi-cial alliance which allows scholars to properly conceive post-colonial agency. Since the mid-1980s versions of this secular anti-imperialism have influenced discourses of modern South Asian studies both as an area specialism and in its role as an archive for the study of South Asian religions.

However, if this form of critical theory was supposed to provide a corrective to the West's continuing will-to-power, it has, through the denegation of religion in favour of historicism, simply reinstated the very Hegelianism that it set out to remove. The idea that historicism in itself can provide the proper element for think-ing about post-colonial agency crucially fails to account for several things. First, it fails to acknowledge the extent to which the conceptualization of religion and his-tory are mutually imbricated in Hegel's thought (a problem that will be more fully explored later in this paper).

Second, as Chakrabarty rightly points out, it overlooks the deep ties that bind historicism as a mode of thought to the formation of political modernity in India – a political modernity that is no less religious than it is secular. Consider for example the almost cathartic return of religion and religious traditions as legitimate and democratic vehicles for voicing cultural, political and existential concerns – indeed, in some cases as the only means for articulating life-worlds that were colonized and translated as religion, repressed by secular modernity, but which continue to simultaneously adopt and resist the aporetic space created by the translatability and untranslatability of religion. Historicist thought can only conceive of this return of religion as an inherent failure or incompleteness of the transition to capitalism and modernity that is characteristic of countries like India.

Thirdly (the contemporary rhetorics of multidisciplinarity and multicultural-ism notwithstanding) the sub-discipline of South Asian religions remains unable to respond to the effects of demographic changes on pedagogy and classrooms. Whereas in the 1960s and 1970s students, researchers and teachers were drawn largely from the host communities in Europe and North America, the discipline is populated today by increasing numbers of diasporic South Asians whose cultural affiliation is as much Western as it is Eastern. The crucial difference that this makes is that their interventions in the academy are governed by an understanding of their lifeworld which, far from being restricted to South Asian particularity, is in fact inscribed by a sense of universality imparted by the unhindered translatability of religion. Consequently there is an increasingly vocal demand from diasporic South Asians to be regarded as more than mere producers of empirical data in relation to a theoretically active West. Or for South Asian phenomena to be turned into resources for contemporary critical thought. Stated more crudely: why can the turn towards critical and cultural theory not be done using Indian religious phenomena/materials/thinking?

Notwithstanding the numerous recent exorcisms of Hegel, this paper argues for a re-examination of Hegel's texts on India and Indian religion, specifically his *Lectures on the Philosophy of Religion (LPR)*. For it is these texts rather than the more widely read *LPH*, that not only anticipate the emergence of the area studies concept or formations such as South Asian religions, but also provide the conceptual matrix which keeps these disciplines safely protected from theoretical movements in religious studies. Although post-colonial theorists such as Ronald Inden, Gayatri Spivak, and more recently Pheng Cheah have attempted to locate this conceptual matrix in Hegel's *LPH*, these texts merely reveal its outer contours. Its inner mechanism remains remarkably resistant to exposure due to a belief that underpins the very means by which these scholars seek to conceptualize the break with impe-rialism. As William Hart has convincingly shown, this belief, attributable in the first place to Karl Marx, also provides the impetus behind secular post-colonial theorizing (Hart 2000: 151). Marx neatly summarized it as follows: "the criticism of religion is the premise of all criticism". Stated otherwise, critical thinking can only begin with a displacement of religion or the religious by historicism. What secular post-colonial theory fails to acknowledge, however, is that Marx's stand-point was not only anticipated by Hegel but that it was problematized in the *LPR from the standpoint of religion*! Indeed Hegel's perpetual struggle to theorize what Chakrabarty calls the "transition to capital" revolved around the question concerning the *difference* between religion and history (Chakrabarty 2000: 46). The evidence for this can be found in the relatively neglected second part of the *LPR* (which deals with Determinate Religions) and specifically the transition from the 1824 to the 1827 *LPR* text where Hegel can be found attempting to articulate the problem of transition from universal to particular in terms of a transparent relation between religion and history, but more significantly as far as this paper is concerned, *in the context of a discussion on the proper place of India and Indology within the emerging discourse of Wissenschaft*. Though largely overlooked by the dominant narratives in the humanities, the discourse of Indology is more closely linked to the re-conceptualization of religion and history in the nineteenth century, and more importantly to the continuing disengagement between theory and Indic phenomena, than is given credit for. To properly examine this link it will therefore be necessary to question the accepted narratives of Indology and to re-situate them in relation to the co-emergence of universal and particular knowledge formations.

Indology, Race Theory and the (Re-)Conceptualization of Religion(s)

The accepted narratives concerning the rise of Indology credit figures such as Sir William Jones and his contemporaries Charles Wilkins, Nathaniel Halhed, and H.T. Colebrook with the institutionalisation of Orientalism as a "scientific" research tradition. It is often forgotten, however, that these men straddled and worked within the intellectual parameters of two major movements in European cultural thinking: the tail end of Enlightenment Deism and the birth of racial theories for classifying the human species. Thus, well before they had embarked on their Orientalist endeavours, Jones et al were already heir to a considerable body of isolated writings and accounts of India and its natives produced mainly by Jesuit missionaries such as Robert de Nobili (1577–1656) and Abraham Roger (1663), the Lutheran missionary Bartholomaus Ziegenbalg (1682–1719), the British diplomats Alexander Dow and J. Holzwell (1761–1767), and as one of the contemporary readers of Dow and Holzwell, the French *philosophe* Voltaire.[2] Their remarks are clearly influenced by the generally benign deistic outlook of the late seventeenth and early eighteenth centuries. Running like a thread through these reports is the idea that Indians, despite their fall into idolatry and superstition, once possessed a monotheistic belief in the One highest and most perfect being. Constant references to the "natural light of reason" or "basic human reason" which they felt the natives possessed, were necessary for the missionaries serving both as a bridge and as the basis for the possibility of receiving Christian revelation. As Ziegenbalg states in his main work *Genealogie der malabarischen Gotter*: "These heathens recognize from the light of nature that there is a God, a truth which they did not need the Christians to teach them" (Halbfass 48), a view that is echoed by Voltaire who took a more radical stand, professing that India is the home of religion in its oldest and purest form: "the Brahmins.... could establish religion only on the basis of universal reason." (Halbfass 57). Nevertheless, and again there is broad unanimity in this theme, the Indians had fallen from the pure religion of natural reason of which they were the first possessors, into the degenerate religion represented by the Puranic tradition: "In spite of the knowledge that there is only one single divine being, these heathens have nonetheless allowed themselves to be seduced by the devil and their ancient poets into believing in a multitude of gods..." (Halbfass 48). Thus Jones et al. inherited a long prevalent view of India which had been used to illustrate a key motif of deism, namely, the fall and decline of civilization via the eclipse of the "natural light of reason" through superstition, dogma and ritualism. Stated differently, the decay of religion from a state of pristine (Vedic) monotheism into heathen polytheism occurred by a loss of reason.

Far from challenging the inherited view of an original Indian Ur-monotheism, Jones' work in comparative linguistics, for which he is chiefly remembered, actually appeared to confirm this view. On the basis of an affinity between the verb roots of Sanskrit, Latin and Greek Jones postulated "a common ancestral origin" for these languages. From this Jones conjectured that the European and Indian races may have sprung from a common source. The question of the origins of the European peoples had been the subject of intense speculation, no more so than at academic centres such as Göttingen where, at about the same time that Jones' work was published, Blumenbach was expounding his new classification of human races. Blumenbach work was not only based partly on Linnaeus' earlier typology of natural life forms as is often thought. More importantly Blumenbach was indebted to Kant for a conceptual articulation of race in terms of teleological principles.[3] When translations of Jones' work reached a German readership, it was but a short step to link the idea of an ultimate proto-language (Indo-European) with Blumenbach's theory of an Aryan Caucasian proto-race from which are descended the Indian Brahmins as well as the modern European races. In another important paper "On the Origin and Families of Nations" Jones was able to bring this new element of linguistic precision to racial speculation, arguing that there was

> [i]ncontestable proof.... that the first race of Persians and Indians, to whom we may add the Romans and Greeks, the Goths, and the old Egyptians or Ethiops, originally spoke the same language and professed the same popular faith. (Halbfass 1988: 60–61)

It would appear that for Jones and other Orientalists of his generation, there was no real contradiction between a *religious* ideology based on monotheism and the natural light of reason, and an overtly *racial* ideology centered on the belief in pure and original stocks of languages/peoples. In other words, race, religion and the possession of reason were not only seen as compatible but each was able to justify the other. Although the existing idea of an Indian Ur-monotheism/language/race blended well with Orientalist translations of Sanskrit classics to generate the myth of an Indian Golden Age, Jones could not easily avoid the contradiction between the once glorious past of the Hindus and their present 'degenerate' and 'abased' state, except by distinguishing their "primitive religion and languages" which had not changed and which "prevail to this day with more or less their ancient purity" from their "arts" "government" and "knowledge" which have become debased. Jones' belief in an Indian Ur-monotheism and language thus came close to a version of monogenesis – the belief that humanity and therefore civilisation came from a single source – shared by philosophers such as Kant. For Kant the appeal of monogenesis lay not only in its conformity to the Biblical account of the beginnings of humanity, but that it lent itself, via the notion of universal reason, to discussions of "human fraternity" (Bernasconi 2001: 11). Somewhat ironically, therefore, the facile overlap between the concepts of race, Ur-monotheism and an Ur-sprache in the monogenetic hypothesis became, in the context of the late eighteenth century, a resource for "liberals" who needed to justify colonialism.

As is well know Jones' translations of Indian classics generated enthusiasm in England and in Germany. The academic results of this enthusiasm were the establishment of many chairs of Sanskrit and Oriental Studies, and the creation of a disciplinary base which in alliance with Germanic studies might have threatened the monopoly of Latin and Greek studies as the only ancient languages relevant to the European identity and its conceptual framework (Bernal 1987: 237–239). Although these new academic studies were based initially in Britain, it seems that before the 1820s the 'liberal' form of Orientalism inspired by William Jones was replaced by more aggressive styles of representing the nature of Indic phenomena. To mention but two: a more 'progressive' i.e. historicist frame of narrating non-Western others exemplified by James Mills' enormously influential *History of British India*. Mill's *History* and his espousal of Utilitarian ideology coincided with and reflected the new mood of economic and military expansion of British interest in India. The other being a new wave of uncompromising missionary activity led by the Serampore Baptists William Ward, Joshua Marshman and William Carey who produced new translations and more comprehensive empirical work, the most influential of which was Ward's monumental *Mythology and Religion of the Hindoos*. What needs to be noted for the purposes of our study is that although these new developments in the early nineteenth century provided a serious challenge to the prevalent Deistic notions of an original Indian monotheism and an Indian Golden Age, these developments alone were not sufficient to displace the Deist paradigm. Although it is rarely acknowledged the displacement of Deism in relation to Orientalist studies was achieved through the kind of ideological/political alliance mentioned earlier. In this case a supra-national alliance between English Utilitarian historiography and missionary translations on the one hand, and on the other, new developments in German philosophizing about the nature of religion. The ideological bridge for this alliance was a combined British–German (Protestant) opposition to monogeneticism. That is to say, an alliance between *historicism* – which supported the opposite ideal of polygeneticism or the belief in multiple and distinct origins and by implication evolution of the races of man – and *a new theory of religion*. Because this debate is reflected most powerfully by the way in that Indology was developed and reformulated within the leading German academic institutions such as Jena, Heidelberg, Göttingen, Tübingen and of course Berlin, I shall focus mostly on the German effort.

The German reshaping of Indology was articulated at the intersection of a series of intellectual debates that were occurring simultaneously during the early nineteenth century including the theorisation of religion, aesthetics and the history of philosophy. Much of this activity which was centred particularly in Germany during the 1790s around two parallel movements. First, what Bernard Reardon describes as the "intellectual rekindling of Christianity both Protestant and Catholic without parallel since high middle ages" (Perkins 1999: 357). Secondly, the growth of national consciousness motivated in particular by a need felt by leading European intellectuals to respond to a proliferating knowledge of Oriental religions and cultures particularly as this was presented through its most effective vehicle, the new discipline of Indology (Bernal 1987; Perkins 1999). As Wilhelm Halbfass notes the newly discovered Indological materials affected European understandings of philosophy, the history of philosophy and, more directly, the relationship between religion and philosophy (Halbfass 1988: 83). Indology was in its formative stage during the very period in which the history and historiography of philosophy were assuming new forms, particularly in the work of Schelling and his antipode, Hegel. Despite their common concern for rethinking the European and Christian traditions, their respective responses to the "Oriental Enlightenment" are motivated by opposing desires, which, for argument's sake, can be referred to as orientalist and occidentalist.[4] Nowhere are these opposing desires better manifested than in the battle for ideological supremacy between the respective systems of Hegel and Schelling. This battle which began in the early 1800s with Hegel's critiques of Schelling's *Identitatsphilosophie* and *Naturphilosphie* heated up considerably in the early 1820s following Hegel's arrival at the University of Berlin and the dissemination of his lecture courses on Aesthetics, History and Religion – all of which engaged in some form or other with newly available Indological materials. Schelling's defence of pantheism and his juxtaposition of Indian ideas with discussions of European philosophy and religion, had already exercised considerable influence beyond Berlin and certainly beyond the field of philosophy. Though caricatured as an Indomaniac, Schelling's engagement with India was propelled less by any love for India than by a desire to present a radically different way of perceiving Europe, a difference that is not necessarily imported from a foreign source but is already at the heart of European identity. By contrast, for Hegel, whose thinking was more in tune with the interlinked currents of nationalism and imperialism sweeping across Europe at the time, India and pantheism needed to be kept intellectually and culturally at a safe distance from the West. For Hegel knowledge of the Orient needed to be systematically ordered and controlled. The most effective way to do this was to suture any gaps present in the growing databank of knowledge about Oriental cultures, thereby keeping the possibility of any harmful influence at a safe distance. The problem was how this was to be done intellectually and in a way that removed the threat of Oriental religions and at the same time the threat of those like Schelling who colluded with such ideas. In short, the debate between Hegel and Schelling, as well as the shift in the direction of Indological research, can be traced to a change in the framework for conceptualising religion(s) which itself is redefined through the encounter with Indology, given that what was at stake in the

Occidentalist (re)defining of religion was the place and status of European identity as essentially Christian.

The Unbearable Proximity of the Orient

Perhaps the best example of this process in Hegel's *oeuvre* Part 2 of his posthumously published Berlin *Lectures on the Philosophy of Religion* (hereafter *LPR*). As well as constituting his most sustained encounter with Indian thinking, the Berlin lecture course in its published form represents a deepening of his critique and consequent philosophical estrangement from the Jena Romantics and Schelling in particular. But more importantly it represents the clearest articulation of a new form of classification based on the connection between two interconnected themes: *race/ethnicity/nation* on the one hand and *ontotheology* on the other. The former refers to a desired separation of the European/Greek/Christian group of religions from the Oriental and African groups on racial grounds. According to this racial classification non-European cultures had to be excluded from the history of philosophy and from the possibility of their ever having received a revelation in the first place. Revelation was linked to historico-spiritual evolution. Ontotheology refers to a way of thinking about determinate religions in terms of their classification within a particular order of civilisation, a process that is entirely governed by theologico-political considerations. The interconnection between these two themes is elaborated within a long discussion of the proper constitution of the first two stages of the dialectic: the stage of Primal Unity as we see it in natural or immediate religion, and the stage of Representation as seen in artistic or determinate religions, i.e. religions as they are manifested in history. For Hegel, accounting for the difference between these two stages of the dialectic will be pivotal to his classification of Oriental religions in contradistinction to Western-European religions, and thus not only to what constitutes the boundary between East and West, but also to the line separating pre-history from history, indeed to the very conception of what religion and history are.

A close reading of Hegel's key moves in this lecture course reveals three main concerns. First, the "need" to establish a firm theoretical standard for thinking about religion in general. Second, to use this standard as the basis for bringing the growing diversity of Oriental religions into some kind of manageable order. Third, by ordering them to counter the influence of Indophiles such as Schelling in whose philosophy the prevailing definition of God/religion brought the origins of Oriental and Occidental civilizations unbearably close, such that the dominant vantage point of Euro-Christian identity based on its exclusionary claims to history, reason and metaphysics, not to mention the colonial enterprise itself, would be threatened. To even suggest the possibility of coevalness between true metaphysical thinking and the type of thinking possessed by Orientals would render the very source of Western thinking as impure.[5]

The clearest articulation of Hegel's concern can be seen in the transition from the 1824 to 1827 lecture course and most noticeably in the long discussions about the proper constitution of the first two stages of the dialectic: the stage of primal unity associated with religions of nature exemplified by Oriental religions, and the stage of artistic religion exemplified by Graeco-Roman religions (Hegel 1987: 144–148). For Hegel the need to rationally account for a qualitative difference between these two stages was crucial both in order to justify a cultural boundary between India and Europe, and for any systematic classification of the religions of other nations or races. The entire argument in this section revolves around the problem of beginning. More specifically the problem of *identifying* the nature of this beginning which is also the "original condition of mankind" (Hegel 1987: 147).

Co-origination, or, the Difference Between Religion and History

The dilemma for Hegel was how to classify Indic culture *as* religion and yet keep it outside of history which properly speaking belonged to the West. There were two obstacles here. First, there was an abundance of seemingly compelling evidence relating to the antiquity of Sanskrit as the source of Indo-Aryan languages and race. Backed by the philological authority of Sir William Jones and the philosophical arguments of Schlegel and Schelling amongst others, this evidence tended to suggest that Orient and Occident shared the same origin, given which there could then be no moral justification either for the colonisation of India or for placing Indian religions outside the pale of history.

The second obstacle was more complex in that it stemmed from Hegel's attempt in Part 1 ("The Concept of Religion in General") to define "what religion is" in and through thought itself. According to this definition: "Religion is the consciousness of the true that has being in and for itself without limit and universally: this is an *elevation*, a *rising above*, a reflecting upon, a *passing over* from what is immediate, sensible" (Hegel 1987: 115–117). In other words the kind of thinking that is proper to religion had to be grounded in a principle that was not merely subjective but objective and universal. Thinking about religion had to be grounded in a *pure* movement, a *pure* transition. Pure in the sense that such movement must not leave any trace in time. It must not rely for its movement on anything outside of itself. Such movement, which is effectively the definition of transcendence, also comprises the essence of historicism, the impulse to historicise, and insofar, belongs to the West. Transcendental historicity – having history, being able to define "what history is" and yet to remain outside of history in the sense of not being affected by it – defines what it means to be Western as opposed to an Oriental.

But here was the problem. To be classifiable as religion the Indian had to have progressed from a stage where it was not-yet religion. In as much as the antiquity of Indian religion was regarded as unchallenged even by Hegel, the real problem was that the emergence of history, or the first moment of the *aufhebung*, appeared to coincide with the emergence of Indian religion. By Hegel's own definition, Indian culture insofar as it was defined as religion or religious, also showed a progression in consciousness (i.e. movement, elevation, transition) thus allowing it to be demarcated at the stage of primal unity which corresponds to the 'moment' when history begins. To his distaste Hegel was confronted by the possibility of a *coincidence* between the origination of religion in India and the origination of history. It was clearly difficult to avoid the necessity of a "first moment" of the *aufhebung*. Which is to say, however, that the essence of transition necessary for Indian religions to emerge and the essence of transition necessary for history to emerge, appeared to be the same. Moreover, both appeared to have definite origins *in time*.

This was not merely incidental to the 1824 *LPR* course. It was also an issue in his vastly more popular *LPH* course which Hegel had formulated and delivered a year earlier than the religion seminars. In one of the key chapters of the *LPH* (Hegel 1956 *passim*) tackles head on "the topic of how the origin of history is to be conceived". The problem, which he contests, is that the discovery of Sanskrit projected as an incontestable fact the idea of a bond between Germanic and Indic peoples and cultures. But for Hegel this event had to be kept outside history. Whereas the seemingly more secular *LPH* text manages to side step the issue of Indian religion's origination, the 1824 *LPR* text finds itself entangled in the issue of the *co*-origination of history and religion. Two possibilities now suggested themselves. Either, the origin is contaminated by cultural difference, in the sense that two or more cultures share the same origin, in which case the *aufhebung* is supplementary to nature (from which it follows that domination as the work of the *aufhebung*, belongs not so much to the domain of nature as it does to the domain of culture). Or, the co-existence of two different *aufhebungs*, two different essences of transition: one that corresponds to the continuum of transitions that we call history or historical knowledge, and one that corresponds to the *original transition* from nature which defines "what religion is".

Although both choices are distasteful to Hegel, the second is potentially more threatening as far as the construction of systematic knowledge is concerned. For any knowledge to count as scientific there must be *consistency* between the *continuum* of transitions that corresponds to historical knowledge of religions, and the *original* transition that corresponds to the concept of Religion. The essence of the two *aufhebungs* – concept of religion versus the history of religions – must be qualitatively consistent throughout; which of course derives from the very definition of essence as that which is unique, one, and only one. To entertain the possibility that there are different kinds of essences would mean that the concept of *aufhebung* itself is flawed. An imperfection in the *aufhebung* would not only jeopardise the basis of knowledge itself, it would bring Indian religions unbearably close to the origin of history. Yet Hegel needed to keep India as far as possible from this origin in order to protect not only the West's claim to superiority in conceptual knowledge (what we today call Eurocentrism) but also its central mechanism behind its conceptual superiority: the idea of unhindered translatability between cultures. Logically speaking, the latter simply collapses into the former. An imperfect *aufhebung* implies an imperfect origin: original *co*-existence, the original plurality of cultures. What is especially interesting about the 1824 course is that Hegel will opt for the second choice and will try to qualify the very definition of *aufhebung* rather than allow India into history. Clearly what was at stake in demarcating history and India and religion, was the conceptual purity of European identity.

Linking the Aufhebung to the Ontological Proof for God's Existence

Hegel's resolution to this problem was to implement a move originally formulated in his 1812 *Science of Logic* where the ontological proof for God's existence, with its implicit assumption of the identity of being and thinking, is made the central criterion for thinking about religion as such and the phenomenal appearance of determinate religions during the course of human history. This move allowed Hegel to think *philosophically* about religion in general and *historico-phenomenologically* (that is to say empirically) about other religion*s* and thus to classify them based on the degree to which a particular culture was capable of thinking God's existence, which in turn is measured by its distance from the ontological proof as the ultimate standard for measuring the progress of religion(s) in world history. As a result it was now possible to classify Indic phenomena under the category 'religion' (the idea of divinity was clearly there) but still keep it outside history. The Indian idea of divinity was as yet "confused", "monstrous", "terrifying", "idolatrous", "absurd", "erroneous". Clear evidence for Hegel that Hindu thinking was limited to thinking nothingness. To think nothingness was to think improperly about God's existence. History could *begin* only when a culture became capable of thinking properly about God.

What emerges in the transition to the 1827 lectures is not simply an improved system for describing other religions and therefore a precursor to the phenomeno-logical method (which remains one of the primary tools in the modern study of South Asian religions) but a specific device which prefigures the very possibility of phenomenology itself, namely an ontotheological schema – indeed Hegel's own reworking of ontotheology – which ensures the production of stereotypical versions of Hinduism. With the ontological proof providing the law for thinking about reli-gion – *God cannot not be thought, therefore God cannot be nothing or thought as nothing* – the schema consists in a prior operation of marking out a visual time-chart upon which any culture encountered by the ontological proof is automatically compared and fixed in its proper place.

This time-chart is of course the basis of the modern disciplines that we know as the history or phenomenology of religions (or the comparative study of religions) whose primary axis is drawn automatically by the Hegelian narrative itself. As Gayatri Spivak points out in her perceptive readings of Hegel on the *Srimadbhag-vadgita*, "Hegel places all of history and reality on a diagram. By reading-off the diagram the law of motion of history is made visible as the Hegelian morphology is fleshed out" (Spivak 1999: 39). Spivak rightly suggests that what we have in Hegel's narrative is not an epistemo*logy* i.e. an account of how individual subjects produce religion, but an epistemo*graphy*, a graduated diagram of how knowledge comes into being. Whereas in the West the proof of God's existence provides the ontological law for thinking about God's existence as an exclusion of the nihil, Oriental religions by comparison, i.e. by automatically reading off the epistemograph, have not sufficiently evolved to this stage of thinking. As is well known the *LPH* marks out a similar time-chart as the path of world-historical progress, where the spirit of each nation (*Volksgeist*) embodies the world spirit in a given epoch. But whereas in the *LPH* the work of ontotheology forms the subtext of Hegel's narrative, the *LPR* is a more rounded statement in which ontotheology is history and history is ontotheology. Accordingly each epoch on the graduated diagram correlates spatially to a bounded localised configuration. Each configuration is designated as a quasi-cartographical realm. Thus the spatial boundaries of a nation/culture corresponds to its level of spirituality-cum-historicity. By this logic cultures that are mired in an existence that remains bound to a particular area can only have a limited life span on the time-chart of world history. They can only exist today as static, frozen objects i.e. as *phenomena* to be known and studied by conceptually more advanced cultures. They become raw material, empirical data that can only be fully understood and retrieved by those who possess the conceptual means.

   Although it is often overlooked the ontotheological nature of the Hegelian epistemograph, mediated through the two new disciplines Philosophy of Religion and the *Religionswissenschaft* (what is now called the History of Religions) whose essential form Hegel had outlined in the *LPR*, exerted a theoretical and practical influence with important consequences for future intellectual encounters between India and Europe. Brief mention will be made of the two most relevant ones: (i) the colonial reconstitution of Indology and related to this (ii) the post-colonial reproduction of native informancy through the enunciation of re-imagined "religious traditions".

The Reconstitution of Indology

The second phase of Indological research after the 1860s focused mainly on the translation and exegesis of North Indian *bhakti* or devotional texts and traditions by a new generation of Indologists trained at institutions such as Tübingen, Göttingen and Berlin where Hegel's ideas continued to set the tone for thinking about religion long after his death. In contradistinction to the previous phase dominated by British Indologists which had found philosophy but no true religion in Hinduism, this 'post-Hegelian' generation of Indologists were now able to identify *bhakti* as the "only true religion of the Hindus" (Sharma 1986: 83; Dalmia 1996: 396–399). This important shift in perception was made possible by a new framework for thinking about religions that was at the same time *ontotheological* (allowing the Indologist access to Indian thinking about God's existence), and *phenomenological* (allowing them to introduce classificatory distinctions i.e. the correct degree of historical distance between different phenomena). An important consequence of this new standpoint was that it allowed Indologists to remain committed to a Euro-Christian standpoint given that many of them were also active missionaries, and yet claim scientific or disinterested status for their work. Consequently for the first time in Western intellectual history terms such as theism, Monotheism and Pantheism became standardized world-historical categories for classifying non-Western cultures. They became formulaic concepts imposing a logic of the stereotype into the activity of thinking about religion and religions.

Although the new distinction between pantheism and monotheism overtakes earlier traditions of distinguishing between heathens and Christians, a more important issue arises here than a merely improved procedure for classification. Given that this world-historical categorization (mono-versus pan-theism) is part of the colonial procedure for managing the multiplicity of new religions that were flooding the knowledge market – one that finds it most comprehensive expression in Hegel's various Berlin lecture courses and will only be refined in Husserl's version of phenomenology – is there not a transparent slippage from its application to religion versus religions to the concept of culture versus cultures? That is to say, isn't the *mono-* versus *pan*-theism distinction as it comes to be understood after Hegel, effectively also the basic measure of what counts *most* as culture in the multi-cultural frame despite its supposedly secular-humanist framing. If these world-historical categories are simply part and parcel of the evolution of metaphysical thinking, it brings into visibility the historico-comparative (or phenomenological) enterprise as an apparatus that has continued to protect Western secular-humanism either from a cross-fertilisation of ideas or a radical questioning of its ground, both of these possibilities being caricatured as the approach of 'Eastern' nihilism. Eric Alliez points to precisely this problem in his important work *Capital Times*. Alliez qualifies the notion that historico-comparative phenomenology as a tool for encountering non-Western cultures is a purely modern development reflecting the separation between religion and secularism. Instead, for Alliez, phenomenology must be regarded as a continuation of the tradition of distancing non-Christian otherness inaugurated by St. Augustine's treatment of time and consciousness in Book IX of the *Confessions*. As a result our modern sense of phenomenological positioning, as elaborated in the tradition of comparativism that runs from Augustine through Hegel and Husserl to Eliade, "in its most dynamic effects must be considered the ultimate process of covering over the Christian conception of the world" (Alliez 1996: 134). If Alliez is right then the positioning of cultural multiplicity can be conceptually traced to the manner in which Augustinian theology has distanced and installed its non-Christian interlocuters.

The Comparative Imaginary & the Manufacture of Native Informancy

Though rarely acknowledged the ontotheological schema exerts an oblique influence on the formation of colonial and post-colonial subjectivity. One reason for this is the prevailing dogma in the social sciences about the nature of communication between colonizer to colonized. This dogma dictates that knowledge simply 'diffuses' from colonizer to the native elites. The native elites then 'internalized' new knowledges (the ontotheological or historico-comparative schema being one example) which duly facilitated a 'dialogue' or fluent exchange of ideas between colonizer and colonized. Clearly this model of dialogue as fluent exchange between two equal ('free') minds is part of a social science ideology of historicism grounded in a hermeneutics of trust and goodwill. It is a hermeneutic that serves the purpose of (re)writing social history and, in so far, requires a subject-object or historico-comparative horizon to be already in place. Thus, in the case of colonized Indians, if a subject or agent of history is not immediately recognizable, historians can give back agency on behalf of the natives.

A more realistic model would suggest that the work of internalizing the ontotheological schema is itself a subjective technology involving a process of *co-figuration* between the cultures of the colonized (self) and colonizer (other). As a subjective technology the mechanism of co-figuration is automatically comparative, that is, the subject is concretized through an availability of terms for comparison ('history' 'religion' etc.) in which the familiar and the foreign are rendered representable (Sakai 1997: 34, 59–64). But the relation to the self cannot be determined unless the relation to the other has already been determined beforehand as an interlocutor, a witness who confirms the concretization of one's own self. Properly speaking, then, prior to any "politics of recognition" the self that is capable of responding to the figure of the West as its other, has to be figured out. As a result the ontotheological schema is also practical in that it fashions the shape of desire of those influenced by it. One is seduced into reading one's self-positioning in history as an autonomy, a standpoint from which one perceives oneself to be *equal* to others and at the same time *free* to assert the distinctness of one's identity. But this equality, freedom and perceived cultural difference is an illusion bought at the cost of conceding the very concept of reality to the phantasmatic figure of the West. In effect this concession amounts to no more than the manufacture of native-informancy through the self-imposed task of "confirming and policing the West's own boundaries in the very act of invoking, on behalf of its interlocutors, the promise of global translation of *religio*" (Derrida 1998: 29–30). It is not therefore difficult to understand why even today, Hindu/Sikh/Muslim interlocuters to the philosophy of religion continue to be seduced into acknowledging the standpoint of this discipline as the condition for the 'authentic' enunciation of their own religious identity. Yet in responding to one's ascription as Sikh/Hindu/Muslim, one runs the risk of simply reproducing oneself as a native-informant to the philosophy of religion and therefore re-enacting the colonial mirroring that was first played out in the Anglo-vernacular mission schools in mid-nineteenth century India. But if, as Derrida incessantly reminds us, one must still respond, the question then becomes *how* to respond? How is one to respond *critically* to a discipline whose self-constitution is based on a fundamental repression of otherness?

Reading Comparativism in the Study of Religion(s) as a Spectrology of "the West"

My reasons for linking the representation of Indic religious phenomena to the continuing influence of Hegel should now be clearer. What alarmed Occidentalists such as Hegel in the early nineteenth century was a discovery which threatened to undermine the configuration of positions that legitimates "Western man's" claim to be historically different from "the Rest". Moreover, this threat continues to surface in the production of knowledge and in the pedagogical strategies deployed to represent Indic phenomena in the two main divisions of religious studies: the philosophy of religion (PR) and the history of religions (HR) (of which South Asian religions is a specialist sub-field). The division between HR and PR corresponds respectively to the classical pedagogical analogues *humanitas* and *anthropos*. As the evolution of these analogues suggests, the former refers to those who engage in knowledge production about religion through a self-reflective knowing that tries to set the conditions of knowing thereby transforming both the constitution of the object/phenomenon and the subjective conditions of knowing. The latter refers to those who participate primarily as suppliers of raw data or factual knowledge. As Naoki Sakai convincingly argues, however, the *humanitas/anthropos* distinction goes further than epistemic transactions. It also implies a distinction between two types of humanity. Humanity in the sense of *humanitas* has come to designate Western or European humanity to be distinguished from the rest of humanity as long as we insist on the "historical difference" of "the West" (Naoki 2001: 75). Indeed, humanity in the sense of *humanitas* authorizes the very distinction of the West from what Stuart Hall calls "the Rest", or, as Dipesh Chakrabarty refers to it, the West's sense of historical difference from the Indic. However, the West's sense of "historical difference" is itself anything but historical. As I have argued above, this sense of "historical difference" represses the historical. It is a manifestation of the putative unity of the West which is not in time. Thus while it imposes historical difference in relation to others, it escapes or transcends the temporal by defining the very sense of transition or movement, since time is of course nothing but movement. It is therefore a denial of the possibility that Western and Indic phenomena can co-exist *in time*.

It follows, then, that the historicism proper to the West's sense of "historical difference" is theological in nature. It is a transcendental historicity that remains operative in both PR and HR. This is certainly the case in the PR which not only asserts the historical difference between Western and Eastern religions more strongly, but in doing so inadvertently eradicates the challenge of diversity – perhaps the very challenge that inaugurated PR as a discipline – through self-inoculation. Surprisingly, though, HR – the very discipline which supposedly combats theology to allow religious and cultural diversity to be manifested – in reality suppresses diversity more insidiously than PR and theology.

As I have shown above, the historicist and secular (impartiality) claims of HR can only operate on the basis that the theological nature of the Indic phenomenon is determined in advance. This resonates with Tomoko Masuzawa's claim that the "origin-logic" operative in the modern study of religions is typified by the kind of HR programs conceived by Mircea Eliade (Masuzawa 1994: 166–169). Indeed it can be shown that Hegel's task of determining a particular religion's elevation (*aufhebung*) is repeated Eliade's project of illuminating the "genius" or "religious creativity" that can be ascribed to Indians and Indic phenomena. Indians are historical and creative but without being conscious of it. The Indic phenomenon thus continues to be conceptualized as remaining in dreamtime, a primitive, non-modern phenomenon in danger of becoming extinct, but which can be saved from total extinction by the safe haven provided by the HR. Clearly, the HR scholar's prerogative of knowing the elevation/creativity of the Indic phenomenon depends on his ability to simultaneously access its origin and to be able to distance himself from this quest. To paraphrase Masuzawa, the historian of religion imputes an irrepressible desire for origins to all religions and religious peoples yet *at the same time* absolves himself from the effects of this desire by saying that the question of origin is of no concern for the HR, because this discipline has progressed beyond it Hegelian beginnings to the realization that it is impossible to reach the origin of religion (Masuzawa 1994: 14). It is not a problem for the HR. Yet in the same breath this very discipline legitimizes the quest for origins on the basis that every religion must by definition have an origin from which it was first elevated, and that the retrieval of this origin is of ultimate concern for some other people but not for "us". In other words, the HR scholar must be an expert at disavowing the possibility of co-existence, of the co-origination of such phenomena with modernity. In short, the oft-repeated difference between HR and PR is both over-determined and misleading. They are in fact two sides of the same coin, driven by a logic of self-innoculation.

In light of the forgoing argument it is helpful to rephrase my earlier question (Is it be possible to theorize religion using Indic phenomena?) in the following ways: Can the subject of South Asian religions, normally regarded as a particular, be regarded as something that actively shares in the universal? Can we consider South Asian religious phenomena sharable with the rest of humanity? My excavation of the history of this problem has shown that these questions are moot given that the Indic and European bodies have *historically* shared and partaken of the universal specifically in that encounter which led to the construction of the comparative imaginary. What forces us to separate the Indic and the Western in terms of particular and universal is the act of disavowing the memory of this encounter. Perhaps what's needed then are ways of halting the compulsion to repeat this disavowal, though such a move is far from discarding the comparative enterprise. Rather it calls attention to new ways of theorizing the comparative enterprise that go beyond the ontotheological schema which not only frames the "historical difference" of "the West", but also continues to underpin the way in which disciplines such as PR and HR relate to Indic phenomena. Naoki Sakai is justified in calling for a new form of comparative cultural theory which would redefine the economy of the humanistic disciplines. The economy he has in mind would not be driven either by the logic of "co-figuration" (Kant) or by the logic of "historical difference" (Hegel).[6] Though unaware of its implications for the study of religion(s), what Sakai hints at is "a form of theorizing that is attentive to the trans-cultural dissemination of global traces with theoretical knowledge produced in geo-politically specific locations and which explores how theories are themselves transformed by their practical effects when they are performed in other sites" (Sakai 2001: 91).

Notes

1 See for example: Ronald Inden: "Orientalist Constructions of India", *Modern Asian Studies* 20.3, 1986, pp. 401–446; Johannes Fabian; Tejaswini Niranjan: *Siting Translation: History, Post-structuralism and the Colinal Context*, California University Press, 1992 (chapter I); Gayatri Spivak: *A Critique of Post-colonial Reason: Towards a History of the Vanishing Present*, Chapter I, Harvard University Press, 1999; Wilhem Halbfass*: India an Europe: An Essay in Philosophical Understanding*, Motilal Banarsidas, New Delhi, 1988 (pp. 84–100); Fred Dallmayr: *Beyond Orientalism: Essays in Cross-Cultural Encounter*, Princeton University Press, 1996, (pp. 84–97); Pheng Cheah: "Universal Areas: Asian Studies in a World in Motion" in *Traces 1: A Multilingual Journal of Cultural Theory and Practice*, pp. 37–70. Pheng Cheah's essay, while neither on the subject of Indology nor religion, nevertheless targets Hegel's *LPH* texts in a very illuminating critique that has a great deal of resonance with this paper.
2 Wilhelm Halbfass, *India and Europe: An Essay in Philosophical Understanding*, (Indian Edition: Motilal Banarsidas, Delhi, 1990), pp. 36–54.
3 See Bernasconi, Race.
4 I am aware that Orientalists were not necessarily Indophiles. Rather this distinction is only meant to highlight the opposing tendencies within European thought itself.
5 For a more detailed argument see my *Religion, Language and Subjectivity: Translating Cultures Between East and West*, Manchester University Press (forthcoming).
6 In a sense both "co-figuration" and "historical difference" can be seen as rivalrous modes of comparison (not dissimilar in its effects to the politics of recognition) organized by an assumed belief in the symmetry and equivalence between autonomous entities and therefore regulated by the putative unity of "the West".

References

Alliez, Eric. 1996. *Capital Times: Tales from the Conquest of Time*, translated by G. Van Den Abbeele. Minneapolis, MN: University of Minnesota Press.
Ansell-Pearson, Keith (ed.). 1997. *Edward Said and the Gravity of History: Cultural Readings of Imperialism*. London: Lawrence & Wishart.
Bernal, Martin. 1987. *Black Athena: The Afroasiatic Roots of Classical Civilization* (Vol. 1). London: Vintage.
Bernasconi, Robert (ed.). 2001. *Race*. Oxford: Blackwell.
Chakrabarty, Dipesh. 2000. *Provincializing Europe: Post-colonial Thought and Historical Difference*. Princeton, NJ/Oxford: Princeton University Press.
Dalmia, Vasudha. 1996. *The Nationalisation of Hindu Traditions: Bharatendu Harischandra and Nineteenth Century Banaras*. New Delhi: Oxford University Press.
Davaney, Sheila Greeve. 2002. Rethinking Theology and Religious Studies. *Religious Studies, Theology and the University: Conflicting Maps, Changing Terrains*, edited by L. Cady and D. Brown. Albany: State University of New York Press.
Derrida, Jacques. 1998. *Religion*. Cambridge: Polity.

Halbfass, Wilhelm. 1988. *India and Europe: An Essay in Philosophical Understanding*. New Delhi: Motilal Banarsidas.

Hart, William. 2000. *Edward Said and the Religious Effects of Culture*. Cambridge: Cambridge University Press.

Hegel, George Wilhelm Friedrich. 1956. *The Philosophy of History*, translated by J. Sibree. New York: Dover. (*LPH*)

Hegel, George Wilhelm Friedrich. 1987. *Lectures on the Philosophy of Religion. Vol. 3: Determinate Religion*, translated by R.F. Brown, P.C. Hodgson and J.M. Steward. Los Angeles, CA: University of California Press. (*LPR*)

Hegel, George Wilhelm Friedrich. 1988. *Introduction to the Philosophy of History*, translated by L. Rauch. Indianapolis, IN: Hackett.

King, Richard. 1999. *Orientalism and Religion: Post-colonial Theory, India and the Mystic East*. London/New York: Routledge.

Marriott, McKimm. 1976. Interpreting Indian Society: A Monistic Alternative to Dumont's Dualism. *Journal of Asian Studies* 36:89–95.

Masuzawa, Tomoko. 1994. *In Search of Dreamtime: The Quest for the Origin of Religion*. Chicago, IL/London: University of Chicago Press.

Perkins, Mary Anne. 1999. *Nation and Word: Religious and Metaphysical Language in European National Consciousness*. Aldershot: Ashgate.

Pollock, Sheldon. 2000. Indology, Power and the Case of Germany. *Orientalism: A Reader*, edited by A.L. Macfie. Edinburgh: Edinburgh University Press.

Sakai, Naoki. 1997. *Translation and Subjectivity: On Japan and Cultural Nationalism*. Minneapolis, MN: Minnesota University Press.

Sakai, Naoki. 2001. "Dislocation of the West and the Status of the Humanities." *Traces: A Multilingual Journal of Cultural Theory and Translation* 1:71–94.

Sharma, Krishna. 1986. *Bhakti and the Bhakti Movement*. New Delhi: Motilal Banarsidas.

Spivak, Gayatri Chakravorty. 1999. *The Critique of Post-colonial Reason: Toward a History of the Vanishing Present*. Cambridge, MA: Harvard University Press.

Taylor, Mark C (ed.). 1999. *Critical Terms for Religious Studies*. Chicago, IL/London: Chicago University Press.

Part III
"America"

The Meaning and Function of Religion in an Imperial World

Nelson Maldonado-Torres

Again, a son's condition is most perfect when the son, as far as his nature allows, reproduces the perfection of the father. Mankind is the son of the heavens, which is perfect in all its works... Therefore mankind's condition is most perfect when it reproduces the perfection of the heavens, so far as human nature allows. And just as the heavens are governed and directed in every movement by a single mover, which is God... so, if our argument has been correct, mankind is at its best when all its movements and intentions are governed by one Prince as its sole mover and with one law for its direction.

Hence it is obvious that the world's well-being demands a Monarch or single government known as the Empire.

Dante Alighieri, *The Monarch*

Abstract It is fairly evident today that the modern Western theory of religion has been intimately connected with the critique or defense of Christianity in a context imperialism and increased secularism. Most analyses have focused on the tensions between Christianity and secular ideas, while a critique of the workings of the theory of religion in relation to imperialism has been more recent. This essay contributes to these more recent efforts by offering a Fanonian sociogenic analysis of religion in an imperial world. It brings out the necessity to consider intersubjectivity and spatiality as relevant coordinates to study religion and the theory of religion in the West. The analysis is grounded on Frantz Fanon's critique of ontology and his descriptions of the imperial/colonial context, in critical dialogue with the work of L. Feuerbach, GWF Hegel, and F. Nietzsche. A Fanonian approach insists on the centrality of intersubjective relations and dynamics of power that can only be understood by illuminating the constitutive role of spatial relations among regions and subjects that conform the modern world.

Things take precise forms and meanings according to their order and position. If the human and social sciences are so complicated, it is precisely because they do not deal only with things, but also with a multidimensional order of things that allows each one of its elements to get the most varied meanings and functions. Things appear to us, but, as Husserl notes, only from certain angles and shades. Meanings of a thing may remain hidden and only appear as we struggle with our position or locus of enunciation. Then, sometimes, we begin to see new unforeseeable dimensions

P. Bilimoria and A.B. Irvine (eds.), *Postcolonial Philosophy of Religion.*
© Springer Science+Business Media B.V. 2009

of the thing and the order to which it belongs. This paper is an attempt to reveal certain aspects of the meaning of theistic religion in the "order of things" known as Empire.[1] With Empire, I do not refer solely to historical expressions of imperialism, but, more exactly, to an Imperial order of things linked to modalities of human existence and to intersubjective relations inserted in processes of recognition that give rise and sustain a fundamental condition of lordship and bondage.[2] This perspective has not found much attention in the field of the study of religion, particularly in the theory of religion. I attempt here also to articulate reasons and reveal methodological limitations that animate or foment this remarkable *forgetfulness* of the question of Empire.

This essay has two parts: the first is an attempt to elucidate the religion of Empire with reference to the work of Ludwig Feuerbach and Frantz Fanon; the second deals with the dismissal of imperiality in Western critiques of religion. Nietzsche's ideas about asceticism and his discourse about the "death of God" are central in the discussion. A form of critical reflection aware of the significance of intersubjective relations to the formation of subjectivity and human reality (viz. Feuerbach), as well as the integration of spatiality as a coordinate of reflection in critical discourses (viz. Nietzsche, Feuerbach, and Hegel) are called for as necessary components of a theory of religion that aims to reveal the traces of Empire in our varied and multiple religious expressions.

The Religion of Empire and the Unmasking of Imperial Man

Ludwig Feuerbach's approach to the study and critique of religion occupies a prominent place not only in the history of the philosophy and theory of religion, but also in the formative process of critical perspectives that dominated the arena during the twentieth century. His theory of religion is today considered, however, much as a historical artifact, a rather simplistic view undoubtedly overcome by the many sophisticated analyses pursued by what is today known as 'Religious Studies.' I suspect, in contrast, that this field still shares fundamental philosophical presuppositions with Feuerbach, and that we have not considered carefully the ways in which Feuerbach's work gives rise to tensions that may lead us to develop more complicated accounts of religion. I will attempt here to show the relevance of the problem of Empire and imperialism for the study of religion through a Fanonian critique of Feuerbach and Hegel. Such a critique begins with an elucidation of Feuerbach's work.

The Overcoming of Spirit and Man

Van A. Harvey claims that Feuerbach's theory of religion underwent significant changes in the writings after *The Essence of Christianity*. Harvey finds in Feuerbach's later works a turn away from the logic of Hegelian Spirit, to a more materialistically oriented philosophy that recognizes the ultimate tension between two poles: subjectivity and Nature. There are antecedents of this in the *Essence*, where Feuerbach suggests that the awareness of the otherness of nature and the world is predicated on a previous contact with "a sensuously perceived Thou" (see Harvey 1995: 36). As Feuerbach puts it, "[t]he first object of man is man. The sense of Nature... is a later product" (quoted in Harvey 1995: 36). From these passages Harvey highlights the emphasis on embodiment implicit in the I-Thou encounter, and the strong idea of Nature. Yet these crucial ideas only appear scattered throughout the *Essence*, still subordinated to the theme of (infinite) consciousness. For Harvey, this represents no less than a failure, leading Feuerbach to revert to the Hegelian concern with consciousness and falling short of the implications of his own materialist turn (see p. 37). So Harvey turns to praise the late Feuerbach for his uncovering of two fundamental and irreducible poles of experience in relation to which dependence, egoism, the drive to happiness, and other basic modes of intersubjective relations and religious attitudes will be explained.

This move has some advantages over the typical idealistic Hegelian strategy, but I will not repeat here what Harvey articulates so eloquently in his text. What is interesting for me is that, in attempting to overcome the limits of the Hegelian paradigm of consciousness, Feuerbach and Harvey concentrate on the traditional bipolarity of Man and Nature, and do not develop the more interesting and innovative view, advanced in the *Essence*, that the sense of Nature is mediated by the intersubjective relation of man and man. This idea is, indeed, treated by Hegel in the *Phenomenology* under the rubric of the dialectic of lordship and bondage. It therefore seems that Feuerbach's more radical turn away from the Hegelian paradigm of consciousness in his later writings led him to an equal dismissal of the centrality and radicality of intersubjectivity in the achievement of recognition.[3] His conception of the exteriority of nature as a "pole" of experience precisely seems to acquire strength only at the expense of a proper consideration of the constitutive force of intersubjective struggles for recognition. Feuerbach's overcoming of Hegel's philosophy of Spirit appears thus only as relative, since his reliance on general conceptions of Man and Nature clearly reflect the presence of a rather strong idealistic vein.[4] He would certainly have developed a more complicated view if he had considered seriously the Hegelian arguments for the idea that a direct relation with objects does not provide an adequate basis for recognition.[5] By ignoring this and other related points Feuerbach's theory fails to give adequate expression to one of the more fundamental Hegelian insights, that the subject itself, and not only a projected God, is traversed and constituted by intersubjective forces. We, therefore, have to be careful with Harvey's celebration of Feuerbach's refashioning of his theory. By privileging the binary I/Non-I, it simply becomes impossible for Feuerbach to uncover the significance of imperial modes of relations, let alone consider the ways in which the projection of God may be motivated by interests of recognition that appear in intersubjective contexts defined by relations of lordship and bondage. It is true that Hegel's philosophy of Spirit also falls short of exploring the extent to which imperial and colonial relations determine the meaning and function of the projected God. This, however, is to be expected since, on the one hand, Hegel does not share a projectionist conception of religion, and second, since his account of the struggle for recognition is subsumed into the dialectical trajectory of Spirit. But this is precisely why Feuerbach's departure from Hegel and his conception of the primacy of the I-Thou encounter in the *Essence* are so significant. They bring out the possibility to approach the question over the meaning and function of religion from the perspective of the struggle for recognition.

A similar, yet, I would argue, more consistent challenge to Hegel's ontological approach is found in the work of the prominent Martiniquean radical intellectual, Frantz Fanon. In his beautifully written and insightful *Black Skin, White Masks* he writes:

> As long as the black man is among his own, he will have no occasion, except in minor internal conflicts, to experience his being through others. There is of course the moment of "being for others," of which Hegel speaks, but *every ontology is made unattainable in a colonized and civilized society*. It would seem that this fact has not been given sufficient attention by those who have discussed the question. In the *Weltanschauung* of a colonized people there is an impurity, a flaw that outlaws any ontological explanation. Someone may object that this is the case with every individual, but such an objection merely conceals a basic problem. Ontology – once it is finally admitted as leaving existence by the wayside – does not permit us to understand the being of the black man. For not only must the black man be black; he must be black in relation to the white man. (1967a: 110, italics mine)

In contexts dominated by colonial relations of power, Fanon asserts, blackness becomes a relational term that represents an area of exclusion from the reign of humanity. Blackness comes to represent something like the anti-thesis of being, or, using Heideggerian parlance, the veritable house of *non*-being. Ontology, the 'science of being,' thus finds limits in this context. It is significant to note that Fanon defines this context not only as colonial, but also as civilized, as if for him civilization were also mounted on relations of subordination that would make ontology untenable – as if civilization itself had imperial dimensions. This idea would make his argument take more general forms than often thought about, becoming at the same time, a general critique of ontology and a theory about the constitution of the most cherished ideals of sociality predicated by Western Man.

The Fanonian critique of ontology gives expression to a most fascinating reversal: while for Hegel the dialectic of master and slave becomes a moment in the development of Spirit and cannot be properly understood without reference to it, for Fanon, it is precisely the existence of relations of subordination akin to this dialectic that makes reference to Spirit and subordination to its logic inadequate. For Fanon, the concrete existence of the master/slave relation transforms the structures of Being and meaning to such an extent that ontology does not make any sense if it does not change its tune and turn to the description of "lived-existence" – rather than insisting on portraying and revealing the meaning and destiny of Spirit.[6] Non-existential ontology appears in this light not only inadequate to spell out the specificities of imperial, colonial, and civilized contexts, but also extremely conservative, if not even oppressive, as it, in its blindness, would tend to mask, hide, or reduce the significance of the existential tensions and the power relations that operate in Empire and in contexts with imperial traces. It is for this reason that, for Fanon, beyond a "science of being" we must engage in a science of the relations between being and non-being, describing how the exclusion from being is performed and how non-being is lived or experienced.[7]

Fanon's critique of ontology is motivated by the particular existential expressions found in contexts where the I-Thou relation appears rather as a relation between a master and a slave. For him, reference to Man or to Spirit would only tend to erase the significance of this intersubjective constitution of subjectivity. Fanon clearly follows the road not taken by Feuerbach, thus offering a new context wherein to pursue the question of the meaning and structure of religion. And since, as Fanon makes clear, the paradigmatic geo-political expression of the intersubjective struggle of lordship and bondage is found in imperialism and colonialism, this analysis takes the form of an inquiry into the meaning and structure of religion in an Imperial World.

God and the Self-recognition of Imperial Man

The existential-phenomenological examination of colonialism pursued by Frantz Fanon in *Black Skin* demonstrates how the perverse vertical distance between subjects characteristic of slavery finds new grounds and levels of expression in the colonial relation. For the colonized, Fanon writes, the colonizer "is not only The Other but also the master" (p. 138). Imperialism appears in Fanon's writings as the institutional and geopolitical re-inscription of the master/slave relation. Empire becomes the world of the master, and the colonial territory the world of the slave. Two distinct spaces, two worlds apart, yet, deeply connected by relations of subjection and forced submission.[8] This condition gives rise to unique existential and semiotic forms which Fanon will tirelessly attempt to make explicit. This project makes a confrontation with Hegel inevitable.

As we have seen, Fanon argues that in imperialism one finds forms of bondage with existential dimensions that cannot be spelled out in relation to the Hegelian dialectic of master and slave. In a footnote to *Black Skin* Fanon writes:

I hope I have shown that here the master differs basically from the master described by Hegel. For Hegel there is reciprocity; here the master laughs at the consciousness of the slave. What he wants from the slave is not recognition but work.

In the same way, the slave here is in no way identifiable with the slave who loses himself in the object and finds in his work the source of his liberation.

The Negro wants to be like the master.

Therefore he is less independent than the Hegelian slave.

In Hegel the slave turns away from the master and turns toward the object.

Here the slave turns toward the master and abandons the object. (pp. 220–221)

In contexts defined by Empire and colonialism, Fanon argues, the relation between lordship and bondage becomes unusually complicated. In an Imperial World, lordship is the position of a privileged self that does not even turn towards the slave to achieve recognition. The reason for this is that in this context the slave does not function or is recognized as an Other. The colonized loses all ontological weight in the eyes of the colonizer. On the other hand, the colonized or colonial sub-alter,[9] Fanon adds, does not turn to the Thing or transform fear into work, but only desires to be like the master.[10]

The drama with which we began the explorations with Feuerbach and Hegel has been now seriously complicated. In the light of the Fanonian critique of Hegel, the limitations of Feuerbach's work relate not only to the absence of a proper thematization of the intersubjective constitution of subjectivity, but also to the indifference to concrete modes of subjection that shape human subjectivity and generate certain kinds of experiences.[11] With this combined intersubjective and existential turn we must now consider the question of religion and God. This question is particularly important since it throws some light on a problem that emerges with Fanon's account of the colonial instantiation of the relation between lordship and bondage. If the master/slave dialectic is not overcome by other forms of Spirit, but remains as a constant explicative factor of human relations defined by the experience of imperialism and colonialism, then we must ask how is it that the master, who in the colonial relation does not look for recognition from the slave, achieves recognition and sustains his position as master. How is it that the master can occupy and sustain his role as privileged self without his being recognized by an other? I suggest that in an Imperial World God becomes the privileged Other who recognizes the master as master and thus helps to sustain the imperial order of things.

The idea that God plays a fundamental role in the self-recognition of Imperial Man finds support in Feuerbach's own writings, since for him the projection of God is tied to the satisfaction of desires for recognition. But recognition for Feuerbach primarily takes place, as we have seen, in the interactions between I and Non-I, while I see it rather, along with Fanon, in contexts defined by historical and structural forms of subjection. The most direct and significant consequence of this turn is that God can no longer be seen as a projection of Human Subjectivity stimulated by feelings of dependence in relation to Nature, but rather as a projection of either master or slave in relation to the continuity or rupture with a context that sustains the division between lordship and bondage, that is, of Empire. This means that the projection of God does not work so much in function of the pacification of Nature, but in terms of the tensions brought up by Empire. To give analytical primacy to the relations between an over-encompassing and impersonal objective pole and an equally indeterminate subjective pole, would mean in this context to render obscure the strength of intersubjective relations of power in the constitution of whatever is taken as Man or Nature. From Feuerbach's perspective also follows the idea of a Religion that arises out of Man's intrinsic subjective tensions and dealings with Nature. This perspective does not offer the necessary resources to make explicit the role of religion in an imperial context. For it simply ignores that religion is politically charged with the most varied meanings, and that conceptions of God become no less than a whole field of political tensions. In an imperial context one never finds God, but the God of the master or the God of the slave. Usually the slave has no other possibility than to turn to the religion of the master, since the master has wiped out or at least strongly devalued the religions of the slave.[12] Then we find a God with two faces. God becomes a site of contestation, the field of an incessant ontological struggle. Monotheism takes the form of Manicheism as the Imperial World becomes a quasi-cosmological context divided by the ontological principles of darkness and light.[13]

In an Imperial context the dominant God is the God of the master. The very existence of Empire is proof of this. In Empire, God becomes the privileged Other who alone can provide authentic recognition to the Imperial Self. The continued existence of this Self testifies to the dominance of this God. God and Man become immediate proofs of the existence of each other. Their existence takes a tautological form. In no other context is the assertion that Man is made in the image of God more literal than in an Imperial World. And the reason for this is clear: in an Imperial World the idea of God is strongly overdetermined as it ceases to make exclusive reference to the divine as such, and begins to function as the projection of Imperial Man. As Feuerbach would put it, it is not that God makes Man to his likeness, but that Man projects God out of his desire for recognition. This reversal has a clear consequence, that the otherness of God is extremely qualified in this context. God becomes the Other who is still part of the Same. God, as the projection of Imperial Man, becomes not so much an Other as an Alter-Ego. God is Master like the master. And, in fact, only a master can provide authentic recognition to another master. The *difference* implicit in the Monotheistic conception of God as the wholly-Other, to what I refer as the trans-ontological difference, is violated and God becomes a most fundamental element in the sustenance of Empire. This is only a first step in the general transmutation of meaning that the order of things undergoes in an Imperial context.

The violation of the difference between God and Man is one side of a more complicated and terrifying violation. This becomes more clear once we consider that in the act of projection there are two simultaneous processes: on the one hand, God takes the shape of Man, while on the other, Man takes God-like features. In short, Imperial Man takes the shape of God. But the reduction of the difference between God and Man is now reversed and augmented to such an extent that Imperial Man is taken to be qualitatively superior to other human beings. The subjugation of the slave rather than the alienation of Man becomes the first evidential and experiential element of the projection. A logic of sub-alteration is contained in the process of recognition of Imperial Man. God recognizes Man, Man takes the shape of God, and then others come to be *seen* as the very incarnation of Evil.[14] This logic does not respond so much to interests in the conciliation with Nature, as, more fundamentally, to interests in the subordination of other human beings. Imperial Man is no pagan. He does not divinize nature, but rather becomes himself God so as to enslave others. Idolatry becomes egolatry, a perverse egolatry that works in function of the rejection of otherness. At the end, narcissism becomes homicidal, and the "Thou shall not kill" is transformed into a project of identity based on the principle "I kill, therefore I am."[15]

The proper recognition of lordship is achieved, or so I have argued, through a double violation of alterity. The interrelation of such violations is clear since the reduction of the alterity of God represents only a step in a project that culminates in obscuring and transgressing the meaning of human alterity, making it part of the homicidal logic of sub-alterity. Thus, in Empire, the phenomenological features of divinity are complicit with the degradation of peoples to a sub-human level. The projection of God is only part of a more general project that intends the collapse of the world of alterity into the world of sameness and the subjugation of otherness. In this kind of world the space between subjects is altered, leaving no space to authentic communication, ethical interaction, and dialogue, but only to imposition and domination.[16] The one under the sight and control of Imperial Man is forced to live in conditions where his worth augments in direct relation to his self-evisceration, that is, to the devaluation of his own body, identity, and culture. Assimilation becomes an intended reality of the structure. Since Imperial Man structurally and semiotically functions as God, the holy call to imitate God becomes an explicit act of violation. Conversion is clearly crucial to this obscure logic of identity, though it takes unique forms. The colonial logic of conversion is designed to make the colonized fail, since he will never be recognized as Lord.[17] Race plays a crucial role here, as the exteriority of the skin becomes the most basic medium through which the perverse difference of sub-alterity is raised and sustained. Through the body and skin the colonized is maintained *in her and his place*.[18] As a result, the body is lived by the colonized not only as a prison, but as an inescapable sign of murder. The codification of the skin by Imperial Man becomes much like the opposite of the biblical tale, it is a mark that signals the place where the homicidal plagues of Empire must fall.

Empire appears in this light as a project that aims at the systematic eradication of difference and otherness through annihilation or assimilation. The world of Empire is the world of Sameness and its structure takes the form of Totality. Imperial Man claims rights of ownership everywhere. His cosmopolitanism works in function of his power. That is, the whole world becomes his habitat as his rights are said to inhere in things. Being is thus coextensive with him. Wherever *there is* (*il y a*) he is, so Imperial Man cannot escape being.[19] Imperial Man is *present* everywhere, and *presence* becomes his more characteristic ontological and temporal condition. The future, as the irruption of the new, is kept from challenging the present and it becomes, as it were, only the emanation of the present. Fanon alludes to this when he points out that Empire represents "a motionless movement where gradually dialectic is changing into the logic of equilibrium" (1991: 314).

The link between *presence* and the *present* points to a fundamental relation between spatiality and temporality. As Lévinas has argued, "maintenant" (*now*) is precisely "main-tenant" (*having at hand*) – (1983: 112). The logic of possession defines a mode of temporality that aims to take the shape of the always present.[20] The "hand that takes" traverses the distance of space and brings the "thing" into its presence. Empire represents in many ways the highest exponential expression of this modality at the concrete historical level. Empire is the organized attempt to take the logic of possession to its most consistent level, making Imperial Man Omnipresent by making the whole world, including other human beings living in it, a field of ever possible explorations and acts of possession.[21] Imperial Man invests its time in acts of classification and division of space and human beings.[22] The interest in preserving the temporality of the present takes sadistic dimensions: one must classify and maintain distant those who fundamentally one would like to see – *annihilated*. The temporality of the present finds its climax and most consistent expression in homicide, torture, and genocide.[23] Temporality is then radically altered by the mutation of human space into inhuman space – communication is the mode of the first, homicide the mode of the second. Spatiality interrupts the flow of time as it enters into the logic of segregation. The segregation of people into different spaces may be seen as either the continuation or the refutation of Babel. After Imperial Man reaches the pinnacles of divinity he creates a distance between himself and others similar to that found between himself and God. Having learned how to transgress the divine space, however, Imperial Man creates a space much more insurmountable and difficult to conquer.[24] Spatiality and temporality, therefore, take precise meanings in Empire. They both are inserted in an order of things that works in function of a process of recognition that ends up sub-alterizing a group of human beings while ascribing divine features to others.

The sustenance of Empire and the recognition of Imperial Man demand a quasi-ontological transformation of the world. The notion of God is crucial to understand Empire not only because God is necessary to provide recognition to Imperial Man, but more significantly, because Empire itself may be taken as Man's most consistent attempt to be God. Structurally, Imperial Man functions like God in an Imperial World.[25] His lived experience, shaped by an imperial process of recognition, also takes theological dimensions. The Sartrean idea that Man fundamentally desires to be God clearly takes literal connotations in an Imperial World. Imperial Man represents perhaps the most successful attempt in this direction, a subject whose desire to be God outweighs the desire to be recognized as human. The desire to be superior to Others and to dominate them appears thus to be a motivating factor of the projection of God by Imperial Man. Indeed, God and the bondsman are the two poles by virtue of which the master constructs the edifice, both at the imaginary and at the concrete level, that will allow him to give to his existence the shape of the necessary and all-important. Imperial Man wants to become necessary Man, a man whose existence is ontologically justified. The divine, the social, and the realm of things cannot but testify to the necessity of his being. Empire is this order of things whereby Man is elevated to the status of God.

The notion of the desire to be God brings a paradoxical element in view: while the master wants to be God he still needs God as an Other who can recognize him as master. This means that, at least under the basic initial conditions of recognition, the master can never truly occupy the position of God. This tension clarifies much of what is behind traditional critiques of religion, a critique that most often than not begins and finishes without questioning Empire and its God. My suspicion is that while atheism and discourses on the "death of God" may be effective against certain trends of religious beliefs and, indeed, open new venues towards more humane modes of valuation, the transparency of Empire and of imperial modes of relations and existential postures posit a limit to the radical critical component and to the humanistic dimension of these theories. I will discuss this in reference to the philosophy of Friedrich Nietzsche.

Towards a Post-Imperial Critique of the Critique of Religion

Nihilism, asceticism, and the "death of God" are perhaps the most central ideas of Nietzsche's philosophy. For Nietzsche, the import of these ideas makes it impossible to subordinate them under the impressive forms of any speculative system. While for Hegel the two attitudinal positions of asceticism and nihilism express partial and one-sided moments of Spirit, for Nietzsche, asceticism is said to pervade the whole of Western Civilization and nihilism appears as the decisive dominant feature of Modern Europe.[26] While, in harmony with Hegel's revelation, Nietzsche sees in nihilism the most consistent result of asceticism, for the latter, the overcoming of this moment cannot be accomplished in a spectacular reconciliation between ethos, state, and subject, but rather in the full realization of nihilism, and in the striving towards an heroic personality. For this reason, while for Hegel the "death of God" reflects a tragic moment, for Nietzsche this becomes a moment for celebration and the opening of the possibility for new modes of valuation.[27]

The centrality of asceticism and nihilism in Nietzsche's thought becomes most obvious in his "genealogical" account of forms of valuation that, according to him, have dominated the European mindset. For Nietzsche, these forms of valuation are ascetic in character and could not have another origin than what he designates as a "slave revolt in morality." Such a revolt, for Nietzsche, began with the Jews, whose priestly Judaism represents for him the epitome of an ascetic mode of self-consciousness.[28]

> It was the Jews who, with awe inspiring consistency, dared to invert the aristocratic value-equation (good = noble = powerful = happy = beloved of God) and to hang on to this inversion with their teeth, the teeth of the most abysmal hatred (the hatred of impotence), saying "the wretched alone are the good; the poor, impotent, lowly alone are the good..., and you, the powerful and noble are on the contrary the evil, the cruel, the lustful....... One knows *who* inherited this Jewish revaluation....... with the Jews there begins *the slave revolt in morality*: that revolt which has a history of two thousand years behind it and which we no longer see because it – has been victorious. (1967: 34)

For Nietzsche, these Jews, along with "the descendants of every kind of European and non-European slavery, and especially of the entire pre-Aryan populace – they represent the *regression* of mankind!" (p. 43, §11). Their regressive revolt begins, according to Nietzsche, when their *ressentiment* finally "becomes creative and gives birth to values" (p. 36, §10). Morality in Europe becomes thus the morality of slaves.

In his 'genealogy' Nietzsche found a persuasive way to convey the powerful grip of decadent modes of valuation in the European mindset and cultural formations. Since the slave mode of valuation is identified with a priestly consciousness the notion of the "death of God" signals, as we have seen, the promise of a new dawn. Slavery and priesthood are related by Nietzsche to dependent and reactive behavior, so the notion of the "death of God" takes the more general meaning of the vanishing of the comfort of dependence and the possibility of unleashing the creative powers of a repressed aristocratic consciousness. In this way Nietzsche's 'genealogy' offers both a diagnosis and a cure to the disease of European Man. This diagnosis and cure represent, indeed, an original account clearly differing from the diagnosis offered by Hegel in the *Phenomenology*.

Yet there is a profound connection between Nietzsche's *Genealogy* and Hegel's *Phenomenology*. Although these texts are not presented as straightforward historical accounts, they advance the idea that history and temporal succession are the most fundamental grounds on which European consciousness has been formed. Both Nietzsche and Hegel dismantle, dissect, and attempt to clarify the condition of Europe with reference to structures of thought and behavior distilled through time. For Hegel it was clear that "Spirit necessarily appears in Time" and that History is "Spirit emptied out into Time." (p. 487, §801; p. 492, §808). Time, for him, appears "as the destiny and necessity of Spirit" (p. 487, §801). It is because of Time and History that the occurrence in diverse spatial locations can become part of the complicated, yet single drama of Spirit. Time unifies the distant. Temporality overcomes the limits of spatiality. Both the *Genealogy* and the *Phenomenology* participate in what I would refer to as a *forgetfulness* of space, as a subordination of space to time.[29] This point is directly linked to Nietzsche and Hegel's respective conceptions of the relation between lord and bondsman.

The subordination of Space to Time makes clear why both Hegel and Nietzsche are unable to consider the particular ways in which the master/slave dialectic is inscribed in the spatial contours of Empire. It is this that explains why Nietzsche examines the ways in which European Man is enslaved by an ascetic morality that animates the history of Western civilization, but does not consider how, in Empire, the same European Man behaves like a master in relation to colonized non-European human beings. The strong focus on temporality also adds support to the already traditional conception of a European humanity, daughter of its own triumphant history, whose virtues and pathologies can be clearly identified in relation to that history. This perspective works in function of the erasure of the philosophical significance of spatiality and of its determinant role in the constitutive process of European subjectivity.[30] The questions of how European Man has constructed his self in relation to space, and how the resulted self-understanding has played a significant role in the mapping of the entire world do not find a space in philosophical discourses that entertain their thoughts constantly with "temporality" and "historicity."

The preceding considerations suggest that there is more at stake in Hegel's philosophy of Spirit than the all-too-well known problem with the alleged violation of the individual person – a dominant problem in the tradition of continental philosophy and in contemporary political theory. Indeed, discourses focused on the question of individuality also prove themselves limited when they do not include a consideration of the constitutive dimension of the concrete spatial instantiation of the relation between lord and bondsman. In Nietzsche, for instance, we find an interesting combination of an effort to rescue individuality from the chains of tradition and from historical determinations with the more positive notion of history in his genealogy. This combination reveals that Nietzsche reflects about individuality first and foremost in the light of the condition of European Man – the privileged "subject" of the genealogy. This over-determination of philosophical debates about the relation between the individual and history is arguably still found today in the debate between liberalism and communitarianism.[31] What is significant in these and other similar debates is the erasure of the significance of space in the constitution of the European/North-American experience and the patent lack of consideration of questions and concerns that originate in the *border* and in the other side of the border where the condition of slavery is experienced as ordinary. These debates should not be abandoned, but complicated in the light of the coordinates of spatiality. In this case, the traditional triad of History (Time/History/Tradition) would no longer be simply opposed to that of Individuality (Experience/Subjectivity/Freedom). Rather they would have to be problematized and reconceived in the light of the triad of Spatiality (Space/Nation/Empire). History, Subjectivity, and Spatiality become the basic coordinates of Post-Imperial theorizing.[32] The introduction of the coordinate of spatiality implicit in the phenomenological features of Empire reveals how the traditional notion of the "death of God" is easily incorporated by the master in the logic that allows him to continue occupying his position as Lord. I will now examine more carefully how this logic operates and unfolds.

Recognition, the Dead God, and the New Project(ion)s of Empire

In an Imperial World, I argued above, the meaning and function of God are greatly determined by Imperial Man's desires for recognition. God becomes a projection that serves to recognize the master as master and to collaborate in the politics that sustain the regime of spatiality characteristic of Empire. The master, however, in being recognized by God the Master, becomes a servant. To be sure this servitude is not totally negative, since it allows Imperial Man to conceive colonization and murder as altruistic acts made in the service of God. Indeed, this servitude is crucial for the initial impetus of Empire. It not only allows Imperial Man to exercise his power with good conscience, but also encourages the exercise of imperial power and the extension of Imperial Civilization by conceiving of these actions in terms of a divine mission. Yet servitude does not fit entirely well with the consciousness of the master, and he will ultimately come to *resent* God for this. The projection of God by Imperial Man, while it allows the master to be recognized as master and thus to legitimate a morality of aggression (towards the colonized other), simultaneously becomes the source of an ascetic form of valuation and existence. The ascetic mode of valuation that for Nietzsche appeared so encompassing can be traced back, in this phenomenological exploration of Empire, to the master and not to the slave. Or, to be more precise, one should perhaps say, to the master as slave (of the god that he projected). This phenomenological configuration helps to explain why asceticism, in the perverse dimensions that Nietzsche observed, combines an attitude of self-submission and hate. Asceticism often works as a discipline of control in the interest of the subordination and dehumanization of Others. Indeed, Imperial Man submits himself to this ascetic mode of existence only insofar as this appears indispensable to sustain a regime of power that maintains him as Lord and others as slaves. As other mechanisms and ideologies of subordination develop, and as *ressentiment* against

God augments we will see the emergence of a strong skepticism and indifference in regard to God and the birth of discourses centered on the alleged "death of God." Nihilism will not be too high a price to pay for the acquired efficiency in sustaining Empire – although this nihilism will soon be overcome by new imperial forms of valuation.

Asceticism and nihilism gradually become the most urgent problems for Imperial Man, indeed, for him, the basic problems of Humanity. The enslaved part of humanity (the colonized), however, has other kind of fears and concerns as they are confronted not only with other aspects of Imperial Divinity, but with Imperial Man himself. This slavery of the slave is, indeed, more terrifying than the slavery of the master. The burden of subjectivity suffered by Imperial Man under the dominance of God becomes murder and violence in the colonial context. And, while Imperial Man may be conceived as an oppressed being, the colonized remains out of the boundaries of being altogether. The most amazing feat is then attempted. The master attempts to persuade the slave that his challenge too consists in evading asceticism and overcoming nihilism. In this way, the proclamation of the freedom of "Humanity" is positively charged with the lived condition of the master in its attempt to break lose of the yoke of holy servitude. The notion of Man then becomes a plausible candidate to assume the position of God, as it also becomes a *projection* of Imperial Man. Imperial Man, in any case, has achieved much simply by foreclosing the possibility that the slave reflect upon the meaning of things according to the exigencies posed by his own condition. He has thus foreclosed one major source for the possible transformation of the critique of God into a Post-Imperial critique of God, one that aims to uncover the ways in which religion becomes complicit with Empire, murder, and violation. Empire truly reaches its climax when it accomplishes this feat, making everyone think their reality through the questions posed by the dilemmas of Empire to Imperial Man.

Many are the subtle and varied forms in which the need to achieve self-recognition in a context without God has found expression. God may be dead, but it is clear that Imperial Man and the imperiality of power are still rising by virtue of new and varied acts of projection.[33] Imperial Man found new ways to sustain his position as Lord and to achieve what only God seemed able to offer, recognition as Master. I already mentioned abstract notions of Humanity or Man as projections of Imperial Man in his effort to erase the significance and constitutive power of relations of lordship and bondage. Along with the notion of Humanity, concepts of Nation and Race, as well as ideas about the System or Market have also come to fill the space left by God.[34] It is not incidental that general skepticism along with ideas about the "death of God" emerged precisely when Europe came to be more consistently formed by Nation States in the nineteenth century – Nietzsche certainly being on this a child of his time.[35] God became more and more dispensable in the process of recognition. And, in fact, once Nation States are formed imperialism finds more effective ways to legitimize itself than religion. The Nation and the Race become central for the identity of Imperial Man as Man, and for the idea of superiority. Then eugenics, phrenology, and the social sciences take the place of religious ideals and creeds in the legitimization of Empire.[36] The divinization of the System and the theological dimensions of the Market also contribute to sustain relations of slavery in a world without God.[37] Ideologies like conservatism and neo-liberalism, with their respective beliefs in the preservation of the system or the sustained increase of the market, offer justification to sacrificial modes of relations that assure the position of the master as the only one lord.[38] To the "egolatrous" projection of Imperial Man to Abstract Man, the idolatrous relation with the System or Market is added as another form of sustaining power and recognition after the "death of God." In the contemporary world, economy becomes the new theology. The logic of the market likewise becomes a new form of theodicy.[39] From here the life and hunger of millions sustain an inhuman system unconditionally defended by Imperial Man.

Idolatry and the sacrificial religiosity of the World-System seem to be related not to a "slave revolt in morality," but to a "master revolt" against God and against obsolete forms of domination.[40] The imperial order of things is structured so as to hide this dimension of our contemporary reality, and ignores that human existence is lived between the poles of lordship and bondage. This notion implicitly refers to the truism that *"the master is the master of the slave and the slave is the slave of the master."* This means that whatever the problems of the master are can't be understood without examining his condition as master in relation to a slave, and that whatever the slave *can't be* has to be spelled out in relation to an examination of the Imperial World. Reference to Man or to Humanity as a single neutral entity, and reference to subjective conditions spelled out according to the internal process of particular historical conditions, must be problematized by a recognition of spatiality and the colonial difference.[41] The intellectual production of those who share a space or history with the master will remain limited if it is not complicated enough to make clear how the *sub-alterical logic* of the relation between master and slave makes of all of us – *less than humans*. The times call for an inter-relational way of thinking aimed to bring about the final overcoming of Empire. The theory and philosophy of religion have much to contribute to this task and cannot, given the many ways in which theories of religion have been complicit with Empire, remain neutral.

Notes

1 This phenomenology of Empire, that is, of a World dominated by imperial modes of recognition, highlights what from a more functionalist perspective may be referred to as an "imperial order of things." Though the reference to the work of Michel Foucault is obvious, I focus here on the phenomenological side of the rather complex exploration into the meaning and structure of Empire, leaving the explicit engagement with his work and his critique of phenomenology to a more comprehensive work in process. Ann Stoler's work on the "colonial order of things" may be taken not only as a possible complementary inquiry into the structure of the imperial/colonial relation, but also as a paradigmatic critical engagement with Foucault that makes clear the "forgetfulness" of the colonial experience in his work (see Stoler 1995). Anibal Quijano has made important contributions to the task of reflecting about power, both national and global, from the perspective of colonial relations (see Quijano 1995, 1997, 2000).

2 Lewis R. Gordon pursues a similar approach in his phenomenological study of bad faith in an Anti-black World (see Gordon 1995). Gordon's work relates to this essay in many ways, some

of which I make explicit in a larger work in progress entitled *Against War: Views from the Underside of Modernity*. Edward Said's work on the relations between culture and imperialism also provides, from a less phenomenological and a more Foucaultian direction, a significant background to understand my approach to the relation between Empire and religion (see Said 1993).

3 The themes of intersubjectivity and recognition have become particularly relevant for recent studies on Hegel. For an excellent work coming from the tradition of the Frankfurt School see Honneth (1996). See also Williams (1992, 1997).

4 In sharp contrast, Honneth provides a sophisticated internal criticism of Hegel's philosophy of Spirit in the light of Hegel's own insights on the nature of intersubjective struggle.

5 The irreducible and constant appearance of the object over and against the satisfaction of Desire is at the basis of the Hegelian claim. Hegel's point is that Desire cannot be really satisfied in this condition and the split between self-consciousness and the object is maintained. By this and other auxiliary arguments Hegel will then conclude, "*Self-consciousness achieves its satisfaction only in another self-consciousness*" (p. 110, §175, italics in original text). Recognition can then only occur for Hegel at the level of self-consciousness.

6 Ronald A.T. Judy submits the related idea that "the unrealizability of ontology in the bifurcated colonial society is not a call for the abandonment of ontology," but that it rather represents the "need to realize ontology by returning it to existence" (p. 60). I believe, in contrast, that the challenge to ontology is part of a more general critique of Hegel's philosophy of Spirit that Judy seems to ignore when he then argues that Fanon's "critique of ontology is that in setting aside existence, it [ontology] excludes whatever form of consciousness attends the black in the becoming of absolute spirit" (p. 60). This statement indicates that, for Judy, Fanon still subscribes to the general agenda of finding a space in the becoming of Spirit. While my treatment of Fanon's work takes a different direction, I nonetheless believe that it is possible to illuminate dimensions of Fanon's work with reference to modes of argumentation related to the general outlines of Hegel's philosophy of Spirit. Sekyi-Otu provides an outstanding example of this.

7 Fanon clearly becomes the paradigmatic philosopher of what I call the sub-alterical difference, an ontological dimension "forgotten" by Heidegger in his many explorations on Being and the ontological difference.

8 The spatial configuration of Empire is a central component of the Manichean form of valuation and reality produced by Imperialism. This condition penetrates and divides settler colonies accordingly. About these Fanon writes, "A world divided into compartments, a motionless, Manicheistic world, a world of status: the statue of the general who carried out the conquest, the statue of the engineer who built the bridge; a world which is sure of itself, which crushes with its stones the backs flayed by whips: this is the colonial world" (1991: 65–66).

9 I coin the term "sub-alter" to highlight the condition of someone whose alterity is made to play a significant role in contexts of subjugation. The colonial Other is not so much an Other, as a sub-alterized or sub-alterical Other, a subject whose being and meaning have been altered to such an extent that her or his alterity works mainly in function of a system of subordination. This idea is not exactly the same as the one conveyed by the recognized and most used term subaltern, with its immediate ring to questions of class and status. Sub-alter, rather focuses on the existential and ontological dimensions of subordination, as well as on the very conditions of possibility for there to be subalternity in the first place.

10 For a recent analysis on the relation between Hegel and Fanon's accounts of the "dialectic" between master and slave see Turner (1996). Perhaps the most fundamental divergence between Turner's account and the approach that I take here consists in that while for him Fanonian dialectics represents only a variant from Hegel's, in my view there are important points where Fanon's existential phenomenology clearly challenges basic methodological premises of Hegelian dialectics and philosophy of Spirit.

11 Enrique Dussel's work concentrates largely on this problem, revealing ways in which modern European subjectivity has been shaped by the experience of conquest and colonization. For a succinct elaboration of this dimension of his life-long project see Dussel (1996).

12 The eradication of the religions of the slave most often occurs only, if at all, when the master ends up killing the slave. In such cases, though not merely in them, the religion in question becomes an object of archaeological *research*, and religious artifacts are decoratively *organized* and *exhibited* in museums. The position of the Master is, indeed, partly defined by the monopoly of *research*, *organization* and *exhibition*, which become, in such monopolized form, trademarks of the Imperial World.

13 Manicheism is a fundamental concept in Fanon and Gordon's analyses of colonial and racist contexts.

14 The logic of the process of recognition of lordship ends up creating a Manichean context where the native of colonial territories, or slave, is rendered as Evil. Fanon develops this point in relation to his phenomenological description of the colonial world: "The colonial world is a Manichean world. It is not enough for the settler to delimit physically, that is to say with the help of the army and the police force, the place of the native. As if to show the totalitarian character of colonial exploitation the settler paints the native as a sort of quintessence of evil. Native society is not simply described as a society lacking in values. It is not enough for the colonist to affirm that those values have disappeared from, or still better never existed in, the colonial world. The native is declared insensible to ethics; he represents not only the absence of values, but the negation of values. He is, let us dare to admit, the enemy of values, and in this sense he is the absolute evil" (1991: 41).

15 Dussel argues that European subjectivity is formed by the similar principle, "I conquer, therefore I am" (1996: 133). The notion of homicide is also central to Dussel's work. "The project of the dominant system is imposed univocally to all.... Whoever resists is kidnapped, imprisoned, tortured... killed." And, interestingly enough, he concludes, "The dialectic of master and slave is not yet possible because the slave disappears from the horizon: he is dead" (Dussel 1985: 64, my translation.).

16 The contrast between communication and imposition is central to Fanon's work. Conquest for him implies a combination of imposition and murder: "Expropriation, spoliation, raids, objective murder, are matched by the sacking of cultural patterns, or at least condition such sacking. The social panorama is destructed; values are flaunted, crushed, emptied. The lines of force, having crumbled, no longer give direction. In their stead a new system of values is imposed, not proposed, but affirmed, by the heavy weight of cannons and sabers" (Fanon 1967b: 33–34). For a related but quite different rendering of these themes see Todorov (1992).

17 Fanon offers several descriptions of these failures of assimilation in the first chapters of *Black Skin*. "The Negro and Language," the first chapter of the book, is a striking analysis of how the attempt to erase certain inflections from the accent never allows the colonized to become or be recognized as something else than what his skin indicates.

18 In relation to this, see Fanon's reflections on the epidermal schema (1967a: 111–112), and Gordon's phenomenological examination of the body in bad faith (pp. 97–103).

19 Empire, indeed, appears in many ways to obey the impulses of a return to a primordial condition of a total anonymity that allows no escape. Something similar to this is what Lévinas understands by "il y a." See Lévinas (1987: 44–51).

20 In this light it is no coincidence that in an Anti-black world "the black body lives as Absence," while "the white body is presumed to live itself as Presence" (Gordon 1995: 100).

21 The very mapping of the world testifies to the geo-political dimensions of coloniality. See Mignolo (2000).

22 Said (1979) and Mignolo (2000) provide extraordinary accounts of the relation between violence, classification, and the conception of space from a post-colonial and a post-Occidental perspective respectively.

23 Fanon offers persuasive arguments to sustain the thesis that "torture is inherent in the whole colonialist configuration" (Fanon 1967b: 64).

24 Gordon calls attention to this in his phenomenology of an Anti-Black World: "From the standpoint of the black in an antiblack world, God is a desire that can never truly be satisfied – the desire to be white" (p. 149).

25 Imperial Man aspires to be God, and structurally takes the place of God – that is, becomes normative – but he *cannot* be God and must remain conscious of that impossibility. This idea is crucial in Gordon's existential analysis of the role of God in an Antiblack world: "If the black *is* human, and whiteness is above blackness, then to be white is tantamount to being a god. The white is aware of this ideal. But every white is simultaneously aware of not being this ideal. To *be* white requires the choice of whiteness as a project" (p. 147). The internal tensions in the process of recognition give rise to unexpected developments that will be considered in the second section of the essay.

26 It was indeed Hegel, before Nietzsche, who linked religious asceticism and the nihilism of the "death of God." These two dimensions become in the *Phenomenology* intrinsic elements of what Hegel refers to as the Unhappy Consciousness (see pp. 132–133, §119; p. 455, §§752–753).

27 Compare Hegel (p. 455, §§752–753) with Nietzsche (1974: 279–280, §343) where, in a paragraph entitled, "The Meaning of Our Cheerfulness," Nietzsche characterizes the "death of God" as the "greatest recent event in Europe."

28 For a critical account of the relation between asceticism, slavery, and the Jews in Hegel and Nietzsche see Yovel (1998).

29 This argumentation owes much to Mignolo. See also Sekyi-Otu's analysis of "Antidialectic as Space" (1996: 72–86).

30 In direct contrast to philosophical positions that tend to erase the significance of spatiality we find Dussel arguing that "[a] great part of the achievements of modernity were not exclusively European but grow from a continuous dialectic of impact and counter-impact, effect and counter-effect, between modern Europe and its periphery, even in that which we could call the constitution of modern subjectivity" (Dussel 1996: 132–133).

31 This is clearly suggested by Dussel's critique of Charles Taylor (see Dussel 1996).

32 Fanon and Dussel's work are clearly fundamental in this field.

33 It is not fortuitous that Michael Hardt and Antonio Negri (2000) use the term "Empire" to refer to the new form of sovereignty that emerged with the new global order (p. xi). Their work makes patently clear the initial intuition of the present essay and of a series of works in the same vein, that our world is not only "postmodern" but imperial as well, and that it is time to analyze carefully the manifold structure of the imperiality of power in the old, modern, and contemporary world.

34 Sylvia Wynter provides sophisticated analyses on how the projection of Man as the ideal to which all humans should aspire and its relations with race and nation. See Wynter (1990).

35 We must not ignore that for Hegel the development of Spirit culminates in the appearance of speculative philosophy on the one hand, and on the Nation State on the other.

36 For an analysis of the ways in which scientific knowledge and the scientific discipline is historically marked by a profound relation with Empire see Said (1979). Immanuel Wallerstein offers a similar account but in relation to Nationalism. See Wallerstein (1991).

37 Dussel refers to the theological dimensions of the system when he writes: "The truth is that there comes a time when every system becomes a totality, it becomes structurally auto-sufficient. Religion, as a group of symbolic mediations and ritual gestures, as an explicative doctrine of the world and in reference to the absolute. . . , comes to be an essential moment of this 'self-closure' of the system. The totalization of the system is a process of divinization" (Dussel 1980: 105, §§2.3.1–2.3.2, my translation). See also Dussel (1993). Franz Hinkelammert, the German economist and philosopher of liberation has pursued, along with the group in the Ecumenical Department of Investigations in Costa Rica where he works, a critique of the links of the market with a sacrificial idolatrous religiosity. See, especially, the proceedings of a conference with René Girard, edited by the theologian, Hugo Assmann (Assmann 1991).

38 On the notion of conservatism and liberalism as ideologies of the modern world system see Wallerstein (1995: 72–92). For an account of the sacrificial logic in Western thought, particularly, as it shows itself in neo-liberal economics see Hinkelammert (1998, 2003).

39 See Gordon's illuminating remarks on the secularization of theodicy in light of the challenged found by Du Bois in his scientific descriptions of black folk (Gordon 2000: 67–68).

40 For an account of the basic principles and fundamental ideas of world-system theory see
    Wallerstein (1974, 1979).
41 For the definition and development of the term "colonial difference" see Mignolo (2000: 3–
    126).

References

Assmann, Hugo, ed. 1991 Sobre ídolos y sacrificios: René Girard con teólogos de la liberación
    [On idols and sacrifices: René Girard with liberation theologians]. San José, Costa Rica:
    Departamento Ecuménico de Investigaciones.
Dussel, Enrique. 1980. Filosofía ética latinoamericana, vol. 5: Arqueológica latinoamericana, una
    filosofía de la religion antifetichista. Bogotá, Colombia: Universidad de Santo Tomas.
Dussel, Enrique. 1985. Filosofía de la liberación. 3ra ed. Buenos Aires, Argentina: Ediciones La
    Aurora.
Dussel, Enrique. 1993. Las metaforas teológicas de Marx. Estella, Navarra (Spain): Editorial Verbo
    Divino.
Dussel, Enrique. 1996. "Modernity, Eurocentricism, and Trans-Modernity: In Dialogue with
    Charles Taylor." The Underside of Modernity: Apel, Ricoeur, Taylor and the Philosophy of Lib-
    eration. Trans. and ed. by Eduardo Mendieta, pp. 129–159. Atlantic Highlands, NJ: Humanities
    Press.
Fanon, Frantz. 1967a. Black Skin, White Masks. Trans. by Charles Lam Markmann. New York:
    Grove Press.
Fanon, Frantz. 1967b. Toward the African Revolution: Political Essays. Trans. by Haakon
    Chevalier. New York: Groove Press.
Fanon, Frantz. 1991. Wretched of the Earth. Trans. by Constance Farrington. New York: Grove
    Press.
Feuerbach, Ludwig. 1989. The Essence of Christianity. Trans. by George Eliot. Buffalo, NY:
    Prometheus.
Gordon, Lewis. 1995. Bad Faith and Anti-black Racism. New Jersey: Humanities Press.
Gordon, Lewis. 2000. Existentia Africana: Understanding African Existential Thought. New York:
    Routledge.
Hardt, Michael and Antonio Negri. 2000. Empire. Cambridge, MA: Harvard University Press.
Harvey, Van A. 1995. Feuerbach and the Interpretation of Religion. Cambridge: Cambridge
    University Press.
Hegel, Georg Wilhelm Friedrich. 1977. Phenomenology of Spirit. Trans. by A.V. Miller. Oxford:
    Oxford University Press.
Hinkelammert, Franz J. 1998. Sacrificios humanos y sociedad occidental: Lucifer y la bestia.
    3rd ed. San José, Costa Rica: Departamento Ecuménico de Investigaciones.
Hinkelammert, Franz J. 2003. Solidaridad o suicidio colectivo. Heredia, Costa Rica: Ambientico
    Ediciones.
Honneth, Axel. 1996. The Struggle for Recognition: The Moral Grammar of Social Conflicts.
    Trans. by Joel Anderson. Cambridge,MA: MIT Press.
Judy, Ronald A.T. 1996. "Fanon's Body of Black Experience." Fanon: A Critical Reader.
    Ed. by Lewis R. Gordon, T. Denean Sharpley-Whiting, and Renée T. White, pp. 53–73.
    Oxford/Cambridge, MA: Blackwell.
Lévinas, Emmanuel. 1983. Beyond Intentionality. Trans by. Kathleen McLaughlin. Philosophy in
    France Today. Ed. by Alan Montefiore, pp. 100–115. Cambridge: Cambridge University Press.
Lévinas, Emmanuel. 1987. Time and the Other. Trans. by Richard A. Cohen. Pittsburgh, PA:
    Duquesne University Press.
Mignolo, Walter D. 2000. Local Histories/Global Designs: Coloniality, Subaltern Knowledges, and
    Border Thinking. Princeton, NJ: Princeton University Press.

Nietzsche, Friedrich. 1967. On the Genealogy of Morals and Ecce Homo. Trans. by Walter Kaufmann and R.J. Hollingdale. New York: Vintage Books.
Nietzsche, Friedrich. 1974. The Gay Science. Trans. by Walter Kaufmann. New York: Vintage Books.
Quijano, Anibal. 1995. Modernity, Identity, and Utopia in Latin America. In The Postmodernism Debate in Latin America, ed. by John Beverly, Michael Arona and José Oviedo, pp. 201–216. Durham, NC: Duke University Press.
Quijano, Anibal. 1997. Colonialidad del Poder, cultura y conocimiento en América Latina. Anuario Mariateguiano 9(9): 113–121.
Quijano, Anibal. 2000. Coloniality of Power, Eurocentrism, and Latin America. Nepantla: Views from South 1, no. 3: 533–80.
Said, Edward. 1979. Orientalism. New York: Random House.
Said, Edward. 1993. Culture and Imperialism. New York: Vintage Books.
Sekyi-Out, Ato. 1996. Fanon's Dialectic of Experience. Cambridge, MA/London: Harvard University Press.
Stoler, Ann Laura. 1995. Race and the Education of Desire: Foucault's History of Sexuality and the Colonial Order of Things. Durham, NC/London: Duke University Press.
Todorov, Tzvetan. 1992. The Conquest of America: The Question of the Other. Trans. by Richard Howard. New York: HarperCollins.
Turner, Leo. 1996. "On the Difference between the Hegelian and Fanonian Dialectic of Lordship and Bondage." Fanon: A Critical Reader. Ed. by Lewis R. Gordon, T. Denean Sharpley-Whiting, and Renée T. White, pp. 134–151. Oxford/Cambridge, MA: Blackwell.
Wallerstein, Immanuel. 1974. The Modern World System: Capitalist Agriculture and the Origins of the European World Economy in the Sixteenth Century. New York: Academic Press.
Wallerstein, Immanuel. 1979. The Capitalist World-Economy. Cambridge/Paris: Cambridge UP, and Editions de la Maison des Sciences de l'Homme.
Wallerstein, Immanuel. 1991. Unthinking Social Science: The Limit of Nineteenth Century Paradigms. Cambridge: Polity Press.
Wallerstein, Immanuel. 1995. "Three Ideologies or One? The Pseudobattle of Modernity." After Liberalism, pp. 72–92. New York: The New Press.
Williams, Robert R. 1992. Recognition: Fichte and Hegel on the Other. Albany, NY: State University of New York Press.
Williams, Robert R. 1997. Hegel's Ethics of Recognition. Berkeley, CA/Los Angeles, CA: University of California Press.
Wynter, Sylvia. 1990. On Disenchanting Discourse: 'Minority' Literary Criticism and Beyond. In The Nature and Context of Minority Discourse. Ed. by Abdul P. Jan Mohamed & David Lloyd, pp. 432–469. New York: Oxford University Press.
Yovel, Yirmiyahu. 1998. Dark Riddle: Hegel, Nietzsche, and the Jews. University Park, PA: The Pennsylvania State University Press.

Cultural Participation and Postcoloniality: A U.S. Case Study

Andrew B. Irvine

Abstract The chapter discusses ways of imagining cultural authority. Part I out-lines Samuel Fleischacker's liberal theory that cultures are "authoritative traditions" posited for coherent moral action. Part II evaluates this proposal through an exami-nation of the writings of two U.S. Latino theologians, Roberto S. Goizueta and Ada Mara Isasi-Díaz. They articulate a practice of culture neglected by Fleischacker but constitutive of the (marginalized) cultural authority of U.S. Latinos, namely '*mes-tizaje*': belonging to several cultures and not fully to any. Attending to '*mestizaje*', the hidden prejudices of liberal egalitarianism can be addressed constructively for the sake of enhanced cultural participation.

Introduction

In a recent essay, Homi Bhabha considers the possibility of a postcolonial theory of culture. Bhabha claims that cultural critics like himself have, on account of the so-called 'culture wars,' been pressed into facing 'the full frontal reality of the idea of "Culture" itself' (Bhabha 1996: 5). So impressed, Bhabha offers a witty and ironic consideration of the culture debate between liberal and conservative positions – the debate that is the scandalous exposé to which cultural pluralism *hors texte* has been reduced. Analyses of the changing configurations of disenfranchisement and resis-tance are stock-in-trade of postcolonial criticism, but publicity-earning declarations about 'Culture' itself (and so values, identity, etc.) have largely promoted a 'liberal' or 'conservative' reclamation of the status quo ahead of listening to the colonial dis-possessed – in the U.S.A., 'books of virtues' and formulae of 'cultural literacy' come to mind. Bhabha muses how one can genuinely ask what ends (suspicion of teleo-logical frameworks notwithstanding) are realizable, and worthwhile, with regard to our culture(s) in postcolonial societies.

The present reflection enters into postcolonial discussion of culture that might yet allow for equitable, participatory social practices better than do regnant essentialist concepts. It draws heavily from U.S. situations and commentators and therefore is something of a report on and synthesis of recent, disparate attempts to disturb the representation that aligns 'the culture wars' along an axis of liberal/conservative

P. Bilimoria and A.B. Irvine (eds.), *Postcolonial Philosophy of Religion.*   213
© Springer Science+Business Media B.V. 2009

hegemony. Part I comprises a rehearsal of the intellectual pedigree of a modern notion of culture as traced by Samuel Fleischacker in his *Ethics of Culture* and an outline of Fleischacker's theory that cultures are best understood as 'authoritative traditions' posited for the sake of coherent moral action. An evaluation of this proposal follows in Part II. This evaluation is carried out primarily by way of an engagement with writings of two U.S. Hispanic/Latino theologians, Roberto Goizueta and Ada María Isasi-Díaz. Their work articulates a practice of culture neglected by Fleischacker, but constitutive of Latina and Latino life, namely *mestizaje*. In fact, a guiding concern of the paper is with how faithfully the practice of *mestizaje* may be raised/reduced to a theory of culture.

Part I: Fleischacker and Culture as a Moral Posit

The most succinct characterization of 'the idea of Culture itself' in Samuel Fleischacker's *Ethics of Culture* is that a culture is an authoritative tradition (Fleischacker 1994: 21). More expansively:

> ... the distinguishing mark of cultures, the instantiation of Leibniz's 'internal principle,' will be their authoritative traditions. Paradigmatically, a culture, as a unique and energizing force in the individual lives of some society, will comprise an oral or written text, passed down and interpreted from generation to generation, which explains and manages a distinctive set of actions (ibid.: 141; the reference to Leibniz will be explained).

Fleischacker's book sets out a mediating approach to the idea of culture, between moral universalism (at highest pitch in Kant's categorical imperative) and cultural relativism (of a sort that claims all ethical questions are *only* rightly resolvable by referring to 'folk wisdom' and the like). For a rich ethical life adequate to the detailed, unpredictable demands of an 'empirical' life, moral universals are so few and so vague, if they even are truly universal, that they cannot nurture. (Notice that the separation of the ethical and the empirical already indicates much about the path Fleischacker will take.) On the other hand, modern anthropological scrutiny of the different ways people of different cultures actually live has yielded, by and large, philosophical scepticism about the integrity of those ways. Moreover, in face of colonialism and/or later cultural pluralism, traditional values (by which I refer more to those enacted in lives than to those invoked in 'culture wars') have entered into crisis. Fleischacker accepts the critique of moral universalism on the one hand but reconstrues culture as an ethical notion rather than as a useful idea for grouping empirical data. He argues that the idea of (a) culture is what permits ordinary people, beset by the myriad details and demands of living, to act in a consistent, coherent way. The idea of a culture is a moral code, 'an oral or written text. . . .'

Fleischacker's proposal owes much to his account of the modern history of the idea of culture (cf. ibid.: 115–148). That account focuses on a struggle over modes of authority, between a culture of Christendom in decline and the flourishing culture of Enlightenment. One specific contest involved clashing attitudes towards religion. Religion was widely understood among the Enlightened as a way to render ethical concerns vivid, especially to those who could not bring reason to bear upon them. However, whereas Descartes' earlier, expedient accord with 'the laws and the customs of my country' tolerated religion even as he pursued radical doubt (Descartes 1988 [1637]: 31), radical Enlightenment critiques of religion – that religion is a form of inhumane oppression and an obstruction to rational political order – were quickly fomented. With minor refinement such attitudes became a modernist gospel: 'positive religion' was superseded by the superior dictates of the truly worthy absolute, Reason.[1]

By the late eighteenth century there were moves 'to back away from the original Enlightenment hope of banishing everything not explicitly rational from human thought and action' (Fleischacker 1994: 119). Romanticism, common-sensism and anti-rationalism were various redeployments of cultural logistics within the prevailing Enlightenment culture. In Fleischacker's account, though, the worthiest of the vanguard was Gotthold Lessing (1729–1781), whom he dissociates from those other movements. Lessing's strategy, he says, was to understand an individual's reason in a social, historical context, such that mature (rational) knowledge and action depends as much upon the ways in which the individual learns from society as upon what is learned:

> Lessing reflected on this subject in terms of religion, but we need to remember that 'religion,' for him and his contemporaries, was not a set of dogmas and rituals, but the presuppositions and prescriptions of a communal way of living – such that 'natural religion' was simply rational morality. This is actually a very old way of using the word, common in the pre-Christian era, but it points in a direction by which 'nation' and 'culture' could come to take over the place of 'religion.' (ibid.: I have suppressed a footnote by Fleischacker)

(Whether the civic and imperial functions of the Hellenistic divine panoply, operating among elites and also among *hoi polloi* all over the Roman Mediterranean to secure personal, familial and broader social integration, are consonant with the interests of Enlightenment-style 'rational morality' seems at least questionable. Fleischacker does not elaborate a justification.)

The point with respect to Lessing is that Lessing was not simply seeking a return to a medieval, 'precritical' heteronomy. Therefore, it is warranted to expand upon Fleischacker's allusion to pre-Christian times (specifically pre-Christian Roman culture) by explicitly relating the ideas of Lessing and his contemporaries to the classical sense of 'religion' as *religio*, re-ligation, a binding back together[2]; all the more so as social disruption in Europe became increasingly aggravated in the closing years of the eighteenth century:

> For those for whom natural religion went morally bankrupt in the French Revolution, while return to historical religion still threatened to bring back all the superstitions and irrational doctrines that the Enlightenment had worked so hard to discredit, 'nation,' 'folk,' and eventually 'culture' became first the preferred and then the sole terms for socially shared ways of life ('religion' then reverted to designating one aspect of those ways of life). (ibid.: 119–120)[3]

The three terms just introduced (nation, folk, culture) signal Fleischacker's turn to the thought of Lessing's younger friend, Johann Gottfried Herder (1744–1803). Those words were for Herder suggestive of a new, humanistic *religio*. He hoped they would serve as normative restraints on historical religion in the communal life of human beings. Indeed those ideas were the *real* source of communal life, whereas religion, more often than not, had bound communal well-being to the whims of inhumane authority. By a sort of containment strategy relegating religion to being but 'one aspect of those ways of life,' (that is, by reconceiving religion as a cultural system, to use Clifford Geertz's phrase) the irrational excesses of religious ambition could at last be reined in and reformed so that it would more faithfully express its ground in the greater, re-ligating norm of the *Volksgeist*.

Herder's notion of the *Volk*, a distinctive national-ethnic community, and the *Volksgeist*, the spiritual principle animating and ordering the *Volk*, has been fundamental for later theories of cultural relativism. Herder, says Fleischacker, 'construed these *Völker* strictly on the basis of Leibniz's monadology. Each *Volk* constitutes a coherent and unique perspective on the world – "singular, wonderful, inexplicable, ineradicable" – with its own internal principle' (p. 121; Fleischacker's footnote suppressed). Still in accordance with Leibniz's doctrine, Herder 'envisioned the highest good as a product of the free development of and interaction among all *Völker* in the world.' (p. 124). On the other hand, nationalist ideologies more inclined to separatism have also stood indebted to Herder's thought. Yet what a variety of formerly colonized nations have attained in terms of ethical dignity is hardly unmitigated good. When the results are more than ambiguous they are often abhorrent, as with FBI involvement in terrorism in Puerto Rico, under Hoover's directorship.[4] Admittedly, most of those interactions have not been 'free,' as Herder idealized, and so such situations do not necessitate a total repudiation of nationalism. Nonetheless, they manifest that 'culture' and 'nation' are no less likely channels for will to power than was religion for those who endured the French Terror.

Fleischacker frames the problem in the following way. Cultural relativism that takes its inspiration from Herder's vision of the inestimable worth of every culture has no sufficient reason to prevent its becoming cultural totalitarianism. So, for instance, the Nazi appetite for *lebensraum* exploited the potential perversity in the Herderian cultural vision. Indeed, it gave the lie to the faith that religious will was grounded in cultural reason: the resurrection of Germany under Nazism entailed programmatic repression and killing of religionists who did not identify their religious devotion with devotion to the *Volk*, who did not join their will to the Party's. Fleischacker delves for reasons for this crisis in an unresolved ambiguity in Herder's thought: is the *Volksgeist* 'spiritual' and thus knowable only to folk who are 'in the spirit' (compare this with Leibniz's 'windowless' monads); or is it materially available and thus to outsiders and insiders alike? If the latter is true then cross-cultural understanding would seem to be possible. That might suggest to the Enlightenment mind that cultural differences are merely 'positive' – like religious differences. Cultural difference would be merely a matter of facts. There would be no spiritual truths at stake that would demand respect as a precondition of true cultural interaction. In Fleischacker's words:

> If a group's internal principle is something metaphysical, then it may well be important, and definitive of the group, but it can have nothing to do with the empirical world, which means that neither science nor politics need pay any attention to it. Metaphysical principles will

neither show up in anthropological studies nor be affected by political actions.... If, on the other hand, internal principles are something natural, it is hard to see why they too should not participate in the flux embracing all natural things (p. 139).[5]

Concretely, Herder's dilemma implies that there is no practical limitation to national-cultural megalomania except some person or persons act to restrict such aggrandizement. The relevant factor in such a scenario is not cultural identity after all (that would entail concomitant recognition of others, so giving ethical importance to the situation) but use of power. In other words, total cultural disintegration – genocide – can be a mere technical matter. Despite Herder's trust that cultural interaction *per se* would instil the spiritual-ethical norms of mutual participation and respect, his view disallows these making any appearance which would bind or re-ligate the interested groups, unless a power-contest is invoked. Even if an arbitrating authority were introduced to circumvent violent conflict, from the perspective of the *Völker* involved that authority's actions could only be heteronomous. The good will of reason succumbs to the wiles of will to power.

That breakdown of participation amounts to a betrayal of the Enlightenment *raison d'etre*, autonomy. As in the statement just quoted, Fleischacker claims that Herder's 'metaphysical' construal of culture leads nowhere in the empirical world; that, in such a case, *Volksgeist* is realized only by the exercise of force, and will be always falsely realized because of the necessarily Pyrrhic nature of this conquest of empirical relativity. The spirit is upheld, either transcendentally through unbending duty to what, in fact, have been shown to be historically relative traditions, or by a leap into cultural truth as subjectivity. Neither of these options, fundamentalism and essentialism respectively, honours the experience of pluralized culture.[6]

In response to the trajectory taken after Herder's doctrine of culture Fleischacker retrieves authority from the Enlightenment roll of the fallen. Fleischacker rein-terprets authority as a differential undergirding cultural pluralism from *within* all particular cultures. The advantage he claims for his interpretation is that the very idea of (a) culture then involves an ethical orientation to others. The key is to view cultural or national identity as a necessary posit for coherent action, rather than as either a 'metaphysical' or an 'empirical' essence requiring ever-greater realization: 'As Kant has shown, in order to act we need to suppose that each of us has a uni-fied self capable of free action, and (although Kant did not say this) in the context of each specific action we need to presuppose that our unified selves have specific characteristics from which specific decisions can flow.' Extending the point to a notion of culture, then, 'It may well be true, as Herder recognized, that we also need to presuppose a unified "group self," with specific characteristics, against which our specific acts can be judged and individual selves defined' (p. 141).

Cultures are such 'presuppositions' by which we judge ourselves. It is crucial to Fleischacker's conception, however, that the posit of culture be normative *only* for action: it is a pure practical posit, and a topic for neither theoretical understanding nor empirical observation (p. 137).[7] What this means is that traditions, the behav-ioral canons and counsels of a culture that might be considered manifestations of the *Volksgeist*, nevertheless require to be taken 'on faith' to have authority. With Less-ing, Fleischacker sees that the Enlightenment project of universalizing necessary truths of reason *needed* a supplement; namely, the various 'positive' folkways in which one learns what constitutes reasonable action amongst the participants of a *particular* community. A person cannot demonstrate the rational necessity of these ways. Rather, one assents to them (more to the point, is raised in them) as a cultural tradition, as one's particular communal *ethos*, in faith.

Always and only from within such bounds is ethical action possible at all (p. 54). The culturally-acquired values and interests that channel our ethical activities are not evident except in specific contexts of action, but that does not mean they are transparent to the actor: most people most of the time make ethically defensible choices 'on faith.' It is because they are busy acting according to traditional values and interests that they do not also evaluate those values and interests. Traditions relieve mere individuals of some of the responsibility for metaethics, so freeing them to act in pursuit of the good they trust those values and interests serve.[8] In fact, there are no mere individuals: every person has been shaped by traditional expectations, processes and materials.

To summarize the discussion thus far, then, faith in tradition is the act or relation wherein persons posit culture. Now, Fleischacker claims, the heart of that relationship is authority. The character of authority and of the authoritative person checks the absolutization of cultural faith-claims by keeping the claims tied to personal participation. Faith in the relationship of authority is a peculiar form of good will which, Fleischacker seems to think, outflanks the wiles of will to power. With Hannah Arendt, Fleischacker asserts 'that true authority entails the absence of both force and persuasion.'

> [T]he relationship of authority is quintessentially the relationship of teacher to student, parent to child, priest, and perhaps God, to worshiper: if genuine, it marks a place where status and interests do not matter and where a concerned and observant public (the 'spectators' of Arendt's polis) is not at all welcome.... Authority proper is a powerless way of bringing about submission, and the individual who accepts it submits only to the truth – although since it is, after all, not persuasion, to an unclearly known, disguised, or otherwise partially hidden truth (p. 84).

As the comments of Latino theologians will suggest to us in more detail in Part II, this account of authority tends toward the 'metaphysical,' in Fleischacker's own sense of the word. Nevertheless, the point bears some weight in terms of the goal of Fleischacker's argument. If such authority can obtain, then culture can be said to be something that flows from the mutual, participatory life of a group of people. This preserves something of what Herder understood by his idea of *Volksgeist*. On the other hand, since the continuation of authority is tied to the quality of individual acts measured against the background of an ongoing history of acts (that is, measured against a tradition) the identity of a culture is neither self-evident nor justifiably imposed on other people who understand themselves differently. Thus the traditional ways of a culture are not impervious to the claims of reason, pure or otherwise.

Fleischacker characterizes traditions in their authoritative influence as a kind of 'idol':

> A project or institution that a society is pursuing too busily to reflect on might be called an 'idol,' with all the Baconian, as well as Old Testament, connotations of that word. It is

an idol because it stands in, unshakably and unquestionably, for the full as well as the true good, but it is also an idol because it has something good about it and draws its strength from the piece of moral purpose it embodies. Idols serve the individual as markers for interests he or she can legitimately pursue (p. 89).

In view of the direction of this paper, it is noteworthy that Fleischacker adopts a metaphor with such strong religious roots to speak about culture. Indeed, he is con-vincing in his claim that the intellectual descent of the cultural conceptions he tracks is directly from Western theology (p. 211). Perhaps more curious is that he chooses the word, 'idol' and not one associated with it, 'icon.' Perhaps the latter is tied too specifically to Christian theology. Still, Fleischacker does not explicitly respond to Hebrew scripture's vituperative rhetoric concerning idols, even though the attacks on idolatry by Ancient Israel's prophets are precisely models for a hermeneutic of suspicion that might have important application to Fleischacker's idea of authority. Suppose the following situation: if a 'project or institution,' shared by a community as a tradition, is enacted in a dramatically different way or under drastically altered conditions or to dubiously traditional ends, then who is able – let alone qualified – to exercise reflective judgment when the 'idol' seems to fail to represent and realize the good for which it once stood? Fleischacker answers, 'It is in the passing down of these standards [of ethical action] that ... there is a need for authority' (p. 90). An authority is:

> ... a person who can think about values without losing faith in them. Authorities tend to be people who, while immersed in the practical world, have more opportunity than others to think about action; who, in that thought, see the possibility of abandoning ethics to which such speculation often leads; but who, either despite this possibility or after passing through it for a while, come to enslave themselves to a particular set of values nevertheless. It is only in and by this extra-ordinary commitment that they are able to see the world from an evaluative standpoint at all – in their speculative thought alone, that standpoint seems unintelligible. But because their commitment is so consciously chosen, because it is not an enslavement out of habit, they are also able, as it were, to see 'around' the values they have chosen, to understand the alternatives to them and hence the specific differences they make to how one finds one's way about the world, better than those who merely live the values without examining them. Authorities on a set of values are usually people a little farther removed from the life of those values than the people who consult them. At least in thought, they are more aware of – and that means, given the nature of practical awareness, more tempted by – alternatives to the way of living for which they speak than those who come to them to avoid such alternatives (p. 91).

Thus, an authority is one who serves and preserves the idols that enable culturally distinctive practices to go on within and across generations.[9]

Fleischacker develops his case with subtlety and detail but in the end he does not resolve Herder's problem but rather compounds it. In a pluralistic situation, the half-sensed arbitrariness of traditional ways of doing things calls for a normative authority to make action ethically credible and intelligible. Fleischacker says that the solution is to submit to the authorities of cultures construed as rule-based vari-ants on moral universals. Cultures consist in more than regulative ideals, however. Even if one abstracts a 'culture' from the people through whom it lives empirically, one is left with more and less than a (moral) code. Clifford Geertz has shown as much, both in his criticisms of Lévi-Strauss and in his own procedures. Fleischacker criticizes Geertz for theorising culture as unending interpretation, yet his own 'positing' model does not circumvent the interpretative demand. Authoritative cultural figures relieve some of the burden of self-interpretation lying upon ordinary, traditional folk; the relationship of authority is neither as transparent nor as innocent as Fleischacker would have it, though. Supposedly ordinary, traditional folk are still involved in interpreting and evaluating the circumstances, pattern and results of an authority's actions, in order to work out what authority means for them, what ends authority serves, and so on.[10] If a society senses a need for some sort of normative authority in order to deal with its own pluralism then, to truly deal with the plurality, it is necessary to at least consider whether the authority does respond to plural norms, and what those norms might be. Apparently, Fleischacker settles instead for maintaining faith not merely in the authority, but in the goodwill of the authority as well. Under this ethic the problem of recognition between self and other is diverted. Instead of something like an ongoing dialectic between the lives of folk and an evolving idea – or, rather, ethos – of a *Volk*, which is what Fleischacker seems to want to promise, his ethic of cultures becomes instead a matter of folk's identification with the supreme idol, the authority. Folks are to join their will to power.[11] Fleischacker's acquiescence makes sense given that his theory suggests the line between cultural authority and authoritarianism is essentially voluntary: a virtual outsider, the authority is restrained only by the binding power of his or her own self-enslavement.[12] Authority is here vested in an Enlightenment-style subject, or in an identity modelled on the subject. An authority is recognized because of his or her accomplishment. Thus, self takes precedence over other.

Acquiescence need not make so much sense if Fleischacker's voluntarism is challenged, though. Fleischacker does make moves in this direction, criticizing social contract theory in vague terms (pp. 76–77). Furthermore, at points he argues that at all times an authority only holds his or her authority through an ethically prior submission *to* authoritative precedent: 'Only by submitting to authority can one achieve authority, and that means, among contemporaries in the same social setting, submitting to the texts of previous generations' (p. 113). The claim in more detail is as follows: first remember that an idol is only a stand-in 'for the full as well as the true good' (p. 89); then the full and true good, as Fleischacker rightly affirms, 'is mysterious[,] not because it is nonempirical, but because it is essentially a project for action, hence something that remains incomplete as long as there remain actions to take' (p. 66).[13] So:

> Authorities stand between the general good to which our ethical beliefs ultimately refer and the particular feelings and ways of living by which we try to realize that good. This is a standing-between like the standing between living values and reflecting on them, with the difference that one of the two poles here is not only incommensurable with the other but intrinsically beyond a full grasp. Authorities should thus not suppose they fully grasp the ultimate good any more than ordinary agents should ... (p. 95).

Fleischacker's conception of culture as authoritative tradition is probably as good as can be proposed within a voluntarist scheme. It carefully offers reasons for persons in positions of authority to take caution against self-aggrandisement. But those reasons remain matters of (good)will for the person concerned. They do not arise intrinsically out of participation in the relationship of authority. Such an arising would be reminiscent of Herder's hope for a 'multicultural' enriching of all the world's cultures. Fleischacker shows why Herder's theory is flawed, but I do not think that Herder's hope of a kind of 'metaphysical' recognition must be thought discredited on account of Kant's conclusions regarding metaphysics; Fleischacker's 'pure practical theory' of culture as deposited will is not a better alternative than Herder's for fostering just and participatory societies in culturally plural situations. In action it would be as easily perverted as was Herder's.

The Kantian approach to metaphysics is largely the source of these problems for Fleischacker. That this is the case may be understood from the following quotation, concerning the kind of thinking appropriate to a cultural authority: 'The pleasure of reflection [Kant's 'disinterested satisfaction,' which Fleischacker extends from the third critique into the ethical domain] requires only the sensations of an object, not the object itself, and is indeed disrupted by any desire we have for the object since desire presupposes a concept' (p. 102). The truth of the other is not deemed relevant to the 'pleasure' of cultural engagement (one thinks of tourists, ogling through bus-windows and camera lenses, with money to spend and nothing to learn). Fleischacker's authority thinks about specific practices and so on, and reflects on overall images of the community's good, but may not think a concept of the good that could in any way enlighten one regarding whether the ethical *religio* of his or her culture actually participates in a good beyond its own bounds. Folks in such a situation could not know whether they had anything to offer to others. They could assume an isolationist stance, or impose their values upon others, but (putting it rather abstractly) they simply could not consider whether 'the good' as they conceive it is *true*.

'Moral truth' such as Fleischacker can write about, is a matter of *fit* between reflective poles, of suitability or taste – an aesthetic concern – and not a concern of referential faithfulness. (And moral truth is that, even if not only that.) Consequently, Fleischacker winds up lacking the kind of 'seriousness' about the subjects who provide him with the material of his theory that Paul Rabinow has advanced as a requisite for ethically defensible cultural studies (Rabinow 1983). In fact, Fleischacker can be criticized in the terms of his own discourse, for while he asserts the value of a certain kind of confident thinking that endorses one's own culture's pursuit of the good, by detaching it from any ontological participation it gradually subsides into cultural relativism of the sort Fleischacker sought to counter.

Part II: *Mestizaje*. Latino Refractions Through Culture and Religion

One way to bring out this inadequacy in Fleischacker's theory is by attending to Latinos in the United States. I will proceed by examining a culturally particular conception of cultural identity, *mestizaje*.[14] *Mestizaje* is being richly reflected upon in the work of Latina and Latino theologians in the USA who, during the last 20 years or so, have returned increasingly to the popular religious experience of US Hispanics as the place from which and into which their theological work takes form.[15]

A core sense of the *mestizo* experience as articulated by US Latino and Latina theologians is a feeling of belonging to several cultures and not fully to any of them. A poem by the Cuban-born New Yorker, Lourdes Casal, serves as a kind of epitome of this 'struggle' to Ada María Isasi-Díaz (1993 1993: vii). Cuban-born Roberto Goizueta identifies with an unnamed New York-born Puerto Rican writer 'who, when asked whether she felt more at home in New York or in Puerto Rico, responded "I feel most at home on the airplane"' (1995: 6). Further instances of this experiential resonance abound.[16]

Both Goizueta and Isasi-Díaz use the notion of mestizaje to schematize the historical experience of U.S. Latinos. I suggest a fivefold function is fulfilled though the mestizo paradigm. First, mestizaje summons up a history of dispossession beginning with the Spanish *conquista* of the fifteenth and sixteenth centuries and the cultural confluence it precipitated, and continuing into the present and a so-called 'second mestizaje' involving both Latinos and that U.S. culture that contrasts itself with 'people of color.' Second, it supports a biblical hermeneutic based on a typological connection between Latinos and the Galilean-centred activity of Jesus of Nazareth with and among poor and outcast folk. Third, it functions as an expression of a preferential option for the poor, to use the parlance of liberation theology. Fourth, mestizaje encapsulates a kind of eschatological hope for the realization of divine love in a just and participatory, pluralistic (mestizo) human community, prefigured in the globalization of Christianity. Fifth, mestizaje connotes a special role for Latinos, as firstborns of that divine/human community. Through their historical experience as mestizos, Latinos have special insight and ability to foster progress of the divine will in history. Thus, especially in this fifth sense, mestizaje serves as a kind of pan-Latin nationalist symbol, predicated on positive valuation of difference – an unusual nationalist symbol, then.

The fifth sense is most relevant to the current study. To be mestizo is to belong to several cultures and be recognized by none. Yet, as the theologians have claimed, to be 'betwixt and between' is also to be positioned for special insights into those cultures. Mestizo consciousness, as the theologians characterize it, shares many characteristics with Fleischacker's person of authority. For example, Virgilio Elizondo writes: 'Because [Mexican-Americans] are insider-outsiders, they appreciate more clearly the best of the traditions of both groups, while also appreciating the worst of the situation of both. It is precisely in this double identity that they have something of unique value to offer both (1983: 101). Says Goizueta: 'The mestizo/a and exile is a person who, by definition, inhabits the in-between world of "both/and." Indeed, this world is more than a habitat, it is our identity' (1995: 17). Isasi-Díaz and Yolanda Tarango, in a discussion of the difficulty of naming themselves and their community, note that for themselves, at least, 'Hispanics' are 'people who are aware and critically conscious of the place and role we have in this society because of who we are culturally' (1992: xi).

However, traditionally in the U.S. Latinos are not recognized as offering an authoritative reflection on matters of cultural importance. Isasi-Díaz's and Tarango's just-mentioned discussion is set within the horizon of, not just naming, but name-calling; within earshot of the contraction of 'Hispanic' into 'Spic.' The birth-pangs of the new mestizo community are not unambiguously a labour of hope. For authority has been over-determined by other categories, including race.

Over much of its history in the Americas, 'mestizo' has tended to bear a pejorative connotation – something like 'half-breed' in English, inheriting none of the valuable qualities of either parent, being instead a degenerate mistake. Fleischacker's analysis takes inadequate cognizance of this kind of genealogical problem. He does not account for the various forms and functions authority can take. He neglects how easily an 'idol,' in his sense, can become a fetish. Fleischacker's criticisms of the lack of respect that passes for cultural relativism are apt. However, his advancement of authority as the mode of genuine respect seems to lead him not to take the whole breadth of *his own* cultural tradition seriously enough, in particular, its 'masters of suspicion,' Marx, Freud, Nietzsche.[17] An adequate treatment of authority must consider the validity or invalidity of the modern, western theories of ideology, neurosis and resentment – whether treating of authority in western cultures or in non-western ones. Fleischacker's appreciation of subjective will and freedom to choose must be located in its tensions with the wiles of discursive power.

For example, racial stereotypes are loci of authority, too, and exert their power *before* any potential authority-figure can speak, to contract what his or her utterance can mean. Thus, authority figures are not contemporaries of their own thoughts and utterances, anymore than Fleischacker's ordinary traditional folk. Authority figures do not have access to clear channels of communication anymore than the rest of us, even presuming 'good will' on their part. They are (to varying extents which would require investigation in any specific case) positioned by ongoing discourses which are little related to their personal achievements and, moreover, that play a determinative role in constituting the possible sense of what counts as 'achievement.'

Texts, too, are positioned in such ways, so Fleischacker may not avoid the problem by discounting the importance of authoritative human beings in favour of authoritative texts. Racial stereotypes exert their power *before* the 'publication' of authorised oral or written texts. Such overdetermination of authority is not incidental to the meaning of authority, nor is it accidental as if, were it not for the greed and meddling of certain notable (and perhaps well-meaning and admirable, nonetheless) culprits, we would all be 'getting along just fine.' Homi Bhabha forcefully argues, against this kind of liberal normativity, that colonialism is *not* an historical misadventure that befalls a primordially contracted, prevenient community of recognition: liberal social indiscriminacy is not normal. Furthermore, to presume uncritically that it serves as a norm for judging colonialism actually masks colonialist stereotypes.[18] The presumption masks the masks, as it were. Bhabha states:

> The stereotype is not a simplification because it is a false representation of a given reality. It is a simplification because it is an arrested, fixated form of representation that, in denying

the play of difference (that the negation through the other permits), constitutes a problem for the *representation* of the subject in significations of psychic and social relations. ...

... What is denied the colonial subject, both as colonizer and colonized, is that form of negation which gives access to the recognition of difference in the symbolic. It is that possibility of difference and circulation which would liberate the signifier of skin/culture from the signifieds of racial typology, the analytics of blood, ideologies of racial and cultural dominance or degeneration. 'Wherever he goes,' Fanon despairs, 'the negro remains a negro' – his race becomes the ineradicable sign of negative difference in colonial discourse. For the stereotype impedes the circulation and articulation of the signifier of 'race' as anything other than its fixity as racism. We always already know that blacks are licentious, Asiatics duplicitous. ... (Bhabha 1990: 80)[19]

Similarly, U.S. expropriators always already knew that Latinos were lazy, passionate, ignorant, tequila-drinking, etc.

An oft-invoked reason for all these generic 'deficiencies' was Latino mestizaje. Mestizaje could be submitted to the authority of 'the signifieds of racial typology, the analytics of blood, ideologies of racial and cultural dominance or degeneration.' Suzanne Oboler records that

... the justifications of expansionism into Latin America had from early on been furthered by racial explanations that, overtly or otherwise, homogenized the complex and heterogeneous class and racial hierarchies that had evolved over more than three hundred years of Spanish colonial rule. The combined effects of the Monroe Doctrine and the idea of the manifest destiny of the United States contributed toward shaping the boundaries of the American community in relation to the Spanish-speaking populations south of the Rio Grande. Moreover, the creation of the *image* of a unified 'national community' contributed toward erasing the complex differences in the ways that race, culture, and nationality were understood by the Spanish-speaking people who lived in the United States in the years following the Mexican-American War. (1995: 38)

What and how Oboler records exemplifies an important cultural irruption in the present-day U.S.A. To record something is to remember; in Spanish, *recordar*. A growing number of Latina and Latino theologians are 'recording' the experience of their people. The *recuerdos*, memories, are ground for innovative attempts at a liberating, theological retrieval/interruption of the history of colonialism in the Americas. Mestizaje is nowadays a core symbol to many Latino theologians. Mestizaje symbolizes the unique abilities and potential of their communities. The emergence of this mestizo paradigm is generally held to have begun during the 1940s with the Mexican philosopher, José Vasconcelos (1882–1959). Vasconcelos reevaluated the Mexican mestizaje resulting from the conquista, describing it as the birth of '*La Raza Cósmica*.' He imagined this 'Cosmic Race' as a universal community created through the recognition of each participant's particularity.

Drawing upon Vasconcelos' imaginative vision, Roberto Goizueta offers thought-provoking commentaries on mestizaje. Goizueta's efforts are directed to rethinking theological concerns in the context of Latino culture. For instance, he writes:

The relationship between the subject, whether personal or collective, and its constituent communities is not identical ... but dialectical. The subject reflects the communities out of which it was born, yet, as in a prism, that reflection is also a *refraction* [my italics]. This process of refraction has been described by the Latin American philosopher-theologian Juan

Carlos Scannone, who suggests that cultural symbols "'objectively condense" the communitarian common world and open up for each individual member of the community the
possibilities that are enclosed therein and that are then appropriated, arranged, criticized,
reinterpreted, or transformed by each person.' In an authentic community, the identity of
the 'we' does not extinguish the 'I'; the Spanish word for 'we' is *nosotros*,' which literally
means 'we others,' a community of *otros*, or others.[20]

Goizueta, like Fleischacker, is attempting to theorize the interrelation of individuals
to culture. However, whereas Fleischacker essays the theory from an epistemological account focussed on authorities and their influence, Goizueta theorizes from the
intersection of 'I' and 'we' in persons in community. An authoritative tradition is not
presupposed – after all, the 'conquest of the Americas' marks a disruption of tradition and the dispersal of authority. But Goizueta can acknowledge the sense of being
nosotros, a variegated assembly of people whose identity is somewhat paradoxically
tied to that wholesale destruction of pedigree. So, with regard to the problem of what
culture is, instead of Fleischacker's emphasis on the constitution of a culture through
folk reflectively identifying with an authority, Goizueta emphasizes a refractive dispersion of culture in flesh-and-blood persons in community. *There is no* essential
way to document mestizo culture or its members. In connection with this, Goizueta
quotes Scannone: 'the "we" as such is revealed in the irreducibility of the "he" and
the "you" to the "I" ... and that of the "you" and the "I" to the "he"' (1992: 66,
note 8).

(The twin motifs of dispersion and documentation which we introduce here to
thematize Goizueta's contributions plainly resonate with important cultural-political
concerns of Latinos in their complex relations to the U.S., that nation which has
sponsored the destruction and scattering of communities in Latin America while at
the same time offering some hope of liberation and safety – at least for people who
can produce their 'documents.')[21]

Ada María Isasi-Díaz also focusses upon the unusual virtues of thinking culture
through mestizaje:

[M]estizaje for us does not carry the negative connotations associated with miscegenation.
It was and is a natural result of the coming together of different races. It is not the attempt
of one race to make the other disappear – which seems to be the sense given to miscegenation by both African Americans and whites in this country. *Mujerista* theologians affirm
mestizaje as the coming together of different races and cultures in a creative way that necessarily precludes the subordination of one to another; we affirm it as the going forward of
humankind. (1993: 15)[22]

In effect, Isasi-Díaz advocates a willing remembrance and recognition by mestizas
of who they are, in the service of a liberative hope. The voluntaristic aspect is similar to Fleischacker's account of cultural identity, but here the locus of authority is
subtly different. Instead of submitting to the past as the accumulation of what it
would mean to be mestiza, and to figures who act as representatives of that deposit,
Isasi-Díaz conceives the authoritative norm as a futuristic realization of hitherto
unrecognized potential. Recognition of that authority cannot be accepted 'on authority'. Rather, practical thinking *is* praxis. One recognizes authority by participating
in it: 'For Latinas, liberation has to do with becoming agents of our own history ...'
(1993: 35).

This amounts to a yet-to-be-documented *proyecto histórico* (historical project) directed toward:

> ... our liberation and the historical specifics needed to attain it. ... It is a plan that deals with the structures of our churches, as well as with social, political, and economic institutions of society. The articulation of Latinas' *proyecto histórico* presented here is not only an explanation but also a strategy: it aims to help shape Latinas' understandings in our day-to-day struggle to survive, and our identity as a community. This articulation springs from our lived-experience and is a prediction of 'our hopes and dreams toward survival,' of our *lucha* – struggle. (pp. 34–35)[23]

Isasi-Díaz argues that Latinas who understand themselves through the cultural experience of mestizaje find the sense of authority in an historical project, a projected history. She identifies three aspects or elements of Latinas' historical project: *libertad, comunidad de fe* and *justicia*, or freedom, faith community and justice. *Libertad* has to do with the participation of persons as agents of the project. *Justicia* refers to the ideal order toward which the project is directed.

The *comunidad de fe* is the centre of reflection and correction; Isasi-Díaz describes it as 'the aspect of liberation that makes us face sin, both personal and social sin. *Comunidad de fe* is both our goal (rejecting sin) and the community that makes rejecting sin possible' (p. 37). The first aspect is distinct from Enlightenment notions of freedom as individual autonomy, but also differs from Fleischacker's in that it supposes a more oppositional, plural sense of what it is to live in a culture. '[W]e must take great care not to oppose structural change to personal liberation.' The clarification of freedom recurs to the community, emphasizing its character as the field of *la lucha*, the struggle: '... for us, *libertad* involves being aware of the role we play in our own oppression and in the struggle for liberation' (pp. 37–38).

Justicia, explains Isasi-Díaz, is 'a matter of permitting and requiring each person to participate in the production of the goods [not in the strict economic sense] needed to sustain and promote human life.' *Justicia* is guided by an ethics of the preferential option for the poor, long a familiar component of liberation theologies. And in the case of Isasi-Díaz's *mujerista* theology, taking the preferential option leads back to the *comunidad de fe* also, concretely to solidarity with Latinas. Solidarity need not imply a harmonious cultural situation, either, although it does prefer mutual responsibilities to rights:

> Effective solidarity with Latinas is not a matter of agreeing with, being supportive of, or being inspired by our cause. Solidarity starts with recognizing the commonality of responsibilities and interests that all of us have despite differences of race or ethnicity, class, sex, sexual preference, age. ... The two main, interdependent elements of solidarity are mutuality and praxis. Mutuality keeps solidarity from being a merely altruistic praxis by making clear that, if it is true that solidarity benefits the poor and the oppressed, it is also true that the salvation and liberation of the rich and the oppressors depend on it. Solidarity is truly praxis, because in order for a genuine community of interests, feelings, and purposes to exist between the oppressed and the oppressor, there must be a radical action on the part of the oppressors that leads to the undoing of oppression. (pp. 41–42).

Isasi-Díaz's suspicion of altruism is important because it supports the creation of a postcolonial community (although the 'radical action on the part of the oppressors' is, at least initially, in some conflict with the espousal of freedom as the agency of

Latinas' in their own history). As she adds shortly after the passage just quoted, 'This preferential option is not based on our moral superiority' (p. 42). There is here an implicit but nevertheless firm disavowal of any parallel to the 'white man's burden,' and its paternalistic, neo-colonialist modes. Further distinguishing it from the wiles of white colonialism, this preferential option is not based on God's moral superiority, either. This point is to be inferred from Isasi-Díaz's characterization of the third aspect of the *proyecto histórico*, the *comunidad de fe*.

Isasi-Díaz starts that characterization by recognizing:

> ... that Latinas' relationship with the divine is a very intimate one. It is not only a matter of believing that God is with us in our daily struggle, but that we can and do relate to God the same way we relate to all our loved ones. We argue with God, barter with God, get upset with God, are grateful and recompense God, use endearing terms for God. This intimate relationship with God is what is at the heart of our *comunidad de fe*. (p. 39)[24]

Rather than a transcendental relationship of the divine to the human, or one of sheer transcendence, Isasi-Díaz suggests a fundamentally interactional relationship of the divine and the human, with immediate consequence for the life of the community:

> Because Latinas relate intimately to the divine, we know that sin hurts such a relationship. We know that sin, while personal, is not private, for it is something that affects our communities negatively. The reflections of grassroots Latinas about evil give a clear sense of their understanding of sin:
> 'Sin is not a matter of disobedience but of not being for others...' (pp. 39–40).

This *comunidad* is also advocated by Goizueta, in terms of 'incarnated theology.' The distinctiveness of the *comunidad* and its theology begins with a valorization of popular religion in the face of denigration by authoritative church powers. What follows from this contrast is not an outright rejection of ecclesial authority as illegitimate (such that Fleischacker could rightly claim his model is being borne out). It is, rather, a case of popular religious inhabitation of alternative spaces within and alongside official channels of religious authority and power. 'We have to accept, however,' writes Isasi-Díaz, 'that most of the time we will not be able to depend on church structures and personnel to help us develop our communities.'[25]

It should be admitted here that Fleischacker does not exclude all conflict from the practical explication of culture, nor does he anchor culture so firmly to past achievement that the future is irrelevant. Isasi-Díaz's theme of liberative praxis is future-oriented, and so is Fleischacker's ideal of the wholeness of a culture inasmuch as a culture is actualized by its people. But Fleischacker's ideal is primarily a function of his location of culture as transcendental with respect to its people. It is alongside Fleischacker's more liberal, modern view that the mestizo culture concept is disjointed. The transcendental work of culture, that is, tradition, is not whole in mestizo experience. It is plural, exilic, deposited but also deposed, anachronistic. Norms, then, are to be forged in the *proyecto histórico* which is the concrete activity definitive of (the) culture.

Isasi-Díaz is in earnest about the vitality of popular religion for the success of the *proyecto historico*, and criticizes the failure of Anglo-American theological imagination to comprehend its importance. She introduces another view upon the status of

'idols' with regard to their part in the continuance of tradition. The official authorities are of limited value in Latinas' lives, she argues, but the very things which
are suspected as idolatrous by the dominant culture within U.S. society – statues of
Mary and so on – are in fact iconic presentations of the way the world fundamentally
is and/or ought to be. So, for instance, 'Most of us seldom read the Bible and know
instead popularized versions of biblical stories – versions Latinas create to make a
point. One can consider these versions to be distortions, but for us they are "valid"
interpretations, albeit imaginative ones, insofar as they contribute to the liberation
of Latinas' (pp. 46–47).[26] Indeed, the maintenance of Latino culture at all is rooted
in popular religion:

> The evangelizing role that popular religiosity [sic] has had and continues to have among
> Latinas and within the Latino community is instrumental in the struggle for liberation
> because it is a major force in preserving the Latino community.... Latino Christianity and
> culture are alive today thanks to the evangelizing role of popular religiosity through which
> Latinas transmit the religious, cultural, and social values of our people. (p. 49)

In short, Isasi-Díaz resists any identification with an authority that stands as a virtual
outsider. Perhaps the simplest way to draw the distinction from Fleischacker is to
draw attention to the immanent authorization focussed upon 'texts' yet to be written
rather than authority figures contemporary with the culture: 'Salvation history is not
something different from what actually happened to the Jewish people. Salvation
history *is* precisely what happened to them; it has to do with how they interpreted
what happened to them, with the role that God played in their struggles and accomplishments' (pp. 51–52). So salvation history for Latinas now is the primacy of their
own *historico proyecto* over the authority of the past.

Isasi-Díaz' view might be called an 'iconic' view of cultural authority: authority as given with experience rather than being imparted to experience by an 'idol.'
At the same time, this also entails a self-effacement on the part of each 'icon.'
For example, Goizueta writes that: 'One cannot understand U.S. Hispanic popular Catholicism without understanding its essentially incarnational and, therefore,
relational character: Jesus is not simply a spirit "out there" or even "in here"; he is
a truly historical, flesh-and-blood man who *accompanies* us in our lives – as do our
families and friends' (1995: 69).

For Isasi-Díaz, and for Goizueta and for other religious thinkers of mestizaje, the
continued flowering of the community is what is authoritative; *que somos unidos*
('that we are one') is the evidence of the good. They stress the authority of the
marginalized *comunidad*, those who are 'outsiders' not on account of expertise and
privilege but because of rejection and suffering. The authoritativeness of Jesus and
of Mary lies in their otherness as among 'we others,' *nosotros*. Goizueta extols
this sense in recounting the observance of Good Friday by the community of San
Fernando cathedral in San Antonio, Texas. 'There is an abiding sense that we are
strengthened and given new life even in the midst of our common suffering, perhaps
precisely because it is a suffering undertaken in common. When we are standing
alongside Mary in her pain, she is no longer *la Soledad* – and neither are any of us'
(1995: 37). The story of Juan Diego, the poor Indian who encountered the Virgin of

Guadalupe, is an 'authoritative' exemplum of the orientation which the theologians of mestizaje are bringing to their work (pp. 40ff.)

Conclusion

Isasi-Díaz and Goizueta do not flinch from the anguished sides of life as mestizos. Goizueta is perhaps the starker of the two, when he writes:

> The resurrection, then, is not a counterbalance to the cross, but the consequence of our honesty about and fidelity to the historical experience of *mestizaje* as crucifixion. The experience of *mestizaje* has given birth to a new people not in spite of, or alongside our history of suffering, but because, in the midst of that suffering, we – and our ancestors before us – have continued to live, to love, and to hope. (1992: 58)

Then is this theological motif an extreme form of resentment, fit for Nietzsche's despisal? Is it a product of centuries of defeat, of a dearth of heroes and role models who could have provided cultural authority?

It seems rather to be a feature of the in-between location of mestizo culture. Insofar as Latino/as are conscious that they are forced to play roles but that there is a gap between the role and the actuality and between stereotypes and other statuses they have, they are possessed of fine sensitivity to the traditional authorities which are currently failing U.S. society. Many U.S. Hispanic/Latino theologians today are working within a mestizo paradigm to articulate their cultural situation with a theological significance that might strengthen their communities and advance the growth of a genuinely pluralistic culture less beholden to stereotypical 'idols' for negotiating differences.

Samuel Fleischacker has rendered a fine account of the importance of cultural authorities in providing sufficient flexibility for cultures to negotiate differences, but his account is flawed by its Kantian voluntarism and the supposition of cultures as relatively discrete, homogeneous communities. The U.S. Latino mestizaje does not seem to satisfy easily these conditions for the success of Fleischacker's theory of culture. This is not to say that Fleischacker's theory fails altogether. In the theological work taking account of mestizaje, there is not yet any precisely formulated alternative theory of culture. At times, these theologians do enact claims regarding cultural authority that bear out Fleischacker's work: they do recognize certain texts and people, and not others, as 'their' authoritative predecessors; they do emphasize practical subjectivity; they do employ mestizaje as a symbol for strengthening a distinctive, quasi-nationalist identity for Latinos.

However, there also emerge what appear to be significant differences. Roberto Goizueta and Ada María Isasi-Díaz, for instance, contribute to a critique of the transcendental character of authority as Fleischacker portrays it. Fleischacker's notion of culture as pure practical posit nonetheless recurs to the epistemological privilege of authoritative interpreters who stand in a virtual 'outside' of culture. They thereby provide a horizon for cohesion and documentation of the tradition, but have made a rather un-Kantian bound for themselves beyond that horizon. Since ordinary folk are then bounden unto these authorities, the vulnerability of good will to the wiles of will to power remains, despite the liberal displacement of religion as a cultural artefact.

For Goizueta and Isasi-Díaz, the situation of the mestizo, as authoritative, is 'in-between,' both in and between diverse discursive trajectories of pluralized culture. This predicament has social and cultural dimensions, and a lack of precision about the relations of these (and other) dimensions of mestizaje is a challenge still to be clarified by theologians concerned with mestizaje.[27] Nevertheless, this 'in-between-ness' highlights the attempt by Goizueta and Isasi-Díaz to avoid difficulties of voluntarism and subjectivism by turning instead toward the fostering of solidarity as *nosotros*, as *comunidad*, in order to reorganize suffering in such a way as to subvert cultural domination and exclusion.

By learning from the mestizo paradigm it may be possible to identify why so many 'authorities' in the U.S. today fail to engage their pluralized culture. Perhaps this identification would be not merely in an extrinsic critical mode, but also in a positive cultural embodiment, participated already, and open to further mestizaje. But this requires of someone like myself a readiness to give up certain notions of cultural equality which Homi Bhabha has elucidated. Bhabha, for instance, roundly criticizes liberal notions of 'multiculturalism': In a recent essay he writes:

> Liberal discourses on multiculturalism experience the fragility of their principles of 'tolerance' when they attempt to withstand the pressure of revision. In addressing the multicultural demand, they encounter the limit of their enshrined notion of 'equal respect'; and they anxiously acknowledge the attenuation in the authority of the Ideal Observer, an authority that oversees the ethical rights (and insights) of the liberal perspective.... (1996: 54)

Goizueta is similarly suspicious of moves toward multiculturalism in his own ecclesial context, suggesting that: 'such a dialogue will only contribute to the historical marginalization of Latinos and Latinas if not accompanied by an attentiveness to the ways in which the very meaning of self and community are influenced by culture.... under the guise of cultural pluralism, Hispanic culture will be co-opted by the dominant society' (1992: 55). As Bhabha sees it, one problematic aspect of the liberal version of equality is that:

> [a]t the point at which liberal discourse attempts to normalize cultural difference, to turn the presumption of equal cultural respect into the recognition of equal cultural worth, it does not recognize the disjunctive, 'borderline' temporalities of partial, minority cultures. The sharing of equality is genuinely intended, but only so long as we start from a historically congruent space; the recognition of difference is genuinely felt, but on terms that do not represent the historical genealogies, often postcolonial, that constitute the partial cultures of the minority. (1996: 56)

Bhabha's recognition of disjunctive temporalities is astute. The insistence on 'historical congruence' makes possible 'but I wasn't there' arguments: for example, 'But I wasn't there when the U.S. annexed Mexican territory,' offered as an excuse for not caring about today's violation of Mexican immigrants' human rights by U.S. border patrolmen. What recognition there is of 'disjunctive temporalities' and the people who live them is often overlaid by stereotypes: 'Mexican time,' as perpetual procrastination until '*mañana*,' or neocolonial domination as 'underdevelopment,' for instance. Most importantly, the insistence on historical congruence also makes possible the elision of the memory that the U.S. has other histories, the histories of Indian land, Puerto Rican land, Mexican land, African land. Mestizos, bearers of all these memories in their *comunidad*, may call them back to our recognition, re-ligating histories that a colonialist U.S. has sought to relegate for the sake of imbuing its own dates with the aura of manifest destiny.

Notes

1 Supersession served as a mediating position *vis à vis* the church for a thinker such as Locke.
2 Ray L. Hart (1986: 39–41) provides a concise review of variant etymologies of *religio*.
3 In support of this reading of Lessing, note Lessing's 1778 pamphlet, 'Necessary Answer to a Very Unnecessary Question...,' in Lessing (1957: 62–64). Lessing there asserts the fundamental position of the *regula fidei* (not scriptures or apostolic succession) for the Christian church. See also 'The Education of the Human Race' (1777, 1780 [see Chadwick's introduction in ibid. (14–21), on the publication of this essay]) wherein, interestingly, Lessing writes that it was the Jews of the exile in Persia, 'thus enlightened' about the nature of God by contact with Persian thought, who were restored *as a nation*; again, Christ came to Israel because God 'only wished to embrace in such a plan [of further education into reason] that part of the human race which by language, habits, government, and other natural and political relationships, *was already united in itself*' (ibid.: 89, 92, my italics).
4 A brief review can be found in López (1987: 140–150).
5 Fleischacker seems to have Kant's realm of the noumena in mind when characterizing things as 'metaphysical': utterly inaccessible to the understanding of anyone outside of the relevant realm. His position is best represented at p. 140: 'Today metaphysics has been more or less discredited, in part because of Kant, while the distinction between thought apart from action and thought in the course of action retains its force.' This seems a mistaken stance to me. In the American Pragmatist philosophical tradition (and he is familiar with Donald Davidson's thought, at least), Fleischacker would find a rich body of metaphysical thought that avoids Kantian dualism. For example, Charles Sanders Peirce's 1877 essay, 'The Fixation of Belief,' deals with some of the same issues of truth and tradition (see Peirce 1934: 358–387). Fleischacker's own account of the Good is hardly bereft of metaphysical suggestiveness.
6 For a curiously dehistoricized contemporary blend of cultural fundamentalism and essentialism, see Bernstein (1995). For the teenagers interviewed by Bernstein, who 'claim' ethnicity like choosing a cafeteria meal, their cultural essence only exists as they dispose it, usually by imitating historically reduced stereotypes that they value as glamorous.
7 The distinction of doing and knowing seems exorbitant here. Fleischacker attempts to moderate it by discussing ethical 'knowledge' as a kind of gambling. He refers the metaphor to Kierkegaard's idea of 'subjective truth.' For example, '... we might say that our commitment to the factual claims most important to our ethical lives is a sort of bet, and the fact that we must bet on these matters frees us from being strictly bound by what science has to say for and against them. It is in this need for betting that interests come to play a role in our rationality, for what we may rationally bet on is no less a matter of what our stakes are than of the chances we will succeed. The gambler's perspective thus opens up an alternative route to relativism' (p. 34).
8 Fleischacker writes, 'traditions acquire their ethical value precisely by providing us with a working conception of the telos of our lives' (p. 68).
9 Fleischacker comments that he has in mind as a model for the relationship of authority an orthodox rabbi's relation to a congregant seeking a legal decision (pp. 91f.). However, this makes the choice of the image of 'idol' seem yet stranger to me. I do not imagine an orthodox

rabbi would accept that his role is to attend to idols. Particularly where Torah is involved even G_d, who forbids images, studies Torah. I do not note this as invalidating Fleischacker's view of the authoritative relationship, but the apparently unfitting metaphor perhaps indicates a problem with his wider, Kantian background theory concerning the ontological engagement of thinking.

10 Fleischacker's criticism of Geertz (p. 144) is based on a confusion which Geertz warns of: to mistake the object of study with the object itself. Cf. Geertz (1973: 22): 'The locus of study is not the object of study. Anthropologists don't study villages (tribes, towns, neighborhoods ...); they study *in* villages.' For Geertz's understanding of his method, see Geertz (1973: 17–20).

11 In Fleischacker's argument, this power is a good thing. It is power to choose how to live, for which the authority is the exemplar. Obviously, I am insinuating a Nietzschean suspicion into the account of Fleischacker's discourse.

12 Despite proposing texts as the paradigmatic form of cultural authority, Fleischacker's insistence on conceiving of cultural value as a posit forces him to keep returning to the will of human agents as the arbiter of authority.

13 Here again, Fleischacker discloses a Pragmatist sensibility that he does not make the most of.

14 The *Diccionario de la Lengua Española*, Vigésima Edición (1984) defines *mestizaje* as, 'a crossing/interbreeding of different races,' and as 'a collection/community of individuals resulting from this interbreeding.' *Mestizo/mestiza* is a term 'applied to the person born from a father and a mother of different race, and especially to the child of a white man and an Indian woman, or from an Indian man and a white woman.' The verb *mestizar*, derived from *mestizo*, means 'to mix the castes through copulation by individuals who do not belong to the same one.' (My translations.) *Simon and Schuster's International Dictionary* translates *mestizo/mestiza* as 'crossbreed, mongrel, hybrid.'

15 The merits and demerits of 'Hispanic,' 'Latina/o,' and other ethnic denominators lies mostly outside the scope of this paper but has been taken up by numerous commentators. See, for example, Segovia (1995: 62–63). Oboler (1995) offers a book-length multi-layered analysis and discussion of the topic. Regarding the age of the Hispanic/Latino theological movement, I tie it to the 1978 doctoral dissertation of the man generally acknowledged as a trailblazer for Latino theologians, Virgilio P. Elizondo. His *Galilean Journey* (1983), is based on that dissertation.

16 Justo González observes, 'we are no longer Latin Americans living in exile in the United States but Hispanic Americans, people who have no other land than this, but who nevertheless remain exiles' (González 1990: 41). See also Traverzo (1989) and Segovia (1996). The chance that this essay appears to homogenize a variety of theological approaches as 'Latino theology' causes me some anxiety. There is not homogeneity, but there is a great deal of agreement and conversation – solidarity, indeed – among various Latino theologians. On Hispanic/Latino diversity on the theological and religious scene, see Quiñones-Ortiz (1991) and Pineda (1993).

17 Again, see Rabinow (1983). 'Masters of suspicion' is, of course, Paul Ricoeur's well-known appellation for Marx, Nietzsche and Freud.

18 As will be indicated below, Bhabha questions whether Liberal social indiscriminacy is even ideal.

19 Tribal masks have been taken by a variety of white analysts as exemplary of fetishism. *Black Skin White Masks*, the title of Fanon's book discussed by Bhabha, adroitly turns the tables. In this regard, Fanon demonstrates that there is a difference between overdetermination and utter determination – there is real ambiguity and opportunity for resistance. For example, I was lucky enough to witness a peculiarly American display of the overdetermination of race on cable TV on the Fourth of July, 1995. The 'live' performance took place in Texas, as I recall. A middle-aged man with shoulder-length, permed, platinum blonde hair, and wearing jeans, cowboy boots and a stars-and-stripes shirt, the star at an outdoor concert, sang songs about the glory of America and the glory of God. The line that caught my attention ran: 'And I'm proud to be part/of the American Race.' Was he proposing a vision of a 'race' that transcended race, or reiterating a (semi-)conscious white, U.S. suprematism going back to the Puritan massacres

of the Pequot? Would finding ways to activate such ambiguities in the social process enable more astute counteraction of stereotypes?

20 Goizueta (1992: 57, suppressing Goizueta's own footnote). I abstain from commenting in detail on Goizueta's notion of subjectivity here, as it is an area of his thinking where his audience must await greater clarity and consistency.

21 Gregory Nava's film, *El Norte* (Cinecom International Films, 1983; CBS/Fox Video, 1984), is driven by just these dilemmas.

22 *Mujer* is Spanish for woman; *mujerista* theology is allied in intent with African American womanist theology, though with different contextual concerns, of course.

23 Isasi-Díaz quotes from Audre Lorde's (1977) poem, 'Poems are not Luxuries.'

24 I have omitted an original footnote from this quotation. In respect of this statement by Isasi-Díaz, the story of Juan Diego and his encounter with the Virgin of Guadalupe in Mexico, a fundamental encounter in the history of all *mestizo* Christianity in the Americas, also involves what might seem to 'outsiders' like impiety toward the Virgin. See Goizueta (1995: 37–46).

25 Isasi-Díaz remarks the significance of Latin American Base Ecclesial Communities as models of ways forward for Latinos in the U.S. Also, for a nuanced consideration of the phenomenon of 'popularity,' see White (1994).

26 Elizondo (1997) is a good example of the iconic liberating function of elements of Latino popular religion.

27 I have tended to stress, then, an order of social formations within (a) pluralized culture, rather than of different cultures within a society, to accentuate what seems to me a distinctive emphasis in the mestizo paradigm when compared with Fleischacker, although this order is not followed by all Latino theologians.

References

Bernstein, Nell. 1995. Goin' Gangsta, Choosin' Cholita, *Utne Reader* 68: 87–90.

Bhabha, Homi K. 1990. The Other Question: Difference, Discrimination and the Discourse of Colonialism. In *Out There: Marginalization and Contemporary Cultures*, edited by Russell Ferguson et al., pp. 71–87. New York/Cambridge, MA: The New Museum of Contemporary Art/MIT Press.

Bhabha, Homi K. 1996. Culture's In-Between. In *Questions of Cultural Identity*, edited by Stuart Hall and Paul Du Gay, pp. 53–60. London: SAGE.

Descartes, René. 1988 [1637]. Discourse on the Method. In *Selected Philosophical Writings*, translated by John Cottingham, Robert Stoothoff, and Dugald Murdoch, pp. 20–56. Cambridge: Cambridge University Press.

Diccionario de la Lengua Española, Vigésima Edición. Madrid: Real Academia Española, 1984.

Elizondo, Virgilio P. 1983. *Galilean Journey: The Mexican-American Promise*. Maryknoll, NY: Orbis.

Elizondo, Virgilio P. 1997. *Guadalupe: Mother of the New Creation*. Maryknoll, NY: Orbis.

Fleischacker, Samuel. 1994. *The Ethics of Culture*. Ithaca, NY/London: Cornell University Press.

Geertz, Clifford. 1973. *The Interpretation of Cultures*. New York: Basic Books.

Goizueta, Roberto S. 1992. *Nosotros*: Toward a U.S. Hispanic Anthropology. *Listening: Journal of Religion and Culture* 27: 55–69.

Goizueta, Roberto S. 1995. *Caminemos Con Jesús: Toward a Hispanic/Latino Theology of Accompaniment*. Maryknoll, NY: Orbis.

González, Justo. 1990. *Mañana: Christian Theology from a Hispanic Perspective*. Nashville, TN: Abingdon.

Hart, Ray L. 1986. The Dialectic of Home and Homelessness: Religion, Nature, and Home. In *The Critique of Modernity: Theological Reflections on Contemporary Culture*, edited by Julian N. Hartt et al., pp. 35–54. Charlottesville, VA: University Press of Virginia.

Isasi-Díaz, Ada María and Yolanda Tarango. 1992. *Hispanic Women: Prophetic Voice in the Church/Mujer Hispana: Voz Profética en la Iglesia*. Minneapolis, MN: Fortress.

Isasi-Díaz, Ada María. 1993. *En La Lucha/In the Struggle. A Hispanic Women's Liberation Theology*. Minneapolis, MN: Fortress.

Lessing, Gotthold. 1957. *Lessing's Theological Writings*, edited by Henry Chadwick. Stanford, CA: Stanford University Press.

López, Alfred. 1987. *Doña Licha's Island: Modern Colonialism in Puerto Rico*. Boston, MA: South End Press.

Lorde, Audre. 1977. Poems Are Not Luxuries. *Chrysalis* 3: 8.

Nava, Gregory. 1983. *El Norte* (Cinecom International Films, CBS/Fox Video).

Oboler, Suzanne. 1995. *Ethnic Labels, Latino Lives: Identity and the Politics of (Re)Presentation in the United States*. Minneapolis, MN/London: University of Minnesota Press.

Peirce, Charles Sanders. 1934. *Collected Papers*, vol. 5, edited by Charles Hartshorne and Paul Weiss. Cambridge, MA: Harvard University Press.

Pineda, Ana María. 1993. The Challenge of Hispanic Pluralism for the United States Churches. *Missiology: An International Review* 21: 437–442.

Quiñones-Ortiz, Javier. 1991. The *Mestizo* Journey: Challenges for Hispanic Theology. *Apuntes* 11(3): 62–72.

Rabinow, Paul. 1983. Humanism as Nihilism: The Bracketing of Truth and Seriousness in American Cultural Anthropology. In *Social Science as Moral Inquiry*, edited by Norma Haan et al., pp. 52–75. New York: Columbia University Press.

Segovia, Fernando F. 1995. Toward a Hermeneutics of the Diaspora: A Hermeneutics of Otherness and Engagement. In *Reading from This Place. Vol. 1: Social Location and Biblical Interpretation in the United States*, edited by Fernando F. Segovia and Mary Ann Tolbert, pp. 57–73. Minneapolis, MN: Fortress.

Segovia, Fernando F. 1996. In the World but Not of It: Exile as Locus for A Theology of the Diaspora. In *Hispanic/Latino Theology: Challenge and Promise*, edited by Ada María, Isasi-Díaz and Fernando F. Segovia, pp. 195–217. Minneapolis, MN: Fortress.

Traverzo, David. 1989. Towards a Theology of Mission in the U.S. Puerto Rican Migrant Community: From Captivity to Liberation. *Apuntes* 9: 54–57.

White, Robert E. 1994. If It's Official, It Can't Be Popular? Reflections on Popular and Folk Religion. *Journal of Hispanic/Latino Theology* 1: 47–67.

Imperial Somatics and Genealogies of Religion: How We Never Became Secular*

Eduardo Mendieta

Abstract The narrative of Modernity is a fabulous retelling of colonialism and the cultural and ethnic devastation that came along with European imperialism. With the aid of Foucault's genealogical method, the author re-reads the story of alleged social, political, and epistemological advances that propel the West to world-historical pre-eminence as the formation of a complex "autotheodicy" aimed at justifying the depredations of the West on the rest. In particular, the author considers the case of the Inquisition in Spain, and its exportation to the "New World." In the course of this process, "religion" turned into the form of (Western) "science," but the operation remained much the same under either description: an education in self-regard and other-loathing. The supposed secularization of the West is, then, a fable. Religion is the mirror in which modern society must look at itself to discover its own otherness. But it is also in this mirror where its "others" look back.

Introduction

Modernity is the Aesopian name for a violent historical process in which colonialism, genocide, and ecocide went hand in hand with two other fundamental processes: the spiritual conquest of the peoples to be subjugated, and what we can call epistemological gerrymandering.[1] In the 1940s and 1950s of the twentieth century cultural critics argued that whoever wants to speak about Nazism and Fascism must also speak of capitalism. Today, whoever wants to talk about modernity must talk about colonialism and the cultural and ethnic devastation that came along with European imperialism. Whoever wants to theorize modernity, must now only do so by way of acknowledging that the alleged social, political, and epistemological advances that propelled the West forward into the privileged place of the world-historical vanguard, were intricately entwined with, at the very least, three narratives. These narratives, in turn, sought to conceal their colonial underbellies

---

*I use "secular" here in the way that Talal Asad has taught us: being cautious and skeptical of the "other's" religious fundamentalism that as a shibboleth conceals and elides our own – U.S. I mean – fundamentalisms. See Asad (1993, 2003).

P. Bilimoria and A.B. Irvine (eds.), *Postcolonial Philosophy of Religion.*
© Springer Science+Business Media B.V. 2009

and their colonial undersides, by turning their stories into theo-onto-logical theod-icies. The supremacy of the Occident and the subjugation of its "others" was not accidental, but ordained, necessitated, exculpated, and in the last instance, conceived as part of some sort of divine plan.

One of these narratives had to do with the rise of the autonomous, rational, self-expressive subject. This subject had its sources in Christian subjectivity, which conceives of the subject as singular and always subjected to the omniscience of a judging God. This subject also has sources in the Cartesian, Lutheran, and Kantian versions of the Christian subject. The Cartesian influence seeks to establish the subject as an epistemic machine, from which doubt must be expunged, while trans-parency must be absolute. The Lutheran influence establishes the Christian subject as both utterly responsible and just as proportionally at the mercy of an inscrutable Divine grace. The Kantian influence sought to counter the corrosive effects of Carte-sian anxiety and Lutheran psychosis: the Christian subject is now sovereign over what it can legitimately know, for this subject is partly responsible for its consti-tution as an object of knowledge, and it can also be absolutely responsible as it can discover what would be moral with the aid of its reason alone. Autonomy and sovereignty are within the reach of this subject so long as it stays within the bounds of reason.

This narrative about subjectivity and agency is related to another narrative that has to do with religion, or rather the power and role of the religious within the psychic life of the subject and the social life of communities. Perhaps one of the most notorious stories told about the West and modernity has to do with the con-quest of the religious. Modernity is synonymous with the age of reason, which is invidiously juxtaposed to a bygone age of faith. This age of faith has been invari-ably described as an age of darkness, superstition, despotism, ritual and stagnation. Indeed, before the modern state could rise, the grip of the church on both society and the individual had to be, if not dissolved, at the very least loosened and contained. Most importantly, how could Western society distinguish itself, differentially and hierarchically, from those societies it set out to conquer and subjugate, if Western societies were also suffused by the euphoria, passion, atavism, and sacrificial vio-lence that are endemic to all religions? How the West allegedly became secular is a story not just about the containment of religion within the West, but also a story about what distinguishes the West from the rest.

The third narrative that we have to discuss, among the many other narratives that could be foregrounded, has to do with science, credible witnesses, and epistemic trustworthiness. This narrative tells the story of the rise of the scientific mentality, and how a few entrepreneurs, fighting religious fundamentalism and overcoming all kinds of economic and political obstacles, prevailed and so unleashed an epochal revolution. Part and parcel of this narrative is that the epistemological and con-ceptual revolution took place before the advent of the industrial revolution in the nineteenth century, and the emergence of capitalism in the eighteenth century. The narrative about the scientific revolution thus is a story about parthenogenesis and about epistemic purity and autochthony. The story about the scientific originality of the West, which partly justifies its right to colonize other peoples as its scientists are the most reliable, credible, trustworthy, is further complicated by the rise in the nineteenth century of the modern research university in Europe. This modern research university institutionalized an epistemic division of labor (Wallerstein et al. 1996, 2001). The objective world would be studied by the natural sciences. The social world, which is only the present European and American social arrangement, would be studied by the social sciences, i.e. sociology, economics, and political theory. The past would be studied by the humanistic sciences: history, oriental studies, anthropology, and ethnography. In this way, the knowable world was divided into three distinct ontological regions: the objective world, the present, and the past. In this way, the West cut itself off from its coeval and contemporary others. Looking back on this division of labor and the splitting up of the knowable world into three regions one quickly notices that religion does not fit neatly into any of these regions or division of labor. Indeed, one of the primary ways in which sociology was established as a credible discipline that is authorized to study contemporary (European) society, was by the process of the invention of religion, as a social phenomenon, and then the domestication of this subject within a sub-discipline of sociology (Mendieta 2002). The story of how sociology arose to become one of the privileged disciplines of Western epistemology, the one that most loudly and most assuredly argued for the distinctiveness and supremacy of the West over its others, is also a story about how "religion" was both invented and gerrymandered (Mendieta 2001).

These three narratives have been intricately related. The story about the modern, autonomous, sovereign and "unencumbered" subject is also a story about how this subject prevails over religion, or put more precisely, is able to privatize religion. In this way, however, the subject isolated in the solitude of his religiosity, is sundered from his social bonds. If religion is neutralized and relegated to the inner sanctum of isolated subjectivity, then the fountain of social solidarity and cohesion dries up. What can possibly replace it? This was Emile Durkheim's question. On the other hand, if the individual can not appeal to religion as a way to make sense of the world, as a moral compass but also a comprehensive world-view, then the subject is left bereft of moral guidance, or moral certitude. The disenchanted world of modernity is also a world without moral virtues: an iron cage of soulless technocrats. This was Max Weber's problematic. At the same time, as the West sought to celebrate its supremacy and uniqueness vis-à-vis the rest of the world, a world that now it held under its military boot, religion as the detritus and surplus of sociology always returns to haunt the self-certitude and uniqueness of the West. Secularism had hardly been accomplished. In fact, the more technocratic and disenchanted the world became, the more society sought solace and refuge in religion and quasi-religious movements. Religion remains not just an inexhaustible fountain of moral inspiration, but also an uncontainable, and undomesticateable source of both social cohesion and social intolerance.

Religion has continued to haunt the epistemic certitude and assurances of sociology, and Western society, as Exhibit One in the project of secularism, not because it remains other than modern society, not because it is a historical and developmental vestigial organ that it cannot digest, but precisely because religion remains as modern as contemporary society. Religion has not remained past, although it is one of the privileged ways to access the past; nor has it been a conservative force that hinders social progress. Modernity, even as an Aesopian narrative, could not have been possible without religion, and modern religion is through and through an expression of modernity. The enlightenment project's key promissory note, that where religion was, reason would be; where id was, ego would be; where heteronomy was, autonomy would be; turned out to be not just a delusion but, above all, an untenable goal. The elimination or complete assimilation of religion as a precondition for modernity was an untenable project because religion was continuously modernized by the thrust towards modernity, and because modernity was partly made by religion. Religion is the mirror in which modern society must look at itself to discover its own otherness. But it is also in this mirror where its "others" look back.

These narratives, hitherto described in the most general strokes, have at the same time, and with the same deliberation and intent, sought to conceal the ways in which the project of modernity was an imperial and colonial project. Modernity is and remains a dominating project. More concretely, however, we must ask: how have the narratives about the autonomous subject, the conquest and expulsion of religion, and the rise of a sovereign and imposing discipline, concealed and collaborated in the colonial and imperial underside of modernity? How, in other words, have the mirages of autonomy, secularism, and disciplinary prowess and purity, contributed to the performance and enactment of colonialism, genocide and ecocide? In the following, I want to approach these questions from the perspective of Foucault's genealogical method. This method, in turn, will be made to confess its own eurocentrism and complicity in European colonialism, before it can be of any use to the analysis of the dark side of modernity.

Imperial Somatologies

In his book, *Empire as a way of life*, the revisionist historian, William Appleman Williams talks about how Americans have just began their confrontation with "our imperial history, our imperial ethic, and our imperial psychology" (1980: xi). This book summarizes 2 decades of research into the sources of American imperial history. But it is above all a jeremiad, a severe, devastating, but also patriotic, critique of the American Imperial ethos. In our days, Howard Zinn and Noam Chomsky are some of the few public intellectuals to follow in this important tradition of self-critique. *Empire as a way of life* proceeds to articulate the "imperial history" and "imperial ethic" by documenting the ceaseless and intense interventionism that has shaped "American" foreign policy, that is directly linked to an ethic of entitlement, of self-assurance, arrogance, narcissism, and egotism, for which the fundamental assumption is that one must have more than one needs (ibid.: 31). An "imperial ethic" – certainly an oxymoron but etymologically justifiable, even necessary – may best be described as the "colonial mentality." An "imperial ethic" is a way of life, but this way of life is determined by the incommensurate power differentials between master and servant, colonizer and colonized, imperial self and subaltern, in which the lives of the latter are at the absolute, boundless, unquestioned, and naturalized disposal of the former. The life of the servant, colonized, and subaltern is at worst a mere supplement, a disturbance, an annoyance, a statistical invariance, and at best the slave and subaltern are the horizon against which the imperial self measures its omnipotence. If ethics is the response to the other, as suggested by Emmanuel Levinas, summarizing the original insights of the Judeo-Christian tradition, then imperial ethics is a travesty, an affront to ethics as such. Still, ethics is a relation to the other, a response to the other that returns back to the self. The self is figured by this relationship to the other. The "I" sees itself as ethical in the gaze and visage of the other. Lest we privilege the specular, we should also add that the "I" is consti-tuted by its touch of the other, not because the "I" touches the other, but because in touching the other, this "I" touches itself through the other. It is the touch of the other that discloses my own flesh to myself. It is this originary ethical touch that also reveals to us how ethics is always a corporeal encounter, an encounter having to do with bleeding, hungering, mute, mutilated, and lacerated bodies.

But returning to Williams. *Empire as a way of life* is less successful at describing what is or may be "imperial psychology." In all fairness, however, we do get some pointers. Williams suggests that in order to overcome the "imperial" *Weltanschau-ung*, way of life, and all of its preconceptions and prejudices, we must minimize and eventually abandon, "the imperial propensity to externalize evil" (ibid.: 149). The imperial psychology, then, is fundamentally predicated on this psychological mech-anism by means of which the sources of "evil," "tension," "conflict," "problems," and "difficulties" are always externalized, extrojected and externalized. "Empire turns a culture away from its own life as a society or community" (ibid.). Indeed, the imperial way of life is parasitic on its ability to always export its internal cri-sis, and it is the imperial possessions, protectorates, colonies, etc., that become the dumping grounds for all the internal contradictions of the imperial metropolis. How is this imperial psychology made possible? How does it operate on the basic every-day level? And most importantly, how does it distort the relationship of oneself to oneself, of the self to the self, in such a way that something like an imperial self is constituted? The question of imperial psychology is related, then, to how we relate to ourselves by relating to others. This question is about techniques, modalities, forms, practices and technologies of agency and of subjection. These terms already evoke Michel Foucault and the project of a genealogy of the imperial self. But before we turn to such a genealogy, it is necessary that we traverse the path of the education of desire and the *somatology of contempt*, disgust, abjection, and repulsion, which are always linked to exoticization, fascination, reveling, temptation, and desire.

Laura Kipnis's recently published *Against Love: A Polemic* (2003) would be an apt point of departure for a discussion of what I call the somatology of contempt and desire, but it may derail us with its incisive and devastating look at the duplicitous Puritan politics of adultery that have caught the prurient and pornographic imagina-tion of the American polity. Instead, I will proceed by way of a writer Kipnis uses very adroitly, namely Ruth Perry, who is a professor of literature at MIT. In an essay on Jane Austen's portrayal of romantic love, entitled "Sleeping with Mr. Collins," Perry argues that Austen's work is straddled over the chasm between two paradigms, two entirely different ways of thinking and, above all, feeling about sex without love, or unsentimental love. In other words, Perry argues that Austen's work does not yet differentiate between having sex because it is part of the work of being a wife, and having sex only if you have a sentimental and romantic attachment to the person with whom you have sex. Romantic sex is a new invention, one that is made in the eighteenth century, argues Perry. In order, however, to establish romantic sex as the norm, the body and the self had to undergo an education. The education of desire that is exhibited in eighteenth century novels proceeds by way of what Perry calls "sexual disgust." And this is what is invented as a way to establish romantic sex, sentimental sex, as the norm of heterosexuality. Perry writes: "Sexual disgust was an invention of the eighteenth century, one dimension of an evolving sexual identity for women that could control their sexual reactions without interference – whether policing or protective – of a network of kin relations. A somatized relation compelling enough to regulate women's sexual preferences and habits, sexual disgust can hardly be found in the repertoire of earlier English written experience" (Perry 2000: 121).

Sexual disgust is a somatic experience, but note how it is something we are socialized into. We can argue in a Humean way that our inner, psychological, sense of selfhood is trained and socialized from without, by way of the education of our visceral and tactile reactions. Sexual disgust, however, is fundamentally asymmetrical. It is a somatic technology that is aimed at domesticating the bodies and sense of selfhood of women. As Perry puts it jocularly, "no one expects a heterosexual man to be so put off by the vulgar mind or loose morals of an attractive woman as to be unwilling to have sex with her" (ibid.: 123). In fact, male heterosexual subjectivity and corporeality is immune to the pangs of disgust; it is unassailable by the polluting effects of the bodies of those it deems inferior or defective. This is a point that Perry does not labor, but which I think needs to be underscored. Nonetheless, as Perry argues, sexual disgust signals the possibility of two types of violation: bodily and moral. To be touched, to be sexually accosted by a polluting agent is a violation of the body, but also of one's psychological integrity, and above all, moral character. Disgust is simultaneously somatic revulsion, and moral disapproval: a disapproval that cuts both ways: the other is contemptible, while the one, the disgusted one, places itself above and beyond the touch of that one.

Sexual disgust is a visceral response that helps to define the social and moral limits of acceptable behavior. It must be understood as one of the bodily forms of discipline that Foucault has famously explained as providing the invisible regulatory mechanism for policing the most important rules of social reproduction (ibid.: 124).

Sexual disgust is not unlike Jeremy Bentham's panopticon. Through sexual disgust, revulsion, and contempt, we socialize and domesticate our bodies and moral selves into submission to a certain normative and sanctioned sexual behavior. We police ourselves by policing our desire: we introject the disapproval and negative sanctioning of society by deriding others and raising ourselves above them. Perry summarizes her analysis of the uses of sexual disgust when she writes: "A woman's relation to sex was coming to stand for her *integrity* as a woman, to be identified as the expression of her deepest self" (ibid.: 125). The moral integrity of woman is built from *without* while it is policed from *within* by its ability to be disgusted by what it is taught is contemptible and repugnant. Imperial psychology is related to this learned and socialized capacity to be disgusted and revolted, to deride and to feel oneself above that which is contemptible. In fact, and this is what I want to claim here, what Williams called an "imperial psychology" is what Foucault would call a technology of the self, what, in light of Perry, we can call the *imperial somatology of disgust and contempt*. We can now turn to Foucault's genealogy of the imperial self and the technologies of the imperial agent.

On Foucault's Genealogy

The following are important methodological clarifications. We can define genealogy most elementally by way of its etymological sources, and thus we can say that genealogy is the study of the genesis, or source, of our modes of thinking, world-views, *Weltanschauungen*. Genealogy attempts to excavate the origins of our epistemes, or conceptual paradigms, not in order to mitigate skepticism and discontent with our institutions, but rather in order to demonstrate their vulnerability and historicity. At the same time, and principally, genealogy tries to make visible what cannot be seen at first blush. It does this by tracing the nadir in the horizon. Once the limits of what is knowable have been drawn, and the cartographies of episteme lay before us, what is or was unthinkable begins to be profiled not as that which is unconceivable in itself, but as what remains unthinkable so long as we remain rooted in one place, one horizon. Genealogy then is a *critique of impure reason*, or more specifically, it is a transcendental investigation. In other words, genealogy deals with the conditions of possibility, not narrowly conceived as epistemological or even ontological conditions, but more amply, as the conditions of possibility of a form of thinking, of living, of being able to conceive anything at all. Genealogy, like phenomenology, begins with what is most evident; that is, with what is most intimate and familiar, with the instruments and practices of quotidian existence. For this reason, as Foucault made explicit in many places, genealogy is simultaneously an archeology; or in other words, it is an excavation from the surface of the everyday towards the deep of the foundation of the instruments, practices and institutions within which we dwell. To live is to dwell, to inhabit, and we always inhabit dwellings that are practices and habits, which are, simply put, forms of behaving and dealing, of managing and toiling with. Before the world becomes a text and a museum of disposed artifacts, the world is primordially a regime of practices, a *habitus*, forms of dwelling and behaving. Thus, this is what genealogy investigates: the origins of our epistemes in practices or modes of dwelling. Thought itself is a *habitus*. Logos is a dwelling, a *habitus*. And every *habitus* always secretes an armature, an infrastructure that is as much the vehicle of the execution of the *habitus* as it is a result, a detritus.

The prior discussion of genealogy was very general. Now I will discuss it with greater detail and precision. Genealogy, helped by archeology, allows us to query the conditions of possibility of our epistemes, or worldviews, from the perspective of three different but insolubly linked levels (Foucault 1980; Han 2002: especially 73–107). Firstly, genealogy is a genealogy of *institutions*. In Foucault's case, his genealogical exercises dealt with the prison, the clinic, the madhouse, and the psychoanalyst's couch. Every institution, however, is susceptible of a genealogical analysis. A second level of analysis is that of objects and truths that are required by those institutions and sanctioned spaces as a type of conceptual armature. Truths are not discovered, but invented. They are invented as much by the institutions that produce them as they are invented by the discourses that legitimate these institutions. *Genealogy is a transcendental investigation that seeks to elucidate the conditions of possibility of the production of certain truths.* An example: what truth is disclosed by our sexual preferences? What truths tie our desires with our bodies, and the body with the flesh, and this flesh with our souls, and our souls with a certain aptitude or skill to be or not to be a certain type of self? In third place, genealogy allows us to analyzed and excavate the origins of our systems of thought, our epistemes, and paradigms of thinking. To illustrate: Sigmund Freud and the whole psychoanalytic system are linked to a conceptual perspective, both synchronically and diachronically, a conceptual lens that links individual ontogenesis to social phylogenesis, that links the private to the public, that ties desire to quotidian frustration, that displaces the pugnacity of the soul against evil and sin towards the battle of desire with sociality. We could offer similar caricatures of Karl Marx and Charles Darwin. Genealogy, then, allows us to investigate institutions, truths, and discourses.

This way of presenting genealogy as a methodology is not yet sufficiently precise, and most importantly, it conceals the dynamic character of it as a method as well as the dynamic character of that which it studies. Institutions, truths, and the discourses that justify and make indispensable their truth and institutions, are always in processes of transformation, modification, renovation and transmutation. For this reason, we err if we think that genealogy is a methodology of discontinuities, one that toils the zones of rupture in order to precisely indicate the brakes and abysms. No, genealogy is a method that pays attention to areas of discontinuity and epistemological and conceptual ruptures in order to show, to foreground the continuity in the discontinuity. Discontinuity is only thinkable within a continuum that is in transformation. What is yet most objectionable in my presentation above is that it conceals the dynamic and agonistic aspect, to use that Arendtian term, where there is a ceaseless confrontation among forces, forces that dominate and forces that resist. There is only power where there is force to subjugate, but there is only subjugation if there is opposition. Power therefore is not a *prius*, something pure and antecedent to the encounter of forces, prior to the positioning within a horizon of institutions, truths, and discourses. Power circulates; it is exercised, is transmitted, and empowered, given potency, by its very conditions of possibility. For this reason, genealogy is always an analysis of the conditions of possibility of power. Power, however, is always the name of an abstraction, which abstracts precisely from those relations that are made possible by those institutions, truth, and discourses. In order to make even more evident how genealogy as a method is dynamic, and always aims at the heart of dynamic power, at the heart of the regimes that produce power, which produces its truths, we have to speak of techniques of production, of signification, and domination. Genealogy, then, investigates the conditions of possibility of our forms of thinking, conceiving, and imaging, through the investigation of different techniques of the production of truths and objects of truth, techniques of signification, and techniques of domination.

Religion and Racism

Religion is a political technology that determines as much the horizon of the social as the horizon of the subjective. Technology, however, is always given in the plural. For this reason, and lest we fall prey to bad academic habits, we will speak of genealogies of religions, and even more specifically, of the genealogies of different political technologies. When we speak of the political, we are speaking of those habits of behavior and social structures that condition what one, what agents, may or may not be. The political always points in the direction of the agonistic, the agora, and the space within which we are witnesses to the confessions of others and of ourselves. This way of speaking about religion was already implicit in what we said earlier about techniques of signification, and techniques of domination. For a technique is always a political event, a political fact. This is the case not only because a certain force is always required so that certain forms of inhabiting and dwelling are constituted and given form, but principally because every technique becomes a vehicle, the conducting medium, for the transmittal of force as power. Religion is perhaps one of the most important techniques, if not the most important, in the West.

Now, religion is that which, in the etymological lingo, binds us, but that simultaneously, sunders us, from others, ourselves, clearly, and the transcendent, also clearly. Religion is that which conditions an internal and subjective relation, as well as social and objective relations. The genealogical analysis of religion allows us to study in great detail how every conceptual regime, episteme, and paradigm conditions certain forms of subjective and social relations, both always mediated by produced and invented truths. Religion as political technology, the political technology *par excellence*, allows us to see how an entire *Weltanschauung* is a technology of production, signification, and domination. That is to say, religion is always a conglomerate of institutions, objects and truths, and discourses. All of this, in its synchronic and diachronic synergy, produces a world in which certain truths are admissible, and other barely conceivable. The singular virtue that makes of Foucauldian genealogy the absolutely ideal method to study religion is that it allows us to consider how the subject, *the self*, is produced. Religion is a technology for the production of certain types of subjectivity, of the incorporation of the other into ourselves, of our production of subjects by the way we related to others. *Genealogy allows us to understand how it is that the "soul" is the prison of the body, and how it is that the skin confesses the soul, in such a way that the skin and the body always betray the truths that constitute us as subjects.* If the body is a technology of corporalization, embodiment, or corporeal materialization, of subjects, then the skin is the surface where the social touches the subjective, the place where the social is subjectivized. *The skin is the subjectivity of the body*, announces Foucault. *The skin is where I touch myself, when I touch the other and only if I touch the other*. The skin is where I touch myself from out of my subjectivity, from which I see myself but from the other. My subjectivity is always exocentric, and decentered. It is from its periphery that I constitute myself, but always by way of the other. But if the body is produced, by a technology of embodiment, then the skin is also produced. The skin is the surface of the body, on which we discover explicitly how subjectivity is also produced, and particularly, how it is produced by technologies of subjectivization, which are simultaneously techniques of corporalization.[2]

If religion is a political technology, it is so because it is a technology of the production of subjects, a technique of subjectification that is at the same time a technique of embodiment and the production of the skin.[3] Religion produces the skin of the subject, and produces it in certain shades and forms, as desiring flesh, a flesh and skin that betray their desire, their sin, their shame, and contempt. Skin is where the desire for the other betrays us, and where the other's desire also betrays. Religion is then a technique for the production of the skin, of that surface and region where the social touches the subjective, where subjectivity is embodied, and where the social is touched from within. All of this, however, we already knew, although not epistemologically, but as a *habitus*, as a form of behavior and dwelling in the social. We already know very well all of this because religion regiments our bodies, but we do not understand well enough how it is that religion produces our skins, those zones where we encounter ourselves as others and with others. It is precisely here where we can make a transition to the problematic of racism.

Racism produces race, the idea and social construct of race; race is the detritus of an ensemble of practices of racialization (West 1982). Racism is thus a political technology that registers the introduction of new techniques of production, significa-tion, and domination of subjects. For the moment we can only formulate as a thesis without being able to offer sufficient justification or proofs the following affirmation concerning religion and racism: racism extends, transforms and exacerbates religion as a political technology. Racism is parasitic on religion, but at the same time it inau-gurates a new religion: the religion of the body, of the flesh, as a scientific object.[4] Racism, however, not only exacerbates and makes more sophisticated the technolo-gies of subjection, but also the techniques of social domination. Racism is a political technology that inverts the truth that the soul is the prison of the body; now it is the body that is the prison of the soul. Racism produces the techniques that make possi-ble that the body become the prison of the soul, but now as secularized, biologized, scienticized. In fact, it is racism that allows for the secularization of the soul. What is the soul once this has passed through the filter of modernity? It is subjectivity as cognitive capacity; it is the ability to withstand truth as index of intelligence that can be measured in the size of the skull, the weight of the brain, and the color of the skin. Racism is therefore a political technology that allowed the secularization of the Christian subject into the modern subject. Racism is the reverse of Cartesian dualism that allows the disembodiment of the cognitive ego. The one conceals the other; one is the alibi for the other. As such, racism is indispensable for modernity.

In fact, racism is the *sine qua non* of modernity. There is no passage through and to modernity, at least in the West, without the horizons opened up by the techniques that together conform the regimen of racialization.

Genealogically we can appreciate how institutions, truths and objects, and discourses constitute racism. Racism produces and is produced by the institutions of slavery, principally, but also by all the institutions that deal with the control and domination of populations spread over non-contiguous territories. Like religion, racism is auxiliary to the political-military power that make possible empires and nations. Racism produces and is produced by the object of the skin, the chromatic skin of race, the skin as the visible evidence of metaphysical and moral truths. The body, the skin, and race, as synergistic unity of the biological, the social, and the metaphysical, disclose the most profound truths of the subject. Or rather, these truths bind the soul. And it is thus that the body becomes the prison of subjectivity. Finally, racism is produced and produces all the discourses that legitimate the practices of exclusion, of marginalization, of containment, of subjection and control, that operate as much through the scienticization of subjectivity as through the methods of investigation themselves (racialized science). Racism, succinctly then, produces and is produced by all those discourses that are in turn articulated as manifestation of a biological truth. Racism biologizes divine history in the truth of the human species, phylogenesis. The truth of the soul, the truth that the soul gathers and guards, is turned into scientific object: the body as biological entity – as singular unity, but also as totality that aggregates plurality within itself. The racial discourse allows us to segregate within a biological continuum the plurality of human cultures. All are human, but some are more human than others. Each culture is an expression of the human species, but some are more advanced than others. The racial discourse, racism, therefore allows us to translate the Christian teleology into a biological teleology that clearly is only legible if it is read from back to front. Racism, for these reasons, modernizes, transforms, but extends, religion, and just like religion, we can see how racism is a technique for the production of biologized subjectivities, techniques of signification that signify through the scienticized biological body, and that are deployed with the goal of producing dominations that are very specific.

As Foucault noted in his 1976 lectures at the *Collège de France* on the genealogy of racism, racism inverts the dominion over death that characterized the medieval period (Foucault 2003 [These lectures appeared in French only in 1997]). If the power of the sovereign king was the power to put to death, racism makes it possible that we all, as totalized multiplicity, can kill. In fact, racism makes quotidian the killing of the racially abject; it sanctions and secularizes the extermination of the other, the other as racialized flesh and embodiment. But this inversion of the power of the sovereign is possible if we accept that racism is a technology for the production of life. Racism, therefore, is the *litmus test* of modernity in as much as modernity is the ascendancy of a new order, a new episteme, the new paradigm of the biopolitical. Thus, already using Foucault's later language, we can say that racism is the acme of biopolitics, and in fact, it is the first and most originary form in which biopolitics is made evident as a new political regime, a new form of sovereignty and governmentality. Racism is a bridge between the form of the sovereign power that characterized medieval, theocratic imperial power, and the new order of biopolitics. More explicitly, racism allows the transformation of what Foucault called pastoral power, into biopolitical power. Now we are able to see how racism was a catalyst for the transformation of Christianity as political technology underwriting the power of the sovereign, into a political technology that secures the power of society over each and every individual. This last transformation was in turn catalyzed by racism which allowed the transformation of pastoral power into a form of biopower, or power over life, over the life of a people, now thought of as a biological continuum. For biopower, the people is a biological entity, a species, whose well-being became, first and foremost, an obligation of the state, until it becomes a problematic of social hygiene, what was called originally during the seventeenth and eighteenth centuries by the name of the science of policing, in German, *Polizeiwissenschaft*. In this word, the science of police, to translate literally, we find the naked the truth of biopower: the power to police over life, by way of policing over the people. But this policing is not an outrageous and bombastic performance and consumption of power, but rather a routine. To police the body of the people is the mere and most elemental duty of the state of biopower.

We can ask now in order to begin to make good on a series of threads that I have been weaving: how was pastoral power transformed into the power of the modern, welfare state, which is a power that racializes and that is predicated on a racial hierarchy? How is it that sexuality, racism, truth impregnated by racism, are joined in an infernal embrace in such a way that modern subjectivity is suffused by both sexuality and racism? How is it that racism allows not only the secularization of the soul, but also the de-spiritualization of sexuality, in such a way that both can be medicalized and biologized, and as such become object of utmost preoccupation for the state, a biopower sovereignty? These questions allow us now to focus geopolitically on the questions of race, religion and empire. And it is here where we can turn to the Hispanic world of the sixteenth century.

Spiritual Conquest and the Inquisition

During the fifteenth and sixteenth centuries, through the process of imperial unification in the Iberian peninsula, the *Reconquista*, and the expulsion of the Jews, there emerged an institution that was vital to the process of transforming the centralized and executive power of an imperial sovereign into a pastoral power, which then begins to establish the foundations of a biopolitical power; this institution was the Inquisition (Netanyahu 1992, 1997). This had as a goal to maintain the purity of the religion, of belief, of the credo, and eventually, the purity of blood. The rise of modern racism has to be directly linked to the transformation that the Inquisition affected, one that linked orthodoxy to the purity of blood. The primary function of the Inquisition was to track down, to unmask, prosecute and judge heresy, and every violation and infraction against orthodoxy. In the process of the eradication of heresy and heterodoxy, the inquisition became an institution for the preservation of the purity of race. If the genealogical study attends to institutions, truths and objects, and the discourses that produce these truths and objects, then the institution *par excellence* that allows us to observe with great clarity the passage from the medieval to the classical paradigm is without doubt the inquisition. Here we have an institution that is the *locus classicus* where ecclesiastical power is slowly metabolized into secular power, where theological reason is catalyzed into political reason, where canonical bureaucracy gives way to juridical and, later, liberal and legalistic bureaucracy. But it is also here, in this institution, where the people of god become a people as a biological and racial unit, a unit now that underlies and supports a people as a political, juridical, linguistic unity that forms the basis for the genocidal nationalism of modernity. Another extremely important aspect of the inquisition is who can be an agent of it, or, in other words, who can represent this power to discern the purity of both blood and faith. Who can be the agent of the discrimination between the truth and false faith, the pure and impure blood? In other words, how, under the questioning initiated by the Inquisition, can we know who is credible and reliable, and who is duplicitous and untrustworthy? The credible witness, to use Donna Haraway's expression, is one of the most important questions at the core of modernity – the whole scientific project is made possible by our ability to answer this question. In this way, the orthodoxy of belief, and the purity of blood are linked to the possibility of modern science (Haraway 1997: especially chapter I).

Now, if Michel Foucault had been a Latin American, or simply had looked beyond the eighteenth and nineteenth centuries, the second institution he would have treated as paradigmatic of the kind of transformation that gave rise to biopower is the *encomienda*. This was a fundamental institution for the conquest, colonization, and pacification of the so-called New World (Rivera 1992: 113–131). Through the *encomienda* the mission of the territorial and imperial expansion is dignified by the sacred mantle of the mission of conversion. It has to be admitted that it is extremely difficult to distinguish between the evangelizing mission and the imperial design, since the power of the kings was linked to an apostolic and papal sanction, and furthermore, the territories of the new lands that had been *donamos, condedimos et assignamus* (to quote the bull that grants Spain jurisdiction over the new lands) impose on them a mission that has to be assumed with unwavering responsibility. This mission and duty, as blessed and commanded by the church, is to the great benefit and glory of all Christians. But what is incredible about the *encomienda* is that it exhibits in exemplary form the characteristics and virtues of what Foucault called pastoral power. The *encomienda*, that began as the *repartimientos*, became an institution that virtually and ideologically, in the benign sense of the word, has to attend to, take care, educate, evangelize, save, and provide for the bodies and souls of the "Indians," the natives.[5] The *encomienda*, furthermore, allows the transformation of a process of colonization and territorial domination into a spiritual domination of entire peoples. For this reason, the conquest was not merely and principally a territorial conquest, but perhaps most fundamentally a spiritual conquest. Within the *encomienda*, the labor that the Indians performed had the goal of re-educating. This re-education included that the natives abandon their practices and customs, and that they adopt those of the allegedly civilized Europeans, customs that included dress codes, the institution of private property, and even, as Hegel notes in his *Lectures on the Philosophy of World History*, when and where to execute the sexual act.[6] But above all, the *encomendero* assumed a paternal, benign, and sacralized charge, a charge that is taken over in the name of the souls to be saved, but simultaneously is made to the glory of the Spaniards and Christians. This paternalism was eventually transferred to the institution of the slave plantation, where the master did not, allegedly, exploit the slave but where the slave was educated, Christianized, taken care of, and where he or she were granted and socialized into the virtues of discipline, work and spirituality. In this way, the *encomienda* was the prototype for many such institutions: the plantation, the reservation, and the concentration camp. Over the entrances to all these institutions hang, whether *de facto* or only virtually, the motto: *"Arbeit macht Frei."* Today, this very same paternalism lives on, but perhaps without the ideological justification, and thus in an even more arrogant, imperial, and brutal form, without any masks, as in the plenipotentiaries of democracy and liberalism that imposed their civilizing and salvation mission with the boot and the machine gun.

Notes

1 On the spiritual conquest, see Gruzinski (1993) and Rivera (1992), see also León-Portilla (1990). For what I call epistemological gerrymandering, see Mignolo (1995).
2 See Carrette (1999). This is an indispensable resource for understanding how Foucault's work can contribute to our deeper understanding of religion as a technology of embodiment. Another is Brown (1988). See also Bernauer and Carrette (2003).
3 It may be useful to note Foucault's clarification of the concept of "technology." Foucault writes: "[T]here are four major types of these "technologies," each a matrix of practical reason: (1) technologies of production, which permit us to produce, transform, or manipulate things; (2) technologies of sign systems, which permit us to use signs, meanings, symbols, or signification; (3) technologies of power, which determine the conduct of individuals and submit them to certain ends or domination, an objectivizing of the subject; (4) technologies of the self, which permit individuals to effect by their own means or with the help of other a certain number of operations on their own bodies and souls, thoughts, conduct, and way of being, so as to transform themselves in order to attain a certain state of happiness, purity, wisdom, perfection, or immortality. These four types of technologies hardly ever function separately, although each one of them is associated with a certain type of domination" (Foucault 1988: 18).
4 See the first part of Mendieta (2004) on Foucauldian genealogical analysis of racism in the United States; also Stingelin (2003).
5 Criticizing Foucault, while acculturating him to the U.S., Angela Y. Davis notes: "At least four great systems of incarceration could be identified: the reservation system, slavery, the mission system, and the internment camps of World War II" (Davis 1998: 96–107).
6 The passage I have in mind is the following: "I even recollect having read that a clergyman used to ring a bell at midnight to remind them [the natives of the New World] to perform their matrimonial duties, for it would otherwise never have occurred to them to do so" (Hegel 1975: 165).

References

Asad, Talal. 1993. *Genealogies of Religion: Discipline and Reasons of Power in Christianity and Islam*. Baltimore, MD/London: Johns Hopkins Press.

Asad, Talal. 2003. *Formations of the Secular: Christianity, Islam, Modernity*. Stanford, CA: Stanford University Press.

Bernauer, James and Jeremy Carrette (Eds.). 2003. *Michel Foucault and Theology: The Politics of Religious Experience*. Burlington, VT: Ashgate.

Brown, Peter. 1988. *The Body and Society: Men, Women, and Sexual Renunciation in Early Christianity*. New York: Columbia University Press.

Carrette, Jeremy R. 1999. *Foucault and Religion: Spiritual Corporality and Political Spirituality*. London/New York: Routledge.

Davis, Angela Y. 1998. Racialized Punishment and Prison Abolition. In *The Angela Y. Davis Reader*, edited by Joy James, pp. 96–107. Malden, MA: Blackwell.

Foucault, Michel. 1980. Two Lectures. In *Power/Knowledge: Selected Interviews & Other Writings 1972–1977*, edited by Colin Gordon, pp. 78–108. New York: Pantheon.

Foucault, Michel. 1988. Technologies of the Self. In *Technologies of the Self. A Seminar with Michel Foucault*, edited by Luther H. Martin, Huck Gutman, Patrick H. Hutton. Amherst: The University of Massachusetts Press.

Foucault, Michel. 2003. *"Society Must Be Defended" Lectures at the Collège de France 1975–1976*, translated by David Macey. New York: Picador.

Gruzinski, Serge. 1993. *The Conquest of Mexico: The Incorporation of Indian Societies in the Western World 16–18th Centuries*. Cambridge, MA: Blackwell.

Han, Béatrice. 2002. *Foucault's Critical Project: Between the Transcendental and the Historical*, translated by Edward Pile. Stanford, CA: Stanford University Press.

Haraway, Donna J. 1997. *Modest_Witness@Second_Millenium.FemaleMan©_Meets_OncoMouse^TM*. New York: Routledge.

Hegel, Georg Wilhelm Friedrich. 1975. *Lectures on the Philosophy of World History*. London/New York/Melbourne: Cambridge University Press.

Kipnis, Laura. 2003. *Against Love: A Polemic*. New York: Pantheon.

León-Portilla, Miguel. 1990. *Endangered Cultures*. Dallas: Southern Methodist University Press.

Mendieta, Eduardo. 2001. Society's Religion: The Rise of Social Theory, Globalization and the Invention of Religio. In *Religions/Globalizations*, edited by Dwight N. Hopkins, Lois Ann Lorentzen, David Batstone, Eduardo Mendieta, pp. 46–65. Durham, NC: Duke University Press.

Mendieta, Eduardo. 2002. Religion y Sociologia. In *El Estudio de la Religion*, Vol. 1. of the *Enciclopedia Iberoamericana de Religiones*, edited by Francisco Diez de Velasco y Francisco García Bazán, pp. 103–120. Madrid: Trotta.

Mendieta, Eduardo. 2004. Plantations, Ghettos, Prisons: US racial geographies. *Philosophy & Geography* 7: 43–59.

Mignolo, Walter. 1995. *The Darker Side of the Renaissance: Literacy, Territoriality, & Colonization*. Ann Arbor, MI: The University of Michigan Press.

Netanyahu, Benzion. 1992. *The Origins of the Inquisition in Fifteenth Century Spain*. New York: Random House.

Netanyahu, Benzion. 1997. *Toward the Inquisition: Essays on Jewish and Converso History in Late Medieval Spain*. Ithaca, NY/London: Cornell University Press.

Perry, Ruth. 2000. Sleeping with Mr. Collins. *Persuasions: The Jane Austen Journal* 22: 119–135.

Rivera, Luis N. 1992. *A Violent Evangelism: The Political and Religious Conquest of the Americas*. Louisville, KY: Westminster John Knox Press.

Stingelin, Martin (Ed.). 2003. *Biopolitik und Rassismus*. Frankfurt am Main: Suhrkamp.

Wallerstein, Immanuel et al. 1996. *Open Up the Social Sciences: Report of the Gulbenkian Commission on the Restructuring of the Social Sciences*. Stanford, CA: Stanford University Press.

Wallerstein, Immanuel et al. 2001. *The End of the World as We Know It: Social Science for the Twenty-First Century*. Minneapolis, MN: University of Minnesota Press.

West, Cornel. 1982. A Genealogy of Modern Racism. In *Prophesy Deliverance! An Afro-American Revolutionary Christianity*, pp. 47–65. Philadelphia, PA: The Westminster Press.

Williams, William Appleman. 1980. *Empire as a Way of Life: An Essay on the Causes and Character of America's Present Predicament Along with a Few Thoughts About an Alternative*. New York: Oxford University Press.

De-colonial Jewish Thought and the Americas

Santiago E. Slabodsky[1]

"Among the millions of human beings who encountered misery and death, the Jews alone experienced a total dereliction." (Levinas 1990a: 11)

"[A problem for Jewish Thought today is] the arrival on the historical scene of those under-developed Afro-Asiatic masses who are strangers to the sacred history that forms the heart of the Judaic-Christian world." (Levinas 1990a: 58–59)

Abstract This essay voices a de-colonial reading of peripheral Judaism. The de-colonial discourse reconfigures the racial, political, and epistemological alliances that were put in place after the Holocaust. By departing from the limitations of one of the most influential post-1945 European Jewish intellectuals, Emmanuel Levinas, I show the need to return to a narrative of Jewish thought that neither reduces racial suffering exclusively to the Jewish case, nor tries to incorporate Judaism within the Western canon. A de-colonial reading shows that through the historical interrelation, hybridization, and common social struggle with, or within, other others, Judaism can complement other contemporary proposals and confront the ethical and political dilemmas of the post-1945 American Jewish narrative.

I

It was only a few years before the establishment of concentration camps in Argentina and 20 years before the quincentenary of the beginning of the extermination of original peoples in Latin-America. In those days of the early 1970s, a young Argentinean philosopher, Enrique Dussel, felt an affinity for the work of Emmanuel Levinas, a Lithuanian Jewish thinker whose work, mostly written in France, was "dominated by the presentiment and the memory of the Nazi horror" (Levinas 1990a: 291). Dussel recalls gathering in 1972 in Louvain:

a group of students together to talk with Levinas. I asked: "What about the fifteen million Indians slaughtered during the conquest of America and the thirteen millions Africans who were made slaves, aren't they the other you are speaking about? ... " What of all of us who are not Semitic? Levinas looked at me and said: 'That is something for you to think about... I see all of you as hostages.' I did not know [whether or not] he was insulting us by making this observation. (Dussel 1999: 123–127; cf. Dussel 1973: 111–113)

P. Bilimoria and A.B. Irvine (eds.), *Postcolonial Philosophy of Religion.*
© Springer Science+Business Media B.V. 2009

Given such a confusing answer, why was Dussel – and many other third-world thinkers – attracted to Levinas, whose major activity until his late 50s was being director of the colonial and universalist *Ecole Normale Israelite Orientale*?[2] What Levinas offered Dussel was a step beyond the merely negative critique of the false universality generated by the West. Indeed, the rabbinical Levinas, in opposition to the Jewish atheistic school of Frankfurt, charts the path for the production of knowledge from an-other place, and from other sources. Effectively, Levinas introduces "some barbarism in the language of philosophy" (Levinas 1998[1974]: 178).

Levinas aims to demonstrate that "western history and our philosophy of history announce the realization of a humanist ideal while ignoring the vanquished, the victims, and the persecuted, as if they were not significant" (Levinas 1990a: 170). He confronts the "imperial ontology" that "digests otherness into sameness" (Levinas 1969: 127–129). Dislocating the center of western thought, he claims that the 'Ego' (the I, the Greek, the totality, or, even more interestingly, the West) ignores a previous commitment to an ethical relationship with the other that precedes the constitution of the subject and his/her 'economy' (understood as the law, the dominion, the authority of the Ego) guided by his/her wishes and natural drives (Levinas 1969: 109–118).

The other, preceding the Self, resides in an unreachable distance from the Ego's power. This distance is described as height. The excessively impoverished, destitute, and naked other evades capture by the Self, resisting the Ego's drive to know, and thereby to possess. This interruption, prior to cognition, is a traumatic reminder to the Self of a debt that cannot be discharged. The impossibility of reaching the other, who resides beyond the economy of the Ego, in exteriority, reverses the understanding of being hostage. In Levinas' thinking the Ego (supposedly powerful) is the hostage of the other (supposedly weak). The Ego becomes obsessed with the other (Levinas 1998[1974]: 117–121).

However, Dussel points out a problem with the content of Levinas' understanding of exteriority or otherness. Philosophy (the Greek) is represented as the kingdom of ontology, the empire of violence and suppression of alterity. In opposition to this stands the Hebrew, the elusive, anarchical thinking that permits the existence of an-otherness that is not subsumed by the same. In other words, it is the ethical stand of Judaism that antecedes and resists Christianity.[3] Along this line, Levinas writes that, in opposition to the history of the West, "the history of Israel invites us to create a new anthropology, a new history, and perhaps, by bringing about the end of Western triumphalism" (Levinas 1990: 171). Israel does not stand as the victim of history but as a collective of those who, having suffered it, refuse to accept its judgment. Jews stand outside history – not because of their eternity (as per Levinas' forerunner, Franz Rosenzweig), but because of their history of suffering and their ethical choice to defend sufferers (Levinas 1990c: 181–202).[4]

For Levinas, however, only the Jews are the source for this anarchical thinking: "Among the millions of Human beings who encountered misery and death, the Jews alone experienced a total dereliction" (Levinas 1990a: 11). If the Hebrew is the paradigm of otherness one may ask whether there is any space for other others. Dussel reads Levinas and reflects:

> Between the hostage and the victim appears the "Third Party." In my case the Third Party
> was the Europe that held as hostage those of us who comprised a small group of teachers
> and students from South America. The system, the totality is justice (or injustice).

Responsibility for the other obligates me to search in the prevailing system or Totality for the causes of the victimization of the victim, and this is the critical moment
of ethics as such (Dussel 1994: 1–16).

According to Levinas, the third party disrupts the encounter between the Self
and the other, paradigmatic of the ethical relationship. It is no mere inference that
the encounter, for Levinas, is between a European conversation between Christian
and Jew. Now there are competitive others who also claim an ethical relationship.
These other others are referred to by Levinas as the third party. In response to the
third party, Levinas abandons the anarchical ethical relationship for a system of liberal justice that can respond to multiple demands (Levinas 1998: 50–52). While the
confrontation of Judaism and the West is a radical dislocation, relations between
other others and the West should be judged within the liberal framework. Whereas
the Jew's refusal to accept history is a return to the ethical, the same resistance of
other others violates the ethical possibility to the extent that the other others become
hostages (paradoxically, Egos and not others). Following this line of thought, we
can understand why, for Levinas, "the arrival on the historical scene of those under-
developed Afro-Asiatic masses who are strangers to the sacred history that forms
the heart of the Judaic-Christian world" threatens that "Judaic-Christian world"
(Levinas 1990a: 58–59). The "Afro-Asiatic masses" deprive Judaism of its exclusivity. Levinas was apparently unable to recognize the extreme destitution and the
ethical resistance of third parties (or masses).

Dussel's critique marks a fundamental turning point not only in non-Jewish
deconstructions of Levinas' dialogical formulation, but also in liberation and decolo-
nial readings of the eurocentrism of radical European thought in general.[5] Dussel's
Philosophy of Liberation takes up the spirit of Levinas and goes beyond it, leaving the limitations of Levinas behind, by thinking of ethical responsibility in terms
of structural situations and finding alternative sources to think from an-other place
(Dussel 1985).

Yet, another question arises. Have *Jewish* intellectuals confronted the disturbing
fact that one of their most influential representatives reproduces the very colonial and euro/ego-centric project that oppressed the Jews from 1492 to 1942 (i.e.,
between the expulsion and the extermination)? After all, Levinas simultaneously
limits the suffering to Jewish people and incorporates *the Jew* into the white and
western project of a sacred Judaic-Christian world.[6] Furthermore, to what degree is
Levinas' inability to acknowledge what I call the *other others* (or third party) related
to, first, Western post-Holocaust philo-Semitism and philo-Zionism, and second,
the canonical Jewish formulation of "otherness" after 1945?[7] Is Levinas, perhaps in
spite of himself, recognizing that after a process of 50 years that began roughly in
1945–1948, Jews have become white and western? Have the Jews, in other words,
abandoned their ethical height and became fearful hostages?[8]

Despite deep engagement with Levinas in the North American (and European)
academy, mainstream liberal, institutional Judaism has insulated itself from these

questions, raised from the 1970s liberationist and de-colonial movements. There were several lost opportunities for this reflection to take place. But the relationship between liberationist critiques and Jewish suffering has been repeatedly avoided, with the exception of a few Jewish thinkers such as Marc Ellis, Dan Cohn-Sherbok, and Michael Lowy, none of whom have directly developed our question.[9]

One of the most interesting of the aforementioned lost opportunities took place when a reform Argentinean Rabbi, Leon Klenicki, become director of interfaith dialogue at the Anti-Defamation League/B'nai Brith, New York. Without even analyzing the possible conversation between liberationism and modern Judaism, Klenicki accused all liberation theologians of ignorance of Jewish history and explicit anti-Semitism. Klenicki, an official voice in the post-1945 liberal Jewish-Christian dialogue, in charge of the relations with liberation theology, is still trapped by a constellation that sees anti-Semitism in any Christian voice that attempts to present the limitation of a Jewish proposal. I contend that this has been the official Jewish position toward the liberationist critique until today (Klenicki 1983: 37).

However, Dussel's primary confrontation with Levinas is not over Levinas' Judaism, but over his post-1945 Jewish Euro/Ego-centrism. If Levinas had written his work before 1945, Klenicki's accusations would deserve consideration in the case of Dussel and other liberationists. Nevertheless, the post-1945 Jewish engagement with the white and western world leads us to recognize the validity of liberationist voices. In other words, while the presentation of the Jew as the other in western history before 1945 is an interesting analytical tool, to assert it after 1945 is an insult to the suffering of the other others; as it unfolds, our argument will bear particularly on the plight of Palestinians.[10]

II

I will try to contextualize the problem of Jewish exclusivism in relation to the position of Jews in modernity before and after 1945 to understand the implications of the claim before and after the Holocaust. Diverse and opposite schools of thought have defined modernity with the attempt of implicitly installing a particular narrative of this period. On the one hand, one group of scholars describes modernity as the attempt at a worldwide extension of civil rights, democracy and freedom of conscience to equal human beings. This tendency places the beginning of the period in the seventeenth and eighteenth centuries' double European revolution (Taylor 1989; Dubnow 1967–1973). On the other hand, an opposing group of scholars describes modernity as the attempt to install a global market that, through oppression, genocide, and a hegemonic colonial and coloniality of knowledge, guarantees capitalist material accumulation. This group's narrative places the turning point of the period in the conquest of America, which initiates the continent's incorporation to the global market in the sixteenth century (Quijano and Wallerstein 1992; Slabodsky 2004).

Under either one or the other narrative, in spite of what many thinkers such as a Jewish-born Karl Marx believe – that there is a "natural suitability" between modernity and Judaism and that modern society itself "became Jewish"[11] – Jews, both as a people and as individuals, arrived at the supposed turning point of modernity under let us say problematic conditions. In the first version, Jews received their civil rights (as individuals – certainly not as Jews) during the French revolution only after 3 years of heated debates – 1792–,[12] while the second version highlights that Jews were expelled from the center of power only 2 days before the departure of Cristobal Colón to the Americas-1492-.[13] Whereas the first narrative must recount that the same nation-state that made a claim for "liberty, equality and fraternity" was divided by the anti-Semitic Dreyfus affair less than 100 years after its inauguration, (Hyman 1998: 91–114) the second narrative must recall that the first anti-Semitic event (an act that was not only religiously, but also racially, anti-Jewish) took place in June, 1511, when the New Christian, even some of the most devoted of them, were excluded and persecuted for the inability to obtain a "proof of blood." (Netanyahu 1995: 975–980)

The image of *the Jew* and the structural anti-Semitism (on its racial connotations since the sixteenth century) become a crucial component of the coloniality of knowledge from then until Auschwitz. In those places where there were Jews, their image was manufactured creating of *her* an almost ontological figure which hybridization was an impossible (Kalmar and Penslar 2006: xix). In those places without Jewish population, they were created as it happened under Spanish, French, British, and Dutch colonizations from South-America to Africa to China (Parfit 2006: 51–67; Xun 2006: 68–89). The relationship between the need for anti-Semitism in the development of the relationship between modernity and capitalism was eloquently developed by Max Horkheimer in the following way:

> This is how it is with the Jews… despite all the fundamental differences between the Committee of Public Safety and the leaders of the Third Reich, which can be confronted with surprising parallels, the practice of both springs from the political necessity: to preserve control of the means of production for those groups which already own them… the same rationality of economics … has now pronounced judgment on the Jews… The same economic necessity, that irrationality created the army of the unemployed has now turned, in the form of carefully considered regulations, against entire minority groups. (Horkheimer 2005: 236–237)

Horkheimer (this time in tandem with Theodor Adorno) concludes claiming a few years later that "anti-Semitism has proved immune to the charge of inadequate profitability." According to the critical theorists: "its usefulness for the rulers is evident. It serves as a distraction for the masses, a cheap means of corruption." (Horkheimer and Adorno 2002: 139). Anti-Semitism has been a structural part of the capitalist racialization process from 1492 to 1789 to 1942.

The existence of a Jewish reaction to this capitalist racialization has been documented by several authors. Isaac Deustcher reflects that there is a hidden tradition of confrontation with modernity of a group of thinkers that comprehend intellectuals such as Moses Hess, Rosa Luxemburg, Leon Trotsky, and Georg Lukacs. According to Deustcher these thinkers do not set themselves apart from Judaism, but they create an internal heretic trend that has been transforming the tradition to the extent that their solidarity with the oppressed becomes the center of Jewish thought and existence. In his words, Deustcher sees himself as: "a Jew by force of my unconditional solidarity with the persecuted and exterminated" (Deutscher 1969: 56–57).

In the same line of thought Jean-Paul Sartre, in a work that will be strongly influential for cultural studies in North-America, recommends "the Jew" to answer "authentically" to their condition assuming the problem and engaging from this position with the liberation of all the others (Sartre 1995: 136–139). This position will be critically taken later on by Tunisian Jew Albert Memmi, perhaps one of the most forgotten de-colonial thinker (thinker), to explain the problem of both Jewish self-rejection and self-acceptation what makes the Jewish existence and 'impossible condition.' Even in this context, the Jew still has a final social(ist) goal (Memmi 1973).

However, some may argue that this solidarity beyond borders (very different from the proposal of Levinas) should be restricted to the non-Jewish Jews (i.e. those who saw Judaism too constraint and rejected a self-identification with it). However, as Michael Lowy and David Myers have demonstrated, the elective affinity of liberationist/libertarian thought and Jewish messianism and/or counter-modern historicism can be also extended to thinkers such as the neo-Kantian Hermann Cohen, the existentialist theologian who renewed Jewish philosophy Franz Rosenzweig (perhaps the most problematic case), the dialogical philosopher and Hassidic influenced Martin Buber, and the creator of the academic study of Jewish mysticism Gershom Scholem.[14] After all, it may be true, that there is a as "the natural suitability" between Judaism and radical trends (Fishman 1983: 143–145). Even if those include those who believe that in Jewish sources there may be an alternative source of knowledge and are the forerunners of Levinas.

Nevertheless, this elective affinity seems to die in Auschwitz, and especially after the rise of the hegemonic post-Holocaust Judeo-Christian readings of the Holocaust. Levinas is being caught in this transition. The knowledge is still produced in central Europe, but applied in the North-American context, the new center of Jewish power. In other words, the official narrative of the Holocaust in Euro/American-centric colonial proposals disrupted the Jewish subversion of the modern project that understands the conflictive imperialistic nature of modernity (Steiner 1988: 154). What in France was a problem in the public sphere, in North-America transcends it.

Post-Holocaust Judeo-Christian theology (with the exception of courageous thinkers such as Richard L. Rubenstein and Hannah Arendt) understands the Holocaust and the slogan, *Never Again*, as a license for Jews to survive even if their allies are their former enemies, and it implies not only participating in the reproduction of eurocentric epistemology, but also, for example, in a U.S.-centric crusade in the Middle East premised on a Clash of Civilizations. The reception of Levinas in North-America should be understood under this dynamic. The exclusivism of Jewish suffering is a path for the incorporation of Judaism into the Western world.

The dominant stream of Post-Holocaust Jewish theology, led by Emil Fackenheim, who understands Jewish empowerment as a 614th *mitzvah* added to the canonical 613th commandments of the rabbinical system of law, and by the holocaustic novelist, Elie Wiesel, who strongly supports the U.S. interventions in Afghanistan and Iraq, carries a consequence that would shock even these, its leading authors: If Jewish empowerment is necessary to protect post-Holocaust Jews then so, inevitably, is the oppression of other people (i.e. Palestinians).[15] In other words, this narrative reproduces not only Levinas's narrow view of the other as the Jew, but also its consequence: that the only solution for anti-Semitism is the non-acknowledgement of other others in history.[16] The line of thought employed by Klenicki earlier in our article, finds at home within this line of thought.

Tragically, this narrative carries difficulties not only for the other others, but also for Jews – peripheral Jews, at least. A certain alliance of conservatives and liberal sectors of the American Jewish establishment has supported a zealous American policy that includes the sponsorship of Latin American dictatorships in the 1960s and 1970s as part of a *Real Politik* understanding of the world-system. One of the cruelest governments of this process, the Argentine *Proceso de Reorganización Nacional*, should have been a test case for this sector of Judaism. From 1976 to 1983, the PRN 'disappeared' 30,000 voices and bodies, 13% of them Jews. Yet Jews account for less than 1% of Argentina's population.[17] The necessity to disrupt the dominant Post-Holocaust Jewish theological narrative is not caused only by the suffering of the other, but also by the suffering of American Jewry's brothers and sisters.[18]

After all, it may have been right Deustcher when he reflected that the major problem of Judaism after the Second War World is that "the world has compelled the Jews to embrace the nation state" to the extent that the insecure Jew, mostly represented as in Europe as an almost feminine weak figure become the stars of national security from Henry Kissinger to William Cohen to Madeline Albright (Deutscher 1969: 41). Therefore, before 1945 there is a not-so-hidden line of Jewish thought that understands that solidarity should not be restricted to what Rosa Luxemburg calls the "tears of the Ghetto" (Luxemburg 1995: 374–375). However, after 1945, the situation of the Jews in post-war Europe, Israel, and especially Latin-America let the Jewish exclusivism to emerge in a context of empowerment. They were others before 1945 who were exclusivist. But now the exclusivism is practiced in possession of power. This exclusivism is the prelude of Jewish inclusion into the *Judeo-Christian world*.

III

A variety of schools of thought have argued that, during the twentieth century, the center of the coloniality of knowledge passed from Europe to North America. The production of knowledge is still shared. But its application takes place in a new context. The problem is not where knowledge is generated, but how it is globally applied. Have Jewish counter-modern thinkers of this new location confronted Levinas's limitation, re-evaluated post-1945 Judaism, and welcomed the pre-1945 heritage? In the new scenario, and without a practical euro-centric pretension, limited but provocative groups of contemporary American Jewish scholarship have confronted, consciously or not, this post-1945 problematic Jewish relation with the other. I now analyze the proposals of three schools of thought that, confronting this problem situate themselves in three totally different places on the philosophical and political spectrum. They are traditional/liberal Postmodern Jewish philosophy, progressive Multicultural Judaism, and radical Jewish Liberation Theology.

A first Jewish school of thought that addresses Levinas' thought, and could be seen as the source of an alternative understanding to the neo-colonial depiction of otherness is Postmodern Jewish Philosophy. Originally emerging from authors such as Eugene Borowitz (Borowitz 1991), the latest generation of this thought has only recently developed in America under the name of *Textual Reasoning*, or *Postmodern Jewish Philosophy* (PJP) and is led by thinkers such as Peter Ochs from the University of Virginia, Robert Gibbs from the University of Toronto, and Steven Kepnes from Colgate University. This school of thought is usually associated with a return to the traditional texts through (partial) rejection of the modern western philosophical canon. Its project is to embrace both central post-Holocaust Jewish dialogic formulations (Buber's *I-Thou* relationship; Levinas' *exteriority*) in order to criticize modernity's inability, among other problems, to recognize the suffering of others.[19]

In fact, PJP is an interesting source to draw from in order to better understand Levinas because it claims him as a post-modern Jewish thinker (i.e. one of them) (Kepnes et al. 2001: 29–35, 42–46). Does PJP confront Dussel's critique of Levinas, and its ethical and political consequences? The school calls for a renunciation of modern values in order to engage with an alternative Judaism (Kepnes et al. 2001: 11). Furthermore, it understands that what makes postmodern Jewish thought truly Jewish is the Jewish praxis that leads to concrete actions (Kepnes et al. 2001: 11–12). On the one hand, this is a very promising starting point. First, philosophy as a reflection on practice allows for thinking about a renewal of the rabbinical orthopraxis which led to a dynamic interpretation of the law not only as ethical obligation, but as *halakah* – guide, or way of life. This school allows for confronting alterity in each practical situation, and re-evaluating Jewish understanding in order to construct a dialogical approach to the other toward a rabbinical end: *tikkun olam*, the reconstruction of the world that recognizes God and human beings as partners in creation and redemption. Second, the re-evaluation of traditional sources through a postmodern Jewish hermeneutic allows a recovery of the spirit of exteriority that was broken by post-Holocaustic thought. Renewed reflection on texts that were created in a context of exteriority allows a special sensibility toward other outsiders.

On the other hand, I have two interrelated concerns regarding the proposal of this group of scholars. The first is some members' negation of the existence of a crucial formative event in modern Judaism: "the event of the Holocaust does not generate the term of our discourse… We do not want to begin with the Holocaust agenda…I want to say again that for me, 'postmodern' is not historical" (Ochs in Kepnes et al. 2001: 40–41). If Jewish philosophers reject the possibility to think of the Holocaust as a formative event, they are missing a crucial component of contemporary Jewish discourses. The Holocaust should be confronted not only for the philosophical doubts that it carries, but also because this event is crucial in the formation of a new Judeo-Christian narrative that lead to eliminating the suffering of non-Jews. By eliminating the historical dimension of the Jewish proposal they abandon the step already taken by Levinas.

Second, Judaism in the twenty-first century, far from being a powerless exteriority, has become a crucial part of the white powerful totality. Hence, this school of thought seems to be applying teachings generated within a community in times of lack of power (Jewish people between 70 BCE and 1945) in a period of empowerment (after 1945). A de-colonial reading of modern Judaism understands that the political and ethical consequences in the generation of a particular colonial epistemology are different whether this community belongs to the center or to the exteriority. Whether or not this difference is acknowledged, the stigma of being sufferers in times of empowerment would silence the sufferings of real sufferers because of attempts to prevent the suffering of people of the center who still consider themselves the powerless exteriority. Probably the accusation of anti-Semitism endured by each thinker who supports Palestinian rights emerges from the latter construction which PJP involuntarily reproduces (Keppes et al. 2001: 41–42). Nevertheless, the school is still an interesting source because of its openness to the utilization of *post-methodologies* that focus on otherness for the analysis of modern Jewish thought.

I have called the second school of thought *Multicultural Judaism.* It is usually placed somewhere on the center-left wing of the political spectrum (depending on whether it is discussed by liberal, progressive or radical thinkers). It is associated, ideologically and practically, with the activist movement of renewal led by Rabbis Arthur Waskow and Michael Lerner from the popular movement *Tikkun.* The most comprehensive collection of articles reflecting on this trend was compiled by David Biale from UC-Davis, Michael Galchinsky of Millsaps College, and Susannah Heschel from Dartmouth College in 1998, although Sander Gilman its most solid and cutting edge representative. This school of thought is comprised of a vast and diverse group of scholars, often linked to activist movements, who have tried to confront the dilemmas raised for Jews by modernity in general, and the U.S. in particular. Indeed, the name, Multicultural Judaism, probably should be followed with an interrogation mark (Multicultural Judaism?), because what unifies this group of scholars is more the question regarding Judaism and multicultural societies than an answer to the question.

Multicultural Judaism recognizes its strong ties with the spirit of the 1960s and early 1970s: the Civil Rights movements, the New Left, radical student movements, and anti-Vietnam War protests. On the one hand, as heirs of this spirit (that our next school of thinkers will connect with *the Prophetic discourse*), the members of this group usually abstain from formulating general statements that could leave a voice outside the group. In other words, they recognize as crucial to scholarship the incorporation of all voices: the exteriority, the third parties, and even the Ego. On the other hand, they recognize the failure of the Enlightenment to naturally open an inclusive society for all ethnicities and cultures. Hence, the central problem of this school is to debate the extant limitations in the project of creating a new multicultural society, and the degree to which members of each culture should resign their heritage in order to engage with a multicultural totality (Biale et al. 1998: 1–11). In a related move, proponents of Multicultural Judaism investigate why incorporation into multicultural modernity has been more ambivalent for Jews than for others – depending on the author, other cultures, peoples, ethnicities, nations, or religions.

The trend of Multicultural Judaism is valuable for a de-colonial project in several respects; first, for trying to think through, and sometimes (problematically?) beyond, differences from an inclusive framework. Second, it not only crosses disciplines in the humanities (departments of comparative literature, women's studies, and intellectual history are scholarly centers of Multicultural Jewish thought), but it also has been working, at least for the last 20 years, with a method of textual analysis that breaks the monopoly of conservative and/or rabbinical voices reflected in the ancient, medieval and early modern Jewish texts. Indeed, it is not surprising that *close others*, such as Jewish feminist thinkers confronting the patriarchy and misogyny of rabbinical interpretation, usually find their place among this diverse, rich and provocative trend of thought (Seidman in Biale et al. 1998: 185–211). Third, this trend is useful for thinking through literary criticism on how to approach the other. It would be a natural bridge between postmodern Judaism and postcolonial Judaism because it incorporates elements of both: it shares certain concepts regarding methodology and material of analysis with the first, and regarding ideology, an area of study and a project with the second.

Although it is difficult to pin-down a precise conception of the other from within the Multicultural Jewish trend because of the diversity of the school, the consensus among its members is that society is composed by different others and that there is equivalence among these others. This is a useful starting point from which to examine the inadequacy of the category of exteriority for thinking about Judaism. In other words, this group of scholars disrupts the Judeo-centric reading of history. The problem with this school is one of narrowness (which may be worked out in the future); in other words, their reflection focuses on American problems. It is possible to transpose their reflection, to some extent, to bear on Western and Central Europe. However, the multicultural framework is hardly to be applied in South Africa, Argentina, Israel, or Eastern Europe.

Nevertheless, some may argue that some thinkers of this school, notably the provocative Gilman (now at Emory University) has placed special attention on what he calls "Border Communities" or "Communities on the Frontier" (Gilman and Shain 1999: 1–25; Gilman 2003: 1–31). Gilman seems to be opening the path for other scholars of multicultural Judaism. Nevertheless, closer attention to his proposal reveals a complication. His proposal is to analyze a Jewish history and culture without centers. But we ask whether the other communities can defy the preeminence of the American Jewry (or American academy) in defining the characteristics of diasporic Judaism. To what extent can a border historiography that does not recognize the economical, cultural and political power of American Jewish scholarship even hear other communities than the American, which (unlike South-Africa, the current exterior model) do not write in English? Is it true that one out of ten experiences related are not English-speakers (when the quantity of Jewish communities in the third-world do not follow this pattern), but to what extent a non-English-speaker case can generate a historiographical model?

Hence, it is possible that, perhaps unwittingly, this group of scholars is incorporating Jews who are still exterior into the totality, reproducing the same path opened by Levinas, and with it the coloniality of knowledge. If this is the case, it is probably possible for Multicultural Judaism to eventually overcome this dilemma. However, a de-colonial Jewish thought which does not center around social problems inside the U.S./UK, or in the small remaining English-speaking Diaspora, seeks to bypass this dilemma entirely.

A third school of thought is represented by a variety of Jewish radical thinkers. Indeed, it includes works by authors who have been accused by certain groups of *Jewish Jews* of being *anti-Semitic or self-hating Jews*. I will focus on one of the thinkers of this trend, whose work is crucial for understanding the problem of the other in Jewish scholarship. Marc Ellis, an eclectic and, provocative Jewish thinker, and the founder of American Jewish Liberation Theology, was professor and director of the Peace and Justice graduate program of the Catholic missionary school of Maryknoll, where he became acquainted with Latin American, Black, Feminist and Asian Liberation Theologies. Ellis' *Toward a Jewish Liberation Theology*, was published in 1987. Ellis confronts the hegemonic narratives of the Holocaust, arguing that there should be another way to engage with the other others. Ellis defies the *unholy alliance* of the Jews and Christendom (i.e. a similar concept of what Anibal Quijano will understand as the coloniality of power), and harshly criticizes the empowerment and militarization of Jewish life *after Auschwitz*. Indeed, in the last 20 years, his *theology of solidarity* confronts what he believes is *the issue* of post-Holocaust theology: Israel and its relationship with Palestinians (Ellis 1994, 1997).

Two main questions would be addressed to American Jewish Liberation Theology. Is its focus on Israel-Palestine (a place where no more than a quarter of Jews live) inclusive enough to be a comprehensive praxis and starting point for a Jewish understanding of the other? Probably the answer of the trend would be that it is impossible to talk about modern Judaism without referring to Israel, the Holocaust and their connections. The second question would be asked by PJP. Postmodern Jewish philosophers have defined what makes their philosophy *truly Jewish*, namely the praxis that emerges from their readings of Jewish rabbinical writings. However, what makes Jewish Liberation Theology *truly Jewish*? From where does this trend approach otherness? This last question would be seen as an obstacle for a Jewish scholar who is more concerned with the letter than the spirit of Jewish thought. Nevertheless, American Jewish Liberation Theology offers one of the few non-essentialist interpretations of modern Judaism because it incorporates a complex matrix of voices that allow Jews, in spite of being part of the center and recognizing themselves as white and western, to engage with discourses that emerge from subaltern peoples. In other words, it acknowledges its centric location of knowledge, but attempts to work beyond it.

As we have seen, Jewish American scholarship presents several possibilities for an alternative to the hegemonic modern Judaism. However, none of them reflects directly on the coloniality of knowledge and its links with Jewish history and thought. The three schools surveyed are provocative sources, but they do not completely transcend Levinas's limitations because they do not connect Jewish otherness with the construction of the post-Holocaust epistemology of knowledge. In other words, there is no clear relation between the exclusivism of Jewish suffering and the racial incorporation of Judaism into the Western Canon. Furthermore, in line with Gustavo Gutierrez's understanding of "the German master of knowledge," "philosophy rises only at sundown" (Gutierrez 1995: 9). The historical experience precedes any philosophical and theological speculation.

IV

I will trace, therefore, a colonial praxis that helps Judaism to return to what seems to be lost in the current framework. It is necessary to rediscover and to reevaluate sources of hidden Judaism, which we are led to precisely by following the steps of subaltern and postcolonial scholars (Spivak 1988: 3–33). This approach allows us to accept the validity of Dussel's criticism of Levinas, but presents a *Jewish* alternative as a resolution. The intention of this section is to re-discover three discredited, hidden, and silenced Jewish projects, understanding them as sources for returning to and going beyond the liberative Jewish European exteriority.

In this section I aim to overcome both Jewish exclusivism of suffering and Jewish incorporation into the Western model through cases of interrelation, hybridization and common struggle of Jews with or within other others. First, I will explore the new limits for inter-religious conversation starting from the historical example of hidden relations between Jews and the *Andean Indians*. Second, I will assert the impossibility of a complete installation of a world Jewish narrative that pretends to consider Jews in the service of neo-colonial forces in Latin America through the case of the *Colonia Sousa* of the Dominican Republic. Finally, I will reflect on the construction of a praxis for Latin American Jewish Liberation Theology through the experience of the Argentine Jewish social justice movement, *Masorti*.[20]

The first source, the *Indian Jews* of sixteenth century Peru, forces into question the Jewish modern politics of alliance and identity after Auschwitz.[21] During the first years of the sixteenth century, Antonio Montezinos-Levi, a *marrano* escaping from the Inquisition, traveled to the mountains of *Los Andes* and revealed his true identity to his native interlocutor. According to his story, his conversation partner then revealed to Montezinos-Levi his true identity also: he was part of the tribe of Reuben, one of the lost ten tribes of Israel. He not only narrated the same story that Montezinos-Levi knew from his ancestors, but also prayed one of the two main Jewish *tefilot*, or prayers, the *Shema Israel* (Feirstein 1993: 16–19).

Montezinos-Levi's story (as one among many Jews who encountered Indian Jews) is deliciously provocative, but it should not surprise us. During medieval times there were dozens of messianic heralds asseverating that they knew how to find the lost Israelites' tribes, "beyond the river *Sambation*" (Feierstein 1993: 21); and in modern times there are hundreds of versions of the origins of the first inhabitants of the America continent, from the wonderful *Atlantida* in colonial times to sympathetic aliens during the 1960s and 1970s (Feierstein 1993: 23).

This time, however, the story might have an interesting colonial turn. In 1523, a Spanish priest of the Dominican order started to proclaim the veracity of these stories. It may have been that the story would be useful to the conquistadors: if the Indians were Jews, then they were humans born with original sin, which *invites* the conquistador to evangelize the Indians/Jews in order to redeem them, even (as was happening to Jews in Europe at the same time) with torments if judged necessary. Nevertheless, the name of the Dominican may cause surprise: Fray Bartolome de Las Casas – the same Las Casas who championed native rights, and who is one of the most important influences on Latin American Christian liberation theology.[21]

A few years later, in 1650, Rabbi Menashe Ben Israel, Baruch Spinoza's teacher and a well-known Jew from the *Portuguese Nation* (a numerous group of Jews who, after the expulsion from Spain, fled first to Portugal and after four generations of persecution settled in Amsterdam), published an entire study proclaiming the veracity of the story. His book, as well as the more contemporary interpretation of the few people who researched the case, would show that, perhaps, the connection between twelfth century B.C.E. Jews and (for example) Mesoamerican Chapanecas was not a total falsification (ben Israel 1987) Current scholarship on the subject has demonstrated that Jews and Indians were seen as allied enemies by the empire, which confused one with the other. Indians were seen escaping reserves to join the ranks of infidels led by Jews, and Indian witches declared themselves Jewish (Silverblatt 2004).

I suggest that this case can be read as an interrelated re-appropiation of identities. Both Indian and Jews were *recovering'* (or *reinventing*) identities after 2 centuries of evangelization and persecution by the conquistador and the Inquisition. Indians could have identified with Jews since they represented the natural nemesis of Christianity. The Jews were a people that anteceded and resisted the empire (anticipation and resistance is, not coincidentally, central for Levinas' depiction of otherness). Jews could have felt compelled to identify themselves with Indians since they confirmed the messianic aspiration of Jewish resistance. Diverse Native groups were becoming Indian Jews, and former *marranos* were opening Jewishness to the Indians as a means to confront the empire.

The story of the Indian-Jews has not been a source for a de-colonial Judaism, but this is not because of its uncertain veracity of the bond. Rather, it is because it may show an early interrelation between Jews and other others. If brought into the open debate, would this source not challenge the exclusive religious dialogue between Jews and Christians and open up to a conversation among others for whom modernity started with being persecuted by the first empire and its global institution of repression, *el imperio Español* and *el Santo Oficio de la Inquisición?* Whether or not we accept that post-1945 Judaism became white and western, this source is a challenge to the new status because it recognizes that Jews might enjoy stronger ties with the oppressed of the Americas than the *conquistadors*. This case would be a source of identification with third-world peoples that would defy the hegemonic modern, white Jewish perspective, not only in the Americas, but also in Asia, Europe, and, especially, the Middle East.

The second source is the *Colonia Sousa*. In 1938 when nearly all the nations of the world closed their doors to Jewish refugees from Europe, the General Rafael Trujillo, a Dominican trained by US marines who became dictator of *República Dominicana* in 1930 and remained formally or informally in power until his assassination in 1961, decided to open immigration. Trujillo granted around 5,000 visas, and finally received more than 600 German and Austrian Jews. The refugees founded a colony in the maritime port of Sousa. With the help of a well-known Jewish institution, the Agro-American Jewish Joint Distribution Committee, and despite their class origin (most of them were young professionals), they created a flourishing agricultural and livestock cooperative that took the name *Productos Sousa*.[22]

The main question posed by the success of the *Colonía Sousa* is why Trujillo was so *generous* as to invite those Jews to integrate into Dominican society. Fostering the establishment of the Colonía Sousa was *a priori* useful for each party involved. Trujillo, who had massacred thousands of Haitians and other Afro-Caribbeans only a year before, recognized an opportunity to *upgrade* the island's skin color. The Jews of the Agro-American Jewish Joint Distribution Committee, living in the emerging center of colonial power, remembered their responsibility to their relatives. To the American government, it was an opportunity to show to the Jewish community its solidarity without either receiving immigrants (cf. the 1938 Saint Louis' tragedy when a ship with Jewish refugees was forced to return to Europe and most of the Jews, many of them children, were killed in the Holocaust) or being contaminated by the European conflict (or by the Jews).[23] Finally, it was useful to the Central European Jews because, quite simply, they saved their lives.

The case of the *Colonía Sousa* shows how he logic peculiar to a colonial power sometimes fails in the colonies. In Jewish scholarship, the case has been a footnote in the texts, when it has not simply been ignored. Why? The case was elaborated as a model: a Jewish organization at the colonial center supports, ideologically and financially, the installation of a Jewish settlement in the periphery, as it has done in the rest of Latin America (as it was the original plan of Herzl for a Jewish state in the Middle East, West Africa, and to a lesser extent Latin-America).[24]

However, an astute Trujillo extended visas almost entirely to young males. Naturally, most of them married with local women. On the one hand, it was Trujillo's triumph in order to *upgrade* the skin color of his population. On the other hand, Jews committed the most important Jewish modern sin: exogamy and also, presumably, assimilation. Moreover, the same generation subsequently tried to immigrate to the United States, thereby to commit the most important Jewish modern sin of peripheral areas (as Polish, Israeli, and Argentinean immigrants well know): becoming equal citizens of the colonial power, and through the support of a zealous board of American Jewry.

This double transgression (exogamy and immigration to the Colonial Power) made the *Colonía Sousa* project a triumph for almost all involved: Trujillo, who attracted whites, the American government, which diverted the problem of German

Jews, and lastly, the group of refugees who escaped with their lives. Only the Jewish American community, through the thwarted zeal of its immigration lobby, suffered a defeat. However, this case is exemplary for showing that colonial locations give rise to their own logic, and that what is intended to be a model case for the empowerment of a modern hegemonic Judaism would instead become a source for an alternative Judaism.

Consequently, Colonia Sousa is a source for a de-colonial Judaism because this means that the construction of a white and western identity for Jews is not possible to apply worldwide. Jews become hybrids even when they are early recognized as white and there are used to hide racial crimes. The American Jewish influence would be important in order to open the doors, but the praxis of the group of Jews once in the periphery generates its own logic and gives rise to hybrid understandings of the world. The possible exogamy with oppressed people would be one generator of new borders of thought, rendering both Jewish exclusivism and the limitation of Jewish dialogue to Europe/North-America impossible.

The third source, *Masorti*, an activist religious liberationist movement that emerged in the 1960s in Argentina and spread though all Latin America, demonstrates that the south is a favorable setting for not only for rejecting the colonial network, but also constructing a Jewish Liberation Theology, source for a de-colonial Judaism. *Masorti* is the Latin-American branch of North-America conservative/reform Judaism that, under the leadership of the Rabbi Marshall T. Meyer, became radical once it developed in Latin-America.

Let me begin with what will seem like a diversion. In 1983, 1 year after the beginning of the collapse of the Argentine military dictatorship and its genocide, Leon Klenicki, the aforementioned Argentine rabbi who became director of Inter-religious Relations of the Anti-Defamation League of B'nai-Brith in New York, published an article entitled "The Theology of Liberation: A Latin American Jewish Exploration." In this article, Klenicki not only attacks Liberation Theologians, but also, and especially, an unknown (at least in 1983) Jewish Liberation Theology.[25] Was someone offering a Jewish Liberation Theology that ought to be silenced? Why does Klenicki not name it? I am not aware of any research that explains the motives of this article.

In 1959, Marshall T. Meyer, an American rabbi and opponent of the US interventions in Asia arrived in Argentina, intending to stay for 2 or 3 years in order to avoid his service as a chaplain for the US army. As in the case of the *Colonía Sousa*, Meyer arrived under the umbrella of an American Jewish institution, this time the World Council of Synagogues (Weil 1988: 7–10). In 1985, more than 25 years later, he finally left Argentina after serving as the only non-Argentinean member of CONADEP, the truth commission that investigated the disappearance of 30,000 voices and bodies during the military genocide. Despite the Argentinean Jewish board's conciliatory strategy toward *the Proceso de Reorganización Nacional*, Meyer was one of the most relevant religious activists against the dictatorship (Trachman 1998: 27–33). In addition, he founded the only Latin American rabbinical seminary, with the aim of breaking the *civilizational mission spirit* of northern Judaism by generating an *autochthonous leadership*. Today, almost half

of the Jewish communities in Latin America are part of this movement (Slabodsky
and Kandel 2001: 14–17).

A few years after the article of Klenicki, and after the work of Ellis and Cohn-
Sherbok on a Jewish Liberation Theology, Meyer reflected:

> Today, in Latin America, there is a class struggle. As a result of my association with the
> struggle for Human Rights, I was denominated the communist or red rabbi.... many Jews
> see themselves involved in a type of a Jewish Liberation Theology.... these actions would
> be supported with the argument that the first liberation theologians were the prophets of
> Israel. (Meyer 1987: 6)[26]

In spite of some voices that have tried to reflect on the work of *Masorti* in Latin
America, the movement has been overlooked by Jewish English-speaking scholarship worldwide.[27] *Masorti* implies a radical change in Jewish praxis and thought. It
became the first Jewish modern movement that, *as a movement*, struggled against
the oppression of a complete population as part of this population. In terms recalling Dussel's critique of Levinas, the movement struggled for *all* the others including
themselves. The movement was able to justify its actions through a reformulation
of the "Jewish trinity" (Torah, God and Israel):

> According to my teacher's lessons, one leg in the Torah and the other in the street.
> (Trachman 1998: 46)

> In Judaism the world has not been created, it is an ongoing process, and you and I, and
> every human being is invited to participate with God in the re-creation. All too often, human
> beings choose destruction, hatred, killing, bigotry, racism, prejudice.... I have no right to
> be silent in the face of injustice! I cannot claim to believe in God and remain inactive when
> God's image is destroyed... when Humans are denigrated, humiliated and persecuted, the
> sanctity of human life is threatened everywhere. (Trachman 1998: 52)

> I am a Zionist. I think the peace process in the Middle East is, perhaps, the most important
> task that I, as an American, a Jew and a Zionist can undertake within the Jewish arena....
> There must be peace if there is to be an Israel congruent with the Values of Jewish History.
> There must be an end to occupied territories if the Jewish soul is to remain intact. (Trachman
> 1998: 54)

Analyzing these three reflections invites us to recognize two clear and connected
aspects in each of them. The first part of each quotation reflects the consensus of
the liberal synagogue rabbinical paradigm and the second part advocates a liberation theology that emerges not only from the immediate context, but also from what
Marc Ellis calls a 'dissident Prophetic Jewish line of thought.' The first part of each
quotation reflects Meyer's consensus with rabbinical sources: (1) oral and written
Torah is orthopraxis and a guide to life (*halakah*); (2) God and human beings are
partners in the creation and redemption (*tikun olam*); and (3) there is a natural connection between Israel as a people and Israel as a land (*Zionut*). However, the most
provocative lesson is the second part of each statement: (1) Torah means a structural condition of struggle ("one leg in the street"); (2) the connection between God
and human beings is a first step in the struggle against social injustice, which is the
rejection and profanation of Divinity; and (3) Zionism is not an unconditional support to Israel policies but rather an imperative in support of *any* (national) oppressed
group – occupation and oppression of the other risks the loss of the "Jewish soul." In

this light, we can easily recognize why *Masorti* was a risk for the neo-colonial epistemology of knowledge expressed in Klenicki's attack on an anonymous "Jewish Theology of Liberation."

Masorti becomes a source for De-colonial Liberationist Judaism because it generates, from peripheral and from subaltern centers, a reformulation of the basic understandings of Jewish action and, in second place, faith. Though Judaism has resisted formulating a creed and has tried to reject the different attempts of a "code of faith" (such as the attempt of Aristotelian inspired Maimonides in the twelfth century), after the Holocaust Judaism has adopted Emil Fackenheim's new commandment ("Jews should survive in order to forbid a posthumous victory of Hitler without regard of the obstacles") as its canonical new creed. While for Marc Ellis this commandment is a source for the moral suicide, *Masorti* works in parallel to offer an alternative practice. In *Masorti*, the new commandment seems to be "You are witness of my struggle for all the others."

V

In this article I explored a de-colonial answer for two of the more problematic issues of contemporary Jewish thought. I refer to its complicity with the Western canon through the reduction to otherness to the intra-European Jewish case and the final incorporation of the Jew into the American white, central and Western world. Latin-American peripherial Judaism can develop from its original experience a framework of analysis that exceeds what can be offered by discourses in central locations. For this reason I contend that de-colonial Judiasm should be analyzed next to other parallel projects (i.e. Post-modern, Multicultural and Liberationist Judaisms) in order to confront the political and ethical dilemmas of post-1945 Jewish thought. Thus Judaism will recover its height and will cease to be held hostage by those 'Afro-Asiatic(-American)' masses that, according to Levinas, subvert the sacred history of an only recently constituted Judeo-Christian tradition.

Notes

1 This paper was delivered to a session of the Annual Meeting of the American Academy of Religion in 2003 and its core has not changed since then. I am deeply indebted to Marc Ellis and Nelson Maldonado-Torres for their help through the writing of different versions of this presentation in Waco and Durham, to Enrique Dussel for his welcoming reception of this essay, to Andrew Irvine for his very helpful revisions of my English and interest to publish a version of my presentation since Atlanta, and to Paula Schwebel for her careful reading of the last version. For space constraints I will cite English sources when there are available.
2 See the recent biography of Emmanuel Levinas as director of school which mission was to spread universal cultural knowledge to North-African French speaking Jewish communities in Salomon Malka (2006: 84–106).

3 For those interested in Jewish philosophy, please see the interconnection between the interpretation of binary ideal types (Hebrew and Greek) and Rosenzweig's influence in Robert Gibbs (1992: 155–175).

4 See the development of Rosenzweig's conception of Judaism as eternal life outside political history in Franz Rosenzweig (1985: 298–335).

5 On the exploration of the influence of Levinas in Latino thought in English see the collection of articles in Linda Martin Alcoff and Eduardo Mendieta (2000). Of particular importance are the Introduction written by the editors and the essays by Walter Mignolo and Michael Barber. To this collection should be added the dissertation completed by Nelson Maldonado-Torres in 2002. The only reference to this encounter I could find within Jewish thought is Robert Gibbs's acknowledgment of the existence of this influence. See Gibbs (1992: 229).

6 See the critical positions of George Salemohamed (1992: 93–97) and Howard Caygill (2002: 159–203).

7 This question has been explored by Marc Ellis (2002: 1–17).

8 An excellent overview of the social and political reasons of the Jewish incorporation into the white framework in the US can be found in the work of Karen Brodkin. See Brodkin (1988).

9 Unfortunately these thinkers are rarely grouped within the same line of thought. See Ellis (1987, 2004), Cohn Sherbok (1984, 1987), and Löwy (1996, 2004).

10 The work of Howard Caygil (2002) is extremely informative, but it develops a critical intellectual biography and does not analyze what are the consequences of this reading for Jewish thought.

11 For the development of the problem of Marxist theory on the Jews see Karl Marx (1978: 35, 45), Abraham Leon (1970) and Enzo Traverso (1993).

12 See the logic of modern departure from the French Revolution in Paul Mendes-Flohr and Jeudha Reinharz (1995: 117–121).

13 See the active role of 'the Jew' in the creation of the new colonial world as described by Walter Mignolo (2002: 21, 29).

14 Of special is importance the definition and survey of Liberationist Jews in Michael Lowy (1988: 1–26) (1988: 1–26) and David Myers (2003: 33–67, 68–105).

15 See the beginning of this line of thought: Elie Wiesel (1967, 1977), Emil Fackenheim (1970, 1982), and Irvin Greenberg (1977).

16 See the opposite line of thought: Richard Rubenstein (1966), Ellis (1986), and Chmiel (2001).

17 I developed this case in Santiago Slabodsky and Victoria Kandel (2001: III, 3–17).

18 Paradoxically and tragically, one of the most important voices of the defense of Argentineans' desaparecidos was Elie Wiesel. See how he present himself at the web-page of his own foundation: http://www.eliewieselfoundation.org/ElieWiesel/ElieWieselBio.htm

19 These thee cases were already developed in an article I wrote in Spanish: Slabodsky (2003: 72–93).

20 I will utilize the term "Indian" following Irene Silverblatt's suggestion of the recovering of Indianess as an anti-imperial resource. See Silverblatt (1995: 283–286).

21 The role of Bartolome de las Casas for liberation theology can be never overemphasized. Just as an example the center for research and social work lead by Gustavo Gutierrez, founder of the movement, takes his name. http://www.cbc.org.pe/. See also Gutierrez (1995: xxvii–xxxv).

22 Unfortunately the case has been just a footnote in the books of Jewish history. See, for example Sachar (1993: 540, 548).

23 The concept of liberation from the contaminated Europe has permeated the new American Jewish whiteness. See, for example, the development showed by Henry Kissinger (1994: 21–28) and also the idea of fratricide rivalry between pure American and contaminated European Jews in Marshall Sklare (1955:23–25).

24 The original plan of Herzl was rejected by Bernard Lazare specifically for this reason: Herzl intended to create a settler colony with persecuted Jews financed by major philanthropist Jewish organizations. See Herzl's political proposal (1972) and his more seductive novel (Herzl). The critiques can be found in Bernard Lazare (1967) and during contemporary times Edward Said (1992).

25 The article (Klenicki 1983: 37–45) was further discussed by Jewish (Cohn Sherbok 1984) and Christian (O'Hare 1990) intellectuals which lead Klenicki to defend his position (Klenicki 1990). Nevertheless, nobody attempted to answer why he was confronting a Jewish liberation theology four years before Marc Ellis wrote his *Toward a Jewish Theology of Liberation* (1987).

26 The reflection is the most comprehensive expression of several articles of Marshall T. Meyer that were published between 1970 and 1985 by Latin American Rabbinical Seminary's journal *Majshavot*. The main point is that his reflection comes from a practice what converts the experience in praxis for a Jewish Theology of Liberation. Among the few works on the subject in English we can mention Trachman (1998) and Freund (1992, 1994). The former dean of the seminary, Prof. Daniel Fainstein, finished in Spanish a related dissertation two years ago: Fainstein (2006).

27 The motto "*Atem Edim*," "You are my witnesses" has become the official motto of the Seminary since years prior the struggle for Human Rights.

References

Alcoff, Linda and Eduardo Mendieta. 2000. *Thinking from the Underside of History*. Cumnor Hill: Rowman & Littlefield.

Biale, David, Michael Glachinsky and Susannah Heschel. 1998. *Insiders/Outsiders, American Jews and Multiculturalism*. Berkeley, CA: University of California Press.

Borowitz, Eugene. 1991. *Renewing the Covenant: A Theology for the Postmodern Jew*. Philadelphia, PA: Jewish Publication Society.

Brodkin, Karen. 1988. *How Jews Became White Folks and What That Says About Race in America*. New Brunswick, NJ: Rutgers University Press.

Caygill, Howard. 2002. *Levinas and the Political*. London/New York: Routledge.

Chmiel, Marc. 2001. *Elie Wiesel and the Politics of Moral Leadership*. Philadelphia, PA: Temple University.

Cohn-Sherbok, Daniel. 1984. Latin American Theology and Jewish–Christian Dialogue: A reply to Leon Klenicki. *American Jewish Archives* 36: 57–61.

Cohn-Sherbok, Daniel. 1987. *On Earth as It Is on Heaven: Jews, Christians, and Liberation Theology*. Maryknoll, NY: Orbis.

Deutscher, Isaac. 1969. *Non-jewish Jew and Other Essays*. New York: Oxford University Press.

Dubnow, Simon. 1967–1973. *History of the Jews*. South Brunswick, NJ: T. Yoseloff.

Dussel, Enrique. 1973. *America Latina, Dependencia y Liberación*. Buenos Aires: Garcia Cambeiro.

Dussel, Enrique. 1985. *Philosophy of Liberation*. Maryknoll, NY: Orbis.

Dussel, Enrique. 1999. Sensibility and Otherness in Emmanuel Levinas. *Philosophy Today* 37: 123–127.

Ellis, Marc. 1987. *Toward a Jewish Theology of Liberation*. Maryknoll, NY: Orbis.

Ellis, Marc. 1986. *Faithfulness in the Age of the Holocaust*. Amity: Amity House.

Ellis, Marc. 1994. *Ending Auschwitz: The Future of Jewish and Christian Life*. Louisville: Westminister/John Knox Press.

Ellis, Marc. 1997. *Unholy Alliance. Religion and Atrocity in Our Time*. Minneapolis, MN: Fortress Press.

Ellis, Marc. 2002. The Next Fifty Years: Remembering the Holocaust and the Future of Jewish Life at the Dawn of the 21st Century. Recent Essay on *The Holocaust, Israel/Palestine and the Future of the Jewish People*. Waco, TX: Center for American and Jewish Studies.

Ellis, Marc. 2004. *Toward A Jewish Theology of Liberation: The Challenge of the 21st Century*. Waco, TX: Baylor University Press.

Fackenheim, Emil. 1970. *God's Presence in History: Jewish Affirmation and Philosophical Reflections*. New York: New York University Press.

Fackenheim, Emil. 1982. *To Mend the World: Foundations of Future Jewish Thought*. New York: Schocken.

Fainstein, Daniel. 2006. Secularización, profecía y liberación: la desprivatización de la religión en el pensamiento judío contemporáneo. Un estudio comparativo de sociología histórica e historia intellectual. Doctoral dissertation, Universidad Nacional Autónoma de México.

Feierstein, Ricardo. 1993. *Historia de los Judios Argentinos*. Buenos Aires: Planeta.

Fishman, Arey. 1983. Moses Hess on Judaism and Its Aptness for Socialist Civilization. *Journal of Religion* 63: 136–152.

Freund, Richard. 1992. The Rabbinical Seminary of Latin America: The First Thirty Years. *Conservative Judaism* 44: 67–78.

Freund, Richard. 1994. '*Somos Testigos* – We Are Witnesses': The Jewish Theology of Liberation of Rabbi Marshall T Meyer. *Conservative Judaism* 47: 46–52.

Gibbs, Robert. 1992. *Correlations Between Rosenzweig and Levinas*. Princeton, NJ: Princeton University Press.

Gilman, Sander. 2003. *Jewish Frontiers: Essays on Bodies, Histories and Identities*. New York: Palgrave Macmillian.

Gilman, Sander and Milton Shain. 1999. *Jewries at the Frontier.Accomodation, Identity, Conflict*. Urbana, IL/Chicago, IL: University of Illinois Press.

Greenberg, Irvin. 1977. *Cloud of Smoke, Pillar of Fire: Judaism, Christianity and Modernity After the Holocaust*. New York: Ktav.

Gutierrez, Gustavo 1995. A Theology of Liberation: History, Politics, Salvation. Maryknoll, NY: Orbis.

Herzl, Theodor. 1972. The Jewish State. An Attempt at a Modern Answer for the Jewish Question. London: Pordes.

Herzl, Theodor. 1987. *Old New Land*. New York: M. Wiener.

Horkheimer, Max. 2005 [1938]. The Jews and Europe. In *The Frankfurt School on Religion*, edited by Eduardo Mendieta, pp. 25–241. New York: Routledge.

Horkheimer, Max and Theodor Adorno. 2002 [1944/1947]. Elements of Anti-semitism. In *Dialectics of Enlightenment*, pp. 137–172. Stanford, CA: Stanford University Press.

Hyman, Paula. 1998. *The Jews of France*. Berkeley, CA: University of California Press.

Israel, Mannasse ben. 1987 [1650]. *The Hope of Israel*. New York: Oxford University Press.

Kalmar, Ivan and Derek Penslar. 2006. *Orientalism and the Jews*. Hanover, PA: University Press of New England.

Kissinger, Henry. 1994. *Diplomacy: The History of Diplomacy and Balance of Power*. New York: Simon & Schuster.

Klenicki, Leon. 1983. The Theology of Liberation: A Latin American Jewish Exploration. *American Jewish Archives H.U.C* 35: 37–45.

Klenicki, Leon. 1990. I Stand My Ground. *Cross Currents: Religion and Intellectual Life* 40(3): 117–123.

Kepnes, Steven, Peter Ochs, and Robert Gibbs. 2001. *Reasoning After Revelation: Dialogues in Postmodern Jewish Philosophy*. Boulder, CO: Westview.

Lazare, Bernard. 1967. *Anti-semitism, Its History, and Causes*. London: Briton.

Leon, Abraham. 1970. *The Jewish Question: A Marxist Interpretation*. New York: Pathfinder.

Levinas. Emmanuel. 1969 [1961]. *Totality and Infinity*. Pittsburgh, PA: Duquesne University Press.

Levinas, Emmanuel. 1990a. *Difficult Freedom*. Baltimore, MD: The Johns Hopkins University Press.

Levinas, Emmanuel. 1990b. *Nine Talmudic Readings*. Bloomington, IN: Indiana University Press.

Levinas, Emmanuel. 1990c [1960]. *Between Two Worlds (The Way of Franz Rosenzweig)*. Baltimore, MD: The Johns Hopkins University.

Levinas, Emmanuel. 1998 [1974]. *Otherwise than Being*. Pittsburgh, PA: Duquesne University Press.

Löwy, Michael. 1988. *Redemption and Utopia. Jewish Libertarian Thought in Central Europe*. Stanford, CA: Stanford University Press.

Löwy, Michael. 1996. *The War of Gods: Religion and Politics in Latin-America*. London/New York: Verso.

Löwy, Michael. 2005. *Walter Benjamin in Fire alarm: Reading Walter Benjamin's on the Concept of History*. London/New York: Verso.

Luxemburg, Rosa. 1995. Letter to Mathilda Wurm, February 16, 1916. In *The Jew in the Modern World. A Documentary History*, edited by Paul Mendes Flohr and Jehuda Reinharz, pp. 261–262. New York: Oxford University Press.

Maldonado-Torres, Nelson. 2002. Thinking from the Limits of Being. Levinas, Fanon, Dussel and the Cry of Ethical Revolt. Doctoral dissertation, Brown University.

Malka, Salomon. 2006. *Emmanuel Levinas. His Life and Legacy*. Pittsburgh, PA: Duquesne University Press.

Marx, Karl. 1978. On the Jewish Question. In *Early Writings*, pp. 34–45. New York: Vintage.

Memmi, Albert. 1973. *The Liberation of the Jew*. New York: Viking.

Meyer, Marshall. 1987. Consideraciones sobre América Latina. *Majsahvot* 26: 5–27.

Mignolo, Walter. 2000. *Local Histories/Global Designs*. Princeton, NJ: Princeton University Press.

Myers, David. 2003. *Resisting History: Historicism and Its Discontents in German–Jewish Thought*. Princeton, NJ: Princeton University Press.

Netanyahu, Benzion. 1995. *The Origins of the Inquisition in the Fifteenth Century*. New York: Random House.

O'Hare, Padraic. 1990. Liberation Theology: Romantic Ideology? Teacher or Contempt. An exchange Between Padraic O'Hare and Leon Klenicki. *Cross Currents* 40(1): 109–119.

Parfitt, Tudor. 2006. The Use of the Jew in the Colonial Discourse. In *Orientalism and the Jews*, edited by Ivan Kalmar and Derek Penslar, pp. 51–67. Hanover, NJ: University of New England Press.

Quijano, Anibal and Immanuel Wallerstein. 1992. Americanity as a Concept, or the Americas in the Modern-World System. *International Social Sciences Journal* 134: 549–557.

Rosenzweig, Franz. 1985. *The Star of Redemption*. Notre Dame: Notre Dame University Press.

Rubenstein, Richard. 1966. *After Auschwitz*. Indianapolis, IN: Bobbs Merrill.

Sachar, Howard. 1993 *A History of the Jews in America*. New York: Vintage.

Salemohamed, George. 1992. Levinas: From Ethics to Political Theology. *Economy and Society* 21: 87–102.

Said, Edward. 1992. *The Question of Palestine*. New York: Vintage.

Sartre, Jean-Paul. 1995. *The Jew and the Anti-semite: An Exploration of the Etiology of Hate*. New York: Schocken.

Silverblatt, Irene. 1995. Becoming Indians in the Central Andes of the Seventeenth Century. In *After Colonialism: Imperial Histories and Post-colonial Displacement*, edited by Gyan Prakash, pp. 279–298. Princeton, NJ: Princeton University Press.

Silverblatt, Irene. 2004. *Modern Inquisitions: Peru and the Colonial Origins of the Colonial World*. Durham, NC: Duke University Press.

Sklare, Marshall. 1955. Judaism: An American Jewish Movement. Glencoe: Free Press.

Slabodsky, Santiago. 2004. Relocalizando Sinai en Los Andes. Especificidad Latinoamericana en un duelo Judio Post-Holocausto: Liberacionismo Judio vs. Judaismo Constantiniano. *Majshavot.*. Ano XL No 4: 72–94.

Slabodsky, Santiago and Victoria Kandel. 2001. Religion & Particularism: Latin-American Specificity in the Emergence of Liberal Religious Judaism. *Religión y Sociedad/ASRLA* III: 3–17.

Spivak, Gayatri Chakravorty. 1988. Subaltern Studies: Deconstructing Historiography. In *Subaltern Studies*, edited by Gayatri Charavorty Spivak and Ranjit Guha, pp. 3–33. Delhi: Oxford University Press.

Steiner, George. 1988. The Long Life of Metaphor: An Approach to the Shoa. In *Writing and the Holocaust*, edited by Beryl Lang, pp. 154–172. New York: Holmes & Meyer.

Taylor, Charles. 1989. *Sources of the Self. The Making of the Modern Identity*. Cambridge, MA: Harvard University Press.

Trachman, Gerdy. 1998. Marshall Meyer, Rabbi who Changed the Face of Latin American Jewry. Baltimore, MD: Baltimore Hebrew University.

Traverso, Enzo. 1993. The Marxists and the Jewish Question: The History of a Debate, 1843–1943. Atlantic Highland, NJ: Humanities.

Weil, Adolfo 1988. *Origenes del Judaismo Conservador*. Argentino, Buenos Aires: Ediciones del Seminario Rabinico Latinoamericano.

Wiesel, Elie. 1967. *The Gates of the Forest*. New York: Avon.

Wiesel, Elie. 1977. *Dimensions of the Holocaust*. Evanston, IL: Northwestern University Press.

Xun, Zhou. 2006. The 'Haifeng Jew' Hoax: Constructing the 'Chinese Jew.' In *Orientalism and the Jews*, edited by Ivan Kalmar and Derek Penslar, pp. 68–89. Hanover, NJ: University of New England Press.

Enduring Enchantment: Secularism and the Epistemic Privileges of Modernity

Walter D. Mignolo

Abstract Common wisdom has it that secularism dominated the project of the second modernity (the Enlightenment) and ended with the enchanted world that the very rhetoric of secularism used to displace theology and to convert religion in a field of study. I argue that indeed secularism implanted its own secular enchantment in the very act of undermining theological and religious enchantment. Secular epistemology took the place of theological epistemology in a double imperial move: it asserted secular epistemology over theological one in the internal history of the West; and discredited all non-Western epistemologies by inventing concepts such as tradition, myth, cosmologies, beliefs, etc. Secular epistemology created the new enchantment masked under the rhetoric of the irresistible and unavoidable progress of history and of (Western) idea of modernity.

There are enduring enchantments that, created by the self-defining discourse of modernity, acquired an ontological dimension beyond the discourse itself. "Modernity" has, in these enduring enchantments, a double role. On the one hand it is one of a series of oppositions: for example, modernity/tradition, colony/modernity. On the other hand, it names the paradigm which reproduces and maintains those oppositions. My thesis is that the self-conception of the European Renaissance was expressed, basically, in a temporal and spatial matrix corresponding to a religious and alphabetic/historiographic imaginary which was supported by the invention of the printing press. This matrix was transformed in the late eighteenth century as the alphabetic/historiographic imaginary was replaced by the emergence of a new type of discourse, political economy (Heilbroner 1992; Rothschild 2001).

Political economy came into the picture with a geopolitical concept of time, which displaced, in the West, the hegemony of the Christian idea of time and of space. Christianity told the story of humankind from its origins in God's creation and distributed space in three continents, each of them attributed to one of Noah's sons: Asia to Sem, Africa to Ham, and Europe to Japhet (Hay 1968; Bartlett 1993). This secularization of time paralleled, interestingly enough, the emergence of political economy. Toward the end of the eighteenth century, Adam Smith had no doubt about the "advancement" of colonized sites (places) with the help of the colonial countries. Today, the rhetoric is that "technology will lift poverty." At the end of the eighteenth century the rhetoric ran like this:

P. Bilimoria and A.B. Irvine (eds.), *Postcolonial Philosophy of Religion.*
© Springer Science+Business Media B.V. 2009

> The colony of a civilized nation which takes possession either of a waste country, or of one so thinly inhabited, that the natives easily give place to the new settlers, advances more rapidly to wealth and greatness than any other human society. The colonists carry out with them a knowledge of agriculture and other useful arts, superior to what can grow up of its own accord in the course of many centuries among savage and barbarous nations. They carry out with them too the habit of subordination, some notion of the regular government which takes place in their own country, of the system of laws which supports it, and of regular administration of justice, and naturally establish something of the same kind of the new settlement. (Smith 2000: 609)

Thus, the colonists not only "carried out with them" all those aspects that Adam Smith enumerated. More importantly, they carried with them the *conceptualization* of what they carried with them, that is, that which Smith here conceives but already as naturalized. Thus it *became* natural that Karl Marx, little more than half a century after Adam Smith, should understand the sixteenth and seventeenth centuries as a period of primitive accumulation. By doing so, he reinforced both the temporal direction of the history of capitalism to its point of arrival in the "mother country" (Marx's expression), and re-articulated the temporal relations within the colonies. Said Marx:

> In Western Europe, *the homeland of political economy*, the process of primitive accumulation has more or less been accomplished. Here the capitalist regime has either directly subordinated to itself the whole of the nation's production, or, where economic relations are less developed, it has at least indirect control of those social layers which, although they belong to the antiquated mode of production, still continue to exist side by side with it in a state of decay. To this ready-made world of capital, the political economist applies the notions of law and of property inherited from a pre-capitalist world, with all the more anxious zeal and all the greater unction, the more loudly the facts cry out in the face of his ideology. (Marx 1976: 931)

However, Marx adds, "it is otherwise in the colonies" (ibid.). In the colonies the capitalist regime "constantly comes up against the obstacle presented by the producer, who, as owner of his own conditions of labor, employs that labor to enrich himself instead of the capitalist" (ibid.: 931–932).

Most likely Marx was thinking about Indians in South Asia under British rule. However, the conceptualization of economics based on the laws that Smith and Marx expounded had its foundation in religious discourse, also based on the law, established three centuries before Marx but under different economic and colonial conditions. That is, what Marx called Europe's "primitive accumulation" (which made Europe, for him, the "homeland of political economy") was caused by the transformation of mercantile capitalism in the sixteenth century due to the "discovery of America." What Marx was referring to, but not naming as such, was apparently "*colonial* (primitive) accumulation."

Marx was very much imbued with the already entrenched belief in the linear march of time, and the progress of universal history. But the accumulation of capital that resulted from the exploitation of the silver and gold mines in Potosí, Zacatecas and Ouro Preto by Spaniards and Portuguese, as well as the exploitation of the Caribbean lands – and of African Slaves – in the French, British, and Dutch plantations, was not the same as the accumulation in Europe itself, that is, that kind of accumulation that (since Europe was the "homeland of political economy") had been already accomplished.

For one thing, race was not a significant element in *modern* (that is, intra-European) accumulation, while it was the essence of *colonial* accumulation. Indeed, race became a foundational category in the organization and the exploitation of labor in colonial accumulation, while class became the foundational category in modern accumulation.[1] Lewis Gordon pointed out the same phenomenon from a different perspective:

> In Europe, class is so indigenous to its environment that it emerges even in European efforts to socialism. One can "feel" class in Europe as one can feel the air that one breathes. In the U.S., however [and, I add, in the Americas including the Caribbean], the effort to escape (yet retain) Europe took the form of homogenizing European identities into a whiteness framed on the premise of racially falling being. Race, then, became an endemic motive of the New World, and that is why one can "feel" race here as one can the air that one breathes.... (Gordon 2001: 74)

Now, both Smith and Marx underlined the extreme relevance of the "discovery" of the Cape of Good Hope in 1488, and of the Americas thereafter, to the history of capital (first commercial and then industrial). The first "discovery" allowed Christian Europe to establish commercial relations with the economic centers of China and India. The "discovery" of America brought gold, silver and goods from the Caribbean plantations to Europe and, later, to "Western Europe" (Holland, England, France, Germany). Certainly, Smith and Marx made their remarks in a secular prose that contrasted with the triumphal enunciation by which Francisco de Gomara, historian of Hernan Cortes's conquest of Mexico, framed the discovery of America in the history of the Christian Western World. For Gomara, the discovery of America (he does not pay attention to the Cape of Good Hope) was, without a doubt, the most extraordinary event in the history of the world, since its very creation was by the will of God. In the dedication of his *Hispania Vitrix* to Charles V, Francisco de Gomara states:

> La mayor cosa despues de la creacion del mundo sacando la encarnacion y muerte del que lo crio, es el descubrimiento de Indias.... Quiso Dios descobrir las Indias en vuestro tiempo y a vuestros vasallos, para que las convirtiesedes a su santa ley.... Comenzaron las conquistas de Indios acabada la de los moros, porque siempre guerreasen espanioles contra infieles.

> The most important event after the creation of the World, beyond the incarnation and death of its Creator, was the discovery of the Indies.... It was God's will to discover the Indies during your time and the time of your vassals so the Indies can be converted into his Sacred Law.... The conquest of the Indies began once the conquests of the Moors ended, and that is because it was God's will that Spaniard be always at war with the infidels. (Gómara 1946 [1552]: xx, my translation)

Bringing a Spanish and Christian historian to this picture may seem farfetched. I hope to show that it is not.

Smith and Marx transformed the "foundational" discourse of enduring enchantment, from the language of Christian historiography, law and rhetoric, to the language of political economy. Furthermore, Smith and Marx were not looking at the discovery of America from the perspective of the Spanish empire, be it in triumphal mode like Gomara's, or critical like Bartolomé de Las Casas's. The transformed discourse did, however, carry over the enchantments of the discovery of America, in both Smith's consideration of (colonial) commerce, and Marx's treatment of (colonial) primitive accumulation.

The excesses committed by Spanish *"conquistadores,"* so well exploited later on by England and France in order to take over the colonial power enjoyed by Spain in the sixteenth and seventeenth centuries, had its own criticism among Spanish missionaries as well. It is well known that Bartolomé de Las Casas was used by the promoters of the "Black Legend" to show how bad things were in the Spanish colonies, such that even Spaniards like Las Casas were horrified (Gerbi 1958: 129–195).

We are no longer persuaded, today, by the rhetoric used by an imperial power against another imperial power. If Bartolomé de Las Casas was the activist who denounced the abuses of the *"conquistadores,"* Francisco de Vitoria and the Salamanca school established, starting around 1539, a system of international law based on the universal perspective of Christianity. Vitoria and the Salamanca school did not invent the law, of course. They worked seriously, though, to put in place a system of international law that would acknowledge the "rights" of the Indians as well as of the Spanish. For instance, the Indians' right to keep their property was one of the fundamental issues explored and defended by Vitoria. The rights of the Spaniards to be in Indian territory and preach Christianity were also defended. While Spaniards, according to Vitoria, did not have the right to expropriate Indians' property, Indians had no right to exclude Spaniards from their territory and even less to stop them from spreading Christianity.[2] Political economy was not yet in place when Vitoria was active, and economic issues were subsumed under historical, religious and legal discourses. The situation was quite different from what Smith and Marx were looking at in the eighteenth and nineteenth centuries. And yet, in different ways, Vitoria, Smith and Marx embodied the existing power relations which they, from different perspectives, pretended thoroughly to criticize.

In the case of Vitoria, the Indians whose rights were being defended had no opportunity to voice their opinions about the rights they were supposed to have. In the case of Smith, the critique was directed toward the areas of the world that needed colonialism for their own advancement toward "modernity" (the precise word not being used by Smith, although its spirit was implied). And Marx condemned the exploitation of the capitalist mode of production. Everything was decided – whether in the discourse of theological law or of political economy – without any say from the rest of the world. In this sense, the three great critics indeed embodied the power relations of which they pretended to be critical.

Due to the worldwide expansion of Christian, Liberal and Marxist discourses, we are in a similar position still today. There is no longer even the possibility of attaining and pretending to be a meta-critical voice from the left that condemns all the failures of leftist-like discourses, pretending to find a place uncontaminated from the embodiment of existing power relations; no possibility of finding a place, finally, in which, like God, everybody else could be criticized by the embodiment of the existing power relations. This is why I argue, instead, for *border thinking*, as one possible way of breaking the enchantments of capitalism, figured in the vicious circularity of its internal critiques.[3]

During the European Renaissance, people around the world were mainly located in space, not in time. Christianity did not conceive of the "infidels" as being less developed, or behind in time. The "denial of coevalness" (Johannes Fabian's lucid term) emerging from the European Enlightenment, and particularly in G.W.F. Hegel's philosophy of history would have been nonsensical in the Renaissance. The infidels were not primitive or distant in time. Rather, they were in distant geographical places, like India, or in different spheres of belief, as with the Moors or the Jews. Christians did not classify the world in terms of a point of arrival in time, *the* point of arrival at History, but rather in space. (There was a temporal point of arrival, but it was the Final Judgement, not some present age as in later, secular history.) The Christian map was drawn in consonance with Christian narratives of origin. The names of the three sons of Noah served to locate continents, therefore people, and also to rank the continents in relation to Japheth, Noah's preferred son. Japheth was located in the West, in the lands of Western Christians. Shem and Ham were located in Asia and Africa, respectively.

It was during the eighteenth century and the European Enlightenment that people outside of Europe began to be located in time. The secular idea of "primitives" replaced that of "infidels." By the time Hegel wrote his lectures on the philosophy of history, the East (with respect to Europe) of the world was situated *in the past*. It was where history began, but was no longer dwelling. China, India, and Japan no longer co-existed with Europe. They belonged to a different "time." The *present* of History was located in Europe. Hegel's denial of coevalness established the dividing line between "modernity" and "tradition"; but the distinction between both was created by the discourse of "modernity," not by the discourse of "tradition." "Tradition" *did not have* its own discourse. It was created by the discourse of, the discourse which defined, "modernity." In fact, "tradition" was an invention very much like "modernity," a necessary invention in order to define "modernity" and to locate it in Europe, in "Western Europe," in England, France and Germany. But of course what really counts is not that it was an invention, but rather the geopolitical order and the historical consequences of such an invention.

During the Renaissance the distinction between *les anciens* and *les modernes* was established within European history. *Les anciens* referred to Europe's own past, in contrast to "primitives," who belonged to history outside of Europe, conceived either as past history (China, India), or as future history (America), or as without history (Africa). Hegel's was the canonical narrative of both the space–time matrix established in the European Renaissance, and the transformed matrix of the European Enlightenment. Thus, Hegel (with the help of Kant) set the stage for the enduring enchantments being discussed here.

Secular thinkers criticized religion that became the "opium of the people." Yet, Christianity remained complicit with secular critique, since Christianity could not be placed at the same level, as "opium of the people," with Islam, Buddhism, Hinduism, or even Judaism! The complicity between secularism and Christianity is clear today in the enactment of international relations and global politics. Some religion had to be superior to others, even if "faith" cannot be maintained at the same level as "reason." The Palestine–Israel conflict is of course not unrelated to the tensions, the complicity, and the hatred generated by the imaginary of the modern/colonial world, and its articulation of differences and hierarchies. And all the talk on the "clash of civilization" is very much the natural consequence of the invention of modernity and tradition. It is then necessary to replace "tradition" with *coloniality*, the latter being a place of enunciation from where the invention of modernity can be disclosed, and its "natural" underpinning revealed.

The modern/colonial world was founded and sustained through a geopolitical organization of the world that, in the last analysis, stood on an ethno-racial foundation (Quijano 2000; Mignolo 2000a: 3–48). In the sixteenth century, "race" did not yet have the meaning it acquired in the eighteenth and nineteenth centuries. However, the racial classifications from the eighteenth century on, based on skin color rather than blood purity, cannot be understood without the former.[4] The transformation from blood purity to skin color parallels the transformation from the hegemony of religious discourses grounded in faith to the hegemony of secular discourses grounded in reason. The persistence of bodies of knowledge distributed between "enchanted spaces" and "modern places," between traditional and modern knowledge, between African philosophy and philosophy *tout court*, demonstrates the flexibility of modernity in implementing coloniality of power and, therefore, Western racism. In "modern space," epistemology was first Christian and then White. In "enchanted places," wisdom (and *not* epistemology) was, to begin with, non-Christian (one of the reasons why Christianity remained complicit with its secular philosophical critics), and also, later on, "colored." Islam, for instance, became a colored religion. Christianity, particularly Protestant Christianity, became whiter after the reformation (Allen 1994: 1–26, 71–90).

One can surmise that the persistence of binary classifications then is due to two interrelated factors. On the one hand, and as I already mentioned, Christianity is a member of the set of World Religions, and a particular contributor to World History. Simultaneously, Christianity is the epistemic location that created and implanted such classification. None of the other members in the set of World Religions, none of the other contributors to World History, has provided an equally powerful and enduring classification. In this regard, Christianity and modernity (and, I should add, postmodernity) share the privilege of a double location. First, in virtue of being one among many of a set of religions, and one among many of a set of historical epochs, and second, by being the only religion, and the only historical epoch, from which all other religions and historical epochs are established. Their enchantments will endure, in spite of work by critics of the Empire, who in spite of ourselves/themselves remain embodied in the imperial relations of power. Christianity and its aftermath, secular epistemology, had the privilege of being part of the totality enunciated, and at the same time the universal place of enunciation (while being able to make-believe that the place of enunciation was a non-place). Consequently, the order of the enunciator was the natural order of the world, and the world, alas, was organized in dichotomous hierarchies.

The "Other" in space, time, belief, skin color, or place of birth was of a particular kind. The "Other" was a part of humanity in the world that, until then, was unknown to the Christian Europeans, who promptly began debating questions such as the justice of war against this Other, or the rights of the people to property and autonomy. Modernity and tradition did not yet constitute a binary opposition. Nor did myth and history, although the "lack of history" Spaniards attributed to the Indians would become, later on, filled by the category of myth. State and community were not in opposition since the concept of the state, in the sixteenth century, was of a religion-state and not a nation-state as it would become conceptualized in secular eighteenth century. The opposition between emotion and reason was not yet in place for several reasons, one of which is that while "emotion" became a necessary component of the secular conceptualization of the subject-ego, endowed with reason, it was not a distinctive feature of the individual believer, endowed with faith and injected with fear toward God. The distinction between the former and the latter is related to, and parallels, the difference between the religion-state and the nation-state, between communities of believers and communities of citizens. The secular concept of reason was conceptualized, in part, through the distinction between primary and secondary qualities, by the detachment of the body from the mind, and by the erasure of secondary qualities from the pure work of reason, which Immanuel Kant theorized with such intensity (Eze 1997).

Now, although the existing dichotomies are the result of the mobilization of a discourse that, under the name and the positive value of "modernity," produces colonial differences to disqualify the opposing binary that it creates, the devalued set in the paradigm yet may give rise to several possible outcomes. The first possibility is to accept that one is traditional, that one does not measure up to the standard of "rationality," that one has mythic narrative but not history, that one is black and not white, etc. This outcome is passive acceptance of an inferior condition. A second possibility is to affirm the values that have been devalued and negated by the discourse of modernity. This outcome is clearly anti-modern, and may end up in a fundamentalistic defense of what modernity has devalued. The third option is one that accepts, first, that double consciousness is a condition of the colonial paradigm, and second, that the colonial paradigm consists of a set of binary oppositions resulting from the implementation of coloniality of power. Double consciousness is a necessary condition for the mobilization of *border thinking*. By definition, border thinking is beyond the national discourses of bounding, territorial states (that is, what are often called *nation-states*). Border thinking may lead us to critical cosmopolitanism as an intellectual, political and ethical project (Mignolo 2000b).

If we agree that the paradigm of binary oppositions such as modernity/tradition is a business of the second and secular modernity, that is, the modernity of Western Europe (mainly England, France and Germany after the Reformation), then the stories I have been telling about the European Renaissance become situated in *pre*-modernity or in the *early* modern period (as the French historians from the Annales School would say). Thus, the way is paved for a modern period in the same narrow geopolitical line as the rest of the Eurocentric concept of historical time. This modern concept of historical time silenced the rest of the world, by assuming the superiority of the "present," and of a type of "human being," that was based in the ideal of the Renaissance, that is, an ideal based in the paradigmatic example of certain white males.[5]

Once we are aware of the narrow frame of mind implanted by intellectuals of the second modernity, it is not surprising that Michel Foucault, for instance, locates the beginning of the discourse on war and race in 1630. This corresponds to the beginning of the biopolitics of the Europe of nations, not to the biopolitics of the constitution of Europe as such, as discussed in the sixteenth century, mainly by Vitoria and the Salamanca school, as they constructed a framework for global relations – and for the making of the colonial difference. The debate on the justice of war against the Indians occupied the entire sixteenth century in Spain, indeed in Europe at large. But *that* "Europe," the Europe of the sixteenth century, is *traditional* – not the modern Europe Foucault is interested in talking about.

In other words, the Thirty Years War in Europe (in the middle of which Foucault locates the beginning of the discourse of bio-politics) *presupposes* the consolidation of Europe through the colonial Christian missions and the reformation (Foucault 1977: 217–239 [March 17, 1976]; I am working from the Spanish translation, *Defender la sociedad*, by Horacio Pons). It presupposes, also, the wealth provided by the gold and silver of Potosí and Zacatecas and the Caribbean plantations, and the consolidation of the French and English economies through exploitation of the Caribbean plantations, the massive transportation of slaves, and the foundation of European nations, which would eventually emerge between the Peace of Westphalia (1648) and the post-Napoleonic colonial expansion. This racial war, that is, the war of England and France against Spain, was certainly a war of imperial conflicts and of racial categorization among and between European emerging nations, as Kant made clear (Kant 1996).

The common knowledge seldom appears articulated in a prose clear and concise as that of a recent editorial of the International Society for the Study of European Ideas:

> In the seventeenth century what had been known as Christendom became Europe and a new civilization came into being: European civilization. From then onwards Europe mirrored itself not only in its Greco-Roman legacy and its Judeo-Christian religion but also in the world's other civilizations discovered by European travelers.[6]

This image takes Western Europe as the heart of Europe, as Hegel did. For someone who does not identify him-or herself with European civilization, though, history can begin someplace else. For example:

> Toward the end of the fifteenth century what had been known as Tawantinsuyu, Anahuac and Abya-Yala by the inhabitants of what is today the Andean Region, Mexico and Panama respectively, but also what is today the Insular Caribbean, became *Indias Occidentales*, and then *America*, and then *Latin America*. A new civilization was born of the Christian and Castilian colonization, a civilization that was reproduced later on in Africa and in Asia by the European civilization that was born in the seventeenth century. A civilization of diversity, this "colonial/post-colonial civilization" characterizes itself by the diversity of local histories emerging from the encounter between Christian Spain and European civilization with America, Africa and Asia. The European civilization, as described above, did not leave its marks in the Caribbean until after the French revolution. From the early seventeenth century to the end of the eighteen century French and British presence in the Caribbean was

fully devoted to plantation economy rather than to the civilizing mission. The colonial/post-colonial civilization has received several names: transmodernity, subaltern modernities, or alternative modernities.[7]

The enduring enchantment of modernity's binary oppositions seems to be related to the enduring image of a European civilization, and of European history told from the perspective of Europe itself. Europe is not only the center (that is, the center of space and the point of arrival in time). It also has the epistemic privilege of being the center of enunciation. And in order to maintain the epistemic privilege it is necessary, today, to assimilate to the epistemic perspective of modernity and accuse emerging epistemologies of claiming epistemic privileges! The logic of "ethnic" food seems to be at work in epistemology as well. The only non-ethnic food in any European or U.S. fair would be precisely the food that is identified with European (but not "eastern European") or U.S. cuisine. All other food has the "privilege" of being "ethnic," and so related to tradition, folklore, popular culture, etc. Capitalism moved from Europe to the U.S., then to Japan, and now to China. Epistemology, though, apparently remains located in Europe, which is simultaneously the non-place of transparently universal enunciation. The complementary relations between the accumulation of capital and the accumulation of knowledge created the conditions for a self-definition of modernity. To be modern is either to assimilate to the self-fashioning of modernity, or to oppose it from the perspective of modernity itself (as with the opposition opened up by Marxism). Therefore, the dichotomies ranged according to modern spaces and enchanted places reproduce themselves under different masks.

Let us review some of their foundations. The temporal matrix pronounced the Middle Ages as the necessary "before" to justify the need of a "re-naissance" (Maravall 1963, 1972, 1973). The spatial matrix organized the difference between Christianity, on the one hand, and pagans and infidels on the other. The argument that I have developed until now addresses two interrelated issues which are embedded in the enduring oppositions that can be traced back to the European Renaissance and to the invention of America (O'Gorman 1958).

One, as I already mentioned, is the legitimization of a self-endowed double role enjoyed by the first set of terms of the binary oppositions being discussed in the issue of the *Journal of Medieval and Early Modern Studies*, devoted to the (temporal) decolonization of the Middle Ages. This indirectly led me to think of the need to "decolonize traditions colonized by modernity."[8] Each term implies the other. Modernity, for example, implies *West*, *reason*, *history*, *state*, and *rationality*. *Rationality* implies *modernity*, *West*, etc. Each term is part of the enunciated, but all of them are, at the same time, pervasively and invisibly, the foundation of the classification itself, that is, of what I am calling the enunciation.

What we have here is a different version of the coloniality of power, since the second set of terms are part of the colonization of time within Europe itself and the colonization of space *and* time in the colonial world outside Europe. The terms in the complementary side of the paradigm (*tradition*, *ritual*, *myth*, *community* and *emotion*) also are implied in each other. But, contrary to the first set of terms in the paradigm, none of them are part of the enunciation. They all have been relegated to the enunciated only.

What is invisible in this paradigm are perhaps the reasons for its enduring enchantment, namely, the workings of the "coloniality of power" and, therefore, the fact that the discourse of modernity (the enunciation) that defined modernity (the enunciated) was successful in hiding the fact that there cannot be modernity without coloniality. If coloniality, then, becomes the place of the enunciation, the second set of terms in the paradigm (colony, ritual, tradition, etc.) loses its passive role of being the supporting actor of a triumphant self-defined modernity.

The European Renaissance provided the logic upon which the philosophers of the European enlightenment could first build and later modify the logic related the content of modernity and of tradition. The binary oppositions that we are exploring were articulated during and after the European Enlightenment and consisted of "filling in the blanks" of a "before" in European history in relation to which the Renaissance was conceived precisely as Renaissance. The notion of newness began to be associated with modernity. The "before" was the period to which the pagans and infidels were assigned, and pagans and infidels were defined as such by the rhetoric of Christianity. In other words, there was not such a thing as infidels without the rhetoric of Christianity appointing itself as the measuring stick for the classification of people according to their beliefs. When the Indians of the "New World" (and here we have the newness in space) came into the picture, a new dimension of the difference emerged, and it was that difference that became one of the pillars of the very modernity/coloniality, of the modern/colonial world.

Pagans and infidels in time, and in a shared territory, had to be dealt with as infidels in space and in an alien territory. West and East, Occident and Orient came into the picture. The Spanish possessions were divided between *Indias Occidentales* (the Americas) and *Indias Orientales* (the Philippines and Moluccas), as I have already mentioned (Mignolo 1995; Migolo 1998; Rafael 1993). Occidentalism in the sixteenth century became the necessary grounding to conceive Orientalism in the eighteenth century (Coronil 1996; also Coronil 2000; Mignolo 1995). The geographical paradigm for the establishment of a series of "lacks" and "wrongs" was established according to Christian religious and secular epistemic frames. Briefly, the European Renaissance established the matrix for a double colonization, of time and of space.

The colonization of time resulted in the invention of the Middle Ages in European history. The colonization of space meant, on the one hand, the expulsion of the Moors and the Jews from Christian Spain, and on the other hand, the conquest of the *Indias Occidentales* upon the "discovery" of a New World.

The spatial colonial difference emerged toward the end of the fifteenth through the sixteenth centuries. The triumph of Christianity over the Moors and the Jews in late fifteenth century Spain laid out the foundations of the enduring paradigm of binary oppositions, and of the epistemic privilege of modern (western, Christian) epistemology, which has held from the Renaissance to today. Jews and Moors, on the one hand, embraced the wrong God and the wrong beliefs. The American Indians, on the other, were not on the intellectual horizon of Christianity. Therefore, they were distinguished by their "lacks" rather than their "wrongs."

For instance, they lack alphabetical writing, and therefore do not have history. They worship plants and nature, and therefore do not have religion. They lack the logical way of reasoning established by the Christian thinkers of Medieval Europe. Although the Aztecs' and Incas' social organization impressed the Spaniards very much, they did not have a conception of their lack of logical explicitness compared to, say, Roman Law. Or, at least, the Spaniards were unable to see the logic underlying Aztec and Inca social organization.

In the Caribbean the scenario is more complex. In the first place, this is due to the extermination of the native population. In the second, it owes to the arrival of massive contingents of African slaves. Antiguan philosopher, Paget Henry, has recently mapped the imperial/colonial conditions under which an Afro-Caribbean philosophy emerged. According to him, "the original content of Caribbean philosophy emerged as a series of extended debates over projects of colonial domination between four major social groups: Euro-Caribbeans, Amerindians, Indo-Caribbeans and Afro-Caribbeans" (Henry 2000).

In any case, the colonial difference in the Andes, Mesoamerica and the Caribbean is the foundation of both the colonial differences created by colonial discourses, and the differential colonial accumulation that ensued from that historical foundational moment. The binary oppositions, which are indeed the colonial difference created from the epistemic privilege of colonial modernities, are the conditions under which subjectivities have been formed in the process of differential colonial accumulation.

To imagine possible futures beyond the enduring enchantments of the differential colonial accumulation of binary oppositions would imply a redressing in the direction in which the coloniality of power has been implemented in the past 500 years. And that process is already taking place. It is not, however, a project consisting of a mere reversal of the epistemic privilege of modernity, that is, of displacing the privileges from the first set of the paradigm to the second set. It would consist of taking advantage of the double-consciousness that emerges, out of necessity, in all those subjectivities that have been formed under the second set of terms.

For instance, belonging to a world that has been classified as traditional and irrational means that any attempt to mobilize from that position will have to assume that the conditions of being irrational and traditional have been allocated from the epistemic privilege of a mythical space/time called modernity. However, since the epistemic privilege goes hand-in-hand with its hegemony, its displacement implies subsuming the first set of terms in the paradigm into the second, by making of the latter a locus of enunciation as legitimate as the first. This is the epistemic operation I have conceptualized as "border thinking," "border gnosis," or border epistemology (Mignolo 2000a).

Thus, there are three important "attitudes" influencing developments in the South and North Atlantic, prior to the European Enlightenment, without which the Enlightenment itself and what followed can be only partially understood.

The first attitude is doubly articulated, in the invention of the Middle Ages in the Renaissance, and in the victory of Christianity over the Jews and the Moors at the end of the fifteenth century in Castile.

The second attitude is formed through the discourse of the invention of America, and the verbalization of the colonial difference in three different and interrelated domains. One domain was the notion of human being, which seemed to need revision due to the appearance of the "Indians" in the European consciousness. This need gave rise to the "right of peoples," widely discussed in the school of Salamanca and in Europe in general. The right of peoples was indeed the conceptualization of the right of the other, and was the first expression of international law in the modern/colonial world. The second domain was related to conversion, and to the brutal campaign that took the name of the "extirpation of idolatry." The extirpation of idolatry was a process of, as Manuel Moreno Fraginals puts it, "deculturation" (Moreno Fraginals 1999: 24–29). Deculturation consists of a conscientious process of economic exploitation, through which those in power proceed to "remove" knowledges and memories of a given human group. These processes facilitate, according to Moreno Fraginals, the expropriation of natural resources of a territory in which the human group in question dwells and, at the same time, the use of the human community as a cheap, unqualified labor force. Deculturation has been common since the early colonization of the New World, the main targets having been Amerindians and African slaves (ibid.: 25–26).

The third attitude was constituted by Spanish missionaries and men of letters appointing themselves to write the history that, they claimed, Amerindians did not have.

In these three parallel and complementary processes there were of course mixed positions. At one end of the spectrum were those who considered Amerindians subhuman, and who justified war, dispossession of property, and the extirpation not only of "idolatry," but of memories and knowledges. At the other end were those who recognized the humanity of Amerindians, yet could not overcome the belief that, *as* humans, they were still inferior to the Spaniards.

These three attitudes prevailed during the sixteenth and the seventeenth centuries. The eighteenth century was a scenario of radical changes, both in the re-articulation of the colonial difference, and in the inventions of the South of Europe and the imperial difference. It is during this century that the dichotomies under consideration were put in place. Furthermore, a new set of actors entered into the game, the so-called *criollos* in the Spanish colonies, who began to voice their position vis a vis the previous Spanish colonial discourse, and also the emergent colonial discourses put in place by French, British and German intellectuals. This pre-Enlightenment moment informed the Enlightenment so much that it is known in the history of Latin America as "The Debate Over the New World." Yet it continues to be ignored by European historians of the Enlightenment and their followers.

I will concentrate on three major issues in the configuration of this new scenario. First, there was the radical displacement from a Spanish discourse about *las Indias Occidentales*, to French, British and German discourses on the "New World." The New World acquired at this moment a new meaning, and this displacement impinged directly on the idea of modernity and tradition. In the sixteenth century, the idea of the "New World" (introduced, incidentally, by the Italian intellectual Pietro Martir d'Anghiera, who was living in Spain at the time of the Columbus and Vespucci voyages) meant that a world unknown to Europeans became visible. The distinction in the sixteenth century was between the "New World" (*Indias Occidentales*, then later, "America") and the "Old World" (that is, Asia, Africa and Europe, in Christian cosmography). By the eighteenth century, the idea of the New World was taken by European intellectuals like Buffon, de Paw, and the Abbé Reynal to entail, first, literal "newness," and second, to be associated with "youth," "immaturity," and "weakness," in contrast to the Old World, which was thought to have matured, physically, mentally, and spiritually. Within this tradition, it is unsurprising that Hegel should assert history moves from East to West. While Asia is the past, and Europe the present, the "youth" of America designed "her" as the future and continuity of European history (Gerbi 1958: 47–101).

Secondly, the Debate Over the New World was, during the eighteenth century, the main expression of colonial discourse, although it has not been much acknowledged by historians beyond Latin America. The contact between Europe and the East was, since the early fourteenth century, basically commercial. However, while commercial contacts between European and Asian cities had been significant in the self-definition of Christendom and Europe up to the sixteenth century, from the sixteenth century on both European and Christian self-definition was performed on the basis of the colonial discourse, which was being built upon the emerging Atlantic commercial circuits (Abu-Lughod 1989). It was those Atlantic commercial circuits (carrying gold and silver from Zacatecas and Potosí for Spain, and Ouro Preto for the Portuguese; sugar, coffee, and tobacco from the Caribbean plantations for the French and the British) in which European cities found an impressive source of wealth.

Furthermore, in the sixteenth century the Atlantic commercial circuit was controlled totally by the Spanish and Portuguese. It was only in the seventeenth century that the Dutch, French and English made their presence felt, particularly in the Caribbean, with the massive slave trade needed for the plantations. The Dutch East India Company and its English rival, the East India Company did not generate the wealth provided by the Caribbean plantations, either for the Dutch or the English. Nor was commerce with the East Indies during the sixteenth and the seventeenth centuries complemented by a colonial discourse, like the one put in place (mainly by the Spaniards) in the sixteenth and seventeenth centuries, followed by the French in the eighteenth century. The discourse of the "civilizing mission", as global design, and "orientalism" as a scholarly discourse justifying – albeit indirectly – the need of the civilizing mission, were put in place toward the end of the eighteenth and during the nineteenth centuries. There were also a series of historical circumstances that should be taken into account to understand these changes. The industrial revolution, the French revolution, and the end of the Napoleonic era, created the condition for the expansions – mainly of France and England in Asia and Africa. There was a totally different *ethos*, at this point, compared to that of either the French or British Caribbean and North American possessions in the seventeenth century.

Third, the word, *colony*, which originates from the early Roman Empire, is a term employed in the measurement of lands and city planning that involved both *mensores* (for the measurement and planning of urban spaces) and *agrimensores* (for the measurement and planning of country spaces). Curiously enough, Rome borrowed these administrative practices not only from the Greeks, but also from other "Eastern" practices beyond (Nicolet 1991: 90). In any event, the word, "colony," moved into Western vernacular languages, carrying with it the meaning it had in Latin as it was employed in the administration of the Roman Empire. Thus, colony did not become related to modernity until later on, after a substantial transformation of its meaning.

One can surmise that the colonies were similar to the communities that the Inca and Aztec "Empires," totally independent of the influence of the Roman Empire, annexed to the central administration of Tawantinsuyu in the Andes, and of Anahuac in Mesoamerica, today Mexico and Guatemala. Thus, the arrival of the Spaniards produced a significant change in that the two Empires, Aztec and Inca, became "colonies" of Spain. Therefore, the foundation of the modern/colonial world meant that "empires" became "colonies." And, of course, "colonies" also became everything under colonial administration.

In 1532 the Spanish Crown began a process of mapping and describing the territories or colonies under their possessions, as the *mensores* and *agrimensores* had done for ancient Rome. The results were known as *relaciones geograficas de Indias*. But the most important thing here is that the colonies in question were not established in a space already known, the *orbis terrarum*, or *oikoumene*, but in a *(the)* New World (O'Gorman 1958). When Charles became Emperor of both Spain and Europe in 1516, the colonies in Europe and those in the New World were clearly distinguished. A crucial distinction was that the original inhabitants of the New World, and the enslaved Africans brought there, did not have the same civil position (nor, later on, the same citizenship) as the inhabitants of Europe. Thus the colonies of the New World were distinguished precisely by implementation of the colonial difference.

The colonial difference in the New World was twice articulated during the sixteenth and the seventeenth centuries, as I already mentioned. First by Spaniards like Francisco de Gómara, who held that their discovery of the New World was the most significant event in World History since the creation of the world, then by French and German intellectuals like Hegel, who trooped the newness of the "New World" so as to treat its inhabitants and their history as if they did not exist until "discovered" by Europeans!

A third articulation came with the discourse of the "civilizing mission," and of "orientalism" in particular. The idea of scientific and industrial revolutions became clear signs of modernity. The conviction that technology and the sciences inspired among European intellectuals and men of state replaced convictions of religion and the *studia humanitates* during the period between the Renaissance and the Enlightenment. Thus, the current meaning of the modernity/colony oppositional pairing, and of the related binaries, was put in place. And this story is also helpful in understanding modern and colonial accumulation.

Let us now sketch the emergence of a worldwide double consciousness, consequence of the imperial and hegemonic imaginary of the modern/colonial world in its successive transformations. I introduced this topic earlier in the essay. There are two significant moments that deserve attention. The first took place toward the end of the sixteenth and the beginning of the seventeenth centuries in Tawantinsuyu and Anahuac. A significant number of indigenous intellectuals in both places had to deal with a situation involving the replacement of their memories, social organization, and way of life with those being implanted by the newcomers.

The experience was not named as W.E.B. Du Bois named the experience of the "souls of black folk" at the beginning of the twentieth century. Yet the feeling was similar. A word, *nepantla*, was invented by Nahuatl-language speakers to describe their situation: it meant "being between two worlds" (of course while knowing that the power relations of these two worlds were not symmetrical). Clearly, double consciousness was in place, albeit with a different name. I am not arguing here who was the first to have double consciousness. Rather, I am trying to demonstrate the continual articulation and rearticulation of the colonial difference.

In those who are at the receiving end (that is, those who are identified with tradition, ritual, myth, community, *etcetera*), the colonial difference always generates a double consciousness, whether they assimilate in silence or protest the situation. The endurance of enchantments in the time of modernity can be explained by the fact that modernity, rationality, history, state, *etcetera*, are still taken as reference points of an *arrival*, even if modernization is detached from westernization. "Modernization without westernization" is a formula embraced by many non-Western intellectuals and state officers. However, it is not clear that by modernization they mean justice, equality, health and education for all, and a fair distribution of wealth. Indeed, "Modernization without westernization" seems often to imply instead an *overcoming* of the "traditional" organization of society, a technological upgrade.

The desire for modernization is always a desire emanating from "traditional," "Third World," or "post-colonial" countries – in other words, from the side of the *colonized*. The societies that did the *colonizing* do not have to become modern. (Their problem is to remain modern. Thus, England became a post-colonial country after its decolonization in Africa and Asia, but we do not hear any claim for the modernization of England. We do hear, however, many claims from, for example, Indian progressive intellectuals who embrace the project of modernity, although not necessarily as Jurgen Habermas would have it) (See, for example, Chatterjee 1998).

Thus, there is a Catch 22 in the opposition of modernity/tradition, inasmuch as the categories of tradition, ritual, myth, community, and so on, are not realities, but categories constructed to make possible the self-defining discourse of modernity. One set of terms in the oppositional paradigm describes the exteriority created by the opposing set of terms, which are modernity's points of reference for its own arrival. The exteriority is not outside modernity, but is being created by an interiority. This is precisely the colonial condition that promotes the emergence of double consciousness, and border thinking. The point here is that modernity and its categories are not only members of the binary oppositions enunciated, but are also key to an actual enunciation of the oppositions. In this regard, the binary oppositions we are discussing correspond to an enduring colonial logic, which has structured and motivated Western epistemology from the Renaissance to today. That is to say, the paradigm of opposition is not being articulated from a neutral perspective, uncontaminated by the terms of the opposition. The paradigm *defines* modernity, in moderns' very act of conceiving their time *as* an epoch, *as* a point of arrival in European history. Moreover, this paradigm also became the universal locus of enunciation. When a regional locus of enunciation becomes universal, it acquires the force of controlling its own criticism.

In the past few decades, it has become customary to argue in favor of the epistemic potential implied in the genealogy of knowledges that have been subalternized from the perspective of modern epistemology. Some of those who argued in favor of the political and epistemic legitimacy of subaltern voices have been accused (by modern or postmodern, right- and left-wing intellectuals) of defending an "epistemic privilege" of the des-empowered, and thus of confusing epistemology with political sloganeering. In my view, the debate framed in those terms reveals that the only privileged episteme continues to be that of *modern epistemology*. Subaltern perspectives of course are not endowed with an epistemic privilege. They do not need that privilege, for what subaltern perspectives have is an epistemic potential, a potential grounded in what – for modern epistemology – has been silence and darkness: the silence of those epistemically disinherited by and through the emancipation claims of modernity (think of the Haitian revolution, for instance), and the darkness to which the world was reduced in order to sustain modernity's epistemic privilege, *the* enduring enchantment.

Philosophers from the Arab-Islamic world have been dealing with the problem of tradition and modernity, asking how to imagine possible futures building from what is alive today in both "tradition" and "modernity," that is, in the tradition of the Arab-Islamic world and in the tradition of European modernity. Mohamed al-Jabri is one of these philosophers.

For al-Jabri, the great Ibn Rushd, or Averroës, is a model for carrying out this task (Al-Jabri 1994, 1999).[9] On both the Christian-Latin and Islamic-Arabic sides of the Middle Ages, philosophers built on the physics of Aristotle. But what happened since then? Descartes built his philosophy upon Galileo's physics and, later on, Kant "advanced" over Descartes by building his philosophy upon Newton's physics. Later, Bachelard follow suit by building on quantum physics and the theory of relativity. The bearers of the "temporal tradition" of European modernity built upon and inscribed their own past into their present. As we have already seen, the colonization of the Middle Ages initiated the inscription of the past of modernity.

In the Arabic-Islamic world, by contrast, what happened was the historical and epistemic rupture between Ibn Sina (Avicenna) and Averroës.[10] Averroës would be then the equivalent of Descartes in the history of Arab-Islamic philosophy. According to al-Jabri, Averroës, "entered history because [he] broke with the Aviccenianism of 'oriental' philosophy. . . . He also broke with the manner in which theoretical thinking – both theological and philosophical – had addressed the critical relationship between religion and philosophy." But, al-Jabri continues, Averroës did not limit himself to "rupture." He also offered the possibilities of a "carry-on spirit" (Al-Jabri 1999: 123).

Thus, the point of articulation today, from the perspective of Arabic-Islamic philosophy, consists of a double task. One is to evaluate their own "tradition," and the other is to articulate their modern present with the hegemony of European modernity. Thus, the question is no so much, what is modern and what is traditional, but rather, what is the structure of power, and of the coloniality of power, when it comes to the face-to-face of two modernities, one, secular European with a Christian/Latin foundation, and expressed in the hegemonic languages of colonialism and imperialism, and the other religious with a secular will, and that needs to be expressed in Arabic *and* in the languages of European modernity? (The reverse process does not apply. Modern European philosophers do not need to express themselves in Arabic. Arabic, from the perspective of Europe, is a language needed to study the Arabic-Islamic world but not to do philosophy, or other practices of knowledge.)

Al-Jabri rescues Averroës's method for dealing with the past, with a new will to implement it. Averroës's method consisted in separating the "instrument" and the "faith." Al-Jabri quotes Averroës, noting that for Averroës the "Other" was the (non-Muslim) philosophers of Ancient Greece. Therefore, he was able to make a distinction in the reason of the Other between instrument and subject matter, method and belief:

> [I]t is clear that for our purposes (i.e., the rational study of beings) we must resort to the theses of our precursors in this field, irrespective of whether or not the latter were of our own faith. One does not ask the instrument, e.g., the knife used in the ritual sacrifice, whether or not it belonged to one of our fellow Muslims in order to make a judgment on the validity of the sacrifice. One asks of it only to be of suitable use. By those who are not fellow Muslims, we mean those among the ancient ones who had pondered over these questions long before the birth of Islam. Under the circumstances, since all the laws of reasoning (logic and method) have already been perfectly laid down by the ancient ones, we ought to draw from their books by the handful, to find out what they have said about that. If it happens to be correct, we shall welcome it with open arms; if it were to contain something incorrect, we shall make sure to note it. (ibid.: 127)

Al-Jabri concludes from this excerpt, first, to read the contemporary past as Averroës read his, namely the Ancient Greek philosophers, and second, to apply the same criteria in reading the contemporary Other in space, in particular the hegemonic texts of European modernity. This al-Jabri calls the "Averroist spirit." He explains:

> I simply mean this: It must be made present in our thought, in our esteem and in our aspirations in the same way that the Cartesian spirit is present in French thought or that the spirit of empiricism, inaugurated by Locke and by Hume, is present in English thought, we would be bound to answer that only one thing has survived in each case. We could refer to it as the Cartesian spirit in France providing specificity to French thought, or the empiricist providing specificity to English thought. *Let us therefore construct our specificity upon what is ours and is particular rather than foreign to us.* (ibid.: 128)

Al-Jabri is aware that in the Arab-Islamic world there are intellectuals who would prefer to go the other way: to bring European modernity to bear upon "traditional" Islam. He argues that it is erroneous to imagine the future in that direction, because:

> [W]hen we ask the Arabs to assimilate European liberalism, we are in effect asking them to incorporate into their consciousness a legacy that is foreign to them with the themes that it raises, the problematic that it poses, and the languages in which it is expressed; a legacy which therefore does not belong in their history. A nation can only bring back to its consciousness a tradition that belongs to it, or something that pertains to that tradition. *As*

*for the human legacy in general, with its universal attributes, a nation always experiences
it within its own tradition and not outside of it.* (ibid.: 129)

Let me make a couple of final comments. I believe that Al-Jabri's invitation to
revamp Averroës's method would be embraced by many other intellectuals in the
peripheral modernities of the modern/colonial world. I also believe that there will
be a significant number of post-modern and North-Atlantic intellectuals who would
scratch their heads when they read the complicity between the "spirit," "nation,"
and "tradition" in the prose of an Arab-Islamic intellectual, even if he is a progressive one. And they, the North Atlantic modern and post-modern intellectuals, may
be right to do so. But complicities between the "spirit," "nation," and "tradition"
should concern us equally in the "tradition of European modernity" as in the "tradition of the Arabic-Islamic world," or indeed in traditions of other worlds occupying
similar, subaltern positions in relation to Europe, and the epistemic hegemony of
North Atlantic modernity.

Notes

1 This is the crucial point of the articulation of the modern/colonial world that Anibal Quijano has
   been theorizing since the late 1980s. According to Quijano, "The project being developed under
   the name of 'coloniality of power' refer to the overall frame of power, established worldwide
   since the sixteenth century, with the formation of the Atlantic commercial circuit and the so-
   called 'Discovery of America.' Such overall frame has been constituted by the articulation
   of two fundamental axes. One of them was a system of domination of the subjectivity and
   establishment of authority, based and crossed by the idea of 'race' as the basic criteria of social
   and cultural classification of the entire planet. This is the 'racial frame of the coloniality of
   power.' The second was a system of control and exploitation of labor based in the articulation
   of all known systems of exploitations related to capitalism (for instance, social relation of the
   exploitation of waged labor) and, consequently, of the market. Given the dominant function of
   economy in this configuration it could be called 'the capital frame of the coloniality of power'"
   (personal communication, April 2004, during a meeting of the collective modernity/coloniality
   at the University of California, Berkeley). Coloniality of power, it emerges for Quijano, is the
   moment in which the 'racial frame' and the 'capital frame' work in tandem and complement
   each other. See Quijano (2000); see also Lander (2000).
2 For an overview on these issues see Perez Luño (1992). This topic, which has been, and continues to be, extensively discussed in Spain, Europe and Latin America, recently has received
   the attention of postcolonial legal studies. For a generally well informed, although somewhat
   superficial (in the context of the existing debate published in Spanish) presentation in English,
   see Anghie (1999).
3 I have analyzed this overarching discourse of the modern/colonial world as "occidentalism."
   See Mignolo (2000a). For an earlier formulation of this critique see Coronil (1996).
4 For a brilliant analysis of the reconfiguration of "racial" classifications in eighteenth century
   secular philosophy see Eze (1997).
5 On the racial configuration of the concept of "human being" in European history and philosophy, and on the ethical, political and epistemic consequences of such configuration, see
   Trouillot (1995) and Gordon (2001: 62–95).
6 Editorial from *History of European Ideas*, the official journal of the International Society for
   the Study of European Ideas, sponsored by the European Cultural Foundation. I am quoting
   from vol. 6, a special issue devoted to Europe and its Encounter with the Amerindians. With

the exception of the article by Rolena Adorno, the entire issue is unidirectional and monotropic. That is, there is no concern about the Anahuac, say, or the Tawantinsuyu, and their encounter with the Europeans. The indigenous people do not count because their function was precisely to be there, in order for European narratives to build up Europe and Europeans as "modern," and the Indians as "traditional." Here we have a revealing trick, or strategy, as to how "tradition" is a construction of "modernity," and not a reality in itself. "Tradition" is the exteriority, the outside as created by and from the perspective of the inside.

7 This text is, of course, my own revision of the text from *History of European Ideas*.
8 See the special issue of the *Journal of Medieval and Early Modern Studies* 30/3 (Dagenais and Greer 2000). While "decolonization" was introduced to map the movements of "independence" from Europe in Latin America, Asia and Africa, and was, therefore, implicitly spatial, the "independence" from the Middle Ages in the Renaissance is implicitly temporal. However, and in retrospective, the European Renaissance put in place two kind of colonial matrix: temporal (colonizing the Middle Ages) and spatial (colonizing the Americas, and then Asia and Africa). The "double colonization" during the Renaissance allowed, for example, colonization of the memories as well as the space of the Amerindians. That is, "traditions" were invented temporally in Europe and spatially in America, Asia and Africa. For further analysis, see Mignolo (1995).
9 The 1999 text is an abridged translation into English of the work from 1994.
10 I note, in passing, that when I type here, "Aristotle," nothing happens. However, when I type "Avicenna" and "Averroës," the electronic thesaurus does not recognize them, and offers other word possibilities: Avicenna and Averroës are out of the memory of (Western) modernity.

References

Abu-Lughod, Janet. 1989. *Before European Hegemony. The World System, AD 1250–1350*. New York: Oxford University Press.
Al-Jabri, Mohamed 'Abed. 1994. *Introduction à la critique de la raison arabe*. Paris: Editions la Découverte; Institut de Monde Arabe.
Al-Jabri, Mohamed 'Abed. 1999. *Arab-Islamic Philosophy. A Contemporary Critique*. Translated by Aziz Abbassi. Austin, TX: University of Texas.
Allen, Theodore W. 1994. *The Invention of the White Race*. Vol. 1: *Racial Oppression and Social Control*. London/New York: Verso.
Anghie, Antony. 1999. Francisco de Vitoria and the Colonial Origins of International Law. In *Laws of the Postcolonial*, eds. Eve Darian-Smith and Peter Fitzpatrick, 89–108. Ann Arbor, MI: University of Michigan Press.
Bartlett, Robert. 1993. The Expansion of Latin Christendom. In *The Making of Europe. Conquest, Colonization and Cultural Change*, 950–1350. Princeton, NJ: Princeton University Press.
Chatterjee, Partha. 1998. Talking About Our Modernity in Two Languages. In *A Possible India: Essays in Political Criticism*, 263–285. Delhi/Calcutta: Oxford University Press.
Coronil, Fernando. 1996. Beyond Occidentalism. Toward Non-imperial Geohistorical Categories. *Cultural Anthropology* 11: 52–87.
Coronil, Fernando. 2000. Towards a Critique of Globalcentrism: Speculations on Capitalism's Nature. *Public Culture* 12(2): 23–53.
Dagenais, John and Margaret Greer (eds.). 2000. Decolonizing the Middle Ages. Special issue of *The Journal of Medieval and Early Modern Studies* 30: 3.
Eze, Emmanuel Chukwudi. 1997. The Color of Reason: The Idea of 'Race' in Kant's Anthropology. In *Postcolonial African Philosophy. A Critical Reader*, ed. E. C. Eze, 103–140. London: Blackwell.
Foucault, Michel. 1977. *Il faut défendre la societé. Cours au Collége de France, 1975–1976*. Paris: Seuil.

Gerbi, Antonello. 1958. *La disputa del Nuevo Mundo*. Translated from the Italian by Antonio Alatorre. México.

Gómara, Francisco de. 1946 [1552]. *Hispania Vitrix*. Madrid.

Gordon, Lewis. 2001. *Existentia Africana: Understanding African Existential Thought*. New York: Routledge.

Hay, Denys. 1968. The Medieval Notion of Europe and Its People. In *Europe. The Emergence of an Idea*, second edition. Edinburgh: Edinburgh University Press.

Heilbroner, Robert. 1992. The Worldly Philosophers. In *The Lives, Times and Ideas of the Great Economic Thinkers*, sixth edition. New York: Simon & Schuster.

Henry, Paget. 2000. *Caliban's Reason. Introducing Afro-Caribbean Philosophy*. New York/London: Routledge.

Kant, Immanuel. 1996. *Anthropology from a Pragmatic Point of View*. Trans. Victor Lyle Dowdell. Carbondale, IL/Edwardsville, IL: Southern Illinois University Press.

Lander, Edgardo, ed. 2000. *La colonialidad del saber: eurocentrismo y ciencias sociales. Perspectivas latinoamericanas*. Buenos Aires: Consejo Latinoamericano de Ciencias Sociales. The complete text may be accessed on-line via http://www.biblioteca.clacso.edu.ar/.

Maravall, José Antonio. 1963. *Los factores de la idea de progreso en el Renacimiento español: discurso leído él día 31 de marzo de 1963 en el acto de su recepción pública*. Madrid.

Maravall, José Antonio. 1972. *Estado moderno y mentalidad social (siglos XV a XVII)*. Madrid.

Maravall, José Antonio. 1973. *Estudios de historia del pensamiento español*. 2. ed. Madrid: Ampliada.

Marx, Karl. 1976. *Capital*, vol. 1. London/New York: Pelican.

Mignolo, Walter D. 1995. *The Darker Side of the Renaissance. Literacy, Territoriality and Colonization*. Ann Arbor, MI: University of Michigan Press.

Mignolo, Walter D. 1998. Postoccidentalismo: el argumento desde América Latina. *Cuadernos Americanos* 67: 143–165.

Mignolo, Walter D. 2000a. *Local Histories/Global Designs*. Princeton, NJ: Princeton University Press.

Mignolo, Walter D. 2000b. The Many Faces of Cosmo-Polis: Border Thinking and Critical Cosmopolitanism. *Public Culture* 12: 721–748.

Moreno Fraginals, Manuel. 1999. *La historia como arma y otros estudios sobre esclavos, ingenios y plantaciones*. Barcelona: Editorial Crítica.

Nicolet, Claude. 1991. *Space, Geography, and Politics in the Early Roman Empire*. Ann Arbor, MI: University of Michigan Press.

O'Gorman, Edmundo. 1958. *La invención de América. El universalismo de la cultura occidental*. Ciudad de México: Fondo de Cultura Economica.

Perez Luño, Antonio-Enrique. 1992. La polémica sobre el Nuevo Mundo. In *Los clásicos españoles de la Filosofía del Derecho*. Madrid.

Quijano, Anibal. 2000. Coloniality of power, knowledge and Latin America. *Nepantla: Views from South* 1: 3.

Rafael, Vicente. 1993. *Contracting Colonialism: Translation and Christian Conversion in Tagalog Society Under Early Spanish Rule*. Durham, NC: Duke University Press.

Rothschild, Emma. 2001. *Economic Sentiments: Adam Smith, Condorcet and the Enlightenment*. Cambridge, MA: Harvard University Press.

Smith, Adam. 2000. *The Wealth of Nations*. New York: Penguin Classics.

Trouillot, Michel-Rolph. 1995. *Silencing the Past: Power and the Production of History*. New York: Beacon.

Part IV
Uneasy Intersections

"Uneasy Intersections": Postcolonialism, Feminism, and the Study of Religions*

Grace Jantzen

Abstract Feminists, in their efforts to reconstruct a heavily masculinist philosophy of religion, have developed insights that can also help the discipline recognize tedious reaffirmations of its history with respect to Eurocentric colonizations of other peoples. Specifically, the chapter discusses ceasing to speak for and about others, redescribing self in terms of "new" categories made evident in the experience of colonized peoples, and destabilizing the structural force of "Western" theological norms in the study of religions. The author essays to what extent feminist insights can be appropriated to the study of religion in relation to postcolonial discourse. Specific

> We cannot content ourselves with reaffirming a certain history, a certain memory of the origins or the Western history of philosophy (Mediterranean or central-European, Greco-Roman-Arab or Germanic), nor can we be content with opposing or opposing denial to this memory and to these languages; rather we must try to displace the fundamental schema of this problematic by carrying ourselves beyond the old, tiresome, wearing, wearying opposition between Eurocentrism and anti-Eurocentrism. (Derrida 2002: 336)

In other words, we're in a rut. And we need to get out of it. And when you're in a hole – or a rut – stop digging! The scholarship of religions among English speaking academics has been dominated by demarcations of the discipline which embody and reinforce what is considered proper to religions and their study. But since a central questions in the philosophy of religions is precisely the question of how the phenomenon of religion/s can best be understood, such demarcations of the discipline neatly ensure from the outset what sorts of conclusions will be possible. And so we dig the rut deeper.

---

* [Editors' note]: Prof. Jantzen died untimely before this volume could be brought to publication. She had no significant opportunity to revise her essay, which was presented at a session on "Postcolonial Theory and the Philosophy of Religion(s)" at the Annual Meeting of the American Academy of Religion, in Toronto in 2002. We have retained its style and tone. The title-phrase, "uneasy intersections," comes from Donaldson and Kwok (2002: 28).

P. Bilimoria and A.B. Irvine (eds.), *Postcolonial Philosophy of Religion.*   295
© Springer Science+Business Media B.V. 2009

But if digging is an exercise in futility, so is the idea that we could somehow rise above it all and see religions from some universal vantage point. Pigs might fly, but we can't. We are stuck in the situatedness of our own language and culture, and if we are going to make progress in our understanding of religions and their construction, there is no place to start from other than where we are.

So where are we? Well, that depends on who 'we' are: it is a pronoun guaranteed to mystify by its putative inclusivity, thereby becoming yet another (ever so courteous) technology of power, more useful for digging deeper ruts than for finding ways out of them. So let me be specific. Some of us, including myself, are feminists, mostly of the white Anglo-American educated and privileged variety. In order to be here at all, to be taken seriously as feminist academics, we have had to work hard to rethink the discipline and to contribute to its reshaping. We have had to overcome our own internalized sense of gender inferiority without either trying to be 'one of the boys' or becoming anti-men. We have had to deal with those – mostly but not only men – who think that gender has no place in questions of scholarship, since its aim and its highest achievement is unsituated universal truth: an assumption very often situated squarely in rank if unacknowledged misogyny. However, although a few such people are still with us, most scholars of religion know better by now than to be explicit in their exclusion of women, and hardly anyone would refuse on principle to consider gender significant. The huge struggle for feminist scholars of religion now has changed from tackling open misogyny to dealing with the issue of all those scholars who pay lip service to the importance of gender considerations, make all the right noises, succeed in convincing themselves of their progressive attitudes, and then manage to exclude or sideline gender in their actual work.[1] It isn't their specialty, they say; or they haven't yet got around to studying women's writings on the subject even though (oh, of course!) they know how important it is; or they are interested in the general (read 'male') arguments rather than specifically gendered interpretations. The excuses from well-intentioned academics of bad conscience are wearyingly unoriginal. The work of reshaping the discipline so that it stops reinforcing institutionalized sexism is very far from complete.

My purpose today, though, is not to harangue scholars of religion for ignoring or marginalizing gender. Rather, my purpose is to take some of the lessons feminists have learned and tools we have developed in our efforts to increase gender awareness, and to show how they could also be used to rethink the study of religion in relation to postcolonial discourse. What I am suggesting is that feminists in our efforts to reconstruct a heavily masculinist philosophy of religion have developed insights that can also help the discipline out of its tedious reaffirmations of its history and help to displace its fundamental schema: a ladder to climb out of the rut. What are the shifts of consciousness and method that have been necessary to effect the change of paradigm from a masculinist approach to philosophy of religion to an approach that takes gender seriously? To what extent can these shifts be appropriated to the study of religion in relation to postcolonial discourse?

On Shutting Up

Central to a feminist approach to the study of religion is the insistence that women find a voice and be allowed to speak for ourselves; that we set an agenda that includes what is important for us rather than be told by men what we should think about and how we should think about it. For many of us this was a new experience. We had everything to learn, both in terms of our own self-confidence and in terms of method and content. We needed some space and time to work at this in women-only groups: groups in which we got out of the male gaze and did not have to feel instantly accountable to masculinist criteria for our often hesitant experiments. To our surprise, we quickly discovered that our male friends and colleagues often found this deeply threatening (even while belittling what we were doing). It was as if they worried that if once they lost control, all hell might break loose. What did they think we were!? They told us that unless men were included our scholarship wouldn't be sound; that the methods of the discipline were independent of gender; that we would be marginalized as academics (and sometimes they saw to it that we were). Men who had hitherto shown very little interest in our work suddenly were desperate to be invited if a meeting was advertised as 'women only'.

And sometimes we agreed. And far too often, before we knew what was happening, the men had hijacked the agenda. We were spending the whole meeting explaining to them why gender was important, how the discipline was biased against it – basic feminist principles which they often were there to resist. Now, *of course* it was important to involve men in raising gender consciousness; *of course* the discussion needs to include everyone. But it does not have to include everyone *all the time*. If one group has been – or has felt – dominated by the other, then it is crucially important that that group be given the space it needs to find its own voice and develop the confidence to use it, without the powerful group constantly pointing out flaws and pitfalls (just to save problems, of course!) Separatism is not a long term goal; but it may be a short term strategy. Those men who were unthreatened by it and did what they could to encourage and enable women-only groups were enormously valued.

Now the parallel with the study of religion/s is obvious. A lot of so-called interreligious dialogue is set up by western academics, and implicitly or explicitly carries a western academic agenda. The same is true for the study of religion/s. The main topics are taken for granted: the existence and nature of God/s, the question of revelation or scripture, the figures of central religious leaders, religious experience, issues of ethics and ritual, the understanding of salvation. These are taken as the most significant religious issues, and therefore are the focus also of discussions relating to philosophy of religion. But clearly they also demarcate the boundaries of the discipline according to western assumptions. The question is, are we open to having those assumptions destabilized? What if some of the main concerns of the 'others' with whom 'we' want to dialogue or whom 'we' want to understand (hear the scare quotes) have to do with, say, relationship to the land, or issues of greed or violence? Of course we could quickly subsume these 'topics' under western categories of ecology or ethics rather than allow the demarcations of the discipline to shift. The same thing happened when philosophers took over feminist concerns about gender into a small section of the epistemology of personal identity, or, as in a recent book entitled *God, the Big Questions*,[2] gender concerns are relegated to a small section at the back called 'alternative voices'.

The point is that just as it is unconscionable for men to dictate to women what 'philosophy of religion' should be, whether by loud arrogance or by the sort of exquisite courtesy that nevertheless effectively silences a feminist agenda, so also it is outrageous that a white western paradigm should be imposed as a universal or normative account of the discipline. I suggest that the first and most important lesson for the study of religion/s in relation to 'nonwestern' demarcations of the subject is to allow plenty of space and respectful silence that enables others to find their voices. And if we find this threatening and feel a need to keep some kind of control (possibly in the name of ensuring adequate academic standards) then we need to take a long hard look at ourselves.

Who Speaks for Whom?

Closely related to issues of enabling space and respectful silence is the question of who speaks for whom. Again there is a parallel with gender issues. As feminists began to teach and publish, and our classes and books were well received, a few men tried to shut down courses or write damning reviews, but far more began to get the point. Before we knew it, men started to offer courses on feminism or present women's issues in their own writings. It was a strange mixture: some men were clearly just jumping on a bandwagon; but many others taught and wrote with good intentions. But good intentions, notoriously, pave the way to hell; sometimes the effect was that women were not offered academic appointments or publishing contracts because that area of the curriculum was 'already taken care of' by men. The parallels with western scholars of religion speaking for our nonwestern counterparts are too obvious to need spelling out.

Now, *of course* feminists want men to take gender seriously: to think and teach and write about gender. But often 'gender issues' get treated as though they were 'women's issues': as though women are gendered while men are normatively human. Thus for example the *Blackwell Companion to Postmodern Theology* (Ward 2001), in many respects an excellent book, has a substantial section on 'Gender' to which however every one of the contributors is female: the many male contributors to the book then largely ignore the implications of gender for their own discussions. What is needed is not for men to discuss women's issues, though it will of course help if they take them seriously, but for men to notice that they themselves are also gendered. Where this is happening, where men are looking seriously at their own masculinity, highly interesting and effective work is being done. It is perhaps not coincidental that much of this intersects with Queer Theory: I think of the work of James Nelson (1988), and, more recently, Daniel Boyarin (1997). Unfortunately such studies are still relatively rare in the study of religion. One of the most effective masculinist technologies of power is simply to be silent about – to fail to investi-gate – the implications of their own masculinist assumptions for their study; it is perfectly possible to combine this well-intentioned avowals of the importance of 'gender' where 'gender' translates as 'women'.

Similarly. I suggest that western study of religion needs to take a hard look, not so much at alterity, as at our own investment in 'sameness', and the technologies of power that we use to reinforce and impose our 'normativity'. This will certainly involve respectful listening to the voices of 'others' and taking what they say seri-ously. What I am questioning is how much 'we' need to speak for 'them': they are quite capable of speaking for themselves as long as we don't take up all the airtime. What we do need to do is to start to notice what we ourselves look like.

The parallel with gender is important; so also is the parallel with race. Robert Dyer (1997), in his excellent book *White*, shows what happens when white people problematize our own whiteness rather than pontificate about race as though race is about Blacks and 'people of colour' – as if we are not! (And yet a person who was literally white would be very ill indeed!) Once we begin to notice how frag-ile and unstable this whiteness is, and how it has protected itself from threat by (often silent) insistence on its normativity, questions of race relations never look the same again. Just as our understanding of issues of race is greatly increased by thus turning the spotlight on ourselves, and just as men get the point of feminism when they problematize their own masculinity, so also, I suggest, our (western) under-standing of our own philosophy of religion and the demarcations of the discipline will be creatively transformed by rethinking it in relation to voices from elsewhere that articulate the oppressions which western study of religion has imposed upon them. Some examples are already available: I think of the work of Talal Asad (1993) on the "reasons of power in Christianity and Islam" a book even more significant now than when it was written; or Richard King's (1999) work on the imposition of categories of western mysticism on to India; or Lionel Jensen's (1997) work on *Manufacturing Confucianism*. Important as these works are, they call out for very much more; moreover in common with most writings by men on religion they hardly engage with issues of gender.[3] Given the ways in which western scholars have con-structed the 'alterities' of nonwestern 'religions', how should we now reconsider our 'sameness'?

Instabilities

What are some of the areas of instability that emerge when we begin to look at ourselves in terms of our putative 'sameness', our complicity in repressions? Here again I believe that gender parallels are instructive, not least because Eurocentric culture has frequently feminized other cultures while seeing itself as stereotypically masculine: active, strong, and rational. Therefore its cultural oppression, including the oppressions in the study of religions, is of a piece with its gender oppressions. Both are rooted in a notion of what counts and what does not count as normatively human.

Now in the west what has counted as normatively human has been constructed in relation to what has counted as normatively divine. The philosophy of religion in the west has largely assumed a male, 'omni-everything' God: as a bishop wrote in *Church Times* a few years ago, 'God is a relatively genderless male deity:' we need only add that he is also white. It is of course always immediately added that God does not have a body, and therefore has neither colour nor gender. But lurking behind the denial is the imaginary: the body that God does not have is male and white.

Again, there has been widespread agreement in western study of religion, sometimes explicit and sometimes tacit, that monotheism is the highest form of religion and should receive the most attention. Often it is made the standard by which other approaches are measured: they are 'primitive' or 'advanced' in a neo-Hegelian (or neo-Darwinian) imaginary of progress. This leaves out of account any serious consideration of polytheisms, nature divinities, pantheisms, or other understandings of the divine, while at the same time it reinforces the conviction that the One, the Same, is of higher value than alterities. Moreover in the west religion itself is separated off from something called the 'secular'. How would the demarcations of our discipline need to be altered once this separation is questioned? What sorts of control are we operating by continuing to hold this assumption, and at whose expense?

Again, feminist philosophers have been pointing out for some time the extent to which the west prides itself on models of rationality which are rooted in masculinist assumptions.[4] These models, which focus on the primacy of justified true beliefs, are the foundation of western science and technology, and are deeply interwoven with issues of mastery and power. At least since the Enlightenment, prominent strands of the study of religion in the west has accepted this model of rationality, and has demarcated religion as essentially about true beliefs: indeed a religious person can be designated simply as a 'believer'. But when we take a hard look at ourselves in the light of how our attitudes and practices might be oppressing others, surely this preoccupation with beliefs and their justification as the most important thing about religion must come up for scrutiny. Not only does the fixation on beliefs in itself betoken attitudes of power, but it also distracts attention from such things as the importance of ritual, of connection with the earth, of community, and of beauty. How if we were to allow the boundaries of the discipline to be destabilized in ways that challenged the primacy of beliefs and the preoccupation with epistemology, and that lifted up beauty, the earth, and its peoples?

Finally, I have argued elsewhere that western masculinist philosophy of religion (and western culture more generally) has been preoccupied with death and mortality, and has characterized religion largely in terms of 'salvation' understood as life in heaven after death. This mortality is seen as deriving from our maternal origin; and salvation is found in 'rebirth' according to the will of the 'Father'. The preoccupation with mortality can be shown to be deeply interwoven in the drives to conquest and colonialism, and the 'globalatinization' which characterizes the west. In contrast to that necrophilic approach, I have suggested the importance of natality as a concept of at least as great importance for understanding our humanity as is mortality, a concept which takes seriously our maternal connection. Now, if we engage properly with postcolonial discourses in the study of religion, might it be the case that the focus of religion will be a question of flourishing on earth at least as much as anything to do with heaven? And if that is so, how will it stand with those economies, whether monetary or intellectual, which promote only our own flourishing while not caring about those on whose silenced labour and blood this western dominance is maintained? At whose expense is our study of religion?

Notes

1 One indication of this is a check of the bibliography of books and articles: male scholars often ignore what women have written on a subject, whereas female scholars cite books and articles by both genders. The point in terms of this paper is that the same thing happens in relation to books and articles by people from 'non-Western' contexts: western scholars statistically do not take them as serious scholarship.
2 [Editors' note]: Prof. Jantzen presumably was referring to Stump and Murray (1999). In fact, the final section of that volume is titled, "How should religious, gender, and ethnic diversity affect our thinking about religion?" Incidentally, it includes Prof. Jantzen's essay, "What's the Difference? Knowledge and Gender in (Post)Modern Philosophy of Religion."
3 Of the three, only Richard King discusses feminism at all, and he does so in a brief section (1999: 111–116) showing parallels between the 'othering' of women and the postcolonial subject in masculinist discourse. He does not however take further the issues this raises up, and continues as though the topic had not been mentioned.
4 See for example Lloyd (1993) and Code (1991).

References

Asad, Talal. (1993) *Genealogies of Religion: Discipline and Reasons of Power in Christianity and Islam*. Baltimore, MD/London: Johns Hopkins University Press.
Boyarin, Daniel. (1997) *Unheroic Conduct: The Rise of Heterosexuality and the Invention of the Jewish Man*. Berkeley, CA/London: University of California Press.
Code, Lorraine. (1991) *What Can She Know? Feminist Theory and the Construction of Knowledge*. Ithaca, NY: Cornell University Press.
Derrida, Jacques. (2002) *Negotiations: Interventions and Interviews 1971–2001*. Ed. and trans. Elizabeth Rottenberg. Stanford, CA: Stanford University Press.
Donaldson, Linda and Kwok Pui-Lan (eds.). (2002) *Postcolonialism, Feminism, and Religious Discourse*. New York/London: Routledge.
Dyer, Richard. (1997) *White*. London: Routledge.
Jensen, Lionel M. (1997) *Manufacturing Confucianism: Chinese Traditions and Universal Civilization*. Durham, NC/London: Duke University Press.
King, Richard. (1999) *Orientalism and Religion: Postcolonial Theory, India and 'The Mystic East'*. London/New York: Routledge.
Lloyd, Genevieve. (1993) *The Man of Reason: 'Male' and 'Female' in Western Philosophy*. Second edition. London/New York: Routledge.
Nelson, James B. (1988) *The Intimate Connection: Male Sexuality, Masculine Spirituality*. Philadelphia, PA: Westminster.
Stump, Eleonore and Murray, Michael J. (eds.). (1999) *Philosophy of Religion: The Big Questions*. Oxford: Blackwell.
Ward, Graham (ed.). (2001) *Blackwell Companion to Postmodern Theology*. Oxford: Blackwell.

Postcolonial Discontent with Postmodern Philosophy of Religion

Purushottama Bilimoria

> After the beginning there appeared some stranger texts
> West's Orientalism objectified the corpus's otherness
> And Modernity's philology rendered their syntax as his own;
> Thence followed the postmodern disruption of the *aporia*
> Re-citing the alterity and the *ousia* of the Other's face;
> But it awaited the hybrid-angst of postcolonialism's site
> Whence the interrupted texts begin miming an-other meaning.
>
> *Authorless Revelation*

Preamble

If we are to have a relational view of taxonomy and discourse – the explosive myth of contextualization and positionality – then 'sites' should also bear out their relative differences. There are '*in* sites' and there are '*out* sites' (ones you see and ones you don't), and borderzones in-between. The present chapter is located in this unchartered borderzone, though its critique is intended to be 'radical' without the frothy ambiguities, equivocations, hybrid-speakages more usually than not associated with the two 'sites' I wish here to bring into confrontation. What are these sets of 'sites'?

First though a brief remark on the term 'sites' or 'site' (in the singular). The Latin root '*situ*', semantically linked to the Greek '*topos*', denotes a fixed position where an object, structure or tissue is placed or where something occurs. In geographical and architectural usage its reference is usually to the place, space, location, setting or situatedness of a very particular or distinctive structure or tissue in an open-ended plot that also marks it off from similar 'site' elsewhere. If another structure is erected or imposed in that particular spot then the site is said to have been erased. There could be related parallel or deeper, invisible structures or 'locale', (the session next door) that remain out of sight (out of this site, i.e. in another place). In other contexts, the latter may acquire connotations of care and securedness (*home*, community, nation) the sacred and mythical (land, ritual altar, location of the temple as *ikos*), moral or ethical ('life-world', 'form of life', *dharma* as that which holds), surrogate or virtual (dreamspace, doughnut hole, cyberspace, web-sites), or quasi-mystical (Heidegger's 'locale of the truth of Being', totality, absence), cosmological (*dharmakāya*, infinite empty space or nothingness), even metaphysical (Omni-Presence, Void or Absolute *Nothingness, śūnyatā*).

In modernist discourse, sites and places presented newer apertures or frontiers awaiting discovery, appropriation and settlement, i.e. colonization. Like a new home, all structures and constructions were full of new hopes, simply if one could amass them and hold the pieces together in a large warehouse, empire or imperial emprise as it were, and universalize them. In postmodernism critique 'sites' acquire other metaphorical nuances, although these are problematized as well, with more subjective tonalities such as memories, dreams, textual and celluloid productions, social tensions, etc., entering the descriptive picture. But more usually than not the 'sites' in postmodern contextualization are still particularities and differences that evoke the Humean sentiments or judgment of sanguine approval or disapproval, hope or its lapses, potential recovery or future redemption, even where these stand de-constructed and 'ring foul' or may look hollow in due course. One moves on to another site.

However (and here is the rub) the metaphorical associations of 'site' of the third kind that critics like Talpade Mohanty, Spivak, Bhutalia, Bharucha hounds me to are almost compulsively those of 'disturbance, agitation, violence, rupture' (Bharucha 1998: 169), i.e. sites of contestations where there are real, *actual*, not such textual, contextual or virtual victims, where the 'site' in-between is disfigured with blood and pain of the depraved, the wretched and the fallen. They don't simply exist by default on the margins of the page; they actually cease to exist when another makes a claim for their 'site', their 'locale', and dispossess their 'culture', their ideals, hopes and aspirations. There are no escape routes from such sites. One stands damned or condemned; or one struggles back. This is the violence of the 'site'; the anger of subjectivities clashing over the right to their deprived or stolen 'sites', and so on. For this one turns to the critique of postcoloniality incomplete as it may be, as all promising projects or agendas are. Postcoloniality or postcolonialism (inter-changeable forms), is both a 'site' (set of 'sites') and a set of developing reflections, and a determined critique from a particular positionality, and – I can't resist repeat-ing Amartya Sen's suggestive addition to Spivak's search for a name – of 'reason' (hence was born, *'A Critique of Postcolonial Reason'*).

After discussing two nuances of postmodernism, I present an outline of the Postcolonial Condition and its own internal theorizing or the kinds of concerns articulated in its struggle to overcome the burden of colonialism, and in the sev-eral dis/ruptures experienced under this latter condition. We may begin with Fanon and wade through a number of now welcome critiques of orientalism and colo-nialism, such as Said drawing on Foucault, to Gayatri Spivak, Ashis Nandy, Partha Chatterjee, Leela Gandhi, Appadurai among others.

In the second part of the discussion I will move to the main task before me which is to offer some reflections on the growing discontent in the postcolonial quarters with the discourses of modernity and especially of postmodernism and some of its familiar sites, since the difference or distance marking the two broad temporal movements from the positionality of those doubly crossed or condemned, as it were, to the inclusive borderzones of alterity, appears about as wide and redemptively real as the land-mined trespass on the borders of Kosovo, the camps of Albania, a brimming Macedonia, and a confused NATO raining down from the clouds above.

I will analyze these reflections and offer or re-iterate arguments to deepen the problematic, and make pleas against the allures of celebrative complacency that habitually reinscripts itself in the quiescent halls of the academe and the Rortyian comforts of pragmatic theorizing from the supposed gaze of nowhere, i.e. the liberaldom in the First World of late twentieth century and its echoes in neo-modernisms of other worlds.

What Is Postmodernism?

Might we though begin in the beginning with some general definitions, so that unlike gods we don't come to expect the self-same sacrifice from each temple totem-pole as we race through the virtual landscape. Postmodernism is – true to its own advocacy of diversity and *difference* – difficult to define. We shall present two approaches to postmodernism as a theory and a practice. The first takes us back to its historical genesis and the second to some critical formulations and revisioning in the light of the question of the 'other'. So to the first.

Postmodernism, first coined in the context of architecture to mark a critique of modernism and an end to a long tradition of modern architecture that had dominated its imaginary since the onset of modernity, roughly with the dawning of the Enlightenment, its concomitant capitalist and industrial revolutions, so as to move its aesthetics towards the avant-garde. The idea of postmodernism – *after-modernism* – began to have an unwitting impact in areas outside the revisioning of the concrete jungle, across the disciplines of literary studies and criticism, history, political theory, philosophy, the arts, anthropology and even psychoanalysis, and the performative arts. The damning critique of modernity and its Enlightenment legacy of Reason's supremacy, but including remnants of Christian morality and heavy-duty metaphysical thinking since Plato and Aristotle, harnessed at the hands of the modernist *philosophies* such as Rousseau, Kant, Hegel, the Mills, Locke and Weber, to name a few in the league, came under the scrutiny and assault from a number of non-analytical forays into these fields of thought and praxis. Drawing on phenomenology and a disenchantment with positivism of the Vienna Circle and the so-called linguistic turn that ensued with Russell, Wittgenstein and Frege, the frameworks and tools of analysis hitherto dominant and in some ways taken for granted were ravaged for their essentialism and absolutist presuppositions. Among these leading (anti-)gurus providing the rich ammunitions for the critiques was Nietzsche with his ideas of Nothingness, a call for transvaluation of values and his bitter attack on the narcissism of the Age of Reason and the decadence of the Christian West which he took to have defined the trajectory of the Enlightenment epistemes; and in the background was Kierkegaard, followed by Husserl (to an extent), Sartre and indeed Heidegger, who set out to put aside the sacred metaphysics of Being and inserted instead temporality in thinking about human beingness and its thrownness in the world with the eventuality of death. Also questioned here was the seeming amorality of modernity in as much as the Age of Reason with its liberal predilections that emerged from the Enlightenment critique of the earlier moralistic Protestant heritage imbued in the sternness of Reformation making space for a less hamstrung morality (amoral since not entirely immoral judged by the Enlightenment's own standards).

Postmodernism – the sign of the times – came to be defined as a condition in contrast to the absolutist foundations on which much of modernity's thinking appeared to have been based. Hence the newfound 'condition' served as the forum from which to launch a whole array of damning questioning of the assumptions informing the bulwark of traditionalism and the work of reason, logic, linguistic or neo-positivist conceptual framework and faith in historicism and capitalism alike. The metaphysics underpinning these theoretical practices came to be identified as logocentricism, the idea that reason can solve all of humanity's questions and problems, through a mode of theorizing which is elitist, reifying, universalizing, totalizing, speculative and even totalitarian. The critique extends to the reliance upon logocentricism in its myriad manifestations, such as in the liberal political establishment and its 'force of law' with its utilitarian violence, to deliver the goods of truth, justice, and values in an age of crisis – the crisis of reason, the horrors of world wars, imperialism, colonialism, the women's question in the face of patriarchy, the rights of the marginalized other, and so on, – came increasingly under the hammer of the hermeneutics of suspicion.

One looked not for a position but in the spirit of the Buddhist Nāgārjuna's equally damning critique of Hindu-Brahmanical ritualised obstinacy a millennium back of the fetishism with foundationalism, unassailable or absolute positions, and an image of culture that was unmalebale as the steel and glass façades erected across the metropolitan geographies, the class structures and imperatives of a market-driven economic ideology. Everything, its seemed, was up for grabs. This message, incredulous to many, however did herald a significant intellectual movement and even had an impact, perhaps in part triggered, the 1968 May uprisings across the campuses of Europe and America where students, workers, and intellectuals united in solidarity to attempt to 'pull down the walls' of the establishment and the portals also of their ivory-tower representatives perpetrating the myths of the Enlightenment and ideologies of capitalism gone out of control. Short-lived though, its impact nonetheless flowed into the so-called counter-cultural movement and alternative thinking and experimental life-styles we now see heavily commercialized and re-absorbed into the corporate market economy and its scintillating media culture.

On the theoretical side, postmodernism's alignment with three or four methodological currents as forms of critiques – in Walter Benjamin's sense of 'passing judgment on the present with an eye toward the realization of a future as a way of undoing the errors of the past' are important to mention here if only because the demarcation of labour and internal tensions between and among these disparate intellectual movements are often blurred or occluded. And these are: the Frankfurt School of critical theory associated largely with Jüngen Habermas and poststructuralist theory, in particular Foucault's discursive genealogies, the deconstruction forays of Derrida, and feminist deconstructive performatives. While Derrida's deconstructive strategy has been celebrated with high-point of a doctrinaire of difference, *difference*, and multiplicity of valences or significations in any work of representation (from text, textuality, history to film and postcard), Habermas in particular questions the very presence of the term — *post* — as a sign of the problem being addressed rather than an epistemological and political solution disclaimed in these intellectual fads, something that might however pass in time, as all trends do. Habermas in his influential work *The Philosophical Discourse of Modernity* (1985) criticizes what he saw as Foucault's attack on the principle of the Enlightenment, arguing that because Foucault's version of poststructuralist theory hollowed out reason, the result of his theoretical stance could only be unreason or the authoritarian decision-ism of the legal theorist Carl Schmitt. Such an attack on reason, Habermas warned, would put the whole Enlightenment project of critique at risk, in particular the much needed critique of ideology (*a la* Ricoeur) which Habermas revised through discursive action theory in order to take into account postmodernity. Foucault had, he argued, demolished the possibility of a knowing subject who might be capable of resistant action by heeding Nietzsche's call "for historical understanding to sever the roots of dilapidated historicism from historicism... such a move leaves resistant subjects with no affirmative position or agency for making a difference and bringing about change in the historical conditions apart from 'interrupting it within discursive genealogies'." (see Bilimoria 2008a). But for now it needs to be said that Habermas actually underestimated Foucault's attempt to historicize the liberatory potential of Kantian practical critique – Habermas's own pet self-acclaim – by developing a methodology that could take into account postmodernity, a methodology as Hansen notes, based not on the reversal of the *ratio* – as reason-, but on breaching, or counterforce situated at the "dilapidated frontiers of the old episteme" (or reason or historicized reason). This form of resistant methodology, or *ethos*, also informs other poststructuralist thinking, in particular Judith Butler's performative feminism, and postcolonialism.

A second point of the critique bears on the issue of relativism. The intriguing response to the postmodern revolution (if one wants to call it that) was the charge of 'relativism', that is to say, if your critique questions foundationalism in epistemology or knowledge-and-truth making and all positions are questioned for their inherent falsity or cul-de-sac, and no claim has any finality, then you are suggesting that all claims are relative: one truth, or one's truth is as good as another's and all positions are relative, or as good and solid, or as weak and shaky, as another position, or an-other's position. (Even the mute or silenced other, such as women and the colonized or displaced indigenous people, the inanimate environment and animals included, have any voice at all, or are heeded for their point-of-view.) In other words, there is no such thing as 'God's-eye view' or an Archimedean point of view from which to judge anything: whether in epistemology or in the areas of morality or ethics, etc. All truths are value-laden, and all values are culturally-constructed and relative to a particular group and period in history: there are no absolute values. One cannot take an ethical stance for all stances are flawed in the end. This is relativism at its best or worst. Postmodernism's reformulation often attributed – albeit falsely – to the American philosopher Richard Rorty whose antifoundationalist strategy leaned more towards 'conversation', paved some way towards belief in relativism. It may be noted that Rorty himself preferred to call his theory a (post)modern version of pragmatism, since he reduced much of Enlightenment projects such as universalism, ideological critique, and moral philosophy to contingent language games, and ironies or even irenic hang-overs, whose truth can no longer be justified, except through particular, albeit strained forms of reasoning. Identity politics seizes on such contingencies and runs with it, dismissing the cultural left and socialism as viable alternatives to a fumbling liberalism, which Rorty believes is the only reasonable option available to the West even in its deepest despair over the apparent failure of democracy (Rorty 1995).

Both the contentions in respect of the postmodern critiques I have briefly outlined above fray into the discourse of postcolonialism in one way or another, especially when postcolonialism turns its armor on the excesses of postmodernism with which it nevertheless shares some common critical grounds. But this is not entirely the case as postcolonialism shares more with poststructuralism and its critique of both modernity and postmodernism, even as it builds on Foucault's deshistoricization and the possibility of a resistant agency in what Homi Bhabha has dubbed the discursive 'third pace', or Gayatri Spivak has called 'the *post* in post*colonialism*' – at least outside the field of literature – and this is more aligned to poststructuralism and critical theory than to the *post*-in postmodernism. It is because of its commitment to this Foucaldian *ethos* and constant questioning of the trappings of normativity, that it is able to turn the critique on its own, so to speak, offspring, or its native informants, who loose the plot somewhere and become complicitious purveyors and perpetrators of the project of colonialism in its smooth transition into neocolonialism, nationalism, fundamentalism, theological revisionism, and so on, which really is tantamount to a betrayal of Kantian practical reason.

So now a quick cook's tour of postcolonialism: what do the terms postcolonialism (hyphenated and unhyphenated), postcolonialism, postcoloniality (and variations in-between) signify? We need not be too concerned with the niceties here, which is best left to students of 'postcolonial literature' and unreformed colonialists who parade themselves as *bona fide* postcolonialists in some campus quarters, when they would be better placed addressing grassroots issues of neocolonialism or the hitherto unbroken sinews of (internal) colonialism long after the masters have abandoned the territory they once thought their own preserve etc., whether in India or in Indonesia, Africa or the Americas.

Indeed, a thoroughgoing postcolonial critique (reference volume on Spivak on Critique of Postcolonial Reason) does not spare that kind of dabbling in postcolonial theory either.

The intellectual history of postcolonialism can be traced to the tensed dialectic between poststructuralism (for its theories) and Marxism (for its politics), especially Foucault's incursions into the discourse of history or, better, historicism as practiced in the Western academy. But we should also mention the seminal insights of Franz Fanon who drew attention to the plight of the Other as the colonized subject and the wretched of the earth. Fanon's work on the racialized psychiatry of the French colonial regime in Algiers paved the way for a deep questioning of the representation of the colonizer-colonized, master–slave, "us and them", 'normal and other', 'superior'/'inferior' binaries by problematizing the prevailing paradigm of the burden of the white man, beaconing the urgency of a reversal or unloading of the burden in the opposite direction: the slavish colonized, the other, might have something to say (however muted the voice or their speech) and teach the over-zealous and 'high civilization' backed master in the ethos of subjectivity and multiple ways of forging identity in the troubled terrain of imperialism's reach into the other and her systematic subjugation. Couple to this, Foucault's insight into the complicated inter-looping relationship between knowledge and power, the power of history and Western epistemologies not least as a means of social control. Foucault's application of this shattering insight of genealogical archeology that carries out a systematic excavation of layers of buried 'epistemes' becomes instructive at this point. Genealogy is the study of the genesis, or source, of our modes of thinking, world-views, of Weltanschauung, and its objective is to unearth the origins of our epistemes or conceptual paradigms in order to demonstrate their vulnerability and historicity. At the same time genealogy tries to make visible what cannot be seen at first blush. In the regard it is a critique of 'impure reason' (see Mendietta's chapter in this volume), or a transcendental investigation, much like phenomenology, particularly in respect of its strategy of *epoché*, the bracketing out of ontology and judgments about truth or falsity of the claim or belief or doctrine under investigation. Genealogy, aided by an archeology of knowledge-forms, allows an investigator to quiz the conditions of possibility of our epistemes, or worldviews and theories that support the same, from the different perspectives, especially of what he called institution, discourse and truth, in short 'culture', which is central to establishing hegemony. Thus his own genealogical exercises dealt with the genesis and inner workings of the prison (the idea of discipline and punish-ment), the clinic, the madhouses and ('lunatic') asylums, sexuality, the self, and the psychoanalyst's couch (Sharma 1993). Every institution and its own peculiar history, every text and authorial or canonical stamping can be subjected to genealogical analysis. But what trumps the force of subjugation in the relations made possible by institution, discourse and truth is power or the force of domination. The same power feeds on itself and grows in time, amassing more power and thereby empowers its hegemonic controllers, who transmit the power to an institution and knowledge-form that will perpetrate its ideology and strengthen its conditions of possibility.

Let us go a step further, and consider how power relations have the ability to create, define and represent cultures, especially of cultures of the others, of others indeed. Drawing on Foucaldian methodology and relation between power and knowledge. Edward Said's thesis of Orientalism brought this issue to the fore. Europe or the Occidental abrogates to, expropriates and authorises to itself the representation (in text but also in commerce and governance) of its silent other, in the image of its own invulnerable essence and universalising self (subject), but Said at the same time dismissed that there was such a space or geography or reality as the Orient or the East and other than the crisis of the Palestianians there was no political reality to be to too fuzzed about, at least outside of the European texts. One can say a lot more about representation of the exotic other in literature and grand narratives or discourse formations of the elite Eurocentricism and in its romanticised, depoliticised depiction of the other, its history, philosophies, religions, and law etc., that produces replacement realities and hybrid traditions – indeed hybridity – through texts; and Gandhi's questioning of the linear progress of Western modernity, with its handmaiden of industrialism and rabid colonisation of the non-Western world, needs to be mentioned also. To be sure, Gandhi endorsed some key ideas of modernity, but held the West responsible for not practicing in the colonies what it had been preaching for centuries. His relationship to modernity was dialogic, not exactly antagonistic, as a number of scholars have pointed out. But for his idea of nationhood, or nationalism, to which he was not entirely averse, he believed India, unlike the West, could draw from native religions, which had preached *ahiṃsā* (non-injury), and such inclusive practices. In short, the 'elegance' and 'relative simplicity', and academic elitism, of Said's thesis however blocked out the outsider from an effective participation in the deconstruction of colonialism and imperialism, and the global restructuring that becomes imperative in the wake of, yes, post-colony phase (meaning by this particular term merely that the discourse – not necessarily the process – of colonialism and the play of power and knowledge inherent to this discourse – has been laid bare, recognised for what it is and is placed on notice; heretofore a new discourse is essential that will begin to bear apart first the discourse and through a certain politics, or resistant agency, work to undo the errors of this past inflicted upon the other world. This new, supplemental discourse, that builds on Said's Orientalism but also, deepens the political urgency of Marxism (or its Asian/African/Indian versions that have had a fiery success among the left in the third world, except perhaps in Indonesia, where radical Islamic neo-modernism has played a similar role instead) and poststructuralist and deconstructive thinking, especially of the Frankfurt School (Habermas, Althusser, Adorno, et al.), feminist performatives, and continental philosophy and crosscultural thought.

Postmodernism Revisited

We now turn to the promised second definitional nuance of postmodernism in the light of the foregoing discussion. Cahoone summarizes postmodernism in terms of five prominent sites of criticism: *presence* or presentation (versus representation and construction), *origin* (versus phenomenon), *unity* (versus plurality), and *transcendence* of norms (versus their immanence). It typically offers analysis of phenomena through *constitutive otherness*, i.e. contextualization and positionality of what has been rendered peripheral by the Enlightenment sensibilities (Cahoone 1996: 14). Apart from its own origins in structuralism, which it seeks to go past or *post-*, i.e. jump a few steps forward and indeed complicate the interdependence of constituent phenomena, the crucial act of postmodernism is (as everyone here knows) its denial of the *transcendence*, i.e. totalizing essentialism and universalism of norms, in particular truth, rationality, modal semantics, the good, purity, idealized beauty, and all utopic salvations. The upshot of this hermeneutic of suspicion is that these norms are heretofore to be seen as products of and immanent in the processes of discourse and social formations – on the model of the plot and play in rites of narration, or signature to a text – within a set of relations that owe nothing to an outside objective realm, such as a God's aperture or the 'view from nowhere', or to any other privileged and privileging position for that matter. All normative claims are thus rendered problematic, especially the claims of those who exercise these within the safety and security of their own fortified discourse, closures, or power. But the analysis is also sensitive to elements that are 'marginalized', disenfranchised, and repressed, i.e. that and those who are under-represented and as such are already outside or the 'other' to the dominant norms and ascriptions (or ritual in-scriptions) of the privileged groups.

In terms a program for emancipation of the 'other' and overturning the processes that continue or perpetuate their otherness, postmodernists appear to be divided: some claiming that a complete overhaul of the repressive forces through revolutionary, intensely nationalistic and violent rebellion, is not feasible; while others prefer to *soften* (sing softly) the literary and philosophical or overly doctrinaire inheritances from modernity as a way of rendering 'repressive forces more diverse and fluid' (Cahoone 1996: 17) and making do with a liberal solidarity strengthened through piece-meal communitarian reforms, and so on.

For our present purposes, it is significant to underscore the *political* implications of postmodernism, which Cahoone begins to outline but which, I believe, needs confrontation from places or sites still far afield (or yet another extreme of the usual analytical, discursive partner in the comforts of academe – then that marked by, say, the Habermas–Gadamer–Ricoeur frank–furt debate, Rorty–Bernstein–Putnam ex-brooklyn chatters, Derrida–Searle incontinental exchanges, etc.) (This is Cahoone:) 'Its – postmodernism's – most well-known political manifestation is the attempt to make contemporary culture acknowledge and respond to "difference", or "otherness," under the names of *feminism*. . . and *multiculturalism*. Most poststructuralists, feminists, and multiculturalists are associated with the left. But others are not, like Richard Rorty, who has labelled himself a "postmodernist bourgeois liberal". Indeed. Some critics from the left have criticized postmodernism for just this, viz., that it opens the way to reactionary forces or to an acquiescence in the status quo, by undermining the modernist justifications for left political reform. Hence Jurgen Habermas once called the French poststructuralists the "Young Conservatives" I almost read, "not-so-young-now conversationists on behalf of *man*-kind". There is nothing confusing about this diversity; it is arguable that postmodernism by itself need not lead in any particular political direction. Its political usefulness lies in criticizing any established authority (Habermas 1985: 19). Another way of putting the reticence is to suggest, pushing past Raymond Williams' well-known distinction markers, that postmodernism – as Aijaz Ahmad and others have said repeatedly of Said's classic *Orientalism* – is largely an exercise in "indicative" deconstruction, and while its gesture toward "subjunctive" and "performative" enactments are laudable inasmuch as it permits lifting the limits and pressures – the (Rawlsian-adorned) 'veil' – of erstwhile ideological reproductions, it remains fundamentally stalemated by the (accompanying) rise of right-wing governments and movements throughout the Anglo-American-NATO-ed world, and is even implicated in the demise of leftist movements (in part – so Aijaz Ahmad insists – through sentimental identification with flaky forms of ecological doomsdayism and 'third worldism' (1992: 191ff.).

But this patience is running out; there are those who don't locate themselves either on the right or left (they have not that literary-leisure nor time), and demand more decisive action informed by a more radical understanding of the world that has been impacted by a discourse of imperialism and history of lived colonialism, of the private versus public, of worlds at wars, invented oppressions of other kinds, and forged new collusions between tradition and modernity – all of which in unison have privileged a much greater kind of civil or public irrationality than known before in human experience and which far outweigh the accomplishments of all claims to rationality by any measure. Postmodernism – as Walter Benjamin said also of phenomenology and history – epistemologically falls short, beyond the pale-hued rhetoric or linguistic inversions, of deeply understanding these bastard children of history *and* empathizing beyond self-congratulatory condescension with the vastly different experiences of women, class (read, out-class or caste) formations, of the indigenous or native, among others, who have grown up and lived under such conditions. Postmodernism also fails to effectively participate in the intellectual and social activism movements felt necessary – or which get generated almost instinctually – in the ghettoed predicament of the victims and muted voices of the utterly and indefinitely *other*-ed, namely the colonized and the continuing traces or consequences of colonialism in the lives of the postcolonial (then and now).

I think the last paragraph also brings to relief the 'reasoning' apparatus in postcolonialism in this conversation, though it will help to refine the critique of (i.e. from the locale of) postcolonial rationality coming as it does from the great granddaughter of the Mahatma who was among the first moderns to have, as it were, kicked the cricket-size ball 'past the colonial post'. Here is Leela Gandhi: "For all its animosity, the colonial encounter produced a rich body of thought which concerned itself with a visionary commitment to the end of all institutional suffering. Much of this thought began with a critique of 'Western civilization', but its aim – in so doing – was to instigate a reform within the very structures of Western rationality. Thus Gandhi's uncompromising repudiation of modernity emphasised the transcultural benefits of a non-violent sociality. The oppressors, he maintained, had to be liberated from their own worst selves." (Gandhi 1998: 137).

Part I

With this as the preamble, I wish to move quickly to Part I which looks at some theoretical underpinnings of postcolonialism.

There has been an explosion of work recently in postcolonial theorizing, which on the one hand appears to continue the Postmodern critical interrogation of modernity (the cultural sweep of European Enlightenment with its logocentric disciplinary forays or the complex relation of knowledge to the portals of power) even as the Postcolonial Condition celebrates difference, diversity and diasporic hybridity. While on the other hand, Postcolonialism expresses a degree of ambivalence even outraged impatience with Postmodern theorizing precisely because of the latter's inability to reach out to those 'others' in the borderzones, i.e. those displaced and muted in the invisible zone we might call the 'subaltern topoi' or subaltern alterity. As with history, in social and political realities also, there are not just minority or marginalized people and discourses (though they too), but those that are subordinated (to use Dipesh Chakrabarty's term; see also his *Provincializing Europe* (2000; see also Chakrabarty 2002, 2007)), looked upon as 'immature' with only the more primitive or aboriginal sensibilities (Kant), if not a less developed or cultured rational spirit (Hegel) or institutional capacities (Weber), and those who are wittingly or unwittingly forgotten (Nandy), ruptured, or simply borderlined in their alterity (Bhabha 1994; Sharma 1998). What do we mean by these characterizations or caricatures?

As we saw earlier, Fanon was perhaps one of the earliest writers to trace the effects of colonialism on the subjugated subject and the role of culture within the de/colonization process. There was racism of the more vulgar kind (in which physiology played an intricate part – recall phrenology) and there was 'cultural racism' which was a much more sophisticated and subtle discourse, with its reference to values, means of production, behavioural codes, and aesthetic and sexual management, all of which were deemed to be lacking in their fullest expression in the constitution of the native, i.e. the indigenous tribes, nomads and even those recognized to have mastered hydraulic civilizations (such as the Chinese and Indians in Asia). The native was an inferior species in this theory, not simply on account of the diminutive size of the cortex but because of certain inherent psychological and moral deficiencies. Effective colonization led by well-meaning missionaries, modernists, men of the sciences, would remove this lingering curse of the pre-modern, and herald the colonies into the new era of progress, civility and individuation. Fanon observed that where colonial rule was stable the apparent propensity to laziness and endemic violence on the part of the native was channelled into self-hatred and muscular tension. Thus settler colonialism created a mythology about the alienating culture of the native which both justified and perpetuated the ruse of modernity (see McCulloch 1996: 134). In time, even socialism, or Marx's utopian vision, becomes 'part of the prodigious adventure of the European spirit' (Fanon 1990: 253; Gandhi 1998: 72).

Ashis Nandy, an Indian postcolonial critic *par excellence*, transposes this indictment to the South Asian context. He describes the phenomenon as the construction of the 'intimate enemy', both in the sense of the inner struggle to transform the residual ritual-possessed self as well as the internalized hatred of the colonial-Western Enlightenment economy, which stands now as the site of conflict or clash between two cultures whirling, as it were, in the head of the native (Nandy 1998). In many ways, this muted social psyche of the post-colonized even after absorbing Enlightenment values of liberty and autonomy has not been liberated from this fractured condition. Hence the postcolonial theorist asks, of what avail is postmodernism to the need of the late hour in this unique struggle against the onslaught and persistent trace of modernity?

Is There *Difference* Outside of Postmodernism?

So there is this particular site of identity that might be said to elude the concerns of the Postmodern Condition and it cries out for a voice and liberation beyond the panacea of salvation offered up in the play of narratives (*a la* Rorty), or in the violence of critical theory (Heidegger, Frankfurt School), or in the inter-disciplinary trackings (ubiquitously between philosophy with cultural studies). There is nevertheless a shared common ground, contextual and positional *affinity* between Postmodernism and Postcoloniality, particularly in the celebrative gestures of difference, the moments of hermeneutic suspicion, and the phenomenological act of bracketing out onto-theological presuppositions from descriptive/discursive language, including indeed the ontology of violence and sporadic mini-holocausts experienced in the living history of the wholly other (*tout autre*) in their very otherness. The borders between these two moments of critical engagement in the current temporal space are undoubtedly porous, notwithstanding Postcolonialism's worries about the distantly consoling but never arriving-in-time face of the infinite totality, or indeterminable universality, *that* (w)Holy Other, and of the privileging of, to be sure, the desubstantialized Greco-European-Hebrew sacrificial remnants (*survivance*, as in Buddhist 'after-death') of an apophatic negative an-khoral atheology of Dr. Derrida, The Disincarnation i.e., Second Unbecoming, Saint Jacques: "Deconstruction is a certain faith". But to what end? One might ask again, is it to messianically void the "impoverished *ousia* of the third world"? and to drag its destabilizing fundamentalisms to the charming clinical couch of detraditionalized scholastic doctors (meaning, de-sensitized to *other*-world echoing an uncorrected typo elsewhere particularities)? (cf. Caputo, *Prayers and Tears of J-D*, 1997: 54–55, 141, 149, 152 respectively). Avatar-Mahatma Jacques' own colonial past (in Algiers) and his postcolonial absented presence (in Paris@California) remains mysteriously occluded and de-authorialized, unlike his deconstructionist strategy and, now predictably, akhoral theology.

What appears to have been replaced by Enlightenment's metaphysic of logocentrism is a variant of the eighteenth century reductionist epistemes of philology, etymology, demythologization, recontextualization, and de-theologization plus narrative transplants or retelling of the story by anyone other than the afflicted, i.e. the muted subaltern: 'Can the subaltern speak?' was rightly not intended to be trivially rhetorical; but it gains more force, when it reads 'Can the subaltern *act* in her silence?'. What is lacking here, according to Postcolonial theorists, is a decisive and radical countermovement to the continuing project of modernity in its dis/guises as variants of modernism, including neo-modernisms, enacted mostly in distant locations (i.e. away from the urbanized metropolis of the Western world but nonetheless impacted by it). (Of course radical feminists have expressed similar concerns.) In other words, the social and political edge of solidarity, activism, decisive action (other than a platitudinous theory of pragmatism), is not forthcoming from the self-reclaimed "sites of politics" (Derrida in Caputo 1997) of Postmodernism precisely because the subordinated other (in the borderzones and which could be very large majorities or entire civilizations) elude the noncondescending gaze even of Postmodernism whose agenda, it is claimed by Postcolonial theorists, has already in some ways been prefigured in the project of Europe's efforts at Universal Enlightenment.

Turning this disquisition into a rhetorical question, one would ask: How deep and disruptive is the space of difference in which otherness of the third kind is not swallowed up, between modernism and its deviant child? Perhaps there has to be a healthy hermeneutic of suspicion not just for all things 'modern' but also of all pretensions to the '*post-*' as one is of, say, the excesses of poststructuralism, of post-independent rhetoric and indeed even of *postcolonial* abstractions which are fast-forwarding towards yet another exotic, somewhat deorientalized though to be sure commodified servings, in the ever-curious intellectual marketplace of the West's own making. And so in half self-confessing tone Leela Gandhi notes in own Preface to *Postcolonial Theory, a critical introduction*: "Postcolonialism continues to render *non-Western* knowledge and culture as 'other' in relation to the normative 'self' of Western epistemology and rationality" (Gandhi 1998: ix).

While I personally consider such contentions to be somewhat exaggerated, there is I believe some truth in the steps taken by the Postcolonial Critique to either deepen the Postmodern Critique or to move further towards uncovering those neglected experiences of oppression, political annihilation, ecological devastation, gender blundering, and multinational corporatization increasingly visited upon third world countries as indeed upon 'third worlded' communities/groups within the so-called first and second worlds. So I wish to pause and continue to analyze the *sites* of contestation between Postmodern and Postcolonial theorists to highlight the indictment of the borderzoned Other.

Let me say something about my use of the clause 'deorientalised though to be sure commodified servings'. Orientalism as Said had articulated it was simply too crude and one-sided theory about the representation and containment of the worlds of the other – mostly in Said's case the Arabic-Palestinian Middle Eastern world – by the Europeans through their recovery and appropriation of the literary life-world, scholarship and economic withal of the distant other. So the so-called Oriental world, the dark self-reflection of Europe's own ambivalent soul, is nothing but the construct of the European mind: there is no real place called the Orient, it is like a steamed up tourist or pilgrim destination, i.e. entirely virtual like your cyberspace, and by the same token there is no Oriental self or the confused *desi* (countryman-gone-abroad) that has as it were been spun off as a by-product of the imperial-colonial process and its aftermath. Whereas the Indian critique of the same phenomenon in the subcontinental context has recognized beyond a perfunctory celebrative 'hybridized' entity agonized over in the nineteenth century by Babus, is shown to be a 'joint production' in a matching 'see-me-as-you' contest. Ashis Nandy gets across this imaginary most forcefully and lucidly thus: "The world usually knows India as it has been constructed by the modern Indians in collaboration with specialist western scholarship on India. Orientalism is frequently a joint 'dream work' where the defences and cultural 'armour' of the West is matched by the self-representation and self-engineering of the modernizing West." (1998: 105). In some ways, this is the irrupted self also in constant inner dialogue with him/herself, and it is unpredictably though calculatively both a friend and a foe of modernity. What does this do for postmodernism when it arrives at his/her doorstep? In one-half of postmodernism's self-representation she sees her own foe being graciously dismembered; of the other half, she scans, interprets and assesses the self-same friend in *modernity* which she has come to increasing suspect and hermetically distanced, except for short-term instrumental, pragmatic and economic individualism gains which modernity is best at delivering, bilaterally, and indeed has continued to in the extended hegemony of its political-economic globalization turn – even as this threatens the erasure of local, indigenous, old world 'oriental' cultures. In this respect, Indian-born critiques serve up a deorientalized bilingually curried commodity labeled 'the postcolonial discourse; inflammable'. And that embeds a not-so-overt challenge for postmodernism in as much as it externalizes a challenge to modernity, both in its local and global vestures, in its ideological disliberative or disempowering prowess as well as in its withholding or retentively self-deprecating or (patently nostalgic-)self indulgent critical theorizing born of failed utopian dreams – such as the redemptive promises (still) offered by capitalism, or its half-cousin socialist communism, the progressive secularization process, and the infusion of imperial bureaucracy or monolithic institutions – nowadays overpowered by a ruthless marketplace self promoting economic rationalism (read, multinational corporate culture) and media-managed rhetoric. Such then are, if you will, the gripes of postcolonialism when it turns the mirror around on to modernity's supposed other or *bête noire*.

In the next section I will deal clinically with the pernicious effects of the internalizing of the colonial ideology on the public and political culture of its own people, in respect of the frozen praxis of nationalism, nation-state, progress, rationality and secularism, which are really the prerogative of neo-modernisms of sorts. I won't get through them all though.

Let us speak of the third world more generally. Consider the observations of Pauline Rosenau: 'On the surface post-modernism appears primarily of interest to the West and of little concern in the Third World' (citing Cahoone). She continues: 'But a closer look reveals that modern social and political movements in the Third World are giving way to new forms of political expression; in some cases what emerges is very much of an affirmative post-modern character. If modernity has failed the Third World, post-modernism appears to in all its diversity and permissiveness to permit and encourage a selective attention to the past and an eclectic re-construction of the present.' (Rosenau 1992: 152). On the face of it, this attempted linkage is simplistic, romantic and appropriative. One wonders if a discourse of difference were ever possible outside of and independent of postmodernism, and whether postmodernism is as affirmatively encouraging of political expressions and engaged social movements as made out here? In this vein, she continues, 'Post-modern themes – including anti-Enlightenment views, anti-modern attitudes, a return to fundamentalist indigenous spirituality, anti-science sentiments, and opposition to modern technology – are generating a growing interest throughout the Third World' (Rosenau 1992: 153). Since when have these (or at least some of 'themes') become properties of postmodernism? Modernity has had its own difficulties and equivocations with each of the positively nuanced counterfactuals, and those who suffered inexorably as a consequence of the undergirding universalism, have voiced concerns far longer than the gurus of postmodernism have been, so to say, at it. At one point in her narrative Rosenau aligns re-configured third world movements as having an opening toward anti-systemic and anti-democratic post-modern movements. This would be patently false and a bone of grave contention on the part of postcolonial critics when they turn their question, to give instance, onto Rorty's offering of liberalism in lieu of democracy to disillusioned postmodernists and third world apaches alike. (A little later for that.) But there is a negative underside to third world-postmodernism that concerns the author.

Rosenau complains that third world postmodernists are intellectually contradictory. She cites as an instance the rejection of western truth claims only to be matched by an equally forceful assertion of their own superior truth-claims: They denounce any voice for the colonizer referring to the adage 'Can the Subaltern Speak?'. But rather than deconstruct and dismiss it, "they seek to replace it with an equally hegemonic, though indigenous, author." Here she turns to Gayatri Spivak, "an Indian feminist post-modernist (who) criticizes the way modern authors represent the Third World."

This is garbled and tendentious. Spivak has become more circumspect since exploding this particular colonial myth, but it is disingenuous not to see the hard difference being driven at by her analysis and project, which only in a very loose sense can be called post-modern; and yet it is modern values that are supposed to enable questioning of many traditional social institutions in the third world that post-modern relativism and tolerance encourage. In other words, post-modernism might become complicitous in third world's claim to legitimate many traditional practices that might be oppressive, as it reestablishes the subservience, notably of women – insinuating the Islamic dress etiquettes as and traditional marriage roles as instances – by an unreconstructed patriarchy. Well, if this is all true, then post-modernism ought to step aside, and let indigenous-framed criticism of the excesses of traditionalism emerge. One might just find that some of the values promoted by modernity (perhaps re-echoing some scholastic strains within their own erstwhile past) are of enduring appeal and a needed armory for reforming social structures that have either remained fossilized, or institutionalized through colonial interventions to serve an entirely arbitrary or hegemonic end. Instances of such values would be a more dispassionate approach to current problems, the discourse of rights and citizenship moderated with responsibility, and indeed emancipatory democracy inasmuch as this ideal remains to be accomplished anywhere.

Part II

The second contention that I canvass in this paper grows out of these 'developing world' critiques and considers how some cultures or regions previously brought under or at least faced with the threat of Imperial European Enlightenment-cum-Secularism had pre-empted the stakes and embarked upon the process of modernization before it had its full Weberian swing in the West. This is particularly true of eighteenth to nineteenth century Arabic Islamic and the subcontinental regions (under Abduh, Afghani, Wahab, Sayeed Ahmed Khan, Rammohun Roy). The blend of indigenous 'modernisms' constructed here however retained a strong element of the imaginary of traditional orthodoxy and left much space for growth of native, culturally-specific consciousness, 'science', legal system, intellectual maturity and economic and social well-being. With increasing pressures from colonial forces and in the aftermath of the World Wars, disenchanted leaders in these regions moved to a revision of modernism toward neo-modernisms (e.g. with Iqbal, Fazrul Rahman, Nasution), which pre-date and share many of the symptoms of postmodernism of sorts, such as ambiguity, relativism of values, and in-countenance at the death of the nation-state ideology.

But these movements have not been particularly empowering or liberating; rather, they have tended to create new internal orientalized elites (as in Indonesia and Malaysia and several Middle Eastern nations, Pakistan and so on), and they stand in the way of greater freedom for the greatest number; they are anti-democratic and anti-disciplinary even in the liberal senses of the terms. Take the case of neo-modernist Islam in South-east Asia. Orthodox Islam had never previously been a major force in either Indonesia or Malaysia prior to colonialism; in fact, the powerful kings modelled themselves on the rajas-sultans of India, and drew liberally from Brahmanised Buddhistic-animistic and moderately Muslim ideologies for their state-craft for centuries and their culturally diverse Bahaasa-speaking people only later clustered into the two large regions, like other spoils of feuding-European imperialists. But the suppression suffered under European rule inversely impacted the importance of Islam for regional and increasingly central politics. What other ideology could stand up to the implicative assaults of a Christianizing imperialism? As in the subcontinent, it was Muslim intellectuals who organized themselves into nationalist pressure-groups and dealt the first blow. As these countries moved towards independence, they looked for a model of the nation-state more suitable to their cultural and ethnic sensibilities. The framework for an 'internally modernizing Islam' which would play a large role in molding, but not monopolize or hog, the revisioned nation-state and its instruments, came from the exiled Pakistani Muslim modernist, Fazrul Rahman. Rahman afterwards taught in Chicago where Indo-Malay students came to study under him and took back with them the resounding message of what has now come to be known as the *Pancashila*. This quasi-secularized set of five token principles or gestures supposedly underwrote pluralism and democracy consistent with the 'ethnic, religious, racial', diversity of the archipelago, especially in its constitutional adoption in Indonesia with Sukarno, a self-made neo-modernist himself (though his own personal leanings were slanted towards animistic Hindu governance accentuated by a Tito-style militarianism). As an attenuated 'rule of law' staked further control under the protection of military or quasi-secular leaders in Indonesia and Malaysia, Muslim leaders felt under pressure to create an alternative force to challenge this order. In part this has been the basis of crisis in Indonesia, where the student movement, which cries out for democracy, real secularism, rights and an end to corrupt privileges amassed by the ruling elite, especially under Suharto, has joint forces with a resurgent Islam which sees itself as going beyond the earlier neo-modernist compromises so that people could have a greater share and say in the powerhouse of the two nations which together have the largest Muslim population anywhere in the world. The neo-modernists king-pins have gone into a modernist habit of bringing their real and potential rivals, especially if they appear to speak for democracy, ethnic autonomy (as in the case of East Timorese Nobel Peace laureates), or for Islamic and ethnic-linguistic power-sharing, of impeaching or charging them with subverting the sacrosanct 'rule of law' on grounds of their alleged private sexual misconduct and other such unthinkable crimes. That is how the staunch neo-modernist Mahatir has dealt with Anwar Ibrahim in Malaysia.

So, what I am saying is that, third world (or even the large rich nations that do not feature in the OECDs ranking of 'Western industrialized developed nation-state' category), have spawned their own 'postmodern' tropes – which others have called 'neo-modernism', with almost the singular exception of the overdetermined juxtaposition by Aziz Ahmed (the Pakistani journalist) of 'postmodern' with Islam to describe an imagined outgrowth of Islam, notwithstanding the several shades of fundamentalism that ripple through the Muslim world, as it confronts Samuel Huntington's dominant civilization in the clash. A Postmodern Islam? (Parodying the Nietzschean trace elsewhere in Heidegger): Too late for modernism, and too early for postmodernism! Why not simply a Postcolonial Muslim Critique, before any such large almost meaningless grand narratives are promulgated echoing the growing appeal to globalization (which is a substitute for modernist universalism), fashion (an apologia for hard tradition), and dissimulation of real identities? This is also quite contrary to the lived experiences (e.g. of women and different ethnic communities) in Al-Azmeh's so-called postmodern Islamic state, which indeed, much like Arjun Appaduria's 'productions of locality' in the melting pot of privileged diasporic long-distance resistances to the moribund discourses of tradition and the 'naturalised' order of modernity, may only be found in potholes of immigrant communities, in South Hall, Middlesex, Toronto, Montreal, New Jersey and maybe Atlanta!

In any case, neo-modernism constitutes a still-born surrogate ideology, even if it is an engendered species. It does not look terribly healthy, it produces its own reign of terror (think of the massacre of East Timorese 'separatists' and ethnic-cleansing of Indonesian Chinese), or it easily falls prey to the imperial reaches of a culture- and difference-blind globalization (the multinational projects of population-growth control as a supposed way of alleviating poverty in the third world). One may well speak, again as Appadurai (1997) does so eloquently alongside his ironic and witty antipatriot who also grew up in the hybrid metropolis of Mumbai (now given over to fundamentalism of another sort), of other subjectivities, caste mobilizations and new ethnicities forged through the global accessibility of multilingual/intracultural infrastructures of massified-media and electronic communications, whose software wizards and Big Apple-stores' security-monitor boys are scattered across the silicon valleys of California, New Jersey and Bangalore talking over mobile cellulars in Samiri-Indian tongues, are mostly displaced celluloid diasporic Indians anyway.

And as Rastom Bharucha has rightly observed, such 'Virtual struggle... is an illusion, an abdication of direct confrontation', describing it virtually as 'the voyeuristic site of a privileged global intelligentsia, who can afford to surf the possibilities of resistance through mediated discourses, transmitted from the trouble spots of third world into the padded cells of first world intellectual production' of, among other fracturous identities, in Benedict Anderson's latest adage to 'imagined communities', to whit, 'long-distance nationalism' (Bharucha 1998: 171, 178). In India, the 'electronic *avatar*' is either in the form of the Muslim-beating communalist saviour touted in the hands of a monolingual resurgent nationalist fundamentalism (whether secular or Hindu), or he is the sky-god exploited by the globalist, indeed utterly tradition-blind (unless it helps the viewer-ratings and mitigates court charges), media-tycoons like Rupert Murdoch, whose global transpervestite reaches through satellite, sky TV, and journalese raggery certainly do not reflect 'the power of mass literacy' in any linguistically or philosophically significant sense, nor do they augur for 'large-scale productions of ethnic affinity' as far as some of the postcolonial critics are aware. Incipient Urdu language-programs and fledgling print-media mostly in northern India, that attracts no state support despite a U.P. constitutional decree, would scantly feature in the global wizardry of 'ethnic affinity' or empowered imaginary of the marginalized.

These are realities, then, that in the virtualization of history, culture, religion and politics, are driven to the borderlines of otherness as a consequence of the normative and aesthetic abdication of modernity from these troubled locations; and the ambiguous interplay of the two post-modernisms (eastern–western) here leaves much to be desired, or is submerged to the persistent traces and desires of modernity. As Aziz Al-Azmeh poignantly puts it:

> For historical reality and the position within modernity of postmodernism are substituted virtual realities of the present, the past and the Other, among which stands out the virtual reality of collective well-being in a West riven with structural crisis, unemployment and social stresses sublimated in a triumphalism of the moment. (Al-Azmeh 1993: 23)

Third world postmodernisms – and here I would like to count in certain forms of subaltern nationalism, as also certain tendencies within Subaltern studies, and possibly again also the hybridity-diasporic celebratory mood prevailing in Chicago – tend to re-orientalize and offer themselves up as subjects for aesthetic authentication (an-other commodification) of modernism, its institutionalized scrambling over discourse and theory, and the closure this entails. Thus, the rootless, homeless, 'go-glow' jholi-wagging-Ānandic, diasporic and self-exiled self-styled postcolonial-subalternist descendants of the yet suffering third world ancestral tribes, and who otherwise stand to make theory and gains out of this supposed lamentable condition, rightly become a bane of discontent of the postcolonial (still) downunder (in the borderzone alterity sense). (Bilimoria 2007b)

Unconcluding Part III

Last but not least, a few words on the disquisition of postmodernism and democracy and the public good. Rorty's 'liberal ironism' calls for jettisoning of the public from the private or local realms, because the former is a logocentric discourse of pain and humiliation and the latter a language of self-creation, historicized self-understanding, poetic narrative, and a centreless web of beliefs and desires freed from the centre/periphery binary, etc. (Rorty 1989: 135). With this goes the universal claims of democracy, human rights, justice, and matters of public concern – at least in any foundational or enduring sense. What is left is participatory bourgeois intellectualism or a tolerant liberal utopic solidarity negotiated through images realized in fluid communities without rootedness in metaphysics, tradition or transcendental epistemology for that matter (Grange 1997: 304). (It went uncommented but in a cross-cultural symposia on justice and democracy Rorty was booed by feminists, third world activists and those others who continue to experience or witness pain and humiliation, but for whom the consolation prize of 'private' 'self-creation' of 'the aesthetic life' as the desirable mode of existence, or better subsistence, is no more than an olive branch nor *neem*. As Roby Rajan notes with added irony: "The quest for private perfection is coupled with a 'public morality' of liberal individualism which is to provide the necessary stable framework of social organization to pursue the good life. The aim of a just and free society is 'letting its citizens be as privatistic, irrationalistic, and aestheticist as they please so long as they do it on their own time.' " (Nandy in Lal 1996: 190, inside quote is given from Rorty 1989: xiv). All this is permitted of course precisely in places or sites where the environment is in tethers, when Java irrupts, wives are burnt, girl-childs are sold for booty, Bosnians and Kosovo-Albians are ethnically-cleansed by Serbs unwittingly abetted or driven under by NATO's larger Euro-globalist agenda, when Aboriginal and indigenous people everywhere are silenced when they fight for their rights; otherwise their own dispossession lingers irreconciled, and so on. The Muslim wants bread, and the postmodernist like the fundamentalist gives him hope and faith, and a ticket for a couch with a 'view from/to nowhere'.

Rosie Braidotti (1997) among other feminists likewise call for a non-relativist epistemological and ethical position, albeit that is suitable to postmodernity in a gendered perspective. But she too opts for a position derived from Deleuzian nomadic subjectivity, which is all very-well for a first-second generation Italian born in Melbourne and lecturing in Rome, Utrecht and widely in the States. The aboriginal who feels possessed by and sacredly rooted in her ancestral soil, community, tradition, and locally-nomadic tribes does not have this option open to her, for then the judgment of the settler legal descendants of John Locke, viz, *terra nullius* ('land not inhabited by anyone but for some exiting nomadic footprints'!) would be vindicated. Rorty's a-democratic tolerant liberalism of otherness without colonial difference echoes (Rorty 1995), and links inexorably with, Irigaray's complaint against Levinas to the effect, that Otherness without sexual difference is a masked form of self-sameness (Braidotti 1997: 7–12). An improbable self-identity made-in-Euromerica in the *aporia* of the other (*Oneself as Another*), even where one goes beyond Ricoeur in being able to name the Other/other (*l'Autre*, *l'autrui*), only further alienates the other, ethically, just as Levinas's interests in the feminine other almost stood inverted (from 1947 to 1974). The other person bears the relation of the father to his son, a paternal God and his subjects, etc. (Pamela Sue Anderson in *Feminist Philosophy of Religion*). The trace, *ousia*, the face and mask of the other remains buried, even in the naming. A hermeneutic of the other begins when the irruption comes from the site of the other, when she re-traces the constituted alterity – otherness – for her/himself, and process her own ethical response to the other-maker. But 'home' is a long-way away from textually-enacted freedoms. She breathes heavily, but holds her word (as God does in the *Genesis*: he creates first and talks After-words.) (See Jantzen's chapter in this volume.) Neither Cartesian certainty nor divinity's love may be at her disposal. But unlike Levinisian Other (the Unnamed) this other is not infinite in dimension; the objectified subject has a fragile condition barely surviving in the 'terminal' nation-state (Appadurai 2006).

Postcolonialism therefore has an array of legitimate grievances against postmodernism for not having addressed issues more centrally concerning the manifestations of imperialism, globalization, corporate multinational political economy, and a persistent Eurocentricism in many areas. To be sure, these manifestations are visited in postmodern discourses, but by the same token the decisive strategy to subvert the internalized colonial practices and rectify the looses or the continuing remnants in other forms, is conspicuous by its absence. The impulse toward theory *qua* theory does not always deliver or is found to be liberating unless accompanied with action and empowering resistant agency. Thus Foucault did not address issues of third-world subjugation and representation, since his preoccupation was with Europe's historicity in respect of its own follies and foibles, and not necessarily its impact on the larger world or elsewhere than in Europe's internal spaces, which is an insufferable lacuna. Hence the need for a 'third space' of theory and practice, which a self-critical postcolonialism tries to instill or inscript through its own conditions of possibility and mode of deconstructive performative. (Bilimoria, Prabhu; Sharma 2007a)

I wish to conclude this chapter with a brief discussion of the possible areas of application of the creative suspicions of postcolonialism in the lived context. The examples I draw upon take in seriously both particular hermeneutic of tradition and the critique of ideology, which become paradigmatic in postcolonial critiques of Western ethnocentrism and other (more indigenist) kinds of author-itarian elitism. To take up the latter first, one could argue that the impersonal, abstract, ahistorical, atemporal concept of "Brahman" much dear to Vedānta philosophy is a "dead" metaphor, inasmuch as it is grounded in eidos, logos, and ousia and therefore has its life or sustaining significance entirely within the discourse of metaphysics (as Heidegger would say of all grand metaphors of the subject). A culture or rather ideology of brahmanical hegemony and renunciative restraint bordering on the obsessive denial of the lived experience, was built or idealized on the basis of this dominant and powerful transcendental signifier. Its social praxis legitimated the rule of the priest, a strident and pervasive caste hierarchy, marginalization of women, the under-class and foreigners as others. A wondrous evocation that may have arisen in the poetic musings of the Vedic (nomadic Āryan) bards, which in the altar of later Vedic sacrificial fire is transmuted into a substantive being (in the dis-guise of language), and which finally under the anvil of speculative philosophy ascends to assume the throne on highest rungs of metaphysics. Thus Brahman stands to be de-structured, dismantled, disseminated, deconstructed by being subjected to the same rigours of the hermeneutic of suspicion and critical ideology as Ricoeur has suggested. It may then be possible to recover the latent and to reanimate the tradition in more creative ways than has occurred either through the revivalism of neo-Vedānta or the Romanticism of nineteenth century philological Indology (see Bilimoria 2008a and the Subaltern chapter in this volume).

The last remark brings me the second example. The large body of texts produced and translated in Europe since around the sixteenth century on the cultures, prevalent literature, and peoples inhabiting the vast landmass to the east and south-east of Europe has nowadays been recognized to be suffused with "orientalism." This marks a peculiar hermeneutical act which the West ingressed upon the East. More specifically, the discourse of Orientalism underscores the willful romantic construct of the East (the Orient or Asia) in the imagination of the West as Europe's "other," and destined to be converted, civilized and controlled by the burgeoning Western religious, economic and political might. But if we leave out any part, conscious or complicitous, involved in the formation of the text or the supplemental discourse we could be doing grave "epistemic violence" to the text. An incisive judgment along these lines has, for instance, been said of the nineteenth century British Raj's novel statutory judgment on *satī*, the Indian practice of widow burning, as constituting a legal "crime," which however failed to register the social motivations of the Hindu patriarchal order that perpetrated this culturally aberrant practice for so long (Spivak 1999). It is not as though such a censor was not possible within the Hindu and Pan-Indian tradition itself; indeed, there was evidence in traditional moral texts against such practices and indigenous leaders had rallied against the act on the grounds that *satī* violated women's rights: but is that tantamount to a criminal act under English Common Law?

By focusing on the discourse of postcolonialism (after Orientalism) we understand better the Occidental-West, its logocentrism, and its failure to bring about genuine dialogue with the East and generate authentic methods for reading, translating and understanding the "other." The same can be said about the early British settlers' judgment that the colonies of *terra australis* were not inhabited by any people (thus rendered as *terra nullius*) because the nomadic native Aborigines appeared not to have cultivated the land or invested any labor in it or asserted an instrumental interest in it. It took Ernie Mabo to challenge this "interpretation" of another tradition in place. This massive legal and political prejudice, in the Gadamarian sense, is finally turned back on the incoming tradition for its own self-reflection, and to demonstrate that it misjudged "interest" in individualistic-utilitarian rather than in communicative-communitarian terms; and it perhaps paves the way for corrective reparation or "Reconciliation" of First and Second-Third Nations' respective claims.

Third World studies and feminist movements more widely have capitalized on such insights and trans-boundary critiques, which was given a heavy political emphasis by Foucault's theorizing premised on the generalization that all knowledge is inextricably linked with power (and power is invariably corrupting). They have advocated, and developed methods for a re-reading and "de-construction" therefore of much of the past history and "civilizing" or literary productions, translatory enactments, etc. resulting from the basically liberal-individualistic, imperial and patriarchy-propelled intrusions into the lives of women, slaves, marginalized groups, the "other," the outcastes, and the colonized subjects, both within the history of Western-European societies but more damagingly in various countries throughout the world. History might be more authentic and closer to the truth were its voices to emerge, as it were, "from below" rather than from the pens of the privileged, the elite, the experts, and bow-tied academic researchers who have a vested interest (unwittingly perhaps) in perpetuating certain myths – "paradigm" – of the dominant cultural force in a society or tradition at large. The requisite hermeneutics for (re-)writing history from below has been technically popularized by South Asian radical social theorists as the "Subaltern" stance or voices of the submerged subject-positions.

Last but not least, cross-cultural philosophers of religion have claimed that the Western invention of the sub-discipline or discourse of philosophy of religion with its expectations of a solid, irrefutable and logically profound "proof" (or, for that matter, "disproof") of the existence of God has triggered much unnecessary anguish, mimicry, and irreparable damage among non-Western, non-Christian peoples. When directed at the "other" this trenchant discourse has in part also helped erode local traditions, folk understandings, indigenous hermeneutics, law and social wisdom developed over many centuries in non-Western religious cultures by which they have sustained themselves. Such and more sophisticated critical analyses have arisen in recent years from movements in philosophy and the human sciences, particularly from Europe and now increasingly influential in North America, India, and Australasia. And this brings me to the third example which questions the trope of radical pluralism common among theologians who been exhausted by the barrage of attacks on their apologetic defences of 'exclusivism', 'inclusivism' and variations in-between.

The conventional discourse on religious pluralism has hitherto been framed in terms of the encounter of Christianity with "other" or "non-Christian" religions and the kind of response Christians might or might not make to people of non-Christian persuasion in all their diversity and complexity. The positions and attitudes adopted within the pluralist ('dialogue-ic') paradigm have ranged from forms of 'exclusivism' (that all religions have some worth, but Christianity offers the only valid path, *extra ecclesiam nulla salus*), 'inclusivism' (that other religions have great spiritual depth and revelations, but are not sufficiently salvific), and 'pluralism' (that the truth-content of faith can have a variety of articulations each of which is legitimate), with shades in-between. Ernest Troeltsch, William Hocking and Paul Tillich first suggested the idea of pluralism, although with differing interpretations and implications of the claim to finality or normativity for Christians. The consensus in more recent times seems to gravitate towards *pluralism* in one or the other of its interpretations. The more popular understanding of religious pluralism, as articulated by W C Smith, John Hick, Paul Knitter, D'Costa among others, maintains that "other religions are equally salvific paths to God, and Christianity's claim that it is the only path (exclusivism), or the fulfilment of other paths (inclusivism) should be rejected for good theological and phenomenological grounds" (Bilimoria 1999).

In other words, the traditional universalism and absolutism attached to the Christian position is bracketed and the independent validity of other religions – even in their "otherness" or *alterity* – is now recognised. Much thought has been given as to how the differences between religions, the great diversity of beliefs, practices, rites and symbolisms, might be reconciled or a *rapprochement* brought about among them. And there has been much optimism about learning from other religions and the mutual enrichment or upliftment that can be experienced anew in "dialogues and conversations" with people whose religious instincts appear not to have been scorched by centuries of internal theological disputes, doubts and argumentations, and by the rapid shifts that the modern (beginning with Western) societies have made towards secularism, scientism and technocratic utopianism.

A corollary of this mitigated position is a more radical form of pluralism which argues that the established and dogmatic traditions should turn over to and enmesh (integrate) themselves as much as practicable with the currency of other, possibly less dogmatic, ("world" and "primal") traditions with radically different (maybe more ancient) historical roots and wealth of outlook on nature, on the human condition, on the cosmos, on liberation, and so on.

While during the colonial-imperial phase the distant and marginalised traditions were infiltrated, expropriated and recast to look more like the dominant tradition (e.g. Christianity in Hindu–Muslim India, typified in Raimon Panikkar's earlier *The Hidden Christ of India*), the trend now is to reverse the process and appropriate the "other" traditions into one's own tradition in the *inter-religious* context. Pluralism becomes a means of preserving the old in the guise of the new or the other.

This task, it is urged, is a matter of some urgency now that there is widespread recognition of the historical contingency of every cultural artefact – as surely religion is one – as well as our growing awareness of the unavoidable "prejudices" and the questionable assumption undergirding the privileged or paradigmatic access to the "Ultimate" claimed in each religion. Together the religions may be able to heal the scars left by the clashes of disparate cultures, and inject some sanity, hope and insightful wisdom towards preventing nature and humankind from the threat of "human-engendered destruction" (HED), if not also work toward the betterment of all sentient beings as indeed the goal of each religion appears, in principle at least, to be absolutely committed to. This would seem to be the challenge of what goes under the rubric of 'radical pluralism', which, while it acknowledges the historical relativity of each religion, nevertheless accedes to the intrinsic intentionality or drift towards the essential truth, the *telos*, as well as submitting to the fundamental integrity, insights, virtues and spirituality of each tradition. Even if the form of relativism it implicitly admits to is merely 'provisional', there appears to prefigure here an assumption that truth might just be plural; or, more likely, that truth is one but that it conceals itself behind a kaleidoscopic facade. This is exactly the thrust and, we trust, the force of the critique developed from the chapter on "What is the 'Subaltern' of" to the *Afterword* that follows; and so this is a good place to bring to a closure the present *post-logue* - with another poem (actually a posted notice not so far from Moses Hall).

Berkeley Modern-Posts

FOUND DOG
Black lab, white underbelly, curly tail
Seeking owner, howls at night
Well taken care of, strayed into
Spruce & Arc Streets, North Berkeley
Call: Jerry O'Garcia 1-008-Subaltern
Will return by UPS-VET (F.O.B)

FOUND GOD
White male, black underbelly, hairy tale
Seeking disciples, hysterical by day
Kept unkempt, wondered into
Bruce & Arche Avenues, North Bay Area
Call: Faristha O'Gibreal 1-800-Prealtern
Will return by FedExp-SKYPE (C.O.D)

References

Ahmad, Aijaz. (1992). *In Theory: Classes, Nations, Literatures*. London: Verso.
Al-Azmeh, Aziz. (1993). *Islam and Modernities*. London: Verso.
Anderson, Pamela Sue. (2004). *Feminist Philosophy of Religion*. London: Routledge.
Appadurai, Arjun. (1997). *Modernity at Large*. Minneapolis, MN: University of Minnesota Press.
Appadurai, Arjun. (2006). *Fear of Small Numbers*. Durham, NC: Duke University Press.
Bhabha, Homi. (1994). *The Location of Culture*. London: Routledge.
Bharucha, Rastom. (1998). *Economic and Political Weekly*. Vol. XXXII, No. 4, January 24–30, pp. 167–181.
Bilimoria, Purushottama. (1999). A Problem for (Onto-theos) Radical Pluralism. In *Philosophy of Religion: Toward a Global Perspective*, edited by GE Kessler, pp. 575–582. Belmont, CA: Wadsworth Press.
Bilimoria, Purushottama, Renuka Sharma and Joseph Prabhu (eds.). (2007). *Indian Ethics Classical and Contemporary*. Aldershot: Ashgate; New Delhi: Oxford University, 2008.

Bilimoria (2007a), Dismantling normativity in Indian ethics – from Vedic altarity to the *Gītā's* alterity', in Youru Wang (ed.), *The Ethical Dimension And Deconstruction Normative Ethics In Asian Traditions*, NY/London: Routledge, pp. 33–74.

Bilimoria (2007b). Transglobalism of Self-Exiled Hindus: The Case of Australia. *Religion Compass*, Vol. 1, No. 2, pp. 305–328.

Bilimoria (2008a), Dialogic Fecundation of Western Hermeneutics and Hindu Mīmāṃsā in the Critical Era. In R. Sherma and A. Sharma (eds.) *Hermeneutics and Hindu Thought Towards a Fusion of Horizons*. Dordrecht: Springer, pp. 43–76.

Bilimoria, Purushottama (2008b). *Śabdapramāṇa: Word and Knowledge as Testimony in Indian Philosophy*. New Delhi: D K Printworld.

Braidotti, Rosie. (1997). Nomadic Subjects: Feminist Postmodernism as Antirelativism. *Justice and Democracy: Cross Cultural Perspectives*, edited by Ron Bontekoe and Marietta Stepaniants. Honolulu, HI: University of Hawaii Press.

Cahoone, Lawrence (ed.). (1996). *From Modernism to Postmodernism an Anthology*. Cambridge, MA: Blackwell.

Caputo, John D. (1997). *The Prayers and Tears of Jacques Derrida: Religion Without Religion*. Bloomington, IN: Indiana University Press.

Chakrabarty, Dipesh. (2000). *Provincialzing Europe: Postcolonial Thought and Historical Difference*. New York: Princeton University Press.

Chakrabarty, Dipesh. (2002). *Habitations of Modernity: Essays in the Wake of Subaltern Studies*. Chicago, IL: University of Chicago Press.

Chakrabarty, Dipesh (ed.). (2007). *From the Colonial to the Postcolonial: India and Pakistan in Transition*. New York: Oxford University Press.

Fanon, Franz. (1990). *The Wretched of the Earth*. New York: Grove Press.

Gandhi, Leela. (1998). *Postcolonial Theory: An Introductory Text*. Sydney: Allen & Unwin.

Grange, Joseph. (1997). In *Justice and Democracy: Cross Cultural Perspectives*. Bontekoe, Ron and Marietta Stepaniants. (eds.) Honolulu: University of Hawaii Press.

Habermas, Jurgern. (1985). *The Philosophical Discourse of Modernity*. Cambridge, MA: MIT Press.

Lal, Vinay. (1995–1996). Plural Worlds, Ashis Nandy and the Post-Columbian Future Multiple Selves. Special Edition of *Emergences* 7/8, Group for Composite Studies, UCLA.

McCulloch, Jock. (1996). *Colonial Psychiatry and the African Mind*. Melbourne: Cambridge University Press.

Nandy, Ashis. (1998). *Return from Exile*. Delhi: Oxford University Press.

Rorty, Richard. (1989). *Contingency, Irony and Solidaarity*. Cambridge/New York: Cambridge University Press.

Rorty, Richard. (1995). Questions to Emmanuel Levinas, Yale *French Studies*, No. 87.

Rosenau, Pauline Vaillancourt. (1992). *Postmodernism and the Social Sciences Insights, Inroads and Intrusions*. Princeton, NJ: Princeton University Press.

Sharma, Renuka. (1993). *Understanding the Concepts of Empathy and Its Foundation in Psychoanalysis*. Lewiston, NY: Edwin Meller.

Sharma, Renuka. (1998). *The Other Revolution: Ngo and Feminist Perspectives from South East Asia* in Naari Studies in Gender, Culture and Society: East; West, No. 3. Delhi: Indian Books Centre.

Spivak, Gayatri Chakravorty. (1999). *A Critique of Postcolonialism*. Cambridge, MA: Harvard University Press.

Afterword: Religion and Philosophy between the Modern and Postmodern

Kenneth Surin

The essays in this volume are guided by a shared premise, namely, that philosophy of religion in the western tradition has thus far been vitiated by its failure to take into account the direct impact and the somewhat less visible implications of the 'colonial difference' that inflects the major intellectual traditions of the west. Any form of reflection that purports to be intellectually credible has thus to take this 'colonial difference' into consideration, and in so doing specify and analyze in its many and varied expressions 'the difference(s)' made by this 'colonial difference' for the contemporary philosophy of religion. By doing this, a philosophy of religion attuned to these postcolonial times will of course be following in the footsteps of other intellectual fields which have sought in their several and complex ways to be heedful of the phenomena associated with this 'colonial difference': cultural anthropology (Lila Abu-Lughod, Talal Asad, James Clifford, James Ferguson, Nicholas Dirks, Ann Stoler, inter alia), history (Dipesh Chakrabarty, Partha Chatterjee, Jack Goody, inter alia), literary theory (Edward Said, Gayatri Chakravorty Spivak, Homi Bhabha, Walter Mignolo, inter alia), political theory (Achille Mbembe, Mahmood Mamdani, David Scott, Timothy Mitchell, inter alia), psychoanalytic theory (Frantz Fanon), philosophy (Enrique Dussel, Kwame Anthony Appiah, Akeel Bilgrami, inter alia), and so on.

The essays lend themselves to a certain kind of provisional grouping. Those by Bilimoria, Jantzen, King, Maldonado-Torres, and Mignolo deal with an array of methodological issues primarily; Ellis, Garfield, Arvind Mandair, Paranjape, Sugirtharajah, and Yadav are concerned with versions of subalternity that impinge more or less on Hinduism (though Indology is the primary focus of some of the essays in this group); Navdeep Mandair focuses on Sikhism; Slabodsky on Judaism; and Mendieta and Irvine engage with the Latin American or Hispanic American recension of subalternity. Two caveats are in order here. Firstly, not all the essays are explicit in their broaching of the theme of subalternity – in some cases this theme underlies an argument rather than serving as that particular argument's explicit focus. Secondly, in all the essays there are discussions which range well beyond the theme of subalternity, thus we find in the preceding pages disquisitions on modernity and postmodernity, ideology, theologies, identity formation, ethnicity, the natures of the textual canon, hermeneutics, western and eastern epistemologies, the philosophy of history, the constitution of disciplinary fields, cultural politics, religious histories, universalism as a concept, political authority and legitimacy, local histories, philology, the history of ideas, globalization theory, orientalism as an intellectual enterprise, imperial formations, religious sectarianism, sacred texts, the nature of postcoloniality, the field of religious studies, the structures of intellectual transmission (and in making this brief enumeration I have barely scratched the surface, as they say). It should be obvious from the foregoing that a response competent enough to do justice to the details of all the essays in this volume is simply impossible – hardly anyone can presume the degree of expertise needed to undertake a full engagement with each and every one of these essays. My response is therefore unavoidably partial and selective.

I share in principle the collective reservations of our essayists regarding the failures and oversights of a previous mode of scholarly engagement (placed here under the label of 'coloniality') with respect to the practices and convictions of those generally deemed to be the adherents of religious traditions that were deemed not to belong to 'the West'. The failures on the part of this by now increasingly outdated scholarship (though when one thinks of someone like Bernard Lewis and his somewhat favorable reception in the US, this disparaging characterization of scholars like Lewis by us may need to be qualified to reckon with the often sympathetic response on the part of America's ruling political elites), guided as it was in its mainsprings by the impulses of this regnant 'coloniality,' are many: they range from outright racism to unquestioned and unwarranted notions of cultural and 'civilizational' superiority (Samuel Huntington is cited in these pages as a case in point), all the way down to sheer ignorance and intellectual opportunism and laziness (the two sometimes go hand in hand!), at times of the crassest and most vicious variety. Then of course there is an epistemically-sanctioned unthinkability – the very factors that conduced, systemically, to making (say) Athenian slavery and the American slavery of its southern states 'thinkable' and thus acceptable to their citizens, also served in uneven and complex ways to deactivate, and thus render 'unthinkable', any kind of systemically-enabled and principled opposition to this slavery (so that the equivalent of an epistemic shift was required before this slavery came to be regarded as objectionable).

Let me begin with a consideration that in my view needs to be observed by all who participate in these crucially important debates, and especially those who pronounce swiftly in the 'civilizational' or 'west versus the rest' debates so prevalent in the mass media these days in order to deny plausibility to those (like the writers in this volume and myself) who are disposed to be skeptical of great empires and their associated structures of intentions.[5]

We need here to distinguish adequately between the concepts of a theory of culture/'civilization'/religion, the concepts intrinsic to a (particular) culture/'civilization'/religion, and that culture/'civilization'/religion in its barest empirical or material conditions. A theory of culture (and so forth) is something which is produced or created no less than its putative object. It is a practice, just as cultures/'civilizations'/religions are multi-linear ensembles of practices. A theory, to be more precise, is a practice of concepts. A theory of culture/'civilization'/religion is not 'about' culture/'civilization'/religion, but about the concepts that culture/

'civilization'/religion generate, concepts that are themselves related in more or less complex ways to other practices, and so on. A theory, in short, operates on the concepts integral to the practical expression of this or that culture/'civilization'/religion.

A theory of culture does not therefore impinge directly on the sheerly empirical phenomena constituting culture, but on the concepts of culture, which however are no less practical, actual or effective than culture itself. (This is simply another way of registering in a way that is as unavoidable as it is problematic that scarcely deniable affectivity of 'thought' with which the 'idealist' philosophical traditions have always been impressed, but which their materialist counterparts have found embarrassing or insusceptible of adequate description and analysis or else reducible in principle to something more fundamental and compelling, namely, 'matter'.) Culture's concepts are not given in the assemblages of practices that constitute it, and yet they are culture's concepts, not theories about culture. Every culture generates for itself its own 'thinkability' (and concomitantly its own 'unthinkability' as the obverse of this very 'thinkability'), and its concepts are constitutive of that 'thinkability'. Another way of making this point would be to say that a culture has to secrete its myriad expressivities precisely in order to be able to be what it is, and that its concepts – in ways that are inevitably selective, limiting, and even arbitrary – are the thematizations or representations of these expressivities. Or, more generally, the concepts of a culture (or a religion or a 'civilization') are its expressivities rendered in the form of that culture's (or that religion's or that 'civilization's') 'thinkability'.

Theories of culture (or religion or 'civilization'), by contrast are theories produced by reflection on the natures, functions, and so forth, of these expressivities. They operate on a culture's (or a religion's or a 'civilization's') 'thinkability'. It is fine and salutary to ask the question 'What is culture?' but there is another kind of question to be asked as well, in this case 'What is (a) theory of (culture)?' Culture itself is an immensely varied and complex practice of signs and images, whose theory philosophers of culture and others must produce, but produce precisely as conceptual practice. No theoretical determination, no matter how subtle or thorough, can on its own constitute the concepts of culture. As indicated, these concepts are expressed in advance and independently of theoretical practice. Theorists, qua theorists, can only traffic in theories of culture (or religion or 'civilization').

The concepts that theorists deal with can function in more than one field of thought, and even in a single domain it is always possible for a concept to fulfill more than one function. Each variable of thought is of course defined by its own internal variables, variables which have a complex relation to their external counterparts (such as historical periods, political and social conditions and forces, even the sheer physical state of things). (It is tempting here to understand this complexity in terms that are akin to Althusser's sense of the 'overdetermined' relation between formations.) It follows that a concept comes into being or ceases to be effective only when there is a change of function and/or field. Functions for concepts must be created or abolished for them to be generated or eliminated, and new fields must be brought into being in order for concepts to be rendered irrelevant or invalid.

All the above seems like a long drawn-out clearing of the throat. But the usefulness of the distinctions made above becomes evident when we realize that a culture's 'expressivities' in themselves have nothing at all to do with the 'idea' (the theory, that is) of (a) culture: many cultures, both now and in the past, have organized their 'expressivities' through such concepts as *umran* (plenitude, fullness), *fortuna*, 'divine election', 'cosmic harmony', 'providence', *moira*, etc., all of these being concepts of a religious, or metaphysical, or cosmological provenance that do not necessarily overlap with notions that have specifically to do with the notion of 'culture' and in some cases even that of 'religion'. Of course, the fact that a particular culture comes to formulate its expressivities through a concept like 'divine election' is potentially very significant, ceteris paribus, for the 'ideas' we (as theorists of culture or religion) may form of it as a cultural or religious formation, but the concept 'divine election' in and of itself is not a theoretical object belonging to our 'idea' of culture or religion qua 'culture' or 'religion', even though it may happen to be a part, and a very important one at that, of the 'expressivity' of the culture or religion in question. The medieval Muslims who used *umran* as the pivotal concept for their characterizations of a life worth living, the ancient Greeks and early modern Italians who invoked, respectively, the concepts of *moira* or *fortuna* for similar purposes, were instantiating, however indirectly, components of the expressivities of their particular cultures or religions, but they were not thereby trafficking in anything that had putatively to do with 'culture' or 'religion' as a theoretical object. But this is as it should be, and all theorists of culture and religion can only deal in theories, and not with the 'expressivities' themselves.

The expressivities of a culture or religion stand as a kind of exteriority to the theory of culture or religion, and in so doing function from the beginning as irremovable etiolations of the ambitions of cultural or religious description.[6] The theorist of culture or religion who makes this principle an essential part of her intellectual baggage will acknowledge, as a formal condition of engaging in such description, that she cannot presume that the expressivities of the culture or religion in question will be exhaustively encompassed by her descriptions. This principle, or something like it, is ostensibly at work in several of the essays in this volume: Irvine's 'mestizo' paradigm, Slabodsky's 'internal heretical trend within Judaism', Eduardo Mendieta's 'imperial somatology of disgust and contempt', or Sugirtharajah's notion of a (merely) 'textualized Hunduism'. But this principle is implicit in all the other essays as well, since they all engage, albeit in different ways and in different contexts, with the phenomena associated with forms of cultural 'membership' (my use of this blandly neutral term is deliberate) that are not however accompanied by the appropriate kind of 'recognition'. The expressivities of those hamstrung by this predicament of subalternity – 'we really belong, but alas there is no recognition of us' – forcibly remind the cultural critic or religious scholar of something she should have known all along, namely, that expressivities will always display an ingrained recalcitrance when confronted with the enterprises of cultural and religious description.

At the same time it has to be acknowledged that the thesis, advanced by a number of our essayists, regarding subaltern epistemologies can take two forms: one is advanced here, and maintains that the subaltern is always in the position of the one who is denied recognition; the other goes further and insists that subalterns occupy a special and distinctive position in the cultures they inhabit, a unique position which affords them singular insights into the cultures in question. This second kind of claim exemplifies a version of so-called standpoint theory, that is, the theory whose fundamental premise is that different positions in social or cultural space will give the occupants of those positions a particular and special kind of knowledge of that society or culture, knowledge that is contingent upon one's being placed at that particular position, and thus not available in principle to those who are not so positioned. The position of the subaltern is thus necessarily and unavoidably one of difference if not active opposition.

These two sets of claims – (1) that the expressivities of culture function insurmountably as a kind of exteriority to the enterprise of cultural description; and (2) that by virtue of her position in the normative culture the subaltern has, decisively, a relation of difference and even antagonism to that culture, a differential relation that manifests itself both interpretively and politically (i.e. 'standpoint theory') – while quite different in their respective implications and theoretical provenances, are not necessarily incompatible. In fact, if anything they complement each other, whilst of course they should not be conflated. Standpoint theory militates against any assumption that a culture is a relatively homogeneous totality. At the same time the lack of commensurability between the expressivities of culture and religion precludes confident talk of such notions as that of a 'culture's pursuit of the good': the inability of description to catch up with expressivity makes it impossible for the cultural or religious theorist to characterize a pursuit of this kind as the pursuit of the 'good' of a whole culture. For, as has been argued, the cultural or religious theorist is never in a position to use her descriptions to capture a culture's expressivities, even when these expressivities give the appearance of having to do with something like the pursuit of 'the good'. A certain kind of theoretical asceticism is enjoined here, because any theorist or philosopher of culture persuaded that it makes sense to talk of the 'good of a whole culture' needs to consider the histories of other cultures and the possibilities afforded by these cultures – after all, the Muslim contemporaries of Ibn Khaldun (AD 1332/AH 732–AD 1406/AH 808) spoke of the life worth living in terms of the concept *umran* and not that of 'the good'.

Another important strand of thought present in these essays concerns the often unacknowledged affinity that the key concepts of the western philosophy of religion – necessity, universality, analyticity, a priority, the *ens realissimum*, the transcendent, etc. – have with a disowned or sloughed-off preceding Christian theology. Even a 'cross-cultural' philosophy of religion of a kind that flourished until the last decade or so reappropriated these concepts even as it revised them for a 'cross-cultural' or 'comparative' context. When this was done by philosophical practitioners belonging to non-Christian traditions (Judaism, Islam, Hinduism, Buddhism, and Sikhism), the adherence to the lexicons and conceptual armatures of this regnant western philosophy resulted in a kind of self-imposed tutelage on the part of these practitioners – the outcome was, unavoidably, the philosophical equivalent of 'subalternity'. The only way to avoid a subordination (whether explicitly avowed or merely tacit) to the dominant western philosophical paradigm is for this 'cross-cultural' philosophy of religion to undergo a 'decolonization of thought', and this endeavor is the focal-point of many of the essays in this volume. One way of undertaking this 'decolonization of thought' is for the philosopher of religion to be ceaselessly aware of the always specific and never generic standpoint from which a particular kind of thinking is generated. This is a salutary insight, but it poses important questions of its own.

One such question arises from the very context supplied by a philosophy that purports to be 'cross-cultural' in its orientation, or to operate in a context whose defining feature is the permeability of cultural boundaries and barriers. In such a context, and some would say that this is precisely the situation that goes by the name of 'postcoloniality', the cultures of 'others' no longer lie on the other side of the putative border or barrier between those (other) cultures and 'our' culture. Instead, this border has become internal, it is endlessly shiftable, and is everywhere and nowhere at the same time. The erstwhile impermeable barrier between cultures has become more like a translucent screen or piece of netting that separates them, reminding one in the process of the distinction that Hegel made in the *Wissenschaft der Logik* between two kinds of exteriority to a concept or definition, that is, the insurmountable 'barrier' (*Schranke*) and the more permeable 'limit' (*Grenze*). Or in terms of our discussion, whereas there had once been 'barriers' between cultures, there are now, in the dispensation that some call 'postcoloniality', only 'limits'. Irrevocable historical and cultural transformations have termed ostensible 'barriers' between cultures into mere 'limits'.

However, if cultural 'barriers' have become shiftable and perhaps even ephemeral 'limits', it becomes harder to tell the difference between a 'real Indian religious or philosophical tradition' and an 'ersatz Indian religious or philosophical tradition'. Here we encounter something like Hegel's problem of the difficulty of providing a specification of a concept in terms of its internal determinations (i.e. within its 'limits'). And so while the presence of a conceptual 'barrier' (*Schranke*) between being an Indian tradition and being a Japanese tradition and being a French tradition, etc., makes the difference between them relatively easy to undertake – according to Hegel, we simply use the operation of negation, hence to be English is not to be French, not to be Nigerian, not to be Cuban, not to be Japanese, etc. But when we seek to grasp the concept 'being English' within its limits (in Hegel's admittedly technical sense of 'limit') the internal determinations of this concept become much harder to specify. What marks someone as 'being English' when there are so many individuals who appear to qualify for this designation? Being born in England? But many well-known English persons were born outside England – of literary figures alone, Rudyard Kipling was born in what is now Pakistan, William Makepeace Thackeray was born in India, J.G Ballard was born in China, Tom Stoppard was born in what was then Czechoslovakia. What about being a subject of the Queen of England? But Australians and New Zealanders are also subjects of the Queen of England. Eating roast beef and Yorkshire pudding? But what about the English people who happen to be vegetarians from birth? Liking televised darts, cricket, snooker, sheepdog trials, and (lawn) bowls? One will still find quite a few English men and women who will declare a profound distaste for these activities, whether televised or not. The distinction between 'playing at being

English' and 'being really English' becomes impossible to maintain at the level of the limit (*Grenze*), and there is ample vindication for Hegel's point that the full set of internal determinations of any concept, when apprehended at its 'limit', can only be approached asymptotically – one may be English or Indian or Kenyan, but in an irreducible sense, no one is fully and completely English or Indian or Kenyan. One is in effect only 'sufficiently' English or Indian or Kenyan, and desire, fantasy, and socially-imposed contrivance have to do the rest, as writers on race, ethnicity, and nationality from different fields and theoretical orientations such as Benedict Anderson, Anthony Appiah, Etienne Balibar, and Slavoj Žižek have been telling us.

It is true of course that traditions, especially when they show themselves to be exceptionally durable, have 'identities' that, in principle, are less prone to alteration or mutation than the 'identities' of persons or such things as quarks, countries, or songs. But even so traditions can and do undergo more or less significant transformations, especially in situations where they have to make concessions to rival or alternative traditions belonging to cultures that are more powerful and more prestigious (the essays in this volume register the tendency on the part of non-western traditions to capitulate philosophically to their western counterparts). What matters here, then, are the asymmetries of power that fuel the making of such concessions, and in so far as it is one of the central concerns of a theory of subalternity to provide an account of these asymmetries, it is right for a contemporary philosophy of religion to be submitted to a 'decolonization of thought'.

However, while the perspective of a 'decolonization of thought' may make it possible for these intellectual capitulations to be identified and be seen for what they really are, the means of their rectification may turn out to be elusive, the subaltern studies perspective notwithstanding. What should one do, apart from doing the obvious things like giving up all attempts, attempts which are at once implausible and meretricious (as some of these essays amply demonstrate), to formulate, say, a Hindu version of the *ens realissimum*, or to seek a Buddhist resolution of the 'problem of evil' (as if some Buddhist thinker could be summoned as the ideal conversation partner for Leibniz or Richard Swinburne), or to conceptualize Jahweh in terms of the Hegelian Absolute, or to 'find' that Nbgbrjuna or Gangeza anticipated some thesis of Wittgenstein's or Quine's? Maybe this is all we can, and possibly need, to do, that is, exercise an unsparing intellectual vigilance in the face of this philosophical colonialism, with its numerous intellectual sleights of hand.

For of course several perspectives can be taken on this philosophical subalternity. One viewpoint enjoins an acceptance of standpoint theory to display the ways in which colonially-sanctioned asymmetries of power, with their in-built propensity for the generalization of colonial normativities, affect and constrain the formulation of those metaphysical and epistemological principles deemed to belong to the non-west. Another, as we have just seen, counsels vigilance with regard to the intellectual concessions made, willy-nilly, by those who adapt some non-western tradition of thought to the intellectual norms belonging to the western philosophy of religion. Yet another seeks to retrieve forms of thought and practice overlooked as a consequence of the imposition of a subaltern consciousness – thus the essay by Paranjape in this volume seeks a recuperation of generally overlooked Gnostic traditions. Or one can reverse the intellectual direction of subalternity's typical sub-ordination of the east to the west by using eastern traditions to 'read' their western counterparts (hence the essay by Garfield uses the Buddhist Cittamatra School to analyze western idealism). There is also the attempt to root out an 'internal colonial-ism' perpetrated by the non-western traditions themselves. Accordingly, the essay by Yadav analyzes the role of the ideology of élite Brahmanism (*bhadraloka*) which 'prepared' Hinduism in advance for its subordination to western thought, the one by Slabodsky shows how Jewish intellectuals living in Europe have had a systemic disregard for peripheral Judaisms, and Navdeep Mandair shows how Sikhism made its own internal accommodation to the colonial British depiction of the Sikhs as a 'martial race' (the British endorsing this claim with respect to the Sikhs having pre-sumed in advance that they are themselves, as members of the 'British race', the quintessential exemplars of a 'martial race').

I have barely skimmed the surface of the essays in this wide-ranging and pio-neering collection. We live in a world that is still as much neocolonial as it is postcolonial, so the 'theory' evinced in these essays is perhaps ahead of the painful realities associated with the neocolonial condition. But this is not necessarily a bad thing – as someone once said, the beheading of the King of France could not have happened if Kant had not first discredited, philosophically, the notion that the King is God's representative on earth. A certain kind of philosophical 'beheading' takes place in this collection, and while the fuller implications of this philosophi-cal gesture are still to be reckoned with, this gesture belongs to a movement (call it the 'decolonization of thought' or something similar) that has a magnitude and significance likely to parallel Kant's preceding philosophical 'cut'.

Notes

1 Several of my formulations here have been taken from my earlier, On Not being Sure About the 'Post' in 'Postcolonial': Afterthoughts on Postcolonial Religious Studies, *Sophia* 39(2000), 208–226.

2 Another way of making this point about the difference in principle between the 'expressivity' of a culture and a theory of culture would be to point to the distinction between being presented with a *description* of a particular culture and being presented, 'in actual fact' as it were, with that culture. The theorist of culture brings with her implicitly the historical and intellectual experience which makes her the thinker she is, but that experience may not belong to the place or culture she is studying. Her ideas, and the ways of living to which they apply, may mean she is not at all like the persons who belong to the culture she is endeavoring to describe. It may also mean, conversely, that the members of that culture may not be in a position to recognize her thoughts as being salient or interesting or whatever. There are inherent obstacles to any attempt to visit as 'a theorist' all the reaches of history or even those of a particular culture. The theorist of culture can never therefore be absolutely certain of the precise reach of her theories and concepts, nor that these theories and concepts have any kind of adequate approximation to the expressivities of the culture or cultures in question. My formulations here are indebted to Bernard Williams, 'The End of Explanation?', *The New York Review of Books*, November 19, 1998, 40–44.

Index

CPSIA information can be obtained
at www.ICGtesting.com
Printed in the USA
LVHW011632071222
734757LV00001B/1